XML™ Bible

XML™ Bible

Elliotte Rusty Harold

IDG Books Worldwide, Inc.
An International Data Group Company

Foster City, CA ✦ Chicago, IL ✦ Indianapolis, IN ✦ New York, NY

XML™ Bible

Published by
IDG Books Worldwide, Inc.
An International Data Group Company
919 E. Hillsdale Blvd., Suite 400
Foster City, CA 94404
www.idgbooks.com (IDG Books Worldwide Web site)

ISBN: 0-7645-3236-7

Printed in the United States of America

10 9 8 7 6 5

1B/QU/QR/QQ/IN

Distributed in the United States by IDG Books Worldwide, Inc.

Distributed by CDG Books Canada Inc. for Canada; by Transworld Publishers Limited in the United Kingdom; by IDG Norge Books for Norway; by IDG Sweden Books for Sweden; by IDG Books Australia Publishing Corporation Pty. Ltd. for Australia and New Zealand; by TransQuest Publishers Pte Ltd. for Singapore, Malaysia, Thailand, Indonesia, and Hong Kong; by Gotop Information Inc. for Taiwan; by ICG Muse, Inc. for Japan; by Intersoft for South Africa; by Eyrolles for France; by International Thomson Publishing for Germany, Austria and Switzerland; by Distribuidora Cuspide for Argentina; by LR International for Brazil; by Galileo Libros for Chile; by Ediciones ZETA S.C.R. Ltda. for Peru; by WS Computer Publishing Corporation, Inc., for the Philippines; by Contemporanea de Ediciones for Venezuela; by Express Computer Distributors for the Caribbean and West Indies; by Micronesia Media Distributor, Inc. for Micronesia; by Chips Computadoras S.A. de C.V. for Mexico; by Editorial Norma de Panama S.A. for Panama; by American Bookshops for Finland.

For general information on IDG Books Worldwide's books in the U.S., please call our Consumer Customer Service department at 800-762-2974. For reseller information, including discounts and premium sales, please call our Reseller Customer Service department at 800-434-3422.

For information on where to purchase IDG Books Worldwide's books outside the U.S., please contact our International Sales department at 317-596-5530 or fax 317-572-4002.

For consumer information on foreign language translations, please contact our Customer Service department at 1-800-434-3422, fax 317-572-4002, or e-mail rights@idgbooks.com.

For information on licensing foreign or domestic rights, please phone +1-650-653-7098.

For sales inquiries and special prices for bulk quantities, please contact our Sales department at 800-762-2974 or write to the address above.

For information on using IDG Books Worldwide's books in the classroom or for ordering examination copies, please contact our Educational Sales department at 800-434-2086 or fax 317-572-4005.

For press review copies, author interviews, or other publicity information, please contact our Public Relations department at 650-653-7000 or fax 650-653-7500.

For authorization to photocopy items for corporate, personal, or educational use, please contact Copyright Clearance Center, 222 Rosewood Drive, Danvers, MA 01923, or fax 978-750-4470.

Library of Congress Cataloging-in-Publication Data
Harold, Elliote Rusty.
    XML bible / Elliote Rusty Harold.
        p.   cm.
    ISBN 0-7645-3236-7 (alk. paper)
    1. XML (Document markup language) I. Title.
QA76.76.H94H34   1999   99-31021
005.7'2–dc21   CIP

 is a registered trademark under exclusive license to IDG Books Worldwide, Inc. from International Data Group, Inc.

ABOUT IDG BOOKS WORLDWIDE

Welcome to the world of IDG Books Worldwide.

IDG Books Worldwide, Inc., is a subsidiary of International Data Group, the world's largest publisher of computer-related information and the leading global provider of information services on information technology. IDG was founded more than 30 years ago by Patrick J. McGovern and now employs more than 9,000 people worldwide. IDG publishes more than 290 computer publications in over 75 countries. More than 90 million people read one or more IDG publications each month.

Launched in 1990, IDG Books Worldwide is today the #1 publisher of best-selling computer books in the United States. We are proud to have received eight awards from the Computer Press Association in recognition of editorial excellence and three from Computer Currents' First Annual Readers' Choice Awards. Our best-selling *...For Dummies®* series has more than 50 million copies in print with translations in 31 languages. IDG Books Worldwide, through a joint venture with IDG's Hi-Tech Beijing, became the first U.S. publisher to publish a computer book in the People's Republic of China. In record time, IDG Books Worldwide has become the first choice for millions of readers around the world who want to learn how to better manage their businesses.

Our mission is simple: Every one of our books is designed to bring extra value and skill-building instructions to the reader. Our books are written by experts who understand and care about our readers. The knowledge base of our editorial staff comes from years of experience in publishing, education, and journalism — experience we use to produce books to carry us into the new millennium. In short, we care about books, so we attract the best people. We devote special attention to details such as audience, interior design, use of icons, and illustrations. And because we use an efficient process of authoring, editing, and desktop publishing our books electronically, we can spend more time ensuring superior content and less time on the technicalities of making books.

You can count on our commitment to deliver high-quality books at competitive prices on topics you want to read about. At IDG Books Worldwide, we continue in the IDG tradition of delivering quality for more than 30 years. You'll find no better book on a subject than one from IDG Books Worldwide.

John Kilcullen
Chairman and CEO
IDG Books Worldwide, Inc.

Steven Berkowitz
President and Publisher
IDG Books Worldwide, Inc.

WINNER VIII

Eighth Annual Computer Press Awards ≥1992

WINNER IX

Ninth Annual Computer Press Awards ≥1993

WINNER X

Tenth Annual Computer Press Awards ≥1994

WINNER XI

Eleventh Annual Computer Press Awards ≥1995

IDG is the world's leading IT media, research and exposition company. Founded in 1964, IDG had 1997 revenues of $2.05 billion and has more than 9,000 employees worldwide. IDG offers the widest range of media options that reach IT buyers in 75 countries representing 95% of worldwide IT spending. IDG's diverse product and services portfolio spans six key areas including print publishing, online publishing, expositions and conferences, market research, education and training, and global marketing services. More than 90 million people read one or more of IDG's 290 magazines and newspapers, including IDG's leading global brands — Computerworld, PC World, Network World, Macworld and the Channel World family of publications. IDG Books Worldwide is one of the fastest-growing computer book publishers in the world, with more than 700 titles in 36 languages. The "...For Dummies®" series alone has more than 50 million copies in print. IDG offers online users the largest network of technology-specific Web sites around the world through IDG.net (http://www.idg.net), which comprises more than 225 targeted Web sites in 55 countries worldwide. International Data Corporation (IDC) is the world's largest provider of information technology data, analysis and consulting, with research centers in over 41 countries and more than 400 research analysts worldwide. IDG World Expo is a leading producer of more than 168 globally branded conferences and expositions in 35 countries including E3 (Electronic Entertainment Expo), Macworld Expo, ComNet, Windows World Expo, ICE (Internet Commerce Expo), Agenda, DEMO, and Spotlight. IDG's training subsidiary, ExecuTrain, is the world's largest computer training company, with more than 230 locations worldwide and 785 training courses. IDG Marketing Services helps industry-leading IT companies build international brand recognition by developing global integrated marketing programs via IDG's print, online and exposition products worldwide. Further information about the company can be found at www.idg.com. 1/24/99

Credits

Acquisitions Editor
John Osborn

Development Editor
Terri Varveris

Contributing Writer
Heather Williamson

Technical Editor
Greg Guntle

Copy Editors
Amy Eoff
Amanda Kaufman
Nicole LeClerc
Victoria Lee

Production
IDG Books Worldwide Production

Proofreading and Indexing
York Production Services

About the Author

Elliotte Rusty Harold is an internationally respected writer, programmer, and educator both on the Internet and off. He got his start by writing FAQ lists for the Macintosh newsgroups on Usenet, and has since branched out into books, Web sites, and newsletters. He lectures about Java and object-oriented programming at Polytechnic University in Brooklyn. His Cafe con Leche Web site at `http://metalab.unc.edu/xml/` has become one of the most popular independent XML sites on the Internet.

Elliotte is originally from New Orleans where he returns periodically in search of a decent bowl of gumbo. However, he currently resides in the Prospect Heights neighborhood of Brooklyn with his wife Beth and cats Charm (named after the quark) and Marjorie (named after his mother-in-law). When not writing books, he enjoys working on genealogy, mathematics, and quantum mechanics. His previous books include *The Java Developer's Resource*, *Java Network Programming*, *Java Secrets*, *JavaBeans*, *XML: Extensible Markup Language*, and *Java I/O*.

For Ma, a great grandmother

Preface

Welcome to the *XML Bible*. After reading this book I hope you'll agree with me that XML is the most exciting development on the Internet since Java, and that it makes Web site development easier, more productive, and more fun.

This book is your introduction to the exciting and fast growing world of XML. In this book, you'll learn how to write documents in XML and how to use style sheets to convert those documents into HTML so legacy browsers can read them. You'll also learn how to use document type definitions (DTDs) to describe and validate documents. This will become increasingly important as more and more browsers like Mozilla and Internet Explorer 5.0 provide native support for XML.

About You the Reader

Unlike most other XML books on the market, the *XML Bible* covers XML not from the perspective of a software developer, but rather that of a Web-page author. I don't spend a lot of time discussing BNF grammars or parsing element trees. Instead, I show you how you can use XML and existing tools today to more efficiently produce attractive, exciting, easy-to-use, easy-to-maintain Web sites that keep your readers coming back for more.

This book is aimed directly at Web-site developers. I assume you want to use XML to produce Web sites that are difficult to impossible to create with raw HTML. You'll be amazed to discover that in conjunction with style sheets and a few free tools, XML enables you to do things that previously required either custom software costing hundreds to thousands of dollars per developer, or extensive knowledge of programming languages like Perl. None of the software in this book will cost you more than a few minutes of download time. None of the tricks require any programming.

What You Need to Know

XML does build on HTML and the underlying infrastructure of the Internet. To that end, I will assume you know how to use ftp files, send email, and load URLs in your Web browser of choice. I will also assume you have a reasonable knowledge of HTML at about the level supported by Netscape 1.1. On the other hand, when I discuss newer aspects of HTML that are not yet in widespread use like cascading style sheets, I will cover them in depth.

To be more specific, in this book I assume that you can:

+ Write a basic HTML page including links, images, and text using a text editor.
+ Place that page on a Web server.

On the other hand, I do not assume that you:

+ Know SGML. In fact, this preface is almost the only place in the entire book you'll see the word SGML used. XML is supposed to be simpler and more widespread than SGML. It can't be that if you have to learn SGML first.
+ Are a programmer, whether of Java, Perl, C, or some other language, XML is a markup language, not a programming language. You don't need to be a programmer to write XML documents.

What You'll Learn

This book has one primary goal; to teach you to write XML documents for the Web. Fortunately, XML has a decidedly flat learning curve, much like HTML (and unlike SGML). As you learn a little you can do a little. As you learn a little more, you can do a little more. Thus the chapters in this book build steadily on each other. They are meant to be read in sequence. Along the way you'll learn:

+ How an XML document is created and delivered to readers.
+ How semantic tagging makes XML documents easier to maintain and develop than their HTML equivalents.
+ How to post XML documents on Web servers in a form everyone can read.
+ How to make sure your XML is well-formed.
+ How to use international characters like ζ and щ in your documents.
+ How to validate documents with DTDs.
+ How to use entities to build large documents from smaller parts.
+ How attributes describe data.
+ How to work with non-XML data.
+ How to format your documents with CSS and XSL style sheets.
+ How to connect documents with XLinks and Xpointers.
+ How to merge different XML vocabularies with namespaces.
+ How to write metadata for Web pages using RDF.

In the final section of this book, you'll see several practical examples of XML being used for real-world applications including:

◆ Web Site Design

◆ Push

◆ Vector Graphics

◆ Genealogy

How the Book Is Organized

This book is divided into five parts and includes three appendixes:

I.	Introducing XML
II.	Document Type Definitions
III.	Style Languages
IV.	Supplemental Technologies
V.	XML Applications

By the time you're finished reading this book, you'll be ready to use XML to create compelling Web pages. The five parts and the appendixes are described below.

Part I: Introducing XML

Part I consists of Chapters 1 through 7. It begins with the history and theory behind XML, the goals XML is trying to achieve, and shows you how the different pieces of the XML equation fit together to create and deliver documents to readers. You'll see several compelling examples of XML applications to give you some idea of the wide applicability of XML, including the Vector Markup Language (VML), the Resource Description Framework (RDF), the Mathematical Markup Language (MathML), the Extensible Forms Description Language (XFDL), and many others. Then you'll learn by example how to write XML documents with tags you define that make sense for your document. You'll see how to edit them in a text editor, attach style sheets to them, and load them into a Web browser like Internet Explorer 5.0 or Mozilla. You'll even learn how you can write XML documents in languages other than English, even languages that are written nothing like English, such as Chinese, Hebrew, and Russian.

Part II: Document Type Definitions

Part II consists of Chapters 8 through 11, all of which focus on document type definitions (DTDs). An XML document may optionally contain a DTD that specifies which elements are and are not allowed in an XML document. The DTD specifies the exact context and structure of those elements. A validating parser can read a document and compare it to its DTD, and report any mistakes it finds. DTDs enable document authors to make sure that their work meets any necessary criteria.

In Part II, you'll learn how to attach a DTD to a document, how to validate your documents against their DTDs, and how to write your own DTDs that solve your own problems. You'l learn the syntax for declaring elements, attributes, entities, and notations. You'll see how you can use entity declarations and entity references to build both a document and its DTD from multiple, independent pieces. This allows you to make long, hard-to-follow documents much simpler by separating them into related modules and components. And you'll learn how to integrate other forms of data like raw text and GIF image files in your XML document.

Part III: Style Languages

Part III consists of Chapters 12 through 15. XML markup only specifies what's in a document. Unlike HTML, it does not say anything about what that content should look like. Information about an XML document's appearance when printed, viewed in a Web browser, or otherwise displayed is stored in a style sheet. Different style sheets can be used for the same document. You might, for instance, want to use a style sheet that specifies small fonts for printing, another one that uses larger fonts for on-screen use, and a third with absolutely humongous fonts to project the document on a wall at a seminar. You can change the appearance of an XML document by choosing a different style sheet without touching the document itself.

Part III, describes in detail the two style sheet languanges in broadest use on the Web, Cascading Style Sheets (CSS) and the Extensible Style Language (XSL).

CSS is a simple style-sheet language originally designed for use with HTML. CSS exists in two versions: CSS Level 1 and CSS Level 2. CSS Level 1 provides basic information about fonts, color, positioning, and text properties, and is reasonably well supported by current Web browsers for HTML and XML. CSS Level 2 is a more recent standard that adds support for aural style sheets, user interface styles, international and bi-directional text, and more. CSS is a relatively simple standard that applies fixed style rules to the contents of particular elements.

XSL, by contrast, is a more complicated and more powerful style language that cannot only apply styles to the contents of elements but can also rearrange elements, add boilerplate text, and transform documents in almost arbitrary ways. XSL is divided into two parts: a transformation language for converting XML trees to alternative trees, and a formatting language for specifying the appearance of the elements of an XML tree. Currently, the transformation language is better supported by most tools than the formatting language. Nonetheless, it is beginning to firm up, and is supported by Microsoft Internet Explorer 5.0 and some third-party formatting engines.

Part IV: Supplemental Technologies

Part IV consists of Chapters 16 through 19. It introduces some XML-based languages and syntaxes that layer on top of basic XML. XLinks provides multi-directional hypertext links that are far more powerful than the simple HTML <A> tag. XPointers introduce a new syntax you can attach to the end of URLs to link not only to particular documents, but to particular parts of particular documents. Namespaces use prefixes and URLs to disambiguate conflicting XML markup languages. The Resource Description Framework (RDF) is an XML application used to embed meta-data in XML and HTML documents. Meta-data is information about a document, such as the author, date, and title of a work, rather than the work itself. All of these can be added to your own XML-based markup languages to extend their power and utility.

Part V: XML Applications

Part V, which consists of Chapters 20–23, shows you four practical uses of XML in different domains. XHTML is a reformulation of HTML 4.0 whose out come is valid XML. Microsoft's Channel Definition Format (CDF) is an XML-based markup language for defining channels that can push updated Web-site content to subscribers. The Vector Markup Language (VML) is an XML application for scalable graphics used by Micro-soft Office 2000 and Internet Explorer 5.0. Finally, a completely new application is developed for genealogical data to show you not just how to use XML tags, but why and when to choose them.

Appendixes

This book has two appendixes, which focus on the formal specifications for XML, as opposed to the more informal description of it used throughout the rest of the book. Appendix A provides detailed explanations of three individual parts of the XML 1.0 specification: XML BNF grammar, well-formedness constraints, and validity constraints. Appendix B contains the official W3C XML 1.0 specification published by the W3C. The book also has a third appendix, Appendix C, which describes the contents of the CD-ROM that accompanies this book.

What You Need

To make the best use of this book and XML, you need:

✦ A PC running Windows 95, Windows 98, or Windows NT

✦ Internet Explorer 5.0

✦ A Java 1.1 or later virtual machine

Any system that can run Windows will suffice. In this book, I mostly assume you're using Windows 95 or NT 4.0 or later. As a longtime Mac and Unix user, I somewhat regret this. Like Java, XML is supposed to be platform independent. Also like Java, the reality is somewhat short of the hype. Although XML code is pure text that can be written with any editor, many of the tools are currently only available on Windows.

However, although there aren't many Unix or Macintosh native XML programs, there are an increasing number of XML programs written in Java. If you have a Java 1.1 or later virtual machine on your platform of choice, you should be able to make do. Even if you can't load your XML documents directly into a Web browser, you can still convert them to XML documents and view those. When Mozilla is released, it should provide the best XML browser yet across multiple platforms.

How to Use This Book

This book is designed to be read more or less cover to cover. Each chapter builds on the material in the previous chapters in a fairly predictable fashion. Of course, you're always welcome to skim over material that's already familiar to you. I also hope you'll stop along the way to try out some of the examples and to write some XML documents of your own. It's important to learn not just by reading, but also by doing. Before you get started, I'd like to make a couple of notes about grammatical conventions used in this book.

Unlike HTML, XML is case sensitive. `<FATHER>` is not the same as `<Father>` or `<father>`. The `father` element is not the same as the `Father` element or the `FATHER` element. Unfortunately, case-sensitive markup languages have an annoying habit of conflicting with standard English usage. On rare occasion this means that you may encounter sentences that don't begin with a capital letter. More commonly, you'll see capitalization used in the middle of a sentence where you wouldn't normally expect it. Please don't get too bothered by this. All XML and HTML code used in this book is placed in a monospaced font, so most of the time it will be obvious from the context what is meant.

I have also adopted the British convention of only placing punctuation inside quote marks when it belongs with the material quoted. Frankly, although I learned to write in the American educational system, I find the British system is far more logical, especially when dealing with source code where the difference between a comma or a period and no punctuation at all can make the difference between perfectly correct and perfectly incorrect code.

What the Icons Mean

Throughout the book, I've used *icons* in the left margin to call your attention to points that are particularly important.

Note icons provide supplemental information about the subject at hand, but generally something that isn't quite the main idea. Notes are often used to elaborate on a detailed technical point.

Tip icons indicate a more efficient way of doing something, or a technique that may not be obvious.

CD-ROM icons tell you that software discussed in the book is available on the companion CD-ROM. This icon also tells you if a longer example, discussed but not included in its entirety in the book, is on the CD-ROM.

Caution icons warn you of a common misconception or that a procedure doesn't always work quite like it's supposed to. The most common purpose of a Caution icon in this book is to point out the difference between what a specification says should happen, and what actually does.

The Cross-Reference icon refers you to other chapters that have more to say about a particular subject.

About the Companion CD-ROM

The inside back cover of this book contains a CD-ROM that holds all numbered code listings that you'll find in the text. It also includes many longer examples that couldn't fit into this book. The CD-ROM also contains the complete text of various XML specifications in HTML. (Some of the specifications will be in other formats as well.) Finally, you will find an assortment of useful software for working with XML documents. Many (though not all) of these programs are written in Java, so they'll run on any system with a reasonably compatible Java 1.1 or later virtual machine. Most of the programs that aren't written in Java are designed for Windows 95, 98, and NT.

For a complete description of the CD-ROM contents, you can read Appendix C. In addition, to get a complete description of what is on the CD-ROM, you can load the file index.html onto your Web browser. The files on the companion CD-ROM are not compressed, so you can access them directly from the CD.

Reach Out

The publisher and I want your feedback. After you have had a chance to use this book, please take a moment to complete the IDG Books Worldwide Registration Card (in the back of the book). Please be honest in your evaluation. If you thought a particular chapter didn't tell you enough, let me know. Of course, I would prefer to receive comments like: "This is the best book I've ever read", "Thanks to this book, my Web site won Cool Site of the Year", or "When I was reading this book on the beach, I was besieged by models who thought I was super cool", but I'll take any comments I can get :-).

Feel free to send me specific questions regarding the material in this book. I'll do my best to help you out and answer your questions, but I can't guarantee a reply. The best way to reach me is by email:

elharo@metalab.unc.edu

Also, I invite you to visit my Cafe con Leche Web site at http://metalab.unc.edu/xml/, which contains a lot of XML-related material and is updated almost daily. Despite my persistent efforts to make this book perfect, some errors have doubtless slipped by. Even more certainly, some of the material discussed here will change over time. I'll post any necessary updates and errata on my Web site at http://metalab.unc.edu/xml/books/bible/. Please let me know via email of any errors that you find that aren't already listed.

Elliotte Rusty Harold
elharo@metalab.unc.edu
http://metalab.unc.edu/xml/
New York City, June 1999

Acknowledgments

The folks at IDG have all been great. The acquisitions editor, John Osborn, deserves special thanks for arranging the unusual scheduling this book required to hit the moving target XML presents. Terri Varveris shepherded this book through the development process. With poise and grace, she managed the constantly shifting outline and schedule that a book based on unstable specifications and software requires. Amy Eoff corrected many of my grammatical shortcomings. Susan Parini and Ritchie Durdin, the production coordinators, also deserve special thanks for managing the production of this book and for dealing with last-minute figure changes.

Steven Champeon brought his SGML experience to the book, and provided many insightful comments on the text. My brother Thomas Harold put his command of chemistry at my disposal when I was trying to grasp the Chemical Markup Language. Carroll Bellau provided me with parts of my family tree, which you'll find in Chapter 17.

I also greatly appreciate all the comments, questions, and corrections sent in by readers of my previous book, *XML: Extensible Markup Language*. I hope that I've managed to address most of those comments in this book. They've definitely helped make *XML Bible* a better book. Particular thanks are due to Alan Esenther and Donald Lancon Jr. for their especially detailed comments.

WandaJane Phillips wrote the original version of Chapter 21 on CDF that is adapted here. Heather Williamson, in addition to performing yeoman-like service as technical editor, wrote Chapter 13, *CSS Level 2*, and parts of Chapters 18, 19, and 22. Her help was instrumental in helping me almost meet my deadline. (Blame for this *almost* rests on my shoulders, not theirs.) Also, I would like to thank Piroz Mohseni, who also served as a technical editor for this book.

The agenting talents of David and Sherry Rogelberg of the Studio B Literary Agency (http://www.studiob.com/) have made it possible for me to write more or less full-time. I recommend them highly to anyone thinking about writing computer books. And as always, thanks go to my wife Beth for her endless love and understanding.

Contents at a Glance

Contents

Part II: Document Type Definitions   189

Part IV: Supplemental Technologies   569

Chapter 16: XLinks 571

Chapter 17: XPointers 591

Introducing XML

An Eagle's Eye View of XML

This first chapter introduces you to XML. It explains in general what XML is and how it is used. It shows you how the different pieces of the XML equation fit together, and how an XML document is created and delivered to readers.

What Is XML?

XML stands for Extensible Markup Language (often written as eXtensibleMarkup Language to justify the acronym). XML is a set of rules for defining semantic tags that break a document into parts and identify the different parts of the document. It is a meta-markup language that defines a syntax used to define other domain-specific, semantic, structured markup languages.

XML Is a Meta-Markup Language

The first thing you need to understand about XML is that it isn't just another markup language like the Hypertext Markup Language (HTML) or troff. These languages define a fixed set of tags that describe a fixed number of elements. If the markup language you use doesn't contain the tag you need — you're out of luck. You can wait for the next version of the markup language hoping that it includes the tag you need; but then you're really at the mercy of what the vendor chooses to include.

XML, however, is a meta-markup language. It's a language in which you make up the tags you need as you go along. These tags must be organized according to certain general principles, but they're quite flexible in their meaning. For instance, if you're working on genealogy and need to desc-ribe people, births, deaths, burial sites, families, marriages, divorces, and so on, you can create tags for each of these. You don't have to force your data to fit into paragraphs, list items, strong emphasis, or other very general categories.

The tags you create can be documented in a Document Type Definition (DTD). You'll learn more about DTDs in Part II of this book. For now, think of a DTD as a vocabulary and a syntax for certain kinds of documents. For example, the MOL.DTD in Peter Murray-Rust's Chemical Markup Language (CML) describes a vocabulary and a syntax for the molecular sciences: chemistry, crystallography, solid state physics, and the like. It includes tags for atoms, molecules, bonds, spectra, and so on. This DTD can be shared by many different people in the molecular sciences field. Other DTDs are available for other fields, and you can also create your own.

XML defines a meta syntax that domain-specific markup languages like MusicML, MathML, and CML must follow. If an application understands this meta syntax, it automatically understands all the languages built from this meta language. A browser does not need to know in advance each and every tag that might be used by thousands of different markup languages. Instead it discovers the tags used by any given document as it reads the document or its DTD. The detailed instructions about how to display the content of these tags are provided in a separate style sheet that is attached to the document.

For example, consider Schrodinger's equation:

$$i\hbar \frac{\partial \psi(r,\, t)}{\partial t} = -\frac{\hbar^2}{2m} \frac{\partial^2 \psi(r,\, t)}{\partial x^2} + V(r)\, \psi(r,\, t)$$

Scientific papers are full of equations like this, but scientists have been waiting eight years for the browser vendors to support the tags needed to write even the most basic math. Musicians are in a similar bind, since Netscape Navigator and Internet Explorer don't support sheet music.

XML means you don't have to wait for browser vendors to catch up with what you want to do. You can invent the tags you need, when you need them, and tell the browsers how to display these tags.

XML Describes Structure and Semantics, Not Formatting

The second thing to understand about XML is that XML markup describes a document's structure and meaning. It does not describe the formatting of the elements on the page. Formatting can be added to a document with a style sheet. The document itself only contains tags that say what is in the document, not what the document looks like.

By contrast, HTML encompasses formatting, structural, and semantic markup. <B> is a formatting tag that makes its content bold. <STRONG> is a semantic tag that means its contents are especially important. <TD> is a structural tag that indicates that the contents are a cell in a table. In fact, some tags can have all three kinds of meaning. An <H1> tag can simultaneously mean 20 point Helvetica bold, a level-1 heading, and the title of the page.

For example, in HTML a song might be described using a definition title, definition data, an unordered list, and list items. But none of these elements actually have anything to do with music. The HTML might look something like this:

```
<dt>Hot Cop
<dd> by Jacques Morali, Henri Belolo, and Victor Willis
<ul>
<li>Producer: Jacques Morali
<li>Publisher: PolyGram Records
<li>Length: 6:20
<li>Written: 1978
<li>Artist: Village People
</ul>
```

In XML the same data might be marked up like this:

```
<SONG>
    <TITLE>Hot Cop</TITLE>
    <COMPOSER>Jacques Morali</COMPOSER>
    <COMPOSER>Henri Belolo</COMPOSER>
    <COMPOSER>Victor Willis</COMPOSER>
    <PRODUCER>Jacques Morali</PRODUCER>
    <PUBLISHER>PolyGram Records</PUBLISHER>
    <LENGTH>6:20</LENGTH>
    <YEAR>1978</YEAR>
    <ARTIST>Village People</ARTIST>
</SONG>
```

Instead of generic tags like <dt> and <li>, this listing uses meaningful tags like <SONG>, <TITLE>, <COMPOSER>, and <YEAR>. This has a number of advantages, including that it's easier for a human to read the source code to determine what the author intended.

XML markup also makes it easier for non-human automated robots to locate all of the songs in the document. In HTML robots can't tell more than that an element is a dt. They cannot determine whether that dt represents a song title, a definition, or just some designer's favorite means of indenting text. In fact, a single document may well contain dt elements with all three meanings.

XML element names can be chosen such that they have extra meaning in additional contexts. For instance, they might be the field names of a database. XML is far more flexible and amenable to varied uses than HTML because a limited number of tags don't have to serve many different purposes.

Why Are Developers Excited about XML?

XML makes easy many Web-development tasks that are extremely painful using only HTML, and it makes tasks that are impossible with HTML, possible. Because XML is eXtensible, developers like it for many reasons. Which ones most interest you depend on your individual needs. But once you learn XML, you're likely to discover that it's the solution to more than one problem you're already struggling with. This section investigates some of the generic uses of XML that excite developers. In Chapter 2, you'll see some of the specific applications that have already been developed with XML.

Design of Domain-Specific Markup Languages

XML allows various professions (e.g., music, chemistry, math) to develop their own domain-specific markup languages. This allows individuals in the field to trade notes, data, and information without worrying about whether or not the person on the receiving end has the particular proprietary payware that was used to create the data. They can even send documents to people outside the profession with a reasonable confidence that the people who receive them will at least be able to view the documents.

Furthermore, the creation of markup languages for individual domains does not lead to bloatware or unnecessary complexity for those outside the profession. You may not be interested in electrical engineering diagrams, but electrical engineers are. You may not need to include sheet music in your Web pages, but composers do. XML lets the electrical engineers describe their circuits and the composers notate their scores, mostly without stepping on each other's toes. Neither field will need special support from the browser manufacturers or complicated plug-ins, as is true today.

Self-Describing Data

Much computer data from the last 40 years is lost, not because of natural disaster or decaying backup media (though those are problems too, ones XML doesn't solve), but simply because no one bothered to document how one actually reads the data media and formats. A Lotus 1-2-3 file on a 10-year old 5.25-inch floppy disk may be irretrievable in most corporations today without a huge investment of time and resources. Data in a less-known binary format like Lotus Jazz may be gone forever.

XML is, at a basic level, an incredibly simple data format. It can be written in 100 percent pure ASCII text as well as in a few other well-defined formats. ASCII text is reasonably resistant to corruption. The removal of bytes or even large sequences of bytes does not noticeably corrupt the remaining text. This starkly contrasts with many other formats, such as compressed data or serialized Java objects where the corruption or loss of even a single byte can render the entire remainder of the file unreadable.

At a higher level, XML is self-describing. Suppose you're an information archaeologist in the 23rd century and you encounter this chunk of XML code on an old floppy disk that has survived the ravages of time:

```
<PERSON ID="p1100" SEX="M">
  <NAME>
    <GIVEN>Judson</GIVEN>
    <SURNAME> McDaniel</SURNAME>
  </NAME>
  <BIRTH>
    <DATE>21 Feb 1834</DATE>   </BIRTH>
  <DEATH>
    <DATE>9 Dec 1905</DATE>   </DEATH>
</PERSON>
```

Even if you're not familiar with XML, assuming you speak a reasonable facsimile of 20th century English, you've got a pretty good idea that this fragment describes a man named Judson McDaniel, who was born on February 21, 1834 and died on December 9, 1905. In fact, even with gaps in, or corruption of the data, you could probably still extract most of this information. The same could not be said for some proprietary spreadsheet or word-processor format.

Furthermore, XML is very well documented. The W3C's XML 1.0 specification and numerous paper books like this one tell you exactly how to read XML data. There are no secrets waiting to trip up the unwary.

Interchange of Data Among Applications

Since XML is non-proprietary and easy to read and write, it's an excellent format for the interchange of data among different applications. One such format under current development is the Open Financial Exchange Format (OFX). OFX is designed to let personal finance programs like Microsoft Money and Quicken trade data. The data can be sent back and forth between programs and exchanged with banks, brokerage houses, and the like.

Cross-Reference   OFX is discussed in Chapter 2.

As noted above, XML is a non-proprietary format, not encumbered by copyright, patent, trade secret, or any other sort of intellectual property restriction. It has been designed to be extremely powerful, while at the same time being easy for both human beings and computer programs to read and write. Thus it's an obvious choice for exchange languages.

By using XML instead of a proprietary data format, you can use any tool that understands XML to work with your data. You can even use different tools for different purposes, one program to view and another to edit for instance. XML keeps you from getting locked into a particular program simply because that's what your data is already written in, or because that program's proprietary format is all your correspondent can accept.

For example, many publishers require submissions in Microsoft Word. This means that most authors have to use Word, even if they would rather use WordPerfect or Nisus Writer. So it's extremely difficult for any other company to publish a competing word processor unless they can read and write Word files. Since doing so requires a developer to reverse-engineer the undocumented Word file format, it's a significant investment of limited time and resources. Most other word processors have a limited ability to read and write Word files, but they generally lose track of graphics, macros, styles, revision marks, and other important features. The problem is that Word's document format is undocumented, proprietary, and constantly changing. Word tends to end up winning by default, even when writers would prefer to use other, simpler programs. If a common word-processing format were developed in XML, writers could use the program of their choice.

Structured and Integrated Data

XML is ideal for large and complex documents because the data is structured. It not only lets you specify a vocabulary that defines the elements in the document; it also lets you specify the relations between elements. For example, if you're putting together a Web page of sales contacts, you can require that every contact have a phone number and an email address. If you're inputting data for a database, you can make sure that no fields are missing. You can require that every book have an author. You can even provide default values to be used when no data is entered.

XML also provides a client-side include mechanism that integrates data from multiple sources and displays it as a single document. The data can even be rearranged on the fly. Parts of it can be shown or hidden depending on user actions. This is extremely useful when you're working with large information repositories like relational databases.

The Life of an XML Document

XML is, at the root, a document format. It is a series of rules about what XML documents look like. There are two levels of conformity to the XML standard. The first is *well-formedness* and the second is validity. Part I of this book shows you how to write well-formed documents. Part II shows you how to write valid documents.

HTML is a document format designed for use on the Internet and inside Web browsers. XML can certainly be used for that, as this book demonstrates. However, XML is far more broadly applicable. As previously discussed, it can be used as a storage format for word processors, as a data interchange format for different programs, as a means of enforcing conformity with Intranet templates, and as a way to preserve data in a human-readable fashion.

However, like all data formats, XML needs programs and content before it's useful. So it isn't enough to only understand XML itself which is little more than a specification for what data should look like. You also need to know how XML documents are edited, how processors read XML documents and pass the information they read on to applications, and what these applications do with that data.

Editors

XML documents are most commonly created with an editor. This may be a basic text editor like Notepad or vi that doesn't really understand XML at all. On the other hand, it may be a completely WYSIWYG editor like Adobe FrameMaker that insulates you almost completely from the details of the underlying XML format. Or it may be a structured editor like JUMBO that displays XML documents as trees. For the most part, the fancy editors aren't very useful yet, so this book concentrates on writing raw XML by hand in a text editor.

Other programs can also create XML documents. For example, later in this book, in the chapter on designing a new DTD, you'll see some XML data that came straight out of a FileMaker database. In this case, the data was first entered into the FileMaker database. Then a FileMaker calculation field converted that data to XML. In general, XML works extremely well with databases.

 Cross-Reference Specifically, you'll see this in Chapter 23, *Designing a New XML Application.*

In any case, the editor or other program creates an XML document. More often than not this document is an actual file on some computer's hard disk, but it doesn't absolutely have to be. For example, the document may be a record or a field in a database, or it may be a stream of bytes received from a network.

Parsers and Processors

An XML parser (also known as an XML processor) reads the document and verifies that the XML it contains is well formed. It may also check that the document is valid, though this test is not required. The exact details of these tests will be covered in Part II. But assuming the document passes the tests, the processor converts the document into a tree of elements.

Browsers and Other Tools

Finally the parser passes the tree or individual nodes of the tree to the end application. This application may be a browser like Mozilla or some other program that understands what to do with the data. If it's a browser, the data will be displayed to the user. But other programs may also receive the data. For instance, the data might be interpreted as input to a database, a series of musical notes to play, or a Java program that should be launched. XML is extremely flex-ible and can be used for many different purposes.

The Process Summarized

To summarize, an XML document is created in an editor. The XML parser reads the document and converts it into a tree of elements. The parser passes the tree to the browser that displays it. Figure 1-1 shows this process.

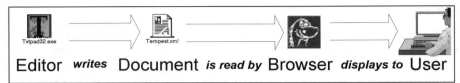

Editor *writes* Document *is read by* Browser *displays to* User

Figure 1-1: XML Document Life Cycle

It's important to note that all of these pieces are independent and decoupled from each other. The only thing that connects them all is the XML document. You can change the editor program independently of the end application. In fact you may not always know what the end application is. It may be an end user reading your work, or it may be a database sucking in data, or it may even be something that hasn't been invented yet. It may even be all of these. The document is independent of the programs that read it.

Note   HTML is also somewhat independent of the programs that read and write it, but it's really only suitable for browsing. Other uses, like database input, are outside its scope. For example, HTML does not provide a way to force an author to include certain required content, like requiring that every book have an ISBN number. In XML you *can* require this. You can even enforce the order in which particular elements appear (for example, that level-2 headers must always follow level-1 headers).

Related Technologies

XML doesn't operate in a vacuum. Using XML as more than a data format requires interaction with a number of related technologies. These technologies include HTML for backward compatibility with legacy browsers, the CSS and XSL stylesheet languages, URLs and URIs, the XLL linking language, and the Unicode character set.

Hypertext Markup Language

Mozilla 5.0 and Internet Explorer 5.0 are the first Web browsers to provide some (albeit incomplete) support for XML, but it takes about two years before most users have upgraded to a particular release of the software. (In 1999, my wife Beth is still using Netscape 1.1.) So you're going to need to convert your XML content into classic HTML for some time to come.

Therefore, before you jump into XML, you should be completely comfortable with HTML. You don't need to be an absolutely snazzy graphical designer, but you should know how to link from one page to the next, how to include an image in a document, how to make text bold, and so forth. Since HTML is the most common output format of XML, the more familiar you are with HTML, the easier it will be to create the effects you want.

On the other hand, if you're accustomed to using tables or single-pixel GIFs to arrange objects on a page, or if you start to make a Web site by sketching out its appearance rather than its content, then you're going to have to unlearn some bad habits. As previously discussed, XML separates the content of a document from the appearance of the document. The content is developed first; then a format is attached to that content with a style sheet. Separating content from style is an extremely effective technique that improves both the content and the appearance of the document. Among other things, it allows authors and designers to work more independently of each other. However, it does require a different way of thinking about the design of a Web site, and perhaps even the use of different project-management techniques when multiple people are involved.

Cascading Style Sheets

Since XML allows arbitrary tags to be included in a document, there isn't any way for the browser to know in advance how each element should be displayed. When you send a document to a user you also need to send along a style sheet that tells the browser how to format individual elements. One kind of style sheet you can use is a Cascading Style Sheet (CSS).

CSS, initially designed for HTML, defines formatting properties like font size, font family, font weight, paragraph indentation, paragraph alignment, and other styles that can be applied to particular elements. For example, CSS allows HTML documents to specify that all H1 elements should be formatted in 32 point cent-ered Helvetica bold. Individual styles can be applied to most HTML tags that override the browser's defaults. Multiple style sheets can be applied to a single document, and multiple styles can be applied to a single element. The styles then cascade according to a particular set of rules.

Cross-Reference

CSS rules and properties are explored in more detail in Chapter 12, *Cascading Style Sheets Level 1*, and Chapter 13, *Cascading Style Sheets Level 2*.

It's easy to apply CSS rules to XML documents. You simply change the names of the tags you're applying the rules to. Mozilla 5.0 directly supports CSS style sheets combined with XML documents, though at present, it crashes rather too frequently.

Extensible Style Language

The Extensible Style Language (XSL) is a more advanced style-sheet language specifically designed for use with XML documents. XSL documents are themselves well-formed XML documents.

XSL documents contain a series of rules that apply to particular patterns of XML elements. An XSL processor reads an XML document and compares what it sees to the patterns in a style sheet. When a pattern from the XSL style sheet is recognized in the XML document, the rule outputs some combination of text. Unlike cascading style sheets, this output text is somewhat arbitrary and is not limited to the input text plus formatting information.

CSS can only change the format of a particular element, and it can only do so on an element-wide basis. XSL style sheets, on the other hand, can rearrange and reorder elements. They can hide some elements and display others. Furthermore, they can choose the style to use not just based on the tag, but also on the contents and attributes of the tag, on the position of the tag in the document relative to other elements, and on a variety of other criteria.

CSS has the advantage of broader browser support. However, XSL is far more flexible and powerful, and better suited to XML documents. Furthermore, XML documents with XSL style sheets can be easily converted to HTML documents with CSS style sheets.

Cross-Reference XSL style sheets will be explored in great detail in Chapter 14, *XSL Transformations*, and Chapter 15, *XSL Formatting Objects*.

URLs and URIs

XML documents can live on the Web, just like HTML and other documents. When they do, they are referred to by Uniform Resource Locators (URLs), just like HTML files. For example, at the URL `http://www.hypermedic.com/style/xml/tempest.xml` you'll find the complete text of Shakespeare's *Tempest* marked up in XML.

Although URLs are well understood and well supported, the XML specification uses the more general Uniform Resource Identifier (URI). URIs are a more general architecture for locating resources on the Internet, that focus a little more on the resource and a little less on the location. In theory, a URI can find the closest copy of a mirrored document or locate a document that has been moved from one site to another. In practice, URIs are still an area of active research, and the only kinds of URIs that are actually supported by current software are URLs.

XLinks and XPointers

As long as XML documents are posted on the Internet, you're going to want to be able to address them and hot link between them. Standard HTML link tags can be used in XML documents, and HTML documents can link to XML documents. For example, this HTML link points to the aforementioned copy of the *Tempest* rendered in XML:

```
<a href="http://www.hypermedic.com/style/xml/tempest.xml">
  The Tempest by Shakespeare
</a>
```

Whether the browser can display this document if you follow the link, depends on just how well the browser handles XML files. Most current browsers don't handle them very well.

However, XML lets you go further with XLinks for linking to documents and XPointers for addressing individual parts of a document.

XLinks enable any element to become a link, not just an A element. Furthermore, links can be bi-directional, multidirectional, or even point to multiple mirror sites from which the nearest is selected. XLinks use normal URLs to identify the site they're linking to.

XLinks are discussed in Chapter 16, *XLinks*.

XPointers enable links to point not just to a particular document at a particular location, but to a particular part of a particular document. An XPointer can refer to a particular element of a document, to the first, the second, or the 17th such element, to the first element that's a child of a given element, and so on. XPointers provide extremely powerful connections between documents that do not require the targeted document to contain additional markup just so its individual pieces can be linked to it.

Furthermore, unlike HTML anchors, XPointers don't just refer to a point in a document. They can point to ranges or spans. Thus an XPointer might be used to select a particular part of a document, perhaps so that it can be copied or loaded into a program.

XPointers are discussed in Chapter 17, *XPointers*.

The Unicode Character Set

The Web is international, yet most of the text you'll find on it is in English. XML is starting to change that. XML provides full support for the two-byte Unicode character set, as well as its more compact representations. This character set supports almost every character commonly used in every modern script on Earth.

Unfortunately, XML alone is not enough. To read a script you need three things:

1. A character set for the script
2. A font for the character set
3. An operating system and application software that understands the character set

If you want to write in the script as well as read it, you'll also need an input method for the script. However, XML defines character references that allow you to use pure ASCII to encode characters not available in your native character set. This is sufficient for an occasional quote in Greek or Chinese, though you wouldn't want to rely on it to write a novel in another language.

Cross-Reference
In Chapter 7, *Foreign Languages and non-Roman Text*, you'll explore how international text is represented in computers, how XML understands text, and how you can use the software you have to read and write in languages other than English.

How the Technologies Fit Together

XML defines a grammar for tags you can use to mark up a document. An XML document is marked up with XML tags. The default encoding for XML documents is Unicode.

Among other things, an XML document may contain hypertext links to other documents and resources. These links are created according to the XLink specification. XLinks identify the documents they're linking to with URIs (in theory) or URLs (in practice). An XLink may further specify the individual part of a document it's linking to. These parts are addressed via XPointers.

If an XML document is intended to be read by human beings — and not all XML documents are — then a style sheet provides instructions about how individual elements are formatted. The style sheet may be written in any of several style-sheet languages. CSS and XSL are the two most popular style-sheet languages, though there are others including DSSSL — the Document Style Semantics and Specification Language — on which XSL is based.

Caution I've outlined a lot of exciting stuff in this chapter. However, honesty compels me to tell you that I haven't discussed all of it yet. In fact, much of what I've described is the promise of XML rather than the current reality. XML has a lot of people in the software industry very excited, and a lot of programmers are working very hard to turn these dreams into reality. New software is released every day that brings us closer to XML nirvana, but this is all very new, and some of the software isn't fully cooked yet. Throughout the rest of this book, I'll be careful to point out not only what is supposed to happen, but what actually does happen. Depressingly these are all too often not the same thing. Nonetheless with a little caution you can do real work right now with XML.

Summary

In this chapter, you have learned some of the things that XML can do for you. In particular, you have learned:

- ✦ XML is a meta-markup language that enables the creation of markup languages for particular documents and domains.

- ✦ XML tags describe the structure and semantics of a document's content, not the format of the content. The format is described in a separate style sheet.

- ✦ XML grew out of many users' frustration with the complexity of SGML and the inadequacies of HTML.

- ✦ XML documents are created in an editor, read by a parser, and displayed by a browser.

- ✦ XML on the Web rests on the foundations provided by HTML, Cascading Style Sheets, and URLs.

- ✦ Numerous supporting technologies layer on top of XML, including XSL style sheets, XLinks, and XPointers. These let you do more than you can accomplish with just CSS and URLs.

- ✦ Be careful. XML isn't completely finished. It will change and expand, and you will encounter bugs in current XML software.

In the next chapter, you'll see a number of XML applications, and learn about some ways XML is being used in the real world today. Examples include vector graphics, music notation, mathematics, chemistry, human resources, Webcasting, and more.

✦　　✦　　✦

An Introduction to XML Applications

In this chapter we'll be looking at some examples of XML applications, markup languages used to further refine XML, and behind-the-scene uses of XML. It is inspiring to look at some of the uses to which XML has already been put, even in this early stage of its development. This chapter will give you some idea of the wide applicability of XML. Many more XML applications are being created or ported from other formats as I write this.

Cross-Reference Part V covers some of the XML applications discussed in this chapter in more detail.

What Is an XML Application?

XML is a meta-markup language for designing domain-specific markup languages. Each XML-based markup language is called an XML application. This is not an application that uses XML like the Mozilla Web browser, the Gnumeric spreadsheet, or the XML Pro editor, but rather an application of XML to a specific domain such as Chemical Markup Language (CML) for chemistry or GedML for genealogy.

Each XML application has its own syntax and vocabulary. This syntax and vocabulary adheres to the fundamental rules of XML. This is much like human languages, which each have their own vocabulary and grammar, while at the same time adhering to certain fundamental rules imposed by human anatomy and the structure of the brain.

XML is an extremely flexible format for text-based data. The reason XML was chosen as the foundation for the wildly different applications discussed in this chapter (aside from the hype factor) is that XML provides a sensible, well-documented format that's easy to read and write. By using this format for its data, a program can offload a great quantity of detailed processing to a few standard free tools and libraries. Furthermore, it's easy for such a program to layer additional levels of syntax and semantics on top of the basic structure XML provides.

Chemical Markup Language

Peter Murray-Rust's Chemical Markup Language (CML) may have been the first XML application. CML was originally developed as an SGML application, and gradually transitioned to XML as the XML standard developed. In its most simplistic form, CML is "HTML plus molecules", but it has applications far beyond the limited confines of the Web.

Molecular documents often contain thousands of different, very detailed objects. For example, a single medium-sized organic molecule may contain hundreds of atoms, each with several bonds. CML seeks to organize these complex chemical objects in a straightforward manner that can be understood, displayed, and searched by a computer. CML can be used for molecular structures and sequences, spectrographic analysis, crystallography, publishing, chemical databases, and more. Its vocabulary includes molecules, atoms, bonds, crystals, formulas, sequences, symmetries, reactions, and other chemistry terms. For instance Listing 2-1 is a basic CML document for water (H_2O):

Listing 2-1: **The water molecule H_2O**

```
<?xml version="1.0"?>
<CML>
  <MOL TITLE="Water">
    <ATOMS>
      <ARRAY BUILTIN="ELSYM">H O H</ARRAY>
    </ATOMS>
    <BONDS>
      <ARRAY BUILTIN="ATID1">1 2</ARRAY>
      <ARRAY BUILTIN="ATID2">2 3</ARRAY>
      <ARRAY BUILTIN="ORDER">1 1</ARRAY>
    </BONDS>
  </MOL>
</CML>
```

The biggest improvement CML offers over traditional approaches to managing chemical data is ease of searching. CML also enables complex molecular data to be sent over the Web. Because the underlying XML is platform-independent, the problem of platform-dependency that plagues the binary formats used by traditional chemical software and documents like the Protein Data Bank (PDB) format or MDL Molfiles, is avoided.

Murray-Rust also created Jumbo, the first general-purpose XML browser. Figure 2-1 shows Jumbo displaying a CML file. Jumbo works by assigning each XML element to a Java class that knows how to render that element. To allow Jumbo to support new elements, you simply write Java classes for those elements. Jumbo is distributed with classes for displaying the basic set of CML elements including molecules, atoms, and bonds, and is available at `http://www.xml-cml.org/`.

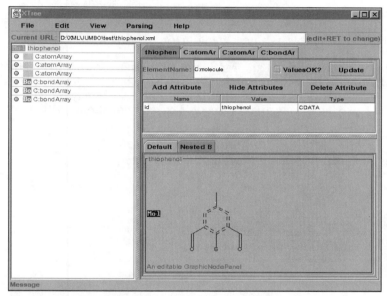

Figure 2-1: The Jumbo browser displaying a CML file

Mathematical Markup Language

Legend claims that Tim Berners-Lee invented the World Wide Web and HTML at CERN so that high-energy physicists could exchange papers and preprints. Personally I've never believed that. I grew up in physics; and while I've wandered back and forth between physics, applied math, astronomy, and computer science over the years, one thing the papers in all of these disciplines had in common was lots and lots of equations. Until now, nine years after the Web was invented, there hasn't been any good way to include equations in Web pages.

There have been a few hacks — Java applets that parse a custom syntax, converters that turn LaTeX equations into GIF images, custom browsers that read TeX files — but none of these have produced high quality results, and none of them have caught on with Web authors, even in scientific fields. Finally, XML is starting to change this.

The Mathematical Markup Language (MathML) is an XML application for mathematical equations. MathML is sufficiently expressive to handle pretty much all forms of math — from grammar-school arithmetic through calculus and differential equations. It can handle many considerably more advanced topics as well, though there are definite gaps in some of the more advanced and obscure notations used by certain sub-fields of mathematics. While there are limits to MathML on the high end of pure mathematics and theoretical physics, it is eloquent enough to handle almost all educational, scientific, engineering, business, economics, and statistics needs. And MathML is likely to be expanded in the future, so even the purest of the pure mathematicians and the most theoretical of the theoretical physicists will be able to publish and do research on the Web. MathML completes the development of the Web into a serious tool for scientific research and communication (despite its long digression to make it suitable as a new medium for advertising brochures).

Netscape Navigator and Internet Explorer do not yet support MathML. Nonetheless, it is the fervent hope of many mathematicians that they soon will. The W3C has integrated some MathML support into their test-bed browser, Amaya. Figure 2-2 shows Amaya displaying the covariant form of Maxwell's equations written in MathML.

On the CD-ROM   Amaya is on the CD-ROM in the browsers/amaya directory.

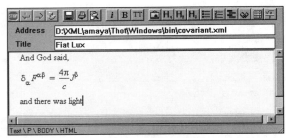

Figure 2-2: The Amaya browser displaying the covariant form of Maxwell's equations written in MathML

The XML file the Amaya browser is displaying is given in Listing 2-2:

Listing 2-2: **Maxwell's Equations in MathML**

```
<?xml version="1.0"?>
<html xmlns="http://www.w3.org/TR/REC-html40"
      xmlns:m="http://www.w3.org/TR/REC-MathML/"
  >
```

```
<head>
<title>Fiat Lux</title>
<meta name="GENERATOR" content="amaya V1.3b" />
</head>
<body>

<P>
And God said,
</P>

<math>
  <m:mrow>
    <m:msub>
      <m:mi>&delta;</m:mi>
      <m:mi>&alpha;</m:mi>
    </m:msub>
    <m:msup>
      <m:mi>F</m:mi>
      <m:mi>&alpha;&beta;</m:mi>
    </m:msup>
    <m:mi></m:mi>
    <m:mo>=</m:mo>
    <m:mi></m:mi>
    <m:mfrac>
      <m:mrow>
        <m:mn>4</m:mn>
        <m:mi>&pi;</m:mi>
      </m:mrow>
      <m:mi>c</m:mi>
    </m:mfrac>
    <m:mi></m:mi>
    <m:msup>
      <m:mi>J</m:mi>
      <m:mrow>
        <m:mi>&beta;</m:mi>
        <m:mo></m:mo>
      </m:mrow>
    </m:msup>
  </m:mrow>
</math>

<P>
and there was light
</P>
</body>
</html>
```

Listing 2-2 is an example of a mixed HTML/XML page. The headers and paragraphs of text ("Fiat Lux", "Maxwell's Equations", "And God said", "and there was light") given in classic HTML. The actual equations are written in MathML, an application of XML.

In general, such mixed pages require special support from the browser, as is the case here, or perhaps plug-ins, ActiveX controls, or JavaScript programs that parse and display the embedded XML data. Ultimately, of course, you want a browser like Mozilla 5.0 or Internet Explorer 5.0 that can parse and display pure XML files without an HTML intermediary.

Channel Definition Format

Microsoft's Channel Definition Format (CDF) is an XML application for defining channels. Web sites use channels to upload information to readers who subscribe to the site rather than waiting for them to come and get it. This is alternately called *Webcasting* or *push*. CDF was first introduced in Internet Explorer 4.0.

A CDF document is an XML file, separate from, but linked to an HTML document on the site being pushed. The channel defined in the CDF document determines which pages are sent to the readers, how the pages are transported, and how often the pages are sent. Pages can either be pushed by sending notifications, or even whole Web sites, to subscribers; or pulled down by the readers at their convenience.

You can add CDF to your site without changing any of the existing content. You simply add an invisible link to a CDF file on your home page. Then when a reader visits the page, the browser displays a dialog box asking them if they want to subscribe to the channel. If the reader chooses to subscribe, the browser downloads a copy of the CDF document describing the channel. The browser then combines the parameters specified in the CDF document with the user's own preferences to determine when to check back with the server for new content. This isn't true push, because the client has to initiate the connection, but it still happens without an explicit request by the reader. Figure 2-3 shows the IDG Active Channel in Internet Explorer 4.0.

CDF is covered in more detail in Chapter 21, *Pushing Web Sites with CDF*.

Internet Explorer 4.0 is on the CD-ROM in the browsers/ie4 directory.

Classic Literature

Jon Bosak has translated the complete plays of Shakespeare into XML. The complete text of the plays is included, and XML markup is used to distinguish between titles, subtitles, stage directions, speeches, lines, speakers, and more.

The complete set of plays is on the CD-ROM in the examples/shakespeare directory.

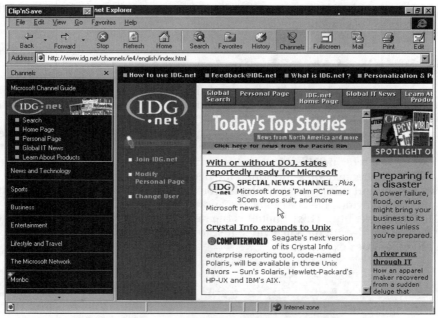

Figure 2-3: The IDG Active Channel in Internet Explorer 4.0

You may ask yourself what this offers over a book, or even a plain text file. To a human reader, the answer is not much. But to a computer doing textual analysis, it offers the opportunity to easily distinguish between the different elements into which the plays have been divided. For instance, it makes it quite simple for the computer to go through the text and extract all of Romeo's lines.

Furthermore, by altering the style sheet with which the document is formatted, an actor could easily print a version of the document in which all their lines were formatted in bold face, and the lines immediately before and after theirs were italicized. Anything else you might imagine that requires separating a play into the lines uttered by different speakers is much more easily accomplished with the XML-formatted versions than with the raw text.

Bosak has also marked up English translations of the old and new testaments, the Koran, and the Book of Mormon in XML. The markup in these is a little different. For instance, it doesn't distinguish between speakers. Thus you couldn't use these particular XML documents to create a red-letter Bible, for example, although a different set of tags might allow you to do that. (A red-letter Bible prints words spoken by Jesus in red.) And because these files are in English rather than the original languages, they are not as useful for scholarly textual analysis. Still, time and resources permitting, those are exactly the sorts of things XML would allow you to do if you wanted to. You'd simply need to invent a different vocabulary and syntax than the one Bosak used that would still describe the same data.

On the CD-ROM The XML-ized Bible, Koran, and Book of Mormon are all on the CD-ROM in the examples/religion directory.

Synchronized Multimedia Integration Language

The Synchronized Multimedia Integration Language (SMIL, pronounced "smile") is a W3C recommended XML application for writing "TV-like" multimedia presentations for the Web. SMIL documents don't describe the actual multimedia content (that is the video and sound that are played) but rather when and where they are played.

For instance, a typical SMIL document for a film festival might say that the browser should simultaneously play the sound file beethoven9.mid, show the video file corange.mov, and display the HTML file clockwork.htm. Then, when it's done, it should play the video file 2001.mov, the audio file zarathustra.mid, and display the HTML file aclarke.htm. This eliminates the need to embed low bandwidth data like text in high bandwidth data like video just to combine them. Listing 2-3 is a simple SMIL file that does exactly this.

Listing 2-3: A SMIL film festival

```
<?xml version="1.0" encoding="ISO-8859-1"?>
<!DOCTYPE smil PUBLIC "-//W3C//DTD SMIL 1.0//EN"
  "http://www.w3.org/TR/REC-smil/SMIL10.dtd">
<smil>
  <body>
    <seq id="Kubrick">
      <audio src="beethoven9.mid"/>
      <video src="corange.mov"/>
      <text src="clockwork.htm"/>
      <audio src="zarathustra.mid"/>
      <video src="2001.mov"/>
      <text src="aclarke.htm"/>
    </seq>
  </body>
</smil>
```

Furthermore, as well as specifying the time sequencing of data, a SMIL document can position individual graphics elements on the display and attach links to media objects. For instance, at the same time the movie and sound are playing, the text of the respective novels could be subtitling the presentation.

HTML+TIME

SMIL operates independently of the Web page. The streaming media pushed through SMIL has its own pane in the browser frame, but it doesn't really have any interaction with the content in the HTML on the rest of the page. For instance, SMIL only lets you time SMIL elements like audio, video, and text. It doesn't let you add timing information to basic HTML tags like <P>, <LI>, or <IMG>. And SMIL duplicates some aspects of HTML, such as how elements are positioned on the page.

Microsoft, along with Macromedia and Compaq, has proposed a semi-competing XML application called Timed Interactive Multimedia Extensions for HTML (or HTML+TIME for short). HTML+TIME builds on SMIL to support timing for traditional HTML elements and features much closer integration with the HTML on the Web page. For example, HTML+TIME lets you write a countdown Web page like Listing 2-4 that adds to the page as time progresses.

Listing 2-4: A countdown Web page using HTML+TIME

```
<html>
  <head><title>Countdown</title></head>
  <body>
    <p t:begin="0" t:dur="1">10</p>
    <p t:begin="1" t:dur="1">9</p>
    <p t:begin="2" t:dur="1">8</p>
    <p t:begin="3" t:dur="1">7</p>
    <p t:begin="4" t:dur="1">6</p>
    <p t:begin="5" t:dur="1">5</p>
    <p t:begin="6" t:dur="1">4</p>
    <p t:begin="7" t:dur="1">3</p>
    <p t:begin="8" t:dur="1">2</p>
    <p t:begin="9" t:dur="1">1</p>
    <p t:begin="10" t:dur="1">Blast Off!</p>
  </body>
</html>
```

This is useful for slide shows, timed quizzes, and the like. In HTML+TIME, the film festival example of Listing 2-3 looks like the following:

```
<t:seq id="Kubrick">
  <t:audio src="beethoven9.mid"/>
  <t:video src="corange.mov"/>
  <t:textstream src="clockwork.htm"/>
  <t:audio src="zarathustra.mid"/>
  <t:video src="2001.mov"/>
  <t:textstream src="aclarke.htm"/>
</seq>
```

It's close to, though not quite exactly the same as, the SMIL version. The major difference is that the SMIL version is intended to be stored in separate files and rendered by special players like RealPlayer, whereas the HTML+TIME version is supposed to be included in the Web page and rendered by the browser. Another key difference is that there are several products that can play SMIL files now, including RealPlayer G2, whereas HTML+TIME-enabled Web browsers do not exist at the moment. However, it's likely that future versions of Internet Explorer will include HTML+TIME support.

There are some nice features and some good ideas in HTML+TIME. However, the W3C had already given its blessing to SMIL several months before Microsoft proposed HTML+TIME, and SMIL has a lot more momentum and support in the third-party, content creator community. Thus it seems we're in for yet another knockdown, drag-out, Microsoft-vs.-everybody-else-in-the-known-universe battle which will only leave third party developers bruised and confused. One can only hope that the W3C has the will and energy to referee this fight fairly. Web development really would be a lot simpler if Microsoft didn't pick up its toys and go home every time they don't get their way.

Open Software Description

The Open Software Description (OSD) format is an XML application co-developed by Marimba and Microsoft for updating software automatically. OSD defines XML tags that describe software components. The description of a component includes the version of the component, its underlying structure, and its relationships to and dependencies on other components. This provides enough information for OSD to decide whether a user needs a particular update or not. If they do need the update, it can be automatically pushed to users, rather than requiring them to manually download and install it. Listing 2-5 is an example of an OSD file for an update to WhizzyWriter 1000:

Listing 2-5: An OSD file for an update to WhizzyWriter 1000

```
<?XML version="1.0"?>
<CHANNEL HREF="http://updates.whizzy.com/updateChannel.html">
  <TITLE>WhizzyWriter 1000 Update Channel</TITLE>
  <USAGE VALUE="SoftwareUpdate"/>
  <SOFTPKG HREF="http://updates.whizzy.com/updateChannel.html"
           NAME="{46181F7D-1C38-22A1-3329-00415C6A4D54}"
           VERSION="5,2,3,1"
           STYLE="MSAppLogo5"
           PRECACHE="yes">
    <TITLE>WhizzyWriter 1000</TITLE>
    <ABSTRACT>
      Abstract: WhizzyWriter 1000: now with tint control!
    </ABSTRACT>
```

```
  <IMPLEMENTATION>
   <CODEBASE HREF="http://updates.whizzy.com/tinupdate.exe"/>
  </IMPLEMENTATION>
 </SOFTPKG>
</CHANNEL>
```

Only information about the update is kept in the OSD file. The actual update files are stored in a separate CAB archive or executable and downloaded when needed. There is considerable controversy about whether or not this is actually a good thing. Many software companies, Microsoft not least among them, have a long history of releasing updates that cause more problems than they fix. Many users prefer to stay away from new software for a while until other, more adventurous souls have given it a shakedown.

Scalable Vector Graphics

Vector graphics are superior to the bitmap GIF and JPEG images currently used on the Web for many pictures including flow charts, cartoons, advertisements, and similar images. However, many traditional vector graphics formats like PDF, PostScript, and EPS were designed with ink on paper in mind rather than electrons on a screen. (This is one reason PDF on the Web is such an inferior replacement for HTML, despite PDF's much larger collection of graphics primitives.) A vector graphics format for the Web should support a lot of features that don't make sense on paper like transparency, anti-aliasing, additive color, hypertext, animation, and hooks to enable search engines and audio renderers to extract text from graphics. None of these features are needed for the ink-on-paper world of PostScript and PDF.

Several vendors have made a variety of proposals to the W3C for XML applications for vector graphics. These include:

- ✦ The Precision Graphics Markup Language (PGML) from IBM, Adobe, Netscape, and Sun.

- ✦ The Vector Markup Language (VML) from Microsoft, Macromedia, Autodesk, Hewlett-Packard, and Visio

- ✦ Schematic Graphics on the World Wide Web from the Central Laboratory of the Research Councils

- ✦ DrawML from Excosoft AB

- ✦ Hyper Graphics Markup Language (HGML) from PRP and Orange PCSL

Each of these reflects the interests and experience of its authors. For example, not surprisingly given Adobe's participation, PGML has the flavor of PostScript but with XML element-attribute syntax rather than PostScript's reverse Polish notation. Listing 2-6 demonstrates the embedding of a pink triangle in PGML.

Listing 2-6: **A pink triangle in PGML**

```
<?xml version="1.0"?>
<!DOCTYPE pgml SYSTEM "pgml.dtd">
<pgml>
  <group name="PinkTriangle" fillcolor="pink">
    <path>
      <moveto x="0" y="0"/>
      <lineto x="100" y="173"/>
      <lineto x="200" y="0"/>
      <closepath/>
    </path>
  </group>
</pgml>
```

The W3C has formed a working group with representatives from the above vendors to decide on a single, unified, scalable vector graphics specification called SVG. SVG is an XML application for describing two-dimensional graphics. It defines three basic types of graphics: shapes, images, and text. A shape is defined by its outline, also known as its path, and may have various strokes or fills. An image is a bitmapped file like a GIF or a JPEG. Text is defined as a string of text in a particular font, and may be attached to a path, so it's not restricted to horizontal lines of text like the ones that appear on this page. All three kinds of graphics can be positioned on the page at a particular location, rotated, scaled, skewed, and otherwise manipulated. Since SVG is a text format, it's easy for programs to generate automatically; and it's easy for programs to manipulate. In particular you can combine it with DHTML and ECMAScript to make the pictures on a Web page animated and responsive to user action.

Since SVG describes graphics rather than text — unlike most of the other XML applications discussed in this chapter — it will probably need special display software. All of the proposed style-sheet languages assume they're displaying fundamentally text-based data, and none of them can support the heavy graphics requirements of an application like SVG. It's possible SVG support may be added to future browsers, especially since Mozilla is open source code; and it would be even easier for a plug-in to be written. However, for the time being, the prime benefit of SVG is that it is likely to be used as an exchange format between different programs like Adobe Illustrator and CorelDraw, which use different native binary formats.

SVG is not fully fleshed out at the time of this writing, and there are exactly zero implementations of it. The first working draft of SVG was released by the World Wide Web Consortium in February of 1999. Compared to other working drafts, however, it is woefully incomplete. It's really not much more than an outline of graphics elements that need to be included, without any details about how exactly those elements will be encoded in XML. I wouldn't be surprised if this draft got pushed out the door a little early to head off the adoption of competing efforts like VML.

Vector Markup Language

Microsoft has developed their own XML application for vector graphics called the Vector Markup Language (VML). VML is more finished than SVG, and is already supported by Internet Explorer 5.0 and Microsoft Office 2000. Listing 2-7 is an HTML file with embedded VML that draws the pink triangle. Figure 2-4 shows this file displayed in Internet Explorer 5.0. However, VML is not nearly as ambitious a format as SVG, and leaves out a lot of advanced features SVG includes such as clipping, masking, and compositing.

Listing 2-7: The pink triangle in VML

```
<html xmlns:vml="urn:schemas-microsoft-com:vml">
  <head>
    <title>
      A Pink Triangle, Listing 2-7 from the XML Bible
    </title>
    <object id="VMLRender"
      classid="CLSID:10072CEC-8CC1-11D1-986E-00A0C955B42E">
    </object>
    <style>
      vml\:* { behavior: url(#VMLRender) }
    </style>
  </head>
  <body>


<div>

  <vml:polyline
    style="width: 200px; height: 200px"
    stroke="false"
    fill="true"
    fillcolor="#FFCCCC"
    points="10pt, 275pt, 310pt, 275pt, 160pt, 45pt">
  </vml:polyline>

</div>
</body>
</html>
```

There's really no reason for there to be two separate, mutually incompatible vector graphics standards for the Web, and Microsoft will probably grudgingly support SVG in the end. However, VML is available today, even if its use is limited to Microsoft products, whereas SVG is only an incomplete draft specification. Web artists would prefer to have a single standard, but having two is not unheard of (think GIF and JPEG). As long as the formats are documented and non-proprietary, it's not out of the question for Web browsers to support both. At the least, the underlying XML makes it a lot easier for programmers to write converters that translate files from one format to the other.

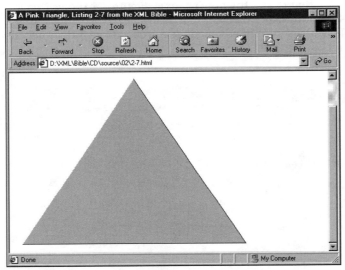

Figure 2-4: The pink triangle created with VML

VML is discussed in more detail in Chapter 22, *The Vector Markup Language.*

MusicML

The Connection Factory has created an XML application for sheet music called MusicML. MusicML includes notes, beats, clefs, staffs, rows, rhythms, rests, beams, rows, chords and more. Listing 2-8 shows the first bar from Beth Anderson's *Flute Swale* in MusicML.

Listing 2-8: **The first bar of Beth Anderson's *Flute Swale***

```
<?xml version="1.0"?>
<!DOCTYPE sheetmusic SYSTEM "music.dtd">
<sheetmusic>
 <musicrow size="one">

   <entrysegment>
```

```
      <entrypart cleff="bass" rythm="fourquarter"
               position="one">
       <molkruis level="plus1" name="f" notetype="sharp"/>
       <molkruis level="plus1" name="c" notetype="sharp"/>
      </entrypart>
    </entrysegment>

    <segment>

     <subsegment position="one">
       <beam size="double">
         <note beat="sixteenth" name="a" level="zero"
             dynamics="mf"/>
         <note beat="sixteenth" name="b" level="zero"></note>
         <note beat="sixteenth" name="c" level="plus1"></note>
         <note beat="sixteenth" name="a" level="zero"></note>
       </beam>
       <beam size="single">
         <note beat="eighth" name="d" level="plus1"/>
         <note beat="eighth" name="c" level="plus1"/>
       </beam>
       <note beat="quarter" name="b" level="zero"/>
       <note beat="quarter" name="a" level="zero"/>
     </subsegment>

    </segment>

   </musicrow>
  </sheetmusic>
```

The Connection Factory has also written a Java applet that can parse and display MusicML. Figure 2-5 shows the above example rendered by this applet. The applet has a few bugs (for instance the last note is missing) but overall it's a surprisingly good rendition.

Figure 2-5: The first bar of Beth Anderson's *Flute Swale* in MusicML

MusicML isn't going to replace Finale or Nightingale anytime soon. And it really seems like more of a proof of concept than a polished product. MusicML has a lot of discrepancies that will drive musicians nuts (e.g., rhythm is misspelled, treble and bass clefs are reversed, segments should really be measures, and so forth).

Nonetheless something like this is a reasonable output format for music notation programs that enables sheet music to be displayed on the Web. Furthermore, if the various notation programs all support MusicML or something like it, then it can be used as an interchange format to move data from one program to the other, something composers desperately need to be able to do now.

VoxML

Motorola's VoxML (http://www.voxml.com/) is an XML application for the spoken word. In particular, it's intended for those annoying voice mail and automated phone response systems ("If your hair turned green after using our product, please press one. If your hair turned purple after using our product, please press two. If you found an unidentifiable insect in the product, please press 3. Otherwise, please stay on the line until your hair grows back to its natural color.").

VoxML enables the same data that's used on a Web site to be served up via telephone. It's particularly useful for information that's created by combining small nuggets of data, such as stock prices, sports scores, weather reports, and test results. The Weather Channel and CBS MarketWatch.com are considering using VoxML to provide more information over regular voice phones.

A small VoxML file for a shampoo company's automated phone response system might look something like the code in Listing 2-9.

Listing 2-9: **A VoxML file**

```
<?xml version="1.0"?>
<DIALOG>
  <CLASS NAME="help_top">
    <HELP>Welcome to TIC consumer products division.
          For shampoo information, say shampoo now.
    </HELP>
  </CLASS>

  <STEP NAME="init" PARENT="help_top">
    <PROMPT>Welcome to Wonder Shampoo
      <BREAK SIZE="large"/>
       Which color did Wonder Shampoo turn your hair?
    </PROMPT>
    <INPUT TYPE="OPTIONLIST">
      <OPTION NEXT="#green">green</OPTION>
      <OPTION NEXT="#purple">purple</OPTION>
      <OPTION NEXT="#bald">bald</OPTION>
      <OPTION NEXT="#bye">exit</OPTION>
    </INPUT>
  </STEP>
```

```
<STEP NAME="green" PARENT="help_top">
  <PROMPT>
    If Wonder Shampoo turned your hair green and you wish
    to return it to its natural color, simply shampoo seven
    times with three parts soap, seven parts water, four
    parts kerosene, and two parts iguana bile.
  </PROMPT>
  <INPUT TYPE="NONE" NEXT="#bye"/>
</STEP>

<STEP NAME="purple" PARENT="help_top">
  <PROMPT>
    If Wonder Shampoo turned your hair purple and you wish
    to return it to its natural color, please walk
    widdershins around your local cemetery
      three times while chanting "Surrender Dorothy".

  </PROMPT>
  <INPUT TYPE="NONE" NEXT="#bye"/>
</STEP>

<STEP NAME="bald" PARENT="help_top">
  <PROMPT>
    If you went bald as a result of using Wonder Shampoo,
    please purchase and apply a three months supply
    of our Magic Hair Growth Formula(TM). Please do not
    consult an attorney as doing so would violate the
    license agreement printed on inside fold of the Wonder
    Shampoo box in 3 point type which you agreed to
    by opening the package.
  </PROMPT>
  <INPUT TYPE="NONE" NEXT="#bye"/>
</STEP>

<STEP NAME="bye" PARENT="help_top">
  <PROMPT>
  Thank you for visiting TIC Corp. Goodbye.
  </PROMPT>
  <INPUT TYPE="NONE" NEXT="#exit"/>
</STEP>

</DIALOG>
```

I can't show you a screen shot of this example, because it's not intended to be shown in a Web browser. Instead, you would listen to it on a telephone.

Open Financial Exchange

Software cannot be changed willy-nilly. The data that software knows how to read has inertia. The more data you have in a given program's proprietary, undocumented format, the harder it is to change programs. For example, my personal finances for the last five years are stored in Quicken. How likely is it that I will change to Microsoft Money even if Money has features I need that Quicken doesn't have? Unless Money can read and convert Quicken files with zero loss of data, the answer is "NOT BLOODY LIKELY!"

The problem can even occur within a single company or a single company's products. Microsoft Word 97 for Windows can't read documents created by some earlier versions of Word. And earlier versions of Word can't read Word 97 files at all. And Microsoft Word 98 for the Mac can't quite read everything that's in a Word 97 for Windows file, even though Word 98 for the Mac came out a year later!

As noted in Chapter 1, the Open Financial Exchange Format (OFX) is an XML application used to describe financial data of the type you're likely to store in a personal finance product like Money or Quicken. Any program that understands OFX can read OFX data. And since OFX is fully documented and non-proprietary (unlike the binary formats of Money, Quicken, and other programs) it's easy for programmers to write the code to understand OFX.

OFX not only allows Money and Quicken to exchange data with each other. It allows other programs that use the same format to exchange the data as well. For instance, if a bank wants to deliver statements to customers electronically, it only has to write one program to encode the statements in the OFX format rather than several programs to encode the statement in Quicken's format, Money's format, Managing Your Money's format, and so forth.

The more programs that use a given format, the greater the savings in development cost and effort. For example, six programs reading and writing their own and each other's proprietary format require 36 different converters. Six programs reading and writing the same OFX format require only six converters. Effort is reduced to $O(n)$ rather than $O(n^2)$. Figure 2-6 depicts six programs reading and writing their own and each other's proprietary format. Figure 2-7 depicts six programs reading and writing the same OFX format. Every arrow represents a converter that has to trade files and data between programs. In Figure 2-6, you can see the connections for six different programs reading and writing each other's proprietary binary format. In Figure 2-7, you can see the same six different programs reading and writing one open XML format. The XML-based exchange is much simpler and cleaner than the binary-format exchange.

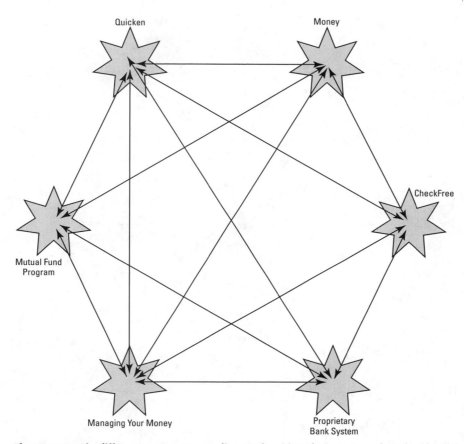

Figure 2-6: Six different programs reading and writing their own and each other's formats

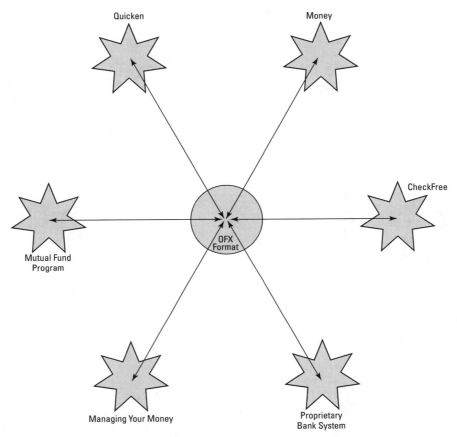

Figure 2-7: Six programs reading and writing the same OFX format

Extensible Forms Description Language

I went down to my local bookstore today and bought a copy of Armistead Maupin's novel *Sure of You*. I paid for that purchase with a credit card, and when I did so I signed a piece of paper agreeing to pay the credit card company $14.07 when billed. Eventually they will send me a bill for that purchase, and I'll pay it. If I refuse to pay it, then the credit card company can take me to court to collect, and they can use my signature on that piece of paper to prove to the court that on October 15, 1998 I really did agree to pay them $14.07.

The same day I also ordered Anne Rice's *The Vampire Armand* from the online bookstore amazon.com. Amazon charged me $16.17 plus $3.95 shipping and handling and again I paid for that purchase with a credit card. But the difference is that Amazon never got a signature on a piece of paper from me. Eventually the credit card company will send me a bill for that purchase, and I'll pay it. But if I did refuse to pay the bill, they don't have a piece of paper with my signature on it showing that I agreed to pay $20.12 on October 15, 1998. If I claim that I never made the purchase, the credit card company will bill the charges back to Amazon. Before Amazon or any other online or phone-order merchant is allowed to accept credit card purchases without a signature in ink on paper, they have to agree that they will take responsibility for all disputed transactions.

Exact numbers are hard to come by, and of course vary from merchant to merchant, but probably a little under 10% of Internet transactions get billed back to the originating merchant because of credit card fraud or disputes. This is a *huge* amount! Consumer businesses like Amazon simply accept this as a cost of doing business on the Net and work it into their price structure, but obviously this isn't going to work for six figure business-to-business transactions. Nobody wants to send out $200,000 of masonry supplies only to have the purchaser claim they never made or received the order. Before business-to-business transactions can move onto the Internet, a method needs to be developed that can verify that an order was in fact made by a particular person and that this person is who he or she claims to be. Furthermore, this has to be enforceable in court. (It's a sad fact of American business that many companies won't do business with anyone they can't sue.)

Part of the solution to the problem is digital signatures — the electronic equivalent of ink on paper. To digitally sign a document, you calculate a hash code for the document using a known algorithm, encrypt the hash code with your private key, and attach the encrypted hash code to the document. Correspondents can decrypt the hash code using your public key and verify that it matches the document. However, they can't sign documents on your behalf because they don't have your private key. The exact protocol followed is a little more complex in practice, but the bottom line is that your private key is merged with the data you're signing in a verifiable fashion. No one who doesn't know your private key can sign the document.

The scheme isn't foolproof — it's vulnerable to your private key being stolen, for example-but it's probably as hard to forge a digital signature as it is to forge a real ink-on-paper signature. However, there are also a number of less obvious attacks on digital signature protocols. One of the most important is changing the data that's signed. Changing the data that's signed should invalidate the signature, but it doesn't if the changed data wasn't included in the first place. For example, when you submit an HTML form, the only things sent are the values that you fill into the form's fields and the names of the fields. The rest of the HTML markup is not included. You may agree to pay $1500 for a new 450 MHz Pentium II PC running Windows NT, but the only thing sent on the form is the $1500. Signing this number signifies what you're paying, but not what you're paying for. The merchant can then send you two gross of flushometers and claim that's what you bought for your $1500. Obviously, if digital signatures are to be useful, all details of the transaction must be included. Nothing can be omitted.

The problem gets worse if you have to deal with the U.S. federal government. Government regulations for purchase orders and requisitions often spell out the contents of forms in minute detail, right down to the font face and type size. Failure to adhere to the exact specifications can lead to your invoice for $20,000,000 worth of depleted uranium artillery shells being rejected. Therefore, you not only need to establish exactly what was agreed to; you also need to establish that you met all legal requirements for the form. HTML's forms just aren't sophisticated enough to handle these needs.

XML, however, can. It is almost always possible to use XML to develop a markup language with the right combination of power and rigor to meet your needs, and this example is no exception. In particular UWI.COM has proposed an XML application called the Extensible Forms Description Language (XFDL) for forms with extremely tight legal requirements that are to be signed with digital signatures. XFDL further offers the option to do simple mathematics in the form, for instance to automatically fill in the sales tax and shipping and handling charges and total up the price.

UWI.COM has submitted XFDL to the W3C, but it's really overkill for Web browsers, and thus probably won't be adopted there. The real benefit of XFDL, if it becomes widely adopted, is in business-to-business and business-to-government transactions. XFDL can become a key part of electronic commerce, which is not to say it *will* become a key part of electronic commerce. It's still early, and there are other players in this space.

Human Resources Markup Language

HireScape's Human Resources Markup Language (HRML) is an XML application that provides a simple vocabulary for describing job openings. It defines elements matching the parts of a typical classified want ad such as companies, divisions, recruiters, contact information, terms, experience, and more. A job listing in HRML might look something like the code in Listing 2-10.

Listing 2-10: A Job Listing in HRML

```
<?xml version="1.0"?>
<HRML_JOB>

  <COMPANY>

    <CO_NAME>IDG Books</CO_NAME>
    <CO_INTERNET_ADDR>
      <CO_HOME_PAGE>http://www.idgbooks.com/</CO_HOME_PAGE>
      <CO_JOBS_PAGE>
        http://www.idgbooks.com/cgi-
bin/gatekeeper.pl?uidg4841:%2Fcompany%2Fjobs%2Findex.html
      </CO_JOBS_PAGE>
    </CO_INTERNET_ADDR>
```

```
</COMPANY>

  <JOB>

    <JOB_METADATA>
      <JOB_LOADED_DT>09/10/1998</JOB_LOADED_DT>
      <JOB_LOADED_URL>
        http://www.idgbooks.com/cgi-
bin/gatekeeper.pl?uidg4841:%2Fcompany%2Fjobs%2Findex.html
      </JOB_LOADED_URL>
    </JOB_METADATA>

    <JOB_DATA>

      <JOB_TITLE>Web Development Manager</JOB_TITLE>

      <JOB_NUMBER_AVAIL>1</JOB_NUMBER_AVAIL>
      <JOB_YEARS_EXP>3</JOB_YEARS_EXP>
      <JOB_DESC>
        This position is responsible for the technical
        and production functions of the Online
        group as well as strategizing and implementing
        technology to improve the IDG Books web sites.
        Skills must include Perl, C/C++, HTML, SQL, JavaScript,
        Windows NT 4, mod-perl, CGI, TCP/IP, Netscape servers
        and Apache server. You must also have excellent
        communication skills, project management, the ability
        to communicate technical solutions to non-technical
        people and management experience.
      </JOB_DESC>

      <JOB_KEYWORDS>
        Perl, C/C++, HTML, SQL, JavaScript, Windows NT 4,
        mod-perl, CGI, TCP/IP, Netscape server, Apache server
      </JOB_KEYWORDS>

      <JOB_TERMS PAY="Salaried" TYPE="Full-time">
        $60,000
      </JOB_TERMS>

      <JOB_LOCATION CITY="Foster City" STATE="California"
        STATE_ABBR="CA" POSTAL_CODE="94404" COUNTRY="USA">
      </JOB_LOCATION>

    </JOB_DATA>

  </JOB>

  <RESPONSE>

    <RESP_EMAIL>cajobs@idgbooks.com</RESP_EMAIL>
    <POSTAL_ADDR ENTITY_TYPE="Response">
```

Continued

Listing 2-10 *(continued)*

```
        <ADDR_LINE_1>Dee Harris, HR Manager</ADDR_LINE_1>
        <ADDR_LINE_2>919 E. Hillsdale Blvd.</ADDR_LINE_2>
        <ADDR_LINE_3>Suite 400</ADDR_LINE_3>
        <CITY>Foster City</CITY>
        <STATE>CA</STATE>
        <POSTAL_CODE>94404</POSTAL_CODE>
      </POSTAL_ADDR>

    </RESPONSE>

  </HRML_JOB>
```

Although you could certainly define a style sheet for HRML, and use it to place job listings on Web pages, that's not its main purpose. Instead HRML is designed to automate the exchange of job information between companies, applicants, recruiters, job boards, and other interested parties. There are hundreds of job boards on the Internet today as well as numerous Usenet newsgroups and mailing lists. It's impossible for one individual to search them all, and it's hard for a computer to search them all because they all use different formats for salaries, locations, benefits, and the like.

But if many sites adopt HRML, then it becomes relatively easy for a job seeker to search with criteria like "all the jobs for Java programmers in New York City paying more than $100,000 a year with full health benefits." The IRS could enter a search for all full-time, on-site, freelance openings so they'd know which companies to go after for failure to withhold tax and pay unemployment insurance.

In practice, these searches would likely be mediated through an HTML form just like current Web searches. The main difference is that such a search would return far more useful results because it can use the structure in the data and semantics of the markup rather than relying on imprecise English text.

Resource Description Framework

XML adds structure to documents. The Resource Description Framework (RDF) is an XML application that adds semantics. RDF can be used to specify anything from the author and abstract of a Web page to the version and dependencies of a software package to the director, screenwriter, and actors in a movie. What links all of these uses is that what's being encoded in RDF is not the data itself (the Web page, the software, the movie) but information about the data. This data about data is called *meta-data*, and is RDF's *raison d'être*.

An RDF vocabulary defines a set of elements and their permitted content that's appropriate for meta-data in a given domain. RDF enables communities of interest to standardize their vocabularies and share those vocabularies with others who may extend them. For example, the Dublin Core is an RDF vocabulary specifically designed for meta-data about Web pages. Educom's Instructional Metadata System (IMS) builds on the Dublin Core by adding additional elements that are useful when describing school-related content like learning level, educational objectives, and price.

Of course, although RDF can be used for print-publishing systems, video-store catalogs, automated software updates, and much more, it's likely to be adopted first for embedding meta-data in Web pages. RDF has the potential to synchronize the current hodge-podge of <META> tags used for site maps, content rating, automated indexing, and digital libraries into a unified collection that all of these tools understand. Once RDF meta-data becomes a standard part of Web pages, search engines will be able to return more focused, useful results. Intelligent agents can more easily traverse the Web to find information you want or conduct business for you. The Web can go from its current state as an unordered sea of information to a structured, searchable, understandable store of data.

As the name implies, RDF describes *resources*. A resource is anything that can be addressed with a URI. The description of a resource is composed of a number of properties. Each property has a type and a value. For example, <DC:Format>HTML</DC:Format> has the type "DC:Format" and the value "HTML". Values may be text strings, numbers, dates, and so forth, or they may be other resources. These other resources can have their own descriptions in RDF. For example, the code in Listing 2-11 uses the Dublin Core vocabulary to describe the Cafe con Leche Web site.

Listing 2-11: An RDF description of the Cafe con Leche home page using the Dublin Core vocabulary

```
<RDF:RDF
  xmlns:RDF="http://www.w3.org/1999/02/22-rdf-syntax-ns#"
  xmlns:DC="http://purl.org/DC/">

  <RDF:Description about="http://metalab.unc.edu/xml/">
    <DC:Creator>Elliotte Rusty Harold</DC:Creator>
    <DC:Language>en</DC:Language>
    <DC:Format>HTML</DC:Format>
    <DC:Date>1999-08-19</DC:date>
    <DC:Type>home page</DC:Type>
    <DC:Title>Cafe con Leche</DC:Title>
  </RDF:Description>

</RDF:RDF>
```

RDF will be used for version 2.0 of the Platform for Internet Content Selection (PICS) and the Platform for Privacy Preferences (P3P) as well as for many other areas where meta-data is needed to describe Web pages and other kinds of content.

XML for XML

XML is an extremely general-purpose format for text data. Some of the things it is used for are further refinements of XML itself. These include the XSL style-sheet language, the XLL-linking language, and the Document Content Description for XML.

XSL

XSL, the Extensible Style Language, is itself an XML application. XSL has two major parts. The first part defines a vocabulary for transforming XML documents. This part of XSL includes XML tags for trees, nodes, patterns, templates, and other elements needed for matching and transforming XML documents from one markup vocabulary to another (or even to the same one in a different order).

The second part of XSL defines an XML vocabulary for formatting the transformed XML document produced by the first part. This includes XML tags for formatting objects including pagination, blocks, characters, lists, graphics, boxes, fonts, and more. A typical XSL style sheet is shown in Listing 2-12:

Listing 2-12: **An XSL style sheet**

```
<?xml version="1.0"?>
<xsl:stylesheet
  xmlns:xsl="http://www.w3.org/TR/WD-xsl"
  xmlns:fo="http://www.w3.org/TR/WD-xsl/FO"
  result-ns="fo">
  <xsl:template match="/">
    <fo:basic-page-sequence >
      <xsl:apply-templates/>
    </fo:basic-page-sequence>
  </xsl:template>

  <xsl:template match="ATOM">
    <fo:block font-size="10pt" font-family="serif"
    space-before="12pt">
      <xsl:value-of select="NAME"/>
    </fo:block>
  </xsl:template>

</xsl:stylesheet>
```

We'll explore XSL in great detail in Chapters 14 and 15.

XLL

The Extensible Linking Language, XLL, defines a new, more general kind of link called an XLink. XLinks accomplish everything possible with HTML's URL-based hyperlinks and anchors. However, any element can become a link, not just A elements. For instance a `footnote` element can link directly to the text of the note like this:

```
<footnote xlink:form="simple" href="footnote7.xml">7</footnote>
```

Furthermore, XLinks can do a lot of things HTML links can't. XLinks can be bi-directional so readers can return to the page they came from. XLinks can link to arbitrary positions in a document. XLinks can embed text or graphic data inside a document rather than requiring the user to activate the link (much like HTML's `<IMG>` tag but more flexible). In short, XLinks make hypertext even more powerful.

XLinks are discussed in more detail in Chapter 16, *XLinks*.

DCD

XML's facilities for declaring how the contents of an XML element should be formatted are weak to nonexistent. For example, suppose as part of a date, you set up `MONTH` elements like this:

```
<MONTH>9</MONTH>
```

All you can say is that the contents of the `MONTH` element should be character data. You cannot say that the month should be given as an integer between 1 and 12.

A number of schemes have been proposed to use XML itself to more tightly restrict what can appear in the contents of any given element. One such proposal is the Document Content Description, (DCD). For example, here's a DCD that declares that `MONTH` elements may only contain an integer between 1 and 12:

```
<DCD>
  <ElementDef Type="MONTH" Model="Data" Datatype="i1"
  Min="1" Max="12" />
</DCD>
```

There are more examples I could show you of XML used for XML, but the ones I've already discussed demonstrate the basic point: XML is powerful enough to describe and extend itself. Among other things, this means that the XML specification can remain small and simple. There may well never be an XML 2.0 because any major additions that are needed can be built out of raw XML rather than becoming new features of the XML. People and programs that need these enhanced features can use them. Others who don't need them can ignore them. You don't need to know about what you don't use. XML provides the bricks and mortar from which you can build simple huts or towering castles.

Behind-the-Scene Uses of XML

Not all XML applications are public, open standards. A lot of software vendors are moving to XML for their own data simply because it's a well-understood, general-purpose format for structured data that can be manipulated with easily available cheap and free tools.

Microsoft Office 2000 promotes HTML to a coequal file format with its native binary formats. However, HTML 4.0 doesn't provide support for all of the features Office requires, such as revision tracking, footnotes, comments, index and glossary entries, and more. Additional data that can't be written as HTML is embedded in the file in small chunks of XML. Word's vector graphics stored in VML. In this case, embedded XML's invisibility in standard browsers is the crucial factor.

Federal Express uses detailed tracking information as a competitive advantage over other shippers like UPS and the Post Office. First that information was available through custom software, then through the Web. More recently FedEx has begun beta testing an API/library that third-party and in-house developers can use to integrate their software and systems with FedEx's. The data format used for this service is XML.

Netscape Navigator 5.0 supports direct display of XML in the Web browser, but Netscape actually started using XML internally as early as version 4.5. When you ask Netscape to show you a list of sites related to the current one you're looking it, your browser connects to a CGI program running on a Netscape server. The data that server sends back is XML. Listing 2-13 shows the XML data for sites related to `http://metalab.unc.edu/`.

Listing 2-13: XML data for sites related to http://metalab.unc.edu/

```
<?xml version="1.0"?>
<RDF:RDF>
<RelatedLinks>
<aboutPage
href="http://info.netscape.com/fwd/rl/http://metalab.unc.edu:80
/*">
```

```
</aboutPage>
<child instanceOf="Separator1"></child>
<child
href="http://info.netscape.com/fwd/rl/http://www.sun.com/"
name="Sun Microsystems">
</child>
<child
href="http://info.netscape.com/fwd/rl/http://www.unc.edu/"
name="Unc">
</child>
<child
href="http://info.netscape.com/fwd/rl/http://sunsite.sut.ac.jp/
" name="SunSITE Japan">
</child>
<child
href="http://info.netscape.com/fwd/rl/http://sunsite.nus.sg/"
name="SunSITE Singapore">
</child>
<child
href="http://info.netscape.com/fwd/rl/http://sunsite.berkeley.e
du/" name="Berkeley Digital Library SunSITE">
</child>
<child
href="http://info.netscape.com/fwd/rl/http://www.sun.com/sunsit
e" name="SunSITE on the net">
</child>
<child
href="http://info.netscape.com/fwd/rl/http://www.sunsite.auc.dk
/" name="SunSITE Denmark">
</child>
<child
href="http://info.netscape.com/fwd/rl/http://sunsite.edu.cn/"
name="SunSITE China">
</child>
<child
href="http://info.netscape.com/fwd/rl/http://sunsite.stanford.o
rg/" name="Stanford University SunSITE">
</child>
<child
href="http://info.netscape.com/fwd/rl/http://www.cdromshop.com/
cdshop/desc/p.061590000085.html" name="SunSITE Archive">
</child>
<child instanceOf="Separator1"></child>
<child instanceOf="Separator1"></child>
<child href="http://home.netscape.com/escapes/smart_browsing"
name="Learn About Smart Browsing...">
</child>
</RelatedLinks>
</RDF:RDF>
```

This all happens completely behind the scenes. The users never know that the data is being transferred in XML. The actual display is a menu in Netscape Navigator, not an XML or HTML page.

This really just scratches the surface of the use of XML for internal data. Many other projects that use XML are just getting started, and many more will be started over the next year. Most of these won't receive any publicity or write-ups in the trade press, but they nonetheless have the potential to save their companies thousands of dollars in development costs over the life of the project. The self-documenting nature of XML can be as useful for a company's internal data as for its external data. For instance, many companies right now are scrambling to try and figure out whether programmers who retired 20 years ago used two-digit dates. If that were your job, would you rather be pouring over data that looked like this:

```
3c 79 65 61 72 3e 39 39 3c 2f 79 65 61 72 3e
```

or like this:

```
<YEAR>99</YEAR>
```

Unfortunately many programmers are now stuck trying to clean up data in the first format. XML even makes the mistakes easier to find and fix.

Summary

This chapter has just begun to touch the many and varied applications to which XML has been and will be put. Some of these applications like CML, MathML, and MusicML are clear extensions to HTML for Web browsers. But many others, like OFX, XFDL, and HRML, go into completely new directions. And all of these applications have their own semantics and syntax that sits on top of the underlying XML. In some cases, the XML roots are obvious. In other cases, you could easily spend months working with it and only hear of XML tangentially. In this chapter, you explored the following applications to which XML has been put to use:

✦ Molecular sciences with CML

✦ Science and math with MathML

✦ Webcasting with CDF

✦ Classic literature

✦ Multimedia with SMIL and HTML+TIME

✦ Software updates through OSD

✦ Vector graphics with both PGML and VML

- ✦ Music notation in MusicML
- ✦ Automated voice responses with VoxML
- ✦ Financial data with OFX
- ✦ Legally binding forms with XFDL
- ✦ Human resources job information with HRML
- ✦ Meta-data through RDF
- ✦ XML itself, including XSL, XLL, and DCD, to refine XML
- ✦ Internal use of XML by various companies, including Microsoft, Federal Express, and Netscape

In the next chapter, you will begin writing your own XML documents and displaying them in Web browsers.

✦   ✦   ✦

Your First XML Document

This chapter teaches you how to create simple XML documents with tags you define that make sense for your document. You'll learn how to write a style sheet for the document that describes how the content of those tags should be displayed. Finally, you'll learn how to load the documents into a Web browser so that they can be viewed.

Since this chapter will teach you by example, and not from first principals, it will not cross all the t's and dot all the i's. Experienced readers may notice a few exceptions and special cases that aren't discussed here. Don't worry about these; you'll get to them over the course of the next several chapters. For the most part, you don't need to worry about the technical rules right up front. As with HTML, you can learn and do a lot by copying simple examples that others have prepared and modifying them to fit your needs.

Toward that end I encourage you to follow along by typing in the examples I give in this chapter and loading them into the different programs discussed. This will give you a basic feel for XML that will make the technical details in future chapters easier to grasp in the context of these specific examples.

Hello XML

This section follows an old programmer's tradition of introducing a new language with a program that prints "Hello World" on the console. XML is a markup language, not a programming language; but the basic principle still applies. It's easiest to get started if you begin with a complete, working example you can expand on rather than trying to start with more fundamental pieces that by themselves don't do anything. And if you do encounter problems with the basic tools, those problems are a lot easier to debug and fix in the context of the short, simple documents used here rather than in the context of the more complex documents developed in the rest of the book.

In this section, you'll learn how to create a simple XML document and save it in a file. We'll then take a closer look at the code and what it means.

Creating a Simple XML Document

In this section, you will learn how to type an actual XML document. Let's start with about the simplest XML document I can imagine. Here it is in Listing 3-1:

Listing 3-1: **Hello XML**

```
<?xml version="1.0" standalone="yes"?>
<FOO>
Hello XML!
</FOO>
```

That's not very complicated, but it is a good XML document. To be more precise, it's a *well-formed* XML document. (XML has special terms for documents that it considers "good" depending on exactly which set of rules they satisfy. "Well-formed" is one of those terms, but we'll get to that later in the book.) This document can be typed in any convenient text editor like Notepad, BBEdit, or emacs.

Cross-Reference   Well-formedness is covered in Chapter 6, *Well-Formed XML Documents.*

Saving the XML File

Once you've typed the preceding code, save the document in a file called hello.xml, HelloWorld.xml, MyFirstDocument.xml, or some other name. The three-letter extension .xml is fairly standard. However, do make sure that you save it in plain text format, and not in the native format of some word processor like WordPerfect or Microsoft Word.

Note   If you're using Notepad on Windows 95/98 to edit your files, when saving the document be sure to enclose the file name in double quotes, e.g. "Hello.xml", not merely Hello.xml, as shown in Figure 3-1. Without the quotes, Notepad will append the .txt extension to your file name, naming it Hello.xml.txt, which is not what you want at all.

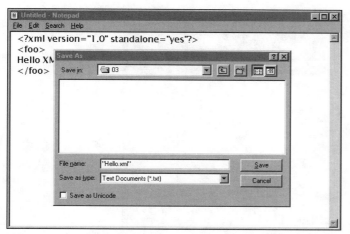

Figure 3-1: A saved XML document in Notepad with the file name in quotes

The Windows NT version of Notepad gives you the option to save the file in Unicode. Surprisingly this will work too, though for now you should stick to basic ASCII. XML files may be either Unicode or a compressed version of Unicode called UTF-8, which is a strict superset of ASCII, so pure ASCII files are also valid XML files.

Cross-Reference UTF-8 and ASCII are discussed in more detail in Chapter 7, *Foreign Languages and non-Roman Text.*

Loading the XML File into a Web Browser

Now that you've created your first XML document, you're going to want to look at it. The file can be opened directly in a browser that supports XML such as Internet Explorer 5.0. Figure 3-2 shows the result.

What you see will vary from browser to browser. In this case it's a nicely formatted and syntax colored view of the document's source code. However, whatever it is, it's likely not to be particularly attractive. The problem is that the browser doesn't really know what to do with the F00 element. You have to tell the browser what it's expected to do with each element by using a style sheet. We'll cover that shortly, but first let's look a little more closely at your first XML document.

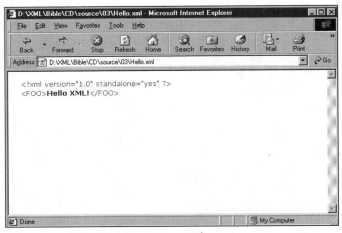

Figure 3-2: hello.xml in Internet Explorer 5.0

Exploring the Simple XML Document

Let's examine the simple XML document in Listing 3-1 to better understand what each line of code means. The first line is the *XML declaration*:

```
<?xml version="1.0" standalone="yes"?>
```

This is an example of an XML *processing instruction*. Processing instructions begin with <? And end with ?>. The first word after the <? is the name of the processing instruction, which is xml in this example.

The XML declaration has version and standalone *attributes*. An attribute is a name-value pair separated by an equals sign. The name is on the left-hand side of the equals sign and the value is on the right-hand side with its value given between double quote marks.

Every XML document begins with an XML declaration that specifies the version of XML in use. In the above example, the version attribute says this document conforms to XML 1.0. The XML declaration may also have a standalone attribute that tells you whether or not the document is complete in this one file or whether it needs to import other files. In this example, and for the next several chapters, all documents will be complete unto themselves so the standalone attribute is set to yes.

Now let's take a look at the next three lines of Listing 3-1:

```
<FOO>
Hello XML!
</FOO>
```

Collectively these three lines form a FOO *element*. Separately, <FOO> is a *start tag*; </FOO> is an *end tag*; and Hello XML! is the *content* of the FOO element.

You may be asking what the <FOO> tag means. The short answer is "whatever you want it to." Rather than relying on a few hundred predefined tags, XML lets you create the tags that you need. The <FOO> tag therefore has whatever meaning you assign it. The same XML document could have been written with different tag names, as shown in Listings 3-2, 3-3, and 3-4, below:

Listing 3-2: **greeting.xml**

```
<?xml version="1.0" standalone="yes"?>
<GREETING>
Hello XML!
</GREETING>
```

Listing 3-3: **paragraph.xml**

```
<?xml version="1.0" standalone="yes"?>
<P>
Hello XML!
</P>
```

Listing 3-4: **document.xml**

```
<?xml version="1.0" standalone="yes"?>
<DOCUMENT>
Hello XML!
</DOCUMENT>
```

The four XML documents in Listings 3-1 through 3-4 have tags with different names. However, they are all equivalent, since they have the same structure and content.

Assigning Meaning to XML Tags

Markup tags can have three kinds of meaning: structure, semantics, and style. Structure divides documents into a tree of elements. Semantics relates the individual elements to the real world outside of the document itself. Style specifies how an element is displayed.

Structure merely expresses the form of the document, without regard for differences between individual tags and elements. For instance, the four XML documents shown in Listings 3-1 through 3-4 are structurally the same. They all specify documents with a single non-empty, root element. The different names of the tags have no structural significance.

Semantic meaning exists outside the document, in the mind of the author or reader or in some computer program that generates or reads these files. For instance, a Web browser that understands HTML, but not XML, would assign the meaning "paragraph" to the tags <P> and </P> but not to the tags <GREETING> and </GREETING>, <FOO> and </FOO>, or <DOCUMENT> and </DOCUMENT>. An English-speaking human would be more likely to understand <GREETING> and </GREETING> or <DOCUMENT> and </DOCUMENT> than <FOO> and </FOO> or <P> and </P>. Meaning, like beauty, is in the mind of the beholder.

Computers, being relatively dumb machines, can't really be said to understand the meaning of anything. They simply process bits and bytes according to predetermined formula (albeit very quickly). A computer is just as happy to use <FOO> or <P> as it is to use the more meaningful <GREETING> or <DOCUMENT> tags. Even a Web browser can't be said to really understand that what a paragraph is. All the browser knows is that when a <P> tag is encountered a blank line should be placed before the next element.

Naturally, it's better to pick tags that more closely reflect the meaning of the information they contain. Many disciplines like math and chemistry are working on creating industry standard tag sets. These should be used when appropriate. However, most tags are made up as you need them.

Here are some other possible tags:

```
<MOLECULE>      <INTEGRAL>
<PERSON>        <SALARY>
<author>        <email>
<planet>        <sign>
<Bill>          <plus/>
<Hillary>       <plus/>
```

```
<Gennifer>      <plus/>
<Paula>         <plus/>
<Monica>        <equals/>
<divorce>
```

The third kind of meaning that can be associated with a tag is style meaning. Style meaning specifies how the content of a tag is to be presented on a computer screen or other output device. Style meaning says whether a particular element is bold, italic, green, 24 points, or what have you. Computers are better at understanding style than semantic meaning. In XML, style meaning is applied through style sheets.

Writing a Style Sheet for an XML Document

XML allows you to create any tags you need. Of course, since you have almost complete freedom in creating tags, there's no way for a generic browser to anticipate your tags and provide rules for displaying them. Therefore, you also need to write a style sheet for your XML document that tells browsers how to display particular tags. Like tag sets, style sheets can be shared between different documents and different people, and the style sheets you create can be integrated with style sheets others have written.

As discussed in Chapter 1, there is more than one style-sheet language available. The one used here is called Cascading Style Sheets (CSS). CSS has the advantage of being an established W3C standard, being familiar to many people from HTML, and being supported in the first wave of XML-enabled Web browsers.

Note As noted in Chapter 1, another possibility is the Extensible Style Language. XSL is currently the most powerful and flexible style-sheet language, and the only one designed specifically for use with XML. However, XSL is more complicated than CSS, not yet as well supported, and not finished either.

Cross-Reference XSL will be discussed in Chapters 5, 14, and 15.

The greeting.xml example shown in Listing 3-2 only contains one tag, <GREETING>, so all you need to do is define the style for the GREETING element. Listing 3-5 is a very simple style sheet that specifies that the contents of the GREETING element should be rendered as a block-level element in 24-point bold type.

Listing 3-5: **greeting.xsl**

```
GREETING {display: block; font-size: 24pt; font-weight: bold;}
```

Listing 3-5 should be typed in a text editor and saved in a new file called greeting.css in the same directory as Listing 3-2. The .css extension stands for Cascading Style Sheet. Once again the extension, .css, is important, although the exact file name is not. However if a style sheet is to be applied only to a single XML document it's often convenient to give it the same name as that document with the extension .css instead of .xml.

Attaching a Style Sheet to an XML Document

After you've written an XML document and a CSS style sheet for that document, you need to tell the browser to apply the style sheet to the document. In the long term there are likely to be a number of different ways to do this, including browser-server negotiation via HTTP headers, naming conventions, and browser-side defaults. However, right now the only way that works is to include another processing instruction in the XML document to specify the style sheet to be used.

The processing instruction is `<?xml-stylesheet?>` and it has two attributes, `type` and `href`. The `type` attribute specifies the style-sheet language used, and the `href` attribute specifies a URL, possibly relative, where the style sheet can be found. In Listing 3-6, the `xml-stylesheet` processing instruction specifies that the style sheet named `greeting.css` written in the CSS style-sheet language is to be applied to this document.

Listing 3-6: **styledgreeting.xml with an xml-stylesheet processing instruction**

```
<?xml version="1.0" standalone="yes"?>
<?xml-stylesheet type="text/css2" href="greeting.css"?>
<GREETING>
Hello XML!
</GREETING>
```

Now that you've created your first XML document and style sheet, you're going to want to look at it. All you have to do is load Listing 3–6 into Mozilla or Internet Explorer 5.0. Figure 3–3 shows styledgreeting in Internet Explorer 5.0. Figure 3–4 shows styledgreeting.xml in an early developer build of Mozilla.

Figure 3-3: styledgreeting.xml in Internet Explorer 5.0

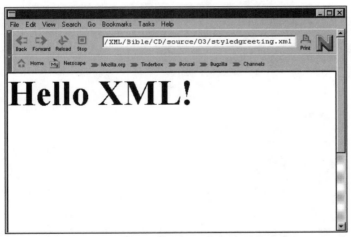

Figure 3-4: styledgreeting.xml in an early developer build of Mozilla

Summary

In this chapter you learned how to create a simple XML document. In particular you learned:

✦ How to write and save simple XML documents.

✦ How to assign to XML tags the three kinds of meaning: structure, semantics, and style.

✦ How to write a CSS style sheet for an XML document that tells browsers how to display particular tags.

✦ How to attach a CSS style sheet to an XML document with an `xml-stylesheet` processing instruction.

✦ How to load XML documents into a Web browser.

In the next chapter, we'll develop a much larger example of an XML document that demonstrates more of the practical considerations involved in choosing XML tags.

✦   ✦   ✦

Structuring Data

In this chapter, we will develop a longer example that shows how a large list of baseball statistics and other similar data might be stored in XML. A document like this has several potential uses. Most obviously it can be displayed on a Web page. It can also be used as input to other programs that want to analyze particular seasons or lineup. Along the way, you'll learn, among other things, how to mark up the data in XML, why XML tags are chosen, and how to prepare a CSS style sheet for a document.

Examining the Data

As I write this (October, 1998), the New York Yankees have just won their 24th World Series by sweeping the San Diego Padres in four games. The Yankees finished the regular season with an American League record 114 wins. Overall, 1998 was an astonishing season. The St. Louis Cardinals' Mark McGwire and the Chicago Cubs' Sammy Sosa dueled through September for the record, previously held by Roger Maris, for most home runs hit in a single season since baseball was integrated. (The all-time major league record for home runs in a single season is still held by catcher Josh Gibson who hit 75 home runs in the Negro league in 1931. Admittedly, Gibson didn't have to face the sort of pitching Sosa and McGwire faced in today's integrated league. Then again neither did Babe Ruth who was widely (and incorrectly) believed to have held the record until Roger Maris hit 61 in 1961.)

What exactly made 1998 such an exciting season? A cynic would tell you that 1998 was an expansion year with three new teams, and consequently much weaker pitching overall. This gave outstanding batters like Sosa and McGwire and outstanding teams like the Yankees a chance to really shine because, although they were as strong as they'd been in 1997, the average opponent they faced was a lot weaker. Of course true baseball fanatics know the real reason, statistics.

That's a funny thing to say. In most sports you hear about heart, guts, ability, skill, determination, and more. But only in baseball do the fans get so worked up about raw numbers. Batting average, earned run average, slugging average, on base average, fielding percentage, batting average against right handed pitchers, batting average against left handed pitchers, batting average against right handed pitchers when batting left-handed, batting average against right handed pitchers in Cleveland under a full moon, and so on.

Baseball fans are obsessed with numbers; the more numbers the better. Every season the Internet is host to thousands of rotisserie leagues in which avid netizens manage teams and trade players with each other and calculate how their fantasy teams are doing based on the real-world performance of the players on their fantasy rosters. STATS, Inc. tracks the results of each and every pitch made in a major league game, so it's possible to figure out that one batter does better than his average with men in scoring position while another does worse.

In the next two sections, for the benefit of the less baseball-obsessed reader, we will examine the commonly available statistics that describe an individual player's batting and pitching. Fielding statistics are also available, but I'll omit them to restrict the examples to a more manageable size. The specific example I'm using is the New York Yankees, but the same statistics are available for any team.

Batters

A few years ago, Bruce Bukiet, Jose Palacios, and myself, wrote a paper called "A Markov Chain Approach to Baseball" (Operations Research, Volume 45, Number 1, January-February, 1997, pp. 14-23, http://www.math.njit.edu/~bukiet/ Papers/ball.pdf). In this paper we analyzed all possible batting orders for all teams in the 1989 National League. The results of that paper were mildly interesting. The worst batter on the team, generally the pitcher, should bat eighth rather than the customary ninth position, at least in the National League, but what concerns me here is the work that went into producing this paper. As low grad student on the totem pole, it was my job to manually re-key the complete batting history of each and every player in the National League. That summer would have been a lot more pleasant if I had had the data available in a convenient format like XML. Right now, I'm going to concentrate on data for individual players. Typically this data is presented in rows of numbers as shown in Table 4-1 for the 1998 Yankees offense (batters). Since pitchers rarely bat in the American League, only players who actually batted are listed.

Each column effectively defines an element. Thus there need to be elements for player, position, games played, at bats, runs, hits, doubles, triples, home runs, runs batted in, and walks. Singles are generally not reported separately. Rather they're calculated by subtracting the total number of doubles, triples, and home runs from the number of hits.

Table 4-1
The 1998 Yankees Offense

Name	Position	Games Played	At Bats	Runs	Hits	Doubles	Triples	Home Runs	Runs Batted In	Strike Walks	Outs	Hit by Pitch
Scott Brosius	Third Base	152	530	86	159	34	0	19	98	52	97	10
Homer Bush	Second Base	45	71	17	27	3	0	1	5	5	19	0
Chad Curtis	Outfield	151	456	79	111	21	1	10	56	75	80	7
Chili Davis	Designated Hitter	35	103	11	30	7	0	3	9	14	18	0
Mike Figga	Catcher	1	4	1	1	0	0	0	0	0	1	0
Joe Girardi	Catcher	78	254	31	70	11	4	3	31	14	38	2
Derek Jeter	Shortstop	149	626	127	203	25	8	19	84	57	119	5
Chuck Knoblauch	Second Base	150	603	117	160	25	4	17	64	76	70	18
Ricky Ledee	Outfield	42	79	13	19	5	2	1	12	7	29	0
Mike Lowell	Third Base	8	15	1	4	0	0	0	0	0	1	0
Tino Martinez	First Base	142	531	92	149	33	1	28	123	61	83	6
Paul O'Neill	Outfield	152	602	95	191	40	2	24	116	57	103	2
Jorge Posada	Catcher	111	358	56	96	23	0	17	63	47	92	0
Tim Raines	Outfield	109	321	53	93	13	1	5	47	55	49	3
Luis Sojo	Shortstop	54	147	16	34	3	1	0	14	4	15	0
Shane Spencer	Outfield	27	67	18	25	6	0	10	27	5	12	0
Darryl Strawberry	Designated Hitter	101	295	44	73	11	2	24	57	46	90	3
Dale Sveum	First base	30	58	6	9	0	0	0	3	4	16	0
Bernie Williams	Outfield	128	499	101	169	30	5	26	97	74	81	1

Note   The data in the previous table and the pitcher data in the next section is actually a somewhat limited list that only begins to specify the data collected on a typical baseball game. There are a lot more elements including throwing arm, batting arm, number of times the pitcher balked (rare), fielding percentage, college attended, and more. However, I'll stick to this basic information to keep the examples manageable.

Pitchers

Pitchers are not expected to be home-run hitters or base stealers. Indeed a pitcher who can reach first on occasion is a surprise bonus for a team. Instead pitchers are judged on a whole different set of numbers, shown in Table 4-2. Each column of this table also defines an element. Some of these elements, such as name and position, are the same for batters and pitchers. Others like saves and shutouts only apply to pitchers. And a few — like runs and home runs — have the same name as a batter statistic, but have different meanings. For instance, the number of runs for a batter is the number of runs the batter scored. The number of runs for a pitcher is the number of runs scored by the opposing teams against this pitcher.

Organization of the XML Data

XML is based on a containment model. Each XML element can contain text or other XML elements called its children. A few XML elements may contain both text and child elements, though in general this is bad form and should be avoided wherever possible.

However, there's often more than one way to organize the data, depending on your needs. One of the advantages of XML is that it makes it fairly straightforward to write a program that reorganizes the data in a different form. We'll discuss this when we talk about XSL transformations in Chapter 14.

To get started, the first question you'll have to address is what contains what? For instance, it is fairly obvious that a league contains divisions that contain teams that contain players. Although teams can change divisions when moving from one city to another, and players are routinely traded at any given moment in time, each player belongs to exactly one team and each team belongs to exactly one division. Similarly, a season contains games, which contain innings, which contain at bats, which contain pitches or plays.

However, does a season contain leagues or does a league contain a season? The answer isn't so obvious, and indeed there isn't one unique answer. Whether it makes more sense to make season elements children of league elements or league elements children of season elements depends on the use to which the data will be put. You can even create a new root element that contains both seasons and leagues, neither of which is a child of the other (though doing so effectively would require some advanced techniques that won't be discussed for several chapters yet). You can organize the data as you like.

Table 4-2
The 1998 Yankees Pitchers

Name	P	W	L	S	G	GS	CG	SHO	ERA	IP	H	HR	R	ER	HB	WP	BK	WB	SO
Joe Borowski	Relief Pitcher	1	0	0	8	0	0	0	6.52	9.2	11	0	7	7	0	0	0	4	7
Ryan Bradley	Relief Pitcher	2	1	0	5	1	0	0	5.68	12.2	12	2	9	8	1	0	0	9	13
Jim Bruske	Relief Pitcher	1	0	0	3	1	0	0	3	9	9	2	3	3	0	0	0	1	
Mike Buddie	Relief Pitcher	4	1	0	24	2	0	0	5.62	41.2	46	5	29	26	3	2	1	13	20
David Cone	Starting Pitcher	20	7	0	31	31	3	0	3.55	207.2	186	20	89	82	15	6	0	59	209
Todd Erdos	Relief Pitcher	0	0	0	2	0	0	0	9	2	5	0	2	2	0	0	0	1	0
Orlando Hernandez	Starting Pitcher	12	4	0	21	21	3	1	3.13	141	113	11	53	49	6	5	2	52	131
Darren Holmes	Relief Pitcher	0	3	2	34	0	0	0	3.33	51.1	53	4	19	19	2	1	0	14	31
Hideki Irabu	Starting Pitcher	13	9	0	29	28	2	1	4.06	173	148	27	79	78	9	6	1	76	126
Mike Jerzembeck	Starting Pitcher	0	1	0	3	2	0	0	12.79	6.1	9	2	9	9	0	1	1	4	1
Graeme Lloyd	Relief Pitcher	3	0	0	50	0	0	0	1.67	37.2	26	3	10	7	2	2	0	6	20
Ramiro Mendoza	Relief Pitcher	10	2	1	41	14	1	1	3.25	130.1	131	9	50	47	9	3	0	30	56
Jeff Nelson	Relief Pitcher	5	3	3	45	0	0	0	3.79	40.1	44	1	18	17	8	2	0	22	35

Continued

Table 4-2 (continued)

Name	P	W	L	S	G	GS	CG	SHO	ERA	IP	H	HR	R	ER	HB	WP	BK	WB	SO
Andy Pettitte	Starting Pitcher	16	11	0	33	32	5	0	4.24	216.1	226	20	110	102	6	5	0	87	146
Mariano Rivera	Relief Pitcher	3	0	36	54	0	0	0	1.91	61.1	48	3	13	13	1	0	0	17	36
Mike Stanton	Relief Pitcher	4	1	6	67	0	0	0	5.47	79	71	13	51	48	4	0	0	26	69
Jay Tessmer	Relief Pitcher	1	0	0	7	0	0	0	3.12	8.2	4	1	3	3	0	1	0	4	6
David Wells	Starting Pitcher	18	4	0	30	30	8	5	3.49	214.1	195	29	86	83	1	2	0	29	163

Note Readers familiar with database theory may recognize XML's model as essentially a hierarchical database, and consequently recognize that it shares all the disadvantages (and a few advantages) of that data model. There are certainly times when a table-based relational approach makes more sense. This example certainly looks like one of those times. However, XML doesn't follow a relational model.

On the other hand, it is completely possible to store the actual data in multiple tables in a relational database, then generate the XML on the fly. Indeed, the larger examples on the CD-ROM were created in that fashion. This enables one set of data to be presented in multiple formats. Transforming the data with style sheets provides still more possible views of the data.

Since my personal interests lie in analyzing player performance within a single season, I'm going to make season the root of my documents. Each season will contain leagues, which will contain divisions, which will contain players. I'm not going to granularize my data all the way down to the level of individual games, innings, or plays — because while useful — such examples would be excessively long.

You, however, may have other interests. If you choose to divide the data in some other fashion, that works too. There's almost always more than one way to organize data in XML. In fact, we'll return to this example in several upcoming chapters where we'll explore alternative markup vocabularies.

XMLizing the Data

Let's begin the process of marking up the data for the 1998 Major League season in XML with tags that you define. Remember that in XML we're allowed to make up the tags as we go along. We've already decided that the fundamental element of our document will be a season. Seasons will contain leagues. Leagues will contain divisions. Divisions will contain teams. Teams contain players. Players will have statistics including games played, at bats, runs, hits, doubles, triples, home runs, runs batted in, walks, and hits by pitch.

Starting the Document: XML Declaration and Root Element

XML documents may be recognized by the XML declaration. This is a processing instruction placed at the start of all XML files that identifies the version in use. The only version currently understood is 1.0.

```
<?xml version="1.0"?>
```

Every good XML document (where the word *good* has a very specific meaning to be discussed in the next chapter) must have a root element. This is an element that completely contains all other elements of the document. The root element's start tag comes before all other elements' start tags, and the root element's end tag comes after all other element's end tags. For our root element, we will use SEASON with a start tag of <SEASON> and an end tag of </SEASON>. The document now looks like this:

```
<?xml version="1.0"?>
<SEASON>
</SEASON>
```

The XML declaration is not an element or a tag. It is a processing instruction. Therefore, it does not need to be contained inside the root element, SEASON. But every element we put in this document will go in between the <SEASON> start tag and the </SEASON> end tag.

This choice of root element means that we will not be able to store multiple seasons in a single file. If you want to do that, however, you can define a new root element that contains seasons. For example,

```
<?xml version="1.0"?>
<DOCUMENT>
  <SEASON>
  </SEASON>
  <SEASON>
  </SEASON>
</DOCUMENT>
```

Naming Conventions

Before we begin, I'd like to say a few words about naming conventions. As you'll see in the next chapter, XML element names are quite flexible and can contain any number of letters and digits in either upper- or lowercase. You have the option of writing XML tags that look like any of the following:

```
<SEASON>
```

```
<Season>
```

```
<season>
```

```
<season1998>
```

```
<Season98>
```

```
<season_98>
```

There are several thousand more variations. I don't really care (nor does XML) whether you use all uppercase, all lowercase, mixed-case with internal capitalization, or some other convention. However, I do recommend that you choose one convention and stick to it.

Of course we will want to identify which season we're talking about. To do that, we should give the SEASON element a YEAR child. For example:

```
<?xml version="1.0"?>
<SEASON>
  <YEAR>
    1998
  </YEAR>
</SEASON>
```

I've used indentation here and in other examples to indicate that the YEAR element is a child of the SEASON element and that the text 1998 is the contents of the YEAR element. This is good coding style, but it is not required. White space in XML is not especially significant. The same example could have been written like this:

```
<?xml version="1.0"?>
<SEASON>
  <YEAR>1998</YEAR>
</SEASON>
```

Indeed, I'll often compress elements to a single line when they'll fit and space is at a premium. You can compress the document still further, even down to a single line, but with a corresponding loss of clarity. For example:

```
<?xml version="1.0"?><SEASON><YEAR>1998</YEAR></SEASON>
```

Of course this version is much harder to read and understand which is why I didn't write it that way. The tenth goal listed in the XML 1.0 specification is "Terseness in XML markup is of minimal importance." The baseball example reflects this goal throughout.

XMLizing League, Division, and Team Data

Major league baseball is divided into two leagues, the American League and the National League. Each league has a name. The two names could be encoded like this:

```
<?xml version="1.0"?>
<SEASON>
  <YEAR>1998</YEAR>
  <LEAGUE>
    <LEAGUE_NAME>National League</LEAGUE_NAME>
  </LEAGUE>
  <LEAGUE>
    <LEAGUE_NAME>American League</LEAGUE_NAME>
  </LEAGUE>
</SEASON>
```

I've chosen to define the name of a league with a LEAGUE_NAME element, rather than simply a NAME element because NAME is too generic and it's likely to be used in other contexts. For instance, divisions, teams, and players also have names.

Cross-Reference

Elements from different domains with the same name can be combined using namespaces. Namespaces will be discussed in Chapter 18. However, even with namespaces, you wouldn't want to give multiple items in the same domain (for example, TEAM and LEAGUE in this example) the same name.

Each league can be divided into east, west, and central divisions, which can be encoded as follows:

```
<LEAGUE>
  <LEAGUE_NAME>National League</LEAGUE_NAME>
  <DIVISION>
    <DIVISION_NAME>East</DIVISION_NAME>
  </DIVISION>
  <DIVISION>
    <DIVISION_NAME>Central</DIVISION_NAME>
  </DIVISION>
  <DIVISION>
    <DIVISION_NAME>West</DIVISION_NAME>
  </DIVISION>
</LEAGUE>
<LEAGUE>
  <LEAGUE_NAME>American League</LEAGUE_NAME>
  <DIVISION>
    <DIVISION_NAME>East</DIVISION_NAME>
  </DIVISION>
  <DIVISION>
    <DIVISION_NAME>Central</DIVISION_NAME>
  </DIVISION>
  <DIVISION>
    <DIVISION_NAME>West</DIVISION_NAME>
  </DIVISION>
</LEAGUE>
```

The true value of an element depends on its parent, that is the elements that contain it as well as itself. Both the American and National Leagues have an East division but these are not the same thing.

Each division is divided into teams. Each team has a name and a city. For example, data that pertains to the American League East can be encoded as follows:

```
<DIVISION>
  <DIVISION_NAME>East</DIVISION_NAME>
  <TEAM>
    <TEAM_CITY>Baltimore</TEAM_CITY>
    <TEAM_NAME>Orioles</TEAM_NAME>
  </TEAM>
  <TEAM>
    <TEAM_CITY>Boston</TEAM_CITY>
```

```
      <TEAM_NAME>Red Sox</TEAM_NAME>
   </TEAM>
   <TEAM>
      <TEAM_CITY>New York</TEAM_CITY>
      <TEAM_NAME>Yankees</TEAM_NAME>
   </TEAM>
   <TEAM>
      <TEAM_CITY>Tampa Bay</TEAM_CITY>
      <TEAM_NAME>Devil Rays</TEAM_NAME>
   </TEAM>
   <TEAM>
      <TEAM_CITY>Toronto</TEAM_CITY>
      <TEAM_NAME>Blue Jays</TEAM_NAME>
   </TEAM>
</DIVISION>
```

XMLizing Player Data

Each team is composed of players. Each player has a first name and a last name. It's important to separate the first and last names so that you can sort by either one. The data for the starting pitchers in the 1998 Yankees lineup can be encoded as follows:

```
<TEAM>
   <TEAM_CITY>New York</TEAM_CITY>
   <TEAM_NAME>Yankees</TEAM_NAME>
   <PLAYER>
      <GIVEN_NAME>Orlando</GIVEN_NAME>
      <SURNAME>Hernandez</SURNAME>
   </PLAYER>
   <PLAYER>
      <GIVEN_NAME>David</GIVEN_NAME>
      <SURNAME>Cone</SURNAME>
   </PLAYER>
   <PLAYER>
      <GIVEN_NAME>David</GIVEN_NAME>
      <SURNAME>Wells</SURNAME>
   </PLAYER>
   <PLAYER>
      <GIVEN_NAME>Andy</GIVEN_NAME>
      <SURNAME>Pettitte</SURNAME>
   </PLAYER>
   <PLAYER>
      <GIVEN_NAME>Hideki</GIVEN_NAME>
      <SURNAME>Irabu</SURNAME>
   </PLAYER>
</TEAM>
```

Note   The tags <GIVEN_NAME> and <SURNAME> are preferable to the more obvious <FIRST_NAME> and <LAST_NAME> or <FIRST_NAME> and <FAMILY_NAME>. Whether the family name or the given name comes first or last varies from culture to culture. Furthermore, surnames aren't necessarily family names in all cultures.

XMLizing Player Statistics

The next step is to provide statistics for each player. Statistics look a little different for pitchers and batters, especially in the American League in which few pitchers bat. Below are Joe Girardi's 1998 statistics. He's a catcher so we use batting statistics:

```
<PLAYER>
  <GIVEN_NAME>Joe </GIVEN_NAME>
  <SURNAME>Girardi</SURNAME>
  <POSITION>Catcher</POSITION>
  <GAMES>78</GAMES>
  <GAMES_STARTED>76</GAMES_STARTED>
  <AT_BATS>254</AT_BATS>
  <RUNS>31</RUNS>
  <HITS>70</HITS>
  <DOUBLES>11</DOUBLES>
  <TRIPLES>4</TRIPLES>
  <HOME_RUNS>3</HOME_RUNS>
  <RBI>31</RBI>
  <STEALS>2</STEALS>
  <CAUGHT_STEALING>4</CAUGHT_STEALING>
  <SACRIFICE_HITS>8</SACRIFICE_HITS>
  <SACRIFICE_FLIES>1</SACRIFICE_FLIES>
  <ERRORS>3</ERRORS>
  <WALKS>14</WALKS>
  <STRUCK_OUT>38</STRUCK_OUT>
  <HIT_BY_PITCH>2</HIT_BY_PITCH>
</PLAYER>
```

Now let's look at the statistics for a pitcher. Although pitchers occasionally bat in the American League, and frequently bat in the National League, they do so far less often than all other players do. Pitchers are hired and fired, cheered and booed, based on their pitching performance. If they can actually hit the ball on occasion too, that's pure gravy. Pitching statistics include games played, wins, losses, innings pitched, earned runs, shutouts, hits against, walks given up, and more. Here are Hideki Irabu's 1998 statistics encoded in XML:

```
<PLAYER>
  <GIVEN_NAME>Hideki</GIVEN_NAME>
  <SURNAME>Irabu</SURNAME>
  <POSITION>Starting Pitcher</POSITION>
  <WINS>13</WINS>
  <LOSSES>9</LOSSES>
  <SAVES>0</SAVES>
  <GAMES>29</GAMES>
  <GAMES_STARTED>28</GAMES_STARTED>
  <COMPLETE_GAMES>2</COMPLETE_GAMES>
  <SHUT_OUTS>1</SHUT_OUTS>
```

```
    <ERA>4.06</ERA>
    <INNINGS>173</INNINGS>
    <HOME_RUNS>148</HOME_RUNS>
    <RUNS>27</RUNS>
    <EARNED_RUNS>79</EARNED_RUNS>
    <HIT_BATTER>78</HIT_BATTER>
    <WILD_PITCHES>9</WILD_PITCHES>
    <BALK>6</BALK>
    <WALKED_BATTER>1</WALKED_BATTER>
    <STRUCK_OUT_BATTER>76</STRUCK_OUT_BATTER>
  </PLAYER>
```

Terseness in XML Markup IS of Minimal Importance

Throughout this example, I've been following the explicit XML principal that "Terseness in XML markup is of minimal importance." This certainly assists non-baseball literate readers who may not recognize baseball arcana such as the standard abbreviation for a walk BB (base on balls), not W as you might expect. If document size is truly an issue, it's easy to compress the files with zip or some other standard tool.

However, this does mean XML documents tend to be quite long, and relatively tedious to type by hand. I confess that this example sorely tempts me to use abbreviations, clarity be damned. If I were to do so, a typical PLAYER element might look like this:

```
<PLAYER>
  <GIVEN_NAME>Joe</GIVEN_NAME>
  <SURNAME>Girardi</SURNAME>
  <P>C</P>
  <G>78</G>
  <AB>254</AB>
  <R>31</R>
  <H>70</H>
  <DO>11</DO>
  <TR>4</TR>
  <HR>3</HR>
  <RBI>31</RBI>
  <BB>14</BB>
  <SO>38</SO>
  <SB>2</SB>
  <CS>4</CS>
  <HBP>2</HBP>
</PLAYER>
```

Putting the XML Document Back Together Again

Until now, I've been showing the XML document in pieces, element by element.
However, it's now time to put all the pieces together and look at the complete
document containing the statistics for the 1998 Major League season. Listing 4-1
demonstrates the complete XML document with two leagues, six divisions, thirty
teams, and nine players.

Listing 4-1: A complete XML document

```
<?xml version="1.0"?>
<SEASON>
  <YEAR>1998</YEAR>
  <LEAGUE>
    <LEAGUE_NAME>National League</LEAGUE_NAME>
    <DIVISION>
      <DIVISION_NAME>East</DIVISION_NAME>
        <TEAM>
          <TEAM_CITY>Atlanta</TEAM_CITY>
          <TEAM_NAME>Braves</TEAM_NAME>
          <PLAYER>
            <SURNAME>Malloy</SURNAME>
            <GIVEN_NAME>Marty</GIVEN_NAME>
            <POSITION>Second Base</POSITION>
            <GAMES>11</GAMES>
            <GAMES_STARTED>8</GAMES_STARTED>
            <AT_BATS>28</AT_BATS>
            <RUNS>3</RUNS>
            <HITS>5</HITS>
            <DOUBLES>1</DOUBLES>
            <TRIPLES>0</TRIPLES>
            <HOME_RUNS>1</HOME_RUNS>
            <RBI>1</RBI>
            <STEALS>0</STEALS>
            <CAUGHT_STEALING>0</CAUGHT_STEALING>
            <SACRIFICE_HITS>0</SACRIFICE_HITS>
            <SACRIFICE_FLIES>0</SACRIFICE_FLIES>
            <ERRORS>0</ERRORS>
            <WALKS>2</WALKS>
            <STRUCK_OUT>2</STRUCK_OUT>
            <HIT_BY_PITCH>0</HIT_BY_PITCH>
          </PLAYER>
          <PLAYER>
            <SURNAME>Guillen</SURNAME>
            <GIVEN_NAME>Ozzie </GIVEN_NAME>
            <POSITION>Shortstop</POSITION>
            <GAMES>83</GAMES>
            <GAMES_STARTED>59</GAMES_STARTED>
            <AT_BATS>264</AT_BATS>
            <RUNS>35</RUNS>
            <HITS>73</HITS>
```

```
    <DOUBLES>15</DOUBLES>
    <TRIPLES>1</TRIPLES>
    <HOME_RUNS>1</HOME_RUNS>
    <RBI>22</RBI>
    <STEALS>1</STEALS>
    <CAUGHT_STEALING>4</CAUGHT_STEALING>
    <SACRIFICE_HITS>4</SACRIFICE_HITS>
    <SACRIFICE_FLIES>2</SACRIFICE_FLIES>
    <ERRORS>6</ERRORS>
    <WALKS>24</WALKS>
    <STRUCK_OUT>25</STRUCK_OUT>
    <HIT_BY_PITCH>1</HIT_BY_PITCH>
  </PLAYER>
  <PLAYER>
  <SURNAME>Bautista</SURNAME>
    <GIVEN_NAME>Danny</GIVEN_NAME>
    <POSITION>Outfield</POSITION>
    <GAMES>82</GAMES>
    <GAMES_STARTED>27</GAMES_STARTED>
    <AT_BATS>144</AT_BATS>
    <RUNS>17</RUNS>
    <HITS>36</HITS>
    <DOUBLES>11</DOUBLES>
    <TRIPLES>0</TRIPLES>
    <HOME_RUNS>3</HOME_RUNS>
    <RBI>17</RBI>
    <STEALS>1</STEALS>
    <CAUGHT_STEALING>0</CAUGHT_STEALING>
    <SACRIFICE_HITS>3</SACRIFICE_HITS>
    <SACRIFICE_FLIES>2</SACRIFICE_FLIES>
    <ERRORS>2</ERRORS>
    <WALKS>7</WALKS>
    <STRUCK_OUT>21</STRUCK_OUT>
    <HIT_BY_PITCH>0</HIT_BY_PITCH>
  </PLAYER>
  <PLAYER>
    <SURNAME>Williams</SURNAME>
    <GIVEN_NAME>Gerald</GIVEN_NAME>
    <POSITION>Outfield</POSITION>
    <GAMES>129</GAMES>
    <GAMES_STARTED>51</GAMES_STARTED>
    <AT_BATS>266</AT_BATS>
    <RUNS>46</RUNS>
    <HITS>81</HITS>
    <DOUBLES>18</DOUBLES>
    <TRIPLES>3</TRIPLES>
    <HOME_RUNS>10</HOME_RUNS>
    <RBI>44</RBI>
    <STEALS>11</STEALS>
    <CAUGHT_STEALING>5</CAUGHT_STEALING>
    <SACRIFICE_HITS>2</SACRIFICE_HITS>
    <SACRIFICE_FLIES>1</SACRIFICE_FLIES>
```

Continued

Listing 4-1 *(continued)*

```
                    <ERRORS>5</ERRORS>
                    <WALKS>17</WALKS>
                    <STRUCK_OUT>48</STRUCK_OUT>
                    <HIT_BY_PITCH>3</HIT_BY_PITCH>
                  </PLAYER>
                  <PLAYER>
                    <SURNAME>Glavine</SURNAME>
                    <GIVEN_NAME>Tom</GIVEN_NAME>
                    <POSITION>Starting Pitcher</POSITION>
                    <WINS>20</WINS>
                    <LOSSES>6</LOSSES>
                    <SAVES>0</SAVES>
                    <GAMES>33</GAMES>
                    <GAMES_STARTED>33</GAMES_STARTED>
                    <COMPLETE_GAMES>4</COMPLETE_GAMES>
                    <SHUT_OUTS>3</SHUT_OUTS>
                    <ERA>2.47</ERA>
                    <INNINGS>229.1</INNINGS>
                    <HOME_RUNS>202</HOME_RUNS>
                    <RUNS>13</RUNS>
                    <EARNED_RUNS>67</EARNED_RUNS>
                    <HIT_BATTER>63</HIT_BATTER>
                    <WILD_PITCHES>2</WILD_PITCHES>
                    <BALK>3</BALK>
                    <WALKED_BATTER>0</WALKED_BATTER>
                    <STRUCK_OUT_BATTER>74</STRUCK_OUT_BATTER>
                  </PLAYER>
                  <PLAYER>
                    <SURNAME>Lopez</SURNAME>
                    <GIVEN_NAME>Javier</GIVEN_NAME>
                    <POSITION>Catcher</POSITION>
                    <GAMES>133</GAMES>
                    <GAMES_STARTED>124</GAMES_STARTED>
                    <AT_BATS>489</AT_BATS>
                    <RUNS>73</RUNS>
                    <HITS>139</HITS>
                    <DOUBLES>21</DOUBLES>
                    <TRIPLES>1</TRIPLES>
                    <HOME_RUNS>34</HOME_RUNS>
                    <RBI>106</RBI>
                    <STEALS>5</STEALS>
                    <CAUGHT_STEALING>3</CAUGHT_STEALING>
                    <SACRIFICE_HITS>1</SACRIFICE_HITS>
                    <SACRIFICE_FLIES>8</SACRIFICE_FLIES>
                    <ERRORS>5</ERRORS>
                    <WALKS>30</WALKS>
                    <STRUCK_OUT>85</STRUCK_OUT>
                    <HIT_BY_PITCH>6</HIT_BY_PITCH></PLAYER>
                  <PLAYER>
                    <SURNAME>Klesko</SURNAME>
                    <GIVEN_NAME>Ryan</GIVEN_NAME>
```

```
      <POSITION>Outfield</POSITION>
      <GAMES>129</GAMES>
      <GAMES_STARTED>124</GAMES_STARTED>
      <AT_BATS>427</AT_BATS>
      <RUNS>69</RUNS>
      <HITS>117</HITS>
      <DOUBLES>29</DOUBLES>
      <TRIPLES>1</TRIPLES>
      <HOME_RUNS>18</HOME_RUNS>
      <RBI>70</RBI>
      <STEALS>5</STEALS>
      <CAUGHT_STEALING>3</CAUGHT_STEALING>
      <SACRIFICE_HITS>0</SACRIFICE_HITS>
      <SACRIFICE_FLIES>4</SACRIFICE_FLIES>
      <ERRORS>2</ERRORS>
      <WALKS>56</WALKS>
      <STRUCK_OUT>66</STRUCK_OUT>
      <HIT_BY_PITCH>3</HIT_BY_PITCH></PLAYER>
<PLAYER>
      <SURNAME>Galarraga</SURNAME>
      <GIVEN_NAME>Andres</GIVEN_NAME>
      <POSITION>First Base</POSITION>
      <GAMES>153</GAMES>
      <GAMES_STARTED>151</GAMES_STARTED>
      <AT_BATS>555</AT_BATS>
      <RUNS>103</RUNS>
      <HITS>169</HITS>
      <DOUBLES>27</DOUBLES>
      <TRIPLES>1</TRIPLES>
      <HOME_RUNS>44</HOME_RUNS>
      <RBI>121</RBI>
      <STEALS>7</STEALS>
      <CAUGHT_STEALING>6</CAUGHT_STEALING>
      <SACRIFICE_HITS>0</SACRIFICE_HITS>
      <SACRIFICE_FLIES>5</SACRIFICE_FLIES>
      <ERRORS>11</ERRORS>
      <WALKS>63</WALKS>
      <STRUCK_OUT>146</STRUCK_OUT>
      <HIT_BY_PITCH>25</HIT_BY_PITCH></PLAYER>
<PLAYER>
      <SURNAME>Helms</SURNAME>
      <GIVEN_NAME>Wes</GIVEN_NAME>
      <POSITION>Third Base</POSITION>
      <GAMES>7</GAMES>
      <GAMES_STARTED>2</GAMES_STARTED>
      <AT_BATS>13</AT_BATS>
      <RUNS>2</RUNS>
      <HITS>4</HITS>
      <DOUBLES>1</DOUBLES>
      <TRIPLES>0</TRIPLES>
      <HOME_RUNS>1</HOME_RUNS>
      <RBI>2</RBI>
```

Continued

Listing 4-1 *(continued)*

```
                <STEALS>0</STEALS>
                <CAUGHT_STEALING>0</CAUGHT_STEALING>
                <SACRIFICE_HITS>0</SACRIFICE_HITS>
                <SACRIFICE_FLIES>0</SACRIFICE_FLIES>
                <ERRORS>1</ERRORS>
                <WALKS>0</WALKS>
                <STRUCK_OUT>4</STRUCK_OUT>
                <HIT_BY_PITCH>0</HIT_BY_PITCH></PLAYER>
      </TEAM>
      <TEAM>
        <TEAM_CITY>Florida</TEAM_CITY>
        <TEAM_NAME>Marlins</TEAM_NAME>
      </TEAM>
      <TEAM>
        <TEAM_CITY>Montreal</TEAM_CITY>
        <TEAM_NAME>Expos</TEAM_NAME>
      </TEAM>
      <TEAM>
        <TEAM_CITY>New York</TEAM_CITY>
        <TEAM_NAME>Mets</TEAM_NAME>
      </TEAM>
      <TEAM>
        <TEAM_CITY>Philadelphia</TEAM_CITY>
        <TEAM_NAME>Phillies</TEAM_NAME>
      </TEAM>
    </DIVISION>
    <DIVISION>
      <DIVISION_NAME>Central</DIVISION_NAME>
      <TEAM>
        <TEAM_CITY>Chicago</TEAM_CITY>
        <TEAM_NAME>Cubs</TEAM_NAME>
      </TEAM>
      <TEAM>
        <TEAM_CITY>Cincinatti</TEAM_CITY>
        <TEAM_NAME>Reds</TEAM_NAME>
      </TEAM>
      <TEAM>
        <TEAM_CITY>Houston</TEAM_CITY>
        <TEAM_NAME>Astros</TEAM_NAME>
      </TEAM>
      <TEAM>
        <TEAM_CITY>Milwaukee</TEAM_CITY>
        <TEAM_NAME>Brewers</TEAM_NAME>
      </TEAM>
      <TEAM>
        <TEAM_CITY>Pittsburgh</TEAM_CITY>
        <TEAM_NAME>Pirates</TEAM_NAME>
      </TEAM>
      <TEAM>
        <TEAM_CITY>St. Louis</TEAM_CITY>
        <TEAM_NAME>Cardinals</TEAM_NAME>
```

```
        </TEAM>
      </DIVISION>
      <DIVISION>
        <DIVISION_NAME>West</DIVISION_NAME>
        <TEAM>
          <TEAM_CITY>Arizona</TEAM_CITY>
          <TEAM_NAME>Diamondbacks</TEAM_NAME>
        </TEAM>
        <TEAM>
          <TEAM_CITY>Colorado</TEAM_CITY>
          <TEAM_NAME>Rockies</TEAM_NAME>
        </TEAM>
        <TEAM>
          <TEAM_CITY>Los Angeles</TEAM_CITY>
          <TEAM_NAME>Dodgers</TEAM_NAME>
        </TEAM>
        <TEAM>
          <TEAM_CITY>San Diego</TEAM_CITY>
          <TEAM_NAME>Padres</TEAM_NAME>
        </TEAM>
        <TEAM>
          <TEAM_CITY>San Francisco</TEAM_CITY>
          <TEAM_NAME>Giants</TEAM_NAME>
        </TEAM>
      </DIVISION>
    </LEAGUE>
    <LEAGUE>
      <LEAGUE_NAME>American League</LEAGUE_NAME>
      <DIVISION>
        <DIVISION_NAME>East</DIVISION_NAME>
        <TEAM>
          <TEAM_CITY>Baltimore</TEAM_CITY>
          <TEAM_NAME>Orioles</TEAM_NAME>
        </TEAM>
        <TEAM>
          <TEAM_CITY>Boston</TEAM_CITY>
          <TEAM_NAME>Red Sox</TEAM_NAME>
        </TEAM>
        <TEAM>
          <TEAM_CITY>New York</TEAM_CITY>
          <TEAM_NAME>Yankees</TEAM_NAME>
        </TEAM>
        <TEAM>
          <TEAM_CITY>Tampa Bay</TEAM_CITY>
          <TEAM_NAME>Devil Rays</TEAM_NAME>
        </TEAM>
        <TEAM>
          <TEAM_CITY>Toronto</TEAM_CITY>
          <TEAM_NAME>Blue Jays</TEAM_NAME>
        </TEAM>
      </DIVISION>
      <DIVISION>
```

Continued

Listing 4-1 *(continued)*

```
            <DIVISION_NAME>Central</DIVISION_NAME>
             <TEAM>
               <TEAM_CITY>Chicago</TEAM_CITY>
               <TEAM_NAME>White Sox</TEAM_NAME>
             </TEAM>
             <TEAM>
               <TEAM_CITY>Kansas City</TEAM_CITY>
               <TEAM_NAME>Royals</TEAM_NAME>
             </TEAM>
             <TEAM>
               <TEAM_CITY>Detroit</TEAM_CITY>
               <TEAM_NAME>Tigers</TEAM_NAME>
             </TEAM>
             <TEAM>
               <TEAM_CITY>Cleveland</TEAM_CITY>
               <TEAM_NAME>Indians</TEAM_NAME>
             </TEAM>
             <TEAM>
               <TEAM_CITY>Minnesota</TEAM_CITY>
               <TEAM_NAME>Twins</TEAM_NAME>
             </TEAM>
        </DIVISION>
        <DIVISION>
            <DIVISION_NAME>West</DIVISION_NAME>
             <TEAM>
               <TEAM_CITY>Anaheim</TEAM_CITY>
               <TEAM_NAME>Angels</TEAM_NAME>
             </TEAM>
             <TEAM>
               <TEAM_CITY>Oakland</TEAM_CITY>
               <TEAM_NAME>Athletics</TEAM_NAME>
             </TEAM>
             <TEAM>
               <TEAM_CITY>Seattle</TEAM_CITY>
               <TEAM_NAME>Mariners</TEAM_NAME>
             </TEAM>
             <TEAM>
               <TEAM_CITY>Texas</TEAM_CITY>
               <TEAM_NAME>Rangers</TEAM_NAME>
             </TEAM>
        </DIVISION>
    </LEAGUE>
</SEASON>
```

Figure 4-1 shows this document loaded into Internet Explorer 5.0.

```
D:\XML\Bible\CD\source\04\1998shortstats.xml - Microsoft Internet Explorer
 File   Edit   View   Favorites   Tools   Help
  ⇦         ⇨       ⊗        ⊡        ⌂         ⊕         ⊡        ⊘
 Back    Forward    Stop    Refresh    Home     Search   Favorites  History
Address  D:\XML\Bible\CD\source\04\1998shortstats.xml

  <?xml version="1.0" ?>
- <SEASON>
   <YEAR>1998</YEAR>
 - <LEAGUE>
    <LEAGUE_NAME>National League</LEAGUE_NAME>
  - <DIVISION>
     <DIVISION_NAME>East</DIVISION_NAME>
   - <TEAM>
      <TEAM_CITY>Atlanta</TEAM_CITY>
      <TEAM_NAME>Braves</TEAM_NAME>
    - <PLAYER>
       <SURNAME>Malloy</SURNAME>
       <GIVEN_NAME>Marty</GIVEN_NAME>
       <POSITION>Second Base</POSITION>
       <GAMES>11</GAMES>
       <GAMES_STARTED>8</GAMES_STARTED>
       <AT_BATS>28</AT_BATS>
       <RUNS>3</RUNS>
       <HITS>5</HITS>
       <DOUBLES>1</DOUBLES>
       <TRIPLES>0</TRIPLES>
       <HOME_RUNS>1</HOME_RUNS>
       <RBI>1</RBI>
       <STEALS>0</STEALS>
 Done                                        My
```

Figure 4-1: The 1998 major league statistics displayed in Internet Explorer 5.0

Even now this document is incomplete. It only contains players from one team (the Atlanta Braves) and only nine players from that team. Showing more than that would make the example too long to include in this book.

On the CD-ROM

A more complete XML document called 1998statistics.xml with statistics for all players in the 1998 major league is on the CD-ROM in the examples/baseball directory.Furthermore, I've deliberately limited the data included to make this a manageable example within the confines of this book. In reality there are far more details you could include. I've already alluded to the possibility of arranging the data game by game, pitch by pitch. Even without going to that extreme, there are a lot of details that could be added to individual elements. Teams also have coaches, managers, owners (How can you think of the Yankees without thinking of George Steinbrenner?), home stadiums, and more.

I've also deliberately omitted numbers that can be calculated from other numbers given here, such as batting average (number of hits divided by number of at bats). Nonetheless, players have batting arms, throwing arms, heights, weights, birth dates, positions, numbers, nicknames, colleges attended, and much more. And of course there are many more players than I've shown here. All of this is equally easy to include in XML. But we will stop the XMLification of the data here so we can move on; first to a brief discussion of why this data format is useful, then to the techniques that can be used for actually displaying it in a Web browser.

The Advantages of the XML Format

Table 4-1 does a pretty good job of displaying the batting data for a team in a comprehensible and compact fashion. What exactly have we gained by rewriting that table as the much longer XML document of Example 4-1? There are several benefits. Among them:

✦ The data is self-describing

✦ The data can be manipulated with standard tools

✦ The data can be viewed with standard tools

✦ Different views of the same data are easy to create with style sheets

The first major benefit of the XML format is that the data is self-describing. The meaning of each number is clearly and unmistakably associated with the number itself. When reading the document, you know that the 121 in <HITS>121</HITS> refers to hits and not runs batted in or strikeouts. If the person typing in the document skips a number, that doesn't mean that every number after it is misinterpreted. HITS is still HITS even if the preceding RUNS element is missing.

Cross-Reference In Part II you'll see that XML can even use DTDs to enforce constraints that certain elements like HITS or RUNS must be present.

The second benefit to providing the data in XML is that it enables the data to be manipulated in a wide range of XML-enabled tools, from expensive payware like Adobe FrameMaker to free open-source software like Python and Perl. The data may be bigger, but the extra redundancy allows more tools to process it.

The same is true when the time comes to view the data. The XML document can be loaded into Internet Explorer 5.0, Mozilla, FrameMaker 5.5.6, and many other tools, all of which provide unique, useful views of the data. The document can even be loaded into simple, bare-bones text editors like vi, BBEdit, and TextPad. So it's at least marginally viewable on most platforms.

Using new software isn't the only way to get a different view of the data either. In the next section, we'll build a style sheet for baseball statistics that provides a completely different way of looking at the data than what you see in Figure 4-1. Every time you apply a different style sheet to the same document you see a different picture.

Lastly, you should ask yourself if the size is really that important. Modern hard drives are quite big, and can a hold a lot of data, even if it's not stored very efficiently. Furthermore, XML files compress very well. The complete major league 1998 statistics document is 653K. However, compressing the file with gzip gets that all the way down to 66K, almost 90 percent less. Advanced HTTP servers like Jigsaw can actually send compressed files rather than the uncompressed files so that network bandwidth used by a document like this is fairly close to its actual information content. Finally, you should not assume that binary file formats, especially general-purpose ones, are necessarily more efficient. A Microsoft Excel file that contains the same data as the 1998statistics.xml actually takes up 2.37 MB, more than three times as much space. Although you can certainly create more efficient file formats and encodings of this data, in practice that simply isn't often necessary.

Preparing a Style Sheet for Document Display

The view of the raw XML document shown in Figure 4-1 is not bad for some uses. For instance, it allows you to collapse and expand individual elements so you see only those parts of the document you want to see. However, most of the time you'd probably like a more finished look, especially if you're going to display it on the Web. To provide a more polished look, you must write a style sheet for the document.

In this chapter, we'll use CSS style sheets. A CSS style sheet associates particular formatting with each element of the document. The complete list of elements used in our XML document is:

```
SEASON
YEAR
LEAGUE
LEAGUE_NAME
DIVISION
DIVISION_NAME
TEAM
TEAM_CITY
TEAM_NAME
PLAYER
SURNAME
GIVEN_NAME
POSITION
GAMES
GAMES_STARTED
AT_BATS
RUNS
```

```
HITS
DOUBLES
TRIPLES
HOME_RUNS
RBI
STEALS
CAUGHT_STEALING
SACRIFICE_HITS
SACRIFICE_FLIES
ERRORS
WALKS
STRUCK_OUT
HIT_BY_PITCH
```

Generally, you'll want to follow an iterative procedure, adding style rules for each of these elements one at a time, checking that they do what you expect, then moving on to the next element. In this example, such an approach also has the advantage of introducing CSS properties one at a time for those who are not familiar with them.

Linking to a Style Sheet

The style sheet can be named anything you like. If it's only going to apply to one document, then it's customary to give it the same name as the document but with the three-letter extension .css instead of .xml. For instance, the style sheet for the XML document 1998shortstats.xml might be called 1998shortstats.css. On the other hand, if the same style sheet is going to be applied to many documents, then it should probably have a more generic name like baseballstats.css.

Cross-Reference

Since CSS style sheets cascade, more than one can be applied to the same document. Thus it's possible that baseballstats.css would apply some general formatting rules, while 1998shortstats.css would override a few to handle specific details in the one document 1998shortstats.xml. We'll discuss this procedure in Chapter 12, *Cascading Style Sheets Level 1*.

To attach a style sheet to the document, you simply add an additional `<?xml-stylesheet?>` processing instruction between the XML declaration and the root element, like this:

```
<?xml version="1.0" standalone="yes"?>
<?xml-stylesheet type="text/css" href="baseballstats.css"?>
<SEASON>
...
```

This tells a browser reading the document to apply the style sheet found in the file baseballstats.css to this document. This file is assumed to reside in the same directory and on the same server as the XML document itself. In other words, baseballstats.css is a relative URL. Complete URLs may also be used. For example:

```
<?xml version="1.0" standalone="yes"?>
<?xml-stylesheet type="text/css"
href="http://metalab.unc.edu/xml/examples/baseballstats.css"?>
<SEASON>
...
```

You can begin by simply placing an empty file named baseballstats.css in the same directory as the XML document. Once you've done this and added the necessary processing instruction to 1998shortstats.xml (Listing 4-1), the document now appears as shown in Figure 4-2. Only the element content is shown. The collapsible outline view of Figure 4-1 is gone. The formatting of the element content uses the browser's defaults, black 12-point Times Roman on a white background in this case.

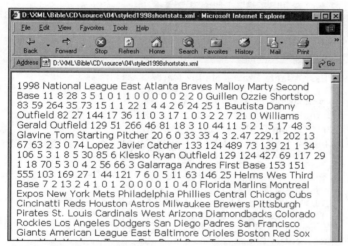

Figure 4-2: The 1998 major league statistics displayed after a blank style sheet is applied

Note You'll also see a view much like Figure 4-2 if the style sheet named by the `xml-stylesheet` processing instruction can't be found in the specified location.

Assigning Style Rules to the Root Element

You do not have to assign a style rule to each element in the list. Many elements can simply allow the styles of their parents to cascade down. The most important style, therefore, is the one for the root element, which is SEASON in this example. This defines the default for all the other elements on the page. Computer monitors at roughly 72 dpi don't have as high a resolution as paper at 300 or more dpi. Therefore, Web pages should generally use a larger point size than is customary. Let's make the default 14-point type, black on a white background, as shown below:

```
SEASON {font-size: 14pt; background-color: white;
        color: black; display: block}
```

Place this statement in a text file, save the file with the name baseballstats.css in the same directory as Listing 4-1, 1998shortstats.xml, and open 1998shortstats.xml in your browser. You should see something like what is shown in Figure 4-3.

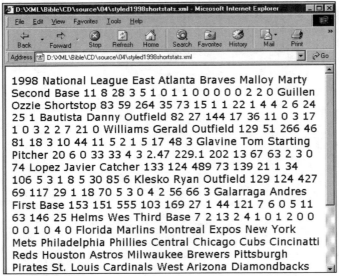

Figure 4-3: Baseball statistics in 14-point type with a black-on-white background

The default font size changed between Figure 4-2 and Figure 4-3. The text color and background color did not. Indeed, it was not absolutely required to set them, since black foreground and white background are the defaults. Nonetheless, nothing is lost by being explicit regarding what you want.

Assigning Style Rules to Titles

The YEAR element is more or less the title of the document. Therefore, let's make it appropriately large and bold — 32 points should be big enough. Furthermore, it should stand out from the rest of the document rather than simply running together with the rest of the content, so let's make it a centered block element. All of this can be accomplished by the following style rule.

```
YEAR {display: block; font-size: 32pt; font-weight: bold;
      text-align: center}
```

Figure 4-4 shows the document after this rule has been added to the style sheet. Notice in particular the line break after "1998." That's there because YEAR is now a block-level element. Everything else in the document is an inline element. You can only center (or left-align, right-align or justify) block-level elements.

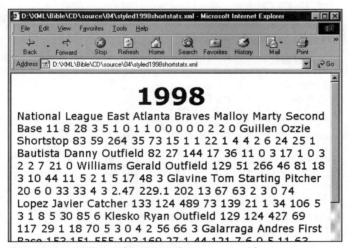

Figure 4-4: Stylizing the YEAR element as a title

In this document with this style rule, YEAR duplicates the functionality of HTML's H1 header element. Since this document is so neatly hierarchical, several other elements serve the role of H2 headers, H3 headers, etc. These elements can be formatted by similar rules with only a slightly smaller font size.

For instance, SEASON is divided into two LEAGUE elements. The name of each LEAGUE, that is, the LEAGUE_NAME element — has the same role as an H2 element in HTML. Each LEAGUE element is divided into three DIVISION elements. The name of each DIVISION—that is, the DIVISION_NAME element—has the same role as an H3 element in HTML. These two rules format them accordingly:

```
LEAGUE_NAME {display: block; text-align: center; font-size:
28pt; font-weight: bold}
DIVISION_NAME {display: block; text-align: center; font-size:
24pt; font-weight: bold}
```

Figure 4-5 shows the resulting document.

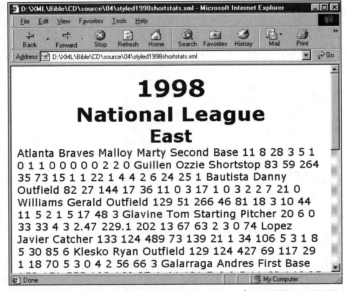

Figure 4-5: Stylizing the LEAGUE_NAME and DIVISION_NAME elements as headings

Note One crucial difference between HTML and XML is that in HTML there's generally no one element that contains both the title of a section (the H2, H3, H4, etc., header) and the complete contents of the section. Instead the contents of a section have to be implied as everything between the end of one level of header and the start of the next header at the same level. This is particularly important for software that has to parse HTML documents, for instance to generate a table of contents automatically.

Divisions are divided into TEAM elements. Formatting these is a little trickier because the title of a team is not simply the TEAM_NAME element but rather the TEAM_CITY concatenated with the TEAM_NAME. Therefore these need to be inline elements rather than separate block-level elements. However, they are still titles so we set them to bold, italic, 20-point type. Figure 4-6 shows the results of adding these two rules to the style sheet.

```
TEAM_CITY {font-size: 20pt; font-weight: bold;
          font-style: italic}
TEAM_NAME {font-size: 20pt; font-weight: bold;
          font-style: italic}
```

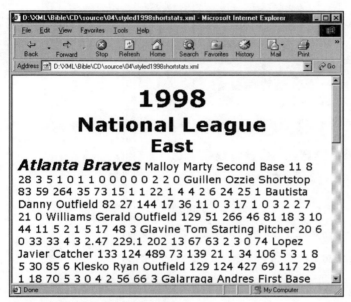

Figure 4-6: Stylizing Team Names

At this point it would be nice to arrange the team names and cities as a combined block-level element. There are several ways to do this. You could, for instance, add an additional TEAM_TITLE element to the XML document whose sole purpose is merely to contain the TEAM_NAME and TEAM_CITY. For instance:

```
<TEAM>
  <TEAM_TITLE>
    <TEAM_CITY>Colorado</TEAM_CITY>
    <TEAM_NAME>Rockies</TEAM_NAME>
  </TEAM_TITLE>
</TEAM>
```

Next, you would add a style rule that applies block-level formatting to TEAM_TITLE:

```
TEAM_TITLE {display: block; text-align: center}
```

However, you really should never reorganize an XML document just to make the style sheet work easier. After all, the whole point of a style sheet is to keep formatting information out of the document itself. However, you can achieve much the same effect by making the immediately preceding and following elements block-level elements; that is, TEAM and PLAYER respectively. This places the TEAM_NAME and TEAM_CITY in an implicit block-level element of their own. Figure 4-7 shows the result.

```
TEAM {display: block}
PLAYER {display: block}
```

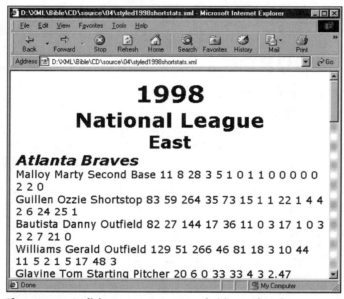

Figure 4-7: Stylizing team names and cities as headers

Assigning Style Rules to Player and Statistics Elements

The trickiest formatting this document requires is for the individual players and statistics. Each team has a couple of dozen players. Each player has statistics. You could think of a TEAM element as being divided into PLAYER elements, and place each player in his own block-level section as you did for previous elements. However, a more attractive and efficient way to organize this is to use a table. The style rules that accomplish this look like this:

```
TEAM {display: table}
TEAM_CITY {display: table-caption}
TEAM_NAME {display: table-caption}
PLAYER {display: table-row}
SURNAME {display: table-cell}
GIVEN_NAME {display: table-cell}
POSITION {display: table-cell}
```

```
GAMES {display: table-cell}
GAMES_STARTED {display: table-cell}
AT_BATS {display: table-cell}
RUNS {display: table-cell}
HITS {display: table-cell}
DOUBLES {display: table-cell}
TRIPLES {display: table-cell}
HOME_RUNS {display: table-cell}
RBI {display: table-cell}
STEALS {display: table-cell}
CAUGHT_STEALING {display: table-cell}
SACRIFICE_HITS {display: table-cell}
SACRIFICE_FLIES {display: table-cell}
ERRORS {display: table-cell}
WALKS {display: table-cell}
STRUCK_OUT {display: table-cell}
HIT_BY_PITCH {display: table-cell}
```

Unfortunately, table properties are only supported in CSS Level 2, and this is not yet supported by Internet Explorer 5.0 or any other browser available at the time of this writing. Instead, since table formatting doesn't yet work, I'll settle for just making TEAM and PLAYER block-level elements, and leaving all the rest with the default formatting.

Summing Up

Listing 4-2 shows the finished style sheet. CSS style sheets don't have a lot of structure beyond the individual rules. In essence, this is just a list of all the rules I introduced separately above. Reordering them wouldn't make any difference as long as they're all present.

Listing 4-2: **baseballstats.css**

```
SEASON {font-size: 14pt; background-color: white;
       color: black; display: block}
YEAR {display: block; font-size: 32pt; font-weight: bold;
      text-align: center}
LEAGUE_NAME {display: block; text-align: center;
             font-size: 28pt; font-weight: bold}
DIVISION_NAME {display: block; text-align: center;
               font-size: 24pt; font-weight: bold}
TEAM_CITY {font-size: 20pt; font-weight: bold;
           font-style: italic}
TEAM_NAME {font-size: 20pt; font-weight: bold;
           font-style: italic}
TEAM {display: block}
PLAYER {display: block}
```

This completes the basic formatting for baseball statistics. However, work clearly remains to be done. Browsers that support real table formatting would definitely help. However, there are some other pieces as well. They are noted below in no particular order:

✦ The numbers are presented raw with no indication of what they represent. Each number should be identified by a caption that names it, like "RBI" or "At Bats."

✦ Interesting data like batting average that could be calculated from the data presented here is not included.

✦ Some of the titles are a little short. For instance, it would be nice if the title of the document were "1998 Major League Baseball" instead of simply "1998".

✦ If all players in the Major League were included, this document would be so long it would be hard to read. Something similar to Internet Explorer's collapsible outline view for documents with no style sheet would be useful in this situation.

✦ Because pitcher statistics are so different from batter statistics, it would be nice to sort them separately in the roster.

Many of these points could be addressed by adding more content to the document. For instance, to change the title "1998" to "1998 Major League Baseball," all you have to do is rewrite the YEAR element like this:

```
1998 Major League Baseball
```

Captions can be added to the player stats with a phantom player at the top of each roster, like this:

```
<PLAYER>
  <SURNAME>Surname</SURNAME>
  <GIVEN_NAME>Given name</GIVEN_NAME>
  <POSITION>Postion</POSITION>
  <GAMES>Games</GAMES>
  <GAMES_STARTED>Games Started</GAMES_STARTED>
  <AT_BATS>At Bats</AT_BATS>
  <RUNS>Runs</RUNS>
  <HITS>Hits</HITS>
  <DOUBLES>Doubles</DOUBLES>
  <TRIPLES>Triples</TRIPLES>
  <HOME_RUNS>Home Runs</HOME_RUNS>
  <RBI>Runs Batted In</RBI>
  <STEALS>Steals</STEALS>
  <CAUGHT_STEALING>Caught Stealing</CAUGHT_STEALING>
  <SACRIFICE_HITS>Sacrifice Hits</SACRIFICE_HITS>
  <SACRIFICE_FLIES>Sacrifice Flies</SACRIFICE_FLIES>
  <ERRORS>Errors</ERRORS>
  <WALKS>Walks</WALKS>
  <STRUCK_OUT>Struck Out</STRUCK_OUT>
  <HIT_BY_PITCH>Hit By Pitch</HIT_BY_PITCH>
</PLAYER>
```

Still, there's something fundamentally troublesome about such tactics. The year is 1998, not "1998 Major League Baseball." The caption "At Bats" is not the same as a number of at bats. (It's the difference between the name of a thing and the thing itself.) You can encode still more markup like this:

```
<TABLE_HEAD>
  <COLUMN_LABEL>Surname</COLUMN_LABEL>
  <COLUMN_LABEL>Given name</COLUMN_LABEL>
  <COLUMN_LABEL>Position</COLUMN_LABEL>
  <COLUMN_LABEL>Games</COLUMN_LABEL>
  <COLUMN_LABEL>Games Started</COLUMN_LABEL>
  <COLUMN_LABEL>At Bats</COLUMN_LABEL>
  <COLUMN_LABEL>Runs</COLUMN_LABEL>
  <COLUMN_LABEL>Hits</COLUMN_LABEL>
  <COLUMN_LABEL>Doubles</COLUMN_LABEL>
  <COLUMN_LABEL>Triples</COLUMN_LABEL>
  <COLUMN_LABEL>Home Runs</COLUMN_LABEL>
  <COLUMN_LABEL>Runs Batted In</COLUMN_LABEL>
  <COLUMN_LABEL>Steals</COLUMN_LABEL>
  <COLUMN_LABEL>Caught Stealing</COLUMN_LABEL>
  <COLUMN_LABEL>Sacrifice Hits</COLUMN_LABEL>
  <COLUMN_LABEL>Sacrifice Flies</COLUMN_LABEL>
  <COLUMN_LABEL>Errors</COLUMN_LABEL>
  <COLUMN_LABEL>Walks</COLUMN_LABEL>
  <COLUMN_LABEL>Struck Out</COLUMN_LABEL>
  <COLUMN_LABEL>Hit By Pitch</COLUMN_LABEL>
</TABLE_HEAD>
```

However, this basically reinvents HTML, and returns us to the point of using markup for formatting rather than meaning. Furthermore, we're still simply repeating the information that's already contained in the names of the elements. The full document is large enough as is. We'd prefer not to make it larger.

Adding batting and other averages is easy. Just include the data as additional elements. For example, here's a player with batting, slugging, and on-base averages:

```
<PLAYER>
<SURNAME>Malloy</SURNAME>
<GIVEN_NAME>Marty</GIVEN_NAME>
<POSITION>Second Base</POSITION>
<GAMES>11</GAMES>
<GAMES_STARTED>8</GAMES_STARTED>
<ON_BASE_AVERAGE>.233</ON_BASE_AVERAGE>
<SLUGGING_AVERAGE>.321</SLUGGING_AVERAGE>
<BATTING_AVERAGE>.179</BATTING_AVERAGE>
<AT_BATS>28</AT_BATS>
<RUNS>3</RUNS>
<HITS>5</HITS>
<DOUBLES>1</DOUBLES>
<TRIPLES>0</TRIPLES>
<HOME_RUNS>1</HOME_RUNS>
<RBI>1</RBI>
```

```
<STEALS>0</STEALS>
<CAUGHT_STEALING>0</CAUGHT_STEALING>
<SACRIFICE_HITS>0</SACRIFICE_HITS>
<SACRIFICE_FLIES>0</SACRIFICE_FLIES>
<ERRORS>0</ERRORS>
<WALKS>2</WALKS>
<STRUCK_OUT>2</STRUCK_OUT>
<HIT_BY_PITCH>0</HIT_BY_PITCH>
</PLAYER>
```

However, this information is redundant because it can be calculated from the other information already included in a player's listing. Batting average, for example, is simply the number of base hits divided by the number of at bats; that is, HITS/AT_BATS. Redundant data makes maintaining and updating the document exponentially more difficult. A simple change or addition to a single element requires changes and recalculations in multiple locations.

What's really needed is a different style-sheet language that enables you to add certain boiler-plate content to elements and to perform transformations on the element content that is present. Such a language exists — the Extensible Style Language (XSL).

 Cross-Reference   Extensible Style Language (XSL) is covered in Chapters 5, 14, and 15.

CSS is simpler than XSL and works well for basic Web pages and reasonably straightforward documents. XSL is considerably more complex, but also more powerful. XSL builds on the simple CSS formatting you've learned about here, but also provides transformations of the source document into various forms the reader can view. It's often a good idea to make a first pass at a problem using CSS while you're still debugging your XML, then move to XSL to achieve greater flexibility.

Summary

In this chapter, you saw examples demonstrating the creation of an XML document from scratch. In particular you learned

- ✦ How to examine the data you'll include in your XML document to identify the elements.
- ✦ How to mark up the data with XML tags you define.
- ✦ The advantages XML formats provide over traditional formats.
- ✦ How to write a style sheet that says how the document should be formatted and displayed.

This chapter was full of seat-of-the-pants/back-of-the-envelope coding. The document was written without more than minimal concern for details. In the next chapter, we'll explore some additional means of embedding information in XML documents including attributes, comments, and processing instructions, and look at an alternative way of encoding baseball statistics in XML.

✦   ✦   ✦

Attributes, Empty Tags, and XSL

Y ou can encode a given set of data in XML in nearly
an infinite number of ways. There's no one right
way to do it although some ways are more right than others,
and some are more appropriate for particular uses. In this
chapter, we explore a different solution to the problem of
marking up baseball statistics in XML, carrying over the
baseball example from the previous chapter. Specifically,
we will address the use of attributes to store information
and empty tags to define element positions. In addition,
since CSS doesn't work well with content-less XML
elements of this form, we'll examine an alternative —
and more powerful — style sheet language called XSL.

Attributes

In the last chapter, all data was categorized into the name of
a tag or the contents of an element. This is a straightforward
and easy-to-understand approach, but it's not the only one.
As in HTML, XML elements may have attributes. An attribute
is a name-value pair associated with an element. The name
and the value are each strings, and no element may contain
two attributes with the same name.

You're already familiar with attribute syntax from HTML. For
example, consider this `<IMG>` tag:

```
<IMG SRC=cup.gif WIDTH=89 HEIGHT=67 ALT="Cup
of coffee">
```

It has four attributes, the SRC attribute whose value is cup.gif, the WIDTH attribute whose value is 89, the HEIGHT attribute whose value is 67, and the ALT attribute whose value is Cup of coffee. However, in XML-unlike HTML-attribute values must always be quoted and start tags must have matching close tags. Thus, the XML equivalent of this tag is:

```
<IMG SRC="cup.gif" WIDTH="89" HEIGHT="67" ALT="Cup of coffee">
</IMG>
```

Note   Another difference between HTML and XML is that XML assigns no particular meaning to the IMG tag and its attributes. In particular, there's no guarantee that an XML browser will interpret this tag as an instruction to load and display the image in the file cup.gif.

You can apply attribute syntax to the baseball example quite easily. This has the advantage of making the markup somewhat more concise. For example, instead of containing a YEAR child element, the SEASON element only needs a YEAR attribute.

```
<SEASON YEAR="1998">
</SEASON>
```

On the other hand, LEAGUE should be a child of the SEASON element rather than an attribute. For one thing, there are two leagues in a season. Anytime there's likely to be more than one of something child elements are called for. Attribute names must be unique within an element. Thus you should not, for example, write a SEASON element like this:

```
<SEASON YEAR="1998" LEAGUE="National" League="American">
</SEASON>
```

The second reason LEAGUE is naturally a child element rather than an attribute is that it has substructure; it is subdivided into DIVISION elements. Attribute values are flat text. XML elements can conveniently encode structure-attribute values cannot.

However, the name of a league is unstructured, flat text; and there's only one name per league so LEAGUE elements can easily have a NAME attribute instead of a LEAGUE_NAME child element:

```
<LEAGUE NAME="National League">
</LEAGUE>
```

Since an attribute is more closely tied to its element than a child element is, you don't run into problems by using NAME instead of LEAGUE_NAME for the name of the attribute. Divisions and teams can also have NAME attributes without any fear of confusion with the name of a league. Since a tag can have more than one attribute (as long as the attributes have different names), you can make a team's city an attribute as well, as shown below:

```
<LEAGUE NAME="American League">
  <DIVISION NAME="East">
   <TEAM NAME="Orioles" CITY="Baltimore"></TEAM>
   <TEAM NAME="Red Sox" CITY="Boston"></TEAM>
   <TEAM NAME="Yankees" CITY="New York"></TEAM>
   <TEAM NAME="Devil Rays" CITY="Tampa Bay"></TEAM>
   <TEAM NAME="Blue Jays" CITY="Toronto"></TEAM>
  </DIVISION>
</LEAGUE>
```

Players will have a lot of attributes if you choose to make each statistic an attribute. For example, here are Joe Girardi's 1998 statistics as attributes:

```
<PLAYER GIVEN_NAME="Joe" SURNAME="Girardi"
  GAMES="78" AT_BATS="254" RUNS="31" HITS="70"
  DOUBLES="11" TRIPLES="4" HOME_RUNS="3"
  RUNS_BATTED_IN="31" WALKS="14" STRUCK_OUT="38"
  STOLEN_BASES="2" CAUGHT_STEALING="4"
  SACRIFICE_FLY="1" SACRIFICE_HIT="8"
  HIT_BY_PITCH="2">
</PLAYER>
```

Listing 5-1 uses this new attribute style for a complete XML document containing the baseball statistics for the 1998 major league season. It displays the same information (i.e., two leagues, six divisions, 30 teams, and nine players) as does Listing 4-1 in the last chapter. It is merely marked up differently. Figure 5-1 shows this document loaded into Internet Explorer 5.0 without a style sheet.

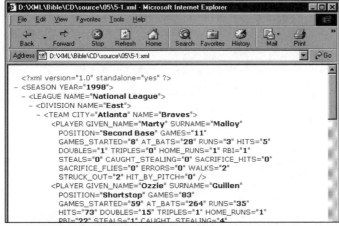

Figure 5-1: The 1998 major league baseball statistics using attributes for most information.

Listing 5-1: **A complete XML document that uses attributes to store baseball statistics**

```
<?xml version="1.0" standalone="yes"?>
<SEASON YEAR="1998">
  <LEAGUE NAME="National League">
    <DIVISION NAME="East">
      <TEAM CITY="Atlanta" NAME="Braves">
        <PLAYER GIVEN_NAME="Marty" SURNAME="Malloy"
          POSITION="Second Base" GAMES="11" GAMES_STARTED="8"
          AT_BATS="28" RUNS="3" HITS="5" DOUBLES="1"
          TRIPLES="0" HOME_RUNS="1" RBI="1" STEALS="0"
          CAUGHT_STEALING="0" SACRIFICE_HITS="0"
          SACRIFICE_FLIES="0" ERRORS="0" WALKS="2"
          STRUCK_OUT="2" HIT_BY_PITCH="0">
        </PLAYER>
        <PLAYER GIVEN_NAME="Ozzie" SURNAME="Guillen"
          POSITION="Shortstop" GAMES="83" GAMES_STARTED="59"
          AT_BATS="264" RUNS="35" HITS="73" DOUBLES="15"
          TRIPLES="1" HOME_RUNS="1" RBI="22" STEALS="1"
          CAUGHT_STEALING="4" SACRIFICE_HITS="4"
          SACRIFICE_FLIES="2" ERRORS="6" WALKS="24"
          STRUCK_OUT="25" HIT_BY_PITCH="1">
        </PLAYER>
        <PLAYER GIVEN_NAME="Danny" SURNAME="Bautista"
          POSITION="Outfield" GAMES="82" GAMES_STARTED="27"
          AT_BATS="144" RUNS="17" HITS="36" DOUBLES="11"
          TRIPLES="0" HOME_RUNS="3" RBI="17" STEALS="1"
          CAUGHT_STEALING="0" SACRIFICE_HITS="3"
          SACRIFICE_FLIES="2" ERRORS="2" WALKS="7"
          STRUCK_OUT="21" HIT_BY_PITCH="0">
        </PLAYER>
        <PLAYER GIVEN_NAME="Gerald" SURNAME="Williams"
          POSITION="Outfield" GAMES="129" GAMES_STARTED="51"
          AT_BATS="266" RUNS="46" HITS="81" DOUBLES="18"
          TRIPLES="3" HOME_RUNS="10" RBI="44" STEALS="11"
          CAUGHT_STEALING="5" SACRIFICE_HITS="2"
          SACRIFICE_FLIES="1" ERRORS="5" WALKS="17"
          STRUCK_OUT="48" HIT_BY_PITCH="3">
        </PLAYER>
        <PLAYER GIVEN_NAME="Tom" SURNAME="Glavine"
          POSITION="Starting Pitcher" GAMES="33"
          GAMES_STARTED="33" WINS="20" LOSSES="6" SAVES="0"
          COMPLETE_GAMES="4" SHUT_OUTS="3" ERA="2.47"
          INNINGS="229.1" HOME_RUNS_AGAINST="13"
          RUNS_AGAINST="67" EARNED_RUNS="63" HIT_BATTER="2"
          WILD_PITCHES="3" BALK="0" WALKED_BATTER="74"
          STRUCK_OUT_BATTER="157">
        </PLAYER>
        <PLAYER GIVEN_NAME="Javier" SURNAME="Lopez"
          POSITION="Catcher" GAMES="133" GAMES_STARTED="124"
          AT_BATS="489" RUNS="73" HITS="139" DOUBLES="21"
          TRIPLES="1" HOME_RUNS="34" RBI="106" STEALS="5"
```

```
        CAUGHT_STEALING="3" SACRIFICE_HITS="1"
        SACRIFICE_FLIES="8" ERRORS="5" WALKS="30"
        STRUCK_OUT="85" HIT_BY_PITCH="6">
      </PLAYER>
      <PLAYER GIVEN_NAME="Ryan" SURNAME="Klesko"
       POSITION="Outfield" GAMES="129" GAMES_STARTED="124"
       AT_BATS="427" RUNS="69" HITS="117" DOUBLES="29"
       TRIPLES="1" HOME_RUNS="18" RBI="70" STEALS="5"
       CAUGHT_STEALING="3" SACRIFICE_HITS="0"
       SACRIFICE_FLIES="4" ERRORS="2" WALKS="56"
       STRUCK_OUT="66" HIT_BY_PITCH="3">
      </PLAYER>
      <PLAYER GIVEN_NAME="Andres" SURNAME="Galarraga"
       POSITION="First Base" GAMES="153" GAMES_STARTED="151"
       AT_BATS="555" RUNS="103" HITS="169" DOUBLES="27"
       TRIPLES="1" HOME_RUNS="44" RBI="121" STEALS="7"
       CAUGHT_STEALING="6" SACRIFICE_HITS="0"
       SACRIFICE_FLIES="5" ERRORS="11" WALKS="63"
       STRUCK_OUT="146" HIT_BY_PITCH="25">
      </PLAYER>
      <PLAYER GIVEN_NAME="Wes" SURNAME="Helms"
       POSITION="Third Base" GAMES="7" GAMES_STARTED="2"
       AT_BATS="13" RUNS="2" HITS="4" DOUBLES="1"
       TRIPLES="0" HOME_RUNS="1" RBI="2" STEALS="0"
       CAUGHT_STEALING="0" SACRIFICE_HITS="0"
       SACRIFICE_FLIES="0" ERRORS="1" WALKS="0"
       STRUCK_OUT="4" HIT_BY_PITCH="0">
      </PLAYER>
    </TEAM>
    <TEAM CITY="Florida" NAME="Marlins">
    </TEAM>
    <TEAM CITY="Montreal" NAME="Expos">
    </TEAM>
    <TEAM CITY="New York" NAME="Mets">
    </TEAM>
    <TEAM CITY="Philadelphia" NAME="Phillies">
    </TEAM>
  </DIVISION>
  <DIVISION NAME="Central">
    <TEAM CITY="Chicago" NAME="Cubs">
    </TEAM>
    <TEAM CITY="Cincinnati" NAME="Reds">
    </TEAM>
    <TEAM CITY="Houston" NAME="Astros">
    </TEAM>
    <TEAM CITY="Milwaukee" NAME="Brewers">
    </TEAM>
    <TEAM CITY="Pittsburgh" NAME="Pirates">
    </TEAM>
    <TEAM CITY="St. Louis" NAME="Cardinals">
    </TEAM>
  </DIVISION>
```

Continued

Listing 5-1 *(continued)*

```
      <DIVISION NAME="West">
        <TEAM CITY="Arizona" NAME="Diamondbacks">
        </TEAM>
        <TEAM CITY="Colorado" NAME="Rockies">
        </TEAM>
        <TEAM CITY="Los Angeles" NAME="Dodgers">
        </TEAM>
        <TEAM CITY="San Diego" NAME="Padres">
        </TEAM>
        <TEAM CITY="San Francisco" NAME="Giants">
        </TEAM>
      </DIVISION>
    </LEAGUE>
    <LEAGUE NAME="American League">
      <DIVISION NAME="East">
        <TEAM CITY="Baltimore" NAME="Orioles">
        </TEAM>
        <TEAM CITY="Boston" NAME="Red Sox">
        </TEAM>
        <TEAM CITY="New York" NAME="Yankees">
        </TEAM>
        <TEAM CITY="Tampa Bay" NAME="Devil Rays">
        </TEAM>
        <TEAM CITY="Toronto" NAME="Blue Jays">
        </TEAM>
      </DIVISION>
      <DIVISION NAME="Central">
        <TEAM CITY="Chicago" NAME="White Sox">
        </TEAM>
        <TEAM CITY="Kansas City" NAME="Royals">
        </TEAM>
        <TEAM CITY="Detroit" NAME="Tigers">
        </TEAM>
        <TEAM CITY="Cleveland" NAME="Indians">
        </TEAM>
        <TEAM CITY="Minnesota" NAME="Twins">
        </TEAM>
      </DIVISION>
      <DIVISION NAME="West">
        <TEAM CITY="Anaheim" NAME="Angels">
        </TEAM>
        <TEAM CITY="Oakland" NAME="Athletics">
        </TEAM>
        <TEAM CITY="Seattle" NAME="Mariners">
        </TEAM>
        <TEAM CITY="Texas" NAME="Rangers">
        </TEAM>
      </DIVISION>
    </LEAGUE>
  </SEASON>
```

Listing 5-1 uses only attributes for player information. Listing 4-1 used only element content. There are intermediate approaches as well. For example, you could make the player's name part of element content while leaving the rest of the statistics as attributes, like this:

```
<P>
   On Tuesday <PLAYER GAMES="78" AT_BATS="254" RUNS="31"
   HITS="70" DOUBLES="11" TRIPLES="4" HOME_RUNS="3"
   RUNS_BATTED_IN="31" WALKS="14" STRIKE_OUTS="38"
   STOLEN_BASES="2" CAUGHT_STEALING="4"
   SACRIFICE_FLY="1" SACRIFICE_HIT="8"
   HIT_BY_PITCH="2">Joe Girardi</PLAYER> struck out twice
   and...
</P>
```

This would include Joe Girardi's name in the text of a page while still making his statistics available to readers who want to look deeper, as a hypertext footnote or tool tip. There's always more than one way to encode the same data. Which way you pick generally depends on the needs of your specific application.

Attributes versus Elements

There are no hard and fast rules about when to use child elements and when to use attributes. Generally, you'll use whichever suits your application. With experience, you'll gain a feel for when attributes are easier than child elements and vice versa. Until then, one good rule of thumb is that the data itself should be stored in elements. Information about the data (meta-data) should be stored in attributes. And when in doubt, put the information in the elements.

To differentiate between data and meta-data, ask yourself whether someone reading the document would want to see a particular piece of information. If the answer is yes, then the information probably belongs in a child element. If the answer is no, then the information probably belongs in an attribute. If all tags were stripped from the document along with all the attributes, the basic information should still be present. Attributes are good places to put ID numbers, URLs, references, and other information not directly or immediately relevant to the reader. However, there are many exceptions to the basic principal of storing meta-data as attributes. These include:

✦ Attributes can't hold structure well.

✦ Elements allow you to include meta-meta-data (information about the information about the information).

✦ Not everyone always agrees on what is and isn't meta-data.

✦ Elements are more extensible in the face of future changes.

Structured Meta-data

One important principal to remember is that elements can have substructure and attributes can't. This makes elements far more flexible, and may convince you to encode meta-data as child elements. For example, suppose you're writing a paper and you want to include a source for a fact. It might look something like this:

```
<FACT SOURCE="The Biographical History of Baseball,
Donald Dewey and Nicholas Acocella (New York: Carroll &amp;
Graf Publishers, Inc. 1995) p. 169">
  Josh Gibson is the only person in the history of baseball to
  hit a pitch out of Yankee Stadium.
</FACT>
```

Clearly the information "The Biographical History of Baseball, Donald Dewey and Nicholas Acocella (New York: Carroll & Graf Publishers, Inc. 1995) p. 169" is meta-data. It is not the fact itself. Rather it is information about the fact. However, the SOURCE attribute contains a lot of implicit substructure. You might find it more useful to organize the information like this:

```
<SOURCE>
  <AUTHOR>Donald Dewey</AUTHOR>
  <AUTHOR>Nicholas Acocella</AUTHOR>
  <BOOK>
    <TITLE>The Biographical History of Baseball</TITLE>
    <PAGES>169</PAGES>
    <YEAR>1995</YEAR>
  </BOOK>
</SOURCE>
```

Furthermore, using elements instead of attributes makes it straightforward to include additional information like the authors' e-mail addresses, a URL where an electronic copy of the document can be found, the title or theme of the particular issue of the journal, and anything else that seems important.

Dates are another common example. One common piece of meta-data about scholarly articles is the date the article was first received. This is important for establishing priority of discovery and invention. It's easy to include a DATE attribute in an ARTICLE tag like this:

```
<ARTICLE DATE="06/28/1969">
  Polymerase Reactions in Organic Compounds
</ARTICLE>
```

However, the DATE attribute has substructure signified by the /. Getting that structure out of the attribute value, however, is much more difficult than reading child elements of a DATE element, as shown below:

```
<DATE>
  <YEAR>1969</YEAR>
  <MONTH>06</MONTH>
  <DAY>28</DAY>
</DATE>
```

For instance, with CSS or XSL, it's easy to format the day and month invisibly so that only the year appears. For example, using CSS:

```
YEAR {display: inline}
MONTH {display: none}
DAY {display: none}
```

If the DATE is stored as an attribute, however, there's no easy way to access only part of it. You must write a separate program in a programming language like ECMAScript or Java that can parse your date format. It's easier to use the standard XML tools and child elements.

Furthermore, the attribute syntax is ambiguous. What does the date "10/11/1999" signify? In particular, is it October 11th or November 10th? Readers from different countries will interpret this data differently. Even if your parser understands one format, there's no guarantee the people entering the data will enter it correctly. The XML, by contrast, is unambiguous.

Finally, using DATE children rather than attributes allows more than one date to be associated with an element. For instance, scholarly articles are often returned to the author for revisions. In these cases, it can also be important to note when the revised article was received. For example:

```
<ARTICLE>
  <TITLE>
    Maximum Projectile Velocity in an Augmented Railgun
  </TITLE>
  <AUTHOR>Elliotte Harold</AUTHOR>
  <AUTHOR>Bruce Bukiet</AUTHOR>
  <AUTHOR>William Peter</AUTHOR>
  <DATE>
    <YEAR>1992</YEAR>
    <MONTH>10</MONTH>
    <DAY>29</DAY>
  </DATE>
  <DATE>
    <YEAR>1993</YEAR>
    <MONTH>10</MONTH>
    <DAY>26</DAY>
  </DATE>
</ARTICLE>
```

As another example, consider the ALT attribute of an IMG tag in HTML. This is limited to a single string of text. However, given that a picture is worth a thousand words, you might well want to replace an IMG with marked up text. For instance, consider the pie chart shown in Figure 5-2.

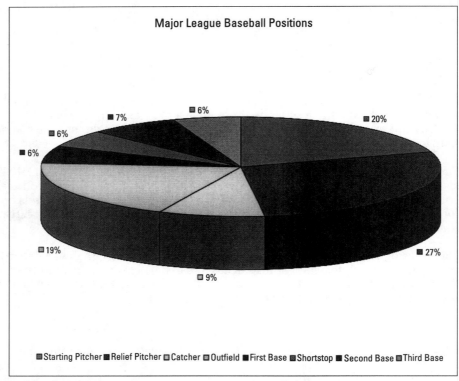

Figure 5-2: Distribution of positions in major league baseball

Using an ALT attribute, the best description of this picture you can provide is:

```
<IMG SRC="05021.gif"
     ALT="Pie Chart of Positions in Major League Baseball"
     WIDTH="819" HEIGHT="623">
</IMG>
```

However, with an ALT child element, you have more flexibility because you can embed markup. For example, you might provide a table of the relevant numbers instead of a pie chart.

```
<IMG SRC="05021.gif" WIDTH="819" HEIGHT="623">
  <ALT>
    <TABLE>
      <TR>
        <TD>Starting Pitcher</TD> <TD>242</TD> <TD>20%</TD>
      </TR>
      <TR>
        <TD>Relief Pitcher</TD> <TD>336</TD> <TD>27%</TD>
      </TR>
      <TR>
        <TD>Catcher</TD> <TD>104</TD> <TD>9%</TD>
      </TR>
      <TR>
        <TD>Outfield</TD> <TD>235</TD> <TD>19%</TD>
      </TR>
      <TR>
        <TD>First Base</TD> <TD>67</TD> <TD>6%</TD>
      </TR>
      <TR>
        <TD>Shortstop</TD> <TD>67</TD> <TD>6%</TD>
      </TR>
      <TR>
        <TD>Second Base</TD> <TD>88</TD> <TD>7%</TD>
      </TR>
      <TR>
        <TD>Third Base</TD> <TD>67</TD> <TD>6%</TD>
      </TR>
    </TABLE>
  </ALT>
</IMG>
```

You might even provide the actual Postscript, SVG, or VML code to render the picture in the event that the bitmap image is not available.

Meta-Meta-Data

Using elements for meta-data also easily allows for meta-meta-data, or information about the information about the information. For example, the author of a poem may be considered to be meta-data about the poem. The language in which that author's name is written is data about the meta-data about the poem. This isn't a trivial concern, especially for distinctly non-Roman languages. For instance, is the author of the Odyssey Homer or Ωμηος? If you use elements, it's easy to write:

```
<POET LANGUAGE="English">Homer</POET>
<POET LANGUAGE="Greek">Ωμηος</POET>
```

However, if POET is an attribute rather than a child element, you're stuck with unwieldy constructs like this:

```
<POEM POET="Homer" POET_LANGUAGE="English"
  POEM_LANGUAGE="English">
  Tell me, O Muse, of the cunning man...
</POEM>
```

And it's even more bulky if you want to provide both the poet's English and Greek names.

```
<POEM POET_NAME_1="Homer" POET_LANGUAGE_1="English"
  POET_NAME_2="Ωμηος" POET_LANGUAGE_2="Greek"
  POEM_LANGUAGE="English">
  Tell me, O Muse, of the cunning man...
</POEM>
```

What's Your Meta-data Is Someone Else's Data

"Metaness" is in the mind of the beholder. Who is reading your document and why they are reading it determines what they consider to be data and what they consider to be meta-data. For example, if you're simply reading an article in a scholarly journal, then the author of the article is tangential to the information it contains. However, if you're sitting on a tenure and promotions committee scanning a journal to see who is publishing and who is not, then the names of the authors and the number of articles they've published may be more important to you than what they wrote (sad but true).

In fact, you may change your mind about what's meta and what's data. What's only tangentially relevant today, may become crucial to you next week. You can use style sheets to hide unimportant elements today, and change the style sheets to reveal them later. However, it's more difficult to later reveal information that was first stored in an attribute. Usually, this requires rewriting the document itself rather than simply changing the style sheet.

Elements Are More Extensible

Attributes are certainly convenient when you only need to convey one or two words of unstructured information. In these cases, there may genuinely be no current need for a child element. However, this doesn't preclude such a need in the future.

For instance, you may now only need to store the name of the author of an article, and you may not need to distinguish between the first and last names. However, in the future you may uncover a need to store first and last names, e-mail addresses, institution, snail mail address, URL, and more. If you've stored the author of the article as an element, then it's easy to add child elements to include this additional information.

Although any such change will probably require some revision of your documents, style sheets, and associated programs, it's still much easier to change a simple element to a tree of elements than it is to make an attribute a tree of elements. However, if you used an attribute, then you're stuck. It's quite difficult to extend your attribute syntax beyond the region it was originally designed for.

Good Times to Use Attributes

Having exhausted all the reasons why you should use elements instead of attributes, I feel compelled to point out that there are nonetheless some times when attributes make sense. First of all, as previously mentioned, attributes are fully appropriate for very simple data without substructure that the reader is unlikely to want to see. One example is the HEIGHT and WIDTH attributes of an IMG. Although the values of these attributes may change if the image changes, it's hard to imagine how the data in the attribute could be anything more than a very short string of text. HEIGHT and WIDTH are one-dimensional quantities (in more ways than one) so they work well as attributes.

Furthermore, attributes are appropriate for simple information about the document that has nothing to do with the content of the document. For example, it is often useful to assign an ID attribute to each element. This is a unique string possessed only by one element in the document. You can then use this string for a variety of tasks including linking to particular elements of the document, even if the elements move around as the document changes over time. For example:

```
<SOURCE ID="S1">
  <AUTHOR ID="A1">Donald Dewey</AUTHOR>
  <AUTHOR ID="A2">Nicholas Acocella</AUTHOR>
  <BOOK ID="B1">
    <TITLE ID="B2">
      The Biographical History of Baseball
    </TITLE>
    <PAGES ID="B3">169</PAGES>
    <YEAR ID="B4">1995</YEAR>
  </BOOK>
</SOURCE>
```

ID attributes make links to particular elements in the document possible. In this way, they can serve the same purpose as the NAME attribute of HTML's A elements. Other data associated with linking—HREFs to link to, SRCs to pull images and binary data from, and so forth—also work well as attributes.

Cross-Reference   You'll see more examples of this when XLL, the Extensible Linking Language, is discussed in Chapter 16, *XLinks*, and Chapter 17, *XPointers*.

Attributes are also often used to store document-specific style information. For example, if TITLE elements are generally rendered as bold text but if you want to make just one TITLE element both bold and italic, you might write something like this:

```
<TITLE style="font-style: italic">Significant Others</TITLE>
```

This enables the style information to be embedded without changing the tree structure of the document. While ideally you'd like to use a separate element, this scheme gives document authors somewhat more control when they cannot add elements to the tag set they're working with. For example, the Webmaster of a site might require the use of a particular DTD and not want to allow everyone to modify the DTD. Nonetheless, they want to allow them to make minor adjustments to individual pages. Use this scheme with restraint, however, or you'll soon find yourself back in the HTML hell XML was supposed to save us from, where formatting is freely intermixed with meaning and documents are no longer maintainable.

The final reason to use attributes is to maintain compatibility with HTML. To the extent that you're using tags that at least look similar to HTML such as <IMG>, <P>, and <TD>, you might as well employ the standard HTML attributes for these tags. This has the double advantage of enabling legacy browsers to at least partially parse and display your document, and of being more familiar to the people writing the documents.

Empty Tags

Last chapter's no-attribute approach was an extreme position. It's also possible to swing to the other extreme— storing all the information in the attributes and none in the content. In general, I don't recommend this approach. Storing all the information in element content— while equally extreme— is much easier to work with in practice. However, this section entertains the possibility of using only attributes for the sake of elucidation.

As long as you know the element will have no content, you can use empty tags as a short cut. Rather than including both a start and an end tag you can include one empty tag. Empty tags are distinguished from start tags by a closing /> instead of simply a closing >. For instance, instead of <PLAYER></PLAYER> you would write <PLAYER/>.

Empty tags may contain attributes. For example, here's an empty tag for Joe Girardi with several attributes:

```
<PLAYER GIVEN_NAME="Joe" SURNAME="Girardi"
   GAMES="78" AT_BATS="254" RUNS="31" HITS="70"
   DOUBLES="11" TRIPLES="4" HOME_RUNS="3"
   RUNS_BATTED_IN="31" WALKS="14" STRUCK_OUT="38"
   STOLEN_BASES="2" CAUGHT_STEALING="4"
```

```
        SACRIFICE_FLY="1" SACRIFICE_HIT="8"
        HIT_BY_PITCH="2"/>
```

XML parsers treat this identically to the non-empty equivalent. This PLAYER element is precisely equal (though not identical) to the previous PLAYER element formed with an empty tag.

```
<PLAYER GIVEN_NAME="Joe" SURNAME="Girardi"
    GAMES="78" AT_BATS="254" RUNS="31" HITS="70"
    DOUBLES="11" TRIPLES="4" HOME_RUNS="3"
    RUNS_BATTED_IN="31" WALKS="14" STRUCK_OUT="38"
    STOLEN_BASES="2" CAUGHT_STEALING="4"
    SACRIFICE_FLY="1" SACRIFICE_HIT="8"
    HIT_BY_PITCH="2"></PLAYER>
```

The difference between <PLAYER/> and <PLAYER></PLAYER> is syntactic sugar, and nothing more. If you don't like the empty tag syntax, or find it hard to read, you don't have to use it.

XSL

Attributes are visible in an XML source view of the document as shown in Figure 5-1. However, once a CSS style sheet is applied the attributes disappear. Figure 5-3 shows Listing 5-1 once the baseball stats style sheet from the previous chapter is applied. It looks like a blank document because CSS styles only apply to element content, not to attributes. If you use CSS, any data you want to display to the reader should be part of an element's content rather than one of its attributes.

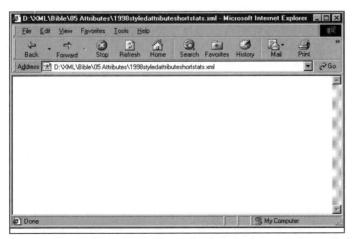

Figure 5-3: A blank document is displayed when CSS is applied to an XML document whose elements do not contain any character data.

However, there is an alternative style sheet language that does allow you to access and display attribute data. This language is the Extensible Style Language (XSL); and it is also supported by Internet Explorer 5.0, at least in part. XSL is divided into two sections, transformations and formatting.

The transformation part of XSL enables you to replace one tag with another. You can define rules that replace your XML tags with standard HTML tags, or with HTML tags plus CSS attributes. You can also do a lot more including reordering the elements in the document and adding additional content that was never present in the XML document.

The formatting part of XSL defines an extremely powerful view of documents as pages. XSL formatting enables you to specify the appearance and layout of a page including multiple columns, text flow around objects, line spacing, assorted font properties, and more. It's designed to be powerful enough to handle automated layout tasks for both the Web and print from the same source document. For instance, XSL formatting would allow one XML document containing show times and advertisements to generate both the print and online editions of a local newspaper's television listings. However, IE 5.0 and most other tools do not yet support XSL formatting. Therefore, in this section I'll focus on XSL transformations.

Cross-Reference   XSL formatting is discussed in Chapter 15, *XSL Formatting Objects*.

XSL Style Sheet Templates

An XSL style sheet contains templates into which data from the XML document is poured. For example, one template might look something like this:

```
<HTML>
  <HEAD>
    <TITLE>
      XSL Instructions to get the title
    </TITLE>
  </HEAD>
  <H1>XSL Instructions to get the title</H1>
  <BODY>
    XSL Instructions to get the statistics
  </BODY>
</HTML>
```

The italicized sections will be replaced by particular XSL elements that copy data from the underlying XML document into this template. You can apply this template to many different data sets. For instance, if the template is designed to work with the baseball example, then the same style sheet can display statistics from different seasons.

This may remind you of some server-side include schemes for HTML. In fact, this is very much like server-side includes. However, the actual transformation of the source XML document and XSL style sheet takes place on the client rather than on the server. Furthermore, the output document does not have to be HTML. It can be any well-formed XML.

XSL instructions can retrieve any data stored in the elements of the XML document. This includes element content, element names, and, most importantly for our example, element attributes. Particular elements are chosen by a pattern that considers the element's name, its value, its attributes' names and values, its absolute and relative position in the tree structure of the XML document, and more. Once the data is extracted from an element, it can be moved, copied, and manipulated in a variety of ways. We won't cover everything you can do with XML transformations in this brief introduction. However, you will learn to use XSL to write some pretty amazing documents that can be viewed on the Web right away.

Cross-
Reference   Chapter 14, *XSL Transformations*, covers XSL transformations in depth.

The Body of the Document

Let's begin by looking at a simple example and applying it to the XML document with baseball statistics shown in Listing 5-1. Listing 5-2 is an XSL style sheet. This style sheet provides the HTML mold into which XML data will be poured.

Listing 5-2: **An XSL style sheet**

```
<?xml version="1.0"?>
<xsl:stylesheet xmlns:xsl="http://www.w3.org/TR/WD-xsl">

  <xsl:template match="/">
    <HTML>
      <HEAD>
        <TITLE>
          Major League Baseball Statistics
        </TITLE>
      </HEAD>
      <BODY>
        <H1>Major League Baseball Statistics</H1>

        <HR></HR>
        Copyright 1999
        <A HREF="http://www.macfaq.com/personal.html">
         Elliotte Rusty Harold
        </A>
```

Continued

Listing 5-2 *(continued)*

```
        <BR />
        <A HREF="mailto:elharo@metalab.unc.edu">
         elharo@metalab.unc.edu
        </A>

       </BODY>
      </HTML>
    </xsl:template>

</xsl:stylesheet>
```

It resembles an HTML file included inside an xsl:template element. In other words its structure looks like this:

```
<?xml version="1.0"?>
<xsl:stylesheet xmlns:xsl="http://www.w3.org/TR/WD-xsl">

  <xsl:template match="/">
    HTML file goes here
  </xsl:template>

</xsl:stylesheet>
```

Listing 5-2 is not only an XSL style sheet; it's also a well-formed XML document. It begins with an XML declaration. The root element of this document is xsl: stylesheet. This style sheet contains a single template for the XML data encoded as an xsl:template element. The xsl:template element has a match attribute with the value / and its content is a well-formed HTML document. It's not a coincidence that the output HTML is well-formed. Because the HTML must first be part of an XSL style sheet, and because XSL style sheets are well-formed XML documents, all the HTML in a XSL style sheet must be well-formed.

The Web browser tries to match parts of the XML document against each xsl:template element. The / template matches the root of the document; that is the entire document itself. The browser reads the template and inserts data from the XML document where indicated by XSL instructions. However, this particular template contains no XSL instructions, so its contents are merely copied verbatim into the Web browser, producing the output you see in Figure 5-4. Notice that Figure 5-4 does not display any data from the XML document, only from the XSL template.

Attaching the XSL style sheet of Listing 5-2 to the XML document in Listing 5-1 is straightforward. Simply add a `<?xml-stylesheet?>` processing instruction with a `type` attribute with value `text/xsl` and an `href` attribute that points to the style sheet between the XML declaration and the root element. For example:

```
<?xml version="1.0"?>
<?xml-stylesheet type="text/xsl" href="5-2.xsl"?>
<SEASON YEAR="1998">
...
```

This is the same way a CSS style sheet is attached to a document. The only difference is that the `type` attribute is `text/xsl` instead of `text/css`.

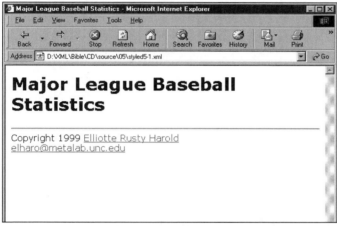

Figure 5-4: The data from the XML document, not the XSL template, is missing after application of the XSL style sheet in Listing 5-2.

The Title

Of course there was something rather obvious missing from Figure 5-4 — the data! Although the style sheet in Listing 5-2 displays something (unlike the CSS style sheet of Figure 5-3) it doesn't show any data from the XML document. To add this, you need to use XSL instruction elements to copy data from the source XML document into the XSL template. Listing 5-3 adds the necessary XSL instructions to extract the YEAR attribute from the SEASON element and insert it in the TITLE and H1 header of the resulting document. Figure 5-5 shows the rendered document.

Listing 5-3: An XSL style sheet with instructions to extract the SEASON element and YEAR attribute

```
<?xml version="1.0"?>
<xsl:stylesheet xmlns:xsl="http://www.w3.org/TR/WD-xsl">

  <xsl:template match="/">
    <HTML>
      <HEAD>
        <TITLE>
          <xsl:for-each select="SEASON">
            <xsl:value-of select="@YEAR"/>
          </xsl:for-each>
          Major League Baseball Statistics
        </TITLE>
      </HEAD>
      <BODY>

      <xsl:for-each select="SEASON">
        <H1>
          <xsl:value-of select="@YEAR"/>
          Major League Baseball Statistics
        </H1>
      </xsl:for-each>

      <HR></HR>
      Copyright 1999
      <A HREF="http://www.macfaq.com/personal.html">
       Elliotte Rusty Harold
      </A>
      <BR />
      <A HREF="mailto:elharo@metalab.unc.edu">
       elharo@metalab.unc.edu
      </A>

      </BODY>
    </HTML>
  </xsl:template>

</xsl:stylesheet>
```

The new XSL instructions that extract the YEAR attribute from the SEASON element are:

```
<xsl:for-each select="SEASON">
  <xsl:value-of select="@YEAR"/>
</xsl:for-each>
```

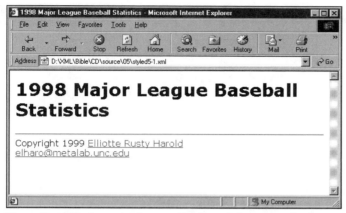

Figure 5-5: Listing 5-1 after application of the XSL style sheet in Listing 5-3

These instructions appear twice because we want the year to appear twice in the output document-once in the H1 header and once in the TITLE. Each time they appear, these instructions do the same thing. `<xsl:for-each select="SEASON">` finds all SEASON elements. `<xsl:value-of select="@YEAR"/>` inserts the value of the YEAR attribute of the SEASON element — that is, the string "1998" — found by `<xsl:for-each select="SEASON">`.

This is important, so let me say it again: `xsl:for-each` selects a particular XML element in the source document (Listing 5-1 in this case) from which data will be read. `xsl:value-of` copies a particular part of the element into the output document. You need both XSL instructions. Neither alone is sufficient.

XSL instructions are distinguished from output elements like HTML and H1 because the instructions are in the `xsl` namespace. That is, the names of all XSL elements begin with `xsl:`. The namespace is identified by the `xmlns:xsl` attribute of the root element of the style sheet. In Listings 5-2, 5-3, and all other examples in this book, the value of that attribute is `http://www.w3.org/TR/WD-xsl`.

Cross-Reference Namespaces are covered in depth in Chapter 18, *Namespaces*.

Leagues, Divisions, and Teams

Next, let's add some XSL instructions to pull out the two LEAGUE elements. We'll map these to H2 headers. Listing 5-4 demonstrates. Figure 5-6 shows the document rendered with this style sheet.

Listing 5-4: An XSL style sheet with instructions to extract LEAGUE elements

```
<?xml version="1.0"?>
<xsl:stylesheet xmlns:xsl="http://www.w3.org/TR/WD-xsl">

  <xsl:template match="/">
    <HTML>
      <HEAD>
        <TITLE>
          <xsl:for-each select="SEASON">
            <xsl:value-of select="@YEAR"/>
          </xsl:for-each>

          Major League Baseball Statistics
        </TITLE>
      </HEAD>
      <BODY>

      <xsl:for-each select="SEASON">
        <H1>
          <xsl:value-of select="@YEAR"/>
          Major League Baseball Statistics
        </H1>

        <xsl:for-each select="LEAGUE">
          <H2 ALIGN="CENTER">
            <xsl:value-of select="@NAME"/>
          </H2>
        </xsl:for-each>

      </xsl:for-each>

      <HR></HR>
      Copyright 1999
      <A HREF="http://www.macfaq.com/personal.html">
       Elliotte Rusty Harold
      </A>
      <BR />
      <A HREF="mailto:elharo@metalab.unc.edu">
       elharo@metalab.unc.edu
      </A>

      </BODY>
    </HTML>
  </xsl:template>

</xsl:stylesheet>
```

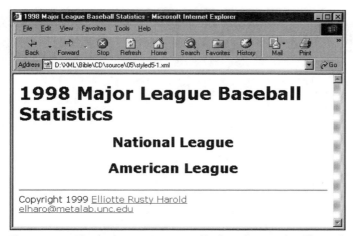

Figure 5-6: The league names are displayed as H2 headers when the XSL style sheet in Listing 5-4 is applied.

The key new materials are the nested `xsl:for-each` instructions

```
<xsl:for-each select="SEASON">
  <H1>
    <xsl:value-of select="@YEAR"/>
    Major League Baseball Statistics
  </H1>

  <xsl:for-each select="LEAGUE">
    <H2 ALIGN="CENTER">
      <xsl:value-of select="@NAME"/>
    </H2>
  </xsl:for-each>

</xsl:for-each>
```

The outermost instruction says to select the SEASON element. With that element selected, we then find the YEAR attribute of that element and place it between `<H1>` and `</H1>` along with the extra text `Major League Baseball Statistics`. Next, the browser loops through each LEAGUE child of the selected SEASON and places the value of its NAME attribute between `<H2 ALIGN="CENTER">` and `</H2>`. Although there's only one `xsl:for-each` matching a LEAGUE element, it loops over all the LEAGUE elements that are immediate children of the SEASON element. Thus, this template works for anywhere from zero to an indefinite number of leagues.

The same technique can be used to assign H3 headers to divisions and H4 headers to teams. Listing 5-5 demonstrates the procedure and Figure 5-7 shows the document rendered with this style sheet. The names of the divisions and teams are read from the XML data.

Listing 5-5: **An XSL style sheet with instructions to extract DIVISION and TEAM elements**

```
<?xml version="1.0"?>
<xsl:stylesheet xmlns:xsl="http://www.w3.org/TR/WD-xsl">

  <xsl:template match="/">
    <HTML>
      <HEAD>
        <TITLE>
          <xsl:for-each select="SEASON">
            <xsl:value-of select="@YEAR"/>
          </xsl:for-each>

          Major League Baseball Statistics
        </TITLE>
      </HEAD>
      <BODY>

      <xsl:for-each select="SEASON">
        <H1>
          <xsl:value-of select="@YEAR"/>
          Major League Baseball Statistics
        </H1>

        <xsl:for-each select="LEAGUE">
          <H2 ALIGN="CENTER">
            <xsl:value-of select="@NAME"/>
          </H2>

          <xsl:for-each select="DIVISION">
            <H3 ALIGN="CENTER">
            <xsl:value-of select="@NAME"/>
            </H3>

            <xsl:for-each select="TEAM">
              <H4 ALIGN="CENTER">
              <xsl:value-of select="@CITY"/>
              <xsl:value-of select="@NAME"/>
              </H4>
            </xsl:for-each>
          </xsl:for-each>

        </xsl:for-each>
      </xsl:for-each>

      <HR></HR>
      Copyright 1999
      <A HREF="http://www.macfaq.com/personal.html">
```

```
      Elliotte Rusty Harold
      </A>
      <BR />
      <A HREF="mailto:elharo@metalab.unc.edu">
      elharo@metalab.unc.edu
      </A>

      </BODY>
    </HTML>
  </xsl:template>

</xsl:stylesheet>
```

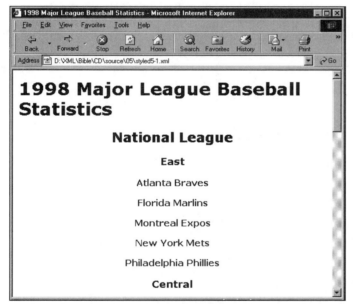

Figure 5-7: Divisions and team names are displayed after application of the XSL style sheet in Listing 5-5.

In the case of the TEAM elements, the values of both its CITY and NAME attributes are used as contents for the H4 header. Also notice that the nesting of the xsl:for-each elements that selects seasons, leagues, divisions, and teams mirrors the hierarchy of the document itself. That's not a coincidence. While other schemes are possible that don't require matching hierarchies, this is the simplest, especially for highly structured data like the baseball statistics of Listing 5-1.

Players

The next step is to add statistics for individual players on a team. The most natural way to do this is in a table. Listing 5-6 shows an XSL style sheet that arranges the players and their stats in a table. No new XSL elements are introduced. The same `xsl:for-each` and `xsl:value-of` elements are used on the PLAYER element and its attributes. The output is standard HTML table tags. Figure 5-8 displays the results.

Listing 5-6: An XSL style sheet that places players and their statistics in a table

```
<?xml version="1.0"?>
<xsl:stylesheet xmlns:xsl="http://www.w3.org/TR/WD-xsl">

  <xsl:template match="/">
    <HTML>
      <HEAD>
        <TITLE>
          <xsl:for-each select="SEASON">
            <xsl:value-of select="@YEAR"/>
          </xsl:for-each>

          Major League Baseball Statistics
        </TITLE>
      </HEAD>
      <BODY>

        <xsl:for-each select="SEASON">
          <H1>
            <xsl:value-of select="@YEAR"/>
            Major League Baseball Statistics
          </H1>

          <xsl:for-each select="LEAGUE">
            <H2 ALIGN="CENTER">
              <xsl:value-of select="@NAME"/>
            </H2>

            <xsl:for-each select="DIVISION">
              <H3 ALIGN="CENTER">
              <xsl:value-of select="@NAME"/>
              </H3>

              <xsl:for-each select="TEAM">
                <H4 ALIGN="CENTER">
                <xsl:value-of select="@CITY"/>
                <xsl:value-of select="@NAME"/>
                </H4>

                <TABLE>
```

```
      <THEAD>
       <TR>
        <TH>Player</TH><TH>P</TH><TH>G</TH>
        <TH>GS</TH><TH>AB</TH><TH>R</TH><TH>H</TH>
        <TH>D</TH><TH>T</TH><TH>HR</TH><TH>RBI</TH>
        <TH>S</TH><TH>CS</TH><TH>SH</TH><TH>SF</TH>
        <TH>E</TH><TH>BB</TH><TH>SO</TH><TH>HBP</TH>
       </TR>
      </THEAD>
     <TBODY>
      <xsl:for-each select="PLAYER">
       <TR>
        <TD>
         <xsl:value-of select="@GIVEN_NAME"/>
         <xsl:value-of select="@SURNAME"/>
        </TD>
        <TD><xsl:value-of select="@POSITION"/></TD>
        <TD><xsl:value-of select="@GAMES"/></TD>
        <TD>
          <xsl:value-of select="@GAMES_STARTED"/>
        </TD>
        <TD><xsl:value-of select="@AT_BATS"/></TD>
        <TD><xsl:value-of select="@RUNS"/></TD>
        <TD><xsl:value-of select="@HITS"/></TD>
        <TD><xsl:value-of select="@DOUBLES"/></TD>
        <TD><xsl:value-of select="@TRIPLES"/></TD>
        <TD><xsl:value-of select="@HOME_RUNS"/></TD>
        <TD><xsl:value-of select="@RBI"/></TD>
        <TD><xsl:value-of select="@STEALS"/></TD>
        <TD>
         <xsl:value-of select="@CAUGHT_STEALING"/>
        </TD>
        <TD>
         <xsl:value-of select="@SACRIFICE_HITS"/>
        </TD>
        <TD>
         <xsl:value-of select="@SACRIFICE_FLIES"/>
        </TD>
        <TD><xsl:value-of select="@ERRORS"/></TD>
        <TD><xsl:value-of select="@WALKS"/></TD>
        <TD>
         <xsl:value-of select="@STRUCK_OUT"/>
        </TD>
        <TD>
         <xsl:value-of select="@HIT_BY_PITCH"/>
        </TD>
       </TR>
      </xsl:for-each>
     </TBODY>
    </TABLE>

</xsl:for-each>
```

Continued

Listing 5-6 *(continued)*

```
            </xsl:for-each>

          </xsl:for-each>
        </xsl:for-each>

        <HR></HR>
        Copyright 1999
        <A HREF="http://www.macfaq.com/personal.html">
         Elliotte Rusty Harold
        </A>
        <BR />
        <A HREF="mailto:elharo@metalab.unc.edu">
         elharo@metalab.unc.edu
        </A>

        </BODY>
      </HTML>
    </xsl:template>

</xsl:stylesheet>
```

Separation of Pitchers and Batters

One discrepancy you might notice in Figure 5-8 is that the pitchers aren't handled properly. Throughout this chapter and Chapter 4, we've always given the pitchers a completely different set of statistics, whether those stats were stored in element content or attributes. Therefore, the pitchers really need a table that is separate from the other players. Before putting a player into the table, you must test whether he is or is not a pitcher. If his POSITION attribute contains the string "pitcher" then omit him. Then reverse the procedure in a second table that only includes pitchers-PLAYER elements whose POSITION attribute contains the string "pitcher".

To do this, you have to add additional code to the xsl:for-each element that selects the players. You don't select all players. Instead, you select those players whose POSITION attribute is not pitcher. The syntax looks like this:

```
<xsl:for-each select="PLAYER[(@POSITION != 'Pitcher')">
```

But because the XML document distinguishes between starting and relief pitchers, the true answer must test both cases:

```
<xsl:for-each select="PLAYER[(@POSITION != 'Starting Pitcher')
  $and$ (@POSITION != 'Relief Pitcher')]">
```

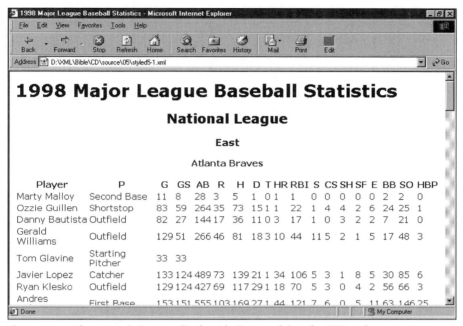

The browser window shows:

1998 Major League Baseball Statistics - Microsoft Internet Explorer

Address: D:\XML\Bible\CD\source\05\styled5-1.xml

1998 Major League Baseball Statistics

National League

East

Atlanta Braves

Player	P	G	GS	AB	R	H	D	T	HR	RBI	S	CS	SH	SF	E	BB	SO	HBP
Marty Malloy	Second Base	11	8	28	3	5	1	0	1	1	0	0	0	0	2	2	0	
Ozzie Guillen	Shortstop	83	59	264	35	73	15	1	1	22	1	4	4	2	6	24	25	1
Danny Bautista	Outfield	82	27	144	17	36	11	0	3	17	1	0	3	2	2	7	21	0
Gerald Williams	Outfield	129	51	266	46	81	18	3	10	44	11	5	2	1	5	17	48	3
Tom Glavine	Starting Pitcher	33	33															
Javier Lopez	Catcher	133	124	489	73	139	21	1	34	106	5	3	1	8	5	30	85	6
Ryan Klesko	Outfield	129	124	427	69	117	29	1	18	70	5	3	0	4	2	56	66	3
Andres	First Base	153	151	555	103	169	27	1	44	121	7	6	0	5	11	63	146	25

Figure 5-8: Player statistics are displayed after applying the XSL style sheet in Listing 5-6.

For the table of pitchers, you logically reverse this to the position being equal to either "Starting Pitcher" or "Relief Pitcher". (It is not sufficient to just change *not equal* to *equal*. You also have to change *and* to *or*.) The syntax looks like this:

```
<xsl:for-each select="PLAYER[(@POSITION = 'Starting Pitcher')
$or$ (@POSITION = 'Relief Pitcher')]">
```

Note   Only a single equals sign is used to test for equality rather than the double equals sign used in C and Java. That's because there's no equivalent of an assignment operator in XSL.

Listing 5-7 shows an XSL style sheet separating the batters and pitchers into two different tables. The pitchers' table adds columns for all the usual pitcher statistics. Listing 5-1 encodes in attributes: wins, losses, saves, shutouts, etc. Abbreviations are used for the column labels to keep the table to a manageable width. Figure 5-9 shows the results.

Listing 5-7: An XSL style sheet that separates batters and pitchers

```
<?xml version="1.0"?>
<xsl:stylesheet xmlns:xsl="http://www.w3.org/TR/WD-xsl">

  <xsl:template match="/">
    <HTML>
      <HEAD>
        <TITLE>
          <xsl:for-each select="SEASON">
            <xsl:value-of select="@YEAR"/>
          </xsl:for-each>

          Major League Baseball Statistics
        </TITLE>
      </HEAD>
      <BODY>

        <xsl:for-each select="SEASON">
          <H1>
            <xsl:value-of select="@YEAR"/>
            Major League Baseball Statistics
          </H1>

          <xsl:for-each select="LEAGUE">
            <H2 ALIGN="CENTER">
              <xsl:value-of select="@NAME"/>
            </H2>

            <xsl:for-each select="DIVISION">
              <H3 ALIGN="CENTER">
              <xsl:value-of select="@NAME"/>
              </H3>

              <xsl:for-each select="TEAM">
                <H4 ALIGN="CENTER">
                <xsl:value-of select="@CITY"/>
                <xsl:value-of select="@NAME"/>
                </H4>

                <TABLE>
                 <CAPTION><B>Batters</B></CAPTION>
                 <THEAD>
                  <TR>
                   <TH>Player</TH><TH>P</TH><TH>G</TH>
                   <TH>GS</TH><TH>AB</TH><TH>R</TH><TH>H</TH>
                   <TH>D</TH><TH>T</TH><TH>HR</TH><TH>RBI</TH>
                   <TH>S</TH><TH>CS</TH><TH>SH</TH><TH>SF</TH>
                   <TH>E</TH><TH>BB</TH><TH>SO</TH>
                   <TH>HBP</TH>
                  </TR>
                 </THEAD>
```

```
<TBODY>
 <xsl:for-each select="PLAYER[(@POSITION
   != 'Starting Pitcher')
  $and$ (@POSITION != 'Relief Pitcher')]">
  <TR>
   <TD>
    <xsl:value-of select="@GIVEN_NAME"/>
    <xsl:value-of select="@SURNAME"/>
   </TD>
   <TD><xsl:value-of select="@POSITION"/></TD>
   <TD><xsl:value-of select="@GAMES"/></TD>
   <TD>
    <xsl:value-of select="@GAMES_STARTED"/>
   </TD>
   <TD><xsl:value-of select="@AT_BATS"/></TD>
   <TD><xsl:value-of select="@RUNS"/></TD>
   <TD><xsl:value-of select="@HITS"/></TD>
   <TD><xsl:value-of select="@DOUBLES"/></TD>
   <TD><xsl:value-of select="@TRIPLES"/></TD>
   <TD>
    <xsl:value-of select="@HOME_RUNS"/>
   </TD>
   <TD><xsl:value-of select="@RBI"/></TD>
   <TD><xsl:value-of select="@STEALS"/></TD>
   <TD>
    <xsl:value-of select="@CAUGHT_STEALING"/>
   </TD>
   <TD>
    <xsl:value-of select="@SACRIFICE_HITS"/>
   </TD>
   <TD>
    <xsl:value-of select="@SACRIFICE_FLIES"/>
   </TD>
   <TD><xsl:value-of select="@ERRORS"/></TD>
   <TD><xsl:value-of select="@WALKS"/></TD>
   <TD>
    <xsl:value-of select="@STRUCK_OUT"/>
   </TD>
   <TD>
    <xsl:value-of select="@HIT_BY_PITCH"/>
   </TD>
  </TR>
 </xsl:for-each>  <!- PLAYER ->
</TBODY>
</TABLE>

<TABLE>
 <CAPTION><B>Pitchers</B></CAPTION>
 <THEAD>
  <TR>
   <TH>Player</TH><TH>P</TH><TH>G</TH>
   <TH>GS</TH><TH>W</TH><TH>L</TH><TH>S</TH>
```

Continued

Listing 5-7 *(continued)*

```
              <TH>CG</TH><TH>SO</TH><TH>ERA</TH>
              <TH>IP</TH><TH>HR</TH><TH>R</TH><TH>ER</TH>
              <TH>HB</TH><TH>WP</TH><TH>B</TH><TH>BB</TH>
              <TH>K</TH>
            </TR>
          </THEAD>
        <TBODY>
        <xsl:for-each select="PLAYER[(@POSITION
          = 'Starting Pitcher')
        $or$ (@POSITION = 'Relief Pitcher')]">
          <TR>
            <TD>
              <xsl:value-of select="@GIVEN_NAME"/>
              <xsl:value-of select="@SURNAME"/>
            </TD>
            <TD><xsl:value-of select="@POSITION"/></TD>
            <TD><xsl:value-of select="@GAMES"/></TD>
            <TD>
              <xsl:value-of select="@GAMES_STARTED"/>
            </TD>
            <TD><xsl:value-of select="@WINS"/></TD>
            <TD><xsl:value-of select="@LOSSES"/></TD>
            <TD><xsl:value-of select="@SAVES"/></TD>
            <TD>
              <xsl:value-of select="@COMPLETE_GAMES"/>
            </TD>
            <TD>
              <xsl:value-of select="@SHUT_OUTS"/>
            </TD>
            <TD><xsl:value-of select="@ERA"/></TD>
            <TD><xsl:value-of select="@INNINGS"/></TD>
            <TD>
            <xsl:value-of select="@HOME_RUNS_AGAINST"/>
            </TD>
            <TD>
              <xsl:value-of select="@RUNS_AGAINST"/>
            </TD>
            <TD>
              <xsl:value-of select="@EARNED_RUNS"/>
            </TD>
            <TD>
              <xsl:value-of select="@HIT_BATTER"/>
            </TD>
            <TD>
              <xsl:value-of select="@WILD_PITCH"/>
            </TD>
            <TD><xsl:value-of select="@BALK"/></TD>
            <TD>
              <xsl:value-of select="@WALKED_BATTER"/>
            </TD>
            <TD>
```

```
                    <xsl:value-of select="@STRUCK_OUT_BATTER"/>
                  </TD>
                 </TR>
               </xsl:for-each>  <!— PLAYER —>
             </TBODY>
           </TABLE>

          </xsl:for-each> <!— TEAM —>
        </xsl:for-each> <!— DIVISION —>
      </xsl:for-each> <!— LEAGUE —>
    </xsl:for-each> <!— SEASON —>


    <HR></HR>
    Copyright 1999
    <A HREF="http://www.macfaq.com/personal.html">
     Elliotte Rusty Harold
    </A>
    <BR />
    <A HREF="mailto:elharo@metalab.unc.edu">
     elharo@metalab.unc.edu
    </A>

    </BODY>
   </HTML>
  </xsl:template>

</xsl:stylesheet>
```

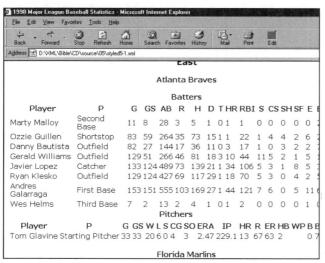

Figure 5-9: Pitchers are distinguished from other players after applying the XSL style sheet in Listing 5-7.

Element Contents and the select Attribute

In this chapter, I focused on using XSL to format data stored in the attributes of an element because it isn't accessible when using CSS. However, XSL works equally well when you want to include an element's character data rather than (or in addition to) its attributes. To indicate that an element's text is to be copied into the output document, simply use the element's name as the value of the select attribute of the xsl:value-of element. For example, consider, once again, Listing 5-8:

```
Listing 5-8greeting.xml<?xml version="1.0" standalone="yes"?>
<?xml-stylesheet type="text/xsl" href="greeting.xsl"?>
<GREETING>
Hello XML!
</GREETING>
```

Let's suppose you want to copy the greeting "Hello XML!" into an H1 header. First, you use xsl:for-each to select the GREETING element:

```
<xsl:for-each select="GREETING">
   <H1>
   </H1>
</xsl:for-each>
```

This alone is enough to copy the two H1 tags into the output. To place the text of the GREETING element between them, use xsl:value-of with no select attribute. Then, by default, the contents of the current element (GREETING) are selected. Listing 5-9 shows the complete style sheet.

Listing 5-9: **greeting.xsl**

```
<?xml version="1.0" ?>
<xsl:stylesheet xmlns:xsl="http://www.w3.org/TR/WD-xsl">
  <xsl:template match="/">
    <HTML>
      <BODY>
        <xsl:for-each select="GREETING">
          <H1>
            <xsl:value-of/>
          </H1>
        </xsl:for-each>
      </BODY>
    </HTML>
  </xsl:template>
</xsl:stylesheet>
```

You can also use `select` to choose the contents of a child element. Simply make the name of the child element the value of the `select` attribute of `xsl:value-of`. For instance, consider the baseball example from the previous chapter in which each player's statistics were stored in child elements rather than in attributes. Given this structure of the document (which is actually far more likely than the attribute-based structure of this chapter) the XSL for the batters' table looks like this:

```
<TABLE>
  <CAPTION><B>Batters</B></CAPTION>
  <THEAD>
   <TR>
    <TH>Player</TH><TH>P</TH><TH>G</TH>
    <TH>GS</TH><TH>AB</TH><TH>R</TH><TH>H</TH>
    <TH>D</TH><TH>T</TH><TH>HR</TH><TH>RBI</TH>
    <TH>S</TH><TH>CS</TH><TH>SH</TH><TH>SF</TH>
    <TH>E</TH><TH>BB</TH><TH>SO</TH><TH>HBP</TH>
   </TR>
  </THEAD>
  <TBODY>
   <xsl:for-each select="PLAYER[(POSITION
   != 'Starting Pitcher')
   $and$ (POSITION != 'Relief Pitcher')]">
    <TR>
     <TD>
      <xsl:value-of select="GIVEN_NAME"/>
      <xsl:value-of select="SURNAME"/>
     </TD>
     <TD><xsl:value-of select="POSITION"/></TD>
     <TD><xsl:value-of select="GAMES"/></TD>
     <TD>
       <xsl:value-of select="GAMES_STARTED"/>
     </TD>
     <TD><xsl:value-of select="AT_BATS"/></TD>
     <TD><xsl:value-of select="RUNS"/></TD>
     <TD><xsl:value-of select="HITS"/></TD>
     <TD><xsl:value-of select="DOUBLES"/></TD>
     <TD><xsl:value-of select="TRIPLES"/></TD>
     <TD><xsl:value-of select="HOME_RUNS"/></TD>
     <TD><xsl:value-of select="RBI"/></TD>
     <TD><xsl:value-of select="STEALS"/></TD>
     <TD>
      <xsl:value-of select="CAUGHT_STEALING"/>
     </TD>
     <TD>
      <xsl:value-of select="SACRIFICE_HITS"/>
     </TD>
     <TD>
      <xsl:value-of select="SACRIFICE_FLIES"/>
     </TD>
     <TD><xsl:value-of select="ERRORS"/></TD>
```

```
<TD><xsl:value-of select="WALKS"/></TD>
<TD>
 <xsl:value-of select="STRUCK_OUT"/>
</TD>
<TD>
 <xsl:value-of select="HIT_BY_PITCH"/>
</TD>
</TR>
</xsl:for-each>  <!— PLAYER —>
</TBODY>
</TABLE>
```

In this case, within each PLAYER element, the contents of that element's GIVEN_NAME, SURNAME, POSITION, GAMES, GAMES_STARTED, AT_BATS, RUNS, HITS, DOUBLES, TRIPLES, HOME_RUNS, RBI, STEALS, CAUGHT_STEALING, SACRIFICE_HITS, SACRIFICE_FLIES, ERRORS, WALKS, STRUCK_OUT and HIT_BY_PITCH children are extracted and copied to the output. Since we used the same names for the attributes in this chapter as we did for the PLAYER child elements in the last chapter, this example is almost identical to the equivalent section of Listing 5-7. The main difference is that the @ signs are missing. They indicate an attribute rather than a child.

You can do even more with the select attribute. You can select elements: by position (for example, the first, second, last, seventeenth element, and so forth); with particular contents; with specific attribute values; or whose parents or children have certain contents or attribute values. You can even apply a complete set of Boolean logical operators to combine different selection conditions. We will explore more of these possibilities when we return to XSL in Chapter 14.

CSS or XSL?

CSS and XSL overlap to some extent. XSL is certainly more powerful than CSS. However XSL's power is matched by its complexity. This chapter only touched on the basics of what you can do with XSL. XSL is more complicated, and harder to learn and use than CSS, which raises the question, "When should you use CSS and when should you use XSL?"

CSS is more broadly supported than XSL. Parts of CSS Level 1 are supported for HTML elements by Netscape 4 and Internet Explorer 4 (although annoying differences exist). Furthermore, most of CSS Level 1 and some of CSS Level 2 is likely to be well supported by Internet Explorer 5.0 and Mozilla 5.0 for both XML and HTML. Thus, choosing CSS gives you more compatibility with a broader range of browsers.

Additionally, CSS is more stable. CSS level 1 (which covers most of the CSS you've seen so far) and CSS Level 2 are W3C recommendations. XSL is still a very early working draft, and won't be finalized until after this book is printed. Early adopters of XSL have already been burned once, and will be burned again before standards gel. Choosing CSS means you're less likely to have to rewrite your style sheets from month to month just to track evolving software and standards. Eventually, however, XSL will settle down to a usable standard.

Furthermore, since XSL is so new, different software implements different variations and subsets of the draft standard. At the time of this writing (spring 1999) there are at least three major variants of XSL in widespread use. Before this book is published, there will be more. If the incomplete and buggy implementations of CSS in current browsers bother you, the varieties of XSL will drive you insane.

However, XSL is definitely more powerful than CSS. CSS only allows you to apply formatting to element contents. It does not allow you to change or reorder those contents; choose different formatting for elements based on their contents or attributes; or add simple, extra text like a signature block. XSL is far more appropriate when the XML documents contain only the minimum of data and none of the HTML frou-frou that surrounds the data.

With XSL, you can separate the crucial data from everything else on the page, like mastheads, navigation bars, and signatures. With CSS, you have to include all these pieces in your data documents. XML+XSL allows the data documents to live separately from the Web page documents. This makes XML+XSL documents more maintainable and easier to work with.

In the long run XSL should become the preferred choice for real-world, data-intensive applications. CSS is more suitable for simple pages like grandparents use to post pictures of their grandchildren. But for these uses, HTML alone is sufficient. If you've really hit the wall with HTML, XML+CSS doesn't take you much further before you run into another wall. XML+XSL, by contrast, takes you far past the walls of HTML. You still need CSS to work with legacy browsers, but long-term XSL is the way to go.

Summary

In this chapter, you saw examples of creating an XML document from scratch. Specifically, you learned:

   ✦ Information can also be stored in an attribute of an element.

   ✦ An attribute is a name-value pair included in an element's start tag.

   ✦ Attributes typically hold meta-information about the element rather than the element's data.

   ✦ Attributes are less convenient to work with than the contents of an element.

✦ Attributes work well for very simple information that's unlikely to change its form as the document evolves. In particular, style and linking information works well as an attribute.

✦ Empty tags offer syntactic sugar for elements with no content.

✦ XSL is a powerful style language that enables you to access and display attribute data and transform documents.

In the next chapter, we'll specify the exact rules that well-formed XML documents must adhere to. We'll also explore some additional means of embedding information in XML documents including comments and processing instructions.

✦　　✦　　✦

Well-Formed XML Documents

✦   ✦   ✦   ✦

In This Chapter

What XML documents
are made of

Markup and
character data

Well-formed XML
in stand-alone
documents

Well-formed HTML

✦   ✦   ✦   ✦

HTML 4.0 has about a hundred different tags. Most of these tags have half a dozen possible attributes for several thousand different possible variations. Because XML is more powerful than HTML, you might think you need to know even more tags, but you don't. XML gets its power through simplicity and extensibility, not through a plethora of tags.

In fact, XML predefines almost no tags at all. Instead XML allows you to define your own tags as needed. However these tags and the documents built from them are not completely arbitrary. Instead they have to follow a specific set of rules which we will elaborate upon in this chapter. A document that follows these rules is said to be *well-formed*. Well-formedness is the minimum criteria necessary for XML processors and browsers to read files. In this chapter, you'll examine the rules for well-formed XML documents and well-formed HTML. Particular attention is paid to how XML differs from HTML.

What XML Documents Are Made Of

An XML document contains text that comprises XML markup and character data. It is a sequential set of bytes of fixed length, which adheres to certain constraints. It may or may not be a file. For instance, an XML document may:

✦ Be stored in a database

✦ Be created on the fly in memory by a CGI program

✦ Be some combination of several different files, each of which is embedded in another

✦ Never exist in a file of its own

However, nothing essential is lost if you think of an XML document as a file, as long as you keep in the back of your mind that it might not really be a file on a hard drive.

XML documents are made up of storage units called *entities*. Each entity contains either text or binary data, never both. Text data is comprised of characters. Binary data is used for images and applets and the like. To use a concrete example, a raw HTML file that includes <IMG> tags is an entity but not a document. An HTML file plus all the pictures embedded in it with <IMG> tags is a complete document.

In this chapter, and the next several chapters, I will treat only simple XML documents that are made up of a single entity, the document itself. Furthermore, these documents are only going to contain text data, not binary data like images or applets. Such documents can be understood completely on their own without reading any other files. In other words they stand alone. Such a document normally contains a standalone attribute in its XML declaration with the value yes, like the one following:

```
<?xml version="1.0" standalone="yes"?>
```

External entities and entity references can be used to combine multiple files and other data sources to create a single XML document. These documents cannot be parsed without reference to other files. These documents normally contain a standalone attribute in the XML declaration with the value no.

```
<?xml version="1.0" standalone="no"?>
```

External entities and entity references will be discussed in Chapter 9, *Entities and External DTD Subsets*.

Markup and Character Data

XML documents are text. Text is made up of characters. A character is a letter, a digit, a punctuation mark, a space, a tab or something similar. XML uses the Unicode character set, which not only includes the usual letters and symbols from the English and other Western European alphabets, but also the Cyrillic, Greek, Hebrew, Arabic, and Devanagari alphabets. In addition, it also includes the most common Han ideographs for the Chinese and Japanese alphabet and the Hangul syllables from the Korean alphabet. For now, in this chapter, I'll stick to English text.

International character sets are discussed in Chapter 7, *Foreign Languages and Non-Roman Text*.

The text of an XML document serves two purposes, character data and markup. Character data is the basic information of the document. Markup, on the other hand, mostly describes a document's logical structure. For example, recall Listing 3-2, greeting.xml, from Chapter 3, repeated on the next page.

```
<?xml version="1.0" standalone="yes"?>
<GREETING>
Hello XML!
</GREETING>
```

Here `<?xml version="1.0" standalone="yes"?>`, `<GREETING>`, and `</GREETING>` are markup. `Hello XML!` is the character data. One of the big advantages of XML over other formats is that it clearly separates the actual data of a document from its markup.

To be more precise, markup includes all comments, character references, entity references, CDATA section delimiters, tags, processing instructions, and DTDs. Everything else is character data. However, this is tricky because when a document is processed some of the markup turns into character data. For example, the markup `&gt;` is turned into the greater than sign character (>). The character data that's left after the document is processed and all of the markup that stands for particular character data has been replaced by the actual character data it stands for is called parsed character data.

Comments

XML comments are almost exactly like HTML comments. They begin with `<!--` and end with `-->` . All data between the `<!-` and `->` is ignored by the XML processor. It's as if it wasn't there. Comments can be used to make notes to yourself or to temporarily comment out sections of the document that aren't ready. For example,

```
<?xml version="1.0" standalone="yes"?>
<!--This is Listing 3-2 from The XML Bible-->
<GREETING>
Hello XML!
<!--Goodbye XML-->
</GREETING>
```

There are some rules that must be followed when using comments. These rules are outlined below:

1. Comments may not come before the XML declaration, which absolutely must be the very first thing in the document. For example, the following is not acceptable:

```
<!--This is Listing 3-2 from The XML Bible-->
<?xml version="1.0" standalone="yes"?>
<GREETING>
Hello XML!
<!--Goodbye XML-->
</GREETING>
```

2. Comments may not be placed inside a tag. For example, the following is illegal:

```
<?xml version="1.0" standalone="yes"?>
<GREETING>
Hello XML!
</GREETING <!--Goodbye--> >
```

3. Comments may be used to surround and hide tags. In the following example, the `<antigreeting>` tag and all its children are commented out; they are not shown when the document is rendered, as if they don't exist:

```
<?xml version="1.0" standalone="yes"?>
<DOCUMENT>
<GREETING>
Hello XML!
</GREETING>
<!--
<ANTIGREETING>
Goodbye XML!
</ANTIGREETING>
-->
</DOCUMENT>
```

Since comments effectively delete sections of text, care must be taken to ensure that the remaining text is still a well-formed XML document. For instance, be careful not to comment out a start tag unless you also comment out the corresponding end tag. For example, the following is illegal:

```
<?xml version="1.0" standalone="yes"?>
<GREETING>
Hello XML!
<!--
</GREETING>
-->
```

Once the commented text is removed what remains is:

```
<?xml version="1.0" standalone="yes"?>
<GREETING>
Hello XML!
```

Since the `<GREETING>` tag is no longer matched by a closing `</GREETING>` tag, this is no longer a well-formed XML document.

4. The two-hyphen string (`--`) may not occur inside a comment except as part of its opening or closing tag. For example, the following is an illegal comment:

```
<!--The red door--that is, the second one--was left open-->
```

This means, among other things, that you cannot nest comments like this:

```
<?xml version="1.0" standalone="yes"?>
<DOCUMENT>
  <GREETING>
```

```
      Hello XML!
    </GREETING>
<!--
   <ANTIGREETING>
      <!--Goodbye XML!-->
   </ANTIGREETING>
-->
</DOCUMENT>
```

It also means that you may run into trouble if you're commenting out a lot of C, Java, or JavaScript source code that's full of expressions like i-- or numberLeft. Generally it's not too hard to work around this problem once you recognize it.

Entity References

Entity references are markup that is replaced with character data when the document is parsed. XML predefines the five entity references listed in Table 6-1. Entity references are used in XML documents in place of specific characters that would otherwise be interpreted as part of markup. For instance, the entity reference < stands for the less-than sign (<), which would otherwise be interpreted as the beginning of a tag.

Table 6-1	
XML Predefined Entity References	
Entity Reference	**Character**
&amp;	&
&lt;	<
&gt;	>
&quot;	"
&apos;	'

Caution In XML, unlike HTML, entity references must end with a semicolon. Therefore, > is a correct entity reference and &gt is not.

Raw less-than signs (<) and ampersands (&) in normal XML text are always interpreted as starting tags and entity references, respectively. (The abnormal text is CDATA sections, described below.) Therefore, less-than signs and ampersands must always be encoded as < and & respectively. For example, you would write the phrase "Ben & Jerry's New York Super Fudge Chunk Ice Cream" as Ben & Jerry's New York Super Fudge Chunk Ice Cream.

Greater-than signs, double quotes, and apostrophes must be encoded when they would otherwise be interpreted as part of markup. However, it's easier just to get in the habit of encoding all of them rather than trying to figure out whether a particular use would or would not be interpreted as markup.

Entity references may also be used in attribute values. For example,

```
<PARAM NAME="joke" VALUE="The diner said,
  &quote;Waiter, There&apos;s a fly in my soup!&quote;">
</PARAM>
```

CDATA

Most of the time anything inside a pair of angle brackets (<>) is markup and anything that's not is character data. However there is one exception. In CDATA sections all text is pure character data. Anything that looks like a tag or an entity reference is really just the text of the tag or the entity reference. The XML processor does not try to interpret it in any way.

CDATA sections are used when you want all text to be interpreted as pure character data rather than as markup. This is primarily useful when you have a large block of text that contains a lot of <, >, &, or " characters, but no markup. This would be true for much C and Java source code.

CDATA sections are also extremely useful if you're trying to write about XML in XML. For example, this book contains many small blocks of XML code. The word processor I'm using doesn't care about that. But if I were to convert this book to XML, I'd have to painstakingly replace all the less-than signs with < and all the ampersands with & as I did in the following:

```
&lt;?xml version="1.0" standalone="yes"?&gt;
&lt;GREETING&gt;
Hello XML!
&lt;/GREETING&gt;
```

To avoid having to do this, I can instead use a CDATA section to indicate that a block of text is to be presented as is with no translation. CDATA sections begin with <![CDATA[and end with]]>. For example:

```
<![CDATA[
<?xml version="1.0" standalone="yes"?>
<GREETING>
Hello XML!
</GREETING>
  ]]>
```

The only text that's not allowed within a CDATA section is the closing CDATA delimiter]]>. Comments may appear in CDATA sections, but do not act as comments. That is, both the comment tags and all the text they contain will be rendered.

Note Since]]> may not appear in a CDATA section, CDATA sections cannot nest. This makes it relatively difficult to write about CDATA sections in XML. If you need to do this, you just have to bite the bullet and use the < and & entity references.

CDATA sections aren't needed that often, but when they are needed, they're needed badly.

Tags

What distinguishes XML files from plain text files is markup. The largest part of the markup is the tags. While you saw how tags are used in the previous chapter, this section will define what tags are and provide a broader picture of how they're used.

In brief, a tag is anything in an XML document that begins with < and ends with > and is not inside a comment or a CDATA section. Thus, an XML tag has the same form as an HTML tag. Start or opening tags begin with a < which is followed by the name of the tag. End or closing tags begin with a </ which is followed by the name of the tag. The first > encountered closes the tag.

Tag Names

Every tag has a name. Tag names must begin with a letter or an underscore (_). Subsequent characters in the name may include letters, digits, underscores, hyphens, and periods. They may not include white space. (The underscore often substitutes for white space.) The following are some legal XML tags:

```
<HELP>
<Book>
<volume>
<heading1>
<section.paragraph>
<Mary_Smith>
<_8ball>
```

Cross-Reference Colons are also technically legal in tag names. However, these are reserved for use with namespaces. Namespaces enable you to mix and match tag sets that may use the same tag names. Namespaces are discussed in Chapter 18, *Namespaces*.

The following are not syntactically correct XML tags:

```
<Book%7>
<volume control>
<1heading>
```

```
<Mary Smith>
<.employee.salary>
```

Note The rules for tag names actually apply to names of many other things as well. The same rules are used for attribute names, ID attribute values, entity names, and a number of other constructs you'll encounter in the next several chapters.

Closing tags have the same name as their opening tag but are prefixed with a / after the initial angle bracket. For example, if the opening tag is `<FOO>`, then the closing tag is `</FOO>`. These are the end tags for the previous set of legal start tags.

```
</HELP>
</Book>
</volume>
</heading1>
</section.paragraph>
</Mary_Smith>
</_8ball>
```

XML names are case sensitive. This is different from HTML where `<P>` and `<p>` are the same tag, and a `</p>` can close a `<P>` tag. The following are *not* end tags for the set of legal start tags we've been discussing.

```
</help>
</book>
</Volume>
</HEADING1>
</Section.Paragraph>
</MARY_SMITH>
</_8BALL>
```

Although both lower- and uppercase letters may be used in XML tags, from this point forward I will mostly follow the convention of making my tags uppercase, mainly because this makes them stand out better in the pages of this book. However, on occasion when I'm using a tag set developed by someone else it will be necessary to adopt that person's case convention.

Empty Tags

Many HTML tags that do not contain data do not have closing tags. For example, there are no `</LI>`, `</IMG>`, `</HR>`, or `</BR>` tags in HTML. Some page authors do include `</LI>` tags after their list items, and some HTML tools also use `</LI>`. However the HTML 4.0 standard specifically denies that this is required. Like all unrecognized tags in HTML, the presence of an unnecessary `</LI>` has no effect on the rendered output.

This is *not* the case in XML. The whole point of XML is to allow new tags to be discovered as a document is parsed. Thus unrecognized tags may not simply be ignored. Furthermore, an XML processor must be able to determine on the fly whether a tag it's never seen before does or does not have an end tag.

XML distinguishes between tags that have closing tags and tags that do not, called *empty tags*. Empty tags are closed with a slash and a closing angle bracket (`/>`). For example, `<BR/>` or `<HR/>`.

Current Web browsers deal inconsistently with tags like this. However, if you're trying to maintain backwards compatibility, you can use closing tags instead, and just not include any text in them. For example,

```
<BR></BR>
<HR></HR>
<IMG></IMG>
```

When you learn about DTDs and style sheets in the next few chapters, you'll see a couple more ways to maintain backward and forward compatibility with HTML in documents that must be parsed by legacy browsers.

Attributes

As discussed in the previous chapter, start tags and empty tags may optionally contain *attributes*. Attributes are name-value pairs separated by an equals sign (=). For example,

```
<GREETING LANGUAGE="English">
  Hello XML!
  <MOVIE SRC="WavingHand.mov"/>
</GREETING>
```

Here the `<GREETING>` tag has a `LANGUAGE` attribute, which has the value *English*. The `<MOVIE>` tag has a `SRC` attribute, which has the value *WavingHand.mov*.

Attribute Names

Attribute names are strings that follow the same rules as tag names. That is, attribute names must begin with a letter or an underscore (_). Subsequent letters in the name may include letters, digits, underscores, hyphens, and periods. They may not include white space. (The underscore often substitutes for whitespace.)

The same tag may not have two attributes with the same name. For example, the following is illegal:

```
<RECTANGLE SIDE="8cm" SIDE="10cm"/>
```

Attribute names are case sensitive. The SIDE attribute is not the same as the side or the Side attribute. Therefore the following is acceptable:

```
<BOX SIDE="8cm" side="10cm" Side="31cm"/>
```

However, this is extremely confusing, and I strongly urge you not to write markup like this.

Attribute Values

Attributes values are also strings. Even when the string shows a number, as in the LENGTH attribute below, that number is the two characters 7 and 2, not the decimal number 72.

```
<RULE LENGTH="72"/>
```

If you're writing code to process XML, you'll need to convert the string to a number before performing arithmetic on it.

Unlike attribute names, there are few limits on the content of an attribute value. Attribute values may contain white space, begin with a number, or contain any punctuation characters (except, sometimes, single and double quotes).

XML attribute values are delimited by quote marks. Unlike HTML attributes, XML attribute values *must* be enclosed in quotes. Most of the time double quotes are used. However, if the attribute value itself contains a double quote, then single quotes may be used. For example:

```
<RECTANGLE LENGTH='7"' WIDTH='8.5"'/>
```

If the attribute value contains both single and double quotes, then the one that's not used to delimit the string must be replaced with the proper entity references. I generally just go ahead and replace both, which is always okay. For example:

```
<RECTANGLE LENGTH='8&apos;7&quot;' WIDTH="10&apos;6&quot;"/>
```

Well-Formed XML in Standalone Documents

Although you can make up as many tags as you need, your XML documents do need to follow certain rules in order to be *well-formed*. If a document is not well-formed, most attempts to read or render it will fail.

In fact, the XML specification strictly prohibits XML parsers from trying to fix and understand malformed documents. The only thing a conforming parser is allowed to do is report the error. It may not fix the error. It may not make a best-faith effort to render what the author intended. It may not ignore the offending malformed markup. All it can do is report the error and exit.

Note

> The objective here is to avoid the bug-for-bug compatibility wars that have hindered HTML, and made writing HTML parsers and renderers so difficult. Because Web browsers allow malformed HTML, Web page designers don't make the extra effort to ensure that their HTML is correct. In fact, they even rely on bugs in individual browsers to achieve special effects. In order to properly display the huge installed base of HTML pages, every new Web browser must support every nuance, every quirk of all the Web browsers that have come before. Customers would ignore any browser that strictly adhered to the HTML standard. It is to avoid this sorry state that XML processors are explicitly required to only accept well-formed XML.

In order for a document to be well-formed, all markup and character data in an XML document must adhere to the rules given in the previous sections. Furthermore, there are several rules regarding how the tags and character data must relate to each other. These rules are summarized below:

1. The XML declaration must begin the document.

2. Elements that contain data must have both start and end tags.

3. Elements that do not contain data and use only a single tag must end with `/>`.

4. The document must contain exactly one element that completely contains all other elements.

5. Elements may nest but may not overlap.

6. Attribute values must be quoted.

7. The characters `<` and `&` may only be used to start tags and entity references respectively.

8. The only entity references which appear are `&amp;`, `&lt;`, `&gt;`, `&apos;` and `&quot;`.

These eight rules must be adjusted slightly for documents that do have a DTD, and there are additional rules for well-formedness that define the relationship between the document and its DTD, but we'll explore these rules in later chapters. For now let's look at each of these simple rules for documents without DTDs in more detail.

Cross-Reference DTDs are discussed in Part II.

#1: The XML declaration must begin the document

This is the XML declaration for stand-alone documents in XML 1.0:

```
<?xml version="1.0" standalone="yes"?>
```

If the declaration is present at all, it must be absolutely the first thing in the file because XML processors read the first several bytes of the file and compare those bytes against various encodings of the string `<?xml` to determine which character set is being used (UTF-8, big-endian Unicode, or little-endian Unicode). Nothing (except perhaps for an invisible byte order mark) should come before this, including white space. For instance, this line is not an acceptable way to start an XML file because of the extra spaces at the front of the line:

```
    <?xml version="1.0" standalone="yes"?>
```

 UTF-8 and the variants of Unicode are discussed in Chapter 7, *Foreign Languages and Non-Roman Text*.

XML does allow you to omit the XML declaration completely. In general, this practice is not recommended. However, it does have occasional uses. For instance, omitting the XML declaration enables you to build one well-formed XML document by combining other well-formed XML documents, a technique we'll explore in Chapter 9. Furthermore, it makes it possible to write well-formed HTML documents, a style we'll explore later in this chapter.

#2: Use Both Start and End Tags in Non-Empty Tags

Web browsers are relatively forgiving if you forget to close an HTML tag. For instance, if a document includes a `<B>` tag but no corresponding `</B>` tag, the entire document after the `<B>` tag will be made bold. However, the document will still be displayed.

XML is not so forgiving. Every start tag must be closed with the corresponding end tag. If a document fails to close a tag, the browser or renderer simply reports an error message and does not display any of the document's content in any form.

#3: End Empty Tags with "/>"

Tags that do not contain data, such as HTML's `<BR>`, `<HR>`, and `<IMG>`, do not require closing tags. However, empty XML tags must be identified by closing with a `/>` rather than just a `>`. For example, the XML equivalents of `<BR>`, `<HR>`, and `<IMG>` are `<BR/>`, `<HR/>`, and `<IMG/>`.

Current Web browsers deal inconsistently with tags like this. However, if you're trying to maintain backwards compatibility, you can use closing tags instead, and just not include any text in them. For example:

```
<BR></BR>
<HR></HR>
<IMG></IMG>
```

Even then, Netscape has troubles with
</BR> (It interprets both as line breaks, rather than only the first.), so unfortunately it is not always practical to include well-formed empty tags in HTML.

#4: Let One Element Completely Contain All Other Elements

An XML document has a root element that completely contains all other elements of the document. This sometimes called the document element instead. Assuming the root element is non-empty (which is almost always the case), it must be delimited by start and end tags. These tags may have, but do not have to have, the name root or DOCUMENT. For instance, in the following document the root element is GREETING.

```
<?xml version="1.0" standalone="yes"?>
<GREETING>
Hello XML!
</GREETING>
```

The XML declaration is not an element. Rather it's a processing instruction. Therefore it does not have to be included inside the root element. Similarly, other non-element data in an XML document like other processing instructions, DTDs, and comments does not have to be inside the root element. But all actual elements (other than the root itself) must be contained in the root element.

#5: Do Not Overlap Elements

Elements may contain (and indeed often do contain) other elements. However, elements may not overlap. Practically, this means that if an element contains a start tag for an element, it must also contain the corresponding end tag. Likewise, an element may not contain an end tag without its matching start tag. For example, the following is acceptable XML:

```
<PRE><CODE>n = n + 1;</CODE></PRE>
```

However the following is not legal XML because the closing </PRE> tag comes before the closing </CODE> tag:

```
<PRE><CODE>n = n + 1;</PRE></CODE>
```

Most HTML browsers can handle this case with ease. However XML browsers are required to report an error for this construct.

Empty tags may appear anywhere, of course. For example,

```
<PLAYWRIGHTS>Oscar Wilde<HR/>Joe Orton</PLAYWRIGHTS>
```

This rule, in combination with Rule 4, implies that for all non-root elements, there is exactly one other element that contains the non-root element, but which does not contain any other element that contains the non-root element. This immediate container is called the *parent* of the non-root element. The non-root element is referred to as the *child* of the parent element. Thus each non-root element always has exactly one parent, but a single element may have an indefinite number of children or no children at all.

Consider Listing 6-1, shown below. The root element is the DOCUMENT element. This contains two state children. The first STATE element contains four children: NAME, TREE, FLOWER, and CAPITOL. The second STATE element contains only three children: NAME, TREE, and CAPITOL. Each of these contains only character data, not more children.

Listing 6-1: Parents and Children

```
<?xml version="1.0" standalone="yes"?>
<DOCUMENT>
  <STATE>
    <NAME>Louisiana</NAME>
    <TREE>Bald Cypress</TREE>
    <FLOWER>Magnolia</FLOWER>
    <CAPITOL>Baton Rouge</CAPITOL>
  </STATE>
  <STATE>
    <NAME>Mississippi</NAME>
    <TREE>Magnolia</TREE>
    <CAPITOL>Jackson</CAPITOL>
  </STATE>
</DOCUMENT>
```

In programmer terms, this means that XML documents form a tree. Figure 6-1 shows Listing 6-1's tree structure as well as why this structure is called a tree. It starts from the root and gradually bushes out to the leaves on the end of the tree.

Trees also have a number of nice properties that make them easy for computer programs to read, though this doesn't matter to you as the author of the document.

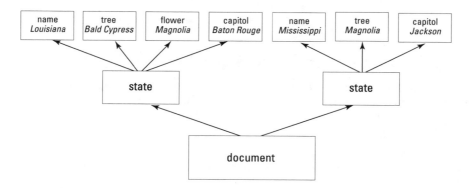

Figure 6-1: Listing 6-1's tree structure

Note

Trees are more commonly drawn from the top down. That is, the root of the tree is shown at the top of the picture rather than the bottom. While this looks less like a real tree, it doesn't affect the topology of the data structure in the least.

#6: Enclose Attribute Values in Quotes

XML requires all attribute values to be enclosed in quote marks, whether or not the attribute value includes spaces. For example:

```
<A HREF="http://metalab.unc.edu/xml/">
```

Note

This isn't true in HTML. For instance, HTML allows tags to contain unquoted attributes. For example, this is an acceptable HTML <A> tag:

```
<A HREF=http://metalab.unc.edu/xml/>
```

The only restriction is that the attribute value must not itself contain embedded spaces.

If an attribute value itself includes double quotes, you may use single quotes to surround the value instead. For example,

```
<IMG SRC="sistinechapel.jpg"
     ALT='And God said, "Let there be light,"
          and there was light'/>
```

If an attribute value includes both single and double quotes, you may use the entity reference ' for a single quote (an apostrophe) and " for a double quote. For example:

```
<PARAM name="joke" value="The diner said,
    &quot;Waiter, There&apos;s a fly in my soup!&quot;">
```

#7: Only Use < and & to Start Tags and Entities

XML assumes that the opening angle bracket always starts a tag, and that the ampersand always starts an entity reference. (This is often true of HTML as well, but most browsers will assume the semicolon if you leave it out.) For example, consider this line,

```
<H1>A Homage to Ben & Jerry's
    New York Super Fudge Chunk Ice Cream</H1>
```

Web browsers will probably display it correctly, but for maximum safety you should escape the ampersand with & like this:

```
<H1>A Homage to Ben &amp; Jerry's New York Super Fudge Chunk
Ice Cream</H1>
```

The open-angle bracket (<) is similar. Consider this common line of Java code:

```
<CODE>    for (int i = 0; i <= args.length; i++ ) { </CODE>
```

Both XML and HTML consider the less-than sign in <= to be the start of a tag. The tag continues until the next >. Thus this line gets rendered as:

```
for (int i = 0; i
```

rather than:

```
for (int i = 0; i <= args.length; i++ ) {
```

The = args.length; i++) { is interpreted as part of an unrecognized tag.

The less-than sign can be included in text in both XML and HTML by writing it as <. For example:

```
<CODE>    for (int i = 0; i &lt;= args.length; i++ ) { </CODE>
```

Well-formed XML requires & to be written as & and < to be written as < whenever they're used as themselves rather than as part of a tag or entity.

#8: Only Use the Five Preexisting Entity References

You're probably familiar with a number of entity references from HTML. For example `&copy;` inserts the copyright symbol ©. `&reg;` inserts the registered trademark symbol ®. However, other than the five entity references already discussed, XML can only use entity references that are defined in a DTD first.

You don't know about DTDs yet. If the ampersand character & appears anywhere in your document, it must be immediately followed by `amp;`, `lt;`, `gt;`, `apos;` or `quot;`. All other uses violate well-formedness.

In Chapter 9, *Entities and External DTD Subsets*, you'll learn how DTDs make it possible to define new entity references that insert particular symbols or chunks of boiler-plate text.

Well-Formed HTML

You can practice your XML skills even before most Web browsers directly support XML by writing well-formed HTML. This is HTML that adheres to XML's well-formedness constraints, but only uses standard HTML tags. Well-formed HTML is easier to read than the sloppy HTML most humans and WYSIWYG tools like FrontPage write. It's also easier for Web robots and automated search engines to understand. It's more robust, and less likely to break when you make a change. And it's less likely to be subject to annoying cross-browser and cross-platform differences in rendering. Furthermore, you can then use XML tools to work on HTML documents, while still maintaining backwards compatibility for readers whose browsers don't support XML.

Real-World Web Page Problems

Real-world Web pages are extremely sloppy. Tags aren't closed. Elements overlap. Raw less-than signs are included in pages. Semicolons are omitted from the ends of entity references. Web pages with these problems are formally invalid, but most Web browsers accept them. Nonetheless, your Web pages will be cleaner, display faster, and be easier to maintain if you fix these problems.

Some of the common problems that Web pages have include the following:

1. Start tags without matching end tags (unclosed elements)
2. End tags without start tags
3. Overlapping elements
4. Unquoted attributes

5. Unescaped <, >, &, and " signs

6. No root element

7. End tag case doesn't match start tag case

I've listed these in rough order of importance. Exact details vary from tag to tag, however. For instance, an unclosed `<STRONG>` tag will turn all elements following it bold. However, an unclosed `<LI>` or `<P>` tag causes no problems at all.

There are also some rules that only apply to XML documents, and that may actually cause problems if you attempt to integrate them into your existing HTML pages. These include:

1. Begin with an XML declaration

2. Empty tags must be closed with a `/>`

3. The only entity references used are `&amp;`, `&lt;`, `&gt;`, `&apos;` and `&quot;`

Fixing these problems isn't hard, but there are a few pitfalls that can trip up the unwary. Let's explore them.

Close All Start Tags

Any element that contains content, whether text or other child elements, should have a start tag and an end tag. HTML doesn't absolutely require this. For instance, `<P>`, `<DT>`, `<DD>`, and `<LI>` are often used in isolation. However, doing this relies on the Web browser to make a good guess at where the element ends, and browsers don't always do quite what authors want or expect. Therefore it's best to explicitly close all start tags.

The biggest change this requires to how you write HTML is probably thinking of `<P>` as a container rather than a simple paragraph break mark. For instance, previously you would probably format the opening of the Federalist Papers like this:

```
To the People of the State of New York:
<P>

AFTER an unequivocal experience of the inefficiency of the
subsisting federal government, you are called upon to
deliberate on a new Constitution for the United States of
America. The subject speaks its own importance; comprehending
in its consequences nothing less than the existence of the
UNION, the safety and welfare of the parts of which it is
composed, the fate of an empire in many respects the most
interesting in the world. It has been frequently remarked that
it seems to have been reserved to the people of this country,
by their conduct and example, to decide the important question,
whether societies of men are really capable or not of
```

```
establishing good government from reflection and choice, or
whether they are forever destined to depend for their political
constitutions on accident and force. If there be any truth in
the remark, the crisis at which we are arrived may with
propriety be regarded as the era in which that decision is to
be made; and a wrong election of the part we shall act may, in
this view, deserve to be considered as the general misfortune
of mankind.
<P>
```

Well-formedness requires that it be formatted like this instead:

```
<P>
To the People of the State of New York:
</P>

<P>
AFTER an unequivocal experience of the inefficiency of the
subsisting federal government, you are called upon to
deliberate on a new Constitution for the United States of
America. The subject speaks its own importance; comprehending
in its consequences nothing less than the existence of the
UNION, the safety and welfare of the parts of which it is
composed, the fate of an empire in many respects the most
interesting in the world. It has been frequently remarked that
it seems to have been reserved to the people of this country,
by their conduct and example, to decide the important question,
whether societies of men are really capable or not of
establishing good government from reflection and choice, or
whether they are forever destined to depend for their political
constitutions on accident and force. If there be any truth in
the remark, the crisis at which we are arrived may with
propriety be regarded as the era in which that decision is to
be made; and a wrong election of the part we shall act may, in
this view, deserve to be considered as the general misfortune
of mankind.
</P>
```

You've probably been taught to think of `<P>` as ending a paragraph. Now you have to think of it as beginning one. This does give you some advantages though. For instance, you can easily assign a variety of formatting attributes to a paragraph. For example, here's the original HTML title of House Resolution 581 as seen on `http://thomas.loc.gov/home/hres581.html`:

```
<center>
<p><h2>House Calendar No. 272</h2>

<p><h1>105TH CONGRESS 2D SESSION H. RES. 581</h1>

<p>[Report No. 105-795]
```

```
<p><b>Authorizing and directing the Committee on the
Judiciary to investigate whether sufficient grounds
exist for the impeachment of William Jefferson Clinton,
President of the United States.</b>
</center>
```

Here's the same text, but using well-formed HTML. The `align` attribute now replaces the deprecated `center` element, and a CSS style attribute is used instead of the `<b>` tag.

```
<h2 align="center">House Calendar No. 272</h2>

<h1 align="center">105TH CONGRESS 2D SESSION H. RES. 581</h1>

<p align="center">[Report No. 105-795]</p>

<p align="center" style="font-weight:bold">
Authorizing and directing the Committee on the Judiciary to
investigate whether sufficient grounds exist for the
impeachment of William Jefferson Clinton,
President of the United States.
</p>
```

Delete Orphaned End Tags and Don't Let Elements Overlap

When editing pages, it's not uncommon to remove a start tag and forget to remove its associated end tag. In HTML an orphaned end tag like a `</STRONG>` or `</TD>` that doesn't have any matching start tag is unlikely to cause problems by itself. However, it does make the file longer than it needs to be, the download slower, and has the potential to confuse people or tools that are trying to understand and edit the HTML source. Therefore, you should make sure that each end tag is properly matched with a start tag.

However, more often an end tag that doesn't match any start tag means that elements incorrectly overlap. Most elements that overlap on Web pages are quite easy to fix. For instance, consider this common problem:

```
<B><I>This text is bold and italic</B></I>
```

Since the `I` element starts inside the `B` element, it must end inside the `B` element. All that you need to do to fix it is swap the end tags like this:

```
<B><I>This text is bold and italic</I></B>
```

Alternately, you can swap the start tags instead:

```
<I><B>This text is bold and italic</B></I>
```

On occasion you may have a tougher problem. For example, consider this fragment from the White House home page (http://www.whitehouse.gov/, November 4, 1998). I've emboldened the problem tags to make it easier to see the mistake:

```
<TD valign=TOP width=85>
<FONT size=+1>
<A HREF="/WH/New"><img border=0
src="/WH/images/pin_calendar.gif"
align=LEFT height=50 width=75 hspace=5 vspace=5></A><br> </TD>
<TD valign=TOP width=225>
<A HREF="/WH/New"><B>What's New:</B></A><br>
</FONT>
What's happening at the White <nobr>House - </nobr><br>
 <font size=2><b>
<!-- New Begin -->
<a href="/WH/New/html/19981104-12244.html">Remarks Of The
President Regarding Social Security</a>
<BR>
<!-- New End -->
 </font>
 </b>
</TD>
```

Here the `<FONT size=+1>` element begins inside the first `<TD valign=TOP width=85>` element but continues past that element, into the `<TD valign=TOP width=225>` element where it finishes. The proper solution in this case is to close the FONT element immediately before the first `</TD>` closing tag; then add a new `<FONT size=+1>` start tag immediately after the start of the second TD element, as follows:

```
<TD valign=TOP width=85>
<FONT size=+1>
<A HREF="/WH/New"><img border=0
src="/WH/images/pin_calendar.gif"
align=LEFT height=50 width=75 hspace=5 vspace=5></A><br>
</FONT></TD>
<TD valign=TOP width=225>
<FONT size=+1>
<A HREF="/WH/New"><B>What's New:</B></A><br>
</FONT>
What's happening at the White <nobr>House - </nobr><br>
 <font size=2><b>
<!-- New Begin -->
<a href="/WH/New/html/19981104-12244.html">Remarks Of The
President Regarding Social Security</a>
<BR>
<!-- New End -->
 </font>
 </b>
</TD>
```

Quote All Attributes

HTML attributes only require quote marks if they contain embedded white space. Nonetheless, it doesn't hurt to include them. Furthermore, using quote marks may help in the future if you later decide to change the attribute value to something that does include white space. It's quite easy to forget to add the quote marks later, especially if the attribute is something like an ALT in an <IMG> whose malformedness is not immediately apparent when viewing the document in a Web browser.

For instance, consider this <IMG> tag:

```
<IMG SRC=cup.gif WIDTH=89 HEIGHT=67 ALT=Cup>
```

It should be rewritten like this:

```
<IMG SRC="cup.gif" WIDTH="89" HEIGHT="67" ALT="Cup">
```

Escape <, >, and & Signs

HTML is more forgiving of loose less-than signs and ampersands than XML. Nonetheless, even in pure HTML they do cause trouble, especially if they're followed immediately by some other character. For instance, consider this email address as it would appear if copied and pasted from the From: header in Eudora:

```
Elliotte Rusty Harold <elharo@metalab.unc.edu>
```

Were it to be rendered in HTML, this is all you would see:

```
Elliotte Rusty Harold
```

The <elharo@metalab.unc.edu> has been unintentionally hidden by the angle brackets. Anytime you want to include a raw less-than sign or ampersand in HTML, you really should use the < and & entity references. The correct HTML for such a line would be:

```
Elliotte Rusty Harold &lt;elharo@metalab.unc.edu&gt;
```

You're slightly less likely to see problems with an unescaped greater-than sign because this will only be interpreted as markup if it's preceded by an as yet unfinished tag. However, there may be such unfinished tags in a document, and a nearby greater-than sign can mask their presence. For example, consider this fragment of Java code:

```
for (int i=0;i<10;i++) {
  for (int j=20;j>10;j—) {
```

It's likely to be rendered as:

```
for (int i=0;i10;j-) {
```

If those are only two lines in a 100-line program, it's entirely possible you'll miss the omission when casually proofreading. On the other hand, if the greater-than sign is escaped, the unescaped less-than sign will hide the rest of the program, and the problem will be easier to spot.

Use a Root Element

The root element for HTML files is supposed to be `html`. Most browsers forgive your failure to include this. Nonetheless, it's definitely better to make the very first tag in your document `<html>` and the very last `</html>`. If any extra text or markup has gotten in front of `<html>` or behind `</html>`, move it between `<html>` and `</html>`.

One common manifestation of this problem is forgetting to include `</html>` at the end of the document. I always begin my documents by typing `<html>` and `</html>`, then type in between them, rather than waiting until I've finished writing the document and hoping that by that point, possibly days later, I still remember that I need to put in a closing `</html>` tag.

Use the Same Case for All Tags

HTML isn't case-sensitive but XML is. I recommend picking a single convention for tag case, either all uppercase or all lowercase, and sticking to it throughout the document. This is easier than trying to remember the details of each tag. I normally pick all lowercase, because it's much easier to type. Furthermore, the W3C's effort to reformulate HTML as an XML application also uses this convention.

Chapter 20, *Reading Document Type Definitions*, will explore the reformulation of HTML in XML in great detail. However, further exploration will have to wait because that effort uses XML techniques you won't learn for several chapters.

Close Empty Tags with a />.

Empty tags are the *bête noir* of converting HTML to well-formed XML. HTML does not formally recognize the XML `<elementname/>` syntax for empty tags. You can convert `<br>` to `<br/>`, `<hr>` to `<hr/>`, `<img>` to `<img/>` and so on quite easily. However, it's a crapshoot whether any given browser will render the transformed tags properly or not.

Do not confuse truly empty elements like `<br>`, `<hr>`, and `<img>` with elements that do contain content but often only have a start tag in standard HTML such as `<p>`, `<li>`, `<dt>`, and `<dd>`.

The simplest solution, and one approved by the XML specification, is to replace the empty tags with start-tag/end-tag pairs with no content. The browser should then ignore the unrecognized end tag. Take a look at the following example,

```
<br></br>
<hr></hr>
<IMG SRC="cup.gif" WIDTH="89" HEIGHT="67" ALT="Cup"></IMG>
```

This seems to work well in practice with one notable exception. Netscape 4.5 and earlier treats </br> the same as <br>; that is, as a signal to break the line. Thus while <br> is a single line break,
</br> is a double line break, more akin to a paragraph mark in practice. Furthermore, Netscape ignores <br/> completely. Web sites that must support legacy browsers (essentially all Web sites) cannot use either
</br> or <br/>. What does seem to work in practice for XML and legacy browsers is the following:

```
<br />
```

Note the space between <br and />. I can't really explain why this works when the more natural variants don't. All I can do is offer it to you as a possible solution if you really care about well-formed HTML.

Use Only the &, <, >, ' and " Entity References

Many Web pages don't need entity references other than &, <, >, ' and ". However, the HTML 4.0 specification does define many more including:

✦ ™ the trademark symbol (™)

✦ © the copyright symbol (©)

✦ ∞ the infinity symbol ∞

✦ π the lower case Greek letter pi, π

There are several hundred others. However, using any of these will make your document not well-formed. The real solution to this problem is to use a DTD. We'll discuss the effect DTDs have on entity references in Chapter 9. In the meantime, there are several short- term solutions.

The simplest solution is to write your document in a character set that has all of the symbols you need, then use a <META> directive to specify the character set in use. For example, to specify that your document uses UTF-8 encoding (a character set we'll discuss in Chapter 7 that contains all the characters you're likely to want) you would place this <META> directive in the head of your document:

```
<META http-equiv="Content-Type"
      content="text/html; charset=UTF-8">
```

Alternately, you can simply tell your Web server to emit the necessary content type header. However, it's normally easier to use the `<META>` tag.

```
Content-Type: text/html; charset=UTF-8
```

The problem with this approach is that many browsers are unlikely to be able to display the UTF-8 character set. The same is true of most other character sets you're likely to use to provide these special characters.

HTML 4.0 supports character entity references just like XML's; that is, you can replace a character by &# and the decimal or hexadecimal value of the character in Unicode. For example:

✦ `&#8482;` the trademark symbol (™)

✦ `&#169;` the copyright symbol (©)

✦ `&#8734;` the infinity symbol ∞

✦ `&#960;` the lower case Greek letter pi, π

HTML 3.2 only officially supports the numeric character references between 0 and 255 (ISO Latin-1) but 4.0 and later versions of Navigator and Internet Explorer do recognize broader sections of the Unicode set.

If you're really desperate for well-formed XML that's backwards compatible with HTML you can include these characters as inline images. For example:

✦ `<img src="tm.gif" width="12" height="12" alt="TM"></img>` the trademark symbol (tm)

✦ `<img src="copyright.gif" width="12" height="12" alt="Copyright"></img>` the copyright symbol (c)

✦ `img src="infinity.gif" width="12" height="12" alt="infinity"></img>` the infinity symbol ∞

✦ `<img src="pi.gif" width="12" height="12" alt="pi"></img>` the lowercase Greek letter pi, π

In practice, however, I don't recommend using these. Well-formedness is not nearly so important in HTML that it justifies the added download and rendering time this imposes on your readers.

The XML Declaration

HTML documents don't need XML declarations. However, they can have them. Web browsers simply ignore tags they don't recognize. From their perspective, the following line is just another tag:

```
<?xml version="1.0" standalone="yes"?>
```

Since browsers that don't understand XML, don't understand the `<?xml?>` tag, they quietly ignore it. Browsers that do understand XML will recognize this as an indication that this document is composed of well-formed XML, and will be treated as such.

Unfortunately, browsers that halfway understand XML may have troubles with this syntax. In particular, Internet Explorer 4.0 for the Mac (but not Netscape Navigator or other versions of IE) uses this as a signal to download the file rather than displaying it. Consequently I've removed the XML declaration from my Web pages.

Follow the Rules

It is not particularly difficult to write well-formed XML documents that follow the rules described in this chapter. However XML browsers are less forgiving of poor syntax than HTML browsers, so you do need to be careful.

If you violate any well-formedness constraints, XML parsers and browsers will report a syntax error. Thus the process of writing XML can be a little like the process of writing code in a real programming language. You write it, then you compile it, then when the compilation fails, you note the errors reported and fix them.

Generally this is an iterative process in which you go through several edit-compile cycles before you first get to look at the finished document. Despite this, there's no question that writing XML is a lot easier than writing C or Java source code, and with a little practice, you'll get to the point at which you have relatively few errors, and you can write XML almost as quickly as you can type.

HTML Clean-Up Tools

There are several tools that will help you clean up your pages, most notably RUWF (Are You Well Formed?) from XML.COM and HTML Tidy from Dave Raggett of the W3C.

RUWF

Any tool that can check XML documents for well-formedness can test well-formed HTML documents as well. However, one of the easiest tools to use is the RUWF well-formedness checker from XML.COM. Figure 6-2 shows this tester. Simply type in the URL of the page you want to check, and RUWF returns the first several dozen errors on the page.

Here's the first batch of errors RUWF found on the White House home page. Most of these errors are malformed XML, but legal (if not necessarily good style) HTML. However, at least one error ("Line 55, column 30: Encountered </FONT> with no start-tag.") is a problem for both HTML and XML.

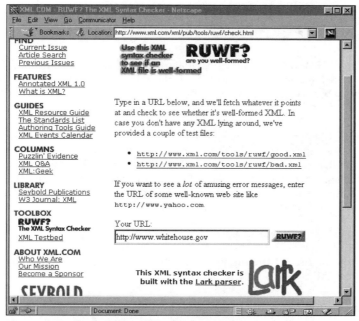

Figure 6-2: The RUWF well-formedness tester

```
Line 28, column 7: Encountered </HEAD> expected </META>
...assumed </META> ...assumed </META> ...assumed </META>
...assumed </META>
Line 36, column 12, character 'O': after AttrName= in start-tag
Line 37, column 12, character 'O': after AttrName= in start-tag
Line 38, column 12, character 'O': after AttrName= in start-tag
Line 40, column 12, character 'O': after AttrName= in start-tag
Line 41, column 10, character 'A': after AttrName= in start-tag
Line 42, column 12, character 'O': after AttrName= in start-tag
Line 43, column 14: Encountered </CENTER> expected </br>
...assumed </br> ...assumed </br>
Line 51, column 11, character '+': after AttrName= in start-tag
Line 52, column 51, character 'O': after AttrName= in start-tag
Line 54, column 57: after &
Line 55, column 30: Encountered </FONT> with no start-tag.
Line 57, column 10, character 'A': after AttrName= in start-tag
Line 59, column 15, character '+': after AttrName= in start-tag
```

HTML Tidy

Once you've identified the problems, you'll want to fix them. Many common problems — for instance, putting quote marks around attribute values — can be fixed automatically. The most convenient tool for doing this is Dave Raggett's command-line program HTML Tidy. Tidy is a character-mode program written in ANSI C that can be compiled and run on most platforms including Windows, Unix, BeOS and the Mac.

On the CD-ROM   Tidy is on the CD-ROM in the directory utilities/tidy. Binaries are included for Windows NT and BeOS. Portable source is included for all platforms. You can download the latest version from `http://www.w3.org/People/Raggett/tidy/`.

Tidy cleans up HTML files in several ways, not all of which are relevant to XML well-formedness. In fact, in its default mode Tidy tends to remove unnecessary (for HTML, but not for XML) end tags like `</LI>` and make other modifications that break well-formedness. However, you can use the `-asxml` switch to specify that you want well-formed XML output. For example, to convert the file index.html to well-formed XML, you would type from a DOS window or shell prompt:

```
C:\> tidy -m -asxml index.html
```

The `-m` flag tells Tidy to convert the file in place. The `-asxml` flag tells Tidy to format the output as XML.

Summary

In this chapter, you learned how to write well-formed XML. In particular, you learned:

✦ XML documents are sequences of characters that meet certain well-formedness criteria.

✦ The text of XML documents is divided into character data and markup.

✦ Comments can document your code with notes to yourself or to temporarily comment out sections of the document that aren't ready.

✦ Entity references allow you to include $<$, $>$, &, ", and ' in your document.

✦ CDATA sections are useful for embedding text that contains a lot of $<$, $>$, and & characters

✦ Tags are anything in an XML document that begins with < and ends with >, and are not inside a comment or CDATA section.

✦ Start tags and empty tags may contain attributes, which describe elements.

✦ HTML documents can also be well-formed with a little extra effort.

In the next chapter, we'll explore how to write XML in languages other than English, in particular in languages that don't look even remotely like English, such as Arabic, Chinese, and Greek.

✦   ✦   ✦

Foreign Languages and Non-Roman Text

The Web is international, yet most of the text you'll find on it is English. XML is starting to change this. XML provides full support for the double-byte Unicode character set, as well as its more compact representations. This is good news for Web authors because Unicode supports almost every character commonly used in every modern script on Earth.

In this chapter, you'll learn how international text is represented in computer applications, how XML understands text, and how you can take advantage of the software you have to read and write in languages other than English.

Non-Roman Scripts on the Web

Although the Web is international, much of its text is in English. Because of the Web's expansiveness, however, you can still surf through Web pages in French, Spanish, Chinese, Arabic, Hebrew, Russian, Hindi, and other languages. Most of the time, though, these pages come out looking less than ideal. Figure 7-1 shows the October 1998 cover page of one of the United States Information Agency's propaganda journals, *Issues in Democracy* (http://www.usia.gov/journals/itdhr/1098/ijdr/ijdr1098.htm), in Russian translation viewed in an English encoding. The red Cyrillic text in the upper left is a bitmapped image file so it's legible (if you speak Russian) and so are a few words in English such as "Adobe Acrobat." However, the rest of the text is mostly a bunch of accented Roman vowels, not the Cyrillic letters they are supposed to be.

The quality of Web pages deteriorates even further when complicated, non-Western scripts like Chinese and Japanese are used. Figure 7-2 shows the home page for the Japanese translation of my book *JavaBeans* (IDG Books, 1997, `http://www. ohmsha.co.jp/data/books/contents/4-274-06271-6.htm`) viewed in an English browser. Once again the bitmapped image shows the proper Japanese (and English) text, but the rest of the text on the page looks almost like a random collection of characters except for a few recognizable English words like JavaBeans. The Kanji characters you're supposed to see are completely absent.

Figure 7-1: The Russian translation of the October 1998 issue of *Issues of Democracy* viewed in a Roman script

These pages look as they're intended to look if viewed with the right encoding and application software, and if the correct font is installed. Figure 7-3 shows *Issues in Democracy* viewed with the Windows 1251 encoding of Cyrillic. As you can see, the text below the picture is now readable (if you can read Russian).

You can select the encoding for a Web page from the View/Encoding menu in Netscape Navigator or Internet Explorer. In an ideal world, the Web server would tell the Web browser what encoding to use, and the Web browser would listen. It would also be nice if the Web server could send the Web browser the fonts it needed to display the page. In practice, however, you often need to select the encoding manually, even trying several to find the exact right one when more than one encoding is available for a script. For instance, a Cyrillic page might be encoded in Windows 1251, ISO 8859-5, or KOI6-R. Picking the wrong encoding may make Cyrillic letters appear, but the words will be gibberish.

Figure 7-2: The Japanese translation of JavaBeans viewed in an English browser

Figure 7-3: *Issues of Democracy* viewed in a Cyrillic script

Even when you can identify the encoding, there's no guarantee you have fonts available to display it. Figure 7-4 shows the Japanese home page for *JavaBeans* with Japanese encoding, but without a Japanese font installed on the computer. Most of the characters in the text are shown as a box, which indicates an unavailable character glyph. Fortunately, Netscape Navigator can recognize that some of the bytes on the page are double-byte Japanese characters rather than two one-byte Western characters.

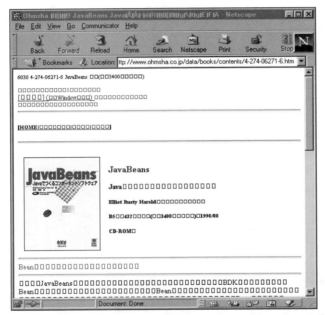

Figure 7-4: The Japanese translation of *JavaBeans* in Kanji without the necessary fonts installed

If you do have a Japanese localized edition of your operating system that includes the necessary fonts, or additional software like Apple's Japanese Language Kit or NJStar's NJWin (http://www.njstar.com/) that adds Japanese-language support to your existing system, you would be able to see the text more or less as it was meant to be seen as shown in Figure 7-5.

Note   Of course, the higher quality fonts you use, the better the text will look. Chinese and Japanese fonts tend to be quite large (there are over 80,000 characters in Chinese alone) and the distinctions between individual ideographs can be quite subtle. Japanese publishers generally require higher-quality paper and printing than Western publishers, so they can maintain the fine detail necessary to print Japanese letters. Regrettably a 72-dpi computer monitor can't do justice to most Japanese and Chinese characters unless they're displayed at almost obscenely large point sizes.

Figure 7-5: The Japanese translation of JavaBeans in Kanji with the necessary fonts installed

Because each page can only have a single encoding, it is difficult to write a Web page that integrates multiple scripts, such as a French commentary on a Chinese text. For a reasons such as this the Web community needs a single, universal character set to display all characters for all computers and Web browsers. We don't have such a character set yet, but XML and Unicode get as close as is currently possible.

XML files are written in Unicode, a double-byte character set that can represent most characters in most of the world's languages. If a Web page is written in Unicode, as XML pages are, and if the browser understands Unicode, as XML browsers should, then it's not a problem for characters from different languages to be included on the same page.

Furthermore, the browser doesn't need to distinguish between different encodings like Windows 1251, ISO 8859-5, or KOI8-R. It can just assume everything's written in Unicode. As long as the double-byte set has the space to hold all of the different characters, there's no need to use more than one character set. Therefore there's no need for browsers to try to detect which character set is in use.

Scripts, Character Sets, Fonts, and Glyphs

Most modern human languages have written forms. The set of characters used to write a language is called a *script*. A script may be a phonetic alphabet, but it doesn't have to be. For instance, Chinese, Japanese, and Korean are written with ideographic characters that represent whole words. Different languages often share scripts, sometimes with slight variations. For instance, the modern Turkish alphabet is essentially the familiar Roman alphabet with three extra letters — ğ, ş, and ı. Chinese, Japanese, and Korean, on the other hand, share essentially the same 80,000 Han ideographs, though many characters have different meanings in the different languages.

 Note   The word *script* is also often used to refer to programs written in weakly typed, interpreted languages like JavaScript, Perl, and TCL. In this chapter, the word *script* always refers to the characters used to write a language and not to any sort of program.

Some languages can even be written in different scripts. Serbian and Croatian are virtually identical and are generally referred to as Serbo-Croatian. However, Serbian is written in a modified Cyrillic script, and Croatian is written in a modified Roman script. As long as a computer doesn't attempt to grasp the meaning of the words it processes, working with a script is equivalent to working with any language that can be written in that script.

Unfortunately, XML alone is not enough to read a script. For each script a computer processes, four things are required:

1. A character set for the script

2. A font for the character set

3. An input method for the character set

4. An operating system and application software that understand the character set

If any of these four elements are missing, you won't be able to work easily in the script, though XML does provide a work-around that's adequate for occasional use. If the only thing your application is missing is an input method, you'll be able to read text written in the script. You just won't be able to write in it.

A Character Set for the Script

Computers only understand numbers. Before they can work with text, that text has to be encoded as numbers in a specified character set. For example, the popular ASCII character set encodes the capital letter 'A' as 65. The capital letter 'B' is encoded as 66. 'C' is 67, and so on.

These are semantic encodings that provide no style or font information. **C**, C, or even *C* are all 67. Information about how the character is drawn is stored elsewhere.

A Font for the Character Set

A font is a collection of glyphs for a character set, generally in a specific size, face, and style. For example, **C**, C, and *C* are all the same character, but they are drawn with different glyphs. Nonetheless their essential meaning is the same.

Exactly how the glyphs are stored varies from system to system. They may be bitmaps or vector drawings; they may even consist of hot lead on a printing press. The form they take doesn't concern us here. The key idea is that a font tells the computer how to draw each character in the character set.

An Input Method for the Character Set

An input method enables you to enter text. English speakers don't think much about the need for an input method for a script. We just type on our keyboards and everything's hunky-dory. The same is true in most of Europe, where all that's needed is a slightly modified keyboard with a few extra umlauts, cedillas, or thorns (depending on the country).

Radically different character sets like Cyrillic, Hebrew, Arabic, and Greek are more difficult to input. There's a finite number of keys on the keyboard, generally not enough for Arabic and Roman letters, or Roman and Greek letters. Assuming both are needed though, a keyboard can have a Greek lock key that shifts the keyboard from Roman to Greek and back. Both Greek and Roman letters can be printed on the keys in different colors. The same scheme works for Hebrew, Arabic, Cyrillic, and other non-Roman alphabetic character sets.

However, this scheme really breaks down when faced with ideographic scripts like Chinese and Japanese. Japanese keyboards can have in the ballpark of 5,000 different keys; and that's still less than 10% of the language! Syllabic, phonetic, and radical representations exist that can reduce the number of keys; but it is questionable whether a keyboard is really an appropriate means of entering text in these languages. Reliable speech and handwriting recognition have even greater potential in Asia than in the West.

Since speech and handwriting recognition still haven't reached the reliability of even a mediocre typist like myself, most input methods today are map multiple sequences of keys on the keyboard to a single character. For example, to type the Chinese character for sheep, you might hold down the Alt key and type a tilde (~), then type *yang*, then hit the enter key. The input method would then present you with a list of words that are pronounced more or less like *yang*. For example:

伴 揚 易 暘 楊 洋 瘍 羊 詳 錫 陽

You would then choose the character you wanted, _. The exact details of both the GUI and the transliteration system used to convert typed keys like *yang* to the ideographic characters like _ vary from program to program, operating system to operating system, and language to language.

Operating System and Application Software

As of this writing, the major Web browsers (Netscape Navigator and Internet Explorer) do a surprisingly good job of displaying non-Roman scripts. Provided the underlying operating system supports a given script and has the right fonts installed, a Web browser can probably display it.

MacOS 7.1 and later can handle most common scripts in the world today. However, the base operating system only supports Western European languages. Chinese, Japanese, Korean, Arabic, Hebrew, and Cyrillic are available as language kits that cost about $100 a piece. Each provides fonts and input methods for languages written in those scripts. There's also an Indian language kit, which handles the Devanagari, Gujarati, and Gurmukhu scripts common on the Indian subcontinent. MacOS 8.5 adds optional, limited support for Unicode (which most applications don't yet take advantage of).

Windows NT 4.0 uses Unicode as its native character set. NT 4.0 does a fairly good job with Roman languages, Cyrillic, Greek, Hebrew, and a few others. The Lucida Sans Unicode font covers about 1300 of the most common of Unicode's 40,000 or so characters. Microsoft Office 97 includes Chinese, Japanese, and Korean fonts that you can install to read text in these languages. (Look in the Fareast folder in the Valupack folder on your Office CD-ROM.)

Microsoft claims Windows 2000 (previously known as NT 5.0) will also include fonts covering most of the Chinese-Japanese-Korean ideographs, as well as input methods for these scripts. However they also promised that Windows 95 would include Unicode support, and that got dropped before shipment. Consequently, I'm not holding my breath. Certainly, it would be nice if they do provide full international support in all versions of NT rather than relying on localized systems.

Microsoft's consumer operating systems, Windows 3.1, 95, and 98, do not fully support Unicode. Instead they rely on localized systems that can only handle basic English characters plus the localized script.

The major Unix variants have varying levels of support for Unicode. Solaris 2.6 supports European languages, Greek, and Cyrillic. Chinese, Japanese, and Korean are supported by localized versions using different encodings rather than Unicode. Linux has embryonic support for Unicode, which may grow to something useful in the near future.

Legacy Character Sets

Different computers in different locales use different default character sets. Most modern computers use a superset of the ASCII character set. ASCII encodes the English alphabet and the most common punctuation and whitespace characters.

In the United States, Macs use the MacRoman character set, Windows PCs use a character set called Windows ANSI, and most Unix workstations use ISO Latin-1. These are all extensions of ASCII that support additional characters like ç and ¿ that are needed for Western European languages like French and Spanish. In other locales like Japan, Greece, and Israel, computers use a still more confusing hodge-podge of character sets that mostly support ASCII plus the local language.

This doesn't work on the Internet. It's unlikely that while you're reading the *San Jose Mercury News* you'll turn the page and be confronted with several columns written in German or Chinese. However, on the Web it's entirely possible a user will follow a link and end up staring at a page of Japanese. Even if the surfer can't read Japanese it would still be nice if they saw a correct version of the language, as seen in Figure 7-5, instead of a random collection of characters like those shown in Figure 7-2.

XML addresses this problem by moving beyond small, local character sets to one large set that's supposed to encompass all scripts used in all living languages (and a few dead ones) on planet Earth. This character set is called Unicode. As previously noted, Unicode is a double-byte character set that provides representations of over 40,000 different characters in dozens of scripts and hundreds of languages. All XML processors are required to understand Unicode, even if they can't fully display it.

As you learned in Chapter 6, an XML document is divided into text and binary entities. Each text entity has an encoding. If the encoding is not explicitly specified in the entity's definition, then the default is UTF-8—a compressed form of Unicode which leaves pure ASCII text unchanged. Thus XML files that contain nothing but the common ASCII characters may be edited with tools that are unaware of the complications of dealing with multi-byte character sets like Unicode.

The ASCII Character Set

ASCII, the American Standard Code for Information Interchange, is one of the original character sets, and is by far the most common. It forms a sort of lowest common denominator for what a character set must support. It defines all the characters needed to write U.S. English, and essentially nothing else. The characters are encoded as the numbers 0-127. Table 7-1 presents the ASCII character set.

Table 7-1
The ASCII Character Set

Code	Character	Code	Character	Code	Character	Code	Character
0	null(Control-@)	32	Space	64	@	96	`
1	start of heading (Control-A)	33	!	65	A	97	a
2	start of text (Control-B)	34	"	66	B	98	b
3	end of text (Control-C)	35	#	67	C	99	c
4	end of transmission (Control-D)	36	$	68	D	100	d
5	enquiry (Control-E)	37	%	69	E	101	e
6	acknowledge (Control-F)	38	&	70	F	102	f
7	bell (Control-G)	39	'	71	G	103	g
8	backspace (Control-H)	40	(	72	H	104	h
9	tab(Control-I)	41	)	73	I	105	i
10	linefeed (Control-J)	42	*	74	J	106	j
11	vertical tab) (Control-K	43	+	75	K	107	k
12	formfeed (Control-L)	44	,	76	L	108	l
13	carriage return (Control-M)	45	-	77	M	109	m
14	shift out (Control-N)	46	.	78	N	110	n
15	shift in (Control-O)	47	/	79	O	111	o
16	data link escape (Control-P)	48	0	80	P	112	p
17	device control 1 (Control-Q)	49	1	81	Q	113	q

Code	Character	Code	Character	Code	Character	Code	Character
18	device control 2 (Control-R)	50	2	82	R	114	r
19	device control 3 (Control-S)	51	3	83	S	115	s
20	device control 4 (Control-T)	52	4	84	T	116	t
21	negative acknowledge (Control-U)	53	5	85	U	117	u
22	synchronous idle (Control-V)	54	6	86	V	118	v
23	end of transmission block (Control-W)	55	7	87	W	119	w
24	cancel (Control-X)	56	8	88	X	120	x
25	end of medium (Control-Y)	57	9	89	Y	121	y
26	substitute (Control-Z)	58	:	90	Z	122	z
27	escape (Control-[)	59	;	91	[	123	{
28	file separator (Control-\)	60	<	92	\	124	|
29	group separator (Control-])	61	=	93	]	125	}
30	record separator (Control-^)	62	>	94	^	126	~
31	unit separator (Control-_)	63	?	95	_	127	delete

Characters 0 through 31 are non-printing control characters. They include the carriage return, the linefeed, the tab, the bell, and similar characters. Many of these are leftovers from the days of paper-based teletype terminals. For instance, carriage return used to literally mean move the carriage back to the left margin, as you'd do on a typewriter. Linefeed moved the platen up one line. Aside from the few control characters mentioned, these aren't used much anymore.

Most other character sets you're likely to encounter are supersets of ASCII. In other words, they define 0 though 127 exactly the same as ASCII, but add additional characters from 128 on up.

The ISO Character Sets

The A in ASCII stands for American, so it shouldn't surprise you that ASCII is only adequate for writing English, and strictly American English at that. ASCII contains no £, ü, ¿, or many other characters you might want for writing in other languages or locales.

ASCII can be extended by assigning additional characters to numbers above 128. The International Standards Organization (ISO) has defined a number of different character sets based on ASCII that add additional characters needed for other languages and locales. The most prominent such character set is ISO 8859-1, commonly called Latin-1. Latin-1 includes enough additional characters to write essentially all Western European languages. Characters 0 through 127 are the same as they are in ASCII. Characters 128 through 255 are given in Table 7-2. Again, the first 32 characters are mostly unused, non-printing control characters.

	Table 7-2						
	The ISO 8859-1 Latin-1 Character Set						
Code	*Character*	*Code*	*Character*	*Code*	*Character*	*Code*	*Character*
128	Undefined	160	non-breaking space	192	À	224	à
129	Undefined	161	¡	193	Á	225	á
130	Bph	162	¢	194	Â	226	â
131	Nbh	163	£	195	Ã	227	ã
132	Undefined	164	¤	196	Ä	228	ä
133	Nel	165	¥	197	Å	229	å
134	Ssa	166	¦	198	Æ	230	æ
135	Esa	167	§	199	Ç	231	ç
136	Hts	168	¨	200	È	232	è
137	Htj	169	©	201	É	233	é
138	Vts	170	ª	202	Ê	234	ê
139	Pld	171	«	203	Ë	235	ë
140	Plu	172	¬	204	Ì	236	ì
141	Ri	173	Discretionary hyphen	205	Í	237	í
142	ss2	174	®	206	Î	238	î

Code	Character	Code	Character	Code	Character	Code	Character
143	ss3	175	¯	207	Ï	239	ï
144	Dcs	176	°	208	Ð	240	ð
145	pu1	177	±	209	Ñ	241	ñ
146	pu2	178	²	210	Ò	242	ò
147	Sts	179	³	211	Ó	243	ó
148	Cch	180	´	212	Ô	244	ô
149	Mw	181	µ	213	Õ	245	õ
150	Spa	182	¶	214	Ö	246	ö
151	Epa	183	·	215	×	247	÷
152	Sos	184	¸	216	Ø	248	ø
153	Undefined	185	¹	217	Ù	249	ù
154	Sci	186	º	218	Ú	250	ú
155	Csi	187	»	219	Û	251	û
156	St	188	1/4	220	Ü	252	ü
157	Osc	189	1/2	221	Ý	253	ý
158	Pm	190	3/4	222	Þ	254	þ
159	Apc	191	¿	223	ß	255	ÿ

Latin-1 still lacks many useful characters including those needed for Greek, Cyrillic, Chinese, and many other scripts and languages. You might think these could just be moved into the numbers from 256 up. However there's a catch. A single byte can only hold values from 0 to 255. To go beyond that, you need to use a multi-byte character set. For historical reasons most programs are written under the assumption that characters and bytes are identical, and they tend to break when faced with multi-byte character sets. Therefore, most current operating systems (Windows NT being the notable exception) use different, single-byte character sets rather than one large multi-byte set. Latin-1 is the most common such set, but other sets are needed to handle additional languages.

ISO 8859 defines ten other character sets (8859-2 through 8859-10 and 8859-15) suitable for different scripts, with four more (8859-11 through 8859-14) in active development. Table 7-3 lists the ISO character sets and the languages and scripts they can be used for. All share the same ASCII characters from 0 to 127, and then each includes additional characters from 128 to 255.

Table 7-3
The ISO Character Sets

Character Set	Also Known As	Languages
ISO 8859-1	Latin-1	ASCII plus the characters required for most Western European languages including Albanian, Afrikaans, Basque, Catalan, Danish, Dutch, English, Faroese, Finnish, Flemish, Galician, German, Icelandic, Irish, Italian, Norwegian, Portuguese, Scottish, Spanish, and Swedish. However it omits the ligatures ij (Dutch), Œ (French), and German quotation marks.
ISO 8859-2	Latin-2	ASCII plus the characters required for most Central European languages including Czech, English, German, Hungarian, Polish, Romanian, Croatian, Slovak, Slovene, and Sorbian.
ISO 8859-3	Latin-3	ASCII plus the characters required for English, Esperanto, German, Maltese, and Galician.
ISO 8859-4	Latin-4	ASCII plus the characters required for the Baltic languages Latvian, Lithuanian, German, Greenlandic, and Lappish; superseded by ISO 8859-10, Latin-6
ISO 8859-5		ASCII plus Cyrillic characters required for Byelorussian, Bulgarian, Macedonian, Russian, Serbian, and Ukrainian.
ISO 8859-6		ASCII plus Arabic.
ISO 8859-7		ASCII plus Greek.
ISO 8859-8		ASCII plus Hebrew.
ISO 8859-9	Latin-5	Latin-1 except that the Turkish letters İ, ı, Ş , ş, Ğ, and ğ take the place of the less commonly used Icelandic letters Ý, ý, Þ, þ, Ð, and ð.
ISO 8859-10	Latin-6	ASCII plus characters for the Nordic languages Lithuanian, Inuit (Greenlandic Eskimo), non-Skolt Sami (Lappish), and Icelandic.
ISO 8859-11		ASCII plus Thai.
ISO 8859-12		This may eventually be used for ASCII plus Devanagari (Hindi, Sanskrit, etc.) but no proposal is yet available.
ISO 8859-13	Latin-7	ASCII plus the Baltic Rim, particularly Latvian.
ISO 8859-14	Latin-8	ASCII plus Gaelic and Welsh.
ISO 8859-15	Latin-9, Latin-0	Essentially the same as Latin-1 but with a Euro sign instead of the international currency sign ¤. Furthermore, the Finnish characters Ž, Š, š, ž replace the uncommon symbols ¦, ¨, ´. And the French Œ, œ, and Ÿ characters replace the fractions 1/4, 1/2, 3/4.

These sets often overlap. Several languages, most notably English and German, can be written in more than one of the character sets. To some extent the different sets are designed to allow different combinations of languages. For instance Latin-1 can combine most Western languages and Icelandic whereas Latin-5 combines most Western languages with Turkish instead of Icelandic. Thus if you needed a document in English, French, and Icelandic, you'd use Latin-1. However a document containing English, French, and Turkish would use Latin-5. However, a document that required English, Hebrew, and Turkish, would have to use Unicode since no single-byte character set handles all three languages and scripts.

A single-byte set is insufficient for Chinese, Japanese, and Korean. These languages have more than 256 characters apiece, so they must use multi-byte character sets.

The MacRoman Character Set

The MacOS predates Latin-1 by several years. (The ISO 8859-1 standard was first adopted in 1987. The first Mac was released in 1984.) Unfortunately this means that Apple had to define its own extended character set called MacRoman. MacRoman has most of the same extended characters as Latin-1 (except for the Icelandic letters Þ, þ, and ð) but the characters are assigned to different numbers. MacRoman is the same as ASCII and Latin-1 in the codes though the first 127 characters. This is one reason text files that use extended characters often look funny when moved from a PC to a Mac or vice versa. Table 7-4 lists the upper half of the MacRoman character set.

Table 7-4 The MacRoman Character Set							
Code	**Character**	**Code**	**Character**	**Code**	**Character**	**Code**	**Character**
128	Ä	160	†	192	¿	224	‡
129	Å	161	°	193	¡	225	·
130	Ç	162	¢	194	¬	226	‚
131	É	163	£	195	√	227	„
132	Ñ	164	§	196	ƒ	228	‰
133	Ö	165	·	197	˜	229	Â
134	Ü	166	¶	198	∆	230	Ê
135	á	167	ß	199	«	231	Á
136	à	168	®	200	»	232	Ë

Continued

Table 7-4 *(continued)*

Code	Character	Code	Character	Code	Character	Code	Character
137	Â	169	©	201	...	233	È
138	Ä	170	™	202	non-breaking space	234	Í
139	Ã	171	´	203	À	235	Î
140	Å	172	¨	204	Ã	236	Ï
141	Ç	173	≠	205	Õ	237	Ì
142	É	174	Æ	206	Œ	238	Î
143	È	175	Ø	207	œ	239	Ó
144	Ê	176	∞	208	–	240	Ô
145	Ë	177	±	209	—	241	Apple
146	Í	178	≤	210	"	242	Ò
147	Ì	179	≥	211	"	243	Ú
148	Î	180	¥	212	'	244	Û
149	Ï	181	µ	213	'	245	ı
150	ñ	182	∂	214	÷	246	ˆ
151	ó	183	Σ	215	◊	247	˜
152	ò	184	∏	216	Ÿ	248	¯
153	ô	185	π	217	Ÿ	249	˘
154	ö	186	∫	218	⁄	250	˙
155	õ	187	ª	219	¤	251	˚
156	ú	188	º	220	‹	252	¸
157	ù	189	Ω	221	›	253	˝
158	û	190	æ	222	fi	254	˛
159	ü	191	ø	223	fl	255	ˇ

The Windows ANSI Character Set

The first version of Windows to achieve widespread adoption followed the Mac by a few years, so it was able to adopt the Latin-1 character set. However, it replaced the non-printing control characters between 130 and 159 with more printing characters to stretch the available range a little further. This modified version of Latin-1 is generally called "Windows ANSI." Table 7-5 lists the Windows ANSI characters.

Code	Character	Code	Character	Code	Character	Code	Character
			Table 7-5				
			The Windows ANSI Character Set				
128	Undefined	136	ˆ	144	Undefined	152	˜
129	Undefined	137	‰	145	'	153	™
130	,	138	Š	146	'	154	š
131	□	139	‹	147	"	155	›
132	„	140	Œ	148	"	156	œ
133	…	141	Undefined	149	•	157	Undefined
134	†	142	Undefined	150	–	158	Undefined
135	‡	143	Undefined	151	—	159	Ÿ

The Unicode Character Set

Using different character sets for different scripts and languages works well enough as long as:

1. You don't need to work in more than one script at once.

2. You never trade files with anyone using a different character set.

Since Macs and PCs use different character sets, more people fail these criteria than not. Obviously what is needed is a single character set that everyone agrees on and that encodes all characters in all the world's scripts. Creating such a set is difficult. It requires a detailed understanding of hundreds of languages and their scripts. Getting software developers to agree to use that set once it's been created is even harder. Nonetheless work is ongoing to create exactly such a set called Unicode, and the major vendors (Microsoft, Apple, IBM, Sun, Be, and many others) are slowly moving toward complying with it. XML specifies Unicode as its default character set.

Unicode encodes each character as a two-byte unsigned number with a value between 0 and 65,535. Currently a few more than 40,000 different Unicode characters are defined. The remaining 25,000 spaces are reserved for future extensions. About 20,000 of the characters are used for the Han ideographs and another 11,000 or so are used for the Korean Hangul syllables. The remainder of the characters encodes most of the rest of the world's languages. Unicode characters 0 through 255 are identical to Latin-1 characters 0 through 255.

I'd love to show you a table of all the characters in Unicode, but if I did this book would consist entirely of this table and not much else. If you need to know more about the specific encodings of the different characters in Unicode, get a copy of

The Unicode Standard (second edition, ISBN 0-201-48346-9, from Addison-Wesley). This 950-page book includes the complete Unicode 2.0 specification, including character charts for all the different characters defined in Unicode 2.0. You can also find information online at the Unicode Consortium Web site at `http://www.unicode.org/` and `http://charts.unicode.org/`. Table 7-6 lists the different scripts encoded by Unicode which should give you some idea of Unicode's versatility. The characters of each script are generally encoded in a consecutive sub-range (block) of the 65,536 code points in Unicode. Most languages can be written with the characters in one of these blocks (for example, Russian can be written with the Cyrillic block) though some languages like Croatian or Turkish may need to mix and match characters from the first four Latin blocks.

Table 7-6
Unicode Script Blocks

Script	Range	Purpose
Basic Latin	0-127	ASCII, American English.
Latin-1 Supplement	126-255	Upper half of ISO Latin-1, in conjunction with the Basic Latin block can handle Danish, Dutch, English, Faroese, Flemish, German, Hawaiian, Icelandic, Indonesian, Irish, Italian, Norwegian, Portuguese, Spanish, Swahili, and Swedish.
Latin Extended-A	256-383	This block adds the characters from the ISO 8859 sets Latin-2, Latin-3, Latin-4, and Latin-5 not already found in the Basic Latin and Latin-1 blocks. In conjunction with those blocks, this block can encode Afrikaans, Breton, Basque, Catalan, Czech, Esperanto, Estonian, French, Frisian, Greenlandic, Hungarian, Latvian, Lithuanian, Maltese, Polish, Provençal, Rhaeto-Romanic, Romanian, Romany, Slovak, Slovenian, Sorbian, Turkish, and Welsh.
Latin Extended-B	383-591	Mostly characters needed to extend the Latin script to handle languages not traditionally written in this script; includes many African languages, Croatian digraphs to match Serbian Cyrillic letters, the Pinyin transcription of Chinese, and the Sami characters from Latin-10.
IPA Extensions	592-687	The International Phonetic Alphabet.
Spacing Modifier Letters	686-767	Small symbols that somehow change (generally phonetically) the previous letter.
Combining Diacritical Marks	766-879	Diacritical marks like ~, ', and ¨ that will somehow be combined with the previous character (most commonly, be placed on top of) rather than drawn as a separate character.

Script	Range	Purpose
Greek	880-1023	Modern Greek, based on ISO 8859-7; also provides characters for Coptic.
Cyrillic	1024-1279	Russian and most other Slavic languages (Ukrainian, Byelorussian, and so forth), and many non-Slavic languages of the former Soviet Union (Azerbaijani, Ossetian, Kabardian, Chechen, Tajik, and so forth); based on ISO 8859-5. A few languages (Kurdish, Abkhazian) require both Latin and Cyrillic characters
Armenian	1326-1423	Armenian
Hebrew	1424-1535	Hebrew (classical and modern), Yiddish, Judezmo, early Aramaic.
Arabic	1536-1791	Arabic, Persian, Pashto, Sindhi, Kurdish, and classical Turkish.
Devanagari	2304-2431	Sanskrit, Hindi, Nepali, and other languages of the Indian subcontinent including Awadhi, Bagheli, Bhatneri, Bhili, Bihari, Braj Bhasha, Chhattisgarhi, Garhwali, Gondi, Harauti, Ho, Jaipuri, Kachchhi, Kanauji, Konkani, Kului, Kumaoni, Kurku, Kurukh, Marwari, Mundari, Newari, Palpa, and Santali.
Bengali	2432-2559	A North Indian script used in India's West Bengal state and Bangladesh; used for Bengali, Assamese, Daphla, Garo, Hallam, Khasi, Manipuri, Mizo, Naga, Munda, Rian, Santali.
Gurmukhi	2560-2687	Punjabi
Gujarati	2686-2815	Gujarati
Oriya	2816-2943	Oriya, Khondi, Santali.
Tamil	2944-3071	Tamil and Badaga, used in south India, Sri Lanka, Singapore, and parts of Malaysia.
Telugu	3072-3199	Telugu, Gondi, Lambadi.
Kannada	3200-3327	Kannada, Tulu.
Malalayam	3326-3455	Malalayam
Thai	3584-3711	Thai, Kuy, Lavna, Pali.
Lao	3712-3839	Lao
Tibetan	3840-4031	Himalayan languages including Tibetan, Ladakhi, and Lahuli.

Continued

Table 7-6 *(continued)*

Script	Range	Purpose
Georgian	4256-4351	Georgian, the language of the former Soviet Republic of Georgian on the Black Sea.
Hangul Jamo	4352-4607	The alphabetic components of the Korean Hangul syllabary.
Latin Extended Additional	7680-7935	Normal Latin letters like E and Y combined with diacritical marks, rarely used except for Vietnamese vowels.
Greek Extended	7936-8191	Greek letters combined with diacritical marks; used in Polytonic and classical Greek.
General Punctuation	8192-8303	Assorted punctuation marks.
Superscripts and Subscripts	8304-8351	Common subscripts and superscripts.
Currency Symbols	8352-8399	Currency symbols not already present in other blocks.
Combining Marks for Symbols	8400-8447	Used to make a diacritical mark span two or more characters.
Letter like Symbols	8446-8527	Symbols that look like letters such as ™ and №.
Number Forms	8526-8591	Fractions and Roman numerals.
Arrows	8592-8703	Arrows
Mathematical Operators	8704-8959	Mathematical operators that don't already appear in other blocks.
Miscellaneous Technical	8960-9039	Cropping marks, braket notation from quantum mechanics, symbols needed for the APL programming language, and assorted other technical symbols.
Control Pictures	9216-9279	Pictures of the ASCII control characters; generally used in debugging and network-packet sniffing.
Optical Character Recognition	9280-9311	OCR-A and the MICR (magnetic ink character recognition) symbols on printed checks.
Enclosed alphanumerics	9312-9471	Letters and numbers in circles and parentheses.
Box Drawing	9472-9599	Characters for drawing boxes on monospaced terminals.
Block Elements	9600-9631	Monospaced terminal graphics as used in DOS and elsewhere.
Geometric Shapes	9632-9727	Squares, diamonds, triangles, and the like.

Script	Range	Purpose
Miscellaneous Symbols	9726-9983	Cards, chess, astrology, and more.
Dingbats	9984-10175	The Zapf Dingbat characters.
CJK Symbols and Punctuation	12286-12351	Symbols and punctuation used in Chinese, Japanese, and Korean.
Hiragana	12352-12447	A cursive syllabary for Japanese
Katakana	12446-12543	A non-cursive syllabary used to write words imported from the West in Japanese, especially modern words like "keyboard".
Bopomofo	12544-12591	A phonetic alphabet for Chinese used primarily for teaching.
Hangul Compatibility Jamo	12592-12687	Korean characters needed for compatibility with the KSC 5601 encoding.
Kanbun	12686-12703	Marks used in Japanese to indicate the reading order of classical Chinese.
Enclosed CJK Letters and Months	12800-13055	Hangul and Katakana characters enclosed in circles and parentheses.
CJK Compatibility	13056-13311	Characters needed only to encode KSC 5601 and CNS 11643.
CJK Unified Ideographs	19966-40959	The Han ideographs used for Chinese, Japanese, and Korean.
Hangul Syllables	44032-55203	A Korean syllabary.
Surrogates	55296-57343	Currently unused, but will eventually allow the extension of Unicode to over one million different characters.
Private Use	57344-63743	Software developers can include their custom characters here; not compatible across implementations.
CJK Compatibility Ideographs	63744-64255	A few extra Han ideographs needed only to maintain compatibility with existing standards like KSC 5601.
Alphabetic Presentation Forms	64256-64335	Ligatures and variants sometimes used in Latin, Armenian, and Hebrew.
Arabic Presentation Forms	64336-65023	Variants of assorted Arabic characters.

Continued

Table 7-6 *(continued)*		
Script	**Range**	**Purpose**
Combining Half Marks	65056-65071	Combining multiple diacritical marks into a single diacritical mark that spans multiple characters.
CJK Compatibility Forms	65072-65103	Mostly vertical variants of Han ideographs used in Taiwan.
Small Form Variants	65104-65135	Smaller version of ASCII punctuation mostly used in Taiwan.
Additional Arabic Presentation Forms	65136-65279	More variants of assorted Arabic characters.
Half-width and Full-width Forms	65280-65519	Characters that allow conversion between different Chinese and Japanese encodings of the same characters.
Specials	65520-65535	The byte order mark and the zero-width, no breaking space often used to start Unicode files.

UTF-8

Since Unicode uses two bytes for each character, files of English text are about twice as large in Unicode as they would be in ASCII or Latin-1. UTF-8 is a compressed version of Unicode that uses only a single byte for the most common characters, that is the ASCII characters 0-127, at the expense of having to use three bytes for the less common characters, particularly the Hangul syllables and Han ideographs. If you're writing mostly in English, UTF-8 can reduce your file sizes by as much as 50 percent. On the other hand if you're writing mostly in Chinese, Korean, or Japanese, UTF-8 can *increase* your file size by as much as 50 percent — so it should be used with caution. UTF-8 has mostly no effect on non-Roman, non-CJK scripts like Greek, Arabic, Cyrillic, and Hebrew.

XML processors assume text data is in the UTF-8 format unless told otherwise. This means they can read ASCII files, but other formats like MacRoman or Latin-1 cause them trouble. You'll learn how to fix this problem shortly.

The Universal Character System

Unicode has been criticized for not encompassing enough, especially in regard to East Asian languages. It only defines about 20,000 of the 80,000 Han ideographs used amongst Chinese, Japanese, Korean, and historical Vietnamese. (Modern Vietnamese uses a Roman alphabet.)

UCS (Universal Character System), also known as ISO 10646, uses four bytes per character (more precisely, 31 bits) to provide space for over two billion different characters. This easily covers every character ever used in any language in any script on the planet Earth. Among other things this enables a full set of characters to be assigned to each language so that the French "e" is not the same as the English "e" is not the same as the German "e," and so on.

Like Unicode, UCS defines a number of different variants and compressed forms. Pure Unicode is sometimes referred to as UCS-2, which is two-byte UCS. UTF-16 is a special encoding that maps some of the UCS characters into byte strings of varying length in such a fashion that Unicode (UCS-2) data is unchanged.

At this point, the advantage of UCS over Unicode is mostly theoretical. The only characters that have actually been defined in UCS are precisely those already in Unicode. However, it does provide more room for future expansion.

How to Write XML in Unicode

Unicode is the native character set of XML, and XML browsers will probably do a pretty good job of displaying it, at least to the limits of the available fonts. Nonetheless, there simply aren't many if any text editors that support the full range of Unicode. Consequently, you'll probably have to tackle this problem in one of a couple of ways:

1. Write in a localized character set like Latin-3; then convert your file to Unicode.
2. Include Unicode character references in the text that numerically identify particular characters.

The first option is preferable when you've got a large amount of text to enter in essentially one script, or one script plus ASCII. The second works best when you need to mix small portions of multiple scripts into your document.

Inserting Characters in XML Files with Character References

Every Unicode character is a number between 0 and 65,535. If you do not have a text editor that can write in Unicode, you can always use a character reference to insert the character in your XML file instead.

A Unicode character reference consists of the two characters &# followed by the character code, followed by a semicolon. For instance, the Greek letter π has Unicode value 960 so it may be inserted in an XML file as π. The Cyrillic character ҷ has Unicode value 1206 so it can be included in an XML file with the character reference Ҷ

Unicode character references may also be specified in hexadecimal (base 16). Although most people are more comfortable with decimal numbers, the Unicode

Specification gives character values as two-byte hexadecimal numbers. It's often easier to use hex values directly rather than converting them to decimal.

All you need to do is include an x after the &# to signify that you're using a hexadecimal value. For example, π has hexadecimal value 3C0 so it may be inserted in an XML file as π. The Cyrillic character ҷ has hexadecimal value 4B6 so it can be included in an XML file with the escape sequence Ҷ. Because two bytes always produce exactly four hexadecimal digits, it's customary (though not required) to include leading zeros in hexadecimal character references so they are rounded out to four digits.

Unicode character references, both hexadecimal and decimal, may be used to embed characters that would otherwise be interpreted as markup. For instance, the ampersand (&) is encoded as & or &. The less-than sign (<) is encoded as < or <.

Converting to and from Unicode

Application software that exports XML files, such as Adobe Framemaker, handles the conversion to Unicode or UTF-8 automatically. Otherwise you'll need to use a conversion tool. Sun's freely available Java Development Kit (JDK) includes a simple command-line utility called native2ascii that converts between many common and uncommon localized character sets and Unicode.

For example, the following command converts a text file named myfile.txt from the platform's default encoding to Unicode

```
C:\> native2ascii myfile.txt myfile.uni
```

You can specify other encodings with the -encoding option:

```
C:> native2ascii -encoding Big5 chinese.txt chinese.uni
```

You can also reverse the process to go from Unicode to a local encoding with the -reverse option:

```
C:> native2ascii -encoding Big5 -reverse chinese.uni chinese.txt
```

If the output file name is left off, the converted file is printed out.

The native2ascii program also processes Java-style Unicode escapes, which are characters embedded as \u09E3. These are not in the same format as XML numeric character references, though they're similar. If you convert to Unicode using native2ascii, you can still use XML character references — the viewer will still recognize them.

How to Write XML in Other Character Sets

Unless told otherwise, an XML processor assumes that text entity characters are encoded in UTF-8. Since UTF-8 includes ASCII as a subset, ASCII text is easily parsed by XML processors as well.

The only character set other than UTF-8 that an XML processor is required to understand is raw Unicode. If you cannot convert your text into either UTF-8 or raw Unicode, you can leave the text in its native character set and tell the XML processor which set that is. This should be a last resort, though, because there's no guarantee an arbitrary XML processor can process other encodings. Nonetheless Netscape Navigator and Internet Explorer both do a pretty good job of interpreting the common character sets.

To warn the XML processor that you're using a non-Unicode encoding, you include an `encoding` attribute in the XML declaration at the start of the file. For example, to specify that the entire document uses Latin-1 by default (unless overridden by another processing instruction in a nested entity) you would use this XML declaration:

```
<?xml version="1.0" encoding="ISO-8859-1" ?>
```

You can also include the encoding declaration as part of a separate processing instruction after the XML declaration but before any character data appears.

```
<?xml encoding="ISO-8859-1"?>
```

Table 7-7 lists the official names of the most common character sets used today, as they would be given in XML encoding attributes. For encodings not found in this list, consult the official list maintained by the Internet Assigned Numbers Authority (IANA) at `http://www.isi.edu/in-notes/iana/assignments/character-sets`.

Table 7-7 Names of Common Character Sets	
Character Set Name	*Languages/Countries*
US-ASCII	English
UTF-8	Compressed Unicode
UTF-16	Compressed UCS
ISO-10646-UCS-2	Raw Unicode
ISO-10646-UCS-4	Raw UCS

Continued

Table 7-7 *(continued)*

Character Set Name	Languages/Countries
ISO-8859-1	Latin-1, Western Europe
ISO-8859-2	Latin-2, Eastern Europe
ISO-8859-3	Latin-3, Southern Europe
ISO-8859-4	Latin-4, Northern Europe
ISO-8859-5	ASCII plus Cyrillic
ISO-8859-6	ASCII plus Arabic
ISO-8859-7	ASCII plus Greek
ISO-8859-8	ASCII plus Hebrew
ISO-8859-9	Latin-5, Turkish
ISO-8859-10	Latin-6, ASCII plus the Nordic languages
ISO-8859-11	ASCII plus Thai
ISO-8859-13	Latin-7, ASCII plus the Baltic Rim languages, particularly Latvian
ISO-8859-14	Latin-8, ASCII plus Gaelic and Welsh
ISO-8859-15	Latin-9, Latin-0; Western Europe
ISO-2022-JP	Japanese
Shift_JIS	Japanese, Windows
EUC-JP	Japanese, Unix
Big5	Chinese, Taiwan
GB2312	Chinese, mainland China
KOI6-R	Russian
ISO-2022-KR	Korean
EUC-KR	Korean, Unix
ISO-2022-CN	Chinese

Summary

In this chapter you learned:

✦ Web pages should identify the encoding they use.

✦ What a script is, how it relates to languages, and the four things a script requires.

✦ How scripts are used in computers with character sets, fonts, glyphs, and input methods.

✦ What character sets are commonly used on different platforms and that most are based on ASCII.

✦ How to write XML in Unicode without a Unicode editor (write the document in ASCII and include Unicode character references).

✦ When writing XML in other encodings, include an `encoding` attribute in the XML declaration.

In the next chapter, you'll begin exploring DTDs and how they enable you to define and enforce a vocabulary, syntax, and grammar for your documents.

✦　　✦　　✦

Document Type Definitions

Document Type Definitions and Validity

XML has been described as a meta-markup language, that is, a language for describing markup languages. In this chapter you begin to learn how to document and describe the new markup languages you create. Such markup languages (also known as *tag sets*) are defined via a document type definition (DTD), which is what this chapter is all about. Individual documents can be compared against DTDs in a process known as validation. If the document matches the constraints listed in the DTD, then the document is said to be valid. If it doesn't, the document is said to be invalid.

Document Type Definitions

The acronym DTD stands for *document type definition*. A document type definition provides a list of the elements, attributes, notations, and entities contained in a document, as well as their relationships to one another. DTDs specify a set of rules for the structure of a document. For example, a DTD may dictate that a BOOK element have exactly one ISBN child, exactly one TITLE child, and one or more AUTHOR children, and it may or may not contain a single SUBTITLE. The DTD accomplishes this with a list of markup declarations for particular elements, entities, attributes, and notations.

Cross-Reference This chapter focuses on element declarations. Chapters 9, 10, and 11 introduce entities, attributes, and notations, respectively.

DTDs can be included in the file that contains the document they describe, or they can be linked from an external URL.

Such external DTDs can be shared by different documents and Web sites. DTDs provide a means for applications, organizations, and interest groups to agree upon, document, and enforce adherence to markup standards.

For example, a publisher may want an author to adhere to a particular format because it makes it easier to lay out a book. An author may prefer writing words in a row without worrying about matching up each bullet point in the front of the chapter with a subhead inside the chapter. If the author writes in XML, it's easy for the publisher to check whether the author adhered to the predetermined format specified by the DTD, and even to find out exactly where and how the author deviated from the format. This is much easier than having editors read through documents with the hope that they spot all the minor deviations from the format, based on style alone.

DTDs also help ensure that different people and programs can read each other's files. For instance, if chemists agree on a single DTD for basic chemical notation, possibly via the intermediary of an appropriate professional organization such as the American Chemical Society, then they can be assured that they can all read and understand one another's papers. The DTD defines exactly what is and is not allowed to appear inside a document. The DTD establishes a standard for the elements that viewing and editing software must support. Even more importantly, it establishes extensions beyond those that the DTD declares are invalid. Thus, it helps prevent software vendors from embracing and extending open protocols in order to lock users into their proprietary software.

Furthermore, a DTD shows how the different elements of a page are arranged without actually providing their data. A DTD enables you to see the structure of your document separate from the actual data. This means you can slap a lot of fancy styles and formatting onto the underlying structure without destroying it, much as you paint a house without changing its basic architectural plan. The reader of your page may not see or even be aware of the underlying structure, but as long as it's there, human authors and JavaScripts, CGIs, servlets, databases, and other programs can use it.

There's more you can do with DTDs. You can use them to define glossary entities that insert boilerplate text such as a signature block or an address. You can ascertain that data entry clerks are adhering to the format you need. You can migrate data to and from relational and object databases. You can even use XML as an intermediate format to convert different formats with suitable DTDs. So let's get started and see what DTDs really look like.

Document Type Declarations

A *document type declaration* specifies the DTD a document uses. The document type declaration appears in a document's prolog, after the XML declaration but before the root element. It may contain the document type definition or a URL identifying the file where the document type definition is found. It may even contain both, in which case the document type definition has two parts, the internal and external subsets.

 Caution

A document type *declaration* is not the same thing as a document type *definition*. Only the document type definition is abbreviated DTD. A document type declaration must contain or refer to a document type definition, but a document type definition never contains a document type declaration. I agree that this is unnecessarily confusing. Unfortunately, XML seems stuck with this terminology. Fortunately, most of the time the difference between the two is not significant.

Recall Listing 3-2 (greeting.xml) from Chapter 3. It is shown below:

```
<?xml version="1.0" standalone="yes"?>
<GREETING>
Hello XML!
</GREETING>
```

This document contains a single element, GREETING. (Remember, `<?xml version="1.0" standalone="yes"?>` is a processing instruction, not an element.) Listing 8-1 shows this document, but now with a document type declaration. The document type declaration declares that the root element is GREETING. The document type declaration also contains a document type definition, which declares that the GREETING element contains parsed character data.

Listing 8-1: **Hello XML with DTD**

```
<?xml version="1.0" standalone="yes"?>
<!DOCTYPE GREETING [
  <!ELEMENT GREETING (#PCDATA)>
]>
<GREETING>
Hello XML!
</GREETING>
```

The only difference between Listing 3-2 and Listing 8-1 are the three new lines added to Listing 8-1:

```
<!DOCTYPE GREETING [
  <!ELEMENT GREETING (#PCDATA)>
]>
```

These lines are this Listing 8-1's document type declaration. The document type declaration comes between the XML declaration and the document itself. The XML declaration and the document type declaration together are called the *prolog* of the document. In this short example, `<?xml version="1.0" standalone="yes"?>` is the XML declaration; `<!DOCTYPE GREETING [ <!ELEMENT GREETING (#PCDATA)> ]>` is the document type declaration; `<!ELEMENT GREETING (#PCDATA)>` is the document type definition; and `<GREETING> Hello XML! </GREETING>` is the document or root element.

A document type declaration begins with `<!DOCTYPE` and ends with `]>`. It's customary to place the beginning and end on separate lines, but line breaks and extra whitespace are not significant. The same document type declaration could be written on a single line:

```
<!DOCTYPE GREETING [ <!ELEMENT GREETING (#PCDATA)> ]>
```

The name of the root element—`GREETING` in this example follows `<!DOCTYPE`. This is not just a name but a requirement. Any valid document with this document type declaration must have the root element `GREETING`. In between the `[` and the `]` is the document type definition.

The DTD consists of a series of markup declarations that declare particular elements, entities, and attributes. One of these declarations declares the root element. In Listing 8-1 the entire DTD is simply this one line:

```
<!ELEMENT GREETING (#PCDATA)>
```

In general, of course, DTDs will be much longer and more complex.

The single line `<!ELEMENT GREETING (#PCDATA)>` (case-sensitive as most things are in XML) is an *element type declaration*. In this case, the name of the declared element is `GREETING`. It is the only element. This element may contain parsed character data (or `#PCDATA`). Parsed character data is essentially any text that's not markup text. This also includes entity references, such as `&amp;`, that are replaced by text when the document is parsed.

You can load this document into an XML browser as usual. Figure 8-1 shows Listing 8-1 in Internet Explorer 5.0. The result is probably what you'd expect, a collapsible outline view of the document source. Internet Explorer indicates that a document type declaration is present by adding the line `<!DOCTYPE GREETING (View Source for full doctype...)>` in blue.

Figure 8-1: Hello XML with DTD displayed in Internet Explorer 5.0

Of course, the document can be combined with a style sheet just as it was in Listing 3-6 in Chapter 3. In fact, you can use the same style sheet. Just add the usual `<?xml-stylesheet?>` processing instruction to the prolog as shown in Listing 8-2.

Listing 8-2: **Hello XML with a DTD and style sheet**

```
<?xml version="1.0" standalone="yes"?>
<?xml-stylesheet type="text/css" href="greeting.css"?>
<!DOCTYPE GREETING [
  <!ELEMENT GREETING (#PCDATA)>
]>
<GREETING>
Hello XML!
</GREETING>
```

Figure 8-2 shows the resulting Web page. This is *exactly* the same as it was in Figure 3-3 in Chapter 3 without the DTD. Formatting generally does not consider the DTD.

Figure 8-2 Hello XML with a DTD and style sheet displayed in Internet Explorer 5.0

Validating Against a DTD

A valid document must meet the constraints specified by the DTD. Furthermore, its root element must be the one specified in the document type declaration. What the document type declaration and DTD in Listing 8-1 say is that a valid document must look like this:

```
<GREETING>
  various random text but no markup
</GREETING>
```

A valid document may not look like this:

```
<GREETING>
  <sometag>various random text</sometag>
  <someEmptyTag/>
</GREETING>
```

Nor may it look like this:

```
<GREETING>
  <GREETING>various random text</GREETING>
</GREETING>
```

This document must consist of nothing more and nothing less than parsed character data between an opening <GREETING> tag and a closing </GREETING> tag. Unlike a merely well-formed document, a valid document does not allow arbitrary tags. Any tags used must be declared in the document's DTD. Furthermore, they must be used only in the way permitted by the DTD. In Listing 8-1, the <GREETING> tag can be used only to start the root element, and it may not be nested.

Suppose we make a simple change to Listing 8-2 by replacing the <GREETING> and </GREETING> tags with <foo> and </foo>, as shown in Listing 8-3. Listing 8-3 is *invalid*. It is a well-formed XML document, but it does not meet the constraints specified by the document type declaration and the DTD it contains.

Listing 8-3: **Invalid Hello XML does not meet DTD rules**

```
<?xml version="1.0" standalone="yes"?>
<?xml-stylesheet type="text/css" href="greeting.css"?>
<!DOCTYPE GREETING [
  <!ELEMENT GREETING (#PCDATA)>
]>
<foo>
Hello XML!
</foo>
```

Note   Not all documents have to be valid, and not all parsers check documents for validity. In fact, most Web browsers including IE5 and Mozilla do not check documents for validity.

A validating parser reads a DTD and checks whether a document adheres to the rules specified by the DTD. If it does, the parser passes the data along to the XML application (such as a Web browser or a database). If the parser finds a mistake, then it reports the error. If you're writing XML by hand, you'll want to validate your documents before posting them so you can be confident that readers won't encounter errors.

There are about a dozen different validating parsers available on the Web. Most of them are free. Most are libraries intended for programmers to incorporate into their own, more finished products, and they have minimal (if any) user interfaces. Parsers in this class include IBM's alphaWorks' XML for Java, Microsoft and DataChannel's XJParser, and Silfide's SXP.

XML for Java: `http://www.alphaworks.ibm.com/tech/xml`

XJParser: `http://www.datachannel.com/xml_resources/`

SXP: `http://www.loria.fr/projets/XSilfide/EN/sxp/`

Some libraries also include stand-alone parsers that run from the command line. These are programs that read an XML file and report any errors found but do not display them. For example, XJParse is a Java program included with IBM's XML for Java 1.1.16 class library in the `samples.XJParse` package. To run this program, you first have to add the XML for Java jar files to your Java class path. You can then validate a file by opening a DOS Window or a shell prompt and passing the local name or remote URL of the file you want to validate to the XJParse program, like this:

```
C:\xml4j>java samples.XJParse.XJParse -d D:\XML\08\invalid.xml
```

Note At the time of this writing IBM's alphaWorks released version 2.0.6 of XML for Java. In this version you invoke only XJParse instead of samples.XJParse. However, version 1.1.16 provides more features for stand-alone validation.

You can use a URL instead of a file name, as shown below:

```
C:\xml4j>java samples.XJParse.XJParse -d
http://metalab.unc.edu/books/bible/examples/08/invalid.xml
```

In either case, XJParse responds with a list of the errors found, followed by a tree form of the document. For example:

```
D:\XML\07\invalid.xml: 6, 4: Document root element, "foo", must
match DOCTYPE root, "GREETING".
D:\XML\07\invalid.xml: 8, 6: Element "<foo>" is not valid in
this context.
<?xml version="1.0" standalone="yes"?>
<?xml-stylesheet type="text/css"  href="greeting.css"?>
<!DOCTYPE GREETING [
  <!ELEMENT GREETING (#PCDATA)>
]>
<foo>
Hello XML!
</foo>
```

This is not especially attractive output. However, the purpose of a validating parser such as XJParse isn't to display XML files. Instead, the parser's job is to divide the document into a tree structure and pass the nodes of the tree to the program that will display the data. This might be a Web browser such as Netscape Navigator or Internet Explorer. It might be a database. It might even be a custom program you've written yourself. You use XJParse, or other command line, validating parser to verify that you've written good XML that other programs can handle. In essence, this is a proofreading or quality assurance phase, not finished output.

Because XML for Java and most other validating parsers are written in Java, they share all the disadvantages of cross-platform Java programs. First, before you can run the parser you must have the Java Development Kit (JDK) or Java Runtime Environment installed. Secondly, you need to add the XML for Java jar files to your class path. Neither of these tasks is as simple as it should be. None of these tools were designed with an eye toward nonprogrammer end-users; they tend to be poorly designed and frustrating to use.

If you're writing documents for Web browsers, the simplest way to validate them is to load them into the browser and see what errors it reports. However, not all Web browsers validate documents. Some may merely accept well-formed documents without regard to validity. Internet Explorer 5.0 beta 2 validated documents, but the release version did not.

Web-based validators are an alternative if the documents are placed on a Web server and aren't particularly private. These parsers only require that you enter the URL of your document in a simple form. They have the distinct advantage of not requiring you to muck around with Java runtime software, class paths, and environment variables.

Richard Tobin's RXP-based, Web-hosted XML well-formedness checker and validator is shown in Figure 8-3. You'll find it at http://www.cogsci.ed.ac.uk/%7Erichard/xml-check.html. Figure 8-4 shows the errors displayed as a result of using this program to validate Listing 8-3.

Brown University's Scholarly Technology Group provides a validator at http://www.stg.brown.edu/service/xmlvalid/ that's notable for allowing you to upload files from your computer instead of placing them on a public Web server. This is shown in Figure 8-5. Figure 8-6 shows the results of using this program to validate Listing 8-3.

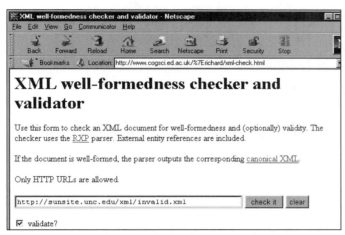

Figure 8-3: Richard Tobin's RXP-based, Web-hosted XML well-formedness checker and validator

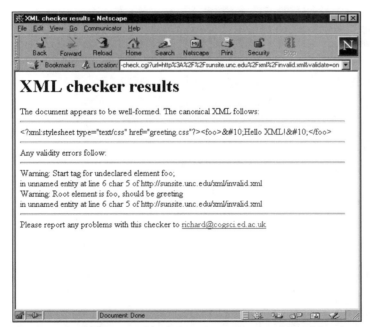

Figure 8-4: The errors with Listing 8-3, as reported by Richard Tobin's XML validator

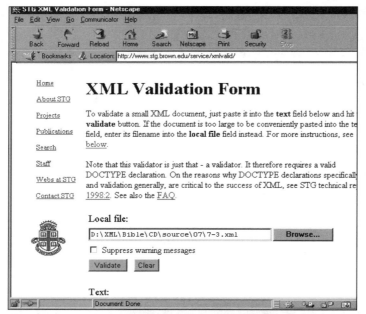

Figure 8-5: Brown University's Scholarly Technology Group's Web-hosted XML validator

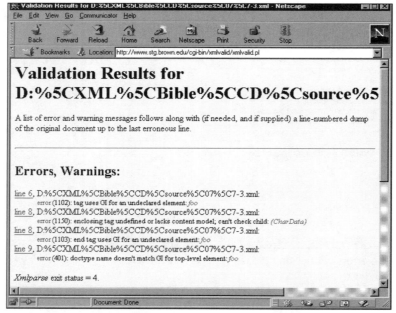

Figure 8-6: The errors with Listing 8-3, as reported by Brown University's Scholarly Technology Group's XML validator

Listing the Elements

The first step to creating a DTD appropriate for a particular document is to understand the structure of the information you'll encode using the elements defined in the DTD. Sometimes information is quite structured, as in a contact list. Other times it is relatively free-form, as in an illustrated short story or a magazine article.

Let's use a relatively structured document as an example. In particular, let's return to the baseball statistics first shown in Chapter 4. Adding a DTD to that document enables us to enforce constraints that were previously adhered to only by convention. For instance, we can require that a SEASON contain exactly two LEAGUE children, every TEAM have a TEAM_CITY and a TEAM_NAME, and the TEAM_CITY always precede the TEAM_NAME.

Recall that a complete baseball statistics document contains the following elements:

SEASON	RBI
YEAR	STEALS
LEAGUE	CAUGHT_STEALING
LEAGUE_NAME	SACRIFICE_HITS
DIVISION	SACRIFICE_FLIES
DIVISION_NAME	ERRORS
TEAM	WALKS
TEAM_CITY	STRUCK_OUT
TEAM_NAME	HIT_BY_PITCH
PLAYER	COMPLETE_GAMES
SURNAME	SHUT_OUTS
GIVEN_NAME	ERA
POSITION	INNINGS
GAMES	HOME_RUNS
GAMES_STARTED	RUNS
AT_BATS	EARNED_RUNS
RUNS	HIT_BATTER
HITS	WILD_PITCHES
DOUBLES	BALK
TRIPLES	WALKED_BATTER
HOME_RUNS	STRUCK_OUT_BATTER

WINS	COMPLETE_GAMES
LOSSES	SHUT_OUTS
SAVES	

The DTD you write needs element declarations for each of these. Each element declaration lists the name of an element and the children the element may have. For instance, a DTD can require that a LEAGUE have exactly three DIVISION children. It can also require that the SURNAME element be inside a PLAYER element, never outside. It can insist that a DIVISION have an indefinite number of TEAM elements but never less than one.

A DTD can require that a PLAYER have exactly one each of the GIVEN_NAME, SURNAME, POSITION, and GAMES elements, but make it optional whether a PLAYER has an RBI or an ERA. Furthermore, it can require that the GIVEN_NAME, SURNAME, POSITION, and GAMES elements be used in a particular order. A DTD can also require that elements occur in a particular context. For instance, the GIVEN_NAME, SURNAME, POSITION, and GAMES may be used only inside a PLAYER element.

It's often easier to begin if you have a concrete, well-formed example document in mind that uses all the elements you want in your DTD. The examples in Chapter 4 serve that purpose here. Listing 8-4 is a trimmed-down version of Listing 4-1 in Chapter 4. Although it has only two players, it demonstrates all the essential elements.

Listing 8-4: **A well-formed XML document for which a DTD will be written**

```
<?xml version="1.0" standalone="yes"?>
<SEASON>
  <YEAR>1998</YEAR>
  <LEAGUE>
    <LEAGUE_NAME>National</LEAGUE_NAME>
    <DIVISION>
        <DIVISION_NAME>East</DIVISION_NAME>
        <TEAM>
          <TEAM_CITY>Florida</TEAM_CITY>
          <TEAM_NAME>Marlins</TEAM_NAME>
          <PLAYER>
            <SURNAME>Ludwick</SURNAME>
            <GIVEN_NAME>Eric</GIVEN_NAME>
            <POSITION>Starting Pitcher</POSITION>
            <WINS>1</WINS>
            <LOSSES>4</LOSSES>
            <SAVES>0</SAVES>
            <GAMES>13</GAMES>
```

```
      <GAMES_STARTED>6</GAMES_STARTED>
      <COMPLETE_GAMES>0</COMPLETE_GAMES>
      <SHUT_OUTS>0</SHUT_OUTS>
      <ERA>7.44</ERA>
      <INNINGS>32.2</INNINGS>
      <HOME_RUNS>46</HOME_RUNS>
      <RUNS>7</RUNS>
      <EARNED_RUNS>31</EARNED_RUNS>
      <HIT_BATTER>27</HIT_BATTER>
      <WILD_PITCHES>0</WILD_PITCHES>
      <BALK>2</BALK>
      <WALKED_BATTER>0</WALKED_BATTER>
      <STRUCK_OUT_BATTER>17</STRUCK_OUT_BATTER>
   </PLAYER>
   <PLAYER>
      <SURNAME>Daubach</SURNAME>
      <GIVEN_NAME>Brian</GIVEN_NAME>
      <POSITION>First Base</POSITION>
      <GAMES>10</GAMES>
      <GAMES_STARTED>3</GAMES_STARTED>
      <AT_BATS>15</AT_BATS>
      <RUNS>0</RUNS>
      <HITS>3</HITS>
      <DOUBLES>1</DOUBLES>
      <TRIPLES>0</TRIPLES>
      <HOME_RUNS>0</HOME_RUNS>
      <RBI>3</RBI>
      <STEALS>0</STEALS>
      <CAUGHT_STEALING>0</CAUGHT_STEALING>
      <SACRIFICE_HITS>0</SACRIFICE_HITS>
      <SACRIFICE_FLIES>0</SACRIFICE_FLIES>
      <ERRORS>0</ERRORS>
      <WALKS>1</WALKS>
      <STRUCK_OUT>5</STRUCK_OUT>
      <HIT_BY_PITCH>1</HIT_BY_PITCH>
   </PLAYER>
</TEAM>
<TEAM>
  <TEAM_CITY>Montreal</TEAM_CITY>
  <TEAM_NAME>Expos</TEAM_NAME>
</TEAM>
<TEAM>
  <TEAM_CITY>New York</TEAM_CITY>
  <TEAM_NAME>Mets</TEAM_NAME>
</TEAM>
<TEAM>
  <TEAM_CITY>Philadelphia</TEAM_CITY>
<TEAM_NAME>Phillies</TEAM_NAME>
</TEAM>
```

Continued

Listing 8-4 *(continued)*

```
      </DIVISION>
      <DIVISION>
         <DIVISION_NAME>Central</DIVISION_NAME>
          <TEAM>
            <TEAM_CITY>Chicago</TEAM_CITY>
            <TEAM_NAME>Cubs</TEAM_NAME>
          </TEAM>
      </DIVISION>
      <DIVISION>
         <DIVISION_NAME>West</DIVISION_NAME>
          <TEAM>
            <TEAM_CITY>Arizona</TEAM_CITY>
            <TEAM_NAME>Diamondbacks</TEAM_NAME>
          </TEAM>
      </DIVISION>
   </LEAGUE>
   <LEAGUE>
     <LEAGUE_NAME>American</LEAGUE_NAME>
     <DIVISION>
        <DIVISION_NAME>East</DIVISION_NAME>
          <TEAM>
            <TEAM_CITY>Baltimore</TEAM_CITY>
            <TEAM_NAME>Orioles</TEAM_NAME>
          </TEAM>
     </DIVISION>
     <DIVISION>
        <DIVISION_NAME>Central</DIVISION_NAME>
          <TEAM>
            <TEAM_CITY>Chicago</TEAM_CITY>
            <TEAM_NAME>White Sox</TEAM_NAME>
          </TEAM>
     </DIVISION>
     <DIVISION>
        <DIVISION_NAME>West</DIVISION_NAME>
          <TEAM>
            <TEAM_CITY>Anaheim</TEAM_CITY>
            <TEAM_NAME>Angels</TEAM_NAME>
          </TEAM>
     </DIVISION>
   </LEAGUE>
</SEASON>
```

Table 8-1 lists the different elements in this particular example, as well as the conditions they must adhere to. Each element has a list of the other elements it must contain, the other elements it may contain, and the element in which it must be contained. In some cases, an element may contain more than one child element of the same type. A SEASON contains one YEAR and two LEAGUE elements. A DIVISION generally contains more than one TEAM. Less obviously, some batters alternate between designated hitter and the outfield from game to game. Thus, a single PLAYER element might have more than one POSITION. In the table, a requirement for a particular number of children is indicated by prefixing the element with a number (for example, 2 LEAGUE) and the possibility of multiple children is indicated by adding (s) to the end of the element's name, such as PLAYER(s).

Listing 8-4 adheres to these conditions. It could be shorter if the two PLAYER elements and some TEAM elements were omitted. It could be longer if many other PLAYER elements were included. However, all the other elements are required to be in the positions in which they appear.

Note

Elements have two basic types in XML. Simple elements contain text, also known as parsed character data, #PCDATA or PCDATA in this context. Compound elements contain other elements or, more rarely, text and other elements. There are no integer, floating point, date, or other data types in standard XML. Thus, you can't use a DTD to say that the number of walks must be a non-negative integer, or that the ERA must be a floating point number between 0.0 and 1.0, even though doing so would be useful in examples like this one. There are some early efforts to define schemas that use XML syntax to describe information that might traditionally be encoded in a DTD, as well as data type information. As of mid-1999, these are mostly theoretical with few practical implementations.

Now that you've identified the information you're storing, and the optional and required relationships between these elements, you're ready to build a DTD for the document that concisely — if a bit opaquely — summarizes those relationships.

It's often possible and convenient to cut and paste from one DTD to another. Many elements can be reused in other contexts. For instance, the description of a TEAM works equally well for football, hockey, and most other team sports.

You can include one DTD within another so that a document draws tags from both. You might, for example, use a DTD that describes the statistics of individual players in great detail, and then nest that DTD inside the broader DTD for team sports. To change from baseball to football, simply swap out your baseball player DTD for a football player DTD.

Cross-Reference

To do this, the file containing the DTD is defined as an external entity. External parameter entity references are discussed in Chapter 9, *Entities*.

Table 8-1
The Elements in the Baseball Statistics

Element	Elements It Must Contain	Elements It May Contain	Element (if any) in Which It Must Be Contained
SEASON	YEAR,	2 LEAGUE	
YEAR	Text		SEASON
LEAGUE	LEAGUE_NAME, 3 DIVISION		SEASON
LEAGUE_NAME	Text		LEAGUE
DIVISION	DIVISION_NAME , TEAM	TEAM(s)	LEAGUE
DIVISION _NAME	Text		DIVISION
TEAM	TEAM_CITY, TEAM_NAME	PLAYER(s)	DIVISION
TEAM_CITY	Text		TEAM
TEAM_NAME	Text		TEAM
PLAYER	SURNAME, GIVEN _NAME, POSITION, GAMES	GAMES_STARTED, AT _BATS, RUNS, HITS, DOUBLES, TRIPLES, HOME_RUNS, RBI, STEALS, CAUGHT_ STEALING, SACRIFICE_HITS, SACRIFICE_FLIES, ERRORS, WALKS, STRUCK_OUT, HIT_ BY_PITCH, COMPLETE _GAMES, SHUT_OUTS, ERA, INNINGS, HIT_ BATTER, WILD_ PITCHES, BALK, WALKED_BATTER, STRUCK_OUT_ BATTER	TEAM
SURNAME	Text		PLAYER
GIVEN_NAME	Text		PLAYER
POSITION	Text		PLAYER

Element	Elements It Must Contain	Elements It May Contain	Element (if any) in Which It Must Be Contained
GAMES	Text		PLAYER
GAMES_STARTED	Text		PLAYER
AT_BATS	Text		PLAYER
RUNS	Text		PLAYER
HITS	Text		PLAYER
DOUBLES	Text		PLAYER
TRIPLES	Text		PLAYER
HOME_RUNS	Text		PLAYER
RBI	Text		PLAYER
STEALS	Text		PLAYER
CAUGHT_STEALING	Text		PLAYER
SACRIFICE_HITS	Text		PLAYER
SACRIFICE_FLIES	Text		PLAYER
ERRORS	Text		PLAYER
WALKS	Text		PLAYER
STRUCK_OUT	Text		PLAYER
HIT_BY_PITCH	Text		PLAYER
COMPLETE_GAMES	Text		PLAYER
SHUT_OUTS	Text		PLAYER
ERA	Text		PLAYER
INNINGS	Text		PLAYER
HOME_RUNS_AGAINST	Text		PLAYER

Continued

Table 8-1 *(continued)*

Element	Elements It Must Contain	Elements It May Contain	Element (if any) in Which It Must Be Contained
RUNS_ AGAINST	Text		PLAYER
HIT_BATTER	Text		PLAYER
WILD_ PITCHES	Text		PLAYER
BALK	Text		PLAYER
WALKED_ BATTER	Text		PLAYER
STRUCK_OUT _BATTER	Text		PLAYER

Element Declarations

Each tag used in a valid XML document must be declared with an element declaration in the DTD. An element declaration specifies the name and possible contents of an element. The list of contents is sometimes called the content specification. The content specification uses a simple grammar to precisely specify what is and isn't allowed in a document. This sounds complicated, but all it really means is that you add a punctuation mark such as *, ?, or + to an element name to indicate that it may occur more than once, may or may not occur, or must occur at least once.

DTDs are conservative. Everything not explicitly permitted is forbidden. However, DTD syntax does enable you to compactly specify relationships that are cumbersome to specify in sentences. For instance, DTDs make it easy to say that GIVEN_NAME must come before SURNAME — which must come before POSITION, which must come before GAMES, which must come before GAMES_STARTED, which must come before AT_BATS, which must come before RUNS, which must come before HITS — and that all of these may appear only inside a PLAYER.

It's easiest to build DTDs hierarchically, working from the outside in. This enables you to build a sample document at the same time you build the DTD to verify that the DTD is itself correct and actually describes the format you want.

ANY

The first thing you have to do is identify the root element. In the baseball example, SEASON is the root element. The !DOCTYPE declaration specifies this:

```
<!DOCTYPE SEASON [

]>
```

However, this merely says that the root tag is SEASON. It does not say anything about what a SEASON element may or may not contain, which is why you must next declare the SEASON element in an element declaration. That's done with this line of code:

```
<!ELEMENT SEASON ANY>
```

All element type declarations begin with <!ELEMENT (case sensitive) and end with >. They include the name of the element being declared (SEASON in this example) followed by the content specification. The ANY keyword (again case-sensitive) says that all possible elements as well as parsed character data can be children of the SEASON element.

Using ANY is common for root elements — especially of unstructured documents — but should be avoided in most other cases. Generally it's better to be as precise as possible about the content of each tag. DTDs are usually refined throughout their development, and tend to become less strict over time as they reflect uses and contexts unimagined in the first cut. Therefore, it's best to start out strict and loosen things up later.

#PCDATA

Although any element may appear inside the document, elements that do appear must also be declared. The first one needed is YEAR. This is the element declaration for the YEAR element:

```
<!ELEMENT YEAR (#PCDATA)>
```

This declaration says that a YEAR may contain only parsed character data, that is, text that's not markup. It may not contain children of its own. Therefore, this YEAR element is valid:

```
<YEAR>1998</YEAR>
```

These YEAR elements are also valid:

```
<YEAR>98</YEAR>
<YEAR>1998 C.E.</YEAR>
<YEAR>
 The year of our lord one thousand,
 nine hundred, &amp; ninety-eight
</YEAR>
```

Even this YEAR element is valid because XML does not attempt to validate the contents of PCDATA, only that it is text that doesn't contain markup.

```
<YEAR>Delicious, delicious, oh how boring</YEAR>
```

However, this YEAR element is invalid because it contains child elements:

```
<YEAR>
  <MONTH>January</MONTH>
  <MONTH>February</MONTH>
  <MONTH>March</MONTH>
  <MONTH>April</MONTH>
  <MONTH>May</MONTH>
  <MONTH>June</MONTH>
  <MONTH>July</MONTH>
  <MONTH>August</MONTH>
  <MONTH>September</MONTH>
  <MONTH>October</MONTH>
  <MONTH>November</MONTH>
  <MONTH>December</MONTH>
</YEAR>
```

The SEASON and YEAR element declarations are included in the document type declaration, like this:

```
<!DOCTYPE SEASON [
  <!ELEMENT SEASON ANY>
  <!ELEMENT YEAR (#PCDATA)>
]>
```

As usual, spacing and indentation are not significant. The order in which the element declarations appear isn't relevant either. This next document type declaration means exactly the same thing:

```
<!DOCTYPE SEASON [
  <!ELEMENT YEAR (#PCDATA)>
  <!ELEMENT SEASON ANY>
]>
```

Both of these say that a SEASON element may contain parsed character data and any number of any other declared elements in any order. The only other such declared element is YEAR, which may contain only parsed character data. For instance, consider the document in Listing 8-5.

Listing 8-5: **A valid document**

```
<?xml version="1.0" standalone="yes"?>
<!DOCTYPE SEASON [
  <!ELEMENT YEAR (#PCDATA)>
  <!ELEMENT SEASON ANY>
]>
<SEASON>
  <YEAR>1998</YEAR>
</SEASON>
```

Because the SEASON element may also contain parsed character data, you can add additional text outside of the YEAR. Listing 8-6 demonstrates this.

Listing 8-6: **A valid document that contains a** YEAR **and normal text**

```
<?xml version="1.0" standalone="yes"?>
<!DOCTYPE SEASON [
  <!ELEMENT YEAR (#PCDATA)>
  <!ELEMENT SEASON ANY>
]>
<SEASON>
  <YEAR>1998</YEAR>
  Major League Baseball
</SEASON>
```

Eventually we'll disallow documents such as this. However, for now it's legal because SEASON is declared to accept ANY content. Most of the time it's easier to start with ANY for an element until you define all of it's children. Then you can replace it with the actual children you want to use.

You can attach a simple style sheet, such as the baseballstats.css style sheet developed in Chapter 4, to Listing 8-6 — as shown in Listing 8-7 — and load it into a Web browser, as shown in Figure 8-7. The baseballstats.css style sheet contains style rules for elements that aren't present in the DTD or the document part of Listing 8-7, but this is not a problem. Web browsers simply ignore any style rules for elements that aren't present in the document.

Listing 8-7: A valid document that contains a style sheet, a YEAR**, and normal text**

```
<?xml version="1.0" standalone="yes"?>
<?xml-stylesheet type="text/css" href="baseballstats.css"?>
<!DOCTYPE SEASON [
  <!ELEMENT YEAR (#PCDATA)>
  <!ELEMENT SEASON ANY>
]>
<SEASON>
  <YEAR>1998</YEAR>
  Major League Baseball
</SEASON>
```

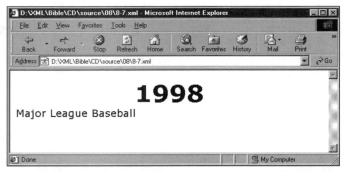

Figure 8-7: A valid document that contains a style sheet, a YEAR element, and normal text displayed in Internet Explorer 5.0

Child Lists

Because the SEASON element was declared to accept any element as a child, elements could be tossed in willy-nilly. This is useful when you have text that's more or less unstructured, such as a magazine article where paragraphs, sidebars, bulleted lists, numbered lists, graphs, photographs, and subheads may appear pretty much anywhere in the document. However, sometimes you may want to exercise more discipline and control over the placement of your data. For example, you could require that every LEAGUE have one LEAGUE_NAME, that every PLAYER have a GIVEN_NAME and a SURNAME, and that the GIVEN_NAME come before the SURNAME.

To declare that a LEAGUE must have a name, simply declare a LEAGUE_NAME element, then include LEAGUE_NAME in parentheses at the end of the LEAGUE declaration, like this:

```
<!ELEMENT LEAGUE (LEAGUE_NAME)>
<!ELEMENT LEAGUE_NAME (#PCDATA)>
```

Each element should be declared in its own <!ELEMENT> declaration exactly once, even if it appears as a child in other <!ELEMENT> declarations. Here I've placed the declaration LEAGUE_NAME after the declaration of LEAGUE that refers to it, but that doesn't matter. XML allows these sorts of forward references. The order in which the element tags appear is irrelevant as long as their declarations are all contained inside the DTD.

You can add these two declarations to the document, and then include LEAGUE and LEAGUE_NAME elements in the SEASON. Listing 8-8 demonstrates this. Figure 8-8 shows the rendered document.

Listing 8-8: **A SEASON with two LEAGUE children**

```
<?xml version="1.0" standalone="yes"?>
<?xml-stylesheet type="text/css" href="baseballstats.css"?>
<!DOCTYPE SEASON [
  <!ELEMENT YEAR (#PCDATA)>
  <!ELEMENT LEAGUE (LEAGUE_NAME)>
  <!ELEMENT LEAGUE_NAME (#PCDATA)>
  <!ELEMENT SEASON ANY>
]>
<SEASON>
  <YEAR>1998</YEAR>
  <LEAGUE>
    <LEAGUE_NAME>American League</LEAGUE_NAME>
  </LEAGUE>
  <LEAGUE>
    <LEAGUE_NAME>National League</LEAGUE_NAME>
  </LEAGUE>
</SEASON>
```

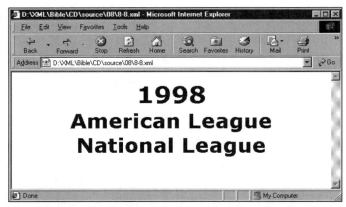

Figure 8-8: A valid document that contains a style sheet, a YEAR element, and two LEAGUE children

Sequences

Let's restrict the SEASON element as well. A SEASON contains exactly one YEAR, followed by exactly two LEAGUE elements. Instead of saying that a SEASON can contain ANY elements, specify these three children by including them in SEASON's element declaration, enclosed in parentheses and separated by commas, as follows:

```
<!ELEMENT SEASON (YEAR, LEAGUE, LEAGUE)>
```

A list of child elements separated by commas is called a sequence. With this declaration, every valid SEASON element must contain exactly one YEAR element, followed by exactly two LEAGUE elements, and nothing else. The complete document type declaration now looks like this:

```
<!DOCTYPE SEASON [
  <!ELEMENT YEAR (#PCDATA)>
  <!ELEMENT LEAGUE (LEAGUE_NAME)>
  <!ELEMENT LEAGUE_NAME (#PCDATA)>
  <!ELEMENT SEASON (YEAR, LEAGUE, LEAGUE)>
]>
```

The document part of Listing 8-8 does adhere to this DTD because its SEASON element contains one YEAR child followed by two LEAGUE children, and nothing else. However, if the document included only one LEAGUE, then the document, though well-formed, would be invalid. Similarly, if the LEAGUE came before the YEAR element instead of after it, or if the LEAGUE element had YEAR children, or if the document in any other way did not adhere to the DTD, then the document would be invalid and validating parsers would reject it.

It's straightforward to expand these techniques to cover divisions. As well as a LEAGUE_NAME, each LEAGUE has three DIVISION children. For example:

```
<!ELEMENT LEAGUE (LEAGUE_NAME, DIVISION, DIVISION, DIVISION)>
```

One or More Children

Each DIVISION has a DIVISION_NAME and between four and six TEAM children. Specifying the DIVISION_NAME is easy. This is demonstrated below:

```
<!ELEMENT DIVISION (DIVISION_NAME)>
<!ELEMENT DIVISION_NAME (#PCDATA)>
```

However, the TEAM children are trickier. It's easy to say you want four TEAM children in a DIVISION, as shown below:

```
<!ELEMENT DIVISION (DIVISION_NAME, TEAM, TEAM, TEAM, TEAM)>
```

Five and six are not harder. But how do you say you want between four and six inclusive? In fact, XML doesn't provide an easy way to do this. But you can say you want one or more of a given element by placing a plus sign (+) after the element name in the child list. For example:

```
<!ELEMENT DIVISION (DIVISION_NAME, TEAM+)>
```

This says that a DIVISION element must contain a DIVISION_NAME element followed by one or more TEAM elements.

Tip   There is a hard way to say that a DIVISION contains between four and six TEAM elements, but not three and not seven. However, it's so ridiculously complex that nobody would actually use it in practice. Once you finish reading this chapter, see if you can figure out how to do it.

Zero or More Children

Each TEAM should contain one TEAM_CITY, one TEAM_NAME, and an indefinite number of PLAYER elements. In reality, you need at least nine players for a baseball team. However, in the examples in this book, many teams are listed without players for reasons of space. Thus, we want to specify that a TEAM can contain zero or more PLAYER children. Do this by appending an asterisk (*) to the element name in the child list. For example:

```
<!ELEMENT TEAM (TEAM_CITY, TEAM_NAME, PLAYER*)>
<!ELEMENT TEAM_CITY (#PCDATA)>
<!ELEMENT TEAM_NAME (#PCDATA)>
```

Zero or One Child

The final elements in the document to be brought into play are the children of the PLAYER. All of these are simple elements that contain only text. Here are their declarations:

```
<!ELEMENT SURNAME (#PCDATA)>
<!ELEMENT GIVEN_NAME (#PCDATA)>
<!ELEMENT POSITION (#PCDATA)>
<!ELEMENT GAMES (#PCDATA)>
<!ELEMENT GAMES_STARTED (#PCDATA)>
<!ELEMENT AT_BATS (#PCDATA)>
<!ELEMENT RUNS (#PCDATA)>
<!ELEMENT HITS (#PCDATA)>
<!ELEMENT DOUBLES (#PCDATA)>
<!ELEMENT TRIPLES (#PCDATA)>
<!ELEMENT HOME_RUNS (#PCDATA)>
<!ELEMENT RBI (#PCDATA)>
<!ELEMENT STEALS (#PCDATA)>
<!ELEMENT CAUGHT_STEALING (#PCDATA)>
<!ELEMENT SACRIFICE_HITS (#PCDATA)>
<!ELEMENT SACRIFICE_FLIES (#PCDATA)>
<!ELEMENT ERRORS (#PCDATA)>
<!ELEMENT WALKS (#PCDATA)>
<!ELEMENT STRUCK_OUT (#PCDATA)>
<!ELEMENT HIT_BY_PITCH (#PCDATA)>
<!ELEMENT COMPLETE_GAMES (#PCDATA)>
<!ELEMENT SHUT_OUTS (#PCDATA)>
<!ELEMENT ERA (#PCDATA)>
<!ELEMENT INNINGS (#PCDATA)>
<!ELEMENT EARNED_RUNS (#PCDATA)>
<!ELEMENT HIT_BATTER (#PCDATA)>
<!ELEMENT WILD_PITCHES (#PCDATA)>
<!ELEMENT BALK (#PCDATA)>
<!ELEMENT WALKED_BATTER (#PCDATA)>
<!ELEMENT WINS (#PCDATA)>
<!ELEMENT LOSSES (#PCDATA)>
<!ELEMENT SAVES (#PCDATA)>
<!ELEMENT COMPLETE_GAMES (#PCDATA)>
<!ELEMENT STRUCK_OUT_BATTER (#PCDATA)>
```

Now we can write the declaration for the PLAYER element. All players have one SURNAME, one GIVEN_NAME, one POSITION, and one GAMES. We could declare that each PLAYER also has one AT_BATS, RUNS, HITS, and so forth. However, I'm not sure it's accurate to list zero runs for a pitcher who hasn't batted. For one thing, this likely will lead to division by zero errors when you start calculating batting averages and so on. If a particular element doesn't apply to a given player, or if it's not available, then the more sensible thing to do is to omit the particular statistic from the player's information. We don't allow more than one of each element for a given player. Thus, we want zero or one element of the given type. Indicate this in a child element list by appending a question mark (?) to the element, as shown below:

```
<!ELEMENT PLAYER (GIVEN_NAME, SURNAME, POSITION, GAMES,
   GAMES_STARTED, AT_BATS?, RUNS?, HITS?, DOUBLES?,
   TRIPLES?, HOME_RUNS?, RBI?, STEALS?, CAUGHT_STEALING?,
   SACRIFICE_HITS?, SACRIFICE_FLIES?, ERRORS?, WALKS?,
   STRUCK_OUT?, HIT_BY_PITCH?, WINS?, LOSSES?, SAVES?,
   COMPLETE_GAMES?, SHUT_OUTS?, ERA?, INNINGS?, EARNED_RUNS?,
   HIT_BATTER?,WILD_PITCHES?, BALK?,WALKED_BATTER?,
   STRUCK_OUT_BATTER?)
>
```

This says that every PLAYER has a SURNAME, GIVEN_NAME, POSITION, GAMES, and GAMES_STARTED. Furthermore, each player may or may not have a single AT_BATS, RUNS, HITS, DOUBLES, TRIPLES, HOME_RUNS, RBI, STEALS, CAUGHT_STEALING, SACRIFICE_HITS, SACRIFICE_FLIES, ERRORS, WALKS, STRUCK_OUT, and HIT_BY_PITCH.

The Complete Document and DTD

We now have a complete DTD for baseball statistics. This DTD, along with the document part of Listing 8-4, is shown in Listing 8-9.

Listing 8-9 only covers a single team and nine players. On the CD-ROM you'll find a document containing statistics for all 1998 Major League teams and players in the examples/baseball/1998validstats.xml directory.

Listing 8-9: A valid XML document on baseball statistics with a DTD

```
<?xml version="1.0" standalone="yes"?>
<!DOCTYPE SEASON [
  <!ELEMENT YEAR (#PCDATA)>
  <!ELEMENT LEAGUE (LEAGUE_NAME, DIVISION, DIVISION, DIVISION)>
  <!ELEMENT LEAGUE_NAME (#PCDATA)>
  <!ELEMENT DIVISION_NAME (#PCDATA)>
  <!ELEMENT DIVISION (DIVISION_NAME, TEAM+)>
  <!ELEMENT SEASON (YEAR, LEAGUE, LEAGUE)>
  <!ELEMENT TEAM (TEAM_CITY, TEAM_NAME, PLAYER*)>
  <!ELEMENT TEAM_CITY (#PCDATA)>
  <!ELEMENT TEAM_NAME (#PCDATA)>
  <!ELEMENT PLAYER (GIVEN_NAME, SURNAME, POSITION, GAMES,
     GAMES_STARTED, WINS?, LOSSES?, SAVES?,
```

Continued

Listing 8-9 *(continued)*

```
       AT_BATS?, RUNS?, HITS?, DOUBLES?, TRIPLES?, HOME_RUNS?,
       RBI?, STEALS?, CAUGHT_STEALING?, SACRIFICE_HITS?,
       SACRIFICE_FLIES?, ERRORS?, WALKS?, STRUCK_OUT?,
       HIT_BY_PITCH?, COMPLETE_GAMES?, SHUT_OUTS?, ERA?, INNINGS?,
       EARNED_RUNS?, HIT_BATTER?, WILD_PITCHES?, BALK?,
       WALKED_BATTER?, STRUCK_OUT_BATTER?)
>
  <!ELEMENT SURNAME (#PCDATA)>
  <!ELEMENT GIVEN_NAME (#PCDATA)>
  <!ELEMENT POSITION (#PCDATA)>
  <!ELEMENT GAMES (#PCDATA)>
  <!ELEMENT GAMES_STARTED (#PCDATA)>
  <!ELEMENT COMPLETE_GAMES (#PCDATA)>
  <!ELEMENT WINS (#PCDATA)>
  <!ELEMENT LOSSES (#PCDATA)>
  <!ELEMENT SAVES (#PCDATA)>
  <!ELEMENT AT_BATS (#PCDATA)>
  <!ELEMENT RUNS (#PCDATA)>
  <!ELEMENT HITS (#PCDATA)>
  <!ELEMENT DOUBLES (#PCDATA)>
  <!ELEMENT TRIPLES (#PCDATA)>
  <!ELEMENT HOME_RUNS (#PCDATA)>
  <!ELEMENT RBI (#PCDATA)>
  <!ELEMENT STEALS (#PCDATA)>
  <!ELEMENT CAUGHT_STEALING (#PCDATA)>
  <!ELEMENT SACRIFICE_HITS (#PCDATA)>
  <!ELEMENT SACRIFICE_FLIES (#PCDATA)>
  <!ELEMENT ERRORS (#PCDATA)>
  <!ELEMENT WALKS (#PCDATA)>
  <!ELEMENT STRUCK_OUT (#PCDATA)>
  <!ELEMENT HIT_BY_PITCH (#PCDATA)>
  <!ELEMENT SHUT_OUTS (#PCDATA)>
  <!ELEMENT ERA (#PCDATA)>
  <!ELEMENT INNINGS (#PCDATA)>
  <!ELEMENT HOME_RUNS_AGAINST (#PCDATA)>
  <!ELEMENT RUNS_AGAINST (#PCDATA)>
  <!ELEMENT EARNED_RUNS (#PCDATA)>
  <!ELEMENT HIT_BATTER (#PCDATA)>
  <!ELEMENT WILD_PITCHES (#PCDATA)>
  <!ELEMENT BALK (#PCDATA)>
  <!ELEMENT WALKED_BATTER (#PCDATA)>
  <!ELEMENT STRUCK_OUT_BATTER (#PCDATA)>

]>
<SEASON>
  <YEAR>1998</YEAR>
  <LEAGUE>
    <LEAGUE_NAME>National</LEAGUE_NAME>
```

```
<DIVISION>
  <DIVISION_NAME>East</DIVISION_NAME>
    <TEAM>
      <TEAM_CITY>Florida</TEAM_CITY>
      <TEAM_NAME>Marlins</TEAM_NAME>
      <PLAYER>
        <GIVEN_NAME>Eric</GIVEN_NAME>
        <SURNAME>Ludwick</SURNAME>
        <POSITION>Starting Pitcher</POSITION>
        <GAMES>13</GAMES>
        <GAMES_STARTED>6</GAMES_STARTED>
        <WINS>1</WINS>
        <LOSSES>4</LOSSES>
        <SAVES>0</SAVES>
        <COMPLETE_GAMES>0</COMPLETE_GAMES>
        <SHUT_OUTS>0</SHUT_OUTS>
        <ERA>7.44</ERA>
        <INNINGS>32.2</INNINGS>
        <EARNED_RUNS>31</EARNED_RUNS>
        <HIT_BATTER>27</HIT_BATTER>
        <WILD_PITCHES>0</WILD_PITCHES>
        <BALK>2</BALK>
        <WALKED_BATTER>0</WALKED_BATTER>
        <STRUCK_OUT_BATTER>17</STRUCK_OUT_BATTER>
      </PLAYER>
      <PLAYER>
        <GIVEN_NAME>Brian</GIVEN_NAME>
        <SURNAME>Daubach</SURNAME>
        <POSITION>First Base</POSITION>
        <GAMES>10</GAMES>
        <GAMES_STARTED>3</GAMES_STARTED>
        <AT_BATS>15</AT_BATS>
        <RUNS>0</RUNS>
        <HITS>3</HITS>
        <DOUBLES>1</DOUBLES>
        <TRIPLES>0</TRIPLES>
        <HOME_RUNS>0</HOME_RUNS>
        <RBI>3</RBI>
        <STEALS>0</STEALS>
        <CAUGHT_STEALING>0</CAUGHT_STEALING>
        <SACRIFICE_HITS>0</SACRIFICE_HITS>
        <SACRIFICE_FLIES>0</SACRIFICE_FLIES>
        <ERRORS>0</ERRORS>
        <WALKS>1</WALKS>
        <STRUCK_OUT>5</STRUCK_OUT>
        <HIT_BY_PITCH>1</HIT_BY_PITCH>
      </PLAYER>
    </TEAM>
    <TEAM>
      <TEAM_CITY>Montreal</TEAM_CITY>
      <TEAM_NAME>Expos</TEAM_NAME>
```

continued

Listing 8-9 *(continued)*

```xml
          </TEAM>
          <TEAM>
            <TEAM_CITY>New York</TEAM_CITY>
            <TEAM_NAME>Mets</TEAM_NAME>
          </TEAM>
          <TEAM>
            <TEAM_CITY>Philadelphia</TEAM_CITY>
            <TEAM_NAME>Phillies</TEAM_NAME>
          </TEAM>
      </DIVISION>
      <DIVISION>
          <DIVISION_NAME>Central</DIVISION_NAME>
          <TEAM>
            <TEAM_CITY>Chicago</TEAM_CITY>
            <TEAM_NAME>Cubs</TEAM_NAME>
          </TEAM>
      </DIVISION>
      <DIVISION>
          <DIVISION_NAME>West</DIVISION_NAME>
          <TEAM>
            <TEAM_CITY>Arizona</TEAM_CITY>
            <TEAM_NAME>Diamondbacks</TEAM_NAME>
          </TEAM>
      </DIVISION>
    </LEAGUE>
    <LEAGUE>
      <LEAGUE_NAME>American</LEAGUE_NAME>
      <DIVISION>
          <DIVISION_NAME>East</DIVISION_NAME>
          <TEAM>
            <TEAM_CITY>Baltimore</TEAM_CITY>
            <TEAM_NAME>Orioles</TEAM_NAME>
          </TEAM>
      </DIVISION>
      <DIVISION>
          <DIVISION_NAME>Central</DIVISION_NAME>
          <TEAM>
            <TEAM_CITY>Chicago</TEAM_CITY>
            <TEAM_NAME>White Sox</TEAM_NAME>
          </TEAM>
      </DIVISION>
      <DIVISION>
          <DIVISION_NAME>West</DIVISION_NAME>
          <TEAM>
            <TEAM_CITY>Anaheim</TEAM_CITY>
            <TEAM_NAME>Angels</TEAM_NAME>
          </TEAM>
      </DIVISION>
    </LEAGUE>
</SEASON>
```

Listing 8-9 is not the only possible document that matches this DTD, however. Listing 8-10 is also a valid document, because it contains all required elements in their required order and does not contain any elements that aren't declared. This is probably the smallest reasonable document that you can create that fits the DTD. The limiting factors are the requirements that each SEASON contain two LEAGUE children, that each LEAGUE contain three DIVISION children, and that each DIVISION contain at least one TEAM.

Listing 8-10: Another XML document that's valid according to the baseball DTD

```
<?xml version="1.0" standalone="yes"?>
<!DOCTYPE SEASON [
  <!ELEMENT YEAR (#PCDATA)>
  <!ELEMENT LEAGUE (LEAGUE_NAME, DIVISION, DIVISION, DIVISION)>
  <!ELEMENT LEAGUE_NAME (#PCDATA)>
  <!ELEMENT DIVISION_NAME (#PCDATA)>
  <!ELEMENT DIVISION (DIVISION_NAME, TEAM+)>
  <!ELEMENT SEASON (YEAR, LEAGUE, LEAGUE)>
  <!ELEMENT TEAM (TEAM_CITY, TEAM_NAME, PLAYER*)>
  <!ELEMENT TEAM_CITY (#PCDATA)>
  <!ELEMENT TEAM_NAME (#PCDATA)>
  <!ELEMENT PLAYER (GIVEN_NAME, SURNAME, POSITION, GAMES,
    GAMES_STARTED, COMPLETE_GAMES?, WINS?, LOSSES?, SAVES?,
    AT_BATS?, RUNS?, HITS?, DOUBLES?, TRIPLES?, HOME_RUNS?,
    RBI?, STEALS?, CAUGHT_STEALING?, SACRIFICE_HITS?,
    SACRIFICE_FLIES?, ERRORS?, WALKS?, STRUCK_OUT?,
    HIT_BY_PITCH?, COMPLETE_GAMES?, SHUT_OUTS?, ERA?, INNINGS?,
    EARNED_RUNS?, HIT_BATTER?, WILD_PITCHES?, BALK?,
    WALKED_BATTER?, STRUCK_OUT_BATTER?)
  >
  <!ELEMENT SURNAME (#PCDATA)>
  <!ELEMENT GIVEN_NAME (#PCDATA)>
  <!ELEMENT POSITION (#PCDATA)>
  <!ELEMENT GAMES (#PCDATA)>
  <!ELEMENT GAMES_STARTED (#PCDATA)>
  <!ELEMENT COMPLETE_GAMES (#PCDATA)>
  <!ELEMENT WINS (#PCDATA)>
  <!ELEMENT LOSSES (#PCDATA)>
  <!ELEMENT SAVES (#PCDATA)>
  <!ELEMENT AT_BATS (#PCDATA)>
  <!ELEMENT RUNS (#PCDATA)>
  <!ELEMENT HITS (#PCDATA)>
  <!ELEMENT DOUBLES (#PCDATA)>
  <!ELEMENT TRIPLES (#PCDATA)>
  <!ELEMENT HOME_RUNS (#PCDATA)>
```

Continued

Listing 8-10 *(continued)*

```
<!ELEMENT RBI (#PCDATA)>
<!ELEMENT STEALS (#PCDATA)>
<!ELEMENT CAUGHT_STEALING (#PCDATA)>
<!ELEMENT SACRIFICE_HITS (#PCDATA)>
<!ELEMENT SACRIFICE_FLIES (#PCDATA)>
<!ELEMENT ERRORS (#PCDATA)>
<!ELEMENT WALKS (#PCDATA)>
<!ELEMENT STRUCK_OUT (#PCDATA)>
<!ELEMENT HIT_BY_PITCH (#PCDATA)>
<!ELEMENT SHUT_OUTS (#PCDATA)>
<!ELEMENT ERA (#PCDATA)>
<!ELEMENT INNINGS (#PCDATA)>
<!ELEMENT HOME_RUNS_AGAINST (#PCDATA)>
<!ELEMENT RUNS_AGAINST (#PCDATA)>
<!ELEMENT EARNED_RUNS (#PCDATA)>
<!ELEMENT HIT_BATTER (#PCDATA)>
<!ELEMENT WILD_PITCHES (#PCDATA)>
<!ELEMENT BALK (#PCDATA)>
<!ELEMENT WALKED_BATTER (#PCDATA)>
<!ELEMENT STRUCK_OUT_BATTER (#PCDATA)>

]>
<SEASON>
  <YEAR>1998</YEAR>
  <LEAGUE>
    <LEAGUE_NAME>National</LEAGUE_NAME>
    <DIVISION>
      <DIVISION_NAME>East</DIVISION_NAME>
        <TEAM>
          <TEAM_CITY>Atlanta</TEAM_CITY>
          <TEAM_NAME>Braves</TEAM_NAME>
        </TEAM>
        <TEAM>
          <TEAM_CITY>Florida</TEAM_CITY>
          <TEAM_NAME>Marlins</TEAM_NAME>
        </TEAM>
        <TEAM>
          <TEAM_CITY>Montreal</TEAM_CITY>
          <TEAM_NAME>Expos</TEAM_NAME>
        </TEAM>
        <TEAM>
          <TEAM_CITY>New York</TEAM_CITY>
          <TEAM_NAME>Mets</TEAM_NAME>
        </TEAM>
        <TEAM>
          <TEAM_CITY>Philadelphia</TEAM_CITY>
          <TEAM_NAME>Phillies</TEAM_NAME>
        </TEAM>
```

```
    </DIVISION>
    <DIVISION>
      <DIVISION_NAME>Central</DIVISION_NAME>
       <TEAM>
         <TEAM_CITY>Chicago</TEAM_CITY>
         <TEAM_NAME>Cubs</TEAM_NAME>
       </TEAM>
    </DIVISION>
    <DIVISION>
      <DIVISION_NAME>West</DIVISION_NAME>
       <TEAM>
         <TEAM_CITY>Arizona</TEAM_CITY>
         <TEAM_NAME>Diamondbacks</TEAM_NAME>
       </TEAM>
    </DIVISION>
  </LEAGUE>
  <LEAGUE>
    <LEAGUE_NAME>American</LEAGUE_NAME>
    <DIVISION>
      <DIVISION_NAME>East</DIVISION_NAME>
       <TEAM>
         <TEAM_CITY>Baltimore</TEAM_CITY>
         <TEAM_NAME>Orioles</TEAM_NAME>
       </TEAM>
    </DIVISION>
    <DIVISION>
      <DIVISION_NAME>Central</DIVISION_NAME>
       <TEAM>
         <TEAM_CITY>Chicago</TEAM_CITY>
         <TEAM_NAME>White Sox</TEAM_NAME>
       </TEAM>
    </DIVISION>
    <DIVISION>
      <DIVISION_NAME>West</DIVISION_NAME>
       <TEAM>
         <TEAM_CITY>Anaheim</TEAM_CITY>
         <TEAM_NAME>Angels</TEAM_NAME>
       </TEAM>
    </DIVISION>
  </LEAGUE>
</SEASON>
```

Choices

In general, a single parent element has many children. To indicate that the children must occur in sequence, they are separated by commas. However, each such child element may be suffixed with a question mark, a plus sign, or an asterisk to adjust the number of times it appears in that place in the sequence.

So far, the assumption has been made that child elements appear or do not appear in a specific order. You may, however, wish to make your DTD more flexible, such as by allowing document authors to choose between different elements in a given place. For example, in a DTD describing a purchase by a customer, each PAYMENT element might have either a CREDIT_CARD child or a CASH child providing information about the method of payment. However, an individual PAYMENT would not have both.

You can indicate that the document author needs to input either one or another element by separating child elements with a vertical bar (|) rather than a comma (,) in the parent's element declaration. For example, the following says that the PAYMENT element must have a single child of type CASH or CREDIT_CARD.

```
<!ELEMENT PAYMENT (CASH | CREDIT_CARD)>
```

This sort of content specification is called a choice. You can separate any number of children with vertical bars when you want exactly one of them to be used. For example, the following says that the PAYMENT element must have a single child of type CASH, CREDIT_CARD, or CHECK.

```
<!ELEMENT PAYMENT (CASH | CREDIT_CARD | CHECK)>
```

The vertical bar is even more useful when you group elements with parentheses. You can group combinations of elements in parentheses, then suffix the parentheses with asterisks, question marks, and plus signs to indicate that particular combinations of elements must occur zero or more, zero or one, or one or more times.

Children with Parentheses

The final thing you need to know about arranging child elements in parent element declarations is how to group elements with parentheses. Each set of parentheses combines several elements as a single element. This parenthesized element can then be nested inside other parentheses in place of a single element. Furthermore, it may then have a plus sign, a comma, or a question mark affixed to it. You can group these parenthesized combinations into still larger parenthesized groups to produce quite complex structures. This is a very powerful technique.

For example, consider a list composed of two elements that must alternate with each other. This is essentially how HTML's definition list works. Each <dt> tag should match one <dd> tag. If you replicate this structure in XML, the declaration of the dl element looks like this:

```
<!ELEMENT dl (dt, dd)*>
```

The parentheses indicate that it's the matched <dt><dd> pair being repeated, not <dd> alone.

Often elements appear in more or less random orders. News magazine articles generally have a title mostly followed by paragraphs of text, but with graphs, photos, sidebars, subheads, and pull quotes interspersed throughout, perhaps with a byline at the end. You can indicate this sort of arrangement by listing all the possible child elements in the parent's element declaration separated by vertical bars and grouped inside parentheses. You can then place an asterisk outside the closing parenthesis to indicate that zero or more occurrences of any of the elements in the parentheses are allowed. For example;

```
<!ELEMENT ARTICLE (TITLE, (P | PHOTO | GRAPH | SIDEBAR
 | PULLQUOTE | SUBHEAD)*, BYLINE?)>
```

As another example, suppose you want to say that a DOCUMENT element, rather than having any children at all, must have one TITLE followed by any number of paragraphs of text and images that may be freely intermingled, followed by an optional SIGNATURE block. Write its element declaration this way:

```
<!ELEMENT DOCUMENT (TITLE, (PARAGRAPH | IMAGE)*, SIGNATURE?)>
```

This is not the only way to describe this structure. In fact, it may not even be the best way. An alternative is to declare a BODY element that contains PARAGRAPH and IMAGE elements and nest that between the TITLE and the SIGNATURE. For example:

```
<!ELEMENT DOCUMENT (TITLE, BODY, SIGNATURE?)>
<!ELEMENT BODY ((PARAGRAPH | IMAGE)*)>
```

The difference between these two approaches is that the second requires an additional BODY element in the document. This element provides an additional level of organization that may (or may not) be useful to the application that's reading the document. The question to ask is whether the reader of this document (who may be another computer program) may want to consider the BODY as a single item in its own right, separate from the TITLE and the SIGNATURE and distinguished from the sum of its elements.

For another example, consider international addresses. Addresses outside the United States don't always follow U.S. conventions. In particular, postal codes sometimes precede the state or follow the country, as in these two examples:

Doberman-YPPAN
Box 2021
St. Nicholas QUEBEC
CAN GOS-3LO

or

Editions Sybex
10/12 Villa Coeur-de-Vey
75685 Paris Cedex 14
France

Although your mail will probably arrive even if pieces of the address are out of order, it's better to allow an address to be more flexible. Here's one address element declaration that permits this:

```
<!ELEMENT ADDRESS (STREET+, (CITY | STATE | POSTAL_CODE
 | COUNTRY)*)>
```

This says that an ADDRESS element must have one or more STREET children followed by any number of CITY, STATE, POSTAL_CODE, or COUNTRY elements. Even this is less than ideal if you'd like to allow for no more than one of each. Unfortunately, this is beyond the power of a DTD to enforce. By allowing a more flexible ordering of elements, you give up some ability to control the maximum number of each element.

On the other hand, you may have a list composed of different kinds of elements, which may appear in an arbitrary order, as in a list of recordings that may contain CDs, albums, and tapes. An element declaration to differentiate between the different categories for this list would look like this:

```
<!ELEMENT MUSIC_LIST (CD | ALBUM | TAPE)*>
```

You could use parentheses in the baseball DTD to specify different sets of statistics for pitchers and batters. Each player could have one set or the other, but not both. The element declaration looks like this:

```
<!ELEMENT PLAYER (GIVEN_NAME, SURNAME, POSITION, GAMES,
   GAMES_STARTED, (( COMPLETE_GAMES?, WINS?, LOSSES?, SAVES?,
   SHUT_OUTS?, ERA?, INNINGS?, EARNED_RUNS?, HIT_BATTER?,
   WILD_PITCHES?, BALK?, WALKED_BATTER?, STRUCK_OUT_BATTER? )
|(AT_BATS?, RUNS?, HITS?, DOUBLES?, TRIPLES?, HOME_RUNS?,
   RBI?, STEALS?, CAUGHT_STEALING?, SACRIFICE_HITS?,
   SACRIFICE_FLIES?, ERRORS?, WALKS?, STRUCK_OUT?,
   HIT_BY_PITCH? ))))>
```

There are still a few things that are difficult to handle in element declarations. For example, there's no good way to say that a document must begin with a TITLE element and end with a SIGNATURE element, but may contain any other elements between those two. This is because ANY may not combine with other child elements.

And, in general, the less precise you are about where things appear, the less control you have over how many of them there are. For example, you can't say that a document should have exactly one TITLE element but that the TITLE may appear anywhere in the document.

Nonetheless, using parentheses to create blocks of elements, either in sequence with a comma or in parallel with a vertical bar, enables you to create complicated structures with detailed rules for how different elements follow one another. Try not to go overboard with this though. Simpler solutions are better. The more complicated your DTD is, the harder it is to write valid files that satisfy the DTD, to say nothing of the complexity of maintaining the DTD itself.

Mixed Content

You may have noticed that in most of the examples shown so far, elements either contained child elements or parsed character data, but not both. The only exceptions were the root elements in early examples where the full list of tags was not yet developed. In these cases, because the root element could contain ANY data, it was allowed to contain both child elements and raw text.

You can declare tags that contain both child elements and parsed character data. This is called *mixed content*. You can use this to allow an arbitrary block of text to be suffixed to each TEAM. For example:

```
<!ELEMENT TEAM (#PCDATA | TEAM_CITY | TEAM_NAME | PLAYER)*>
```

Mixing child elements with parsed character data severely restricts the structure you can impose on your documents. In particular, you can specify only the names of the child elements that can appear. You cannot constrain the order in which they appear, the number of each that appears, or whether they appear at all. In terms of DTDs, think of this as meaning that the child part of the DTD must look like this:

```
<!ELEMENT PARENT (#PCDATA | CHILD1 | CHILD2 | CHILD3 )* >
```

Almost everything else, other than changing the number of children, is invalid. You cannot use commas, question marks, or plus signs in an element declaration that includes #PCDATA. A list of elements and #PCDATA separated by vertical bars is valid. Any other use is not. For example, the following is illegal:

```
<!ELEMENT TEAM (TEAM_CITY, TEAM_NAME, PLAYER*, #PCDATA)>
```

The primary reason to mix content is when you're in the process of converting old text data to XML, and testing your DTD by validating as you add new tags rather than finishing the entire conversion and then trying to find the bugs. This is a good technique, and I do recommend you use it — after all, it is much easier to recognize a mistake in your code immediately after you made it rather than several hours later — however, this is only a crutch for use when developing. It should not be visible to the end-user. When your DTD is finished it should not mix element children with parsed character data. You can always create a new tag that holds parsed character data.

For example, you can include a block of text at the end of each TEAM element by declaring a new BLURB that holds only #PCDATA and adding it as the last child element of TEAM. Here's how this looks:

```
<!ELEMENT TEAM (TEAM_CITY, TEAM_NAME, PLAYER*, BLURB)>
<!ELEMENT BLURB (#PCDATA)>
```

This does not significantly change the text of the document. All it does is add one more optional element with its opening and closing tags to each TEAM element. However, it does make the document much more robust. Furthermore, XML applications that receive the tree from the XML processor have an easier time handling the data when it's in the more structured format allowed by nonmixed content.

Empty Elements

As discussed earlier, it's occasionally useful to define an element that has no content. Examples in HTML include the image, horizontal rule, and break <IMG>, <HR>, and <BR>. In XML, such empty elements are identified by empty tags that end with />, such as <IMG/>, <HR/>, and <BR/>.

Valid documents must declare both the empty and nonempty elements used. Because empty elements by definition don't have children, they're easy to declare. Use an <!ELEMENT> declaration containing the name of the empty element as normal, but use the keyword EMPTY (case-sensitive as all XML tags are) instead of a list of children. For example:

```
<!ELEMENT BR EMPTY>
<!ELEMENT IMG EMPTY>
<!ELEMENT HR EMPTY>
```

Listing 8-11 is a valid document that uses both empty and nonempty elements.

Listing 8-11: **A valid document that uses empty tags**

```
<?xml version="1.0" standalone="yes"?>
<!DOCTYPE DOCUMENT [
  <!ELEMENT DOCUMENT (TITLE, SIGNATURE)>
  <!ELEMENT TITLE (#PCDATA)>
  <!ELEMENT COPYRIGHT (#PCDATA)>
  <!ELEMENT EMAIL (#PCDATA)>
  <!ELEMENT BR EMPTY>
  <!ELEMENT HR EMPTY>
  <!ELEMENT LAST_MODIFIED (#PCDATA)>
  <!ELEMENT SIGNATURE (HR, COPYRIGHT, BR, EMAIL,
```

```
        BR, LAST_MODIFIED)>
]>
<DOCUMENT>
  <TITLE>Empty Tags</TITLE>
  <SIGNATURE>
    <HR/>
    <COPYRIGHT>1999 Elliotte Rusty Harold</COPYRIGHT><BR/>
    <EMAIL>elharo@metalab.unc.edu</EMAIL><BR/>
    <LAST_MODIFIED>Thursday, April 22, 1999</LAST_MODIFIED>
  </SIGNATURE>
</DOCUMENT>
```

Comments in DTDs

DTDs can contain comments, just like the rest of an XML document. These comments cannot appear inside a declaration, but they can appear outside one. Comments are often used to organize the DTD in different parts, to document the allowed content of particular elements, and to further explain what an element is. For example, the element declaration for the YEAR element might have a comment such as this:

```
<!-- A four digit year like 1998, 1999, or 2000 -->
<!ELEMENT YEAR (#PCDATA)>
```

As with all comments, this is only for the benefit of people reading the source code. XML processors will ignore it.

One possible use of comments is to define abbreviations used in the markup. For example, in this and previous chapters, I've avoided using abbreviations for baseball terms because they're simply not obvious to the casual fan. An alternative approach is to use abbreviations but define them with comments in the DTD. Listing 8-12 is similar to previous baseball examples, but uses DTD comments and abbreviated tags.

> **Listing 8-12: A valid XML document that uses abbreviated tags defined in DTD comments**

```
<?xml version="1.0" standalone="yes"?>
<!DOCTYPE SEASON [

  <!ELEMENT YEAR (#PCDATA)>
```

Continued

Listing 8-12 *(continued)*

```
<!ELEMENT LEAGUE (LEAGUE_NAME, DIVISION, DIVISION, DIVISION)>

<!-- American or National -->
<!ELEMENT LEAGUE_NAME (#PCDATA)>

<!-- East, West, or Central -->
<!ELEMENT DIVISION_NAME (#PCDATA)>
<!ELEMENT DIVISION (DIVISION_NAME, TEAM+)>
<!ELEMENT SEASON (YEAR, LEAGUE, LEAGUE)>
<!ELEMENT TEAM (TEAM_CITY, TEAM_NAME, PLAYER*)>
<!ELEMENT TEAM_CITY (#PCDATA)>
<!ELEMENT TEAM_NAME (#PCDATA)>
<!ELEMENT PLAYER (GIVEN_NAME, SURNAME, P, G,
   GS, AB?, R?, H?, D?, T?, HR?, RBI?, SB?, CS?,
   SH?, SF?, E?, BB?, S?, HBP?, CG?, SO?, ERA?, IP?,
   HRA?, RA?, ER?, HB?, WP?, B?, WB?, K?)
>

<!- ======================= ->
<!- Player Info ->
<!- Player's last name ->
<!ELEMENT SURNAME (#PCDATA)>

<!- Player's first name ->
<!ELEMENT GIVEN_NAME (#PCDATA)>

<!- Position ->
<!ELEMENT P (#PCDATA)>

<!-Games Played ->
<!ELEMENT G (#PCDATA)>

<!-Games Started ->
<!ELEMENT GS (#PCDATA)>


<!- ======================= ->
<!- Batting Statistics ->
<!- At Bats ->
<!ELEMENT AB (#PCDATA)>

<!- Runs ->
<!ELEMENT R (#PCDATA)>

<!- Hits ->
<!ELEMENT H (#PCDATA)>

<!- Doubles ->
```

```
<!ELEMENT D (#PCDATA)>

<!- Triples ->
<!ELEMENT T (#PCDATA)>

<!- Home Runs ->
<!ELEMENT HR (#PCDATA)>

<!- Runs Batted In ->
<!ELEMENT RBI (#PCDATA)>

<!- Stolen Bases ->
<!ELEMENT SB (#PCDATA)>

<!- Caught Stealing ->
<!ELEMENT CS (#PCDATA)>

<!- Sacrifice Hits ->
<!ELEMENT SH (#PCDATA)>

<!- Sacrifice Flies ->
<!ELEMENT SF (#PCDATA)>

<!- Errors ->
<!ELEMENT E (#PCDATA)>

<!- Walks (Base on Balls) ->
<!ELEMENT BB (#PCDATA)>

<!- Struck Out ->
<!ELEMENT S (#PCDATA)>

<!- Hit By Pitch ->
<!ELEMENT HBP (#PCDATA)>

<!- ====================== ->
<!- Pitching Statistics ->
<!- Complete Games ->
<!ELEMENT CG (#PCDATA)>

<!- Shut Outs ->
<!ELEMENT SO (#PCDATA)>

<!- ERA ->
<!ELEMENT ERA (#PCDATA)>

<!- Innings Pitched ->
<!ELEMENT IP (#PCDATA)>
```

Continued

Listing 8-12 *(continued)*

```
<!- Home Runs hit Against ->
<!ELEMENT HRA (#PCDATA)>

<!- Runs hit Against ->
<!ELEMENT RA (#PCDATA)>

<!- Earned Runs ->
<!ELEMENT ER (#PCDATA)>

<!- Hit Batter ->
<!ELEMENT HB (#PCDATA)>

<!- Wild Pitches ->
<!ELEMENT WP (#PCDATA)>

<!- Balk ->
<!ELEMENT B (#PCDATA)>

<!- Walked Batter ->
<!ELEMENT WB (#PCDATA)>

<!- Struck Out Batter ->
<!ELEMENT K (#PCDATA)>

<!- ======================= ->
  <!- Fielding Statistics ->
  <!- Not yet supported ->


]>
<SEASON>
  <YEAR>1998</YEAR>
  <LEAGUE>
    <LEAGUE_NAME>National</LEAGUE_NAME>
    <DIVISION>
        <DIVISION_NAME>East</DIVISION_NAME>
          <TEAM>
            <TEAM_CITY>Atlanta</TEAM_CITY>
            <TEAM_NAME>Braves</TEAM_NAME>
            <PLAYER>
            <GIVEN_NAME>Ozzie</GIVEN_NAME>
            <SURNAME>Guillen</SURNAME>
            <P>Shortstop</P>
            <G>83</G>
            <GS>59</GS>
            <AB>264</AB>
            <R>35</R>
            <H>73</H>
```

```
                            <D>15</D>
                            <T>1</T>
                            <HR>1</HR>
                            <RBI>22</RBI>
                            <SB>1</SB>
                            <CS>4</CS>
                            <SH>4</SH>
                            <SF>2</SF>
                            <E>6</E>
                            <BB>24</BB>
                            <S>25</S>
                            <HBP>1</HBP>
                        </PLAYER>
                    </TEAM>
                    <TEAM>
                        <TEAM_CITY>Florida</TEAM_CITY>
                        <TEAM_NAME>Marlins</TEAM_NAME>
                    </TEAM>
                    <TEAM>
                        <TEAM_CITY>Montreal</TEAM_CITY>
                        <TEAM_NAME>Expos</TEAM_NAME>
                    </TEAM>
                    <TEAM>
                        <TEAM_CITY>New York</TEAM_CITY>
                        <TEAM_NAME>Mets</TEAM_NAME>
                    </TEAM>
                    <TEAM>
                        <TEAM_CITY>Philadelphia</TEAM_CITY>
                        <TEAM_NAME>Phillies</TEAM_NAME>
                    </TEAM>
                </DIVISION>
                <DIVISION>
                    <DIVISION_NAME>Central</DIVISION_NAME>
                    <TEAM>
                        <TEAM_CITY>Chicago</TEAM_CITY>
                        <TEAM_NAME>Cubs</TEAM_NAME>
                    </TEAM>
                </DIVISION>
                <DIVISION>
                    <DIVISION_NAME>West</DIVISION_NAME>
                    <TEAM>
                        <TEAM_CITY>Arizona</TEAM_CITY>
                        <TEAM_NAME>Diamondbacks</TEAM_NAME>
                    </TEAM>
                </DIVISION>
            </LEAGUE>
            <LEAGUE>
                <LEAGUE_NAME>American</LEAGUE_NAME>
                <DIVISION>
```

Continued

Listing 8-12 *(continued)*

```
        <DIVISION_NAME>East</DIVISION_NAME>
         <TEAM>
           <TEAM_CITY>Baltimore</TEAM_CITY>
           <TEAM_NAME>Orioles</TEAM_NAME>
         </TEAM>
      </DIVISION>
      <DIVISION>
         <DIVISION_NAME>Central</DIVISION_NAME>
          <TEAM>
            <TEAM_CITY>Chicago</TEAM_CITY>
            <TEAM_NAME>White Sox</TEAM_NAME>
          </TEAM>
      </DIVISION>
      <DIVISION>
         <DIVISION_NAME>West</DIVISION_NAME>
          <TEAM>
            <TEAM_CITY>Anaheim</TEAM_CITY>
             <TEAM_NAME>Angels</TEAM_NAME>
          </TEAM>
       </DIVISION>
    </LEAGUE>
 </SEASON>
```

When the entire Major League is included, the resulting document shrinks from 699K with long tags to 391K with short tags, a savings of 44 percent. The information content, however, is virtually the same. Consequently, the compressed sizes of the two documents are much closer, 58K for the document with short tags versus 66K for the document with long tags.

There's no limit to the amount of information you can or should include in comments. Including more does make your DTDs longer (and thus both harder to scan and slower to download). However, in the next couple of chapters, you'll learn ways to reuse the same DTD in multiple XML documents, as well as break long DTDs into more manageable pieces. Thus, the disadvantages of using comments are temporary. I recommend using comments liberally in all of your DTDs, but especially in those intended for public use.

Sharing Common DTDs Among Documents

Previous valid examples included the DTD in the document's prolog. The real power of XML, however, comes from common DTDs that can be shared among many documents written by different people. If the DTD is not directly included in the document but is linked in from an external source, changes made to the DTD automatically propagate to all documents using that DTD. On the other hand, backward compatibility is not guaranteed when a DTD is modified. Incompatible changes can break documents.

When you use an external DTD, the document type declaration changes. Instead of including the DTD in square brackets, the SYSTEM keyword is followed by an absolute or relative URL where the DTD can be found. For example:

```
<!DOCTYPE root_element_name SYSTEM "DTD_URL">
```

Here `root_element_name` is simply the name of the root element as before, SYSTEM is an XML keyword, and `DTD_URL` is a relative or an absolute URL where the DTD can be found. For example:

```
<!DOCTYPE SEASON SYSTEM "baseball.dtd">
```

Let's convert a familiar example to demonstrate this process. Listing 8-12 includes an internal DTD for baseball statistics. We'll convert this listing to use an external DTD. First, strip out the DTD and put it in a file of its own. This is everything between the opening <!DOCTYPE SEASON [and the closing]> exclusive. <!DOCTYPE SEASON [and]> are not included. This can be saved in a file called baseball.dtd, as shown in Listing 8-13. The file name is not important, though the extension .dtd is conventional.

Listing 8-13: **The baseball DTD file**

```
<!ELEMENT YEAR (#PCDATA)>
<!ELEMENT LEAGUE (LEAGUE_NAME, DIVISION, DIVISION, DIVISION)>

<!-- American or National -->
<!ELEMENT LEAGUE_NAME (#PCDATA)>

<!-- East, West, or Central -->
<!ELEMENT DIVISION_NAME (#PCDATA)>
<!ELEMENT DIVISION (DIVISION_NAME, TEAM+)>
<!ELEMENT SEASON (YEAR, LEAGUE, LEAGUE)>
<!ELEMENT TEAM (TEAM_CITY, TEAM_NAME, PLAYER*)>
<!ELEMENT TEAM_CITY (#PCDATA)>
<!ELEMENT TEAM_NAME (#PCDATA)>
<!ELEMENT PLAYER (GIVEN_NAME, SURNAME, P, G,
    GS, AB?, R?, H?, D?, T?, HR?, RBI?, SB?, CS?,
    SH?, SF?, E?, BB?, S?, HBP?, CG?, SO?, ERA?, IP?,
```

Continued

Listing 8-13 *(continued)*

```
   HRA?, RA?, ER?, HB?, WP?, B?, WB?, K?)
 >

<!— ====================== —>
 <!— Player Info —>
 <!— Player's last name —>
 <!ELEMENT SURNAME (#PCDATA)>

 <!— Player's first name —>
 <!ELEMENT GIVEN_NAME (#PCDATA)>

 <!— Position —>
 <!ELEMENT P (#PCDATA)>

 <!—Games Played —>
 <!ELEMENT G (#PCDATA)>

 <!—Games Started —>
 <!ELEMENT GS (#PCDATA)>


<!— ====================== —>
 <!— Batting Statistics —>
 <!— At Bats —>
 <!ELEMENT AB (#PCDATA)>

 <!— Runs —>
 <!ELEMENT R (#PCDATA)>

 <!— Hits —>
 <!ELEMENT H (#PCDATA)>

 <!— Doubles —>
 <!ELEMENT D (#PCDATA)>

 <!— Triples —>
 <!ELEMENT T (#PCDATA)>

 <!— Home Runs —>
 <!ELEMENT HR (#PCDATA)>

 <!— Runs Batted In —>
 <!ELEMENT RBI (#PCDATA)>

 <!— Stolen Bases —>
 <!ELEMENT SB (#PCDATA)>

 <!— Caught Stealing —>
```

```
<!ELEMENT CS (#PCDATA)>

<!- Sacrifice Hits ->
<!ELEMENT SH (#PCDATA)>

<!- Sacrifice Flies ->
<!ELEMENT SF (#PCDATA)>

<!- Errors ->
<!ELEMENT E (#PCDATA)>

<!- Walks (Base on Balls) ->
<!ELEMENT BB (#PCDATA)>

<!- Struck Out ->
<!ELEMENT S (#PCDATA)>

<!- Hit By Pitch ->
<!ELEMENT HBP (#PCDATA)>

<!- ======================= ->
  <!- Pitching Statistics ->
  <!- Complete Games ->
<!ELEMENT CG (#PCDATA)>

<!- Shut Outs ->
<!ELEMENT SO (#PCDATA)>

<!- ERA ->
<!ELEMENT ERA (#PCDATA)>

<!- Innings Pitched ->
<!ELEMENT IP (#PCDATA)>

<!- Home Runs hit Against ->
<!ELEMENT HRA (#PCDATA)>

<!- Runs hit Against ->
<!ELEMENT RA (#PCDATA)>

<!- Earned Runs ->
<!ELEMENT ER (#PCDATA)>

<!- Hit Batter ->
<!ELEMENT HB (#PCDATA)>

<!- Wild Pitches ->
<!ELEMENT WP (#PCDATA)>
```

Continued

Listing 8-13 *(continued)*

```
<!- Balk ->
<!ELEMENT B (#PCDATA)>

<!- Walked Batter ->
<!ELEMENT WB (#PCDATA)>

<!- Struck Out Batter ->
<!ELEMENT K (#PCDATA)>

<!- ======================= ->
<!- Fielding Statistics ->
<!- Not yet supported ->
```

Next, you need to modify the document itself. The XML declaration is no longer a stand-alone document because it depends on a DTD in another file. Therefore, the standalone attribute must be changed to no, as follows:

```
<?xml version="1.0" standalone="no"?>
```

Then you must change the <!DOCTYPE> tag so it points to the DTD by including the SYSTEM keyword and a URL (usually relative) where the DTD is found:

```
<!DOCTYPE SEASON SYSTEM "baseball.dtd">
```

The rest of the document is the same as before. However, now the prolog contains only the XML declaration and the document type declaration. It does not contain the DTD. Listing 8-14 shows the code.

Listing 8-14: Baseball statistics with an external DTD

```
<?xml version="1.0" standalone="yes"?>
<!DOCTYPE SEASON SYSTEM "baseball.dtd">
<SEASON>
  <YEAR>1998</YEAR>
  <LEAGUE>
    <LEAGUE_NAME>National</LEAGUE_NAME>
    <DIVISION>
        <DIVISION_NAME>East</DIVISION_NAME>
          <TEAM>
              <TEAM_CITY>Atlanta</TEAM_CITY>
              <TEAM_NAME>Braves</TEAM_NAME>
              <PLAYER>
```

```
            <GIVEN_NAME>Ozzie</GIVEN_NAME>
            <SURNAME>Guillen</SURNAME>
            <P>Shortstop</P>
            <G>83</G>
            <GS>59</GS>
            <AB>264</AB>
            <R>35</R>
            <H>73</H>
            <D>15</D>
            <T>1</T>
            <HR>1</HR>
            <RBI>22</RBI>
            <SB>1</SB>
            <CS>4</CS>
            <SH>4</SH>
            <SF>2</SF>
            <E>6</E>
            <BB>24</BB>
            <S>25</S>
            <HBP>1</HBP>
          </PLAYER>
      </TEAM>
      <TEAM>
        <TEAM_CITY>Florida</TEAM_CITY>
        <TEAM_NAME>Marlins</TEAM_NAME>
      </TEAM>
      <TEAM>
        <TEAM_CITY>Montreal</TEAM_CITY>
        <TEAM_NAME>Expos</TEAM_NAME>
      </TEAM>
      <TEAM>
        <TEAM_CITY>New York</TEAM_CITY>
        <TEAM_NAME>Mets</TEAM_NAME>
      </TEAM>
      <TEAM>
        <TEAM_CITY>Philadelphia</TEAM_CITY>
        <TEAM_NAME>Phillies</TEAM_NAME>
      </TEAM>
</DIVISION>
<DIVISION>
    <DIVISION_NAME>Central</DIVISION_NAME>
    <TEAM>
        <TEAM_CITY>Chicago</TEAM_CITY>
        <TEAM_NAME>Cubs</TEAM_NAME>
    </TEAM>
</DIVISION>
<DIVISION>
    <DIVISION_NAME>West</DIVISION_NAME>
    <TEAM>
```

Continued

Listing 8-14 *(continued)*

```
            <TEAM_CITY>Arizona</TEAM_CITY>
            <TEAM_NAME>Diamondbacks</TEAM_NAME>
        </TEAM>
    </DIVISION>
  </LEAGUE>
  <LEAGUE>
    <LEAGUE_NAME>American</LEAGUE_NAME>
    <DIVISION>
        <DIVISION_NAME>East</DIVISION_NAME>
        <TEAM>
          <TEAM_CITY>Baltimore</TEAM_CITY>
          <TEAM_NAME>Orioles</TEAM_NAME>
        </TEAM>
    </DIVISION>
    <DIVISION>
        <DIVISION_NAME>Central</DIVISION_NAME>
        <TEAM>
          <TEAM_CITY>Chicago</TEAM_CITY>
          <TEAM_NAME>White Sox</TEAM_NAME>
        </TEAM>
    </DIVISION>
    <DIVISION>
        <DIVISION_NAME>West</DIVISION_NAME>
        <TEAM>
          <TEAM_CITY>Anaheim</TEAM_CITY>
          <TEAM_NAME>Angels</TEAM_NAME>
        </TEAM>
    </DIVISION>
  </LEAGUE>
</SEASON>
```

Make sure that both Listing 8-14 and baseball.dtd are in the same directory and then load Listing 8-14 into your Web browser as usual. If all is well, you see the same output as when you loaded Listing 8-12. You can now use this same DTD to describe other documents, such as statistics from other years.

Once you add a style sheet, you have the three essential parts of the document stored in three different files. The data is in the document file, the structure and semantics applied to the data is in the DTD file, and the formatting is in the style sheet. This structure enables you to inspect or change any or all of these relatively independently.

The DTD and the document are more closely linked than the document and the style sheet. Changing the DTD generally requires revalidating the document and may require edits to the document to bring it back into conformance with the DTD. The necessity of this sequence depends on your edits; adding elements is rarely an issue, though removing elements may be problematic.

DTDs at Remote URLs

If a DTD is applied to multiple documents, you cannot always put the DTD in the same directory as each document for which it is used. Instead, you can use a URL to specify precisely where the DTD is found. For example, let's suppose the baseball DTD is found at `http://metalab.unc.edu/xml/dtds/baseball.dtd`. You can link to it by using the following `<!DOCTYPE>` tag in the prolog:

```
<!DOCTYPE SEASON SYSTEM
    "http://metalab.unc.edu/xml/dtds/baseball.dtd">
```

This example uses a full URL valid from anywhere. You may also wish to locate DTDs relative to the Web server's document root or the current directory. In general, any reference that forms a valid URL relative to the location of the document is acceptable. For example, these are all valid document type declarations:

```
<!DOCTYPE SEASON SYSTEM "/xml/dtds/baseball.dtd">

<!DOCTYPE SEASON SYSTEM "dtds/baseball.dtd">

<!DOCTYPE SEASON SYSTEM "../baseball.dtd">
```

Note
A document can't have more than one document type declaration, that is, more than one `<!DOCTYPE>` tag. To use elements declared in more than one DTD, you need to use external parameter entity references. These are discussed in the next chapter.

Public DTDs

The `SYSTEM` keyword is intended for private DTDs used by a single author or group. Part of the promise of XML, however, is that broader organizations covering an entire industry, such as the ISO or the IEEE, can standardize public DTDs to cover their fields. This standardization saves people from having to reinvent tag sets for the same items and makes it easier for users to exchange interoperable documents.

DTDs designed for writers outside the creating organization use the `PUBLIC` keyword instead of the `SYSTEM` keyword. Furthermore, the DTD gets a name. The syntax follows:

```
<!DOCTYPE root_element_name PUBLIC "DTD_name" "DTD_URL">
```

Once again, *root_element_name* is the name of the root element. PUBLIC is an XML keyword indicating that this DTD is intended for broad use and has a name. *DTD_name* is the name associated with this DTD. Some XML processors may attempt to use this name to retrieve the DTD from a central repository. Finally, *DTD_URL* is a relative or absolute URL where the DTD can be found if it cannot be retrieved by name from a well-known repository.

DTD names are slightly different from XML names. They may contain only the ASCII alphanumeric characters, the space, the carriage return, the linefeed characters, and the following punctuation marks: -'()+,/:=?;!*#@$_%. Furthermore, the names of public DTDs follow a few conventions.

If a DTD is an ISO standard, its name begins with the string "ISO." If a non-ISO standards body has approved the DTD, its name begins with a plus sign (+). If no standards body has approved the DTD, its name begins with a hyphen (-). These initial strings are followed by a double slash (//) and the name of the DTD's owner, which is followed by another double slash and the type of document the DTD describes. Then there's another double slash followed by an ISO 639 language identifier, such as EN for English. A complete list of ISO 639 identifiers is available from http://www.ics.uci.edu/pub/ietf/http/related/iso639.txt. For example, the baseball DTD can be named as follows:

```
-//Elliotte Rusty Harold//DTD baseball statistics//EN
```

This example says this DTD is not standards-body approved (-), belongs to Elliotte Rusty Harold, describes baseball statistics, and is written in English. A full document type declaration pointing to this DTD with this name follows:

```
<!DOCTYPE SEASON PUBLIC
    "-//Elliotte Rusty Harold//DTD baseball statistics//EN"
    "http://metalab.unc.edu/xml/dtds/baseball.dtd">
```

You may have noticed that many HTML editors such as BBEdit automatically place the following string at the beginning of every HTML file they create:

```
<!DOCTYPE HTML PUBLIC "-//W3C//DTD HTML//EN">
```

Now you know what this string means! It says the document follows a non-standards-body-approved (-) DTD for HTML produced by the W3C in the English language.

Note Technically the W3C is not a standards organization because it's membership is limited to corporations that pay its fees rather than to official government-approved bodies. It only publishes *recommendations* instead of *standards*. In practice, the distinction is irrelevant.

Internal and External DTD Subsets

Although most documents consist of easily defined pieces, not all documents use a common template. Many documents may need to use standard DTDs such as the HTML 4.0 DTD while adding custom elements for their own use. Other documents may use only standard elements, but need to reorder them. For instance, one HTML page may have a BODY that must contain exactly one H1 header followed by a DL definition list while another may have a BODY that contains many different headers, paragraphs, and images in no particular order. If a particular document has a different structure than other pages on the site, it can be useful to define its structure in the document itself rather than in a separate DTD. This approach also makes the document easier to edit.

To this end, a document can use both an internal and an external DTD. The internal declarations go inside square brackets at the end of the <!DOCTYPE> tag. For example, suppose you want a page that includes baseball statistics but also has a header and a footer. Such a document might look like Listing 8-15. The baseball information is pulled from the file baseball.dtd, which forms the external DTD subset. The definition of the root element DOCUMENT as well as the TITLE and SIGNATURE elements come from the internal DTD subset included in the document itself. This is a little unusual. More commonly, the more generic pieces are likely to be part of an external DTD while the internal pieces are more topic-specific.

Listing 8-15: A baseball document whose DTD has both an internal and an external subset

```
<?xml version="1.0" standalone="no"?>
<!DOCTYPE DOCUMENT SYSTEM "baseball.dtd" [
  <!ELEMENT DOCUMENT (TITLE, SEASON, SIGNATURE)>
  <!ELEMENT TITLE (#PCDATA)>
  <!ELEMENT COPYRIGHT (#PCDATA)>
  <!ELEMENT EMAIL (#PCDATA)>
  <!ELEMENT LAST_MODIFIED (#PCDATA)>
  <!ELEMENT SIGNATURE (COPYRIGHT, EMAIL, LAST_MODIFIED)>
]>

<DOCUMENT>
  <TITLE>1998 Major League Baseball Statistics</TITLE>
  <SEASON>
    <YEAR>1998</YEAR>
    <LEAGUE>
      <LEAGUE_NAME>National</LEAGUE_NAME>
      <DIVISION>
        <DIVISION_NAME>East</DIVISION_NAME>
```

Continued

Listing 8-15 *(continued)*

```
        <TEAM>
          <TEAM_CITY>Atlanta</TEAM_CITY>
          <TEAM_NAME>Braves</TEAM_NAME>
        </TEAM>
        <TEAM>
          <TEAM_CITY>Florida</TEAM_CITY>
          <TEAM_NAME>Marlins</TEAM_NAME>
        </TEAM>
        <TEAM>
          <TEAM_CITY>Montreal</TEAM_CITY>
          <TEAM_NAME>Expos</TEAM_NAME>
        </TEAM>
        <TEAM>
          <TEAM_CITY>New York</TEAM_CITY>
          <TEAM_NAME>Mets</TEAM_NAME>
        </TEAM>
        <TEAM>
          <TEAM_CITY>Philadelphia</TEAM_CITY>
        <TEAM_NAME>Phillies</TEAM_NAME>
        </TEAM>
    </DIVISION>
    <DIVISION>
        <DIVISION_NAME>Central</DIVISION_NAME>
        <TEAM>
          <TEAM_CITY>Chicago</TEAM_CITY>
          <TEAM_NAME>Cubs</TEAM_NAME>
        </TEAM>
    </DIVISION>
    <DIVISION>
        <DIVISION_NAME>West</DIVISION_NAME>
        <TEAM>
          <TEAM_CITY>Arizona</TEAM_CITY>
          <TEAM_NAME>Diamondbacks</TEAM_NAME>
        </TEAM>
    </DIVISION>
</LEAGUE>
<LEAGUE>
  <LEAGUE_NAME>American</LEAGUE_NAME>
  <DIVISION>
      <DIVISION_NAME>East</DIVISION_NAME>
        <TEAM>
          <TEAM_CITY>Baltimore</TEAM_CITY>
          <TEAM_NAME>Orioles</TEAM_NAME>
        </TEAM>
    </DIVISION>
    <DIVISION>
        <DIVISION_NAME>Central</DIVISION_NAME>
        <TEAM>
          <TEAM_CITY>Chicago</TEAM_CITY>
```

```
                <TEAM_NAME>White Sox</TEAM_NAME>
            </TEAM>
        </DIVISION>
        <DIVISION>
            <DIVISION_NAME>West</DIVISION_NAME>
            <TEAM>
                <TEAM_CITY>Anaheim</TEAM_CITY>
                <TEAM_NAME>Angels</TEAM_NAME>
            </TEAM>
        </DIVISION>
      </LEAGUE>
    </SEASON>
    <SIGNATURE>
      <COPYRIGHT>Copyright 1999 Elliotte Rusty Harold</COPYRIGHT>
      <EMAIL>elharo@metalab.unc.edu</EMAIL>
      <LAST_MODIFIED>March 10, 1999</LAST_MODIFIED>
    </SIGNATURE>
</DOCUMENT>
```

In the event of a conflict between elements of the same name in the internal and external DTD subsets, the elements declared internally take precedence. This precedence provides a crude, partial inheritance mechanism. For example, suppose you want to override the definition of a PLAYER element so that it can only contain batting statistics while disallowing pitching statistics. You could use most of the same declarations in the baseball DTD, changing the PLAYER element as follows:

```
<!DOCTYPE SEASON SYSTEM "baseball.dtd" [
  <!ELEMENT PLAYER (GIVEN_NAME, SURNAME, P, G,
    GS, AB?, R?, H?, D?, T?, HR?, RBI?, SB?, CS?,
    SH?, SF?, E?, BB?, S?, HBP?)
  >
]>
```

Summary

In this chapter, you learned how to use a DTD to describe the structure of a document, that is, both the required and optional elements it contains and how those elements relate to one another. In particular you learned:

✦ A document type definition (DTD) provides a list of the elements, tags, attributes, and entities contained in the document, and their relationships to one another.

✦ A document's prolog may contain a document type declaration that specifies the root element and contains a DTD. This is placed between the XML declaration and before where the actual document begins. It is delimited by <!DOC-TYPE *ROOT* [and]>, where *ROOT* is the name of the root element.

✦ DTDs lay out the permissible tags and the structure of a document. A document that adheres to the rules of its DTD is said to be valid.

✦ Element type declarations declare the name and children of an element.

✦ Children separated by commas in an element type declaration must appear in the same order in that element inside the document.

✦ A plus sign means one or more instances of the element may appear.

✦ An asterisk means zero or more instances of the element may appear.

✦ A question mark means zero or one instances of the child may appear.

✦ A vertical bar means one element or another is to be used.

✦ Parentheses group child elements to allow for more detailed element declarations.

✦ Mixed content contains both elements and parsed character data but limits the structure you can impose on the parent element.

✦ Empty elements are declared with the EMPTY keyword.

✦ Comments make DTDs much more legible.

✦ External DTDs can be located using the SYSTEM keyword and a URL in the document type declaration.

✦ Standard DTDs can be located using the PUBLIC keyword in the document type declaration.

✦ Declarations in the internal DTD subset override conflicting declarations in the external DTD subset

In the next chapter, you learn more about DTDs, including how entity references provide replacement text and how to separate DTDs from the documents they describe so they can be easily shared between documents. You also learn how to use multiple DTDs to describe a single document.

✦   ✦   ✦

Entities and External DTD Subsets

A single XML document may draw both data and declarations from many different sources, in many different files. In fact, some of the data may draw directly from databases, CGI scripts, or other non-file sources. The items where the pieces of an XML file are stored, in whatever form they take, are called entities. Entity references load these entities into the main XML document. General entity references load data into the root element of an XML document, while parameter entity references load data into the document's DTD.

What Is an Entity?

Logically speaking, an XML document is composed of a prolog followed by a root element which strictly contains all other elements. But in practice, the actual data of an XML document can spread across multiple files. For example, each PLAYER element might appear in a separate file even though the root element contains all 900 or so players in a league. The storage units that contain particular parts of an XML document are called *entities*. An entity may consist of a file, a database record, or any other item that contains data. For example, all the complete XML files in this book are entities.

The storage unit that contains the XML declaration, the document type declaration, and the root element is called the *document entity*. However, the root element and its descendents may also contain entity references pointing to additional data that should be inserted into the document. A validating XML processor combines all the different referenced entities into a single logical document before it passes the document onto the end application or displays the file.

Note   Non-validating processors may, but do not have to, insert external entities. They must insert internal entities.

The primary purpose of an entity is to hold content: well-formed XML, other forms of text, or binary data. The prolog and the document type declaration are part of the root entity of the document they belong to. An XSL style sheet qualifies as an entity, but only because it itself is a well-formed XML document. The entity that makes up the style sheet is not one of the entities that composes the XML document to which the style sheet applies. A CSS style sheet is not an entity at all.

Most entities have names by which you can refer to them. The only exception is the document entity-the main file containing the XML document (although there's no requirement that this be a file as opposed to a database record, the output of a CGI program, or something else). The document entity is the storage unit, in whatever form it takes, that holds the XML declaration, the document type declaration (if any), and the root element. Thus, every XML document has at least one entity.

There are two kinds of entities: internal and external. Internal entities are defined completely within the document entity. The document itself is one such entity, so all XML documents have at least one internal entity.

External entities, by contrast, draw their content from another source located via a URL. The main document only includes a reference to the URL where the actual content resides. In HTML, an `IMG` element represents an external entity (the actual image data) while the document itself contained between the `<HTML>` and `</HTML>` tags is an internal entity.

Entities fall into two categories: parsed and unparsed. Parsed entities contain well-formed XML text. Unparsed entities contain either binary data or non-XML text (like an email message). Currently, unparsed entities aren't well supported (if at all) by most XML processors. In this chapter, we focus on parsed entities.

Cross-Reference   Chapter 11, *Embedding Non-XML Data*, covers unparsed entities.

Entity references enable data from multiple entities to be merged together to form a single document. General entity references merge data into the document content. Parameter entity references merge declarations into the document's DTD. `&lt;`, `&gt;`, `&apos;`, `&quote;`, and `&amp;` are predefined entity references that refer to the text entities `<`, `>`, `'`, `"`, and `&`, respectively. However, you can also define new entities in your document's DTD.

Internal General Entities

You can think of an internal general entity reference as an abbreviation for commonly used text or text that's hard to type. An `<!ENTITY>` tag in the DTD defines an abbreviation and the text the abbreviation stands for. For instance, instead of typing the same footer at the bottom of every page, you can simply define that text as the `footer` entity in the DTD and then type `&footer;` at the bottom of each page. Furthermore, if you decide to change the footer block (perhaps because your email address changes), you only need to make the change once in the DTD instead of on every page that shares the footer.

General entity references begin with an ampersand (&) and end with a semicolon (;), with the entity's name between these two characters. For instance, `&lt;` is a general entity reference for the less than sign (<) The name of this entity is `lt`. The replacement text of this entity is the one character string <. Entity names consist of any set of alphanumeric characters and the underscore. Whitespace and other punctuation characters are prohibited. Like most everything else in XML, entity references are case sensitive.

Cross-Reference   Although the colon (:) is technically permitted in entity names, this character is reserved for use with namespaces, which are discussed in Chapter 18.

Defining an Internal General Entity Reference

Internal general entity references are defined in the DTD with the `<!ENTITY>` tag, which has the following format:

```
<!ENTITY name "replacement text">
```

The *name* is the abbreviation for the *replacement text*. The replacement text must be enclosed in quotation marks because it may contain whitespace and XML markup. You type the name of the entity in the document, but the reader sees the replacement text.

For example, my name is the somewhat excessive "Elliotte Rusty Harold" (blame my parents for that one). Even with years of practice, I still make typos with that phrase. I can define a general entity reference for my name so that every time I type `&ERH;`, the reader will see "Elliotte Rusty Harold". That definition is:

```
<!ENTITY ERH "Elliotte Rusty Harold">
```

Listing 9-1 demonstrates the `&ERH;` general entity reference. Figure 9-1 shows this document loaded into Internet Explorer. You see that the `&ERH;` entity reference in the source code is replaced by `Elliotte Rusty Harold` in the output.

Listing 9-1: The ERH internal general entity reference

```
<?xml version="1.0" standalone="yes"?>
<!DOCTYPE DOCUMENT [

  <!ENTITY ERH "Elliotte Rusty Harold">

  <!ELEMENT DOCUMENT (TITLE, SIGNATURE)>
  <!ELEMENT TITLE (#PCDATA)>
  <!ELEMENT COPYRIGHT (#PCDATA)>
  <!ELEMENT EMAIL (#PCDATA)>
  <!ELEMENT LAST_MODIFIED (#PCDATA)>
  <!ELEMENT SIGNATURE (COPYRIGHT, EMAIL, LAST_MODIFIED)>
]>
<DOCUMENT>
  <TITLE>&ERH;</TITLE>
  <SIGNATURE>
    <COPYRIGHT>1999 &ERH;</COPYRIGHT>
    <EMAIL>elharo@metalab.unc.edu</EMAIL>
    <LAST_MODIFIED>March 10, 1999</LAST_MODIFIED>
  </SIGNATURE>
</DOCUMENT>
```

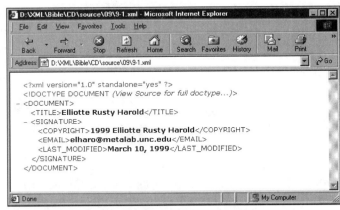

Figure 9-1: Listing 9-1 after the internal general entity reference has been replaced by the actual entity

Notice that the general entity reference, &ERH; appears inside both the COPYRIGHT and TITLE elements even though these are declared to accept only #PCDATA as children. This arrangement is legal because the replacement text of the &ERH; entity reference is parsed character data. Validation is done against the document after all entity references have been replaced by their values.

The same thing occurs when you use a style sheet. The styles are applied to the element tree as it exists after entity values replace the entity references.

You can follow the same model to declare general entity references for the copyright, the email address, or the last modified date:

```
<!ENTITY COPY99 "Copyright 1999">
<!ENTITY EMAIL "elharo@metalab.unc.edu">
<!ENTITY LM "Last modified: ">
```

I omitted the date in the &LM; entity because it's likely to change from document to document. There is no advantage to making it an entity reference.

Now you can rewrite the document part of Listing 9-1 even more compactly:

```
<DOCUMENT>
  <TITLE>&ERH;</TITLE>
  <SIGNATURE>
    <COPYRIGHT>&COPY99; &ERH;</COPYRIGHT>
    <EMAIL>&EMAIL;</EMAIL>
    <LAST_MODIFIED>&LM; March 10, 1999</LAST_MODIFIED>
  </SIGNATURE>
</DOCUMENT>
```

One of the advantages of using entity references instead of the full text is that these references make it easy to change the text. This is especially useful when a single DTD is shared between multiple documents. For example, suppose I decide to use the email address eharold@solar.stanford.edu instead of elharo@metalab.unc.edu. Rather than searching and replacing through multiple files, I simply change one line of the DTD as follows:

```
<!ENTITY EMAIL "eharold@solar.stanford.edu">
```

Using General Entity References in the DTD

You may wonder whether it's possible to include one general entity reference inside another as follows:

```
<!ENTITY COPY99 "Copyright 1999 &ERH;">
```

This example is in fact valid, because the ERH entity appears as part of the COPY99 entity that itself will ultimately become part of the document's content. You can also use general entity references in other places in the DTD that ultimately become part of the document content (such as a default attribute value), although there are restrictions. The first restriction: The statement cannot use a circular reference like this one:

```
<!ENTITY ERH "&COPY99 Elliotte Rusty Harold">
<!ENTITY COPY99 "Copyright 1999 &ERH;">
```

The second restriction: General entity references may not insert text that is only part of the DTD and will not be used as part of the document content. For example, the following attempted shortcut fails:

```
<!ENTITY  PCD     "(#PCDATA)">
<!ELEMENT ANIMAL  &PCD;>
<!ELEMENT FOOD    &PCD;>
```

It's often useful, however, to have entity references merge text into a document's DTD. For this purpose, XML uses the parameter entity reference, which is discussed later in this chapter.

The only restriction on general entity values is that they may not contain the three characters %, &, and " directly, though you can include them via character references. & and % may be included if they're starting an entity reference rather than simply representing themselves. The lack of restrictions means that an entity may contain tags and span multiple lines. For example, the following SIGNATURE entity is valid:

```
<!ENTITY SIGNATURE
  "<SIGNATURE>
      <COPYRIGHT>1999 Elliotte Rusty Harold</COPYRIGHT>
      <EMAIL>elharo@metalab.unc.edu</EMAIL>
      <LAST_MODIFIED>March 10, 1999</LAST_MODIFIED>
   </SIGNATURE>"
>
```

The next obvious question is whether it's possible for entities to have parameters. Can you use the above SIGNATURE entity but change the date in each separate LAST_MODIFIED element on each page? The answer is no; entities are only for static replacement text. If you need to pass data to an entity, you should use a tag along with the appropriate rendering instructions in the style sheet instead.

Predefined General Entity References

XML predefines five general entity references, as listed in Table 9-1. These five entity references appear in XML documents in place of specific characters that would otherwise be interpreted as markup. For instance, the entity reference < stands for the less-than sign (<), which could be interpreted as the beginning of a tag.

For maximum compatibility, you should declare these references in your DTD if you plan to use them. Declaration is actually quite tricky because you must also escape the characters in the DTD without using recursion. To declare these references, use character references containing the hexadecimal ASCII value of each character. Listing 9-2 shows the necessary declarations:

Table 9-1	
XML Predefined Entity References	
Entity Reference	*Character*
&amp;	&
&lt;	<
&gt;	>
&quot;	"
&apos;	'

Listing 9-2: **Declarations for predefined general entity references**

```
<!ENTITY lt    "&#38;#60;">
<!ENTITY gt    "&#62;">
<!ENTITY amp   "&#38;#38;">
<!ENTITY apos  "&#39;">
<!ENTITY quot  "&#34;">
```

External General Entities

External entities are data outside the main file containing the root element/document entity. External entity references let you embed these external entities in your document and build XML documents from multiple independent files.

Documents using only internal entities closely resemble the HTML model. The complete text of the document is available in a single file. Images, applets, sounds, and other non-HTML data may be linked in, but at least all the text is present. Of course, the HTML model has some problems. In particular, it's quite difficult to embed dynamic information in the file. You can embed dynamic information by using CGI, Java applets, fancy database software, server side includes, and various other means, but HTML alone only provides a static document. You have to go outside HTML to build a document from multiple pieces. Frames are perhaps the simplest HTML solution to this problem, but they are a user interface disaster that consistently confuse and annoy users.

Part of the problem is that one HTML document does not naturally fit inside another. Every HTML document should have exactly one BODY, but no more. Server side includes only enable you to embed fragments of HTML—never an entire valid document—inside a document. In addition, server side includes are server dependent and not truly part of HTML.

XML, however, is more flexible. One document's root element is not necessarily the same as another document's root element. Even if two documents share the same root element, the DTD may declare that the element is allowed to contain itself. The XML standard does not prevent well-formed XML documents from being embedded in other well-formed XML documents when convenient.

XML goes further, however, by defining a mechanism whereby an XML document can be built out of multiple smaller XML documents found either on local or remote systems. The parser is responsible for merging all the different documents together in a fixed order. Documents may contain other documents, which may contain other documents. As long as there's no recursion (an error reported by the processor), the application only sees a single, complete document. In essence, this provides client-side includes.

With XML, you can use an external general entity reference to embed one document in another. In the DTD, you declare the external reference with the following syntax:

```
<!ENTITY name SYSTEM "URI">
```

Note   URI stands for Uniform Resource Identifier. URIs are similar to URLs but allow for more precise specification of the linked resource. In theory, URIs separate the resource from the location so a Web browser can select the nearest or least congested of several mirrors without requiring an explicit link to that mirror. URIs are an area of active research and heated debate. Therefore, in practice and certainly in this book, URIs are URLs for all purposes.

For example, you may want to put the same signature block on almost every page of a site. For the sake of definiteness, let's assume the signature block is the XML code shown in Listing 9-3. Furthermore, let's assume that you can retrieve this code from the URL http://metalab.unc.edu/xml/signature.xml.

Listing 9-3: **An XML signature file**

```
<?xml version="1.0"?>
<SIGNATURE>
  <COPYRIGHT>1999 Elliotte Rusty Harold</COPYRIGHT>
  <EMAIL>elharo@metalab.unc.edu</EMAIL>
</SIGNATURE>
```

Associate this file with the entity reference &SIG; by adding the following declaration to the DTD:

```
<!ENTITY SIG SYSTEM "http://metalab.unc.edu/xml/signature.xml">
```

You can also use a relative URL. For example,

```
<!ENTITY SIG SYSTEM "/xml/signature.xml">
```

If the file to be included is in the same directory as the file doing the including, you only need to use the file name. For example,

```
<!ENTITY SIG SYSTEM "signature.xml">
```

With any of these declarations, you can include the contents of the signature file in a document at any point merely by using &SIG;, as illustrated with the simple document in Listing 9-4. Figure 9-2 shows the rendered document in Internet Explorer 5.0.

Listing 9-4: **The SIG external general entity reference**

```
<?xml version="1.0" standalone="no"?>
<!DOCTYPE DOCUMENT [
   <!ELEMENT DOCUMENT (TITLE, SIGNATURE)>
   <!ELEMENT TITLE (#PCDATA)>
   <!ELEMENT COPYRIGHT (#PCDATA)>
   <!ELEMENT EMAIL (#PCDATA)>
   <!ELEMENT SIGNATURE (COPYRIGHT, EMAIL)>
   <!ENTITY SIG SYSTEM
       "http://metalab.unc.edu/xml/signature.xml">
]>
<DOCUMENT>
   <TITLE>Entity references</TITLE>
   &SIG;
</DOCUMENT>
```

Aside from the addition of the external entity reference, note that the standalone attribute of the XML declaration now has the value no because this file is no longer complete. Parsing the file requires additional data from the external file signature.xml.

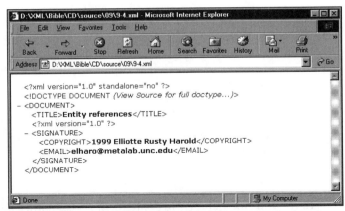

Figure 9-2: A document that uses an external general entity reference.

Internal Parameter Entities

General entities become part of the document, not the DTD. They can be used in the DTD but only in places where they will become part of the document body. General entity references may not insert text that is only part of the DTD and will not be used as part of the document content. It's often useful, however, to have entity references in a DTD. For this purpose, XML provides the *parameter entity reference*.

Parameter entity references are very similar to general entity references—with these two key differences:

1. Parameter entity references begin with a percent sign (%) rather than an ampersand (&).

2. Parameter entity references can only appear in the DTD, not the document content.

Parameter entities are declared in the DTD like general entities with the addition of a percent sign before the name. The syntax looks like this:

```
<!ENTITY % name "replacement text">
```

The name is the abbreviation for the entity. The reader sees the replacement text, which must appear in quotes. For example:

```
<!ENTITY % ERH "Elliotte Rusty Harold">
<!ENTITY COPY99 "Copyright 1999 %ERH;">
```

Our earlier failed attempt to abbreviate (#PCDATA) works when a parameter entity reference replaces the general entity reference:

```
<!ENTITY % PCD "(#PCDATA)">
<!ELEMENT ANIMAL %PCD;>
<!ELEMENT FOOD %PCD;>
```

The real value of parameter entity references appears in sharing common lists of children and attributes between elements. The larger the block of text you're replacing and the more times you use it, the more useful parameter entity references become. For instance, suppose your DTD declares a number of block level container elements like PARAGRAPH, CELL, and HEADING. Each of these container elements may contain an indefinite number of inline elements like PERSON, DEGREE, MODEL, PRODUCT, ANIMAL, INGREDIENT, and so forth. The element declarations for the container elements could appear as the following:

```
<!ELEMENT PARAGRAPH
    (PERSON | DEGREE | MODEL | PRODUCT | ANIMAL | INGREDIENT)*>
<!ELEMENT CELL
    (PERSON | DEGREE | MODEL | PRODUCT | ANIMAL | INGREDIENT)*>
<!ELEMENT HEADING
    (PERSON | DEGREE | MODEL | PRODUCT | ANIMAL | INGREDIENT)*>
```

The container elements all have the same contents. If you invent a new element like EQUATION, CD, or ACCOUNT, this element must be declared as a possible child of all three container elements. Adding it to two, but forgetting to add it to the third element, may cause trouble. This problem multiplies when you have 30 or 300 container elements instead of three.

The DTD is much easier to maintain if you don't give each container a separate child list. Instead, make the child list a parameter entity reference; then use that parameter entity reference in each of the container element declarations. For example:

```
<!ENTITY % inlines
  "(PERSON | DEGREE | MODEL | PRODUCT | ANIMAL | INGREDIENT)*">
<!ELEMENT PARAGRAPH %inlines;>
<!ELEMENT CELL %inlines;>
<!ELEMENT HEADING %inlines;>
```

To add a new element, you only have to change a single parameter entity declaration, rather than three, 30, or 300 element declarations.

Parameter entity references must be declared before they're used. The following example is invalid because the %PCD; reference is not declared until it's already been used twice:

```
<!ELEMENT FOOD %PCD;>
<!ELEMENT ANIMAL %PCD;>
<!ENTITY % PCD "(#PCDATA)">
```

Parameter entities can only be used to provide part of a declaration in the external DTD subset. That is, parameter entity references can only appear inside a declaration in the external DTD subset. The above examples are all invalid if they're used in an internal DTD subset.

In the internal DTD subset, parameter entity references can only be used outside of declarations. For example, the following is valid in both the internal and external DTD subsets:

```
<!ENTITY % hr "<!ELEMENT HR EMPTY>">
%hr;
```

Of course, this really isn't any easier than declaring the HR element without parameter entity references:

```
<!ELEMENT HR EMPTY>
```

You'll mainly use parameter entity references in internal DTD subsets when they're referring to external parameter entities; that is, when they're pulling in declarations or parts of declarations from a different file. This is the subject of the next section.

External Parameter Entities

The preceding examples used monolithic DTDs that define all the elements used in the document. This technique becomes unwieldy with longer documents, however. Furthermore, you often want to use part of a DTD in many different places.

For example, consider a DTD that describes a snail mail address. The definition of an address is quite general, and can easily be used in many different contexts. Similarly, the list of predefined entity references in Listing 9-2 is useful in most XML files, but you'd rather not copy and paste it all the time.

External parameter entities enable you to build large DTDs from smaller ones. That is, one external DTD may link to another and in so doing pull in the elements and entities declared in the first. Although cycles are prohibited—DTD 1 may not refer to DTD 2 if DTD 2 refers to DTD 1—such nested DTDs can become large and complex.

At the same time, breaking a DTD into smaller, more manageable chunks makes the DTD easier to analyze. Many of the examples in the last chapter were unnecessarily large because an entire document and its complete DTD were stored in a single file. Both the document and its DTD become much easier to understand when split into separate files.

Furthermore, using smaller, modular DTDs that only describe one set of elements makes it easier to mix and match DTDs created by different people or organizations. For instance, if you're writing a technical article about high temperature superconductivity, you can use a molecular sciences DTD to describe the molecules involved, a math DTD to write down your equations, a vector graphics DTD for the figures, and a basic HTML DTD to handle the explanatory text.

Note
In particular, you can use the mol.dtd DTD from Peter Murray-Rust's Chemical Markup Language, the MathML DTD from the W3C's Mathematical Markup Language, the SVG DTD for the W3C's Scalable Vector Graphics, and the W3C's XHTML DTD.

You can probably think of more examples where you need to mix and match concepts (and therefore tags) from different fields. Human thought doesn't restrict itself to narrowly defined categories. It tends to wander all over the map. The documents you write will reflect this.

Let's see how to organize the baseball statistics DTD as a combination of several different DTDs. This example is extremely hierarchical. One possible division is to write separate DTDs for PLAYER, TEAM, and SEASON. This is far from the only way to divide the DTD into more manageable chunks, but it will serve as a reasonable example. Listing 9-5 shows a DTD solely for a player that can be stored in a file named player.dtd:

Listing 9-5: A DTD for the PLAYER element and its children (player.dtd)

```
<!- Player Info ->
<!ELEMENT PLAYER (GIVEN_NAME, SURNAME, P, G,
  GS, AB?, R?, H?, D?, T?, HR?, RBI?, SB?, CS?,
  SH?, SF?, E?, BB?, S?, HBP?, W?, L?, SV?, CG?, SO?, ERA?,
  IP?, HRA?, RA?, ER?, HB?, WP?, B?, WB?, K?)
>

<!- Player's last name ->
<!ELEMENT SURNAME (#PCDATA)>

<!- Player's first name ->
<!ELEMENT GIVEN_NAME (#PCDATA)>

<!- Position ->
<!ELEMENT P (#PCDATA)>

<!-Games Played ->
<!ELEMENT G (#PCDATA)>
```

Continued

Listing 9-5 *(continued)*

```
<!-Games Started ->
<!ELEMENT GS (#PCDATA)>


<!- ======================= ->
  <!- Batting Statistics ->
  <!- At Bats ->
  <!ELEMENT AB (#PCDATA)>

  <!- Runs ->
  <!ELEMENT R (#PCDATA)>

  <!- Hits ->
  <!ELEMENT H (#PCDATA)>

  <!- Doubles ->
  <!ELEMENT D (#PCDATA)>

  <!- Triples ->
  <!ELEMENT T (#PCDATA)>

  <!- Home Runs ->
  <!ELEMENT HR (#PCDATA)>

  <!- Runs Batted In ->
  <!ELEMENT RBI (#PCDATA)>

  <!- Stolen Bases ->
  <!ELEMENT SB (#PCDATA)>

  <!- Caught Stealing ->
  <!ELEMENT CS (#PCDATA)>

  <!- Sacrifice Hits ->
  <!ELEMENT SH (#PCDATA)>

  <!- Sacrifice Flies ->
  <!ELEMENT SF (#PCDATA)>

  <!- Errors ->
  <!ELEMENT E (#PCDATA)>

  <!- Walks (Base on Balls) ->
  <!ELEMENT BB (#PCDATA)>

  <!- Struck Out ->
  <!ELEMENT S (#PCDATA)>

  <!- Hit By Pitch ->
  <!ELEMENT HBP (#PCDATA)>
```

```
<!-- ======================= -->
  <!-- Pitching Statistics -->
  <!-- Complete Games -->
  <!ELEMENT CG (#PCDATA)>

  <!-- Wins -->
  <!ELEMENT W (#PCDATA)>

  <!-- Losses -->
  <!ELEMENT L (#PCDATA)>

  <!-- Saves -->
  <!ELEMENT SV (#PCDATA)>

  <!-- Shutouts -->
  <!ELEMENT SO (#PCDATA)>

  <!-- ERA -->
  <!ELEMENT ERA (#PCDATA)>

  <!-- Innings Pitched -->
  <!ELEMENT IP (#PCDATA)>

  <!-- Home Runs hit Against -->
  <!ELEMENT HRA (#PCDATA)>

  <!-- Runs hit Against -->
  <!ELEMENT RA (#PCDATA)>

  <!-- Earned Runs -->
  <!ELEMENT ER (#PCDATA)>

  <!-- Hit Batter -->
  <!ELEMENT HB (#PCDATA)>

  <!-- Wild Pitches -->
  <!ELEMENT WP (#PCDATA)>

  <!-- Balk -->
  <!ELEMENT B (#PCDATA)>

  <!-- Walked Batter -->
  <!ELEMENT WB (#PCDATA)>

  <!-- Struck Out Batter -->
  <!ELEMENT K (#PCDATA)>

<!-- ======================= -->
  <!-- Fielding Statistics -->
  <!-- Not yet supported -->
```

By itself, this DTD doesn't enable you to create very interesting documents. Listing 9-6 shows a simple valid file that only uses the PLAYER DTD in Listing 9-5. By itself, this simple file is not important; however, you can build other, more complicated files out of these small parts.

Listing 9-6: A valid document using the PLAYER DTD

```
<?xml version="1.0" standalone="no"?>
<!DOCTYPE PLAYER SYSTEM "player.dtd">
<PLAYER>
  <GIVEN_NAME>Chris</GIVEN_NAME>
  <SURNAME>Hoiles</SURNAME>
  <P>Catcher</P>
  <G>97</G>
  <GS>81</GS>
  <AB>267</AB>
  <R>36</R>
  <H>70</H>
  <D>12</D>
  <T>0</T>
  <HR>15</HR>
  <RBI>56</RBI>
  <SB>0</SB>
  <CS>1</CS>
  <SH>5</SH>
  <SF>4</SF>
  <E>3</E>
  <BB>38</BB>
  <S>50</S>
  <HBP>4</HBP>
</PLAYER>
```

What other parts of the document can have their own DTDs? Obviously, a TEAM is a big part. You could write its DTD as follows:

```
<!ELEMENT TEAM (TEAM_CITY, TEAM_NAME, PLAYER*)>
<!ELEMENT TEAM_CITY (#PCDATA)>
<!ELEMENT TEAM_NAME (#PCDATA)>
```

On closer inspection, however, you should notice that something is missing: the definition of the PLAYER element. The definition is in the separate file player.dtd and needs to be connected to this DTD.

You connect DTDs with external parameter entity references. For a private DTD, this connection takes the following form:

```
<!ENTITY % name SYSTEM "URI">
%name;
```

For example:

```
<!ENTITY % player SYSTEM "player.dtd">
%player;
```

This example uses a relative URL (player.dtd) and assumes that the file player.dtd will be found in the same place as the linking DTD. If that's not the case, you can use a full URL as follows:

```
<!ENTITY % player SYSTEM
    "http://metalab.unc.edu/xml/dtds/player.dtd">
%player;
```

Listing 9-7 shows a completed TEAM DTD that includes a reference to the PLAYER DTD:

Listing 9-7: **The TEAM DTD (team.dtd)**

```
<!ELEMENT TEAM (TEAM_CITY, TEAM_NAME, PLAYER*)>
<!ELEMENT TEAM_CITY (#PCDATA)>
<!ELEMENT TEAM_NAME (#PCDATA)>
<!ENTITY % player SYSTEM "player.dtd">
%player;
```

A SEASON contains LEAGUE, DIVISION, and TEAM elements. Although LEAGUE and DIVISION could each have their own DTD, it doesn't pay to go overboard with splitting DTDs. Unless you expect you'll have some documents that contain LEAGUE or DIVISION elements that are not part of a SEASON, you might as well include all three in the same DTD. Listing 9-8 demonstrates.

Listing 9-8: The SEASON DTD (season.dtd)

```
<!ELEMENT YEAR (#PCDATA)>
<!ELEMENT LEAGUE (LEAGUE_NAME, DIVISION, DIVISION, DIVISION)>

<!- American or National ->
<!ELEMENT LEAGUE_NAME (#PCDATA)>

<!- East, West, or Central ->
<!ELEMENT DIVISION_NAME (#PCDATA)>
<!ELEMENT DIVISION (DIVISION_NAME, TEAM+)>
<!ELEMENT SEASON (YEAR, LEAGUE, LEAGUE)>
<!ENTITY % team SYSTEM "team.dtd">
%team;
```

Building a Document from Pieces

The baseball examples have been quite large. Although only a truncated version with limited numbers of players appears in this book, the full document is more than half a megabyte, way too large to comfortably download or search, especially if the reader is only interested in a single team, player, or division. The techniques discussed in the previous section of this chapter allow you to split the document into many different, smaller, more manageable documents, one for each team, player, division, and league. External entity references connect the players to form teams, the teams to form divisions, the divisions to form leagues, and the leagues to form a season.

Unfortunately you cannot embed just any XML document as an external parsed entity. Consider, for example, Listing 9-9, ChrisHoiles.xml. This is a revised version of Listing 9-6. However, if you look closely you'll notice that the prolog is different. Listing 9-6's prolog is:

```
<?xml version="1.0" standalone="no"?>
<!DOCTYPE PLAYER SYSTEM "player.dtd">
```

Listing 9-9's prolog is simply the XML declaration with no standalone attribute and with an encoding attribute. Furthermore the document type declaration is completely omitted. In a file like Listing 9-9 that's meant to be embedded in another document, this sort of XML declaration is called a *text declaration*, though as you can see it's really just a legal XML declaration.

Listing 9-9: **ChrisHoiles.xml**

```
<?xml version="1.0" encoding="UTF-8"?>
<PLAYER>
  <GIVEN_NAME>Chris</GIVEN_NAME>
  <SURNAME>Hoiles</SURNAME>
  <P>Catcher</P>
  <G>97</G>
  <GS>81</GS>
  <AB>267</AB>
  <R>36</R>
  <H>70</H>
  <D>12</D>
  <T>0</T>
  <HR>15</HR>
  <RBI>56</RBI>
  <SB>0</SB>
  <CS>1</CS>
  <SH>5</SH>
  <SF>4</SF>
  <E>3</E>
  <BB>38</BB>
  <S>50</S>
  <HBP>4</HBP>
</PLAYER>
```

On the CD-ROM   I'll spare you the other 1,200 or so players, although you'll find them all on the accompanying CD-ROM in the examples/baseball/players folder.

Text declarations must have an encoding attribute (unlike XML declarations which may but do not have to have an encoding attribute) that specifies the character set the entity uses. This allows compound documents to be assembled from entities written in different character sets. For example, a document in Latin-5 might combine with a document in UTF-8. The processor/browser still has to understand all the encodings used by the different entities.

The examples in this chapter are all given in ASCII. Since ASCII is a strict subset of both ISO Latin-1 and UTF-8, you could use either of these text declarations:

```
<?xml version="1.0" encoding="ISO-8859-1"?>
<?xml version="1.0" encoding="UTF-8"?>
```

Listing 9-10, mets.dtd, and Listing 9-11, mets.xml, show how you can use external parsed entities to put together a complete team. The DTD defines external entity references for each player on the team. The XML document loads the DTD using an external parameter entity reference in its internal DTD subset. Then, its document entity includes many external general entity references that load in the individual players.

```
<!ENTITY AlLeiter SYSTEM "mets/AlLeiter.xml">
<!ENTITY ArmandoReynoso SYSTEM "mets/ArmandoReynoso.xml">
<!ENTITY BobbyJones SYSTEM "mets/BobbyJones.xml">
<!ENTITY BradClontz SYSTEM "mets/BradClontz.xml">
<!ENTITY DennisCook SYSTEM "mets/DennisCook.xml">
<!ENTITY GregMcmichael SYSTEM "mets/GregMcmichael.xml">
<!ENTITY HideoNomo SYSTEM "mets/HideoNomo.xml">
<!ENTITY JohnFranco SYSTEM "mets/JohnFranco.xml">
<!ENTITY JosiasManzanillo SYSTEM "mets/JosiasManzanillo.xml">
<!ENTITY OctavioDotel SYSTEM "mets/OctavioDotel.xml">
<!ENTITY RickReed SYSTEM "mets/RickReed.xml">
<!ENTITY RigoBeltran SYSTEM "mets/RigoBeltran.xml">
<!ENTITY WillieBlair SYSTEM "mets/WillieBlair.xml">
```

Figure 9-3 shows the XML document loaded into Internet Explorer. Notice that all data for all players is present even though the main document only contains references to the entities where the player data resides. Internet Explorer resolves external references-not all XML parsers/browsers do.

You can find the remaining teams on the CD-ROM in the directory examples/baseball. Notice in particular how compactly external entity references enable you to embed multiple players.

```
<?xml version="1.0" standalone="no"?>
<!DOCTYPE TEAM SYSTEM "team.dtd" [
  <!ENTITY % players SYSTEM "mets.dtd">
  %players;
]>
<TEAM>
  <TEAM_CITY>New York</TEAM_CITY>
  <TEAM_NAME>Mets</TEAM_NAME>
  &AlLeiter;
```

```
    &ArmandoReynoso;
    &BobbyJones;
    &BradClontz;
    &DennisCook;
    &GregMcmichael;
    &HideoNomo;
    &JohnFranco;
    &JosiasManzanillo;
    &OctavioDotel;
    &RickReed;
    &RigoBeltran;
    &WillieBlair;
</TEAM>
```

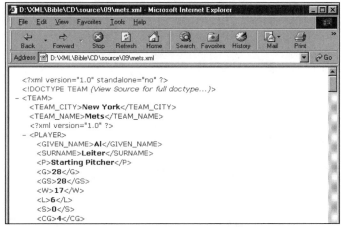

Figure 9-3: The XML document displays all players in the 1998 New York Mets.

It would be nice to continue this procedure building a division by combining team files, a league by combining divisions, and a season by combining leagues. Unfortunately, if you try this you rapidly run into a wall. The documents embedded via external entities cannot have their own DTDs. At most, their prolog can contain the text declaration. This means you can only have a single level of document embedding. This contrasts with DTD embedding where DTDs can be nested arbitrarily deeply.

Thus, your only likely alternative is to include all teams, divisions, leagues, and seasons in a single document which refers to the many different player documents. This requires a few more than 1,200 entity declarations (one for each player). Since DTDs can nest arbitrarily, we begin with a DTD that pulls in DTDs like Listing 9-10 containing entity definitions for all the teams. This is shown in Listing 9-12:

Listing 9-12: **The players DTD (players.dtd)**

```
<!ENTITY % angels SYSTEM "angels.dtd">
%angels;
<!ENTITY % astros SYSTEM "astros.dtd">
%astros;
<!ENTITY % athletics SYSTEM "athletics.dtd">
%athletics;
<!ENTITY % bluejays SYSTEM "bluejays.dtd">
%bluejays;
<!ENTITY % braves SYSTEM "braves.dtd">
%braves;
<!ENTITY % brewers SYSTEM "brewers.dtd">
%brewers;
<!ENTITY % cubs SYSTEM "cubs.dtd">
%cubs;
<!ENTITY % devilrays SYSTEM "devilrays.dtd">
%devilrays;
<!ENTITY % diamondbacks SYSTEM "diamondbacks.dtd">
%diamondbacks;
<!ENTITY % dodgers SYSTEM "dodgers.dtd">
%dodgers;
<!ENTITY % expos SYSTEM "expos.dtd">
%expos;
<!ENTITY % giants SYSTEM "giants.dtd">
%giants;
<!ENTITY % indians SYSTEM "indians.dtd">
%indians;
<!ENTITY % mariners SYSTEM "mariners.dtd">
%mariners;
<!ENTITY % marlins SYSTEM "marlins.dtd">
%marlins;
<!ENTITY % mets SYSTEM "mets.dtd">
%mets;
<!ENTITY % orioles SYSTEM "orioles.dtd">
%orioles;
<!ENTITY % padres SYSTEM "padres.dtd">
%padres;
<!ENTITY % phillies SYSTEM "phillies.dtd">
%phillies;
<!ENTITY % pirates SYSTEM "pirates.dtd">
%pirates;
<!ENTITY % rangers SYSTEM "rangers.dtd">
%rangers;
<!ENTITY % redsox SYSTEM "redsox.dtd">
%redsox;
<!ENTITY % reds SYSTEM "reds.dtd">
%reds;
<!ENTITY % rockies SYSTEM "rockies.dtd">
%rockies;
```

```
<!ENTITY % royals SYSTEM "royals.dtd">
%royals;
<!ENTITY % tigers SYSTEM "tigers.dtd">
%tigers;
<!ENTITY % twins SYSTEM "twins.dtd">
%twins;
<!ENTITY % whitesox SYSTEM "whitesox.dtd">
%whitesox;
<!ENTITY % yankees SYSTEM "yankees.dtd">
%yankees;
```

Listing 9-13, a master document, pulls together all the player sub-documents as well as the DTDs that define the entities for each player. Although this document is much smaller than the monolithic document developed earlier (32K vs. 628K), it's still quite long, so not all players are included here. The full version of Listing 9-13 relies on 33 DTDs and over 1,000 XML files to produce the finished document. The largest problem with this approach is that it requires over 1000 separate connections to the Web server before the document can be displayed.

On the CD-ROM

The full example is on the CD-ROM in the file examples/baseball/players/index.xml.

Listing 9-13: **Master document for the 1998 season using external entity references for players**

```
<?xml version="1.0" standalone="no"?>
<!DOCTYPE SEASON SYSTEM "baseball.dtd" [

    <!ENTITY % players SYSTEM "players.dtd">
    %players;

]>
<SEASON>
  <YEAR>1998</YEAR>
  <LEAGUE>
    <LEAGUE_NAME>National</LEAGUE_NAME>
    <DIVISION>
       <DIVISION_NAME>East</DIVISION_NAME>
        <TEAM>
          <TEAM_CITY>Florida</TEAM_CITY>
          <TEAM_NAME>Marlins</TEAM_NAME>
        </TEAM>
        <TEAM>
          <TEAM_CITY>Montreal</TEAM_CITY>
          <TEAM_NAME>Expos</TEAM_NAME>
```

Continued

Listing 9-13 *(continued)*

```
      </TEAM>
      <TEAM>
        <TEAM_CITY>New York</TEAM_CITY>
        <TEAM_NAME>Mets</TEAM_NAME>
          &RigoBeltran;
          &DennisCook;
          &SteveDecker;
          &JohnFranco;
          &MattFranco;
          &ButchHuskey;
          &BobbyJones;
          &MikeKinkade;
          &HideoNomo;
          &VanceWilson;
      </TEAM>
      <TEAM>
        <TEAM_CITY>Philadelphia</TEAM_CITY>
        <TEAM_NAME>Phillies</TEAM_NAME>
      </TEAM>
    </DIVISION>
    <DIVISION>
      <DIVISION_NAME>Central</DIVISION_NAME>
      <TEAM>
        <TEAM_CITY>Chicago</TEAM_CITY>
        <TEAM_NAME>Cubs</TEAM_NAME>
      </TEAM>
    </DIVISION>
    <DIVISION>
      <DIVISION_NAME>West</DIVISION_NAME>
      <TEAM>
        <TEAM_CITY>Arizona</TEAM_CITY>
        <TEAM_NAME>Diamondbacks</TEAM_NAME>
      </TEAM>
    </DIVISION>
  </LEAGUE>
  <LEAGUE>
    <LEAGUE_NAME>American</LEAGUE_NAME>
    <DIVISION>
      <DIVISION_NAME>East</DIVISION_NAME>
      <TEAM>
        <TEAM_CITY>Baltimore</TEAM_CITY>
        <TEAM_NAME>Orioles</TEAM_NAME>
      </TEAM>
    </DIVISION>
    <DIVISION>
      <DIVISION_NAME>Central</DIVISION_NAME>
      <TEAM>
        <TEAM_CITY>Chicago</TEAM_CITY>
```

```
        <TEAM_NAME>White Sox</TEAM_NAME>
        &JeffAbbott;
        &MikeCameron;
        &MikeCaruso;
        &LarryCasian;
        &TomFordham;
        &MarkJohnson;
        &RobertMachado;
        &JimParque;
        &ToddRizzo;
      </TEAM>
    </DIVISION>
    <DIVISION>
      <DIVISION_NAME>West</DIVISION_NAME>
      <TEAM>
        <TEAM_CITY>Anaheim</TEAM_CITY>
        <TEAM_NAME>Angels</TEAM_NAME>
      </TEAM>
    </DIVISION>
  </LEAGUE>
</SEASON>
```

You do have some flexibility in which levels you choose for your master document and embedded data. For instance, one alternative to the structure used by Listing 9-12 places the teams and all their players in individual documents, then combines those team files into a season with external entities as shown in Listing 9-14. This has the advantage of using a smaller number of XML files of more even sizes that places less load on the Web server and would download and display more quickly. To be honest, however, the intrinsic advantage of one approach or the other is minimal. Feel free to use whichever one more closely matches the organization of your data, or simply whichever one you feel more comfortable with.

Listing 9-14: **The 1998 season using external entity references for teams**

```
<?xml version="1.0" standalone="no"?>
<!DOCTYPE SEASON SYSTEM "baseball.dtd" [

  <!ENTITY angels SYSTEM "angels.xml">
  <!ENTITY astros SYSTEM "astros.xml">
  <!ENTITY athletics SYSTEM "athletics.xml">
  <!ENTITY bluejays SYSTEM "bluejays.xml">
  <!ENTITY braves SYSTEM "braves.xml">
  <!ENTITY brewers SYSTEM "brewers.xml">
  <!ENTITY cubs SYSTEM "cubs.xml">
```

Continued

Listing 9-14 *(continued)*

```
<!ENTITY devilrays SYSTEM "devilrays.xml">
<!ENTITY diamondbacks SYSTEM "diamondbacks.xml">
<!ENTITY dodgers SYSTEM "dodgers.xml">
<!ENTITY expos SYSTEM "expos.xml">
<!ENTITY giants SYSTEM "giants.xml">
<!ENTITY indians SYSTEM "indians.xml">
<!ENTITY mariners SYSTEM "mariners.xml">
<!ENTITY marlins SYSTEM "marlins.xml">
<!ENTITY mets SYSTEM "mets.xml">
<!ENTITY orioles SYSTEM "orioles.xml">
<!ENTITY padres SYSTEM "padres.xml">
<!ENTITY phillies SYSTEM "phillies.xml">
<!ENTITY pirates SYSTEM "pirates.xml">
<!ENTITY rangers SYSTEM "rangers.xml">
<!ENTITY redsox SYSTEM "red sox.xml">
<!ENTITY reds SYSTEM "reds.xml">
<!ENTITY rockies SYSTEM "rockies.xml">
<!ENTITY royals SYSTEM "royals.xml">
<!ENTITY tigers SYSTEM "tigers.xml">
<!ENTITY twins SYSTEM "twins.xml">
<!ENTITY whitesox SYSTEM "whitesox.xml">
<!ENTITY yankees SYSTEM "yankees.xml">

]>
<SEASON>
  <YEAR>1998</YEAR>
  <LEAGUE>
    <LEAGUE_NAME>National</LEAGUE_NAME>
    <DIVISION>
       <DIVISION_NAME>East</DIVISION_NAME>
       &marlins;
       &braves;
       &expos;
       &mets;
       &phillies;
    </DIVISION>
    <DIVISION>
       <DIVISION_NAME>Central</DIVISION_NAME>
       &cubs;
       &reds;
       &astros;
       &brewers;
       &pirates;
    </DIVISION>
    <DIVISION>
       <DIVISION_NAME>West</DIVISION_NAME>
       &diamondbacks;
       &rockies;
       &dodgers;
       &padres;
       &giants;
```

```
      </DIVISION>
    </LEAGUE>
    <LEAGUE>
      <LEAGUE_NAME>American</LEAGUE_NAME>
      <DIVISION>
        <DIVISION_NAME>East</DIVISION_NAME>
        &orioles;
        &redsox;
        &yankees;
        &devilrays;
        &bluejays
      </DIVISION>
      <DIVISION>
        <DIVISION_NAME>Central</DIVISION_NAME>
        &whitesox;
        &indians;
        &tigers;
        &royals;
        &twins;
      </DIVISION>
      <DIVISION>
        <DIVISION_NAME>West</DIVISION_NAME>
        &angels;
        &athletics;
        &mariners;
        &rangers;
      </DIVISION>
    </LEAGUE>
  </SEASON>
```

A final, less likely, alternative is to actually build teams from external player entities into separate files and then combine those team files into the divisions, leagues, and seasons. The master document can define the entity references used in the child team documents. However, in this case the team documents are not usable on their own because the entity references are not defined until they're aggregated into the master document.

It's truly unfortunate that only the top-level document can be attached to a DTD. This somewhat limits the utility of external parsed entities. However, when you learn about XLinks and XPointers, you'll see some other ways to build large, compound documents out of small parts. However, those techniques are not part of the core XML standard and not necessarily supported by any validating XML processor and Web browser like the techniques of this chapter.

Cross-Reference

Chapter 16, *XLinks*, covers XLinks and Chapter 17, *XPointers*, discusses XPointers.

Entities and DTDs in Well-Formed Documents

Part I of this book explored well-formed XML documents without DTDs. And Part II has been exploring documents that have DTDs and adhere to the constraints in the DTD, that is valid documents. But there is a third level of conformance to the XML standard: documents that have DTDs and are well-formed but aren't valid, either because the DTD is incomplete or because the document doesn't fit the DTD's constraints. This is the least common of the three types.

However, not all documents need to be valid. Sometimes it suffices for an XML document to be merely well-formed. DTDs also have a place in well-formed XML documents (though they aren't required as they are for valid documents). And some non-validating XML processors can take advantage of information in a DTD without requiring perfect conformance to it. We explore that option in this section.

If a well-formed but invalid XML document does have a DTD, that DTD must have the same general form as explored in previous chapters. That is, it begins with a document type declaration and may contain ELEMENT, ATTLIST, and ENTITY declarations. Such a document differs from a valid document in that the processor only considers the ENTITY declarations.

Internal Entities

The primary advantage of using a DTD in invalid well-formed XML documents is that you may use internal general entity references other than the five pre-defined references >, <, ", ', and &. You simply declare the entities you want as normal; then use them in your document.

For example, to repeat the earlier example, suppose you want the entity reference &ERH; to be replaced by the string "Elliotte Rusty Harold" (OK, suppose *I* want the entity reference &ERH; to be replaced by the string "Elliotte Rusty Harold") but you don't want to write a complete DTD for your document. Simply declare the ERH entity reference in a DTD, as Listing 9-15 demonstrates. This document is only well-formed, not valid, but perfectly acceptable if you don't require validity.

Listing 9-15: The ERH entity reference in a DTD yields a well-formed yet invalid document

```
<?xml version="1.0" standalone="yes"?>
<!DOCTYPE DOCUMENT [
    <!ENTITY ERH "Elliotte Rusty Harold">
]>
<DOCUMENT>
  <TITLE>&ERH;</TITLE>
```

```
<SIGNATURE>
  <COPYRIGHT>1999 &ERH;</COPYRIGHT>
  <EMAIL>elharo@metalab.unc.edu</EMAIL>
  <LAST_MODIFIED>March 10, 1999</LAST_MODIFIED>
</SIGNATURE>
</DOCUMENT>
```

The document type declaration in Listing 9-15 is very sparse. Aside from defining the ERH entity reference, it simply says that the root element is DOCUMENT. However, well-formedness doesn't even require the document to adhere to that one small constraint. For example, Listing 9-16 displays another document that uses a PAGE root element even though the document type declaration still says the root element should be DOCUMENT. This document is still well-formed, but it's not valid-then again neither was Listing 9-15.

Listing 9-16: **A well-formed but invalid document**

```
<?xml version="1.0" standalone="yes"?>
<!DOCTYPE DOCUMENT [
  <!ENTITY ERH "Elliotte Rusty Harold">
]>
<PAGE>
  <TITLE>&ERH;</TITLE>
  <SIGNATURE>
    <COPYRIGHT>1999 &ERH;</COPYRIGHT>
    <EMAIL>elharo@metalab.unc.edu</EMAIL>
    <LAST_MODIFIED>March 10, 1999</LAST_MODIFIED>
  </SIGNATURE>
</PAGE>
```

It's possible that the DTD may contain other <!ELEMENT>, <!ATTLIST>, and <!NOTATION> declarations as well. All of these are ignored by a non-validating processor. Only <!ENTITY> declarations are considered. The DTD of Listing 9-17 actively contradicts its contents. For instance, the ADDRESS element is supposed to be empty according to the DTD but in fact contains several undeclared child elements. Furthermore, each ADDRESS element is required to have OCCUPANT, STREET, CITY, and ZIP attributes but these are nowhere to be found. The root element is supposed to be DOCUMENT, not ADDRESS. The DOCUMENT element should contain a TITLE and a SIGNATURE, neither of which is declared in the DTD. This document is still well-formed, though very, very invalid.

Listing 9-17: **An extremely invalid, though still well-formed, document**

```
<?xml version="1.0" standalone="yes"?>
<!DOCTYPE DOCUMENT [
   <!ENTITY ERH "Elliotte Rusty Harold">
   <!ELEMENT ADDRESS EMPTY>
   <!ELEMENT DOCUMENT (TITLE, ADDRESS+, SIGNATURE)>
   <!ATTLIST ADDRESS OCCUPANT   CDATA #REQUIRED>
   <!ATTLIST ADDRESS DEPARTMENT CDATA #IMPLIED>
   <!ATTLIST ADDRESS COMPANY    CDATA #IMPLIED>
   <!ATTLIST ADDRESS STREET     CDATA #REQUIRED>
   <!ATTLIST ADDRESS CITY       CDATA #REQUIRED>
   <!ATTLIST ADDRESS ZIP        CDATA #REQUIRED>
]>
<ADDRESS>
  <OCCUPANT>Elliotte Rusty Harold</OCCUPANT>
  <DEPARTMENT>Computer Science</DEPARTMENT>
  <COMPANY>Polytechnic University</COMPANY>
  <STREET>5 Metrotech Center</STREET>
  <CITY>Brooklyn</CITY>
  <STATE>NY</STATE>
  <ZIP>11201</ZIP>
</ADDRESS>
```

External Entities

Non-validating processors may resolve external entity references, but they are not required to. Expat, the open source XML parser used by Mozilla, for instance, does not resolve external entity references. Most others including the one used in Internet Explorer 5.0 do. Non-validating processors may only resolve parsed entities, however. They may not resolve unparsed external entities containing non-XML data such as images or sounds.

External entities are particularly useful for storing boilerplate text. For instance, HTML predefines entity references for the non-ASCII ISO Latin-1 letters that are a little easier to remember than the numeric character entity references. For instance, å is ˚, þ is þ, ý is Ý, and so on. Listing 9-18 is the official ISO DTD that defines these references (with slight modifications to the comments and whitespace to make it fit neatly on the page).

Listing 9-18: **A DTD for the non-ASCII ISO-Latin-1 characters**

```
<!— (C) International Organization for Standardization 1986
    Permission to copy in any form is granted for use with
    conforming SGML systems and applications as defined in
    ISO 8879, provided this notice is included in all copies.
—>
<!— Character entity set. Typical invocation:
    <!ENTITY % ISOlat1 PUBLIC
      "ISO 8879-1986//ENTITIES Added Latin 1//EN//XML">
    %ISOlat1;
—>
<!— This version of the entity set can be used with any SGML
    document which uses ISO 8859-1 or ISO 10646 as its
    document character set. This includes XML documents and
    ISO HTML documents.

    Version: 1998-10-01
—>

<!ENTITY Agrave "&#192;" ><!— capital A, grave accent —>
<!ENTITY Aacute "&#193; "><!— capital A, acute accent —>
<!ENTITY Acirc  "&#194; "><!— capital A, circumflex accent —>
<!ENTITY Atilde "&#195; "><!— capital A, tilde —>
<!ENTITY Auml   "&#196; "><!— capital A, dieresis umlaut —>
<!ENTITY Aring  "&#197; "><!— capital A, ring —>
<!ENTITY AElig  "&#198; "><!— capital AE diphthong ligature—>
<!ENTITY Ccedil "&#199; "><!— capital C, cedilla —>
<!ENTITY Egrave "&#200; "><!— capital E, grave accent —>
<!ENTITY Eacute "&#201; "><!— capital E, acute accent —>
<!ENTITY Ecirc  "&#202; "><!— capital E, circumflex accent —>
<!ENTITY Euml   "&#203; "><!— capital E, dieresis umlaut —>
<!ENTITY Igrave "&#204; "><!— capital I, grave accent —>
<!ENTITY Iacute "&#205; "><!— capital I, acute accent —>
<!ENTITY Icirc  "&#206;" ><!— capital I, circumflex accent —>
<!ENTITY Iuml   "&#207;" ><!— capital I, dieresis umlaut —>
<!ENTITY ETH    "&#208;" ><!— capital Eth, Icelandic —>
<!ENTITY Ntilde "&#209;" ><!— capital N, tilde —>
<!ENTITY Ograve "&#210;" ><!— capital O, grave accent —>
<!ENTITY Oacute "&#211;" ><!— capital O, acute accent —>
<!ENTITY Ocirc  "&#212;" ><!— capital O, circumflex accent —>
<!ENTITY Otilde "&#213;" ><!— capital O, tilde —>
<!ENTITY Ouml   "&#214;"><!—capital O dieresis/umlaut mark—>
<!ENTITY Oslash "&#216;" ><!— capital O, slash —>
<!ENTITY Ugrave "&#217;" ><!— capital U, grave accent —>
<!ENTITY Uacute "&#218;" ><!— capital U, acute accent —>
<!ENTITY Ucirc  "&#219;" ><!— capital U circumflex accent —>
<!ENTITY Uuml   "&#220;" ><!— capital U dieresis umlaut —>
<!ENTITY Yacute "&#221;" ><!— capital Y, acute accent —>
<!ENTITY THORN  "&#222;" ><!— capital THORN, Icelandic —>
```

Continued

Listing 9-18 *(continued)*

```
<!ENTITY szlig   "&#223;" ><!- small sharp s, (sz ligature) ->
<!ENTITY agrave  "&#224;" ><!- small a, grave accent ->
<!ENTITY aacute  "&#225;" ><!- small a, acute accent ->
<!ENTITY acirc   "&#226;" ><!- small a, circumflex accent ->
<!ENTITY atilde  "&#227;" ><!- small a, tilde ->
<!ENTITY auml    "&#228;" ><!- small a dieresis/umlaut mark->
<!ENTITY aring   "&#229;" ><!- small a, ring ->
<!ENTITY aelig   "&#230;" ><!- small ae, diphthong ligature ->
<!ENTITY ccedil  "&#231;" ><!- small c, cedilla ->
<!ENTITY egrave  "&#232;" ><!- small e, grave accent ->
<!ENTITY eacute  "&#233;" ><!- small e, acute accent ->
<!ENTITY ecirc   "&#234;" ><!- small e, circumflex accent ->
<!ENTITY euml    "&#235;" ><!- small e, dieresis or umlaut ->
<!ENTITY igrave  "&#236;" ><!- small i, grave accent ->
<!ENTITY iacute  "&#237;" ><!- small i, acute accent ->
<!ENTITY icirc   "&#238;" ><!- small i, circumflex accent ->
<!ENTITY iuml    "&#239;" ><!- small i, dieresis or umlaut ->
<!ENTITY eth     "&#240;" ><!- small eth, Icelandic ->
<!ENTITY ntilde  "&#241;" ><!- small n, tilde ->
<!ENTITY ograve  "&#242;" ><!- small o, grave accent ->
<!ENTITY oacute  "&#243;" ><!- small o, acute accent ->
<!ENTITY ocirc   "&#244;" ><!- small o, circumflex accent ->
<!ENTITY otilde  "&#245;" ><!- small o, tilde ->
<!ENTITY ouml    "&#246;" ><!- small o, dieresis or umlaut->
<!ENTITY oslash  "&#248;" ><!- small o, slash ->
<!ENTITY ugrave  "&#249;" ><!- small u, grave accent ->
<!ENTITY uacute  "&#250;" ><!- small u, acute accent ->
<!ENTITY ucirc   "&#251;" ><!- small u, circumflex accent ->
<!ENTITY uuml    "&#252;" ><!- small u, dieresis or umlaut ->
<!ENTITY yacute  "&#253;" ><!- small y, acute accent ->
<!ENTITY thorn   "&#254;" ><!- small thorn, Icelandic ->
<!ENTITY yuml    "&#255;" ><!- small y, dieresis or umlaut ->
```

Rather than including Listing 9-18 in the internal subset of your document's DTD, you can simply use a parameter entity reference to link to it, then use the general entity references in your document.

For example, suppose you wanted to put the medieval document Hildebrandslied on the Web in well-formed XML. However since this manuscript is written in German, it uses the non-ASCII characters ê, î, ô, û, and æ.

For maximum portability you can type the poem in ASCII while encoding these letters as the entity references ê, î, ô, û, and æ respectively. However, even if you don't require a valid finished document, you still need a DTD to declare these and any other entity references you may use. The simplest way to get the extra characters you need, is merely to refer to the external DTD of Listing 9-18. Listing 9-19 demonstrates

---

Listing 9-19: A well-formed, invalid document that uses entity references for non ASCII ISO-Latin-1 characters

```
<?xml version="1.0" standalone="no"?>
<!DOCTYPE DOCUMENT [
  <!ENTITY % ISOlat1
     PUBLIC "ISO 8879-1986//ENTITIES Added Latin 1//EN//XML"
            "http://www.schema.net/public-text/ISOlat1.pen">
     %ISOlat1;
]>
<DOCUMENT>
  <TITLE>Das Hildebrandslied, circa 775 C.E. </TITLE>
  <LINE>Ik gih&ocirc;rta dhat seggen,</LINE>
  <LINE>dhat sih urh&ecirc;ttun &aelig;non muot&icirc;n,</LINE>
  <LINE>Hiltibrant enti Hadhubrant untar heriun tu&ecirc;m.
  </LINE>
  <LINE>sunufatarungo: iro saro rihtun,</LINE>
  <COMMENT>I'll spare you the next 61 lines</COMMENT>
</DOCUMENT>
```

The document part consists of well-formed XML using tags made up on the spot. These are not declared in the DTD and do not need to be for a merely well-formed document. However the entity references do need to be declared in the DTD, either in the internal or external subset. Listing 9-19 declares them in the external subset by using the external parameter entity reference %ISOlat1 to load the entities declared in Listing 9-18.

DTDs are also useful for storing common boilerplate text used across a Web site of well- formed XML documents, much as they are for valid XML documents. The procedure is a little easier when working with merely well formed XML documents, because there's no chance that the boilerplate you insert will not meet the constraints of the parent document DTD.

First, place the boilerplate in a file without a DTD, as shown in Listing 9-20.

Listing 9-20: **Signature boilerplate without a DTD**

```
<?xml version="1.0"?>
<SIGNATURE>
  <COPYRIGHT>1999 Elliotte Rusty Harold</COPYRIGHT>
  <EMAIL>elharo@metalab.unc.edu</EMAIL>
</SIGNATURE>
```

Next, write a small DTD as in Listing 9-21 that defines an entity reference for the file in Listing 9-20. Here, I assume that you can locate Listing 9-20 in the file signature.xml in the boilerplate directory at the root level of the Web server, and that you can find Listing 9-21 in the file signature.dtd in the dtds directory at the root level of the Web server.

Listing 9-21: **Signature DTD that defines an entity reference**

```
<!ENTITY SIGNATURE SYSTEM "/boilerplate/signature.xml">
```

Now, you can import signature.dtd in any document, then use the general entity reference &SIGNATURE; to embed the contents of signature.xml in your file. Listing 9-22 demonstrates.

Listing 9-22: **A file that uses &SIGNATURE;**

```
<?xml version="1.0" standalone="yes"?>
<!DOCTYPE DOCUMENT [
  <!ENTITY % SIG SYSTEM "/dtds/signature.dtd">
  %SIG;
]>
<DOCUMENT>
  <TITLE>A Very Boring Document</TITLE>
  &SIGNATURE;
</DOCUMENT>
```

This may seem like one more level of indirection than you really need. For instance, Listing 9-23 defines the &SIGNATURE; entity reference directly in its internal DTD subset, and indeed this does work. However, the additional level of indirection provides protection against a reorganization of a Web site since you cannot only change the signature used on all your pages by editing one file. You can also change the location of the signature used by all your Web pages by editing one file. On the other hand, the more direct approach of Listing 9-22 more easily allows for different signatures on different pages.

Listing 9-23: A file that uses &SIGNATURE; with one less level of indirection

```
<?xml version="1.0" standalone="yes"?>
<!DOCTYPE DOCUMENT [
  <!ENTITY SIGNATURE SYSTEM "/boilerplate/signature.xml">
]>
<DOCUMENT>
  <TITLE>A Very Boring Document</TITLE>
  &SIGNATURE;
</DOCUMENT>
```

Summary

In this chapter, you discovered that XML documents are built from both internal and external entities. . In particular, you learned the following:

✦ Entities are the physical storage units from which the document is assembled.

✦ An entity holds content: well-formed XML, other forms of text, or binary data.

✦ Internal entities are defined completely within the document and external entities draw their content from another resource located via a URL.

✦ General entity references have the form &name; and are used in a document's content.

✦ Internal general entity references are replaced by an entity value given in the entity declaration.

✦ External general entity references are replaced by the data at a URL specified in the entity declaration after the SYSTEM keyword.

✦ Internal parameter entity references have the form %name; and are used exclusively in DTDs.

✦ You can merge different DTDs with external parameter entity references.

✦ External entity references enable you to build large, compound documents out of small parts.

✦ There is a third level of conformance to the XML standard: well-formed, but not valid. This is either because the DTD is incomplete or because the document doesn't meet the DTD's constraints.

When a document uses attributes, the attributes must also be declared in the DTD. The next chapter discusses how to declare attributes in DTDs, and how you can thereby attach constraints to the attribute values.

✦   ✦   ✦

Attribute Declarations in DTDs

Some XML elements have attributes. Attributes contain information intended for the application. Attributes are intended for extra information associated with an element (like an ID number) used only by programs that read and write the file, and not for the content of the element that's read and written by humans. In this chapter, you will learn about the various attribute types and how to declare attributes in DTDs.

What Is an Attribute?

As first discussed in Chapter 3, start tags and empty tags may contain attributes-name-value pairs separated by an equals sign (=). For example,

```
<GREETING LANGUAGE="English">
   Hello XML!
   <MOVIE SOURCE="WavingHand.mov"/>
</GREETING>
```

In the preceding example, the GREETING element has a LANGUAGE attribute, which has the value English. The MOVIE element has a SOURCE attribute, which has the value WavingHand.mov. The GREETING element's content is Hello XML!. The language in which the content is written is useful information about the content. The language, however, is not itself part of the content.

Similarly, the MOVIE element's content is the binary data stored in the file WavingHand.mov. The name of the file is not the content, although the name tells you where the content can be found. Once again, the attribute contains information about the content of the element, rather than the content itself.

Elements can possess more than one attribute. For example:

```
<RECTANGLE WIDTH="30" HEIGHT="45"/>
<SCRIPT LANGUAGE="javascript" ENCODING="8859_1">...</SCRIPT>
```

In this example, the LANGUAGE attribute of the SCRIPT element has the value javascript. The ENCODING attribute of the SCRIPT element has the value 8859_1. The WIDTH attribute of the RECTANGLE element has the value 30. The HEIGHT attribute of the RECT element has the value 45. These values are all strings, not numbers.

End tags cannot possess attributes. The following example is illegal:

```
<SCRIPT>...</SCRIPT LANGUAGE="javascript" ENCODING="8859_1">
```

Declaring Attributes in DTDs

Like elements and entities, the attributes used in a document must be declared in the DTD for the document to be valid. The <!ATTLIST> tag declares attributes. <!ATTLIST> has the following form:

```
<!ATTLIST Element_name Attribute_name Type Default_value>
```

Element_name is the name of the element possessing this attribute. *Attribute_name* is the name of the attribute. *Type* is the kind of attribute-one of the ten valid types listed in Table 10-1. The most general type is CDATA. Finally, *Default_value* is the value the attribute takes on if no value is specified for the attribute.

For example, consider the following element:

```
<GREETING LANGUAGE="Spanish">
  Hola!
</GREETING>
```

This element might be declared as follows in the DTD:

```
<!ELEMENT GREETING (#PCDATA)>
<!ATTLIST GREETING LANGUAGE CDATA "English">
```

The <!ELEMENT> tag simply says that a greeting element contains parsed character data. That's nothing new. The <!ATTLIST> tag says that GREETING elements have an attribute with the name LANGUAGE whose value has the type CDATA—which is essentially the same as #PCDATA for element content. If you encounter a GREETING tag without a LANGUAGE attribute, the value English is used by default.

Table 10-1
Attribute Types

Type	Meaning
CDATA	Character data — text that is not markup
Enumerated	A list of possible values from which exactly one will be chosen
ID	A unique name not shared by any other ID type attribute in the document
IDREF	The value of an ID type attribute of an element in the document
IDREFS	Multiple IDs of elements separated by whitespace
ENTITY	The name of an entity declared in the DTD
ENTITIES	The names of multiple entities declared in the DTD, separated by whitespace
NMTOKEN	An XML name
NOTATION	The name of a notation declared in the DTD
NMTOKENS	Multiple XML names separated by whitespace

The attribute list is declared separately from the tag itself. The name of the element to which the attribute belongs is included in the `<!ATTLIST>` tag. This attribute declaration applies only to that element, which is GREETING in the preceding example. If other elements also have LANGUAGE attributes, they require separate `<!ATTLIST>` declarations.

As with most declarations, the exact order in which attribute declarations appear is not important. They can come before or after the element declaration with which they're associated. In fact, you can even declare an attribute more than once (though I don't recommend this practice), in which case the first such declaration takes precedence.

You can even declare attributes for tags that don't exist, although this is uncommon. Perhaps you could declare these nonexistent attributes as part of the initial editing of the DTD, with a plan to return later and declare the elements.

Declaring Multiple Attributes

Elements often have multiple attributes. HTML's IMG element can have HEIGHT, WIDTH, ALT, BORDER, ALIGN, and several other attributes. In fact, most HTML tags can have multiple attributes. XML tags can also have multiple attributes. For instance, a RECTANGLE element naturally needs both a LENGTH and a WIDTH.

```
<RECTANGLE LENGTH="70px" WIDTH="85px"/>
```

You can declare these attributes in several attribute declarations, with one declaration for each attribute. For example:

```
<!ELEMENT RECTANGLE EMPTY>
<!ATTLIST RECTANGLE LENGTH CDATA "0px">
<!ATTLIST RECTANGLE WIDTH  CDATA "0px">
```

The preceding example says that RECTANGLE elements possess LENGTH and WIDTH attributes, each of which has the default value 0px.

You can combine the two <!ATTLIST> tags into a single declaration like this:

```
<!ATTLIST RECTANGLE LENGTH CDATA "0px"
                    WIDTH  CDATA "0px">
```

This single declaration declares both the LENGTH and WIDTH attributes, each with type CDATA and each with a default value of 0px. You can also use this syntax when the attributes have different types or defaults, as shown below:

```
<!ATTLIST RECTANGLE LENGTH CDATA "15px"
                    WIDTH  CDATA "34pt">
```

Note   Personally, I'm not very fond of this style. It seems excessively confusing and relies too much on proper placement of extra whitespace for legibility (though the whitespace is unimportant to the actual meaning of the tag). You will certainly encounter this style in DTDs written by other people, however, so you need to understand it.

Specifying Default Values for Attributes

Instead of specifying an explicit default attribute value like 0px, an attribute declaration can require the author to provide a value, allow the value to be omitted completely, or even always use the default value. These requirements are specified with the three keywords #REQUIRED, #IMPLIED, and #FIXED, respectively.

#REQUIRED

You may not always have a good option for a default value. For example, when writing a DTD for use on your intranet, you may want to require that all documents have at least one empty `<AUTHOR/>` tag. This tag is not normally rendered, but it can identify the person who created the document. This tag can have NAME, EMAIL, and EXTENSION attributes so the author may be contacted. For example:

```
<AUTHOR NAME="Elliotte Rusty Harold"
  EMAIL="elharo@metalab.unc.edu" EXTENSION="3459"/>
```

Instead of providing default values for these attributes, suppose you want to force anyone posting a document on the intranet to identify themselves. While XML can't prevent someone from attributing authorship to "Luke Skywalker," it can at least require that authorship is attributed to someone by using #REQUIRED as the default value. For example:

```
<!ELEMENT AUTHOR EMPTY>
<!ATTLIST AUTHOR NAME CDATA #REQUIRED>
<!ATTLIST AUTHOR EMAIL CDATA #REQUIRED>
<!ATTLIST AUTHOR EXTENSION CDATA #REQUIRED>
```

If the parser encounters an `<AUTHOR/>` tag that does not include one or more of these attributes, it returns an error.

You might also want to use #REQUIRED to force authors to give their IMG elements WIDTH, HEIGHT, and ALT attributes. For example:

```
<!ELEMENT IMG EMPTY>
<!ATTLIST IMG ALT    CDATA #REQUIRED>
<!ATTLIST IMG WIDTH  CDATA #REQUIRED>
<!ATTLIST IMG HEIGHT CDATA #REQUIRED>
```

Any attempt to omit these attributes (as all too many Web pages do) produces an invalid document. The XML processor notices the error and informs the author of the missing attributes.

#IMPLIED

Sometimes you may not have a good option for a default value, but you do not want to require the author of the document to include a value, either. For example, suppose some of the people posting documents to your intranet are offsite freelancers who have email addresses but lack phone extensions. Therefore, you don't want to require them to include an extension attribute in their `<AUTHOR/>` tags. For example:

```
<AUTHOR NAME="Elliotte Rusty Harold"
        EMAIL="elharo@metalab.unc.edu" />
```

You still don't want to provide a default value for the extension, but you do want to enable authors to include such an attribute. In this case, use #IMPLIED as the default value like this:

```
<!ELEMENT AUTHOR EMPTY>
<!ATTLIST AUTHOR NAME      CDATA #REQUIRED>
<!ATTLIST AUTHOR EMAIL     CDATA #REQUIRED>
<!ATTLIST AUTHOR EXTENSION CDATA #IMPLIED>
```

If the XML parser encounters an <AUTHOR/> tag without an EXTENSION attribute, it informs the XML application that no value is available. The application can act on this notification as it chooses. For example, if the application is feeding elements into a SQL database where the attributes are mapped to fields, the application would probably insert a null into the corresponding database field.

#FIXED

Finally, you may want to provide a default value for the attribute without allowing the author to change it. For example, you may wish to specify an identical COMPANY attribute of the AUTHOR element for anyone posting documents to your intranet like this:

```
<AUTHOR NAME="Elliotte Rusty Harold" COMPANY="TIC"
  EMAIL="elharo@metalab.unc.edu" EXTENSION="3459"/>
```

You can require that everyone use this value of the company by specifying the default value as #FIXED, followed by the actual default. For example:

```
<!ELEMENT AUTHOR EMPTY>
<!ATTLIST AUTHOR NAME      CDATA #REQUIRED>
<!ATTLIST AUTHOR EMAIL     CDATA #REQUIRED>
<!ATTLIST AUTHOR EXTENSION CDATA #IMPLIED>
<!ATTLIST AUTHOR COMPANY   CDATA #FIXED "TIC">
```

Document authors are not required to actually include the fixed attribute in their tags. If they don't include the fixed attribute, the default value will be used. If they do include the fixed attribute, however, they must use an identical value. Otherwise, the parser will return an error.

Attribute Types

All preceding examples have CDATA type attributes. This is the most general type, but there are nine other types permitted for attributes. Altogether the ten types are:

- ✦ CDATA
- ✦ **Enumerated**
- ✦ NMTOKEN
- ✦ NMTOKENS
- ✦ ID
- ✦ IDREF
- ✦ IDREFS
- ✦ ENTITY
- ✦ ENTITIES
- ✦ NOTATION

Nine of the preceding attributes are constants used in the type field, while Enumerated is a special type that indicates the attribute must take its value from a list of possible values. Let's investigate each type in depth.

The CDATA Attribute Type

CDATA, the most general attribute type, means the attribute value may be any string of text not containing a less-than sign (<) or quotation marks ("). These characters may be inserted using the usual entity references (<, and ") or by their Unicode values using character references. Furthermore, all raw ampersands (&)-that is ampersands that do not begin a character or entity reference-must also be escaped as &.

In fact, even if the value itself contains double quotes, they do not have to be escaped. Instead, you may use single quotes to delimit the attributes, as in the following example:

```
<RECTANGLE LENGTH='7"' WIDTH='8.5"'/>
```

If the attribute value contains single and double quotes, the one not used to delimit the value must be replaced with the entity references ' (apostrophe) and " (double quote). For example:

```
<RECTANGLE LENGTH='8&apos;7"' WIDTH="10'6&quot;"/>
```

The Enumerated Attribute Type

The enumerated type is not an XML keyword, but a list of possible values for the attribute, separated by vertical bars. Each value must be a valid XML name. The document author can choose any one member of the list as the value of the attribute. The default value must be one of the values in the list.

For example, suppose you want an element to be visible or invisible. You may want the element to have a VISIBLE attribute, which can only have the values TRUE or FALSE. If that element is the simple P element, then the <!ATTLIST> declaration would look as follows:

```
<!ATTLIST P VISIBLE (TRUE | FALSE) "TRUE">
```

The preceding declaration says that a P element may or may not have a VISIBLE attribute. If it does have a VISIBLE attribute, the value of that attribute must be either TRUE or FALSE. If it does not have such an attribute, the value TRUE is assumed. For example,

```
<P VISIBLE="FALSE">You can't see me! Nyah! Nyah!</P>
<P VISIBLE="TRUE">You can see me.</P>
<P>You can see me too.</P>
```

By itself, this declaration is not a magic incantation that enables you to hide text. It still relies on the application to understand that it shouldn't display invisible elements. Whether the element is shown or hidden would probably be set through a style sheet rule applied to elements with VISIBLE attributes. For example,

```
<xsl:template match="P[@VISIBLE='FALSE']">
</xsl:template>

<xsl:template match="P[@VISIBLE='TRUE']">
  <xsl:apply-templates/>
</xsl:template>
```

The NMTOKEN Attribute Type

The NMTOKEN attribute type restricts the value of the attribute to a valid XML name. As discussed in Chapter 6, XML names must begin with a letter or an underscore (_). Subsequent characters in the name may include letters, digits, underscores, hyphens, and periods. They may not include whitespace. (The underscore often substitutes for whitespace.) Technically, names may contain colons, but you shouldn't use this character because it's reserved for use with namespaces.

The NMTOKEN attribute type proves useful when you're using a programming language to manipulate the XML data. It's not a coincidence that—except for allowing colons—the preceding rules match the rules for identifiers in Java, JavaScript, and many other programming languages. For example, you could use NMTOKEN to associate a particular Java class with an element. Then, you could use Java's reflection API to pass the data to a particular method in a particular class.

The NMTOKEN attribute type also helps when you need to pick from any large group of names that aren't specifically part of XML but meet XML's name requirements. The most significant of these requirements is the prohibition of whitespace. For example, NMTOKEN could be used for an attribute whose value had to map to an 8.3 DOS file name. On the other hand, it wouldn't work well for UNIX, Macintosh, or Windows NT file-name attributes because those names often contain whitespace.

For example, suppose you want to require a state attribute in an <ADDRESS/> tag to be a two-letter abbreviation. You cannot force this characteristic with a DTD, but you can prevent people from entering "New York" or "Puerto Rico" with the following <!ATTLIST> declaration:

```
<!ATTLIST ADDRESS STATE NMTOKEN #REQUIRED>
```

However, "California," "Nevada," and other single word states are still legal values. Of course, you could simply use an enumerated list with several dozen two-letter codes, but that approach results in more work than most people want to expend. For that matter, do you even know the two-letter codes for all 50 U.S. states, all the territories and possessions, all foreign military postings, and all Canadian provinces? On the other hand, if you define this list once in a parameter entity reference in a DTD file, you can reuse the file many times over.

The NMTOKENS Attribute Type

The NMTOKENS attribute type is a rare plural form of NMTOKEN. It enables the value of the attribute to consist of multiple XML names, separated from each other by whitespace. Generally, you can use NMTOKENS for the same reasons as NMTOKEN, but only when multiple names are required.

For example, if you want to require multiple two-letter state codes for a state's attribute, you can use the following example:

```
<!ATTLIST ADDRESS STATES NMTOKENS #REQUIRED>
```

Then, you could have an address tag as follows:

```
<ADDRESS STATES="MI NY LA CA">
```

Unfortunately, if you apply this technique, you're no longer ruling out states like New York because each individual part of the state name qualifies as an NMTOKEN, as shown below:

```
<ADDRESS STATES="MI New York LA CA">
```

The ID Attribute Type

An ID type attribute uniquely identifies the element in the document. Authoring tools and other applications commonly use ID to help enumerate the elements of a document without concern for their exact meaning or relationship to one another.

An attribute value of type ID must be a valid XML name-that is,it begins with a letter and is composed of alphanumeric characters and the underscore without whitespace. A particular name may not be used as an ID attribute of more than one tag. Using the same ID twice in one document causes the parser to return an error. Furthermore, each element may not have more than one attribute of type ID.

Typically, ID attributes exist solely for the convenience of programs that manipulate the data. In many cases, multiple elements can be effectively identical except for the value of an ID attribute. If you choose IDs in some predictable fashion, a program can enumerate all the different elements or all the different elements of one type in the document.

The ID type is incompatible with #FIXED. An attribute cannot be both fixed and have ID type because a #FIXED attribute can only have a single value, while each ID type attribute must have a different value. Most ID attributes use #REQUIRED, as Listing 10-1 demonstrates.

Listing 10-1: A required ID attribute type

```
<?xml version="1.0" standalone="yes"?>
<!DOCTYPE DOCUMENT [
   <!ELEMENT DOCUMENT (P*)>
   <!ELEMENT P (#PCDATA)>
   <!ATTLIST P PNUMBER ID #REQUIRED>
]>

<DOCUMENT>
  <P PNUMBER="p1">The quick brown fox</P>
  <P PNUMBER="p2">The quick brown fox</P>
</DOCUMENT>
```

The IDREF Attribute Type

The value of an attribute with the IDREF type is the ID of another element in the document. For example, Listing 10-2 shows the IDREF and ID attributes used to connect children to their parents.

Listing 10-2: family.xml

```
<?xml version="1.0" standalone="yes"?>
<!DOCTYPE DOCUMENT [
   <!ELEMENT DOCUMENT (PERSON*)>
   <!ELEMENT PERSON (#PCDATA)>
   <!ATTLIST PERSON PNUMBER ID #REQUIRED>
   <!ATTLIST PERSON FATHER IDREF #IMPLIED>
   <!ATTLIST PERSON MOTHER IDREF #IMPLIED>
]>

<DOCUMENT>
  <PERSON PNUMBER="a1">Susan</PERSON>
  <PERSON PNUMBER="a2">Jack</PERSON>
  <PERSON PNUMBER="a3" MOTHER="a1" FATHER="a2">Chelsea</PERSON>
  <PERSON PNUMBER="a4" MOTHER="a1" FATHER="a2">David</PERSON>
</DOCUMENT>
```

You generally use this uncommon but crucial type when you need to establish connections between elements that aren't reflected in the tree structure of the document. In Listing 10-2, each child is given FATHER and MOTHER attributes containing the ID attributes of its father and mother.

You cannot easily and directly use an IDREF to link parents to their children in Listing 10-2 because each parent has an indefinite number of children. As a workaround, you can group all the children of the same parents into a FAMILY element and link to the FAMILY. Even this approach falters in the face of half-siblings who share only one parent. In short, IDREF works for many-to-one relationships, but not for one-to-many relationships.

The ENTITY Attribute Type

An ENTITY type attribute enables you to link external binary data-that is, an external unparsed general entity-into the document. The value of the ENTITY attribute is the name of an unparsed general entity declared in the DTD, which links to the external data.

The classic example of an ENTITY attribute is an image. The image consists of binary data available from another URL. Provided the XML browser can support it, you may include an image in an XML document with the following declarations in your DTD:

```
<!ELEMENT IMAGE EMPTY>
<!ATTLIST IMAGE SOURCE ENTITY #REQUIRED>
<!ENTITY LOGO SYSTEM "logo.gif">
```

Then, at the desired image location in the document, insert the following IMAGE tag:

```
<IMAGE SOURCE="LOGO"/>
```

This approach is not a magic formula that all XML browsers automatically understand. It is simply one technique browsers and other applications may or may not adopt to embed non-XML data in documents.

Cross-Reference   This technique will be explored further in Chapter 11, *Embedding Non-XML Data*.

The ENTITIES Attribute Type

ENTITIES is a relatively rare plural form of ENTITY. An ENTITIES type attribute has a value part that consists of multiple unparsed entity names separated by whitespace. Each entity name refers to an external non-XML data source. One use for this approach might be a slide show that rotates different pictures, as in the following example:

```
<!ELEMENT SLIDESHOW EMPTY>
<!ATTLIST SLIDESHOW SOURCES ENTITIES #REQUIRED>
<!ENTITY PIC1 SYSTEM "cat.gif">
<!ENTITY PIC2 SYSTEM "dog.gif">
<!ENTITY PIC3 SYSTEM "cow.gif">
```

Then, at the point in the document where you want the slide show to appear, insert the following tag:

```
<SLIDESHOW SOURCES="PIC1 PIC2 PIC3">
```

Once again, this is not a universal formula that all (or even any) XML browsers automatically understand, simply one method browsers and other applications may or may not adopt to embed non-XML data in documents.

The NOTATION Attribute Type

The NOTATION attribute type specifies that an attribute's value is the name of a notation declared in the DTD. The default value of this attribute must also be the name of a notation declared in the DTD. Notations will be introduced in the next chapter. In brief, notations identify the format of non-XML data, for instance by specifying a helper application for an unparsed entity.

Cross-Reference   Chapter 11, *Embedding Non-XML Data*, covers notations.

For example, this PLAYER attribute of a SOUND element has type NOTATION, and a default value of MP-the notation signifying a particular kind of sound file:

```
<!ATTLIST SOUND PLAYER NOTATION (MP) #REQUIRED>
<!NOTATION MP SYSTEM "mplay32.exe">
```

You can also offer a choice of different notations. One use for this is to specify different helper apps for different platforms. The browser can pick the one it has available. In this case, the NOTATION keyword is followed by a set of parentheses containing the list of allowed notation names separated by vertical bars. For example:

```
<!NOTATION MP SYSTEM "mplay32.exe">
<!NOTATION ST SYSTEM "soundtool">
<!NOTATION SM SYSTEM "Sound Machine">
<!ATTLIST SOUND PLAYER NOTATION (MP | SM | ST) #REQUIRED>
```

This says that the PLAYER attribute of the SOUND element may be set to MP, ST, or SM. We'll explore this further in the next chapter.

Note   At first glance, this approach may appear inconsistent with the handling of other list attributes like ENTITIES and NMTOKENS, but these two approaches are actually quite different. ENTITIES and NMTOKENS have a list of attributes in the actual element in the document but only one value in the attribute declaration in the DTD. NOTATION only has a single value in the attribute of the actual element in the document, however. The list of possible values occurs in the attribute declaration in the DTD.

Predefined Attributes

In a way, two attributes are predefined in XML. You must declare these attributes in your DTD for each element to which they apply, but you should only use these declared attributes for their intended purposes. Such attributes are identified by a name that begins with xml:.

These two attributes are xml:space and xml:lang. The xml:space attribute describes how whitespace is treated in the element. The xml:lang attribute describes the language (and optionally, dialect and country) in which the element is written.

xml:space

In HTML, whitespace is relatively insignificant. Although the difference between one space and no space is significant, the difference between one space and two spaces, one space and a carriage return, or one space, three carriage returns, and 12 tabs is not important. For text in which whitespace is significant—computer source code, certain mainframe database reports, or the poetry of e. e. cummings, for example— you can use a PRE element to specify a monospaced font and preservation of whitespace.

XML, however, preserves whitespace by default. The XML processor passes all whitespace characters to the application unchanged. The application usually ignores the extra whitespace. However, the XML processor can tell the application that certain elements contain significant whitespace that should be preserved. The page author uses the xml:space attribute to indicate these elements to the application.

If an element contains significant whitespace, the DTD should have an <!ATTLIST> for the xml:space attribute. This attribute will have an enumerated type with the two values, default and preserve, as shown in Listing 10-3.

Listing 10-3: **Java source code with significant whitespace encoded in XML**

```
<?xml version="1.0" standalone="yes"?>
<!DOCTYPE PROGRAM [
  <!ELEMENT PROGRAM (#PCDATA)>
  <!ATTLIST PROGRAM xml:space (default|preserve) 'preserve'>
]>
<PROGRAM xml:space="preserve">public class AsciiTable {

  public static void main (String[] args) {

    for (int i = 0; i &lt; 128; i++) {
      System.out.println(i + "    " + (char) i);
    }

  }

}
</PROGRAM>
```

All whitespace is passed to the application, regardless of whether xml:space's value is default or preserve. With a value of default, however, the application does what it would normally do with extra whitespace. With a value of preserve, the application treats the extra whitespace as significant.

Note Significance depends somewhat on the eventual destination of the data. For instance, extra whitespace in Java source code is relevant to a source code editor but not to a compiler.

Children of an element for which xml:space is defined are assumed to behave similarly as their parent (either preserving or not preserving space), unless they possess an xml:space attribute with a conflicting value.

xml:lang

The xml:lang attribute identifies the language in which the element's content is written. The value of this attribute can have type CDATA, NMTOKEN, or an enumerated list. Ideally, each of these attributes values should be one of the two-letter language codes defined by the original ISO-639 standard. The complete list of codes can be found on the Web at
http://www.ics.uci.edu/pub/ietf/http/related/iso639.txt.

For instance, consider the two examples of the following sentence from Petronius's *Satiricon* in both Latin and English. A sentence tag encloses both sentences, but the first sentence tag has an xml:lang attribute for Latin while the second has an xml:lang attribute for English.

Latin:

```
<SENTENCE xml:lang="la">
  Veniebamus in forum deficiente now die, in quo notavimus
  frequentiam rerum venalium, non quidem pretiosarum sed tamen
  quarum fidem male ambulantem obscuritas temporis
  facillime tegeret.
</SENTENCE>
```

English:

```
<SENTENCE xml:lang="en">
  We have come to the marketplace now when the day is failing,
  where we have seen many things for sale, not for the
  valuable goods but rather that the darkness of
  the time may most easily conceal their shoddiness.
</SENTENCE>
```

While an English-speaking reader can easily tell which is the original text and which is the translation, a computer can use the hint provided by the xml:lang attribute. This distinction enables a spell checker to determine whether to check a particular element and designate which dictionary to use. Search engines can inspect these language attributes to determine whether to index a page and return matches based on the user's preferences.

Too Many Languages, Not Enough Codes

XML remains a little behind the times in this area. The original ISO-639 standard language codes were formed from two case-insensitive ASCII alphabetic characters. This standard allows no more than 26 x 26 or 676 different codes. More than 676 different languages are spoken on Earth today (not even counting dead languages like Etruscan). In practice, the reasonable codes are somewhat fewer than 676 because the language abbreviations should have some relation to the name of the language.

ISO-639, part two, uses three-letter language codes, which should handle all languages spoken on Earth. The XML standard specifically requires two-letter codes, however.

The language applies to the element and all its children until one of its children declares a different language. The declaration of the SENTENCE element can appear as follows:

```
<!ELEMENT SENTENCE (#PCDATA)>
<!ATTLIST SENTENCE xml:lang NMTOKEN "en">
```

If no appropriate ISO code is available, you can use one of the codes registered with the IANA, though currently IANA only adds four additional codes (listed in Table 10-2). You can find the most current list at http://www.isi.edu/in-notes/iana/assignments/languages/tags.

Table 10-2
The IANA Language Codes

Code	Language
no-bok	Norwegian "Book language"
no-nyn	Norwegian "New Norwegian"
i-navajo	Navajo
i-mingo	Mingo

For example:

```
<P xml:lang="no-nyn">
```

If neither the ISO nor the IANA has a code for the language you need (Klingon perhaps?), you may define new language codes. These "x-codes" must begin with the string x- or X- to identify them as user-defined, private use codes. For example,

```
<P xml:lang="x-klingon">
```

The value of the `xml:lang` attribute may include additional subcode segments, separated from the primary language code by a hyphen. Most often, the first subcode segment is a two-letter country code specified by ISO 3166. You can retrieve the most current list of country codes from `http://www.isi.edu/in-notes/iana/assignments/country-codes`. For example:

```
<P xml:lang="en-US">Put the body in the trunk of the car.</P>
<P xml:lang="en-GB">Put the body in the boot of the car.</P>
```

If the first subcode segment does not represent a two-letter ISO country code, it should be a character set subcode for the language registered with the IANA, such as csDECMCS, roman8, mac, cp037, or ebcdic-cp-ca. The current list can be found at `ftp://ftp.isi.edu/in-notes/iana/assignments/character-sets`. For example:

```
<P xml:lang="en-mac">
```

The final possibility is that the first subcode is another x-code that begins with `x-` or `X-`. For example,

```
<P xml:lang="en-x-tic">
```

By convention, language codes are written in lowercase and country codes are written in uppercase. However, this is merely a convention. This is one of the few parts of XML that is case-insensitive, because of its heritage in the case-insensitive ISO standard.

Like all attributes used in DTDs for valid documents, the `xml:lang` attribute must be specifically declared for those elements to which it directly applies. (It indirectly applies to children of elements that have specified `xml:lang` attributes, but these children do not require separate declaration.)

You may not want to permit arbitrary values for `xml:lang`. The permissible values are also valid XML names, so the attribute is commonly given the `NMTOKEN` type. This type restricts the value of the attribute to a valid XML name. For example,

```
<!ELEMENT P (#PCDATA)>
<!ATTLIST P xml:lang NMTOKEN #IMPLIED "en">
```

Alternately, if only a few languages or dialects are permitted, you can use an enumerated type. For example, the following DTD says that the P element may be either English or Latin.

```
<!ELEMENT P (#PCDATA)>
<!ATTLIST P xml:lang (en | la) "en">
```

You can use a `CDATA` type attribute, but there's little reason to. Using `NMTOKEN` or an enumerated type helps catch some potential errors.

A DTD for Attribute-Based Baseball Statistics

Chapter 5 developed a well-formed XML document for the 1998 Major League Season that used attributes to store the YEAR of a SEASON, the NAME of leagues, divisions, and teams, the CITY where a team plays, and the detailed statistics of individual players. Listing 10-4, below, presents a shorter version of Listing 5-1. It is a complete XML document with two leagues, six divisions, six teams, and two players. It serves to refresh your memory of which elements belong where and with which attributes.

Listing 10-4: **A complete XML document**

```
<?xml version="1.0" standalone="yes"?>
<SEASON YEAR="1998">
  <LEAGUE NAME="National League">
    <DIVISION NAME="East">
      <TEAM CITY="Atlanta" NAME="Braves">
        <PLAYER GIVEN_NAME="Marty" SURNAME="Malloy"
          POSITION="Second Base" GAMES="11" GAMES_STARTED="8"
          AT_BATS="28" RUNS="3" HITS="5" DOUBLES="1"
          TRIPLES="0" HOME_RUNS="1" RBI="1" STEALS="0"
          CAUGHT_STEALING="0" SACRIFICE_HITS="0"
          SACRIFICE_FLIES="0" ERRORS="0" WALKS="2"
          STRUCK_OUT="2" HIT_BY_PITCH="0" />
        <PLAYER GIVEN_NAME="Tom" SURNAME="Glavine"
          POSITION="Starting Pitcher" GAMES="33"
          GAMES_STARTED="33" WINS="20" LOSSES="6" SAVES="0"
          COMPLETE_GAMES="4" SHUTOUTS="3" ERA="2.47"
          INNINGS="229.1" HOME_RUNS_AGAINST="13"
          RUNS_AGAINST="67" EARNED_RUNS="63" HIT_BATTER="2"
          WILD_PITCHES="3" BALK="0" WALKED_BATTER="74"
          STRUCK_OUT_BATTER="157" />
      </TEAM>
    </DIVISION>
    <DIVISION NAME="Central">
      <TEAM CITY="Chicago" NAME="Cubs">
      </TEAM>
    </DIVISION>
    <DIVISION NAME="West">
      <TEAM CITY="San Francisco" NAME="Giants">
      </TEAM>
    </DIVISION>
  </LEAGUE>
  <LEAGUE NAME="American League">
    <DIVISION NAME="East">
      <TEAM CITY="New York" NAME="Yankees">
      </TEAM>
```

```
        </DIVISION>
        <DIVISION NAME="Central">
          <TEAM CITY="Minnesota" NAME="Twins">
          </TEAM>
        </DIVISION>
        <DIVISION NAME="West">
          <TEAM CITY="Oakland" NAME="Athletics">
          </TEAM>
        </DIVISION>
    </LEAGUE>
</SEASON>
```

In order to make this document valid and well-formed, you need to provide a DTD. This DTD must declare both the elements and the attributes used in Listing 10-4. The element declarations resemble the previous ones, except that there are fewer of them because most of the information has been moved into attributes:

```
<!ELEMENT SEASON (LEAGUE, LEAGUE)>
<!ELEMENT LEAGUE (DIVISION, DIVISION, DIVISION)>
<!ELEMENT DIVISION (TEAM+)>
<!ELEMENT TEAM (PLAYER*)>
<!ELEMENT PLAYER EMPTY>
```

Declaring SEASON Attributes in the DTD

The SEASON element has a single attribute, YEAR. Although some semantic constraints determine what is and is not a year (1998 is a year; March 31 is not) the DTD doesn't enforce these. Thus, the best approach declares that the YEAR attribute has the most general attribute type, CDATA. Furthermore, we want all seasons to have a year, so we'll make the YEAR attribute required.

```
<!ATTLIST SEASON YEAR CDATA #REQUIRED>
```

Although you really can't restrict the form of the text authors enter in YEAR attributes, you can at least provide a comment that shows what's expected. For example, it may be a good idea to specify that four digit years are required.

```
<!ATTLIST SEASON YEAR CDATA #REQUIRED> <!-- e.g. 1998 -->
<!-- DO NOT USE TWO DIGIT YEARS like 98, 99, 00!! -->
```

Declaring LEAGUE and DIVISION Attributes in the DTD

Next, consider LEAGUE and DIVISION. Each of these has a single NAME attribute. Again, the natural type is CDATA and the attribute will be required. Since these are two separate NAME attributes for two different elements, two separate <!ATTLIST> declarations are required.

```
<!ATTLIST LEAGUE   NAME CDATA #REQUIRED>
<!ATTLIST DIVISION NAME CDATA #REQUIRED>
```

A comment may help here to show document authors the expected form; for instance, whether or not to include the words *League* and *Division* as part of the name.

```
<!ATTLIST LEAGUE   NAME CDATA #REQUIRED>
<!-- e.g. "National League" -->

<!ATTLIST DIVISION NAME CDATA #REQUIRED>
<!-- e.g. "East" -->
```

Declaring TEAM Attributes in the DTD

A TEAM has both a NAME and a CITY. Each of these is CDATA and each is required:

```
<!ATTLIST TEAM NAME CDATA #REQUIRED>
<!ATTLIST TEAM CITY CDATA #REQUIRED>
```

A comment may help to establish what isn't obvious to all; for instance, that the CITY attribute may actually be the name of a state in a few cases.

```
<!ATTLIST TEAM NAME CDATA #REQUIRED>
<!ATTLIST TEAM CITY CDATA #REQUIRED>
<!-- e.g. "San Diego" as in "San Diego Padres"
      or "Texas" as in "Texas Rangers" -->
```

Alternately, you can declare both attributes in a single <!ATTLIST> declaration:

```
<!ATTLIST TEAM NAME CDATA #REQUIRED
               CITY CDATA #REQUIRED>
```

Declaring PLAYER Attributes in the DTD

The PLAYER element boasts the most attributes. GIVEN_NAME and SURNAME, the first two, are simply CDATA and required:

```
<!ATTLIST PLAYER GIVEN_NAME CDATA #REQUIRED>
<!ATTLIST PLAYER SURNAME    CDATA #REQUIRED>
```

The next PLAYER attribute is POSITION. Since baseball positions are fairly standard, you might use the enumerated attribute type here. However "First Base," "Second

Base," "Third Base," "Starting Pitcher," and "Relief Pitcher" all contain whitespace and are therefore not valid XML names. Consequently, the only attribute type that works is CDATA. There is no reasonable default value for the position so we make this attribute required as well.

```
<!ATTLIST PLAYER POSITION    CDATA #REQUIRED>
```

Next come the various statistics: GAMES, GAMES_STARTED, AT_BATS, RUNS, HITS, WINS, LOSSES, SAVES, SHUTOUTS, and so forth. Each should be a number; but as XML has no data typing mechanism, we simply declare them as CDATA. Since not all players have valid values for each of these, let's declare each one implied rather than required.

```
<!ATTLIST PLAYER GAMES            CDATA #IMPLIED>
<!ATTLIST PLAYER GAMES_STARTED    CDATA #IMPLIED>

<!- Batting Statistics ->
<!ATTLIST PLAYER AT_BATS          CDATA #IMPLIED>
<!ATTLIST PLAYER RUNS             CDATA #IMPLIED>
<!ATTLIST PLAYER HITS             CDATA #IMPLIED>
<!ATTLIST PLAYER DOUBLES          CDATA #IMPLIED>
<!ATTLIST PLAYER TRIPLES          CDATA #IMPLIED>
<!ATTLIST PLAYER HOME_RUNS        CDATA #IMPLIED>
<!ATTLIST PLAYER RBI              CDATA #IMPLIED>
<!ATTLIST PLAYER STEALS           CDATA #IMPLIED>
<!ATTLIST PLAYER CAUGHT_STEALING  CDATA #IMPLIED>
<!ATTLIST PLAYER SACRIFICE_HITS   CDATA #IMPLIED>
<!ATTLIST PLAYER SACRIFICE_FLIES  CDATA #IMPLIED>
<!ATTLIST PLAYER ERRORS           CDATA #IMPLIED>
<!ATTLIST PLAYER WALKS            CDATA #IMPLIED>
<!ATTLIST PLAYER STRUCK_OUT       CDATA #IMPLIED>
<!ATTLIST PLAYER HIT_BY_PITCH     CDATA #IMPLIED>

<!- Pitching Statistics ->
<!ATTLIST PLAYER WINS             CDATA #IMPLIED>
<!ATTLIST PLAYER LOSSES           CDATA #IMPLIED>
<!ATTLIST PLAYER SAVES            CDATA #IMPLIED>
<!ATTLIST PLAYER COMPLETE_GAMES   CDATA #IMPLIED>
<!ATTLIST PLAYER SHUTOUTS        CDATA #IMPLIED>
<!ATTLIST PLAYER ERA              CDATA #IMPLIED>
<!ATTLIST PLAYER INNINGS          CDATA #IMPLIED>
<!ATTLIST PLAYER HOME_RUNS_AGAINST CDATA #IMPLIED>
<!ATTLIST PLAYER RUNS_AGAINST     CDATA #IMPLIED>
<!ATTLIST PLAYER EARNED_RUNS      CDATA #IMPLIED>
<!ATTLIST PLAYER HIT_BATTER       CDATA #IMPLIED>
<!ATTLIST PLAYER WILD_PITCHES     CDATA #IMPLIED>
<!ATTLIST PLAYER BALK             CDATA #IMPLIED>
<!ATTLIST PLAYER WALKED_BATTER    CDATA #IMPLIED>
<!ATTLIST PLAYER STRUCK_OUT_BATTER CDATA #IMPLIED>
```

If you prefer, you can combine all the possible attributes of PLAYER into one monstrous <!ATTLIST> declaration:

```
<!ATTLIST PLAYER
   GIVEN_NAME          CDATA #REQUIRED
   SURNAME             CDATA #REQUIRED
   POSITION            CDATA #REQUIRED
   GAMES               CDATA #IMPLIED
   GAMES_STARTED       CDATA #IMPLIED
   AT_BATS             CDATA #IMPLIED
   RUNS                CDATA #IMPLIED
   HITS                CDATA #IMPLIED
   DOUBLES             CDATA #IMPLIED
   TRIPLES             CDATA #IMPLIED
   HOME_RUNS           CDATA #IMPLIED
   RBI                 CDATA #IMPLIED
   STEALS              CDATA #IMPLIED
   CAUGHT_STEALING     CDATA #IMPLIED
   SACRIFICE_HITS      CDATA #IMPLIED
   SACRIFICE_FLIES     CDATA #IMPLIED
   ERRORS              CDATA #IMPLIED
   WALKS               CDATA #IMPLIED
   STRUCK_OUT          CDATA #IMPLIED
   HIT_BY_PITCH        CDATA #IMPLIED

   WINS                CDATA #IMPLIED
   LOSSES              CDATA #IMPLIED
   SAVES               CDATA #IMPLIED
   COMPLETE_GAMES      CDATA #IMPLIED
   SHUTOUTS           CDATA #IMPLIED
   ERA                 CDATA #IMPLIED
   INNINGS             CDATA #IMPLIED
   HOME_RUNS_AGAINST   CDATA #IMPLIED
   RUNS_AGAINST        CDATA #IMPLIED
   EARNED_RUNS         CDATA #IMPLIED
   HIT_BATTER          CDATA #IMPLIED
   WILD_PITCHES        CDATA #IMPLIED
   BALK                CDATA #IMPLIED
   WALKED_BATTER       CDATA #IMPLIED
   STRUCK_OUT_BATTER   CDATA #IMPLIED>
```

One disadvantage of this approach is that it makes it impossible to include even simple comments next to the individual attributes.

The Complete DTD for the Baseball Statistics Example

Listing 10-5 shows the complete attribute-based baseball DTD.

Listing 10-5: The complete DTD for baseball statistics that uses attributes for most of the information

```
<!ELEMENT SEASON (LEAGUE, LEAGUE)>
<!ELEMENT LEAGUE (DIVISION, DIVISION, DIVISION)>
<!ELEMENT DIVISION (TEAM+)>
<!ELEMENT TEAM (PLAYER*)>
<!ELEMENT PLAYER EMPTY>

<!ATTLIST SEASON   YEAR CDATA #REQUIRED>
<!ATTLIST LEAGUE   NAME CDATA #REQUIRED>
<!ATTLIST DIVISION NAME CDATA #REQUIRED>
<!ATTLIST TEAM NAME CDATA #REQUIRED
               CITY CDATA #REQUIRED>


<!ATTLIST PLAYER GIVEN_NAME     CDATA #REQUIRED>
<!ATTLIST PLAYER SURNAME        CDATA #REQUIRED>
<!ATTLIST PLAYER POSITION       CDATA #REQUIRED>
<!ATTLIST PLAYER GAMES          CDATA #REQUIRED>
<!ATTLIST PLAYER GAMES_STARTED  CDATA #REQUIRED>

<!- Batting Statistics ->
<!ATTLIST PLAYER AT_BATS          CDATA #IMPLIED>
<!ATTLIST PLAYER RUNS             CDATA #IMPLIED>
<!ATTLIST PLAYER HITS             CDATA #IMPLIED>
<!ATTLIST PLAYER DOUBLES          CDATA #IMPLIED>
<!ATTLIST PLAYER TRIPLES          CDATA #IMPLIED>
<!ATTLIST PLAYER HOME_RUNS        CDATA #IMPLIED>
<!ATTLIST PLAYER RBI              CDATA #IMPLIED>
<!ATTLIST PLAYER STEALS           CDATA #IMPLIED>
<!ATTLIST PLAYER CAUGHT_STEALING  CDATA #IMPLIED>
<!ATTLIST PLAYER SACRIFICE_HITS   CDATA #IMPLIED>
<!ATTLIST PLAYER SACRIFICE_FLIES  CDATA #IMPLIED>
<!ATTLIST PLAYER ERRORS           CDATA #IMPLIED>
<!ATTLIST PLAYER WALKS            CDATA #IMPLIED>
<!ATTLIST PLAYER STRUCK_OUT       CDATA #IMPLIED>
<!ATTLIST PLAYER HIT_BY_PITCH     CDATA #IMPLIED>

<!- Pitching Statistics ->
<!ATTLIST PLAYER WINS              CDATA #IMPLIED>
<!ATTLIST PLAYER LOSSES            CDATA #IMPLIED>
<!ATTLIST PLAYER SAVES             CDATA #IMPLIED>
<!ATTLIST PLAYER COMPLETE_GAMES    CDATA #IMPLIED>
<!ATTLIST PLAYER SHUTOUTS         CDATA #IMPLIED>
<!ATTLIST PLAYER ERA               CDATA #IMPLIED>
<!ATTLIST PLAYER INNINGS           CDATA #IMPLIED>
<!ATTLIST PLAYER HOME_RUNS_AGAINST CDATA #IMPLIED>
```

Continued

Listing 10-5 *(continued)*

```
<!ATTLIST PLAYER RUNS_AGAINST        CDATA #IMPLIED>
<!ATTLIST PLAYER EARNED_RUNS         CDATA #IMPLIED>
<!ATTLIST PLAYER HIT_BATTER          CDATA #IMPLIED>
<!ATTLIST PLAYER WILD_PITCHES        CDATA #IMPLIED>
<!ATTLIST PLAYER BALK                CDATA #IMPLIED>
<!ATTLIST PLAYER WALKED_BATTER       CDATA #IMPLIED>
<!ATTLIST PLAYER STRUCK_OUT_BATTER   CDATA #IMPLIED>
```

To attach the above to Listing 10-4, use the following prolog, assuming of course that Example 10-5 is stored in a file called baseballattributes.dtd:

```
<?xml version="1.0" standalone="yes"?>
<!DOCTYPE SEASON SYSTEM "baseballattributes.dtd" >
```

Summary

In this chapter, you learned how to declare attributes for elements in DTDs. In particular, you learned the following concepts:

✦ Attributes are declared in an `<!ATTLIST>` tag in the DTD.

✦ One `<!ATTLIST>` tag can declare an indefinite number of attributes for a single element.

✦ Attributes normally have default values, but this condition can change by using the keywords #REQUIRED, #IMPLIED, or #FIXED.

✦ Ten attribute types can be declared in DTDs: CDATA, **Enumerated**, NMTOKEN, NMTOKENS, ID, IDREF, IDREFS, ENTITY, ENTITIES, **and** NOTATION.

✦ The predefined xml:space attribute determines whether whitespace in an element is significant.

✦ The predefined xml:lang attribute specifies the language in which an element's content appears.

In the next chapter, you learn how notations, processing instructions, and unparsed external entities can be used to embed non-XML data in XML documents.

✦   ✦   ✦

Embedding Non-XML Data

Not all data in the world is XML. In fact, I'd venture to say that most of the world's accumulated data isn't XML. A heck of a lot is stored in plain text, HTML, and Microsoft Word-to name just three common non-XML formats. And while most of this data could at least in theory be rewritten as XML—interest and resources permitting—not all of the world's data should be XML. Encoding images in XML, for example, would be extremely inefficient.

XML provides three constructs generally used for working with non-XML data: notations, unparsed external entities, and processing instructions. Notations describe the format of non-XML data. Unparsed external entities provide links to the actual location of the non-XML data. Processing instructions give information about how to view the data.

Caution   The material discussed in this chapter is very controversial. Although everything I describe is part of the XML 1.0 speci-fication, not everyone agrees that it should be. You can cer-tainly write XML documents without using any notations or unparsed external entities, and with only a few simple pro-cessing instructions. You may want to skip over this chapter at first, and return later if you discover a need for it.

Notations

The first problem you encounter when working with non-XML data in an XML document is identifying the format of the data and telling the XML application how to read and display the non-XML data. For example, it would be inappropriate to try to draw an MP3 sound file on the screen.

To a limited extent, you can solve this problem within a single application by using only a fixed set of tags for particular kinds of external entities. For instance, if all pictures are embedded through IMAGE elements and all sounds via AUDIO elements, then it's not hard to develop a browser that knows how to handle those two elements. In essence, this is the approach that HTML takes. However, this approach does prevent document authors from creating new tags that more specifically describe their content; for example, a PERSON element that happens to have a PHOTO attribute that points to a JPEG image of that person.

Furthermore, no application understands all possible file formats. Most Web browsers can recognize and read GIF, JPEG, PNG-and perhaps a few other kinds of image files-but they fail completely when faced with EPS files, TIFF files, FITS files, or any of the hundreds of other common and uncommon image formats. The dialog in Figure 11-1 is probably all too familiar.

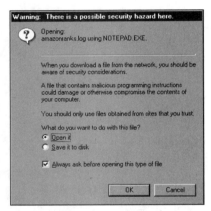

Figure 11-1: What occurs when Netscape Navigator doesn't recognize a file type

Ideally, you want documents to tell the application the format of the external entity so you don't have to rely on the application recognizing the file type by a magic number or a potentially unreliable file name extension. Furthermore, you'd like to give the application some hints about what program it can use to display the image if it's unable to do so itself.

Notations provide a partial (although not always well supported) solution to this problem. Notations describe the format of non-XML data. A NOTATION declaration in the DTD specifies a particular data type. The DTD declares notations at the same level as elements, attributes, and entities. Each notation declaration contains a name and an external identifier according to the following syntax:

```
<!NOTATION name SYSTEM "externalID">
```

The *name* is an identifier for this particular format used in the document. The *externalID* contains a human intelligible string that somehow identifies the notation. For instance, you might use MIME types like those used in this notation for GIF images:

```
<!NOTATION GIF SYSTEM "image/gif">
```

You can also use a PUBLIC identifier instead of the SYSTEM identifier. To do this, you must provide both a public ID and a URL. For example,

```
<!NOTATION GIF PUBLIC
    "-//IETF//NONSGML Media Type image/gif//EN"
    "http://www.isi.edu/in-notes/iana/assignments/media-
types/image/gif">
```

Caution　　There is *a lot* of debate about what exactly makes a good external identifier. MIME types like image/gif or text/html are one possibility. Another suggestion is URLs or other locators for standards documents like http://www.w3.org/TR/REC-html40/. A third option is the name of an official international standard like ISO 8601 for representing dates and times. In some cases, an ISBN or Library of Congress catalog number for the paper document where the standard is defined might be more appropriate. And there are many more choices.

Which you choose may depend on the expected life span of your document. For instance, if you use an unusual format, you don't want to rely on a URL that changes from month to month. If you expect your document to still spark interest in 100 years, then you may want to consider which identifiers are likely to still have meaning in 100 years and which are merely this decade's technical ephemera.

You can also use notations to describe data that does fit in an XML document. For instance, consider this DATE element:

```
<DATE>05-07-06</DATE>
```

What day, exactly, does 05-07-06 represent? Is it May 7, 1906 C.E.? Or is it July 5, 1906 C.E.? The answer depends on whether you read this in the United States or Europe. Maybe it's even May 7, 2006 C.E. or July 5, 2006 C.E. Or perhaps what's meant is May 7, 6 C.E., during the reign of the Roman emperor Augustus in the West and the Han dynasty in China. It's also possible that date isn't in the "Common Era" at all but is given in the traditional Jewish, Muslim, or Chinese calendars. Without more information, you cannot determine the true meaning.

To avoid confusion like this, ISO standard 8601 defines a precise means of representing dates. In this scheme, July 5, 2006 C.E. is written as 20060705 or, in XML, as follows:

```
<DATE>20060705</DATE>
```

This format doesn't match *anybody's* expectations; it's equally confusing to everybody and thus has the advantage of being more or less culturally neutral (though still biased toward the traditional Western calendar).

Notations are declared in the DTD and used in notation attributes to describe the format of non-XML data embedded in an XML document. To continue with the date example, Listing 11-1 defines two possible notations for dates in ISO 8601 and conventional U.S. formats. Then, a required FORMAT attribute of type NOTATION is added to each DATE element to describe the structure of the particular element.

Listing 11-1: **DATE elements in an ISO 8601 and conventional U.S. formats**

```
<?xml version="1.0" standalone="yes"?>
<!DOCTYPE SCHEDULE [

   <!NOTATION ISODATE SYSTEM
     "http://www.iso.ch/cate/d15903.html">
   <!NOTATION USDATE SYSTEM
"http://es.rice.edu/ES/humsoc/Galileo/Things/gregorian_calendar
.html">

   <!ELEMENT SCHEDULE (APPOINTMENT*)>
   <!ELEMENT APPOINTMENT (NOTE, DATE, TIME?)>

   <!ELEMENT NOTE (#PCDATA)>
   <!ELEMENT DATE (#PCDATA)>
   <!ELEMENT TIME (#PCDATA)>

   <!ATTLIST DATE FORMAT NOTATION (ISODATE | USDATE) #IMPLIED>

]>
<SCHEDULE>
  <APPOINTMENT>
    <NOTE>Deliver presents</NOTE>
    <DATE FORMAT="USDATE">12-25-1999</DATE>
  </APPOINTMENT>
  <APPOINTMENT>
    <NOTE>Party like it's 1999</NOTE>
    <DATE FORMAT="ISODATE">19991231</DATE>
  </APPOINTMENT>
</SCHEDULE>
```

Notations can't force authors to use the format described by the notation. For that you need to use some sort of schema language in addition to basic XML—but it is sufficient for simple uses where you trust authors to correctly describe their data.

Unparsed External Entities

XML is not an ideal format for all data, particularly non-text data. For instance, you could store each pixel of a bitmap image as an XML element, as shown below:

```
<PIXEL X="232" Y="128" COLOR="FF5E32" />
```

This is hardly a good idea, though. Anything remotely like this would cause your image files to balloon to obscene proportions. Since you can't encode all data in XML, XML documents must be able to refer to data not currently XML and probably never will be.

A typical Web page may include GIF and JPEG images, Java applets, ActiveX controls, various kinds of sounds, and so forth. In XML, any block of non-XML data is called an *unparsed entity* because the XML processor won't attempt to understand it. At most, it informs the application of the entity's existence and provides the application with the entity's name and possibly (though not necessarily) its content.

HTML pages embed non-HTML entities through a variety of custom tags. Pictures are included with the <IMG> tag whose SRC attribute provides the URL of the image file. Applets are embedded via the <APPLET> tag whose CLASS and CODEBASE attributes refer to the file and directory where the applet resides. The <OBJECT> tag uses its codebase attribute to refer to the URI from where the object's data is found. In each case, a particular predefined tag represents a particular kind of content. A predefined attribute contains the URL for that content.

XML applications can work like this, but they don't have to. In fact, most don't unless they're deliberately trying to maintain some level of backwards compatibility with HTML. Instead, XML applications use an unparsed external entity to refer to the content. Unparsed external entities provide links to the actual location of the non-XML data. Then they use an ENTITY type attribute to associate that entity with a particular element in the document.

Declaring Unparsed Entities

Recall from Chapter 9 that an external entity declaration looks something like this:

```
<!ENTITY SIG SYSTEM "http://metalab.unc.edu/xml/signature.xml">
```

However, this form is only acceptable if the external entity the URL names is more or less a well-formed XML document. If the external entity is not XML, then you have to specify the entity's type using the NDATA keyword. For example, to associate the GIF file logo.gif with the name LOGO, you would place this ENTITY declaration in the DTD:

```
<!ENTITY LOGO SYSTEM "logo.gif" NDATA GIF>
```

The final word in the declaration, GIF in this example, must be the name of a notation declared in the DTD. Notations associate a name like GIF with some sort of external identifier for the format such as a MIME type, an ISO standard, or the URL of a specification of the format. For example, the notation for GIF might look like this:

```
<!NOTATION GIF SYSTEM "image/gif">
```

As usual, you can use absolute or relative URLs for the external entity as convenience dictates. For example,

```
<!ENTITY LOGO SYSTEM "http://metalab.unc.edu/xml/logo.gif"
    NDATA GIF>
<!ENTITY LOGO SYSTEM "/xml/logo.gif" NDATA GIF>
<!ENTITY LOGO SYSTEM "../logo.gif" NDATA GIF>
```

Embedding Unparsed Entities

You cannot simply embed an unparsed entity at an arbitrary location in the document using a general entity reference as you can with parsed entities. For instance, Listing 11-2 is an invalid XML document because LOGO is an unparsed entity. If LOGO were a parsed entity, this example would be valid.

Listing 11-2: An invalid XML document that tries to embed an unparsed entity with a general entity reference

```
<?xml version="1.0" standalone="no"?>
<!DOCTYPE DOCUMENT [
  <!ELEMENT DOCUMENT ANY>
  <!ENTITY LOGO SYSTEM "http://metalab.unc.edu/xml/logo.gif"
    NDATA GIF>
  <!NOTATION GIF SYSTEM "image/gif">
]>
<DOCUMENT>
  &LOGO;
</DOCUMENT>
```

To embed unparsed entities, rather than using general entity references like &LOGO;, you declare an element that serves as a placeholder for the unparsed entity (IMAGE, for example). Then you declare an ENTITY type attribute for the IMAGE element-SOURCE, for example-which provides only the name of the unparsed entity. Listing 11-3 demonstrates.

Listing 11-3: A valid XML document that correctly embeds an unparsed entity

```
<?xml version="1.0" standalone="no"?>
<!DOCTYPE DOCUMENT [

  <!ELEMENT DOCUMENT ANY>
  <!ENTITY LOGO SYSTEM "http://metalab.unc.edu/xml/logo.gif"
    NDATA GIF>
  <!NOTATION GIF SYSTEM "image/gif">
  <!ELEMENT IMAGE EMPTY>
  <!ATTLIST IMAGE SOURCE ENTITY #REQUIRED>

]>
<DOCUMENT>
  <IMAGE SOURCE="LOGO" />
</DOCUMENT>
```

It is now up to the application reading the XML document to recognize the unparsed entity and display it. Applications may not display the unparsed entity (just as a Web browser may choose not to load images when the user has disabled image loading).

These examples show empty elements as the containers for unparsed entities. That's not always necessary, however. For instance, imagine an XML-based corporate ID system that a security guard uses to look up people entering a building. The PERSON element might have NAME, PHONE, OFFICE, and EMPLOYEE_ID children and a PHOTO ENTITY attribute. Listing 11-4 demonstrates.

Listing 11-4: A non-empty PERSON element with a PHOTO ENTITY attribute

```
<?xml version="1.0" standalone="no"?>
<!DOCTYPE PERSON [
  <!ELEMENT PERSON (NAME, EMPLOYEE_ID, PHONE, OFFICE)>
  <!ELEMENT NAME        (#PCDATA)>
  <!ELEMENT EMPLOYEE_ID (#PCDATA)>
  <!ELEMENT PHONE       (#PCDATA)>
  <!ELEMENT OFFICE      (#PCDATA)>
  <!NOTATION JPEG SYSTEM "image/jpg">
  <!ENTITY ROGER SYSTEM "rogers.jpg" NDATA JPEG>
```

Continued

Listing 11-4 *(continued)*

```
  <!ATTLIST PERSON PHOTO ENTITY #REQUIRED>

]>
<PERSON PHOTO="ROGER">
  <NAME>Jim Rogers</NAME>
  <EMPLOYEE_ID>4534</EMPLOYEE_ID>
  <PHONE>X396</PHONE>
  <OFFICE>RH 415A</OFFICE>
</PERSON>
```

This example may seem a little artificial. In practice, you'd be better advised to make an empty PHOTO element with a SOURCE attribute a child of a PERSON element rather than an attribute of PERSON. Furthermore, you'd probably separate the DTD into external and internal subsets. The external subset, shown in Listing 11-5, declares the elements, notations, and attributes. These are the parts likely to be shared among many different documents. The entity, however, changes from document to document. Thus, you can better place it in the internal DTD subset of each document as shown in Listing 11-6.

Listing 11-5: The external DTD subset person.dtd

```
  <!ELEMENT PERSON (NAME, EMPLOYEE_ID, PHONE, OFFICE, PHOTO)>
  <!ELEMENT NAME        (#PCDATA)>
  <!ELEMENT EMPLOYEE_ID (#PCDATA)>
  <!ELEMENT PHONE       (#PCDATA)>
  <!ELEMENT OFFICE      (#PCDATA)>
  <!ELEMENT PHOTO       EMPTY>
  <!NOTATION JPEG SYSTEM "image/jpeg">
  <!ATTLIST PHOTO SOURCE ENTITY #REQUIRED>
```

Listing 11-6: A document with a non-empty PERSON element and an internal DTD subset

```
<?xml version="1.0" standalone="no"?>
<!DOCTYPE PERSON [

  <!ENTITY % PERSON_DTD SYSTEM "person.dtd">
  %PERSON_DTD;
  <!ENTITY ROGER SYSTEM "rogers.jpg" NDATA JPEG>
```

```
]>
<PERSON>
  <NAME>Jim Rogers</NAME>
  <EMPLOYEE_ID>4534</EMPLOYEE_ID>
  <PHONE>X396</PHONE>
  <OFFICE>RH 415A</OFFICE>
  <PHOTO SOURCE="ROGER"/>
</PERSON>
```

Embedding Multiple Unparsed Entities

On rare occasions, you may need to refer to more than one unparsed entity in a single attribute, perhaps even an indefinite number. You can do this by declaring an attribute of the entity placeholder to have type ENTITIES. An ENTITIES type attribute has a value part that consists of multiple unparsed entity names separated by white space. Each entity name refers to an external non-XML data source and must be declared in the DTD. For example, you might use this to write a slide show element that rotates different pictures. The DTD would require these declarations:

```
<!ELEMENT SLIDESHOW EMPTY>
<!ATTLIST SLIDESHOW SOURCES ENTITIES #REQUIRED>
<!NOTATION JPEG SYSTEM    "image/jpeg">
<!ENTITY CHARM SYSTEM     "charm.jpg"    NDATA JPEG>
<!ENTITY MARJORIE SYSTEM "marjorie.jpg" NDATA JPEG>
<!ENTITY POSSUM SYSTEM    "possum.jpg"   NDATA JPEG>
<!ENTITY BLUE SYSTEM      "blue.jpg"     NDATA JPEG>
```

Then, at the point in the document where you want the slide show to appear, you insert the following tag:

```
<SLIDESHOW SOURCES="CHARM MARJORIE POSSUM BLUE">
```

Once again, I must emphasize that this is not a magic formula that all (or even any) XML browsers automatically understand. It is simply one technique browsers and other applications may or may not adopt to embed non-XML data in documents.

Processing Instructions

Comments often get abused to support proprietary extensions to HTML like server side includes, browser-specific scripting languages, database templates, and several dozen other items outside the purview of the HTML standard. The advantage of using comments for these purposes is that other systems simply ignore the extraneous data they don't understand. The disadvantage of this approach is that a document stripped of its comments may no longer be the same document, and that comments intended as mere documentation may be unintentionally processed as input to these proprietary extensions. To avoid this abuse of comments, XML provides the *processing instruction* — an explicit mechanism for embedding information in a file intended for proprietary applications rather than the XML parser or browser. Among other uses, processing instructions can provide additional information about how to view unparsed external entities.

A processing instruction is a string of text between `<?` and `?>` marks. The only required syntax for the text inside the processing instruction is that it must begin with an XML name followed by white space followed by data. The XML name may either be the actual name of the application (e.g., `latex`) or the name of a notation in the DTD that points to the application (e.g., `LATEX`) where `LATEX` is declared like this in the DTD:

```
<!NOTATION LATEX SYSTEM "/usr/local/bin/latex">
```

It may even be a name that is recognized by an application with a different name. The details tend to be very specific to the application for which the processing instruction is intended. Indeed, most applications that rely on processing instructions will impose more structure on the contents of a processing instruction. For example, consider this processing instruction used in IBM's Bean Markup Language:

```
<?bmlpi register demos.calculator.EventSourceText2Int?>
```

The name of the application this instruction is intended for is `bmlpi`. The data given to that application is the string `register demos.calculator.EventSourceText2Int`, which happens to include the full package qualified name of a Java class. This tells the application named `bmlpi` to use the Java class `demos.calculator.EventSourceText2Int` to convert action events to integers. If `bmlpi` encounters this proc-essing instruction while reading the document, it will load the class `demos.calculator.EventSourceText2Int` and use it to convert events to integers from that point on.

If this sounds fairly specific and detailed, that's because it is. Processing instructions are not part of the general structure of the document. They are intended to provide extra, detailed information for particular applications, not for every application that reads the document. If some other application encounters this instruction while reading a document, it will simply ignore the instruction.

Processing instructions may be placed almost anywhere in an XML document except inside a tag or a `CDATA` section. They may appear in the prolog or the

DTD, in the content of an element, or even after the closing document tag. Since processing instructions are not elements, they do not affect the tree structure of a document. You do not need to open or close processing instructions, or worry about how they nest inside other elements. Processing instructions are not tags and they do not delimit elements.

You're already familiar with one example of processing instructions, the `xml-stylesheet` processing instruction used to bind style sheets to documents:

```
<?xml-stylesheet type="text/xsl" href="baseball.xsl"?>
```

Although these examples appear in a document's prolog, in general processing instructions may appear anywhere in a document. You do not need to declare these instructions as child elements of the element they are contained in because they're not elements.

Processing instructions that begin with the string `xml` are reserved for uses defined in the XML standard. Otherwise, you are free to use any name and any string of text inside a processing instruction other than the closing string `?>`. For instance, the following examples are all valid processing instructions:

```
<?gcc HelloWorld.c ?>
<?acrobat document="passport.pdf"?>
<?Dave remember to replace this one?>
```

Note

Remember an XML processor won't necessarily do anything with these instructions. It merely passes them along to the application. The application decides what to do with the instructions. Most applications simply ignore processing instructions they don't understand.

Sometimes knowing the type of an unparsed external entity is insufficient. You may also need to know what program to run to view the entity and what parameters you need to provide that program. You can use a processing instruction to provide this information. Since processing instructions can contain fairly arbitrary data, it's relatively easy for them to contain instructions determining what action the external program listed in the notation should take.

Such a processing instruction can range from simply the name of a program that can view the file to several kilobytes of configuration information. The application and the document author must of course use the same means of determining which processing instructions belong with which unparsed external entities. Listing 11-7 shows one scheme that uses a processing instruction and a PDF notation to try to pass the PDF version of a physics paper to Acrobat Reader for display.

Listing 11-7: **Embedding a PDF document in XML**

```
<?xml version="1.0" standalone="yes"?>
<!DOCTYPE PAPER [

  <!NOTATION PDF PUBLIC
     "-//IETF//NONSGML Media Type application/pdf//EN"
     "http://www.isi.edu/in-notes/iana/assignments/media-
types/application/pdf">

  <!ELEMENT PAPER (TITLE, AUTHOR+, JOURNAL, DATE_RECEIVED,
VOLUME, ISSUE, PAGES)>
  <!ATTLIST PAPER CONTENTS ENTITY #IMPLIED>
  <!ENTITY PRLTAO00000810000240005270000001 SYSTEM

"http://ojps.aip.org/journal_cgi/getpdf?KEY=PRLTAO&amp;cvips=PR
LTAO00000810000240005270000001"
     NDATA PDF>

  <!ELEMENT AUTHOR (#PCDATA)>
  <!ELEMENT JOURNAL (#PCDATA)>
  <!ELEMENT YEAR (#PCDATA)>
  <!ELEMENT TITLE (#PCDATA)>
  <!ELEMENT DATE_RECEIVED (#PCDATA)>
  <!ELEMENT VOLUME (#PCDATA)>
  <!ELEMENT ISSUE (#PCDATA)>
  <!ELEMENT PAGES (#PCDATA)>

]>

<?PDF acroread?>
<PAPER CONTENTS="PRLTAO00000810000240005270000001">
  <TITLE>Do Naked Singularities Generically Occur in
Generalized Theories of Gravity?</TITLE>
  <AUTHOR>Kengo Maeda</AUTHOR>
  <AUTHOR>Takashi Torii</AUTHOR>
  <AUTHOR>Makoto Narita</AUTHOR>
  <JOURNAL>Physical Review Letters</JOURNAL>
  <DATE_RECEIVED>19 August 1998</DATE_RECEIVED>
  <VOLUME>81</VOLUME>
  <ISSUE>24</ISSUE>
  <PAGES>5270-5273</PAGES>
</PAPER>
```

As always, you have to remember that not every processor will treat this example in the way intended. In fact, most won't. However, this is one possible scheme for how an application might support PDF files and other non-XML media types.

Conditional Sections in DTDs

When developing DTDs or documents, you may need to comment out parts of the DTD not yet reflected in the documents. In addition to using comments directly, you can omit a particular group of declarations in the DTD by wrapping it in an IGNORE directive. The syntax follows:

```
<![ IGNORE
  declarations that are ignored
]]>
```

As usual, white space doesn't really affect the syntax, but you should keep the opening <![IGNORE and the closing]]> on separate lines for easy viewing.

You can ignore any declaration or combination of declarations — elements, entities, attributes, or even other IGNORE blocks — but you must ignore entire declarations. The IGNORE construct must completely enclose the entire declarations it removes from the DTD. You cannot ignore a piece of a declaration (such as the NDATA GIF in an unparsed entity declaration).

You can also specify that a particular section of declarations is included — that is, not ignored. The syntax for the INCLUDE directive is just like the IGNORE directive but with a different keyword:

```
<![ INCLUDE
  declarations that are included
]]>
```

When an INCLUDE is inside an IGNORE, the INCLUDE and its declarations are ignored. When an IGNORE is inside an INCLUDE, the declarations inside the IGNORE are still ignored. In other words, an INCLUDE never overrides an IGNORE.

Given these conditions, you may wonder why INCLUDE even exists. No DTD would change if all INCLUDE blocks were simply removed, leaving only their contents. INCLUDE appears to be completely extraneous. However, there is one neat trick with parameter entity references and both IGNORE and INCLUDE that you can't do with IGNORE alone. First, define a parameter entity reference as follows:

```
<!ENTITY % fulldtd "IGNORE">
```

You can ignore elements by wrapping them in the following construct:

```
<![ %fulldtd;
  declarations
]]>
```

The %fulldtd; parameter entity reference evaluates to IGNORE, so the declarations are ignored. Now, suppose you make the one word edit to change fulldtd from IGNORE to INCLUDE as follows:

```
<!ENTITY % fulldtd "INCLUDE">
```

Immediately, all the IGNORE blocks convert to INCLUDE blocks. In effect, you have a one-line switch to turn blocks on or off.

In this example, I've only used one switch, fulldtd. You can use this switch in multiple IGNORE/INCLUDE blocks in the DTD. You can also have different groups of IGNORE/INCLUDE blocks that you switch on or off based on different conditions.

You'll find this capability particularly useful when designing DTDs for inclusion in other DTDs. The ultimate DTD can change the behavior of the DTDs it embeds by changing the value of the parameter entity switch.

Summary

In this chapter, you learned how to integrate your XML documents with non XML data through notations, unparsed external entities, and processing instructions. In particular, you learned the following concepts:

✦ Notations describe the type of non-XML data.

✦ Unparsed external entities are storage units containing non-XML text or binary data.

✦ Unparsed external entities are included in documents using ENTITY or ENTITIES attributes.

✦ Processing instructions contain instructions passed along unchanged from the XML processor to the ultimate application.

✦ INCLUDE and IGNORE blocks specify that the enclosed declarations of the DTD are or are not (respectively) to be considered when parsing the document.

You'll see a lot more examples of documents with DTDs over the next several parts of this book, but as far as basic syntax and usage goes, this chapter concludes the exploration of DTDs. In Part III, we begin discussion of style languages for XML, beginning in the next chapter with Cascading Style Sheets, Level 1.

✦   ✦   ✦

Style Languages

Cascading Style Sheets Level 1

CSS is a very simple and straightforward language for applying styles such as bold and Helvetica to particular XML elements. Most of the styles CSS supports are familiar from any conventional word processor. For example, you can choose the font, the font weight, the font size, the background color, the spacing of various elements, the borders around elements, and more. However, rather than being stored as part of the document itself, all the style information is placed in a separate document called a style sheet. One XML document can be formatted in many different ways just by changing the style sheet. Different style sheets can be designed for different purposes — for print, the Web, presentations, and for other uses — all with the styles appropriate for the specific medium, and all without changing any of the content in the document itself.

What Is CSS?

Cascading Style Sheets (referred to as CSS from now on) were introduced in 1996 as a standard means of adding information about style properties such as fonts and borders to HTML documents. However, CSS actually works better with XML than with HTML because HTML is burdened with backwards-compatibility between the CSS tags and the HTML tags. For instance, properly supporting the CSS `nowrap` property requires eliminating the non-standard but frequently used `NOWRAP` element in HTML. Because XML elements don't have any predefined formatting, they don't restrict which CSS styles can be applied to which elements.

A CSS style sheet is a list of rules. Each rule gives the names of the elements it applies to and the styles it wants to apply to those elements. For example, consider Listing 12-1, a CSS style sheet for poems. This style sheet has five rules. Each rule has a selector — the name of the element to which it applies — and a list of properties to apply to instances of that element. The first rule says that the contents of the POEM element should be displayed in a block by itself (display: block). The second rule says that the contents of the TITLE element should be displayed in a block by itself (display: block) in 16-point (font-size: 16pt) bold type (font-weight: bold). The third rule says that the POET element should be displayed in a block by itself (display: block) and should be set off from what follows it by 10 pixels (margin-bottom: 10px). The fourth rule is the same as the third rule except that it applies to STANZA elements. Finally, the fifth rule simply states that VERSE elements are also displayed in their own block.

Listing 12-1: A CSS style sheet for poems

```
POEM    { display: block }
TITLE   { display: block; font-size: 16pt; font-weight: bold }
POET    { display: block; margin-bottom: 10px }
STANZA  { display: block; margin-bottom: 10px }
VERSE   { display: block }
```

In 1998, the W3C published a revised and expanded specification for CSS called CSS Level 2 (CSS2). At the same time, they renamed the original CSS to CSS Level 1 (CSS1). CSS2 is mostly a superset of CSS1, with a few minor exceptions, which I'll note as we encounter them. In other words, CSS2 is CSS1 plus aural style sheets, media types, attribute selectors, and other new features. Consequently, almost everything said in this chapter applies to both CSS1 and CSS2. CSS2 will be covered in the next chapter as an extension to CSS1.

Parts of CSS Level 1 are supported by Netscape Navigator 4.0 and Internet Explorer 4.0 and 5.0. Unfortunately, they often aren't the same parts. Mozilla 5.0 is supposed to provide no-uncompromising support for CSS Level 1 and most of CSS Level 2. Internet Explorer 5.0 does a better job than Internet Explorer 4.0 but it's still missing some major pieces, especially in regards to the box model and pseudo-elements. I'll try to point out areas in which one or the other browser has a particularly nasty problem.

Attaching Style Sheets to Documents

To really make sense out of the style sheet in Listing 12-1, you have to give it an XML document to play with. Listing 12-2 is a poem from Walt Whitman's classic book of poetry, *Leaves of Grass,* marked up in XML. The second line is the <?xml-stylesheet?> processing instruction that instructs the Web browser loading this document to apply the style sheet found in the file poem.css to this document. Figure 12-1 shows this document loaded into an early alpha of Mozilla.

Listing 12-2: *Darest Thou Now O Soul* marked up in XML

```xml
<?xml version="1.0"?>
<?xml-stylesheet type="text/css" href="poem.css"?>
<POEM>

  <TITLE>Darest Thou Now O Soul</TITLE>
  <POET>Walt Whitman</POET>

  <STANZA>
    <VERSE>Darest thou now O soul,</VERSE>
    <VERSE>Walk out with me toward the unknown region,</VERSE>
    <VERSE>Where neither ground is for the feet nor
            any path to follow?</VERSE>
  </STANZA>
   <STANZA>
     <VERSE>No map there, nor guide,</VERSE>
     <VERSE>Nor voice sounding, nor touch of
            human hand,</VERSE>
     <VERSE>Nor face with blooming flesh, nor lips,
            are in that land.</VERSE>
   </STANZA>
   <STANZA>
     <VERSE>I know it not O soul,</VERSE>
     <VERSE>Nor dost thou, all is blank before us,</VERSE>
     <VERSE>All waits undream'd of in that region,
            that inaccessible land.</VERSE>
   </STANZA>
   <STANZA>
     <VERSE>Till when the ties loosen,</VERSE>
     <VERSE>All but the ties eternal, Time and Space,</VERSE>
     <VERSE>Nor darkness, gravitation, sense,
            nor any bounds bounding us.</VERSE>
   </STANZA>
   <STANZA>
     <VERSE>Then we burst forth, we float,</VERSE>
     <VERSE>In Time and Space O soul,
            prepared for them,</VERSE>
     <VERSE>Equal, equipt at last, (O joy! O fruit of all!)
            them to fulfil O soul.</VERSE>
   </STANZA>

</POEM>
```

The `type` attribute in the `<?xml-stylesheet?>` processing instruction is the MIME type of the style sheet you're using. Its value is `text/css` for CSS and `text/xsl` for XSL.

Cross-Reference   CSS Level 2 is discussed in Chapter 13. XSL is covered in Chapters 14 and 15.

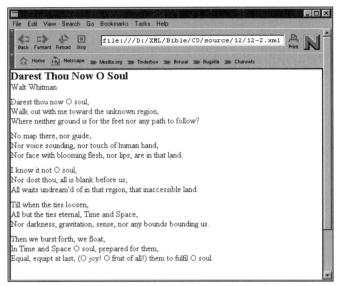

Figure 12-1: *Darest Thou Now O Soul* as rendered by Mozilla

The value of the href attribute in the `<?xml-stylesheet?>` processing instruction is a URL, often relative, where the style sheet is found. If the style sheet can't be found, the Web browser will probably use its default style sheet though some browsers may report an error instead.

You can apply the same style sheet to many documents. Indeed, you generally will. Thus, it's common to put your style sheets in some central location on your Web server where all of your documents can refer to them; a convenient location is the styles directory at the root level of the Web server.

```
<?xml-stylesheet type="text/css" href="/styles/poem.css"?>
```

You might even use an absolute URL to a style sheet on another Web site, though of course this does leave your site dependent on the status of the external Web site.

```
<?xml-stylesheet type="text/css"
    href="http://metalab.unc.edu/xml/styles/poem.css"?>
```

You can even use multiple `<?xml-stylesheet?>` processing instructions to pull in rules from different style sheets. For example:

```
<?xml version="1.0"?>
<?xml-stylesheet type="text/css" href="/styles/poem.css"?>
<?xml-stylesheet type="text/css"
    href="http://metalab.unc.edu/xml/styles/poem.css"?>
<POEM>
...
```

CSS with HTML versus CSS with XML

Although the focus of this book is on XML, CSS style sheets also work with HTML documents. The main differences between CSS with HTML and CSS with XML are:

1. The elements you can attach a rule to are limited to standard HTML elements like P, PRE, LI, DIV, and SPAN.

2. HTML browsers don't recognize processing instructions, so style sheets are attached to HTML documents using LINK tags in the HEAD element. Furthermore, per-document style rules can be included in the HEAD in a STYLE element. For example:

```
<LINK REL=STYLESHEET TYPE="text/css" HREF="/styles/poem.css" >
<STYLE TYPE="text/css">
  PRE { color: red }
</STYLE>
```

3. HTML browsers don't render CSS properties as faithfully as XML browsers because of the legacy formatting of elements. Tables are notoriously problematic in this respect.

Note   Style sheets are more or less orthogonal to DTDs. A document with a style sheet may or may not have a DTD and a document with a DTD may or may not have a style sheet. However, DTDs do often serve as convenient lists of the elements that you need to provide style rules for.

In this and the next several chapters, most of the examples will use documents that are well-formed, but not valid. The lack of DTDs will make the examples shorter and the relevant parts more obvious. However in practice, most of the documents you attach style sheets to will probably be valid documents with DTDs.

Selection of Elements

The part of a CSS rule that specifies which elements it applies to is called a *selector*. The most common kind of selector is simply the name of an element; for instance TITLE in this rule:

```
TITLE { display: block; font-size: 16pt; font-weight: bold }
```

However, selectors can also specify multiple elements, elements with a particular CLASS or ID attribute and elements that appear in particular contexts relative to other elements.

Note   One thing you cannot do in CSS Level 1 is select elements with particular attribute names or values other than the predefined CLASS and ID attributes. To do this, you have to use CSS Level 2 or XSL.

Grouping Selectors

If you want to apply one set of properties to multiple elements, you can include all the elements in the selector separated by commas. For instance, in Listing 12-1 POET and STANZA were both styled as block display with a 10-pixel margin. You can combine these two rules like this:

```
POET, STANZA { display: block; margin-bottom: 10px }
```

Furthermore, more than one rule can apply style to a particular element. So you can combine some standard properties into a rule with many selectors, then use more specific rules to apply custom formatting to selected elements. For instance, in Listing 12-1 all the elements were listed as block display. This can be combined into one rule while additional formatting for the POET, STANZA, and TITLE elements is contained in separate rules, like this:

```
POEM, VERSE, TITLE, POET, STANZA { display: block }
POET, STANZA { margin-bottom: 10px }
TITLE {font-size: 16pt; font-weight: bold }
```

Pseudo-Elements

CSS1 supports two pseudo-elements that can address parts of the document that aren't normally identified as separate elements, but nonetheless often need separate styles. These are the first line and the first letter of an element.

Caution The early betas of Internet Explorer 5.0 and earlier versions of Internet Explorer do not support these pseudo-elements. The early beta of Mozilla 5.0 *does* support them, but only for HTML.

Addressing the First Letter

The most common reason to format the first letter of an element separately from the rest of the element is to insert a drop cap as shown in Figure 12-2. This is accomplished by writing a rule that is addressed with the element name, followed by :first-letter. For example:

```
CHAPTER:first-letter { font-size: 300%;
                       float: left; vertical-align: text-top }
```

Caution As you may notice in Figure 12-2, the "drop" part of the drop cap (float: left; vertical-align: text-top) does not yet seem to work in either the early betas of Mozilla 5.0 or Internet Explorer 5.0, though the size of the initial letter can be adjusted.

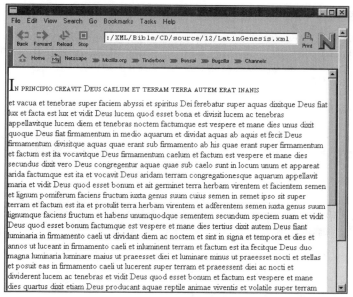

Figure 12-2: A drop cap on the first-letter pseudo element with small caps used on the first-line pseudo-element

Addressing the First Line

The first line of an element is also often formatted differently than the remainder of the text of the element. For instance, it may be printed in small caps instead of normal body text as shown in Figure 12-2. You can attach the :first-line selector to the name of an element to create a rule that only applies to the first line of the element. For example,

```
CHAPTER:first-line { font-variant: small-caps }
```

Exactly what this pseudo-element selects is relative to the current layout. If the window is larger and there are more words in the first line, then more words will be in small caps. If the window is made smaller or the font gets larger so the text wraps differently and fewer words are on the first line, then the words that are wrapped to the next line are no longer in small caps. The determination of which characters comprise the first-line pseudo-element is deferred until the document is actually displayed.

Pseudo-Classes

Sometimes you may want to style two elements of the same type differently. For example, one paragraph may be bold while another has normal weight. To do this, you can add a CLASS attribute to one of the elements, then write a rule for the elements in a given CLASS.

For example, consider a bibliography that contains many CITATION elements. A sample is shown in Listing 12-3. Now suppose you want to color all citations of the work of Alan Turing blue, while leaving the other citations untouched. To do this you have to add a CLASS attribute with a specific value — TURING works well — to the elements to be colored.

Listing 12-3: A bibliography in XML with three CITATION elements

```
<?xml version="1.0" standalone="yes"?>
<?xml-stylesheet type="text/css" href="biblio.css"?>
<BIBLIOGRAPHY>
  <CITATION CLASS="HOFSTADTER" ID="C1">
      <AUTHOR>Hofstadter, Douglas</AUTHOR>.
      "<TITLE>How Might Analogy, the Core of Human Thinking,
        Be Understood By Computers?</TITLE>"
      <JOURNAL>Scientific American</JOURNAL>,
      <MONTH>September</MONTH>
      <YEAR>1981</YEAR>
      <PAGES>18-30</PAGES>
  </CITATION>
  <CITATION CLASS="TURING" ID="C2">
    <AUTHOR>Turing, Alan M.</AUTHOR>
    "<TITLE>On Computable Numbers,
      With an Application to the Entscheidungs-problem</TITLE>"
    <JOURNAL>
      Proceedings of the London Mathematical Society</JOURNAL>,
    <SERIES>Series 2</SERIES>,
    <VOLUME>42</VOLUME>
    (<YEAR>1936</YEAR>):
    <PAGES>230-65</PAGES>.
  </CITATION>
  <CITATION CLASS="TURING" ID="C3">
    <AUTHOR>Turing, Alan M.</AUTHOR>
    "<TITLE>Computing Machinery &amp; Intelligence</TITLE>"
    <JOURNAL>Mind</JOURNAL>
    <VOLUME>59</VOLUME>
    (<MONTH>October</MONTH>
    <YEAR>1950</YEAR>):
    <PAGES>433-60</PAGES>
  </CITATION>
</BIBLIOGRAPHY>
```

Note One of the more annoying aspects of CSS Level 1 is that it makes mixed content more necessary. There's a lot of punctuation in Listing 12-3 that is not really part of the content; for example the parentheses placed around the YEAR element and the quotation marks around the TITLE. These are presentation elements that should be part of the style sheet instead. CSS Level 2 allows extra text such as punctuation to be inserted before and after elements.

The style sheet in Listing 12-4 uses a CLASS selector to color elements in the TURING class blue.

Caution CLASS attributes are supported by IE5 but not by Mozilla as of the milestone 3 release. Mozilla will probably support CLASS attributes by the time it's officially released.

Listing 12-4: A style sheet that colors elements in the TURING class blue

```
BIBLIOGRAPHY { display: block }
CITATION.TURING { color: blue }
CITATION { display: block }
JOURNAL   { font-style: italic }
```

Note In a valid document, the CLASS attribute must be declared as a possible attribute of the styled elements. For example, here's a DTD for the bibliography of Listing 12-3:

```
<!ELEMENT BIBLIOGRAPHY (CITATION*)>
<!ATTLIST CITATION CLASS CDATA #IMPLIED>
<!ATTLIST CITATION ID    ID    #REQUIRED>

<!ELEMENT CITATION   ANY>
<!ELEMENT AUTHOR    (#PCDATA)>
<!ELEMENT TITLE     (#PCDATA)>
<!ELEMENT JOURNAL   (#PCDATA)>
<!ELEMENT MONTH     (#PCDATA)>
<!ELEMENT YEAR      (#PCDATA)>
<!ELEMENT SERIES    (#PCDATA)>
<!ELEMENT VOLUME    (#PCDATA)>
<!ELEMENT PAGES     (#PCDATA)>
```

In general, I do not recommend this approach. You should, if possible, attempt to add additional element markup to the document rather than relying on CLASS attributes. However, CLASS attributes may be necessary when the information you're selecting does not conveniently map to particular elements.

Selection by ID

Sometimes, a unique element needs a unique style. You need a rule that applies to exactly that one element. For instance, suppose you want to make one element in a list bold to really emphasize it in contrast to its siblings. In this case, you can write a rule that applies to the ID attribute of the element. The selector is the name of the element, followed by a # and the value of the ID attribute.

For example, Listing 12-5 is a style sheet that selects the CITATION element from the bibliography in Listing 12-3 with the ID C3 and makes it, and only it, bold. Other CITATION elements appear with the default weight. All CITATION elements are displayed in block fashion and all JOURNAL elements are italicized.

Listing 12-5: A style sheet that makes the CITATION element with ID C3 bold

```
BIBLIOGRAPHY { display: block }
CITATION#C3  { font-weight: bold }
CITATION     { display: block }
JOURNAL      { font-style: italic }
```

Caution   ID selectors are supported by IE5, and by Mozilla for HTML elements, but not XML elements as of the milestone 3 release. Mozilla will probably fully support ID selectors by the time it's officially released.

Contextual Selectors

Often, the formatting of an element depends on its parent element. You can write rules that only apply to elements found inside a named parent. To do this, prefix the name of the parent element to the name of the styled element.

For example, a CODE element inside a PRE element may be rendered in 12-point Courier. However, if the body text of the document is written in 10-point Times, a CODE element that's inline with other body text may need to be rendered in 10-point Courier. The following rules accomplish exactly that:

```
BODY     { font-family: Times, serif; font-size: 10pt }
CODE     { font-family: Courier, monospaced; font-size: 10pt }
PRE      { font-size: 12pt }
PRE CODE { font-size: 12pt }
```

This says that inside the BODY element, the font is 10-point Times. However, inside a CODE element the font changes to Courier, still 10-point. However, if the CODE element is inside a PRE element then the font grows to 12 points.

You can expand this to look at the parent of the parent, the parent of the parent of the parent, and so forth. For example, the following rule says that a NUMBER element inside a YEAR element inside a DATE element should be rendered in a monospaced font:

```
DATE YEAR NUMBER { font-family: Courier, monospaced }
```

In practice, this level of specificity is rarely needed. In cases in which it does seem to be needed, you can often rewrite your style sheet to rely more on inheritance, cascades, and relative units, and less on the precise specification of formatting.

STYLE Attributes

When hand-authoring documents, it's not uncommon to want to apply a particular style one time to a particular element without editing the style sheet for the document. Indeed, you may want to override some standard default style sheet for the document that you can't change. You can do this by attaching a STYLE attribute to the element. The value of this attribute is a semicolon-separated list of style properties for the element. For example, this CITATION uses a STYLE attribute to make itself bold:

```
<CITATION CLASS="TURING" ID="C3" STYLE="font-weight: bold">
  <AUTHOR>Turing, Alan M.</AUTHOR>
  "<TITLE>Computing Machinery &amp; Intelligence</TITLE>"
  <JOURNAL>Mind</JOURNAL>
  <VOLUME>59</VOLUME>
  (<MONTH>October</MONTH>
  <YEAR>1950</YEAR>):
  <PAGES>433-60</PAGES>
</CITATION>
```

If the properties defined in a STYLE attribute conflict with the properties defined in the style sheet, then the properties defined in the attribute take precedence.

Avoid using STYLE attributes if at all possible. Your documents will be much cleaner and more maintainable if you keep all style information in separate style sheets. Nonetheless, there are times when STYLE attributes are too quick and convenient to ignore.

Again, if you use this approach in a valid document, you will need to declare the STYLE attribute in an ATTLIST declaration for the element you're styling. For example:

```
<!ELEMENT CITATION ANY>
<!ATTLIST CITATION CLASS CDATA #IMPLIED>
<!ATTLIST CITATION ID    ID    #REQUIRED>
<!ATTLIST CITATION STYLE CDATA #IMPLIED>
```

Caution   STYLE attributes are supported by IE5, and by Mozilla for HTML elements, but not XML elements as of the milestone 3 release. Mozilla will probably fully support STYLE attributes by the time it's officially released.

Inheritance

CSS does not require that rules be specifically defined for each possible property of each element in a document. For instance, if there is not a rule that specifies the font size of an element, then the element inherits the font size of its parent. If there is not a rule that specifies the color of an element, then the element inherits the color of its parent. The same is true of most CSS properties. In fact, the only properties that aren't inherited are the background and box properties.

For example, consider these rules:

```
P       { font-weight: bold;
          font-size: 24pt;
          font-family: sans-serif}
BOOK    { font-style: italic; font-family: serif}
```

Now consider this XML fragment:

```
<P>
  Michael Willhoite's <BOOK>Daddy's Roommate</BOOK> is
  the #10 most frequently banned book in the U.S. in the 1990s.
</P>
```

Although the BOOK element has not been specifically assigned a font-weight or a font-size, it will be rendered in 24-point bold because it is a child of the P element. It will also be italicized because that is specified in its own rule. BOOK *inherits* the font-weight and font-size of its parent P. If later in the document a BOOK element appears in the context of some other element, then it will inherit the font-weight and font-size of that element.

The font-family is a little trickier because both P and BOOK declare conflicting values for this property. Inside the BOOK element, the font-family declared by BOOK takes precedence. Outside the BOOK element, P's font-family is used. Therefore, "Daddy's Roommate" is drawn in a serif font, while "most frequently banned book" is drawn in a sans serif font.

Often you want the child elements to inherit formatting from their parents. Therefore, it's important not to over-specify the formatting of any element. For instance, suppose I had declared that BOOK was written in 12-point font like this:

```
BOOK { font-style: italic; font-family: serif; font-size: 12pt}
```

Then the example would be rendered as shown in Figure 12-3:

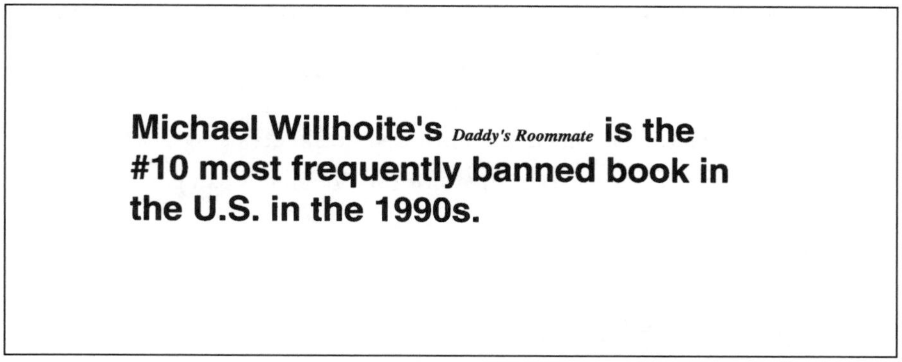

Michael Willhoite's *Daddy's Roommate* **is the #10 most frequently banned book in the U.S. in the 1990s.**

Figure 12-3: The BOOK written in a 12-point font size

You could fix this with a special rule that uses a contextual selector to pick out BOOK elements inside P elements, but it's easier to simply inherit the parent's font-size.

One way to avoid problems like this, while retaining some control over the size of individual elements is to use relative units like ems and ex's instead of absolute units like points, picas, inches, centimeters, and millimeters. An em is the width of the letter *m* in the current font. An ex is the height of the letter *x* in the current font. If the font gets bigger, so does everything measured in ems and ex's.

A similar option that's available for some properties is to use percentage units. For example, the following rule sets the font size of the FOOTNOTE_NUMBER element to 80 percent of the font size of the parent element. If the parent element's font size increases or decreases, FOOTNOTE_NUMBER's font size scales similarly.

```
FOOTNOTE_NUMBER { font-size: 80% }
```

Exactly what the percentage is a percentage of varies from property to property. In the vertical-align property, the percentage is of the line height of the element itself. However in a margin property, a percentage is a percentage of the element's width.

Cascades

It is possible to attach more than one style sheet to a document. For instance, a browser may have a default style sheet which is added to the one the designer provides for the page. In such a case, it's possible that there will be multiple rules that apply to one element, and these rules may conflict. Thus, it's important to determine in which order the rules are applied. This process is called a *cascade*, and is where cascading style sheets get their name.

There are several ways a CSS style sheet can be attached to an XML document:

1. The `<?xml-stylesheet?>` processing instruction can be included in the XML document.
2. The style sheet itself may import other style sheets using `@import`.
3. The user may specify a style sheet for the document using mechanisms inside their browser.
4. The browser provides default styles for most properties.

The @import Directive

Style sheets may contain `@import` directives that load style sheets stored in other files. An absolute or relative URL is used to identify the style sheets. For example,

```
@import url(http://www.w3.org/basicstyles.css);
@import url(/styles/baseball.css);
```

These `@import` directives must appear at the beginning of the style sheet, before any rules. Rules in the importing style sheet always override those in the imported style sheets. The imported style sheets cascade in the order they're imported. Cycles (for example, poem.css imports stanza.css which imports poem.css) are prohibited.

The !important Declaration

In CSS1, author rules override reader rules unless the reader attaches an `!important` declaration to the property. For example, the following rule says that the `TITLE` element should be colored blue even if the author of the document requested a different color. On the other hand, the `font-family` should be `serif` only if the author rules don't disagree.

```
TITLE { color: blue !important font-family: serif}
```

However, author rules may also be declared important. In such a case, the author rule overrides the reader rule.

Note   This is a very bad idea. Readers should always have the option to choose the way they view something. It simply isn't possible to write one style sheet that's appropriate for people using color and black-and-white monitors, the seeing and the sight-impaired, people browsing on 21-inch monitors, television sets, and PDAs. Too many Web designers vastly over-specify their styles, only to produce pages that are completely unreadable on systems that aren't exactly like their own. Fortunately, CSS2 reverses this precedence so that reader rules have the ultimate say.

Cascade Order

Styles are chosen from the available style rules for an element. In general, more specific rules win. For instance, consider this fragment:

```
<OUEVRE>
  <PLAY ID="x02" CLASS="WILDE">
    The Importance of Being Earnest
  </PLAY>
</OUEVRE>
```

The most specific rules are preferred. Thus, one that selected the PLAY element by its ID would be preferred to one that selected the PLAY by its CLASS. A rule that selected the PLAY by its CLASS would be preferred to one that selected PLAY elements contained in OUEVRE elements. Finally, if none of those applied, a generic PLAY rule would be selected. If no selector matches, the value inherited from the parent element is used. If there is no value inherited from the parent element, the default value is used.

If there is more than one rule at a given level of specificity, the cascading order is resolved in the following order of preference:

1. Author declarations marked important.

2. Reader declarations marked important.

3. Author declarations not marked important.

4. Reader declarations not marked important.

5. The latest rule in the style sheet.

Tip Try to avoid depending on cascading order. It's rarely a mistake to specify as little style as possible and let the reader/browser preferences take control.

Comments in CSS Style Sheets

CSS style sheets can include comments. CSS comments are like C's /* */ comments, not like <!− −> XML and HTML comments. Listing 12-6 demonstrates. This style sheet doesn't merely apply style rules to elements. It also describes, in English, the results those style rules are supposed to achieve.

Listing 12-6: **A style sheet for poems with comments**

```
/* Work around a Mozilla bug */
POEM { display:block }

/* Make the title look like an H1 header */
TITLE  { display: block; font-size: 16pt; font-weight: bold }
POET   { display: block; margin-bottom: 10 }

/* Put a blank line in-between stanzas,
   only a line break between verses */
STANZA { display: block; margin-bottom: 10 }
VERSE  { display: block }
```

CSS isn't nearly as convoluted as XML DTDs, Java, C, or Perl, so comments aren't quite as necessary as they are in other languages. However, it's rarely a bad idea to include comments. They can only help someone who's trying to make sense out of a style sheet you wrote and who is unable to ask you directly.

CSS Units

CSS properties have names and values. Table 12-1 lists some of these property names and some of their values.

The names are all CSS keywords. However, the values are much more diverse. Some of them are keywords like the none in display: none or the solid in border-style: solid. Other values are numbers with units like the 0.5in in margin-top: 0.5in or the 12pt in font-size: 12pt. Still other values are URLs like the http://www.idgbooks.com/images/paper.gif in background-image: url(http://www.idgbooks.com/images/paper.gif) or RGB colors like the #CC0033 in color: #CC0033. Different properties permit different values. However, there are only four different kinds of values a property may take on. These are:

1. length
2. URL
3. color
4. keyword

Keywords vary from property to property, but the other kinds of values are the same from property to property. That is, a length is a length is a length regardless of which property it's the value of. If you know how to specify the length of a border, you also know how to specify the length of a margin and a padding and an image. This reuse of syntax makes working with different properties much easier.

Table 12-1 Sample Property Names and Values	
Name	*Value*
display	none
font-style	italic
margin-top	0.5in
font-size	12pt
border-style	solid
color	#CC0033
background-color	white
background-image	url(http://www.idgbooks.com/ images/paper.gif)
list-style-image	url(/images/redbullet.png)
line-height	120%

Length values

In CSS, a length is a scalar measure used for width, height, font-size, word and letter spacing, text indentation, line height, margins, padding, border widths, and many other properties. Lengths may be specified in three ways:

1. Absolute units
2. Relative units
3. Percentages

Absolute Units of Length

Absolute units of length are something of a misnomer because there's really no such thing as an absolute unit of length on a computer screen. Changing a monitor resolution from 640 to 480 to 1600 by 1200 changes the length of everything on your screen, inches and centimeters included. Nonetheless, CSS supports five "absolute" units of length that at least don't change from one font to the next. These are listed in Table 12-2.

	Inch (in)	Centimeters (cm)	Millimeters (mm)	Points (pt)	Picas (pc)
		Table 12-2			
		Absolute Units of Length			
Inch	1.0	2.54	25.4	72	6
Centimeters	0.3937	1	10	28.3464	4.7244
Millimeters	0.03937	0.1	1.0	2.83464	0.47244
Points	0.01389	0.0352806	0.352806	1.0	0.83333
Picas	0.16667	0.4233	4.233	12	1.0

Lengths are given as a number followed by the abbreviation for one of these units:

Inches	in
Centimeters	cm
Millimeters	mm
Points	pt
Picas	pc

The number may have a decimal point (for example, `margin-top: 0.3in`). Some properties allow negative values like -0.5in, but not all do; and even those that do often place limits on how negative a length can be. It's best to avoid negative lengths for maximum cross-browser compatibility.

Relative Units of Length

CSS also supports three relative units for lengths. These are:

1. em: the width of the letter *m* in the current font

2. ex: the height of the letter *x* in the current font

3. px: the size of a pixel (assumes square pixels; all common modern displays use square pixels though some older PC monitors, mostly now consigned to the rubbage bin, do not)

For example, this rule sets the left and right borders of the PULLQUOTE element to twice the width of the letter *m* in the current font and the top and bottom borders to one and a half times the height of the letter *x* in the current font:

```
PULLQUOTE { border-right-width: 2em; border-left-width: 2em;
           border-top-width: 1.5ex; border-bottom-width: 1.5ex }
```

The normal purpose of using ems and ex's is to set a width that's appropriate for a given font, without necessarily knowing how big the font is. For instance in the above rule, the font size is not known so the exact width of the borders is not known either. It can be determined at display time by comparison with the *m* and the *x* in the current font. Larger font sizes will have correspondingly larger ems and ex's.

Lengths in pixels are relative to the height and width of a (presumably square) pixel on the monitor. Widths and heights of images are often given in pixels.

Caution

Pixel measurements are generally not a good idea. First, the size of a pixel varies widely with resolution. Most power users set their monitors at much too high a resolution, which makes the pixels far too small for legibility.

Secondly, within the next ten years, 200 and even 300 dpi monitors will become common, finally breaking away from the rough 72-pixels-per-inch (give or take 28 pixels) de facto standard that's prevailed since the first Macintosh in 1984. Documents that specify measurements in nonscreen-based units like ems, ex's, points, picas, and inches will be able to make the transition. However, documents that use pixel level specification will become illegibly small when viewed on high-resolution monitors.

Percentage Units of Length

Finally, lengths can be specified as a percentage of something. Generally, this is a percentage of the current value of a property. For instance, if the font-size of a STANZA element is 12 points, and the font-size of the VERSE the STANZA contains is set to 150 percent, then the font-size of the VERSE will be 18 points.

URL Values

Three CSS properties can have URL values: `background-image`, `list-style-image`, and the shorthand property `list-style`. Furthermore, as you've already seen, the `@import` rule uses URL values. Literal URLs are placed inside `url()`. All forms of relative and absolute URLs are allowed. For example:

```
DOC { background-image: url (http://www.mysite.com/bg.gif) }
LETTER { background-image: url(/images/paper.gif) }
SOFTWARE { background-image: url(../images/screenshot.gif)}
GAME { background-image: url(currentposition.gif)}
```

You can enclose the URL in single or double quotes, though nothing is gained by doing so. For example:

```
DOC { background-image: url("http://www.mysite.com/bg.gif") }
LETTER { background-image: url("/images/paper.gif") }
SOFTWARE { background-image: url('../images/screenshot.gif')}
GAME { background-image: url('currentposition.gif')}
```

Parentheses, commas, whitespace characters, single quotes (') and double quotes (") appearing in a URL must be escaped with a backslash: '\(', '\)', '\,'. Any parentheses, apostrophes, whitespace, or quotation marks that appear inside the URL (uncommon except perhaps for the space character) should be replaced by URL standard % escapes. That is:

space	%20
,	%2C
'	%27
"	%22
(	%2B
)	%2C

Note CSS defines its own backslash escapes for these characters (\(, \), \,, \', and \"), but these only add an additional layer of confusion.

Color Values

One of the most widely adopted uses of CSS over traditional HTML is its ability to apply foreground and background colors to almost any element on a page. Properties that take on color values include `color`, `background-color`, and `border-color`.

CSS provides four ways to specify color: by name, by hexadecimal components, by integer components, and by percentages. Defining color by name is the simplest. CSS understands these 16 color names adopted from the Windows VGA palette:

- ✦ aqua
- ✦ black
- ✦ blue
- ✦ fuchsia
- ✦ gray
- ✦ green
- ✦ lime
- ✦ maroon

- ✦ navy
- ✦ olive
- ✦ purple
- ✦ red
- ✦ silver
- ✦ teal
- ✦ white
- ✦ yellow

Of course, the typical color monitor can display several million more colors. These can be specified by providing values for the red, green, and blue (RGB) components of the color. Since CSS assumes a 24-bit color model, each of these primary colors is assigned 8 bits. An 8-bit unsigned integer is a number between 0 and 255. This number may be given in either decimal RGB or hexadecimal RGB. Alternately, it may be given as a percentage RGB between 0% (0) and 100% (255). Table 12-3 lists some of the possible colors and their decimal, hexadecimal, and percentage RGBs.

Table 12-3 CSS Sample Colors			
Color	Decimal RGB	Hexadecimal RGB	Percentage RGB
Pure red	rgb(255,0,0)	#FF0000	rgb(100%, 0%, 0%)
Pure blue	rgb(0,0,255)	#0000FF	rgb(0%, 0%, 0%)
Pure green	rgb(0,255,0)	#00FF00	rgb(0%, 100%, 0%)
White	rgb(255,255,255)	#FFFFFF	rgb(100%, 100%, 100%)
Black	rgb(0,0,0)	#000000	rgb(0%, 0%, 0%)
Light violet	rgb(255,204,255)	#FFCCFF	rgb(100%, 80%, 100%)
Medium gray	rgb(153,153,153)	#999999	rgb(60%, 60%, 60%)
Brown	rgb(153,102,51)	#996633	rgb(60%, 40%, 20%)
Pink	rgb(255,204,204)	#FFCCCC	rgb(100%, 80%, 80%)
Orange	rgb(255,204,204)	#FFCC00	rgb(100%, 80%, 80%)

Tip

Many people still use 256 color monitors. Furthermore, some colors are distinctly different on Macs and PCs. The most reliable colors are the 16 named colors.

The next most reliable colors are those formed using only the hexadecimal components 00, 33, 66, 99, CC, and FF (0, 51, 102, 153, 204, 255 in decimal RGBs; 0%, 20%, 40%, 60%, 80%, 100% in percentage units). For instance, 33FFCC is a "browser-safe" color because the red component is made from two threes, the green from two F's, and the blue from two C's.

If you specify a hexadecimal RGB color using only three digits, CSS duplicates them; for example, #FC0 is really #FFCC00 and #963 is really #996633.

Keyword Values

Keywords are the most variable of the four kinds of values a CSS property may take on. They are not generally the same from property to property, but similar properties generally support similar keywords. For instance, the value of border-left-style can be any one of the keywords none, dotted, dashed, solid, double, groove, ridge, inset, or outset. The border-right-style, border-top-style, border-bottom-style, and border-style properties can also assume one of the values none, dotted, dashed, solid, double, groove, ridge, inset, or outset. The individual keywords will be discussed in the sections about the individual properties.

Block, Inline, and List Item Elements

From the perspective of CSS Level 1 all elements are either block-level elements, inline elements, list items, or invisible. (CSS Level 2 adds a few more possibilities.) The type of a given element is set by its display property. This property has four possible values given by keywords:

```
block

inline

list-item

none
```

Note

In CSS Level 1, the default value of the display property is block which means that the item appears in its own box and is separated from other elements in some fashion. However, in CSS Level 2 the default has changed to inline which means that the contents of the element are simply placed sequentially in the text after the previous element. Most Web browsers use the CSS 2 default (inline) rather the CSS 1 default (block).

In HTML, EM, STRONG, B, I, and A are all inline elements. As another example, you can think of EM, STRONG, B, I, and A in this paragraph as inline code elements. They aren't separated out from the rest of the text.

Block-level elements are separated from other block-level elements, generally by breaking the line. In HTML P, BLOCKQUOTE, H1 through H6, and HR are all examples of block-level elements. The paragraphs you see on this page are all block-level elements. Block-level elements may contain inline elements and other block-level elements, but inline elements should only contain other inline elements, not block-level elements.

List item elements are block-level elements with a list-item marker preceding them. In HTML, LI is a list-item element. List items are discussed further in the following section.

Finally, elements with their display property set to none are invisible and not rendered on the screen. Nor do they affect the position of other visible elements on the page. In HTML, TITLE, META, and HEAD would have a display property of none. In XML, display: none is often useful for meta-information in elements.

Consider Listing 12-7, a synopsis of William Shakespeare's *Twelfth Night*. It contains the following elements:

SYNOPSIS	ACT_NUMBER
TITLE	SCENE_NUMBER
ACT	LOCATION
SCENE	CHARACTER

You can do a fair job of formatting this data using only display properties. SYNOPSIS, TITLE, ACT, and SCENE are all block-level elements. ACT_NUMBER, SCENE_NUMBER, LOCATION, and CHARACTER can remain inline elements. Listing 12-8 is a very simple style sheet that accomplishes this.

Listing 12-7: A synopsis of Shakespeare's *Twelfth Night* in XML

```
<?xml version="1.0"?>
<?xml-stylesheet type="text/css" href="12-8.css"?>
<SYNOPSIS>
  <TITLE>Twelfth Night</TITLE>

  <ACT>
    <ACT_NUMBER>Act 1</ACT_NUMBER>
    <SCENE>
      <SCENE_NUMBER>Scene 1</SCENE_NUMBER>
      <LOCATION><CHARACTER>Duke Orsino</CHARACTER>'s palace
      </LOCATION>
    </SCENE>
    <SCENE>
      <SCENE_NUMBER>Scene 2</SCENE_NUMBER>
      <LOCATION>The sea-coast</LOCATION>
    </SCENE>
    <SCENE>
      <SCENE_NUMBER>Scene 3</SCENE_NUMBER>
      <LOCATION><CHARACTER>Olivia</CHARACTER>'s house
      </LOCATION>
    </SCENE>
    <SCENE>
      <SCENE_NUMBER>Scene 4</SCENE_NUMBER>
      <LOCATION><CHARACTER>Duke Orsino</CHARACTER>'s palace.
      </LOCATION>
    </SCENE>
    <SCENE>
      <SCENE_NUMBER>Scene 5</SCENE_NUMBER>
      <LOCATION><CHARACTER>Olivia</CHARACTER>'s house
      </LOCATION>
    </SCENE>
  </ACT>

  <ACT>
    <ACT_NUMBER>Act 2</ACT_NUMBER>
    <SCENE>
      <SCENE_NUMBER>Scene 1</SCENE_NUMBER>
      <LOCATION>The sea-coast</LOCATION>
    </SCENE>
    <SCENE>
      <SCENE_NUMBER>Scene 2</SCENE_NUMBER>
      <LOCATION>A street</LOCATION>
    </SCENE>
```

Continued

Listing 12-7 *(continued)*

```xml
<SCENE>
  <SCENE_NUMBER>Scene 3</SCENE_NUMBER>
  <LOCATION><CHARACTER>Olivia</CHARACTER>'s house
  </LOCATION>
</SCENE>
<SCENE>
  <SCENE_NUMBER>Scene 4</SCENE_NUMBER>
  <LOCATION><CHARACTER>Duke Orsino</CHARACTER>'s palace.
  </LOCATION>
</SCENE>
<SCENE>
  <SCENE_NUMBER>Scene 5</SCENE_NUMBER>
  <LOCATION><CHARACTER>Olivia</CHARACTER>'s garden
  </LOCATION>
</SCENE>
</ACT>

<ACT>
  <ACT_NUMBER>Act 3</ACT_NUMBER>
  <SCENE>
    <SCENE_NUMBER>Scene 1</SCENE_NUMBER>
    <LOCATION><CHARACTER>Olivia</CHARACTER>'s garden
    </LOCATION>
  </SCENE>
  <SCENE>
    <SCENE_NUMBER>Scene 2</SCENE_NUMBER>
    <LOCATION><CHARACTER>Olivia</CHARACTER>'s house
    </LOCATION>
  </SCENE>
  <SCENE>
    <SCENE_NUMBER>Scene 3</SCENE_NUMBER>
    <LOCATION>A street</LOCATION>
  </SCENE>
  <SCENE>
    <SCENE_NUMBER>Scene 4</SCENE_NUMBER>
    <LOCATION><CHARACTER>Olivia</CHARACTER>'s garden
    </LOCATION>
  </SCENE>
</ACT>

<ACT>
  <ACT_NUMBER>Act 4</ACT_NUMBER>
  <SCENE>
    <SCENE_NUMBER>Scene 1</SCENE_NUMBER>
    <LOCATION><CHARACTER>Olivia</CHARACTER>'s front yard
    </LOCATION>
  </SCENE>
  <SCENE>
    <SCENE_NUMBER>Scene 2</SCENE_NUMBER>
    <LOCATION><CHARACTER>Olivia</CHARACTER>'s house
    </LOCATION>
```

```
    </SCENE>
    <SCENE>
      <SCENE_NUMBER>Scene 3</SCENE_NUMBER>
      <LOCATION><CHARACTER>Olivia</CHARACTER>'s garden
      </LOCATION>
    </SCENE>
  </ACT>

  <ACT>
    <ACT_NUMBER>Act 5</ACT_NUMBER>
    <SCENE>
      <SCENE_NUMBER>Scene 1</SCENE_NUMBER>
      <LOCATION><CHARACTER>Olivia</CHARACTER>'s front yard
      </LOCATION>
    </SCENE>
  </ACT>

</SYNOPSIS>
```

Listing 12-8: A very simple style sheet for the synopsis of a play

```
SYNOPSIS, TITLE, ACT, SCENE { display: block }
```

Figure 12-4 shows the synopsis of *Twelfth Night* loaded into Mozilla with the style sheet of Listing 12-8. Notice that in Listing 12-8 it is not necessary to explicitly specify that ACT_NUMBER, SCENE_NUMBER, LOCATION, and CHARACTER are all inline elements. This is the default unless otherwise specified. The display property is not inherited by children. Thus, just because SCENE is a block-level element does not mean that its children SCENE_NUMBER and LOCATION are also block-level elements.

List Items

If you choose the list-item value for the display property, there are three additional properties you can set. These properties affect how list items are displayed. These are:

1. list-style-type

2. list-style-image

3. list-style-position

There's also a shorthand list-style property that lets you set all three in a single rule.

Caution   Internet Explorer 5.0 and Mozilla 5.0 milestone 3 do not yet support `display:`
`list-item`. Mozilla treats list items as simple block-level elements while Internet
Explorer does even worse by treating them as inline elements.

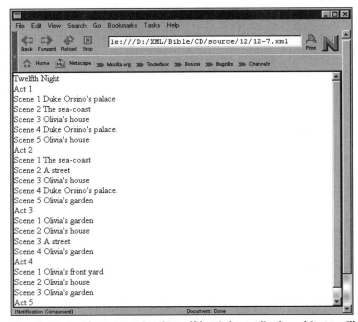

Figure 12-4: The synopsis of *Twelfth Night* as displayed in Mozilla 5.0

The list-style-type Property

The `list-style-type` property determines the nature of the bullet character in
front of each list item. The possibilities are:

    disc

    circle

    square

    decimal

    lower-roman

    upper-roman

    lower-alpha

    upper-alpha

    none

The default is disc. For example, the style sheet in Listing 12-9, which applies to the synopsis in Listing 12-7 defines ACT and SCENE as list items. However, ACT is given no bullet, and SCENE is given a square bullet.

Listing 12-9: A style sheet for a play synopsis that uses list items

```
SYNOPSIS, TITLE { display: block }
ACT { display: list-item; list-style-type: none }
SCENE { display: list-item; list-style-type: square }
```

The list-style-image Property

Alternately, you can use a bitmapped image of your choice loaded from a file as the bullet. To do this you set the list-style-image property to the URL of the image. If both list-style-image and list-style-type are set, the list item will be preceded by both the image and the bullet character. This is rare, however. Listing 12-10 uses a ♥ stored in the file heart.gif as the bullet before each scene (*Twelfth Night* is a romantic comedy after all).

Listing 12-10: A style sheet for a play synopsis that uses the list-style-image property

```
SYNOPSIS, TITLE { display: block }
ACT { display: list-item; list-style-type: none }
SCENE { display: list-item;
        list-style-image: url(heart.gif); list-style-type: none }
```

The list-style-position Property

The list-style-position property specifies whether the bullet is drawn inside or outside the text of the list item. The legal values are inside and outside. The default is outside. The difference is only obvious when the text wraps onto more than one line. This is inside:

- If music be the food of love, play on/Give me excess of it, that, surfeiting,/The appetite may sicken, and so die./That strain again! it had a dying fall:

This is outside:

- If music be the food of love, play on/Give me excess of it, that, surfeiting,/The appetite may sicken, and so die./That strain again! it had a dying fall:

The list-style Shorthand Property

Finally, the list-style property is a short hand that allows you to set all three of the above-described properties at once. For example, this rule says that a SCENE is displayed inside with a heart image and no bullet:

```
SCENE { display: list-item;
        list-style: none inside url(heart.gif) }
```

The whitespace Property

The white-space property determines how significant whitespace (spaces, tabs, line breaks) within an element is. The allowable values are:

    normal

    pre

    nowrap

The default value, normal, simply means that runs of whitespace are condensed to a single space and words are wrapped to fit on the screen or page. This is the normal treatment of whitespace in both HTML and XML.

The pre value acts like the PRE (preformatted) element in HTML. All whitespace in the input document is considered significant and faithfully reproduced on the output device. It may be accompanied by a shift to a monospaced font. This would be useful for much computer source code or some poetry. Listing 12-11 is a poem, *The Altar*, by George Herbert in which spacing is important. In this poem, the lines form the shape of the poem's subject.

Listing 12-11: *The Altar* in XML

```xml
<?xml version="1.0"?>
<?xml-stylesheet type="text/css" href="12-12.css"?>
<POEM>

<TITLE>The Altar</TITLE>
<POET>George Herbert</POET>

<VERSE>    A broken ALTAR, Lord, thy servant rears,</VERSE>
<VERSE>    Made of a heart, and cemented with tears:</VERSE>
<VERSE>    Whose parts are as thy hand did frame;</VERSE>
<VERSE>    No workman's tool hath touched the same.</VERSE>
<VERSE>    No workman's tool hath touched the same.</VERSE>
<VERSE>          A      HEART      alone</VERSE>
<VERSE>          Is    such   a    stone,</VERSE>
<VERSE>          As    nothing     but</VERSE>
<VERSE>          Thy   power   doth   cut.</VERSE>
<VERSE>          Wherefore   each   part</VERSE>
```

```
<VERSE>            Of  my  hard   heart</VERSE>
<VERSE>            Meets  in  this   frame,</VERSE>
<VERSE>            To   praise   thy   name:</VERSE>
<VERSE>   That  if  I  chance  to  hold  my  peace,</VERSE>
<VERSE>   These  stones  to  praise  thee  may  not  cease.</VERSE>
<VERSE>   O  let  thy  blessed   SACRIFICE   be   mine,</VERSE>
<VERSE>   And  sanctify   this   ALTAR   to   be   thine.</VERSE>

</POEM>
```

Listing 12-12 is a style sheet that uses `white-space: pre` to preserve this form. Figure 12-5 shows the result in Mozilla.

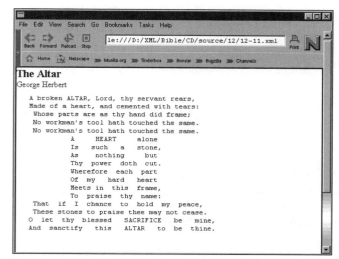

Figure 12-5: *The Altar* by George Herbert with white-space: pre

Caution

Internet Explorer 5.0 does not support `white-space: pre`.

Listing 12-12: **A style sheet for whitespace-sensitive poetry**

```
POEM    { display: block }
TITLE   { display: block; font-size: 16pt; font-weight: bold }
POET    { display: block; margin-bottom: 10px }
STANZA  { display: block; margin-bottom: 10px }
VERSE   { display: block;
          white-space: pre; font-family: monospace }
```

Finally, the nowrap value is a compromise that breaks lines exactly where there's an explicit break in the source text, but condenses other runs of space to a single space. This might be useful when you're trying to faithfully reproduce the line breaks in a classical manuscript or some other poetry where the line breaks are significant but the space between words isn't.

Internet Explorer 5.0 and earlier do not properly support nowrap.

Font Properties

CSS Level 1 supports five basic font properties. These are:

1. font-family
2. font-style
3. font-variant
4. font-weight
5. font-size

Furthermore, there's a font shorthand property that can set all five properties at once.

The font-family Property

The value of the font-family property is a comma-separated list of font names such as Helvetica, Times, Palatino, etc. Font names that include whitespace such as "Times New Roman" should be enclosed in double quotes.

Names may also be one of the five generic names serif, sans-serif, cursive, fantasy, and monospace. The browser replaces these names with a font of the requested type installed on the local system. Table 12-4 demonstrates these fonts.

| | | Table 12-4 | |
| | | **Generic Fonts** | |
Name	**Typical Family**	**Distinguishing Characteristic**	**Example**
Serif	Times, Times New Roman, Palatino	Curlicues on the edges of letters make serif text easier to read in small body type.	The quick brown fox jumped over the lazy dog.

Name	Typical Family	Distinguishing Characteristic	Example
sans-serif	Geneva. Helvetica, Verdana	Block type. often used in headlines.	The quick brown fox jumped over the lazy dog.
Monospace	Courier, Courier New, Monaco, American Typewriter	A typewriter like font in which each character has exactly the same width, commonly used for source code and email.	The quick brown fox jumped over the lazy dog.
Cursive	ZapfChancery	Script font, a simulation of handwriting.	The quick brown fox jumped over the lazy dog.
Fantasy	Western, Critter	Text with special effects; e.g. letters on fire, letters formed by tumbling acrobats, letters made from animals, etc.	THE QUICK BROWN FOX JUMPED OVER THE LAZY DOG.

Because there isn't a guarantee that any given font will be available or appropriate on a particular client system (10-point Times is practically illegible on a Macintosh, much less a Palm Pilot), you'll generally provide a comma-separated list of choices for the font in the order of preference. The last choice in the list should always be one of the generic names. However, even if you don't specify a generic name and the fonts you *do* specify aren't available, the browser will pick something. It just may not be anything like what you wanted.

For example, here are two rules that make the TITLE element Helvetica with a fallback position of any sans serif font; and the rest of the elements Times with fallback positions of Times New Roman, and any serif font.

```
TITLE    { font-family: Helvetica, sans-serif }
SYNOPSIS { font-family: Times, "Times New Roman", serif }
```

Figure 12-6 shows the synopsis loaded into Mozilla 5.0 after these two rules are added to the style sheet of Listing 12-8. Not a great deal has changed since Figure 12-4 Times is commonly the default font. The most obvious difference is that the title is now in Helvetica.

The font-family property is inherited by child elements. Thus by setting SYNOPSIS's font-family to Times, all the child elements are also set to Times except for TITLE whose own font-family property overrides the one it inherits.

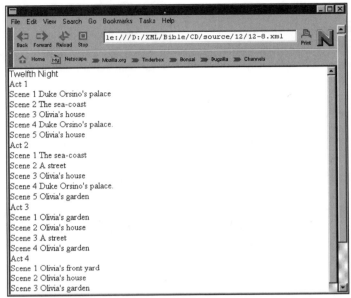

Figure 12-6: The synopsis of *Twelfth Night* with the title in Helvetica

The font-style Property

The font-style property has three values: normal, italic, and oblique. The regular text you're reading now is normal. The typical rendering of the HTML EM element is *italicized*. Oblique text is very similar to italicized text. However, oblique text is most commonly created by a computer following a simple algorithm to slant normal text by a fixed amount. Italicized text generally uses a font hand designed to look good in its slanted form.

This rule italicizes the SCENE_NUMBER:

```
SCENE_NUMBER { font-style: italic}
```

Figure 12-7 shows the synopsis loaded into Internet Explorer 5.0 after this rule is added to the style sheet for the synopsis.

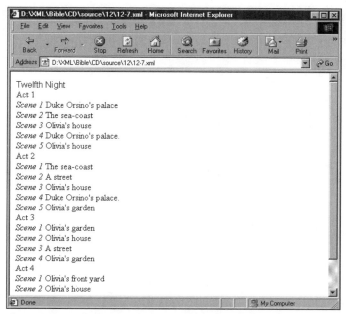

Figure 12-7: The synopsis of *Twelfth Night* with italic scene numbers

The font-variant Property

The font-variant property has two possible values in CSS Level 1, normal and small-caps. The default is normal. Setting font-variant to small-caps replaces lowercase letters with capital letters in a smaller font size than the main body text.

You can get a very nice effect by combining the font-variant property with the first-letter pseudo-element. For example, define the ACT_NUMBER element to have the font-variant: small-caps. Next define the first letter of ACT_NUMBER to have font-variant: normal. This produces act numbers that look like this:

ACT 1

Here are the rules:

```
ACT_NUMBER                { font-variant: small-caps}
ACT_NUMBER:first-letter { font-variant: normal}
```

The second rule overrides the first, but only for the first letter of the act number.

The font-weight Property

The `font-weight` property determines how dark (bold) or light (narrow) the text appears. There are 13 possible values of this property:

```
normal
bold
bolder
lighter
100
200
300
400
500
600
700
800
900
```

Weights range from 100 (the lightest) to 900 (the darkest). Intermediate, non-century values like 850 are not allowed. Normal weight is 400. Bold is 700. The `bolder` value makes an element bolder than its parent. The `lighter` value makes an element less bold than its parent. However, there's no guarantee that a particular font has as many as nine separate levels of boldness.

Here's a simple rule that makes the `TITLE` and `ACT_NUMBER` elements bold.

```
TITLE, ACT_NUMBER { font-weight: bold}
```

Figure 12-8 shows the results in the Mozilla viewer after this rule is added to the style sheet for Listing 12-7.

The font-size Property

The `font-size` property determines the height and the width of a typical character in the font. Larger sizes take up more space on the screen. The size may be specified as a keyword, a value relative to the font size of the parent, a percentage of the size of the parent element's font size, or an absolute number.

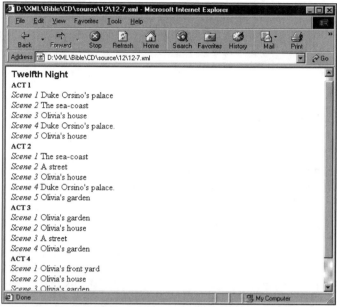

Figure 12-8: The synopsis of *Twelfth Night* with bold title and act numbers

Keyword

Absolute size keywords are:

```
xx-small

x-small

small

medium

large

x-large

xx-large
```

These keywords are the preferred way to set font sizes because they are still relative to the base font size of the page. For instance, if the user has adjusted their default font size to 20 points because they're very near-sighted, all other values here will scale accordingly.

In CSS1, each size is 1.5 times larger than the next smallest size. The default is medium, so if a browser's default is 12 points, then large type will be 18 points, x-large type will be 27 points, and xx-large type will be 40.5 points. By contrast, small type will be 8 points; x-small type will be 5.33 points, and xx-small will be an almost certainly illegible 3.56 points.

Here's the simple rule that makes the TITLE extra large:

```
TITLE    { font-size: x-large }
```

Value Relative to Parent's Font Size

You can also specify the size relative to the parent element as either larger or smaller. For instance, in the following, the SCENE_NUMBER will have a size that is smaller than the font size of its parent SCENE.

```
SCENE_NUMBER { font-size: smaller }
```

There's no definitive rule for exactly how much smaller a smaller font will be or how much larger a larger font will be. Generally, the browser will attempt to move from medium to small, from small to x-small and so forth. The same is true (in the other direction) for larger fonts. Thus, making a font larger should increase its size by about 50 percent, and making a font smaller should decrease its size by about 33 percent, but browsers are free to fudge these values in order to match the available font sizes.

Percentage of Parent Element's Font Size

If these options aren't precise enough, you can make finer adjustments by using a percentage of the parent element's font size. For example, this rule says that the font used for a SCENE_NUMBER is 50% of the size of the font for the SCENE.

```
SCENE_NUMBER { font-size: 50% }
```

Absolute Length Value

Finally, you can give a font size as an absolute length. Although you can use pixels, centimeters, or inches, the most common unit when measuring fonts is points. For example, this rule sets the default font-size for the SYNOPSIS element and its children to 14 points.

```
SYNOPSIS { font-size: 14pt }
```

Caution   I strongly urge you not to use absolute units to describe font sizes. It's extremely difficult (I'd argue impossible) to pick a font size that's legible across all the different platforms on which your page might be viewed, ranging from PDAs to the Sony Jumbotron in Times Square. Even when restricting themselves to standard personal computers, most designers usually pick a font that's too small. Any text that's intended to be read on the screen should be at least 12 points, possibly more.

Figure 12-9 shows the results in Mozilla after these rules are added to the style sheet for Listing 12-7. The text of the scenes is not really bolder. It's just bigger. In any case, it's a lot easier to read.

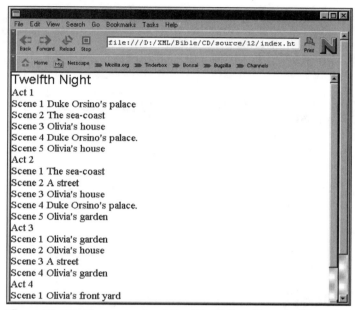

Figure 12-09: The synopsis of *Twelfth Night* with varied font sizes

The font Shorthand Property

The `font` property is a shorthand property that allows the font style, variant, weight, size, and family to be set with one rule. For example, here are two rules for the TITLE and SCENE_NUMBER elements that combine the six separate rules of the previous section:

```
TITLE { font: bold x-large Helvetica, sans-serif }
SCENE_NUMBER { font: italic smaller serif }
```

Values must be given in the following order:

1. One each of style, variant, and weight, in any order, any of which may be omitted

2. Size, which may not be omitted

3. Optionally a forward slash (/) and a line height

4. Family, which may not be omitted

Note If this sounds complicated and hard to remember, that's because it is. I certainly can't remember the exact details for the order of these properties without looking it up. I prefer to just use the individual properties one at a time. It's questionable whether shorthand properties like this really save any time.

Listing 12-13 is the style sheet for the synopsis with all the rules devised so far, using the font shorthand properties. However, since a font property is exactly equivalent to the sum of the individual properties it represents, there's no change to the rendered document.

Listing 12-13: A style sheet for the synopsis with font shorthand

```
SYNOPSIS, TITLE, ACT, SCENE { display: block }
SCENENUMBER { font: italic smaller serif }
TITLE { font: bold x-large Helvetica, sans-serif }
SYNOPSIS { font: 14pt Times, "Times New Roman", serif }
ACTNUMBER { font-variant: small-caps}
ACTNUMBER:first-letter { font-variant: normal}
ACTNUMBER { font-weight: bold}
```

The Color Property

CSS allows you to assign colors to almost any element on a page with the color property. The value of the color property may be one of 16 named color keywords, or an RGB triple in decimal, hexadecimal, or percentages. For instance, the following rules specify that all elements on the page are colored black except the SCENE_NUMBER, which is colored blue:

```
SYNOPSIS { color: black }
SCENE_NUMBER { color: blue}
```

The color property is inherited by children. Thus, all elements in the synopsis except for the SCENE_NUMBER elements will be colored black.

The following rules are all equivalent to the above two. I recommend using named colors when possible, and browser-safe colors when not.

```
SYNOPSIS { color: #000000 }
SCENE_NUMBER { color: #0000FF}
SYNOPSIS { color: rgb(0, 0, 0) }
SCENE_NUMBER { color: rgb(0, 0, 255)}
SYNOPSIS { color: rgb(0%, 0%, 0%) }
SCENE_NUMBER { color: rgb(0%, 0%, 100%)}
```

Background Properties

The background of an element can be set to a color or an image. If it's set to an image, the image can be positioned differently relative to the content of the element. This is accomplished with the following five basic properties:

1. background-color
2. background-image
3. background-repeat
4. background-attachment
5. background-position

Finally, there's a background shorthand property that allows you to set some or all of these five properties in one rule.

Caution   Fancy backgrounds are vastly overused on the Web today. Anything other than a very light background color only makes your page harder to read and annoys users. I list these properties here for completeness' sake, but I strongly recommend that you use them sparingly, if at all.

None of the background properties is inherited. Each child element must specify the background it wants. However, it may appear as if background properties are inherited because the default is for the background to be transparent. The background of whatever element is drawn below an element will show through. Most of the time this is the background of the parent element.

The background-color Property

The background-color property may be set to the same values as the color property. However, rather than changing the color of the element's contents, it changes the color of the element's background on top of which the contents are drawn. For example, to draw a SIGN element with yellow text on a blue background, you would use this rule:

```
SIGN { color: yellow; background-color: blue}
```

You can also set the background-color to the keyword transparent (the default) which simply means that the background takes on the color or image of whatever the element is laying on top of, generally the parent element.

The background-image Property

The background-image property is either none (the default) or a URL (generally relative) where a bitmapped image file can be found. If it's a URL, then the browser will load the image and use it as the background, much like the BACKGROUND attribute of the BODY element in HTML. For example, here's how you attach the file party.gif (shown in Figure 12-10) as the background for an INVITATION element.

```
INVITATION { background-image: url(party.gif) }
```

Figure 12-10: The original, untiled, uncropped background image for the party invitation in Listing 12-14

The image referenced by the background-image property is drawn underneath the specified element, *not* underneath the browser pane like the BACKGROUND attribute of HTML's BODY element.

Note   If the background image is associated with the root element, early betas of Mozilla 5.0 attach the background image to the entire document pane rather than to only the element itself. For all non-root elements, however, the background image applies only to the element it's applied to. The CSS Level 1 specification is not clear regarding whether or not this is acceptable behavior.

Background images will generally not be the exact same size as the contents of the page. If the image is larger than the element's box, the image will be cropped. If the image is smaller than the element's box, it will be tiled vertically and horizontally. Figure 12-11 shows a background image that has tiled exactly far enough to cover the underlying content. Note that the tiling takes place across the element, *not* across the browser window. The XML file for this picture is in Listing 12-14.

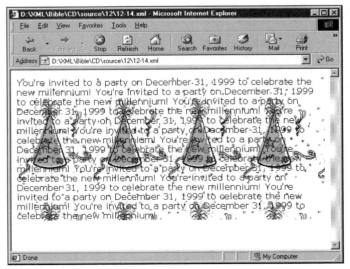

Figure 12-11: A tiled background image

Listing 12-14: A party invitation in XML

```
<?xml version="1.0"?>
<?xml-stylesheet type="text/css" href="party.css"?>
<INVITATION>
You're invited to a party on December 31, 1999 to celebrate the
new millennium! You're invited to a party on December 31, 1999
to celebrate the new millennium! You're invited to a party on
December 31, 1999 to celebrate the new millennium! You're
invited to a party on December 31, 1999 to celebrate the new
millennium! You're invited to a party on December 31, 1999 to
celebrate the new millennium! You're invited to a party on
December 31, 1999 to celebrate the new millennium! You're
invited to a party on December 31, 1999 to celebrate the new
millennium! You're invited to a party on December 31, 1999 to
celebrate the new millennium! You're invited to a party on
December 31, 1999 to celebrate the new millennium! You're
invited to a party on December 31, 1999 to celebrate the new
millennium! You're invited to a party on December 31, 1999 to
celebrate the new millennium!
</INVITATION>
```

The background-repeat Property

The `background-repeat` property adjusts how background images are tiled across the screen. You can specify that background images are not tiled or are only tiled horizontally or vertically. Possible values for this property are:

```
repeat

repeat-x

repeat-y

no-repeat
```

For example, to only show a single party hat on the invitation you would set the `background-repeat` of the INVITATION element to `no-repeat`. Figure 12-12 shows the result. For example:

```
INVITATION { background-image:  url(party.gif);
             background-repeat: no-repeat }
```

To tile across but not down the page, set `background-repeat` to `repeat-x`, as shown below. Figure 12-13 shows the background image tiled across but not down.

```
INVITATION { background-image:  url(party.gif);
             background-repeat: repeat-x }
```

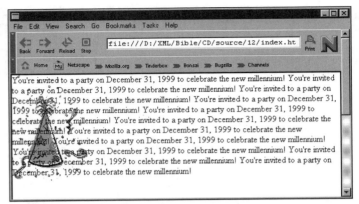

Figure 12-12: An untiled background image

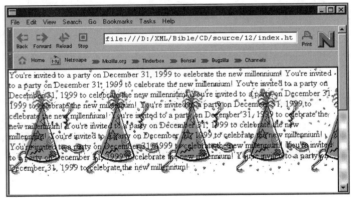

Figure 12-13: A background image tiled across, but not down

To tile down but not across the page, set `background-repeat` to `repeat-y`, as shown below. Figure 12-14 shows the result.

```
INVITATION { background-image:  url(party.gif);
             background-repeat: repeat-y }
```

The background-attachment Property

In HTML, the background image is attached to the document. When the document is scrolled, the background image scrolls with it. With the `background-attachment` property, you can specify that the background be attached to the window or pane instead. Possible values are `scroll` and `fixed`. The default is `scroll`; that is, the background is attached to the document rather than the window.

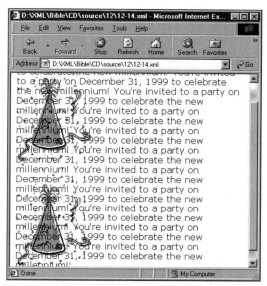

Figure 12-14: A background image tiled down but not across

However, with `background-attachment` set to `fixed`, the document scrolls but the background image doesn't. This might be useful in conjunction with an image that's big enough for a typical browser window but not big enough to be a backdrop for a large document when you don't want to tile the image. You would code this:

```
DOCUMENT { background-attachment: fixed;
           background-repeat: no-repeat }
```

Caution Neither IE5 nor Mozilla supports fixed background images. This feature may be added in later releases. (The CSS1 spec does not require browsers to support fixed backgrounds.)

The background-position Property

By default, the upper-left corner of a background image is aligned with the upper-left corner of the element it's attached to. (See Figure 12-12 for an example.) Most of the time this is exactly what you want. However, for those rare times when you want something else, the `background-position` property allows you to move the background relative to the element.

You can specify the offset using percentages of the width and height of the parent element, using absolute lengths, or using two of these six keywords:

```
top

center

bottom

left

center

right
```

Percentages of Parent Element's Width and Height

Percentages enable you to pin different parts of the background to the corresponding part of the element. The *x* coordinate is given as a percentage ranging from 0% (left-hand side) to 100% (right-hand side). The *y* coordinate is given as a percentage ranging from 0% (top) to 100% (bottom). For example, this rule places the upper-right corner of the image in the upper-right corner of the INVITATION element. Figure 12-15 shows the result.

```
INVITATION { background-image: url(party.gif);
             background-repeat: no-repeat;
             background-position: 100% 0% }
```

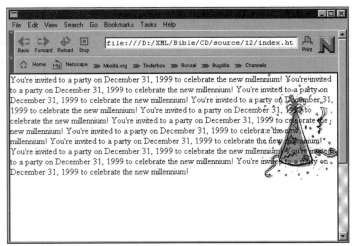

Figure 12-15: A background image aligned with the upper-right corner of the content

Absolute Lengths

Absolute lengths position the upper-left corner of the background in an absolute position in the element. The next rule places the upper-left corner of the background image party.gif one centimeter to the right and two centimeters below the upper-left corner of the element. Figure 12-16 shows the result.

```
INVITATION { background-image: url(party.gif);
             background-repeat: no-repeat;
             background-position: 1cm 2cm }
```

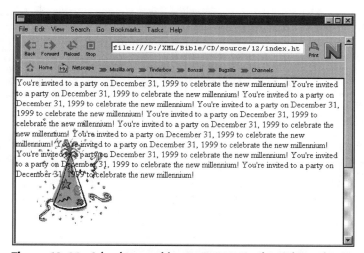

Figure 12-16: A background image 1.0 cm to the right and 2.0 cm below the left-hand corner of the element

Keywords

The top left and left top keywords are the same as 0% 0%. The top, top center, and center top are the same as 50% 0%. The right top and top right keywords are the same as 100% 0%. The left, left center, and center left keywords are the same as 0% 50%. The center and center center keywords are the same as 50% 50%. The right, right center, and center right keywords are the same as 100% 50%. The bottom left and left bottom keywords are the same as 0% 100%. The bottom, bottom center, and center bottom mean the same as 50% 100%. The bottom right and right bottom keywords are the same as 100% 100%. Figure 12-17 associates these with individual positions on an element box.

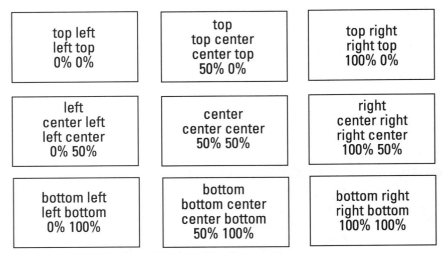

top left left top 0% 0%	top top center center top 50% 0%	top right right top 100% 0%
left center left left center 0% 50%	center center center 50% 50%	right center right right center 100% 50%
bottom left left bottom 0% 100%	bottom bottom center center bottom 50% 100%	bottom right right bottom 100% 100%

Figure 12-17: Relative positioning of background images

For instance, for our running invitation example, the best effect is achieved by pinning the centers together, as shown in Figure 12-18. Here's the necessary rule:

```
INVITATION { background-image: url(party.gif);
             background-repeat: no-repeat;
             background-position: center center }
```

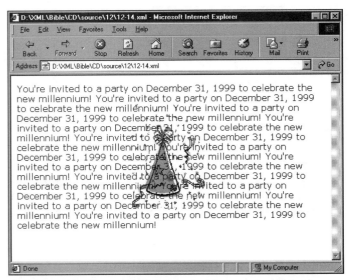

Figure 12-18: An untiled background image pinned to the center of the INVITATION element

If the `background-attachment` property has the value `fixed`, then the image is placed relative to the windowpane instead of the element.

The Background Shorthand Property

The `background` property is shorthand for setting the `background-color`, `background-image`, `background-repeat`, `background-attachment`, and `background-position` properties in a single rule. For example, to set `background-color` to white, `background-image` to party.gif, `background-repeat` to `no-repeat`, and `background-attachment` to `fixed` in the INVITATION element, you can use this rule:

```
INVITATION { background: url(party.gif) white no-repeat fixed }
```

This means exactly the same thing as this longer but more legible rule:

```
INVITATION { background-image: url(party.gif);
             background-color: white;
             background-repeat: no-repeat;
             background-attachment: fixed }
```

When using the `background` shorthand property, values for any or all of the five properties may be given in any order. However, none may occur more than once. For example, the upper-right corner alignment rule used for Figure 12-16 could have been written like this instead:

```
INVITATION { background: url(party.gif) no-repeat 100% 0% }
```

Text Properties

There are eight properties affecting the appearance of text, irrespective of font. These are:

1. `word-spacing`
2. `letter-spacing`
3. `text-decoration`
4. `vertical-align`
5. `text-transform`
6. `text-align`
7. `text-indent`
8. `line-height`

The word-spacing Property

The `word-spacing` property expands the text by adding additional space between words. A negative value removes space between words. The only reason I can think of to alter the word spacing on a Web page is if you are a student laboring under tight page-count limits who wants to make a paper look bigger or smaller than it is.

> **Note**
>
> Desktop publishers love adjusting these kinds of properties. The problem is that all the rules they've learned about how and when to adjust spacing are based on ink on paper, and really don't work when transferred to the medium of electrons on phosphorus (a typical CRT monitor). You're almost always better off letting the browser make decisions about word and letter spacing for you.
>
> If, on the other hand, your target medium *is* ink on paper, then there's a little more to be gained by adjusting these properties. The main difference is that with ink on paper you control the delivery medium. You know exactly how big the fonts are, how wide and high the display is, how many dots per inch are being used, and so forth. On the Web, you simply don't have enough information about the output medium available to control everything at this level of detail.

To change this from the default value of `normal`, you set a length for the property. For example,

```
INVITATION { word-spacing: 1em }
```

Browsers are not required to respect this property, especially if it interferes with other properties like `align: justified`. Internet Explorer 5.0 does not support `word-spacing`, but Mozilla does, as shown in Figure 12-19.

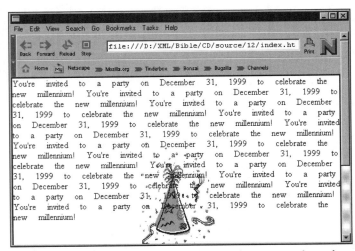

Figure 12-19: The INVITATION element with one em of word spacing

The letter-spacing Property

The letter-spacing property enables you to expand the text by adding additional space between letters. You can make the value negative to remove space between letters. Again, the only reason I can think of to do this on a Web page is to make a paper look bigger or smaller than it really is to meet a length requirement.

To change this from the default value of normal, you set a length for the property. For example:

```
INVITATION { letter-spacing: 0.3em }
```

Since justification works by adjusting the amount of space between letters, changing the letter spacing manually prevents the browser from justifying text.

Browsers are not required to respect this property, especially if it interferes with other properties like align: justified. However both Internet Explorer and Mozilla do, as shown in Figure 12-20.

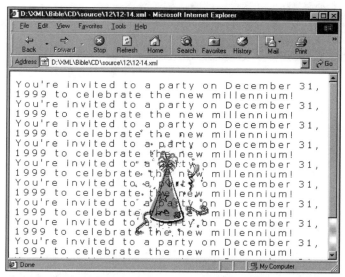

Figure 12-20: The INVITATION element with 0.3em letter spacing

The text-decoration Property

The text-decoration property may have one of the following five values:

```
none
underline
```

```
overline
line-through
blink
```

Except for none, the default, these values are not mutually exclusive. You may for example, specify that a paragraph is underlined, overlined, struck through, and blinking. (I do not, however, recommend that you do this.)

Note   Browsers are not required to support blinking text. This is a good thing.

For example, the next rule specifies that CHARACTER elements are underlined. Figure 12-21 shows the result of applying this rule to the synopsis of *Twelfth Night* in Listing 12-7.

```
CHARACTER { text-decoration: underline }
```

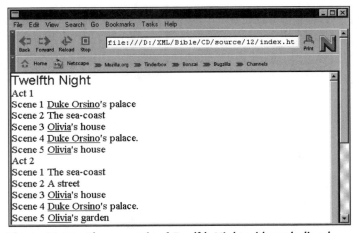

Figure 12-21: The synopsis of *Twelfth Night* with underlined characters

The vertical-align Property

The vertical-align property specifies how an inline element is positioned relative to the baseline of the text. Valid values are:

```
baseline
sub
super
top
```

```
text-top
middle
bottom
text-bottom
```

You can also use a percentage of the line height of the element. The default is `baseline` which lines up the baseline of the element with the baseline of its parent.

The `sub` value makes the element a subscript. The `super` value makes the element a superscript. The `text-top` value aligns the top of the element with the top of the parent element's font. The `middle` value aligns the vertical midpoint of the element with the baseline of the parent plus half the *x*-height. The `text-bottom` value aligns the bottom of the element with the bottom of the parent element's font.

The `top` value aligns the top of the element with the tallest letter or element on the line. The `bottom` value aligns the bottom of the element with the bottom of the lowest letter or element on the line. The exact alignment changes as the height of the tallest or lowest letter changes.

For example, the rule for a footnote number might look like this one that superscripts the number and decreases its size by 20 percent.

```
FOOTNOTE_NUMBER { vertical-align: super; font-size: 80% }
```

The text-transform Property

The `text-transform` property lets you to specify that the text should be rendered in all uppercase, all lowercase, or with initial letters capitalized. This is useful in headlines, for example. The valid values are:

```
capitalize
uppercase
lowercase
none
```

Capitalization Makes Only The First Letter Of Every Word Uppercase Like This Sentence. PLACING THE SENTENCE IN UPPERCASE, HOWEVER, MAKES EVERY LETTER IN THE SENTENCE UPPERCASE. The following rule converts the `TITLE` element in the *Twelfth Night* synopsis to uppercase. Figure 12-22 shows the synopsis after this rule has been applied.

```
TITLE { text-transform: uppercase }
```

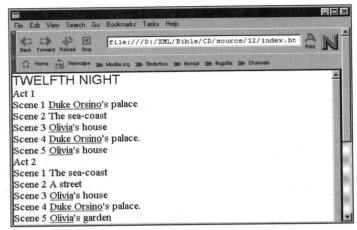

Figure 12-22: The TITLE in the synopsis is now uppercase.

Note

The `text-transform` property is somewhat language-dependent since many languages — Chinese, for example — don't have any concept of an upper- and a lowercase.

The text-align Property

The `text-align` property applies only to block-level elements. It specifies whether the text in the block is to be aligned with the left-hand side, the right-hand side, centered, or justified. The valid values are:

```
left

right

center

justify
```

The following rules center the `TITLE` element in the *Twelfth Night* synopsis and justifies everything else. Figure 12-23 shows the synopsis after these rules have been applied.

```
TITLE { text-align: center }
SYNOPSIS { text-align: justify }
```

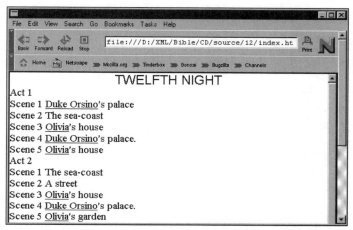

Figure 12-23: The TITLE in the synopsis is centered and the rest of the text is justified.

The text-indent Property

The text-indent property, which applies only to block-level elements, specifies the indentation of the first line of a block with respect to the remaining lines of the block and is given as either an absolute length or a percentage of the width of the parent element. The value may be negative which produces a hanging indent.

Tip   To indent all the lines of an element, rather than just the first, you use the box properties discussed in the next section to set an extra left margin on the element.

For example, the following rule indents the scenes in the synopsis by half an inch. Figure 12-24 shows the synopsis after this rule has been applied.

```
SCENE { text-indent: 0.5in }
```

The line-height Property

The line-height property specifies the distance between the baselines of successive lines. It can be given as an absolute number, an absolute length, or a percentage of the font size. For instance, the following rule double-spaces the SYNOPSIS element. Figure 12-25 shows the *Twelfth Night* synopsis after this rule has been applied.

```
SYNOPSIS { line-height: 200% }
```

Figure 12-24: The SCENE and its children in the synopsis are all indented half an inch.

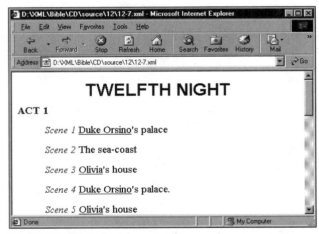

Figure 12-25: A double-spaced synopsis

Double-spacing isn't particularly attractive though so I'll remove it. In the next section, some extra margins are added around individual elements to get a nicer effect. Listing 12-15 summarizes the additions made in this section to the synopsis style sheet (minus the double-spacing).

Listing 12-15: The synopsis style sheet with text properties

```
SYNOPSIS, TITLE, ACT, SCENE { display: block }
SCENE_NUMBER { font: italic smaller serif }
TITLE { font: bold x-large Helvetica, sans-serif }
SYNOPSIS { font: 14pt Times, "Times New Roman", serif }
ACT_NUMBER                { font-variant: small-caps}
ACT_NUMBER:first-letter { font-variant: normal}
ACT_NUMBER { font-weight: bold}
CHARACTER { text-decoration: underline }
TITLE { text-transform: uppercase }
TITLE { text-align: center }
SYNOPSIS { text-align: justify }
SCENE { text-indent: 0.5in }
```

Box Properties

CSS describes a two-dimensional canvas on which output is drawn. The elements drawn on this canvas are encased in imaginary rectangles called boxes. These boxes are always oriented parallel to the edges of the canvas. Box properties enable you to specify the width, height, margins, padding, borders, sizes, and positions of the individual boxes. Figure 12-26 shows how these properties relate to each other.

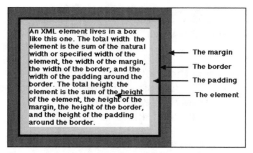

Figure 12-26: A CSS box with margin, border, and padding

Margin Properties

Margin properties specify the amount of space added to the box outside its border. This may be set separately for the top, bottom, right and left margins using the `margin-top`, `margin-bottom`, `margin-right`, and `margin-left` properties. Each margin may be given as an absolute length or as a percentage of the size of the parent element's width. For example, you can add a little extra space between each ACT element and the preceding element by setting ACT's `margin-top` property to 1ex as the following rule and Figure 12-27 demonstrate.

```
ACT { margin-top: 1ex }
```

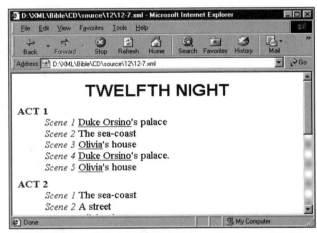

Figure 12-27: The top margin of the ACT element is larger

You can also set all four margins at once using the shorthand `margin` property. For example, you can add extra whitespace around the entire *Twelfth Night* document by setting the margin property for the root-level element (SYNOPSIS in this example) as shown in the next rule. Figure 12-28 demonstrates.

```
SYNOPSIS { margin: 1cm 1cm 1cm 1cm }
```

In fact, this is the same as using a single value for margin, which CSS interprets as being applicable to all four sides.

```
SYNOPSIS { margin: 1cm }
```

Given two `margin` values, the first applies to top and bottom, the second to right and left. Given three `margin` values, the first applies to the top, the second to the right and left, and the third to the bottom. It's probably easier to just use the separate `margin-top`, `margin-bottom`, `margin-right`, and `margin-left` properties.

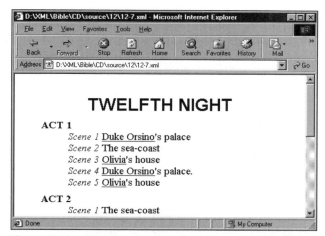

Figure 12-28: One centimeter of whitespace around the entire synopsis

Border Properties

Most boxes won't have borders. They are imaginary boxes that affect the layout of their contents, but are probably not seen as boxes by the readers. However, you can make a box visible by drawing lines around it using the border properties. Border properties let you to specify the style, width, and color of the border.

Border Style

By default, no border is drawn around boxes regardless of the width and color of the border. To make a border visible you must change the `border-style` property of the box from its default value of `none` to one of these values:

```
dotted

dashed

solid

double

groove

ridge

inset

outset
```

The `border-style` property can have between one and four values. As with the `margin` property, a single value applies to all four borders. Two values set top and bottom borders to the first style, right and left borders to the second style. Three values set the top, right and left, and bottom border styles in that order. Four values set each border in the order top, right, bottom, and left. For example, the next rule surrounds the entire SYNOPSIS with a solid border. Figure 12-29 shows the result in Internet Explorer 5.0. In this case, the border has the secondary effect of making the margin more obvious. (Remember, the margin is outside the border.)

```
SYNOPSIS { border-style: solid }
```

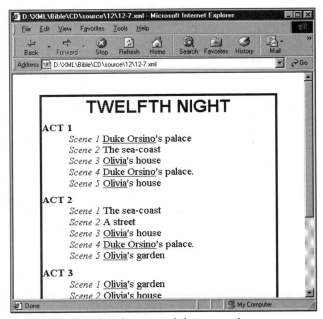

Figure 12-29: A border around the synopsis

Caution   Internet Explorer 5.0 can only display solid borders. The other styles are all drawn as simple, solid borders.

Border Width

There are four border-width properties for specifying the width of the borderline along the top, bottom, right, and left edges of the box. These are:

1. border-top-width
2. border-right-width
3. border-bottom-width
4. border-left-width

Each may be specified as an absolute length or as one of three keywords: `thin`, `medium`, or `thick`. Border widths cannot be negative, but can be zero.

For example, to enclose the `SYNOPSIS` element in a one-pixel wide solid border (the thinnest border any computer monitor can display), you could use the next rule to set these four properties:

```
SYNOPSIS { border-style:        solid;
           border-top-width:    1px;
           border-right-width:  1px;
           border-bottom-width: 1px;
           border-left-width:   1px }
```

If want to set all or several borders to the same width, it's most convenient to use the `border-width` shorthand property. This property can have between one and four values. One value sets all four border widths. Two values set top and bottom borders to the first value, right and left borders to the second value. Three values set the top, right, and left, and bottom widths in that order. Four values set each border in the order top, right, bottom, and left. For example, the following is equivalent to the previous rule:

```
SYNOPSIS { border-style: solid; border-width: 1px }
```

Border Color

The `border-color` property sets the color of between one and four borders. A single value sets all four border colors. Two values set top and bottom borders to the first color, right and left borders to the second color. Three values set the top, right and left, and bottom border colors in that order. Four values set each border in the order top, right, bottom, and left. Valid values are any recognized color name or RGB triplet. For example, to enclose the `SYNOPSIS` element in a one-pixel wide, solid red border, you'd use this rule:

```
SYNOPSIS { border-style: solid;
           border-width: 1px;
           border-color: red }
```

Since this book is printed in black and white, I'll spare you the picture.

Shorthand Border Properties

Five shorthand border properties let you set the width, style, and color of a border with one rule. These are:

1. `border-top`
2. `border-right`
3. `border-bottom`
4. `border-left`
5. `border`

For instance, the `border-top` property provides a width, style, and color for the top border. The `border-right`, `border-bottom`, and `border-left` properties are similar. Omitted properties are set to the value of the parent element. For example, Figure 12-30 shows a two-pixel solid blue border (a horizontal rule if you will) below each act. To achieve this, you would use this rule:

```
ACT { border-bottom: 2px solid blue }
```

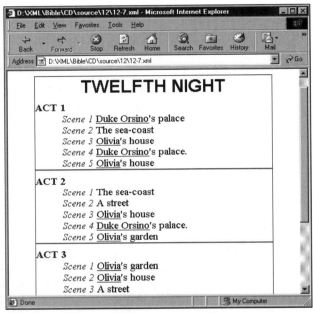

Figure 12-30: A two-pixel, solid bottom border is similar to HTML's HR element.

The `border` property sets all four sides to the specified width, style, and height. For example, this rule draws a three-pixel wide, solid, red border around a CHART element.

```
CHART { border: 3pt solid red }
```

Padding Properties

The padding properties specify the amount of space on the *inside* of the border of the box. The border of the box, if shown, falls between the margin and the padding. Padding may be set separately for the top, bottom, right and left padding using the padding-top, padding-bottom, padding-right, and padding-left properties. Each padding may be given as an absolute length or be a percentage of the size of the parent element's width. For example, you can set off the SYNOPSIS from its border by setting its padding properties as shown in this rule.

```
SYNOPSIS { padding-bottom: 1em;
           padding-top: 1em;
           padding-right: 1em;
           padding-left: 1em }
```

You can also set all four at once using the shorthand padding property. For example, the following rule is the same as the previous one:

```
SYNOPSIS { padding: 1em 1em 1em 1em }
```

In fact, this is the same as using a single value for the padding property, which CSS interprets as applying to all four sides.

```
SYNOPSIS { padding: 1em }
```

Given two padding values, the first applies to top and bottom, the second to right and left. Given three padding values, the first applies to the top, the second to the right and left, and the third to the bottom. It's probably easier to use the separate padding-top, padding-bottom, padding-right, and padding-left properties.

The blue borders below the acts in the synopsis seem a little too close, so let's add an ex of padding between the end of the act and the border with the padding-bottom property, as shown in the following rule. Figure 12-31 shows the result. Generally, it's a good idea to use a little padding around borders to make the text easier to read.

```
ACT { padding-bottom: 1ex }
```

Size Properties

A box can be forced to a given size using the width and height properties. The contents of the box will be scaled as necessary to fit. Although you can use this with text boxes, it's more common and useful with replaced elements like images and applets. The width and the height may be given as an absolute length, as a percentage of the parent element's height and width, or as the keyword auto (the default) to indicate that the browser should use the real size. For example, this rule tries to fit the entire SYNOPSIS element in a 3-inch by 3-inch square.

```
SYNOPSIS { padding: 1em; width: 3in; height: 3in }
```

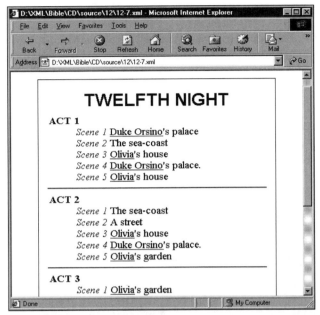

Figure 12-31: Padding makes borders easier on the eye

Figure 12-32 shows the result in Internet Explorer 5.0. When faced with an element that's simply bigger than its box allows, the Internet Explorer constrains the width but expands the height. Mozilla lets the text flow outside the box, possibly overlapping elements below. Browsers deal inconsistently and unpredictably with content that won't fit in a precisely sized box. Therefore, exact sizing is to be eschewed in cross-browser Web design.

If the width is set to an absolute or relative unit, and the height is set to auto, then the height will be adjusted proportionally to the width.

Positioning Properties

By default, block-level elements nested inside the same parent element follow each other on the page. They do not line up side by side or wrap around each other. You can change this with judicious use of the float and clear properties.

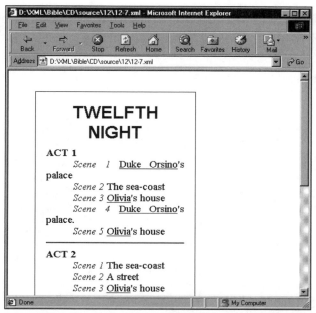

Figure 12-32: A three-inch high by three-inch wide synopsis as viewed in Mozilla

The float Property

The float property, whose value is none by default, can be set to left or right. If the value is left, then the element is moved to the left side of the page and the text flows around it on the right. In HTML, this is how an IMG with ALIGN="LEFT" behaves. If the value is right, then the element is moved to the right side of the page and the text flows around it on the left. In HTML, this is how an IMG with ALIGN="RIGHT" behaves.

There's no standard way to embed images in XML files, so for this example we'll fake it with a background image and some judicious use of CSS properties. Listing 12-16 is a slightly revised party invitation with an empty IMAGE element. Listing 12-17 is a style sheet that sets the party.gif file as the background for IMAGE. It also sets the width and height properties of IMAGE. Finally, it sets float to left. Figure 12-33 shows the result.

Listing 12-16: A party invitation with an empty IMAGE element

```
<?xml version="1.0"?>
<?xml-stylesheet type="text/css" href="12-17.css"?>
<INVITATION>
  <IMAGE />
  <TEXT>
  You're invited to a party on December 31, 1999 to celebrate
  the new millennium! You're invited to a party on December 31,
  1999 to celebrate the new millennium! You're invited to a
  party on December 31, 1999 to celebrate the new millennium!
  You're invited to a party on December 31, 1999 to celebrate
  the new millennium! You're invited to a party on December 31,
  1999 to celebrate the new millennium! You're invited to a
  party on December 31, 1999 to celebrate the new millennium!
  You're invited to a party on December 31, 1999 to celebrate
  the new millennium! You're invited to a party on December 31,
  1999 to celebrate the new millennium! You're invited to a
  party on December 31, 1999 to celebrate the new millennium!
  You're invited to a party on December 31, 1999 to celebrate
  the new millennium! You're invited to a party on December 31,
  1999 to celebrate the new millennium!
  </TEXT>
</INVITATION>
```

Listing 12-17: A style sheet that loads an IMAGE

```
INVITATION { display:block; }
IMAGE { background: url(party.gif) no-repeat center center;
        width: 134px;
        height: 196px;
        float: left; }
TEXT { display: block }
```

The clear Property

The `clear` property specifies whether an element can have floating elements on its sides. If it cannot, the element will be moved below any floating elements that precede it. It's related to the HTML `<BR CLEAR="ALL">` element. The possible values are:

none	right
left	both

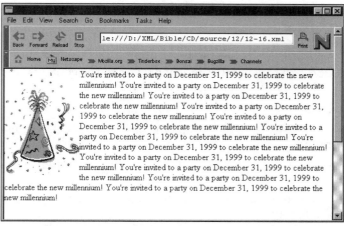

Figure 12-33: The party invitation image floating on the left

The default value, none, causes floating elements to appear on both sides of the element. The value left bans floating elements on the left-hand side of the element. The value right bans floating elements on the right-hand side of the element. The value both bans floating elements on the both sides of the element. For example, suppose you add this rule to the style sheet of Listing 12-17:

```
TEXT { clear: left }
```

Now, although the IMAGE element wants to float on the left of TEXT, TEXT doesn't allow that as is shown in Figure 12-34. IMAGE is still on the left, but now TEXT is pushed down below the image.

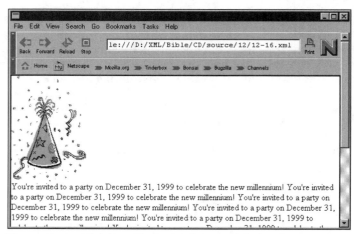

Figure 12-34: The party invitation image with the clear property set to left

Summary

In this chapter, you learned:

✦ CSS is a straightforward language for applying styles to the contents of elements that works well with HTML and even better with XML.

✦ Selectors are a comma-separated list of the elements a rule applies to.

✦ CSS can apply rules to elements of a given type or elements with particular CLASS or ID attributes.

✦ Many (though not all) CSS properties are inherited by the children of the elements they apply to.

✦ If multiple rules apply to a single element, then the formatting properties cascade in a sensible way.

✦ You can include C-like /* */ comments in a CSS style sheet.

✦ Lengths can be specified in relative or absolute units. Relative units are preferred.

✦ The display property determines whether an element is block, inline, or a list item.

✦ Font properties determine the font face, style, size, and weight of text.

✦ Color of elements is given in a 24-bit RGB space in either decimal, hexadecimal, or as percentages.

✦ Background properties include color, image, image position, and image tiling.

✦ Text properties let you adjust line height, word spacing, letter spacing, vertical and horizontal alignment, decoration, and capitalization.

✦ Box properties let you adjust the relative positions and spacing of elements on the page, as well as wrapping borders around elements.

There are some limits to what CSS Level 1 can achieve. First, CSS1 can only attach styles to content that already appears in the document. It cannot add content to the document, even simple content like punctuation marks. Furthermore, it cannot transform the content in any way such as sorting or reordering it. These needs are addressed by XSL, the Extensible Style Language. Even from the perspective of merely formatting content, CSS1 offers less than what you want. Most glaringly, there's no support for tables. And there are other, less-obvious deficiencies. CSS1 cannot handle right-to-left text like Hebrew and Arabic or vertical text such as traditional Chinese. In the next chapter, we'll delve into CSS Level 2, which addresses these and other limitations of CSS1.

✦   ✦   ✦

Cascading Style Sheets Level 2

The Cascading Style Sheets Level 2 (CSS2) specification was published by the W3C in 1998, surpassing CSS Level 1 to make the formatting of XML and HTML documents more powerful than ever. Of course, CSS2 fights the same backwards-compatibility battles with HTML that CSS1 fought. However, with XML, CSS2 can format content on both paper and the Web almost as well as a desktop publishing program like PageMaker or Quark XPress.

Caution

Most of the rules discussed here are not yet implemented by the common browsers. Mozilla should begin implementing some of these styles, but full implementation is still some time away.

What's New in CSS2?

CSS2 incorporates many features that Web developers and designers have long requested from browser vendors. The specification has more than doubled in size from CSS1, and is not only a compilation of changes and new features, but a redraft of the original specification. This makes this specification a single source for all Cascading Style Sheet syntax, semantics, and rules.

On the CD-ROM

The complete CSS Level 2 specification is available on the Web at http://www.w3.org/TR/REC-CSS2 and on the CD in the specs/css2 folder. This is possibly the most readable specification document ever produced by the W3C and is well worth rereading.

It takes some time for popular software to support all new specifications fully, and CSS2 is no exception. As you will discover while reading through this chapter, both Internet Explorer 5.0 and Mozilla are just starting to implement these properties. The ones that have not yet been implemented have been noted for your convenience.

The many new features of CSS2 enable you to more precisely select and format elements in your document. New pseudo-classes and pseudo-elements enable you to select the first child of an element, adjust an element when it receives focus, or control the placement of other elements automatically around specified element selections. Media types let you apply different styles to documents that will appear in different media such as printed pages, computer monitors, and radio broadcasts. Support for paged media like printouts and slide shows has been drastically improved with much stronger control over page breaks. Elements can now be formatted in tables as well as block and inline boxes. Sequences and lists can be automatically numbered and indented. More support is provided for non-Western languages like Arabic and Chinese. And for the first time you can apply aural styles that specify not how a document is rendered, but rather how it is read. In addition, CSS2 changes the implementation of some of CSS1's features.

New Pseudo-classes

Pseudo-classes select elements that have something in common but do not necessarily have the same type. The `:hover` pseudo-class, for example, refers to whichever element the cursor is currently over, regardless of the element's type. CSS2 has seven new pseudo-classes, which are outlined below:

✦ `:first-child`: The `:first-child` pseudo-class selects the first child of an element.

✦ `:focus`: The `:focus` pseudo-class selects the object that has the focus; that is, the one into which input will go if the user types a key on the keyboard.

✦ `:hover`: The `:hover` pseudo-class selects a designated, but not activated object.

✦ `:lang`: The `:lang` pseudo-class selects those elements written in a specific language as identified by the `xml:lang` attribute.

✦ `:first`: The `:first` pseudo-class selects the first page of a document when it is being printed.

✦ `:left`: The `:left` pseudo-class selects the left-hand pages (normally these are the even-numbered pages) of a document printout, as if the hard copy material were going to be in a book.

✦ `:right`: The `:right` pseudo-class selects the right-hand pages (normally these are the odd-numbered pages) of a document printout, as if the hard copy material were going to be bound.

New Pseudo-Elements

Pseudo-elements identify specific elements by information other than what's readily available from the XML input. For example, in CSS1 and CSS2, `:first-line` and `:first-letter` are pseudo-elements that select the first line and letter of an element, even though these aren't necessarily represented by any element.

CSS2 adds two new pseudo-elements, `:after` and `:before`. The `:after` pseudo-element enables you to insert objects after the specified element. These objects can be images, automatic counters, or text. The `:before` pseudo-element enables you to insert objects before a specified element. These objects can also be images, automatic counters, or text.

Media Types

CSS2 defines ten media types in which information is presented such as Braille, computer displays, ink on paper, and television. CSS2 lets you specify different styles for different media. For example, it's more important to use larger fonts for low-resolution computer displays than for 1200 dpi printing.

Paged Media

CSS2 provides control over page breaks and methods of identifying individual pages in a document so that designers can format printed documents, without affecting the appearance of the documents on screen.

Internationalization

As the Internet expands beyond the English- speaking world, more advances are being made in supporting the thousands of languages spoken and written both currently and throughout history. CSS2 adds support for Unicode and bi-directional text so you can style Chinese and Hebrew as easily as English and French.

Visual Formatting Control

CSS2 adds more formatting properties to provide more precise control over the objects that make up a document. You can now specify the absolute positions and dimensions of elements. There are also more display styles to use when creating elements. Shadows can be applied to text. Fonts and colors can be specified as "the same as" a user interface element like a menu item or an icon label. You can change the cursor shown when the pointer moves over different elements.

Tables

Improvements in the `display` property make it easy to treat XML elements as table-like structures, better controlling their alignment.

Generated Content

Automatically generated counters, numbering systems, and list markers enable document authors to force applications to create information on the fly, as the document is being rendered. Numbers can be recalculated on the fly whenever a document changes, rather than having to be painstakingly inserted by hand.

Aural Style Sheets

In an effort to make information dispersal friendlier for all individuals, CSS2 has incorporated specific properties that cover the features of a speech-synthesizing system. These properties enable the document author to control the richness, pitch, and other properties of the speaker's voice for each element within the document.

New Implementations

The CSS2 specification also changes the implementation of some features originally included in CSS1. These include the cascade mechanism, pseudo-classes, and a variety of other properties.

Pseudo-classes and Elements

The :link, :visited, and :active pseudo-classes no longer have to be designated independently of each other, and can be used together.

Inheritance

In CSS1, only some properties were able to inherit values from their parents. In CSS2, all properties can inherit their value from their parent element by setting the value to the keyword inherit. When a property is inherited, the property takes on the same value as the nearest parent element.

Note   Because every property can have the value inherit, I will omit any explanation of this value in the discussions of the individual properties that follow.

Cascade Mechanism

In CSS1 the !important designator can force an author's style sheet to take precedence over a reader's style sheet. CSS2 reverses this precedence so that reader preferences take precedence over author preferences. The default result, when working with both author and reader style sheets, is that the user's style sheet overrides the author's. However, if the author declares a property !important, this adds more force to the specification, making it override the reader's style sheet. However, if the reader also declares a rule !important, this overrides a !important declaration in the author's style sheet. In other words, the reader gets the last word.

Display Property

The default value of the display property is now inline rather than block.

Margins and Padding

In CSS1, some of the margin properties were ignored when other properties were set, for example, margin-right would be ignored if both margin-left and width were set. This decision was independent of the direction of the text and the alignment of the object. CSS2 makes the decision between altering the left or right margin dependent on the direction of the text of the object.

Selecting Elements

Browsers that support CSS2, such as Internet Explorer and Mozilla, can more specifically select an element or object to which a style rule is applied. Using CSS2 you can select elements based upon the pattern they create in the document tree, by simply designating their element name, id, or through a combination of element and attribute settings.

Pattern Matching

CSS2 pattern matching identifies specific elements in the document tree. The syntax of the pattern-matching selector can be anything from a simple element name to a complex system of contextual patterns like those shown in Table 13-1. An element matches a pattern if it meets all of the requirements of the specified pattern. In XML this includes case-sensitivity.

Table 13-1
CSS2 Selector Syntax for Pattern Matching

Syntax	Meaning
*	This is the universal selector, and matches any element.
X	Matches any element by the name of "X".
X Y	Matches any element with the name "Y" that is a descendent of an element with the name "X". For example: all VERSE descendents of SONNET elements.
X > Y	Matches any "Y" element that is a child of an element "X". For example: all VERSE children of a STANZA element.
X:first-child	Matches all "X" elements that are the first child of their parents. For example: the first STANZA element in a SONNET element.
X:link	Matches all "X" elements in a link whose target has not yet been visited.
X:visited	Matches all "X" elements in a link whose target has been visited.
X:active	Matches all "X" elements that are currently selected.
X:hover	Matches all "X" elements that currently have the mouse hovering over them.
X:focus	Matches all "X" elements that currently have the focus of the user either through selection by a mouse, or by being ready to input textual data.
X:lang(*i*)	Matches all "X" elements that are designated to use the human language *i* using the xml:lang attribute.

Continued

Table 13-1 *(continued)*

Syntax	Meaning
X + Y	Matches all "Y" elements whose immediate sibling is an "X" element. For example: a REFRAIN element that is immediately preceded by a STANZA element.
X[attr]	Matches all "X" elements with the "attr" attribute set, no matter what the value of the attribute is. For example: an AUTHOR element with a NAME attribute.
X[attr="string"]	Matches all "X" elements with whose "attr" attribute has the value "string". For example: an AUTHOR element with the DATE attribute with the value 19990723.
X[attr~="string"]	Matches any "X" element whose "attr" attribute is a space-separated list of words of which one is "string".
X[lang|="langcode"]	Matches all "X" elements with the "lang" attribute set to a specific "langcode".
X#myname	Matches any "X" element whose id attribute has the value "myname".

The Universal Selector

The * symbol selects all elements in the document. This enables you to set default styles for all elements. For example, this rule sets the default font to New York:

```
*  { font-face: "New York" }
```

You can combine * with attribute, pseudo-class, and pseudo-element selectors to apply styles to all elements with a specific attribute, attribute value, role, and so forth. For example:

```
*:before      { content: ". " counter(pgraph) ". ";
                counter-increment: pgraph; /*Add 1 to pgraph*/
*[onmouseover] { text-decoration: blink }
```

Tip   If you are using the universal selector with just one other property specification, the * can be omitted. For example,

```
before  { content: ". " counter(pgraph) ". ";
          counter-increment: para }
[onmouseover] { text-decoration: blink }
```

Descendant and Child Selectors

You can select elements that are children or descendents of a specified type of element with child and descendant selectors. For instance, you can select any VERSE element that is contained within a SONNET element, or only those VERSE elements that are direct children of a STANZA element. Consider Listing 13-1, which shows Shakespeare's 21st sonnet in XML.

Listing 13-1: **Shakespeare's 21st sonnet**

```
<?xml version="1.0"?>
<?xml-stylesheet type="text/css" href="shakespeare.css"?>

<SONNET>
  <AUTHOR>William Shakespeare</AUTHOR>
  <TITLE>Sonnet 21</TITLE>
  <STANZA id="st1">
    <VERSE>So is it not with me as with that Muse</VERSE>
    <VERSE>Stirr'd by a painted beauty to his verse,</VERSE>
    <VERSE>Who heaven itself for ornament doth use</VERSE>
    <VERSE>And every fair with his fair doth rehearse;</VERSE>
  </STANZA>
  <STANZA id="st2">
    <VERSE>Making a couplement of proud compare</VERSE>
    <VERSE>With sun and moon, with earth and sea's rich
          gems,</VERSE>
    <VERSE>With April's first-born flowers, and all things
          rare</VERSE>
    <VERSE>That heaven's air in this huge rondure hems.</VERSE>
  </STANZA>
  <STANZA id="st3">
    <VERSE>O, let me, true in love, but truly write,</VERSE>
    <VERSE>And then believe me, my love is as fair</VERSE>
    <VERSE>As any mother's child, though not so bright</VERSE>
    <VERSE>As those gold candles fix'd in heaven's air.</VERSE>
  </STANZA>
  <REFRAIN>
    <VERSE>Let them say more that like of hearsay well,</VERSE>
    <VERSE>I will not praise that purpose not to sell.</VERSE>
  </REFRAIN>
</SONNET>
```

All VERSE elements are descendants of the SONNET element, but not immediate children. Some VERSE elements are immediate children of STANZA elements and some are immediate children of the REFRAIN element. Descendant selectors are made up of two or more element designators separated by a space. A descendant selector of the form SONNET VERSE matches a VERSE element that is an arbitrary descendant of a SONNET element. In order to specify a specific layer of descendant, you need to use the form SONNET * VERSE which forces the VERSE element to be at least a grandchild, or lower descendent of the SONNET element.

To specify an immediate child element, you use the form STANZA > VERSE. This applies the rule only to VERSE elements that are a direct child of a STANZA element, and therefore won't affect any VERSE children of a REFRAIN element.

You can combine both descendant and child selectors to find specific elements. For example the following selector finds all VERSE elements that are the first child of a REFRAIN element that is in turn a descendant of a SONNET element.

```
SONNET REFRAIN>VERSE:first { padding: "2cm" }
```

Applied to Listing 13-1, this rule selects the verse "Let them say more that like of hearsay well,".

Adjacent Sibling Selectors

Adjacent sibling selectors use a + sign between element designators to identify an element that follows another element at the same level of the hierarchy. For example, the following code selects all REFRAIN elements that share a parent with a STANZA element and immediately follow the STANZA element.

```
STANZA+REFRAIN {color:red}
```

Attribute Selectors

Attribute selectors identify specific element/attribute combinations. Place the name of the attribute being matched in square brackets after the name of the element. For example, this rule turns all STANZA elements with a NUMBER attribute red:

```
STANZA[NUMBER]  { color: red }
```

This rule turns all STANZA elements that have a NUMBER attribute red, regardless of the value of that attribute. This includes elements that have a default NUMBER attribute provided by the DTD, but not STANZA elements that don't have a NUMBER attribute.

To test attribute values, you use the same syntax you use to set an attribute value; that is, the name followed by an equals sign, followed by the value in quotes. For instance, to specify that only STANZA elements whose NUMBER attribute has the value 3 should be turned red; you would use this rule:

```
STANZA [NUMBER="3"] { color: red }
```

@rules

@rules do something other than select an element and apply some styles to it. There are five of them:

1. @page: applies styles to a page (as opposed to elements on the page)

2. @import: embeds an external style sheet in the current style sheet

3. @media: groups style rules for attributes that should only be applied to one kind of media

4. @font-face: describes a font used elsewhere in the style sheet

5. @charset: defines the character set used by the style sheet

@page

The @page rule selects the page box. Inside it the designer can specify the dimensions, layout, orientation, and margins of individual pages. The page box is a rectangular area, roughly the size of a printed page, which contains the page area and the margin block. The page area contains the material to be displayed, and the edges of the box provide a container in which page layout occurs between page breaks. Unlike other boxes, page boxes do not have borders or padding, only margins.

The @page rule selects every page of a document. You can use one of the page pseudo-class properties, :first, :left, or :right, to specify different properties for various classes of pages.

Because the @page rule is unaware of the page's content including its fonts, it can't understand measurements in ems and ex's. All other units of measurement are acceptable, including percentages. Percentages used on margin settings are a percentage of the total page box. Margins can have negative values, which place content outside of the area normally accessible by the application or printer. In most cases, the information is simply truncated to the visible or printable area.

@import

The @import rule embeds a specified external style sheet into an existing style sheet. This enables you to build large style sheets from smaller, easier-to-understand pieces. Imported style sheets use a .css extension. For example, the following rule imports the poetry.css file.

```
@import url(poetry.css);
```

@import rules may specify a media type following the name of the style sheet. If no media type is specified, the @import rule is unconditional, and will be used for all media types. For example, the following rule imports the printmedia.css file. The declarations in this style sheet will only be applied to print media.

```
@import url(printmedia.css) print;
```

The next rule imports the continuous.css file that will be used for both computer monitors and/or television display:

```
@import url(continuous.css) tv, screen;
```

Style sheets that are imported into other style sheets rank lower in the cascade than the importing style sheet. For example, suppose shakespeare.css styles a VERSE in the New York font while shakeprint.css styles a VERSE in the Times font. If shakespeare. css imports shakeprint.css, then the verses will be styled in New York. However, if shakeprint.css imports shakespeare.css, then verses will be styled in Times.

@media

Many types of media are used to impart information to readers, and each media type has its own customary styles and formats. You can't very well have a speech synthesizer reading Shakespeare in a monotone, now can you? And italics don't make much sense on a monospaced terminal.

CSS2 allows you to specify different styles for the same element displayed in different media. For example, text is easier to read on the screen if it uses a sans serif font, while text on paper is generally easiest to read if it is written in a serif font. You can enclose style rules intended for only one medium in an @media rule naming that medium. There can be as many @media rules in a document as there are media types to specify. For example, these rules format a SONNET differently depending on whether it's being printed on paper or displayed on a screen.

```
@media print {
   SONNET { font-size: 10pt; font-family: Times, serif }
}
@media screen {
   SONNET { font-size: 12pt;
            font-family: New York, Times New Roman, serif }
}
@media screen, print {
   VERSE { line-height: 1.2 }
}
```

The first two rules define styles specific to the print and screen media types respectively. Since modern computer displays have much lower resolutions than modern printers, it's important to make the font larger on the screen than on the printout and to choose a font that's designed for the screen.

The third rule provides styles that apply to both of these media types. To designate style instructions for multiple media types simultaneously, you simply list them following the @media rule designator, separated by a comma.

Browsers that support CSS2 allow the document author to provide rules governing how a document will be displayed for a particular type of media. For instance, it would likely apply different rules when showing a document on the screen than when sending it to a printer. CSS2 identifies ten media types. These are:

1. all all devices
2. aural (continuous, aural): speech synthesizers
3. braille (continuous, tactile): Braille tactile feedback devices for the sight impaired

4. `embossed` (paged, tactile): paged Braille printers

5. `handheld` (visual): PDAs and other handheld devices such as Windows CE palmtops, Newtons, and Palm Pilots.

6. `print` (paged, visual): all printed, opaque material

7. `projection` (paged, visual): presentation and slide shows, whether projected directly from a computer or printed on transparencies

8. `screen` (continuous, visual): bitmapped, color computer displays

9. `tty` (continuous, visual): dumb terminals and old PC monitors that use a fixed-pitch, monochromatic character grid

10. `tv` (aural/visual): television-type devices, i.e. low-resolution, analog display, color

Browsing software does not have to support all of these types. In fact, I know of no single device that does support all of these. However, style-sheet designers should probably assume that readers will use any or all of these types of devices to view their content.

Of course, the characteristics of individual media change over time. My first printer was 144dpi, but such low-resolution printers should be relatively rare in the 21st century. On the other hand, monitors will eventually reach resolutions of 300 dpi or more; and color printing is rapidly becoming accessible to more and more users.

Some properties are only available with specific media types. For instance, the `pitch` property only makes sense with the aural media type. CSS2 does not specify an all-inclusive list of media types, although it does provide a list of current values for the `@media` rule. These values are not case-sensitive.

@font-face

The `@font-face` rule provides a description of a typeface used elsewhere in the style sheet. It can provide the font's name, a URL from which the font can be downloaded, and detailed information about the metrics of the font that allow a reasonable facsimile to be synthesized. The `@font-face` rule also controls how the software selects the fonts for a document with author-specified fonts. You can suggest identical font matching, intelligent font matching, synthesizing the requested font, downloading the fonts from the server, or rendering the font. These methods are described below:

✦ **Identical Font Matching:** The user's software chooses the local system font with the same family name. Fonts with the same name may not necessarily match in appearance. The font the client is using could have originated from a different source than the font located on the server.

✦ **Intelligent Font Matching:** The software chooses a font that is available on the client system and is closest in appearance to the requested font. This is not an exact match, but it should be close. The font is matched based on font type, whether it uses serifs, its weight, the height of its capital letters, and other font characteristics.

✦ **Font Synthesis:** The Web browser builds a font that closely resembles the designated font, and shares its metrics. When a font is synthesized, it will generally be a closer duplicate than a font found by matching. Synthesis requires accurate substitution and position information in order for all the font characteristics to be preserved.

✦ **Font Download:** The browsing software downloads the font from a specified URL. The process is the same as downloading an image or sound to be displayed with the current document. Users that download fonts will experience delays similar to those that occur when downloading images.

✦ **Font Rendering:** The last alternative for managing fonts is progressive rendering. This is a combination of downloading and matching which enables the browser to create a temporary font so a document's content can be read while the original font downloads. After the "real" font has been downloaded, it replaces the synthesized font in subsequent documents. To avoid having a document rendered twice, your font description must contain the metric information describing the font. The more complete a font's metric information, the less likely a document will need to be re-rendered once the download is complete.

CSS2 enables the document author to specify which of these methods, if any, are used when a designated font is not available on the reading system. The @font-face rule provides a font description, created out of a series of font descriptors, defining detailed information about the fonts to be used on the page. Each font descriptor characterizes a specific piece of information about the font. This description can include a URL for the font, the font family name, and the font size.

Font descriptors are classified into three types:

✦ Those that provide a link between the style sheet usage of the font and its description.

✦ Those that provide a URL for the location of the font or its pertinent information.

✦ Those that provide character information for the font.

The @font-face rule applies only to the fonts specified within the style sheet. You will need one @font-face specification for each font in the style sheet. For example:

```
@font-face { font-family: "Comic Sans";
        src: url(http://metalab.unc.edu/xml/fonts/comicsans)}
@font-face { font-family: "Jester"; font-weight: bold;
            font-style: italic}
TITLE     { font-family: "Comic Sans"}
AUTHOR    { font-family: "Jester", serif}
```

As the software reads this style sheet, it will try to find a set of rules that specify how each element should be rendered. The style sheet sets all TITLE elements to the Comic Sans font family, at the same time it sets all AUTHOR elements to the Jester font. A Web browsing application that supports CSS1 will search for the Comic Sans and Jester font families. If it can't find them, then it will use its default text font for the Comic family, and the specified fall-back serif font for the Jester family. The @font-face rule's font descriptors will be ignored. CSS1 software will be able to safely skip over this command without encountering an error.

Applications that support CSS2 will examine the @font-face rules in an attempt to match a font description to the Comic Sans and Jester fonts. In the above example, the browsing software will find a URL from which it can download the Comic Sans font. If Comic Sans were found on the client system, the software would have used that instead of downloading the font. In the case of Jester, the users software will use one of the matching rules, or the synthesis rule to create a similar font from the descriptors provided. If the Web browser could not find a matching @font-face rule for the font family specified, it would have attempted to match the fonts using the rules specified for CSS1.

CSS2 allows any font descriptor that is not recognized, or useful to the browser, to be skipped. This provides a built-in means for increasing the descriptors in an effort to improve the font substitution, matching, or synthesis rules being used.

@charset

There are three ways to specify the character set in which a style sheet is written, and they take precedence in the following order:

1. An HTTP "charset" parameter in a "Content-Type" field

2. The @charset rule

3. Attributes and properties associated with the document, such as HTML's charset attribute used with the LINK element

Each style sheet can contain a single @charset rule. The @charset rule must appear at the very beginning of the document, and can not be preceded by any other characters. The syntax for using @charset is:

```
@charset "character set name"
```

The character set name specified in this statement must be a name as described in the IANA registry. You can see a partial list of character sets in Table 7-7 in Chapter 7. To specify that a style sheet is written in Latin-1, you would write:

```
@charset "ISO-8859-1"
```

Cross-Reference Character sets are discussed in great detail in Chapter 7, *Foreign Languages and non-Roman Text.*

Pseudo Elements

Pseudo-elements are treated as elements in style sheets but are not necessarily particular elements in the XML document. They are abstractions of certain parts of the rendered document after application of the style sheet; for example, the first line of a paragraph. Pseudo-elements are not case-sensitive, and may only appear directly after the subject of a style-sheet selector. CSS2 introduces two new pseudo-elements: `:after` and `:before`.

The `:before` and `:after` pseudo-elements select the location immediately before and after the element that precedes them. The `content` property is used to put data into this location. For example, this rule places the string ———— between STANZA objects to help separate the stanzas. The line breaks are encoded as `\A` in the string literal:

```
STANZA:after {content: "\A————\A"}
```

As well as a literal string, you can use one of these four keywords as the value of the `content` property:

1. `open-quote`
2. `close-quote`
3. `no-open-quote`
4. `no-close-quote`

The `open-quote` and `close-quote` keywords insert the appropriate quote character for the current language and font (for example, " or '). The `no-open-quote` and `no-close-quote` keywords do not insert any characters, but increment the level of nesting as if quotes were used. With each level of nesting, the quote marks switch from double to single or vice versa.

You can also use the `attr(X)` function as the value of the content property to insert the value of the X attribute before or after the identified element.

Finally, you can insert the current value of an automatic counter using either the `counter()` or `counters()` function. This has two distinct forms: `counter(name)` or `counter(name, style)`. The default style is decimal.

Pseudo Classes

Pseudo-class selectors select elements based on aspects other than the name, attributes or content of the element. For example, a pseudo-class may be based on the position of the mouse, the object that has the focus, or whether an object is a link. An element may repeatedly change its pseudo-classes as the reader interacts with the document. Some pseudo-classes are mutually exclusive, but most can be applied simultaneously to the same element, and can be placed anywhere within an element selector. When pseudo-classes do conflict, the cascading order determines which rules are activated.

:first-child

The :first-child pseudo-class selects the first child of the named element, regardless of its type. For example, in Listing 13-1 the VERSE element whose contents are "So is it not with me as with that Muse" would be the first child of the STANZA element and would be designated by this rule:

```
STANZA:first-child {font-style: bold}
```

:link, :visited, :active

In CSS1 :link, :visited, and :active pseudo-classes are mutually exclusive. In CSS2, :link and :visited are still mutually exclusive (as they logically have to be), but you can use either of these in conjunction with :active. For example, the following code fragment assumes the AUTHOR element has been designated as a link, and alters the colors of the text depending upon the current state of the link. In the following code fragment, an unvisited link is set to red, a visited link will be displayed as gray, and an active link will be shown as lime green while the cursor is being placed over it.

```
AUTHOR:link    { color: "red" }
AUTHOR:visited { color: "gray" }
AUTHOR:active  { color: "lime" }
```

:hover

The :hover pseudo-class selects elements which the mouse or other pointing device is pointing at, but without the mouse button depressed. For instance, this rule colors the AUTHOR element red when the cursor is pointing at it:

```
AUTHOR:hover { color: "red" }
```

The AUTHOR element returns to its normal color when the cursor is no longer pointing at it.

:focus

The :focus pseudo-class refers to the element that currently has the focus. An element has the focus when it has been selected and is ready to receive some sort of text input. The following rule makes the element with the focus bold.

```
:focus { text-style: "bold" }
```

:lang()

The :lang() pseudo-class selects elements with a specified language. In XML this is generally done via the xml:lang attribute and/or the encoding attribute of the XML declaration. The following rule changes the direction of all VERSE elements written in Hebrew to read right to left, rather than left to right:

```
VERSE:lang(he) {direction: "rtl" }
```

:right, :left, :first

The :right, :left, and :first pseudo-classes are only applied to the @page rule. They enable you to specify different styles for the first page of a document, for the left (generally even-numbered) pages of a document, and for the right (generally odd-numbered) pages of a document. For example, these rules specify very large margins:

```
@page:right   { margin-top: 5cm;
                margin-bottom: 5cm;
                margin-left: 7cm;
                margin-right: 5cm }
@page:left    { margin-top: 5cm;
                margin-bottom: 5cm;
                margin-left: 5cm;
                margin-right: 7cm }
@page:first   { margin-top: 10cm;
                margin-bottom: 10cm;
                margin-left: 10cm;
                margin-right: 10cm }
```

The only properties you can set in a rule for these pseudo-classes are the margin properties.

Formatting a Page

The @page selector refers to a page. It's used to set properties that apply to the page itself rather than an individual XML element on the page. Each page of a document has a variety of properties applied to it, including the page size, orientation, margins, and page breaks. These properties cascade to any element placed on the page. Optional pseudo-classes can specify different properties for the first page, right-facing pages, and left-facing pages.

CSS2 makes the reasonable assumption that pages are rectangular. Given that assumption, a page can posses the box properties you're familiar with from CSS1 including margins and size. However, a page box does not have borders or padding since these would naturally fall outside the physical page.

Size Property

In an @page rule, the size property specifies the height and width of the page. You can set the size as one or two absolute lengths or as one of the four keywords auto, portrait, landscape, or inherit. If only one length is given, the page will be a square. When both dimensions are given, the first is the width of the page; the second is the height. For example,

```
@page { size: 8.5in 11in }
```

The auto setting automatically sizes to the target screen or sheet. landscape forces the document to be formatted to fit the target page, but with long sides horizontal. The portrait setting formats the document to fit the default target page size, but with long sides vertical.

Margin Property

The margin property controls the margins of the page—the rectangular areas on all four sides in which nothing is printed. This property is used as a shorthand for setting the margin-top, margin-bottom, margin-right, and margin-left properties separately. These properties are the same as they are for boxes in CSS1. For example, this rule describes an 8.5 by 11 inch page with one-inch margins on all sides.

```
@page { size: 8.5in 11in; margin: 1.0in }
```

Mark Property

CSS2 offers the mark property to place marks on a page delineating where the paper should be cut and/or how pages should be aligned. These marks appear outside of the page box. A page box is simply the viewable area of the document that can be affected by the @page rule. If you were to look at a printed 8 1/2" x11" piece of paper, the page box would be everything inside the printable region on that paper, what we normally think of as the space inside the printer margins. The software controls the rendering of the marks, which are only displayed on absolute page boxes. Absolute page boxes cannot be moved, and are controlled by the general margins of the page. Relative page boxes are aligned against a target page, in most cases forcing the marks off the edge of the page. When aligning a relative page box, you are essentially looking at the page in your mind's eye, and using margin and padding properties to move the printed area of that page about the physical paper.

The mark property has four possible values—crop, cross, inherit, and none—and can only be used with the @page element. Crop marks identify the cutting edges of paper. Cross marks, also known as registration marks, are used to align pages after printing. If set to none, no marks will be displayed on the document. The following rule specifies a page with both crop and cross marks:

```
@page { mark: crop cross}
```

Page Property

As well as using the @page selector to specify page properties, you can attach page properties to individual elements using the page property. To do this you write an @page rule that specifies the page properties, give that @page rule a name, and then use the name as the value of the page property of a normal element rule. For example, these two rules together say that a SONNET will be printed in landscape orientation.

```
@page rotated { size: landscape}
SONNET       { page: rotated}
```

When using the `page` property, it's possible for different sibling elements to specify different page properties. If this happens, a page break will be inserted between the elements. If a child uses a different page layout than its parent, the child's layout will take precedence. For instance, in the following example the two tables are rendered on landscape pages, possibly on the same page if space allows. Because of the layering of the elements in the document, the assignment of the rotated page to the SONNET element is over ridden, and not used.

```
@page narrow   { size: 9cm 18cm}
@page rotated  { size: landscape}
STANZA         { page: narrow}
SONNET         { page: rotated}
```

Page-Break Properties

The `page-break-after` property forces or prohibits the insertion of a page break after the current object. The `page-break-before` property forces or prohibits the insertion of a page break before the current object. The `page-break-inside` property allows or prohibits the insertion of a page break inside the current object. These can be used to keep together paragraphs of related text, headings and their body text, images and their captions, or to keep complete tables on the same page.

When either of these properties is set to `auto`, a page break is neither forced nor prohibited after the current box. A setting of `always` forces a page break. The `avoid` setting prevents a page break from appearing. The `left` and `right` settings force the insertion of either one or two page breaks as necessary in order to force the next page to be either a left- or right-hand page. This is useful at the end of a chapter in a book in which chapters generally start on right-hand pages, even if it leaves blank pages.

The following rule inserts a page break before and after every SONNET element in a document but not inside a sonnet so that each sonnet appears on its own page.

```
SONNET { page-break-before: always;
         page-break-after:  always;
         page-break-inside: avoid }
```

Visual Formatting

CSS2 adds many new formatting features that provide more control over the layout of your XML document. The `display` property has many new values that expand on the basic block and inline types of CSS1. The `cursor` property enables you to identify what sort of cursor to display over your object. You can control the height and width of all object boxes. CSS2 also gives you the ability to modify your document objects' visibility, clipping size, color, font, text shadows, alignment, and control how an object's contents are dealt with if overflow should occur.

Display Property

The expansion of the display property in CSS2 provides more complete layout options, most notably tables. In CSS2, there are 17 possible values of the display property:

inline	table-header-group
block	table-footer-group
list-item	table-row
run-in	table-column-group
compact	table-column
marker	table-cell
table	table-caption
inline-table	none
table-row-group	

Block elements are drawn by adding out space around the objects to place a buffer around their contents. Inline elements work without setting aside separate space. Table elements are various parts of a grid. Inline elements are like a word in a sentence. Their position moves freely as text is added and deleted around them. Block objects are more fixed and at most move up and down but not left and right as content is added before and after it. Block items include such items as tables, lists, and list items. Most display types are just modifications of the main block or inline types.

Inline Objects

Inline object boxes are laid horizontally in a row starting from the top of the containing box of the surrounding page or block element. Between these boxes of horizontal margins, borders, and padding spaces are implemented. You can also align these types of boxes vertically in a variety of ways including character baselines, box bottoms, or box tops.

Note In CSS1, the block value was the default display type of all objects, but that has changed in CSS2. Elements are now automatically displayed as inline unless otherwise designated.

Block Objects

Block objects are laid out vertically, one on top of the other. The first block is laid in the top left corner of the containing block, then the second block is placed below it, also flush against the left edge of the containing block. The vertical distance between each block is defined by the individual block's margin and padding properties. For example, this rule identifies the VERSE, STANZA, and REFRAIN elements as individual blocks. Figure 13-1 shows Listing 13-1 when this rule (and only this rule) is applied. Note that the AUTHOR and the TITLE are on the same line because they are inline by default. However, when a block element follows an inline element, a line break is required after the block element.

```
VERSE, STANZA, REFRAIN  { display: block }
```

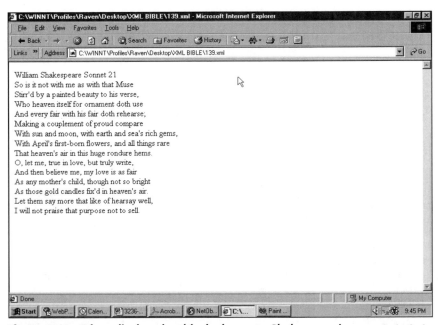

Figure 13-1: When displayed as block elements, Shakespeare's sonnet starts to take on a more normal appearance.

None

The value of none forces the element to not generate a display box of any kind for formatting the content of the element. In other words, the element will not have any effect on the layout of the document. Child and other descendant elements don't generate boxes either, even if the display property is set for them. When display is none, the box is not just invisible; it actually does not exist.

Compact and Run-in Values

The compact and run-in values of the display property identify an element as either a block or an inline box depending on context. Properties used on items declared as these types will be effective based upon their final rendered status. A compact box is placed in the margin of the block box that follows it if it will fit. If the box that follows it is not a block box, or the compact box will not fit in the margin, then it is rendered simply as another block box.

The `run-in` value enables you to format normal block elements as the first inline block of the next block element in the code. If the next element is not a block element, then the run-in element is formatted as a block element.

Marker Value

Setting the `display` property to the `marker` value identifies a block that's formed by content generated in the style sheet rather than copied in from the XML document. This value is only used with the `:before` and `:after` pseudo-elements that have been attached to block-level elements.

Table Display Values

One of the most important new features in CSS2, especially for XML developers who often create tabular structures with tags that look nothing like HTML's table tags, is support for table layout of elements. CSS2 adds support for styling elements as parts of tables using these ten values of the `display` property:

1. `table`
2. `inline-table`
3. `table-row-group`
4. `table-header-group`
5. `table-footer-group`
6. table-row
7. table-column-group
8. table-column
9. table-cell
10. table-caption

For example, setting the `display` property to `table` indicates that the selected element is a block-level container for various smaller children that will be arranged in a grid. The `inline-table` value forces the table to function as an inline object, enabling text to float along its side, and for multiple tables to be placed side by side. The `table-caption` value formats an element as a table caption. The `table-row-group`, `table-header-group`, and `table-footer-group` values create groups of data cells that work as a single row, as if it was defined using the `table-row` value. The `table-column-group` creates a group of data cells that work as a single column that was defined using the `table-column` value. XML elements that appear in table cells have — naturally enough — a `display` property with the value `table-cell`.

For example, if you were to configure a sonnet in a table-like structure, you might set each STANZA and REFRAIN to be a table and each VERSE to be a table row. The style sheet to create this effect might include these three rules:

```
STANZA  { display: table }
REFRAIN { display: table }
VERSE   { display: table-row }
```

Width and Height Properties

The default height of a box in which each element appears is calculated from the combined height of the element's contents. The default width of each element's box is calculated from the combined width of the element's contents or the width of the viewable area on the page or the screen. Inline elements and table elements that contain text always have these automatically calculated dimensions. However, the style-sheet designer can change these defaults for block-level elements and replaced inline elements by specifying values for six properties:

1. min-width
2. max-width
3. min-height
4. max-height
5. height
6. width

The min-height and min-width properties specify the smallest dimensions that the object can be displayed with. The maximum properties are a maximum size for the box regardless of the total size of its contents. The Web browser is free to adjust the size of the box within these limits. However, if height and width are set, then they determine exactly the size of the box.

```
STANZA  { width:  100px;
          Height: 100px }
```

Overflow Property

When the size of a box is precisely specified using the width and height properties, it's entirely possible that its contents may take up more area than the box actually has. The overflow property controls how the excess content is dealt with. This property can be set to one of four values:

1. auto
2. hidden
3. scroll
4. visible

If overflow is set to auto, scroll bars are added if necessary to enable the user to see excess content. If overflow is set to hidden, the excess content is simply truncated. If overflow is set to scroll, scroll bars are added whether there's overflow or not. Finally, if overflow is set to visible, the complete contents are shown, if necessary by overriding the size constraints that were placed on the box.

Figure 13-2 shows the sonnet when the STANZA's overflow property is set to scroll with this rule:

```
STANZA  { overflow:  scroll }
```

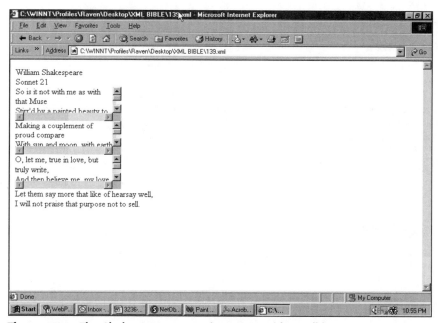

Figure 13-2: The Shakespeare sonnet's stanzas with scroll bars

Clip Property

The clip property identifies the portion of an object's content that will be visible when rendered by the user's software. Generally the clipping region will match the outside borders of the element's box, but the region can be altered. This property applies only to elements with an overflow attribute that is set to a value other than visible.

In CSS2, you can only clip to rectangular regions. Set the clip property to rect(top, bottom, left, right) where top, bottom, left, right are the offsets on each side. If the clipped object still exceeds the viewable area of the browser's window; the contents will be further clipped to fit in the window. The following rule uses the clip property with a STANZA block element:

```
STANZA  { clip: rect(5px, 5px, 5px, 5px);
          overflow: auto }
```

Visibility Property

The visibility property controls whether the contents of an element are seen. The four possible values of this property are:

1. visible

2. hidden

3. collapse

4. inherit

If visibility is set to visible, the contents of the box, including all borders are shown. If visibility is set to hidden, the box's contents borders are not seen. Invisible boxes still take up space and affect the layout of the document. Setting visibility to hidden is not the same as setting display to none.

If visibility is set to collapse, it is the same as hidden for any object, except a table row or column. However, for table rows and columns, it completely hides (as with display: none) the row or column.

Cursor Property

The cursor is the arrow/hand/insertion bar/other icon that indicates the position of the pointer on the screen. A cursor is the visible representation of your mouse's logical position that is displayed on the viewable area of your computer monitor. The cursor property specifies the cursor a user's software should display when a reader moves the mouse over a particular object. CSS2 allows these 16 cursor values:

1. auto: the browser chooses a cursor based on the current context. This is the default value

2. crosshair: a simple cross-hair cursor

3. default: the platform-dependent default cursor, usually an arrow

4. hand: a hand

5. move: crossed arrows indicating something to be moved

6. e-resize: east-pointing arrow (up is north)

7. ne-resize: northeast-pointing arrow

8. nw-resize: northwest-pointing arrow

9. n-resize: north-pointing arrow

10. se-resize: southeast-pointing arrow

11. sw-resize: southwest-pointing arrow

12. s-resize: south-pointing arrow

13. `w-resize`: west-pointing arrow

14. `text`: I-beam

15. `wait`: stop watch, spinning beach ball, hourglass or other icon indicating the passage of time

16. `help`: question mark

The following rule uses the `cursor` property to says that the hand cursor should be used when the pointer is over a `VERSE` element.

```
VERSE    { cursor: hand }
```

You can also use a custom cursor that's loaded from an image file by giving a URL for the image. Generally you'll provide cursors in several formats in a comma-separated list, the last of which is the name of a generic cursor. For example:

```
VERSE { cursor: url("poetry.cur"), url("poetry.gif"), text }
```

Color-Related Properties

CSS2 identifies colors as RGB values in the Standard Default Color Space for the Internet (sRGB). The way these colors are represented varies from browser to browser, but this specification provides an unambiguous and objectively measurable definition of a color's appearance. Web browsers that conform to the standard perform a gamma correction on the colors identified by the CSS2 specification. sRGB identifies a display gamma of 2.2 under most viewing conditions. This means that for most computer hardware, the colors given through CSS2 properties will have to be adjusted for an effective display gamma of 2.2.

> **Note**
> Only colors identified in CSS2 rules are affected. Colors used in images are expected to carry their own color correction information.

Color Property

The `color` property specifies the foreground color for the text content of an element. It may be given as a literal color name like `red` or an RGB value like `#CC0000`. Color names (or values) include `aqua`, `black`, `blue`, `fuchsia`, `gray`, `green`, `lime`, `maroon`, `navy`, `olive`, `purple`, `red`, `silver`, `teal`, `white`, and `yellow`.

The following style rules apply color to three elements, using all three methods of identifying color. It specifies the RGB hex value `#FF0000` for `AUTHOR` elements, all `TITLE` elements to appear in red, and all `VERSE` elements to appear in `rgb(255,0,0)`. These values are all red:

```
AUTHOR   { color: #FF0000}
TITLE    { color: red}
VERSE    { color: rgb(255,0,0) }
```

Gamma Correction

At its most basic, gamma correction controls the brightness of images so they are displayed accurately on computer screens. Images that have not been corrected can appear bleached-out or too dark. In order to make gamma correction easier to understand, let's look at the images displayed on your computer screen.

Practically every computer monitor has a gamma of 2.5. This means that its intensity to voltage curve is roughly a function of the power 2.5. If you send your monitor a message for a specific pixel to have an intensity of x, that pixel will automatically have an intensity of x^2.5 applied to it. Because the range of voltage is between 0 and 1, this means that your pixel's intensity is lower than you wish. To correct this, the voltage to the monitor has to be "gamma corrected."

The easiest way to correct this problem is to increase the voltage before it gets to the monitor. Since the relationship between the voltage and the brightness is known, the signal can be adjusted to remove the effect of the monitor's gamma. When this is done properly, the computer display should accurately reflect the image input. Of course, when you are gamma correcting an image, the light in your computer room, the brightness and contrast settings on your monitor, and your personal taste will also play a role.

When attempting to do gamma correction for the Web, platform idiosyncrasies come into play. Some UNIX workstations automatically correct for gamma variance on their video card, as does the Macintosh, but most PCs do not. This means that an image that looks good on a PC will be too light on a Mac; and when something looks good on a Mac, it will be too dark on a PC. If you are placing colored images or text on the Internet, you can't please all of the people all of the time. Currently, none of the graphic formats used on the Web can encode gamma correction information.

System Colors

CSS2 enables you to specify colors by copying them from the user's native GUI. These system colors can be used with all color-related properties. Style rules based on system colors take into account user preferences, and therefore offer some advantages, including:

1. Pages that fit the user's preferred look and feel.

2. Pages that are potentially more accessible for users with settings that might be related to a disability.

Table 13-2 lists CSS2-system color keywords and their descriptions. Any of the color properties can take on these values.

For example, the following style rule sets the foreground and background colors of a VERSE to the same colors used for the foreground and background of the browser's window.

```
VERSE    { color: WindowText; background-color: Window}
```

Table 13-2
Additional System Colors to Be Used with
All Color-related Properties

System Color-keywords	Description
ActiveBorder	Active window border.
ActiveCaption	Active window caption.
AppWorkspace	Background color of multiple document interface.
Background	Desktop background.
ButtonFace	Face color for three-dimensional display elements.
ButtonHighlight	Dark shadow for three-dimensional display elements (for edges facing away from the light source).
ButtonShadow	Shadow color for three-dimensional display elements.
ButtonText	Text on push buttons.
CaptionText	Text in caption, size box, and scroll-bar arrow box.
GrayText	Grayed (disabled) text. This color is set to #000 if the current display driver does not support a solid gray color.
Highlight	Items selected in a control.
HighlightText	Text of items selected in a control.
InactiveBorder	Inactive window border.
InactiveCaption	Inactive window caption.
InactiveCaptionText	Color of text in an inactive caption.
InfoBackground	Background color for tooltip controls.
InfoText	Text color for tooltip controls.
Menu	Menu background.
MenuText	Text in menus.
Scrollbar	Scroll bar gray area.
ThreeDDarkShadow	Dark shadow for three-dimensional display elements.
ThreeDFace	Face color for three-dimensional display elements.
ThreeDHighlight	Highlight color for three-dimensional display elements.
ThreeDLightShadow	Light color for three-dimensional display elements (for edges facing the light source).
ThreeDShadow	Dark shadow for three-dimensional display elements.
Window	Window background.
WindowFrame	Window frame.
WindowText	Text in windows.

Font Properties

Font properties in CSS1 are fairly complete. CSS2 doesn't add a lot to them. Changes include:

✦ The addition of the `font-size-adjust` property

✦ The scaling factor between the different keyword font sizes (`xx-small`, `x-small small`, `medium`, `large`, `x-large`, `xx-large`) is 1.2, not 1.5

✦ The `font-stretch` property can adjust the kerning

font-size-adjust Property

The legibility of a font is generally less dependent upon the size of the font, than on the value of its *x*-height. The aspect value of a font is the font-size divided by the *x*-height. The higher this number, the more likely it is that a font will be legible when the font is a small size. The lower the aspect value, the more likely it is that the font will become illegible as it is shrunk. When browsers perform straightforward font substitutions that rely solely on the font size, the likelihood that the resulting font will be illegible is greatly increased. The `font-size-adjust` property controls the aspect value of elements that preserve the `x-height` of the first choice font in the substitute font when using the `font-family` property.

The Verdana and Times New Roman fonts provide a good example of this legibility issue. Verdana has an aspect value of .58, while Times New Roman has an aspect value of .46. Therefore, Verdana will remain legible at a smaller size than Times New Roman, but may appear too large if substituted directly for Times New Roman at the same font size.

If the value of the `font-size-adjust` property is `none`, the font's *x*-height is not preserved. If a number is specified, the value identifies the aspect value of the first-choice font, and directs the software to scale the substitution font accordingly. This system helps you force legibility across all platforms, and all supporting applications. The following rules use the `font-size-adjust` property to maintain legibility of fonts while implementing a range of sizes.

```
VERSE  { font-size-adjust: ".58";  }
         font-family: "Verdana, Times New Roman,
                       Helvetica, Arial " ; }
AUTHOR { font-size-adjust: ".46" }
         font-family: "Times New Roman, Goudy Old Style,
                       serif, fantasy"; }
```

font stretch Property

The `font-stretch` property controls the kerning of a font; that is, the amount of space found between two characters in the font. There are 12 legal keyword values for this property:

1. `normal`

2. `ultra-condensed`

3. extra-condensed

4. condensed

5. semi-condensed

6. semi-expanded

7. expanded

8. extra-expanded

9. ultra-expanded

10. wider

11. narrower

12. inherit

The default is normal. The values ultra-condensed through ultra-expanded are organized from most condensed to least condensed. Each is a small change in the horizontal spacing of the text. The values wider and narrower increase or decrease the kerning, without increasing or decreasing it more past the ultra-expanded or ultra-condensed level.

The following style sheet rules use a variety of kernings.

```
TITLE          { font-stretch: "ultra-expanded" }
AUTHOR         { font-stretch: "expanded" }
STANZA         { font-stretch: "ultra-condensed" }
VERSE          { font-stretch: "wider" }
REFRAIN VERSE  { font-stretch: "narrower" }
```

The font Shorthand Property and System Fonts

In CSS1, the font property is a shorthand property that enables you to select font style, variant, weight, size, and family with one rule. In CSS2, the font property may also have one of these six keyword values that match all of a font's properties to the properties of particular elements of the browser user interface or the user's system:

1. caption: the font used for captioned controls like buttons

2. icon: the font that labels icons

3. menu: the font used in menus

4. message-box: the font used for display text in dialog boxes

5. small-caption: the font used for labels on small controls

6. status-bar: the font used in the browser status bar

For example this rule says that a SONNET element will be formatted with the same font family, size, weight, and style as the font the browser uses in its status bar:

```
SONNET { font: status-bar }
```

Text Shadow Property

The text-shadow property applies shadows to text. The value is a comma-separated list of shadow effects to control the order, color, and dimensions of the shadows that are overlaid on the text. Shadows do not extend the size of the block containing the text, but may extend over the boundaries of the block. The stacking level of the shadows is the same as the element itself.

The value of the text-shadow includes a signed length for the offset of the shadow. It may also include a blur radius and a shadow color. The shadow offset is specified with two signed lengths that specify how far out from the text the shadow will extend. The first length specifies the horizontal distance from the text; the second length specifies vertical depth of the shadow. If you apply a negative value to the shadow offsets, the shadow will appear to the left and above the text, rather than below and to the right. An optional third signed length specifies the boundary of the blur effect. A fourth optional value specifies the color of the shadow. For example,

```
TITLE    { text-shadow: red -5pt -5pt -2pt }
AUTHOR   { text-shadow: 5pt 4pt 3pt green }
VERSE    { text-shadow: none }
```

Vertical Align Property

The vertical-align property controls the vertical alignment of text within an inline box that is found within a block element. It's most commonly used with table cells. The eight possible alignment keyword values are:

1. baseline: aligns the baseline of the inline box with the baseline of the block box

2. sub: aligns the baseline of the inline box to the position for subscripts inside the parent block box

3. super: raises the baseline of the inline box to the position for superscripts in the parent's box

4. top: aligns the top of the inline box with the top of the line

5. middle: aligns the midpoint of the inline box with the baseline of the block box, plus half of the x-height of the block box

6. bottom: aligns the bottom of the inline box with the bottom of the line

7. text-top: aligns the top of the inline box with the top of the parent element's font

8. text-bottom: aligns the bottom of the inline box with the bottom of the parent element's font

You can also set the vertical-align property to a percentage that raises (positive value) or lowers (negative value) the box by the percentage of the line height. A value of 0% is the same as the baseline keyword. Finally, you can set vertical-align to a signed length that will raise or lower the box by the specified distance. A value of 0cm is the same as the baseline keyword.

Boxes

When you are using CSS to format a document and its contents, you need to think in terms of boxes with borders and dimensions that hold the contents of an element. These boxes stack together and wrap around each other so that the contents of each element are aligned in an orderly fashion, based on the rules of the style sheets. CSS2 adds new outline properties for boxes, and enables boxes to be positioned in absolute positions on a page, in another box, or in a window.

Outline Properties

CSS2 makes it possible to add outlines to objects. An outline is a lot like a border. However, an outline is drawn over the box. Its width does not add to the width of the box. Furthermore, if a CSS element is non-rectangular (unlikely), the outline around it will also be non-rectangular. Since outlines are not necessarily rectangular, you can not set the left, right, top, and bottom outline separately. You can only affect the entire outline at once.

Outline Style Property

The `outline-style` property sets the style of the outline for the entire box. This functions just like the `border-style` property in CSS1, and has the same 11 possible values with the same meanings:

1. `none`: no line

2. `hidden`: an invisible line that still takes up space

3. `dotted`: a dotted line

4. `dashed`: a dashed line

5. `solid`: a solid line

6. `double`: a double solid line

7. `grooved`: a line that appears to be drawn into the page

8. `ridge`: a line that appears to be coming out of the page

9. `inset`: the entire object (not just the outline line) appears pushed into the document

10. `outset`: the entire object (not just the outline line) appears to be pushed out of the document

11. `inherit`: use the values of the parent

These three rules set the outline styles for the `TITLE`, `AUTHOR`, and `REFRAIN` elements:

```
TITLE   { outline-style: solid }
AUTHOR  { outline-style: outset }
REFRAIN { outline-style: dashed }
```

Outline Width Property

The outline-width property works like the margin-width and border-width properties discussed in Chapter 12. It sets the width of the outline of a box using either an unsigned length or one of these three keywords:

1. thin: about 0.5 to 0.75 points

2. medium: about 1 point

3. thick: about 1.5 to 2 points

For example, this rule outlines the STANZA with a thick outline and the VERSE with a thin one.

```
STANZA      { outline: thick }
VERSE       { outline: thin }
```

Outline Color Property

The outline-color property sets the color of the outline of an element's box. Generally, this is set to either a color name like red or an RGB color like #FF0000. However, it may also have the keyword value invert which inverts the color of the pixels on the screen. (Black becomes white, and vice versa.) For example:

```
TITLE   {  outline-color: #FFCCCC;
           outline-style: inset;
           outline-width: thick}
AUTHOR {  outline-color: #FF33CC}
VERSE  {  outline-color: invert}
```

Outline Shorthand Property

The outline property is a shorthand property that sets the outline width, color, and style for all four edges of a containing box. For example:

```
STANZA      { outline: thin dashed red }
VERSE       { outline: inset }
```

Positioning Properties

CSS2 provides an astonishing amount of control over the position of each object in a document. You can put specific objects or specific types of objects in layers. Each layer can be moved independently of the other layers. The position property determines how objects are arranged and can have one of these four keyword values:

1. static: the default layout

2. relative: objects are offset from their static positions

3. absolute: objects are placed at a specific position relative to the box they're contained in

4. fixed: objects are placed at a specific point in the window or on the page

Relative Positioning

As a document is laid out, the formatter chooses positions for items according to the normal flow of the objects and text. This is essentially the default static formatting of objects used by most document creators. After this has been completed, the objects may be shifted relative to their current position. This adjustment in an object's position is known as relative positioning. By using relative positioning, altering the position of an object has no effect on the objects following it. Thus boxes can overlap, since relatively positioned boxes retain all of their normal flow sizes and spacing.

You can generate a relatively positioned object by setting the `position` property to `relative`. Its offset will be controlled by the `left`, `right`, `top`, and `bottom` properties. By changing these properties with JavaScript you can even move objects and layers on your documents. You can make images or text move, appear and disappear, or change in mid-stream. For example, this rule moves the `TITLE` element 50 pixels up and 65 pixels to the left from where it would normally be.

```
TITLE    { position: relative;  top: 50px;  left: 65px}
```

Absolute Positioning

An absolutely positioned element is placed in reference to the block that contains it. It establishes a new containing block for boxes it contains. The contents of absolutely positioned elements do not flow around other boxes. This may cause them to obscure the contents of other boxes displayed in the document. Absolutely positioned elements have no impact on the flow of their following siblings, so elements that follow an absolutely positioned one, act as if it were not there. For example, this rule puts the top left corner of the `AUTHOR` element 60 pixels down and 140 pixels to the right of the top left corner of the box it's contained in.

```
AUTHOR    { position: absolute;  top: 60px;  left: 140px }
```

Fixed Positioning

Elements with fixed position are placed at coordinates relative to the window or page on which they're displayed. If you are viewing a document composed of continuous media, the fixed box will not move when the document is scrolled. If the fixed box is located on paged media, it will always appear at the end of each page. This enables you to place a footer or header on a document, or a signature at the end of a series of one-page letters. For example, this rule puts the top-left corner of the `REFRAIN` element 300 pixels down and 140 pixels to the right of the top-left corner of the window it's displayed in or the page it's printed on.

```
REFRAIN  { position: fixed;  top: 300px;  left: 140px}
```

Stacking Elements with the Z-Index Property

The `z-index` property controls the stacking order of positioned boxes. To change the default z-index value, you set `z-index` to an integer like 2. Objects with larger z-index values are placed on top of objects with smaller z-index values. Whether the objects on the bottom show through is a function of the background properties of the object on top of them. If the backgrounds are transparent, at least some of what's below will probably show through.

Listing 13-2 is a style sheet that uses absolute positioning with a z-index to create a multi-part overlay of the Shakespearean sonnet. The result is shown in Figure 13-3. It's certainly not as nice as the version that merely allows the browser to lay out the sonnet. Absolute positioning should be used with extreme care. I'd really only recommend it for print media where you'll be distributing the paper that comes out of your printer rather than the electronic files.

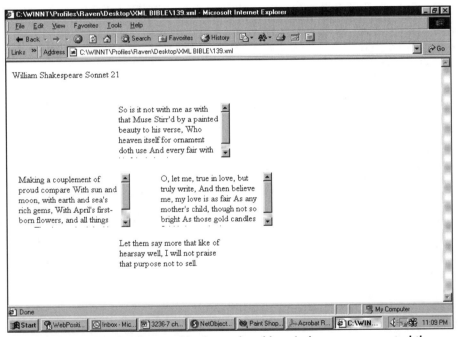

Figure 13-3: Using absolute positioning ordered by z-index, you can control the stacking order of text boxes.

Listing 13-2: **Shakespeare's sonnet with a z-index stylesheet**

```
#st1     { position: absolute;
           top: 160px;
           left:200px;
           height: 100px;
           width:200px;
           overflow: auto;
```

```
              z-index: 2}
#st2    { position: absolute;
          top: 210px;
          left:50px;
          height: 100px;
          width:200px;
          overflow: auto;
          z-index: 3}
#st3    { position: absolute;
          top: 210px;
          left:250px;
          height: 100px;
          width:200px;
          overflow: auto;
          z-index: 4}
REFRAIN { position: absolute;
          top: 300px;
          left:200px;
          height: 100px;
          width:200px;
          overflow: auto;
          z-index: 5}
```

Counters and Automatic Numbering

CSS2 enables you to automatically generate some content. For instance, you can use the style sheet to create outlines that are properly indented with different numbering systems for each level of the outline.

The `counter-increment` property adds one to a counter. The `content` property inserts the current value of a named counter by using either the `counter(`*`id`*`)` or `counter(`*`id, list-style-type`*`)` functions as values. Finally, the `counter-reset` property sets a counter back to 0.

For example, let's suppose you want to number each VERSE in a poem starting from one, but reset the counting in each new STANZA. and the REFRAIN. You can do that with the following rules:

```
VERSE         {counter-increment: verse-num}
STANZA        {counter-reset: verse-num}
REFRAIN       {counter-reset: verse-num}
VERSE:before  {content: counter(verse-num) }
```

You can reset back to a number other than 0 by specifying the integer to reset to after the counter name in `counter-reset`. For example, to reset the counter to -10:

```
VERSE         {counter-reset: verse-num -10}
```

You can also increment by an integer different than 1 by specifying it in `counter-increment` after the counter name. For example,

```
VERSE          {counter-increment: verse-num -1}
```

Finally, the `content` property can have more than one counter, and additional content as well as counters. For instance, these rules number the verses in the form 1.1, 1.2, 1.3, ..., 2.1, 2.2, 2.3, ... where the first number indicates the stanza and the second the verse:

```
VERSE          {counter-increment: verse-num}
STANZA         {counter-reset: verse-num}
STANZA         {counter-increment: stanza-num}
REFRAIN        {counter-reset: verse-num}
REFRAIN        {counter-reset: stanza-num 0}
VERSE:before   {content:
                    counter(stanza-num) "." counter(verse-num) }
```

You're not limited to European numerals either. You can pass a second argument to the `counter()` function to specify a different number format. Available formats include `disc`, `circle`, `square`, `decimal`, `decimal-leading-zero`, `lower-roman`, `upper-roman`, `lower-greek`, `lower-alpha`, `lower-latin`, `upper-alpha`, `upper-latin`, `hebrew`, `armenian`, `georgian`, `cjk-ideographic`, `hiragana`, `katakana`, `hiragana-iroha`, and `katakana-iroha`. For example, to number the verses using Japanese numeral in hiragana, you might write:

```
VERSE:before {content: counter(stanza-num, hiragana)
                    "." counter(verse-num, hiragana) }
```

Aural Style Sheets

Visually impaired users already use special software to read Web pages. In the future, such use is likely to expand to sighted people browsing the Web while talking on cell phones, driving their cars, washing the dishes, and performing other activities in which the eyes and hands have to be directed elsewhere. CSS2 supports new properties to describe how elements are read out loud as well as how they're printed or shown on a screen. The new properties are discussed in the sections that follow. Listing 13-3 is an aural style sheet that identifies specific ways to speak information found in common play-related XML elements.

Listing 13-3: An Aural style sheet for a play or sonnet

```
TITLE, AUTHOR, ACT, SCENE {
        voice-family: narrator;
        stress: 20;
```

```
          richness: 90;
          cue-before: url("ping.au")
   }

.narrator { pause: 20ms;
            cue-before: url("pop.au");
            cue-after: url("pop.au");
            azimuth: 30deg;
            elevation: above }

ACT    { pause: 30ms 40ms } /* pause-before: 30ms;
                               pause-after: 40ms */

SCENE { pause-after: 10ms } /* pause-after: 10ms */

SCENE { cue-before: url("bell.aiff");
        cue-after: url("dong.wav") }

MOOD.sad       { play-during: url("violins.aiff") }
MOOD.funereal  { play-during: url("harp.wav") mix }
MOOD.quiet     { play-during: none }

LINE.narrator       { azimuth: behind } /* 180deg */
LINE.part.romeo     { voice-family: romeo, male }
LINE.part.juliet    { voice-family: juliet, female }
LINE.part.hercules  { azimuth: center-left }
LINE.part.richard   { azimuth: right }
LINE.part.carmen    { volume: x-soft }
LINE.part.muse1     { elevation: 60deg }
LINE.part.muse2     { elevation: 30deg }
LINE.part.muse3     { elevation: level }
```

Speak Property

The speak property determines whether text will be rendered aurally and if so, how. If speak has the value normal, text is spoken using the best available speech synthesis. If speak has the value spell-out, the text is spelled out letter-by-letter, which might be useful for unusual or foreign words a speech synthesizer probably can't handle. The default value is none (for example, just render the content visually and forget about speech synthesis).

Volume Property

The volume property controls the average volume of the speaking voice of the speech synthesizer. This is the median value of the analog wave of the voice, but it's only an average. A highly inflected voice at a volume of 50 might peak at 75. The minimum volume is 0. The maximum volume is 100. Percentage values can also be used, as can any of these six keywords:

1. `silent`: no sound

2. `x-soft`: 0, the minimum audible volume

3. `soft`: about 25

4. `medium`: about 50

5. `loud`: about 75

6. `x-loud`: 100, the maximum comfortable hearing level

Pause Properties

Pauses are the aural equivalent of a comma. They can be used to provide drama, or just to help separate one speaker's voice from another's. They're set in CSS2 with the `pause`, `pause-before`, and `pause-after` properties.

The `pause-before` property specifies the length of time the speech synthesizer should pause before speaking an element's contents. The `pause-after` property specifies the length of time the speech synthesizer should pause after speaking an element's contents. These can be set as an absolute time or as a percentage of the speech-rate property. The `pause` property is shorthand for setting both `pause-before` and `pause-after`. When two values are supplied, the first is applied to `pause-before` and the second is applied to `pause-after`. When only one value is given, it applies to both properties. For example:

```
SCENE { pause-after: 10ms }

/* pause-before: 20ms; pause-after: 20ms */
.narrator { pause: 20ms }

/* pause-before: 30ms; pause-after: 40ms */
ACT    { pause: 30ms 40ms }
```

Cue Properties

Cues are audible clues that alert the listener to a specific event that is about to occur, or has just occurred. Each cue property specifies a URL for a sound file that will be played before or after an element is spoken. The `cue-before` property plays a sound before an element is read. The `cue-after` property plays a sound after an element is read.

The `cue` property is shorthand for setting both `cue-before` and `cue-after`. When two values are supplied, the first is applied to `cue-before` and the second is applied to `cue-after`. When only one value is given, it applies to both properties. For example:

```
ACT, SCENE { cue-before: url("ping.au") }
```

```
.narrator   { cue: url("pop.au") }
SCENE       { cue-before: url("bell.aiff");
              cue-after: url("dong.wav") }
```

Play-During Property

The `play-during` property specifies a sound to be played in the background while an element's content is spoken. The value of the property is URL to the sound file. You can also add one or both of the keywords `mix` and `repeat` to the value. `Mix` tells the speech synthesizer to mix in the parent's `play-during` sound. The `repeat` value tells the speech synthesizer to loop the sound continuously until the entire element has been spoken. The default value is `none`.

Spatial Properties

The spatial properties specify where the sound should appear to be coming from. For example, you can have a document read to you from 3 feet away in a ditch or 100 feet away on a cliff. This is of course limited by the capabilities of the speech synthesizer and audio hardware. Since you can not predetermine the number and location of speakers in use by the document reader, these properties simply identify the desired end result. As the document author, you can't really force the sound to appear to be coming from any particular direction, anymore than you can guarantee that a reader has a color monitor.

Azimuth Property

The `azimuth` property controls the horizontal angle from which the sound appears to come. When you listen to audio through good stereo speakers, you seem to hear a lateral sound stage. The `azimuth` property can be used with this type of stereo system to create angles to the sound you hear. When you add a total surround-sound system using either a binaural headphone or a 5-speaker home theatre setup, the `azimuth` property becomes very noticeable.

The azimuth is specified as an angle between -360° and 360°. A value of `0deg` means that the sound is directly in front of the listener (as are `-360deg` and `360deg`). A value of `180deg` means that the sound is directly behind the listener. (In CSS terminology `deg` replaces the more common ° degree symbol.) Angles are counted clockwise to the listener's right. You can also use one of these nine keywords to specify the azimuthal angle:

1. `center`: 0deg
2. `center-right`: 20deg
3. `right`: 40deg
4. `far-right`: 60deg
5. `right-side`: 90deg
6. `left-side`: 270deg

7. far-left: 300deg

8. left: 320deg

9. center-left: 340deg

You can add the keyword behind to any of these values to set the position to 180deg minus the normal value. For example left behind is the same as 180deg - 320deg = -140deg or 220deg.

A value of leftwards moves the sound an additional 20 degrees to the left, relative to the current angle. This is most easily understood as turning the sound counter-clockwise. So even if the sound is already behind the listener, it will continue to move "left" around the circle. A value of rightwards moves the sound an additional 20 degrees to the right (clockwise) from to the current angle.

Elevation Property

The elevation property controls the apparent height of the speaker above the listener's position. The elevation is specified as an angle between -90° and 90°. It can also be given as one of these five keywords:

1. below   -90deg

2. level   0deg

3. above   90deg

4. higher   10deg above the current elevation (useful with inheritance)

5. lower   10deg below the current elevation (useful with inheritance)

Voice Characteristics Properties

The individual characteristics of the synthesizer's voice can be controlled by adjusting the rate of speech, the voice-family used, the pitch, and the richness of the voice.

Speech Rate Property

The speech-rate property specifies the speaking rate of the speech synthesizer as an approximate number of average sized words per minute. You can supply an integer or one of these five keywords:

1. x-slow: 80 words per minutes

2. slow: 120 words per minute

3. medium: 180 to 200 words per minute

4. fast: 300 words per minute

5. x-fast: 500 words per minute

You can also use the keyword `faster` to add 40 words per minute to the rate of the parent element or `slower` to subtract 40 words per minute from the rate of the parent element.

Voice Family Property

The `voice-family` property is a comma-separated, prioritized list of voice-family names that chooses the voice used for reading the text of the document. It's like the `font-family` property discussed in Chapter 12, but is regarding voices instead of typefaces.

Generic voice values include `male`, `female`, and `child`. Specific names are as diverse as font names and include `Agnes`, `Bruce`, `Good News`, `Hysterical`, `Victoria`, `Whisper`, and many more. These names must be quoted if they do not conform to syntax rules for identifiers, or if they consist of more than one word. For example:

```
LINE.part.romeo { voice-family: Bruce, "Good News", male }
```

Pitch Property

The `pitch` property specifies the frequency the speech synthesizer uses for a particular type of object. To some degree this controls whether a voice sounds male or female. However, it's better to use an appropriate voice-family instead. The value is given in hertz (cycles per second). Female voices are about 120Hz, while typical male voices are in the ballpark of 200Hz. You can also use these keywords to adjust the pitch:

1. `x-low`
2. `low`
3. `medium`
4. `high`
5. `x-high`

The exact frequencies of these keywords depend on the user's environment and selected voice. However, `x-low` is always lower than `low`, which is always lower than `medium`, and so forth.

Pitch Range Property7

The `pitch-range` property specifies the acceptable variations in the speaker's average pitch as a number between 0 and 100. This controls the inflection and variation of the voice used by the speech synthesizer. A value of 0 creates a flat, monotone voice, while 50 is a normal voice, and values above 50 create an exceptionally animated voice.

Stress Property

The `stress` property specifies the level of assertiveness or emphasis that's used in the speaking voice. The default is `50`. The value and effect of this attribute has a different effect in each language being spoken. When used with languages such as English that stress sentence position, you can select primary, secondary, and tertiary stress points to control the inflection that is applied to these areas of the sentence.

Richness Property

The `richness` property specifies the "brightness" of the voice used by the speech synthesizer. The richer the voice, the better its carrying capacity. Smooth voices don't carry far because their wave forms are not as deeply pitched as rich voices. The value is a number between 1 and 100, with a default of 50. Higher values produce voices that carry better, while lower values produce softer voices that are easier to listen to.

Speech Properties

These properties control how the speech synthesizer interprets punctuation and numbers. There are two such properties: `speak-punctuation` property and the `speak-numeral` property.

Speak Punctuation Property

By default punctuation is spoken literally. A statement such as "The cat, Charm, ate all of his food." is read as "The cat comma Charm comma ate all of his food period". However, by setting the `speak-punctuation` property to `none`, none of the punctuation will be spoken. It will, however, have pauses, as would a natural speaking voice. For example, "The cat <pause> Charm <pause> ate all of his food <silence>".

Speak Numeral Property

By default numbers are spoken as a full string. For example, the number 102 would be read "one hundred and two". If, however, you set the `speak-numeral` property to `digits`, each number being will be spoken individually like "one zero two". You can return to the default by setting `speak-numeral` property to `continuous`. If `speak-numeral` is set to `none`, numbers will not be spoken.

Summary

This chapter covered CSS2's features and how to implement them. In this chapter, you learned:

✦ CSS2 is mostly a superset of CSS1, though there are a few differences including a default display type of `inline` instead of `block`.

✦ Internet Explorer 5 and Mozilla only marginally implement CSS2, so don't expect a lot of its features to work flawlessly.

✦ CSS2 has expanded the various selectors that can apply specific properties to particular elements including a universal selector, child selectors, descendant selectors, and sibling selectors.

✦ New @rules have been developed to give document authors more control over their printed documents, including @charset, @page, and @font-face.

✦ CSS2 has seven new pseudo-classes, including :first-child and :hover, to select elements that have something in common, but do not necessarily have the same type.

✦ CSS2 has two new pseudo-elements that let you insert content into the document: :after and :before.

✦ CSS2 has increased the use of the display property, by incorporating values to display elements as all the parts of a table, not at all (none), and as compact or run-in objects.

✦ System colors and systems fonts enable you to create an interface on your XML applications that more closely matches the main system settings on each individual visitors computers.

✦ CSS2 adds aural properties for describing speech, volume, pausing, cues, voice characteristics, and the specification of a sound to be played and where it should be coming from, among other things.

As with CSS1, CSS2 still has many limitations, the most obvious of which is lack of full support from Web browsers, but this should change with time. XSL is still by far the most full-bodied style sheet language for use with XML documents. In the next chapter, you will explore XSL transformations, and see how much farther they can take you.

✦   ✦   ✦

XSL Transformations

The Extensible Style Language (XSL) includes both a transformation language and a formatting language. Each of these, naturally enough, is an XML application. The transformation language provides elements that define rules for how one XML document is transformed into another XML document. The transformed XML document may use the markup and DTD of the original document or it may use a completely different set of tags. In particular, it may use the tags defined by the second part of XSL, the formatting objects. This chapter covers the transformation language half of XSL.

What Is XSL?

The transformation and formatting halves of XSL can function independently of each other. For instance, the transformation language can transform an XML document into a well-formed HTML file, and completely ignore the XSL formatting objects. This is the style of XSL supported by Internet Explorer 5.0, previewed in Chapter 5, and emphasized in this chapter.

Furthermore, it's not absolutely required that a document written in XSL formatting objects be produced by using the transformation part of XSL on another XML document. For example, it's easy to imagine a converter written in Java that reads TeX or PDF files and translates them into XSL formatting objects (though no such converters exist as of summer, 1999).

In essence, XSL is two languages, not one. The first language is a transformation language, the second a formatting language. The transformation language is useful independently of the formatting language. Its ability to move data from one XML representation to another makes it an important component of XML-based electronic commerce, electronic data interchange, metadata exchange, and any application that needs to convert between different XML representations of the same data. These uses are also united by their lack of concern with rendering data on a display for humans to read. They are purely about moving data from one computer system or program to another.

Consequently, many early implementations of XSL focus exclusively on the transformation part and ignore the formatting objects. These are incomplete implementations, but nonetheless useful. Not all data must ultimately be rendered on a computer monitor or printed on paper.

Cross-Reference Chapter 15, *XSL Formatting Objects*, covers the XSL formatting language.

A Word of Caution about XSL

XSL is still under development. The XSL language has changed radically in the past, and will almost certainly change again in the future. This chapter is based on the April 21, 1999 (fourth) draft of the XSL specification. By the time you are reading this book, this draft of XSL will probably have been superseded and the exact syntax of XSL will have changed. I'm hopeful that this chapter won't be too far removed from the actual specification. Nonetheless, if you do encounter inconsistencies, you should compare the examples in this book against the most current specification.

To make matters worse, no software yet implements all of the April 21, 1999 (fourth) draft of the XSL specification, not even the transformation half. All products available now implement different subsets of the current draft. Furthermore, many products, including Internet Explorer 5.0 and XT add elements not actually present in the current draft specification for XSL. Finally, most products that attempt to implement at least part of XSL have non-trivial bugs in those parts they do implement. Consequently, very few examples will work exactly the same way in different software.

Eventually, of course, this should be straightened out as the standard evolves toward its final incarnation, as vendors fix the bugs in their products and implement the unimplemented parts, and as more software is published that supports XSL. Until then you're faced with a choice: you can either work out on the bleeding edge with XSL in its current, incomplete, unfinished state and try to work around all the bugs and omissions you'll encounter; or you can stick with a more established technology like CSS until XSL becomes more solid.

Overview of XSL Transformations

In an XSL transformation, an XSL processor reads both an XML document and an XSL style sheet. Based on the instructions the processor finds in the XSL style sheet, it outputs a new XML document.

Trees

As you learned in Chapter 6, every well-formed XML document is a tree. A tree is a data structure composed of connected nodes beginning with a single node called the root. The root connects to its child nodes, each of which may connect to zero or more children of its own, and so forth. Nodes that have no children of their own are called leaves. A diagram of tree looks much like a genealogical descendant chart that lists the descendants of a single ancestor. The most useful property of a tree is that each node and its children also form a tree. Thus, a tree is a hierarchical structure of trees in which each tree is built out of smaller trees.

The nodes of an XML tree are the elements and their content. However, for the purposes of XSL, attributes, namespaces, processing instructions, and comments must also be counted as nodes. Furthermore, the root of the document must be distinguished from the root element. Thus, XSL processors assume an XML tree contains seven kinds of nodes. These are:

1. The root

2. Elements

3. Text

4. Attributes

5. Namespaces

6. Processing instructions

7. Comments

For example, consider the XML document in Listing 14-1. This shows a periodic table of the elements that I'll use as an example in this chapter. (More properly it shows the first two elements of the periodic table.)

On the CD-ROM

The complete periodic table appears on the CD-ROM in the file allelements.xml in the examples/periodic_table directory.

The root `PERIODIC_TABLE` element contains `ATOM` child elements. Each `ATOM` element houses a variety of child elements providing the atomic number, atomic weight, symbol, boiling point, and so forth. A `UNITS` attribute specifies the units for those elements that have units.

Note

ELEMENT would be a more appropriate choice here than ATOM. However, writing about ELEMENT elements and trying to distinguish between chemical elements and XML elements might create confusion. Thus, at least for the purposes of this chapter, ATOM seemed like the more legible choice.

Listing 14-1: An XML periodic table with two elements, hydrogen and helium

```
<?xml version="1.0"?>
<?xml-stylesheet type="text/xsl" href="14-2.xsl"?>
<PERIODIC_TABLE>

  <ATOM STATE="GAS">
    <NAME>Hydrogen</NAME>
    <SYMBOL>H</SYMBOL>
    <ATOMIC_NUMBER>1</ATOMIC_NUMBER>
    <ATOMIC_WEIGHT>1.00794</ATOMIC_WEIGHT>
    <BOILING_POINT UNITS="Kelvin">20.28</BOILING_POINT>
    <MELTING_POINT UNITS="Kelvin">13.81</MELTING_POINT>
    <DENSITY UNITS="grams/cubic centimeter"><!— At 300K —>
      0.0899
    </DENSITY>
  </ATOM>

  <ATOM STATE="GAS">
    <NAME>Helium</NAME>
    <SYMBOL>He</SYMBOL>
    <ATOMIC_NUMBER>2</ATOMIC_NUMBER>
    <ATOMIC_WEIGHT>4.0026</ATOMIC_WEIGHT>
    <BOILING_POINT UNITS="Kelvin">4.216</BOILING_POINT>
    <MELTING_POINT UNITS="Kelvin">0.95</MELTING_POINT>
    <DENSITY UNITS="grams/cubic centimeter"><!— At 300K —>
      0.1785
    </DENSITY>
  </ATOM>

</PERIODIC_TABLE>
```

Figure 14-1 displays a diagram of this document as a tree. It begins at the top with the root node (not the same as the root element!) which contains two child nodes, the xml-stylesheet processing instruction and the root element PERIODIC_TABLE. (The XML declaration is not visible to the XSL processor and is not included in the tree the XSL processor operates on.) The PERIODIC_TABLE element contains two child nodes, both ATOM elements. Each ATOM element has an attribute node for its STATE attribute, and a variety of child element nodes. Each child element encompasses a node for its contents, as well as nodes for any attributes and comments it possesses. Notice in particular that many nodes are something other than elements. There are nodes for text, attributes, comments, and processing instructions. Unlike CSS1, XSL is not limited to working only with whole elements. It has a much more granular view of a document that enables you to base styles on comments, attributes, processing instructions, and more.

Note Like the XML declaration, an internal DTD subset or DOCTYPE declaration is is not part of the tree. However, it may have the effect of adding attribute nodes to some elements through <!ATTLIST> declarations that use #FIXED or default attribute values.

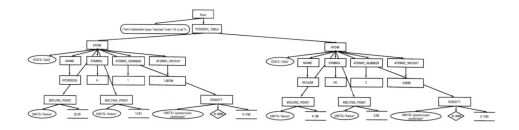

Figure 14-1: Listing 14-1 as a tree diagram

The XSL transformation language operates by transforming one XML tree into another XML tree. The language contains operators for selecting particular nodes from the tree, reordering the nodes, and outputting nodes. If one of these nodes is an element node, then it may be an entire tree itself. Remember that all these operators, both for input and output, are designed for operation on a tree. They are not a general regular expression language for transforming arbitrary data.

XSL Style Sheet Documents

More precisely, an XSL transformation accepts as input a tree represented as an XML document and produces as output a new tree, also represented as an XML document. Consequently, the transformation part of XSL is also called the tree construction part. Both the input and the output must be XML documents. You cannot use XSL to transform to or from non-XML formats like PDF, TeX, Microsoft Word, PostScript, MIDI, or others. You can use XSL to transform XML to an intermediate format like TeXML, then use additional, non-XSL software to transform that into the format you want. HTML and SGML are borderline cases because they're so close to XML. You can use XSL to transform to or from HTML and SGML that meets XML's well-formedness rules. However, XSL cannot handle the wide variety of non-well-formed HTML and SGML you'll encounter on most Web sites and document production systems. The key thing to remember is that XSL transformation language works for XML-to-XML conversions, not for anything else.

An XSL document contains a list of template rules and other rules. A template rule has a pattern specifying the trees it applies to and a template to be output when the pattern is matched. When an XSL processor formats an XML document using an XSL style sheet, it scans the XML document tree looking through each sub-tree in turn. As each tree in the XML document is read, the processor compares it with the pattern of each template rule in the style sheet. When the processor finds a tree that matches a template rule's pattern, it outputs the rule's template. This template generally includes some markup, some new data, and some data copied out of the tree from the original XML document.

XSL uses XML to describe these rules, templates, and patterns. The XSL document itself is an `xsl:stylesheet` element. Each template rule is an `xsl:template` element. The pattern of the rule is the value of the `match` attribute of the `xsl:template` element. The output template is the content of the `xsl:template` element. All instructions in the template for doing things like selecting parts of the input tree to include in the output tree are performed by one or another XSL element. These are identified by the `xsl:` prefix on the element names. Elements that do not have an `xsl:` prefix are part of the result tree.

Cross-Reference
More properly, all elements that are XSL instructions are part of the `xsl` namespace. Namespaces are discussed in Chapter 18, *Namespaces*. Until then, all you have to know is that the names of all XSL elements begin with `xsl:`.

Listing 14-2 shows a very simple XSL style sheet with two template rules. The first template rule matches the root element `PERIODIC_TABLE`. It replaces this element with an `html` element. The contents of the `html` element are the results of applying the other templates in the document to the contents of the `PERIODIC_TABLE` element.

The second template matches `ATOM` elements. It replaces each `ATOM` element in the input document with a `P` element in the output document. The `xsl:apply-templates` rule inserts the text of the matched source element into the output document. Thus, the contents of a `P` element will be the text (but not the markup) contained in the corresponding `ATOM` element. I further discuss the exact syntax of these elements below.

Listing 14-2: An XSL style sheet for the periodic table with two template rules

```
<?xml version="1.0"?>
<xsl:stylesheet
xmlns:xsl="http://www.w3.org/XSL/Transform/1.0">

  <xsl:template match="PERIODIC_TABLE">
    <html>
      <xsl:apply-templates/>
    </html>
  </xsl:template>

  <xsl:template match="ATOM">
    <P>
      <xsl:apply-templates/>
    </P>
  </xsl:template>

</xsl:stylesheet>
```

Where Does the XML Transformation Happen?

There are three primary ways XML documents are transformed into other formats, such as HTML, with an XSL style sheet:

1. The XML document and associated style sheet are both served to the client (Web browser), which then transforms the document as specified by the style sheet and presents it to the user.

2. The server applies an XSL style sheet to an XML document to transform it to some other format (generally HTML) and sends the transformed document to the client (Web browser).

3. A third program transforms the original XML document into some other format (often HTML) before the document is placed on the server. Both server and client only deal with the post-transform document.

Each of these three approaches uses different software, though they all use the same XML documents and XSL style sheets. An ordinary Web server sending XML documents to Internet Explorer 5.0 is an example of the first approach. A servlet-compatible Web server using the IBM alphaWorks' XML enabler exemplifies the second approach. Using the command line XT program to transform XML documents to HTML documents, then placing the HTML documents on a Web server is an example of the third approach. However, these all use (at least in theory) the same XSL language.

In this chapter, I will emphasize the third approach, primarily because at the time of this writing, specialized converter programs like James Clark's XT or IBM's LotusXSL provide the most complete and accurate implementation of the current XSL specification. Furthermore, this provides the broadest compatibility with legacy Web browsers and servers whereas the first approach requires a more recent browser than most users use and the second approach requires special Web server software. In practice, though, requiring a different server is not nearly as onerous as requiring a particular client. You, yourself, can install your own special server software, but you cannot rely on your visitors to install particular client software.

How to Use XT

XT is a Java 1.1 character mode application. To use it, you'll need to have a Java 1.1 compatible virtual machine installed such as Sun's Java Development Kit (JDK) or Java Runtime Environment (JRE), Apple's Macintosh Runtime for Java 2.1 (MRJ), or Microsoft's virtual machine. You'll also need to install a SAX compliant XML parser like James Clark's XP. This is also a Java application.

Note

At the time of this writing, XT can be found at `http://www.jclark.com/xml/xt.html` and . XP can be found at `http://www.jclark.com/xml/xp/index.html`. These URLs are, of course, subject to change as time passes. Indeed, there's no guarantee that XT will be available when you read this. However, although I use XT in this chapter, the examples should work with any XSL processor that implements the tree construction part of the April 21, 1999 working draft of the XSL specification. Another possibility is IBM alphaWorks' LotusXSL, available at `http://www.alphaworks.ibm.com/tech/LotusXSL`. The examples may or may not work with software that implements later drafts of XSL, though I hope they'll be close. I'll post any updates on my own Web site at `http://metalab.unc.edu/xml/books/bible/`.

The Java class containing the main method for XT is `com.jclark.xsl.sax.Driver`. Assuming your Java `CLASSPATH` environment variable includes the xt.jar and sax.jar files (both included in the XT distribution), you can run XT by typing the following at the shell prompt or in a DOS window:

```
C:\> java
    -Dcom.jclark.xsl.sax.parser=com.jclark.xml.sax.CommentDriver
    com.jclark.xsl.sax.Driver 14-1.xml 14-2.xsl 14-3.html
```

This line runs the `java` interpreter, sets the `com.jclark.xsl.sax.parser` Java environment variable to `com.jclark.xml.sax.CommentDriver`, which indicates the fully qualified name of the Java class used to parse the input documents. This class must be somewhere in your class path. Here I've used the XP parser, but any SAX-compliant parser will do. Next comes the name of the Java class containing the XT program's `main()` method, `com.jclark.xsl.sax.Driver`. Finally, there are the names of the input XML document (14-1.xml), the input XSL style sheet (14-2.xsl), and the output HTML file (14-3.html). If the last argument is omitted, the transformed document will be printed on the console.

Tip If you're using Windows and have installed the Microsoft Java virtual machine, you can use a stand-alone executable version of XT instead. This is a little easier to use since it includes the XP parser and doesn't require you to mess around with the CLASSPATH environment variable. With this program, you simply place the xt.exe file in your path, and type:

```
C:\> xt 14-1.xml 14-2.xsl 14-3.html
```

Listing 14-2 transforms input documents to well-formed HTML files as discussed in Chapter 6. However, you can transform from any XML application to any other as long as you can write a style sheet to support the transformation. For example, you can imagine a style sheet that transforms from VML documents to SVG documents:

```
% java
  -Dcom.jclark.xsl.sax.parser=com.jclark.xml.sax.CommentDriver
  com.jclark.xsl.sax.Driver pinktriangle.vml
  VmlToSVG.xsl -out pinktriangle.svg
```

Most other command line XSL processors behave similarly, though of course they'll have different command line arguments and options. They may prove slightly easier to use if they're not written in Java since there won't be any need to configure the CLASSPATH.

Listing 14-3 shows the output of running Listing 14-1 through XT with the XSL style sheet in Listing 14-2. Notice that XT does not attempt to clean up the HTML it generates, which has a lot of whitespace. This is not important since ultimately you want to view the file in a Web browser that trims whitespace. Figure 14-2 shows Listing 14-3 loaded into Netscape Navigator 4.5. Since Listing 14-3 displays standard HTML, you don't need an XML-capable browser to view it.

Listing 14-3: The HTML produced by applying the style sheet in Listing 14-2 to the XML in Listing 14-1

```
<html>

  <P>
    Hydrogen
    H
    1
    1.00794
    20.28
    13.81

      0.0899

  </P>
```

Continued

Listing 14-3 *(continued)*

```
<P>
   Helium
   He
   2
   4.0026
   4.216
   0.95

      0.1785

</P>

</html>
```

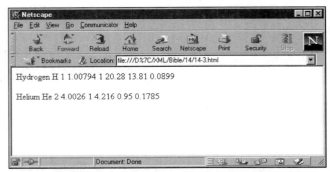

Figure 14-2: The page produced by applying the XSL style sheet in Listing 14-2 to the XML document in Listing 14-1

Direct Display of XML Files with XSL Style Sheets

Instead of preprocessing the XML file, you can send the client both the XML file, and the XSL file that describes how to render it. The client is responsible for applying the style sheet to the document and rendering it accordingly. This is more work for the client, but places much less load on the server. In this case, the XSL style sheet must transform the document into an XML application the client understands. HTML is a likely choice, though in the future some browsers will likely work with XSL formatting objects as well.

Attaching an XSL style sheet to an XML document is easy. Simply insert an `xml-stylesheet` processing instruction in the prolog immediately after the XML declaration. This processing instruction should have a `type` attribute with the value `text/xsl` and an `href` attribute whose value is a URL pointing to the style sheet. For example:

```
<?xml version="1.0"?>
<?xml-stylesheet type="text/xsl" href="14-2.xsl"?>
```

This is also how you attach a CSS style sheet to a document. The only difference here is that the `type` attribute has the value `text/xsl` instead of `text/css`.

Internet Explorer 5.0's XSL support differs from the 4-21-1999 working draft in a number of respects. First of all it expects that XSL elements are in the `http://www.w3.org/TR/WD-xsl` namespace instead of the `http://www.w3.org/XSL/Transform/1.0` namespace, although the `xsl` prefix is still used. Secondly, it does not implement the default rules for elements that match no template. Consequently, you need to provide a template for each element in the hierarchy starting from the root before trying to view a document in Internet Explorer. Listing 14-4 demonstrates. The three rules match the root node, the root element `PERIODIC_TABLE`, and the `ATOM` elements in that order. Figure 14-3 shows the XML document in Listing 14-1 loaded into Internet Explorer 5.0 with this style sheet.

Listing 14-4: The style sheet of Listing 14-2 adjusted to work with Internet Explorer 5.0

```
<?xml version="1.0"?>
<xsl:stylesheet xmlns:xsl="http://www.w3.org/TR/WD-xsl">

  <xsl:template match="/">
    <html>
      <xsl:apply-templates/>
    </html>
  </xsl:template>

  <xsl:template match="PERIODIC_TABLE">
    <xsl:apply-templates/>
  </xsl:template>

  <xsl:template match="ATOM">
    <P>
      <xsl:value-of select="."/>
    </P>
  </xsl:template>

</xsl:stylesheet>
```

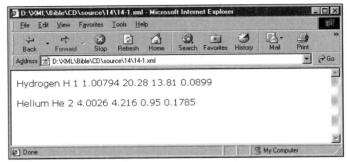

Figure 14-3: The page produced in Internet Explorer 5.0 by applying the adjusted XSL style sheet in Listing 14-4 to the XML document in Listing 14-1

Caution Ideally, you would use the same XML document both for direct display and for pre-rendering to HTML. Unfortunately, XT won't accept the `http://www.w3.org/TR/WD-xsl` namespace and IE5 won't accept the `http://www.w3.org/XSL/Transform/1.0` namespace. Such is life on the bleeding edge as different processors play leapfrog in their support of various parts of the evolving XSL specification.

In the rest of this chapter, I will simply pre-render the file in HTML before loading it into a Web browser.

XSL Templates

Template rules defined by the `xsl:template` element are the most important part of the XSL style sheet. Each template rule is an `xsl:template` element. These associate particular output with particular input. Each `xsl:template` element has a `match` attribute that specifies which nodes of the input document the template is instantiated for.

The content of the `xsl:template` element is the actual template to be instantiated. A template may contain both text that will appear literally in the output document and XSL instructions that copy data from the input XML document to the result. Because all XSL instructions are in the `xsl` namespace (that is they all begin with `xsl:`), it's easy to distinguish between the elements that are literal data to be copied to the output and XSL instructions. For example, here is a template that is applied to the root node of the input tree:

```
<xsl:template match="/">
  <html>
    <head>
    </head>
    <body>
    </body>
```

```
    </html>
  </xsl:template>
```

When the XSL processor reads the input document, the first node it sees is the root. This rule matches that root node, and tells the XSL processor to emit this text:

```
<html>
  <head>
  </head>
  <body>
  </body>
</html>
```

This text is well-formed HTML. Since the XSL document is itself an XML document, its contents—templates included—must be well-formed XML.

If you were to use the above rule, and only the above rule, in an XSL style sheet, the output would be limited to the above six tags. (Actually they're compressed to the equivalent four tags `<html><head/><body/></html>`). That's because no instructions in the rule tell the formatter to move down the tree and look for further matches against the templates in the style sheet.

The xsl:apply-templates Element

To get beyond the root, you have to tell the formatting engine to process the children of the root. In general, to include content in the child nodes, you have to recursively process the nodes through the XML document. The element that does this is `xsl:apply-templates`. By including `xsl:apply-templates` in the output template, you tell the formatter to compare each child element of the matched source element against the templates in the style sheet; and, if a match is found, output the template for the matched node. The template for the matched node may itself contain `xsl:apply-templates` elements to search for matches for its children. When the formatting engine processes a node, the node is treated as a complete tree. This is the advantage of the tree structure. Each part can be treated the same way as the whole. For example, Listing 14-5 is an XSL style sheet that uses the `xsl:apply templates` element to process the child nodes.

> Listing 14-5: **An XSL style sheet that recursively processes the children of the root**

```
<?xml version="1.0"?>
<xsl:stylesheet
xmlns:xsl="http://www.w3.org/XSL/Transform/1.0">

  <xsl:template match="/">
    <html>
```

Continued

> **Listing 14-5:** *(continued)*
>
> ```
>       <xsl:apply-templates/>
>     </html>
>   </xsl:template>
>
>   <xsl:template match="PERIODIC_TABLE">
>     <body>
>       <xsl:apply-templates/>
>     </body>
>   </xsl:template>
>
>   <xsl:template match="ATOM">
>     An Atom
>   </xsl:template>
>
> </xsl:stylesheet>
> ```

When this style sheet is applied to Listing 14-1, here's what happens:

1. The root node is compared with all template rules in the style sheet. It matches the first one.

2. The `<html>` tag is written out.

3. The `xsl:apply-templates` element causes the formatting engine to process the child nodes.

   A. The first child of the root, the `xml-stylesheet` processing instruction, is compared with the template rules. It doesn't match any of them so no output is generated.

   B. The second child of the root, the root element `PERIODIC_TABLE`, is compared with the template rules. It matches the second template rule.

   C. The `<body>` tag is written out.

   D. The `xsl:apply-templates` element in the `body` element causes the formatting engine to process the child nodes of `PERIODIC_TABLE`.

      a. The first child of the `PERIODIC_TABLE` element, that is the Hydrogen `ATOM` element, is compared with the template rules. It matches the third template rule.

      b. The text "An Atom" is output.

      c. The second child of the `PERIODIC_TABLE` element, that is the Helium `ATOM` element, is compared with the template rules. It matches the third template rule.

d. The text "An Atom" is output.

E. The `</body>` tag is written out.

4. The `</html>` tag is written out.

5. Processing is complete.

The end result is:

```
<html><body>


    An Atom


    An Atom


</body></html>
```

The select Attribute

To replace the text "An Atom" with the name of the ATOM element as given by its NAME child, you need to specify that templates should be applied to the NAME children of the ATOM element. To choose a particular set of children instead of all children you supply `xsl:apply-templates` with a `select` attribute designating the children to be selected. In this example:

```
<xsl:template match="ATOM">
  <xsl:apply-templates select="NAME"/>
</xsl:template>
```

The `select` attribute uses the same kind of patterns as the `match` attribute of the `xsl:template` element. For now, we'll stick to simple names of elements; but in the section on patterns for matching and selecting later in this chapter, we'll explore many more possibilities for both `select` and `match`. If no `select` attribute is present, all child elements are selected.

The result of adding this rule to the style sheet of Listing 14-5 and applying it to Listing 14-5 is this:

```
<html><head/><body>

  Hydrogen

  Helium

</body></html>
```

Computing the Value of a Node with xsl:value-of

The `xsl:value-of` element copies the value of a node in the input document into the output document. The `select` attribute of the `xsl:value-of` element specifies which node's value is being taken.

For example, suppose you want to replace the literal text "An Atom" with the name of the `ATOM` element as given by the contents of its `NAME` child. You can replace An Atom with `<xsl:value-of select="NAME"/>` like this:

```
<xsl:template match="ATOM">
  <xsl:value-of select="NAME"/>
</xsl:template>
```

Then, when you apply the style sheet to Listing 14-1, this text is generated:

```
<html><head/><body>

   Hydrogen

   Helium

</body></html>
```

The item whose value is selected, the `NAME` element in this example, is relative to the source node. The source node is the item matched by the template, the particular `ATOM` element in this example. Thus, when the Hydrogen `ATOM` is matched by `<xsl:template match="ATOM">`, the Hydrogen `ATOM`'s `NAME` is selected by `xsl:value-of`. When the Helium `ATOM` is matched by `<xsl:template match="ATOM">`, the Helium `ATOM`'s `NAME` is selected by `xsl:value-of`.

The value of a node is always a string, possibly an empty string. The exact contents of this string depend on the type of the node. The most common type of node is element, and the value of an element node is particularly simple. It's the concatenation of all the parsed character data (but not markup!) between the element's start tag and end tag. For example, the first `ATOM` element in Listing 14-1 is as follows:

```
<ATOM STATE="GAS">
  <NAME>Hydrogen</NAME>
  <SYMBOL>H</SYMBOL>
  <ATOMIC_NUMBER>1</ATOMIC_NUMBER>
  <ATOMIC_WEIGHT>1.00794</ATOMIC_WEIGHT>
  <OXIDATION_STATES>1</OXIDATION_STATES>
  <BOILING_POINT UNITS="Kelvin">20.28</BOILING_POINT>
  <MELTING_POINT UNITS="Kelvin">13.81</MELTING_POINT>
```

```
<DENSITY UNITS="grams/cubic centimeter"><!- At 300K ->
   0.0899
</DENSITY>
</ATOM>
```

The value of this element is shown below:

```
Hydrogen
H
1
1.00794
1
20.28
13.81

   0.0899
```

I calculated that, just by stripping out all the tags and comments. Everything else including whitespace was left intact. The values of the other six node types are calculated similarly, mostly in obvious ways. Table 14-1 summarizes.

Table 14-1 Values of Nodes	
Node Type	**Value**
Root	the value of the root element
Element	the concatenation of all parsed character data contained in the element, including character data in any of the descendants of the element
Text	the text of the node; essentially the node itself
Attribute	the normalized attribute value as specified by Section 3.3.3 of the XML 1.0 recommendation; basically the attribute value after entities are resolved and leading and trailing whitespace is stripped; does not include the name of the attribute, the equals sign, or the quotation marks
Namespace	the URI for the namespace
Processing instruction	the value of the processing instruction; does not include the processing instruction name, `<?` or `?>`
Comment	the text of the comment, `<!--` and `-->` not included

Processing Multiple Elements with xsl:for-each

The `xsl:value-of` element should only be used in contexts where it is unambiguous as to which node's value is being taken. If there are multiple possible items that could be selected, then only the first one will be chosen. For instance, this is a poor rule because a typical `PERIODIC_TABLE` element contains more than one `ATOM`.:

```
<xsl:template match="PERIODIC_TABLE">
  <xsl:value-of select="ATOM"/>
</xsl:template>
```

There are two ways of processing multiple elements in turn. The first you've already seen. Simply use `xsl:apply-templates` with a `select` attribute that chooses the particular elements you want to include, like this:

```
<xsl:template match="PERIODIC_TABLE">
  <xsl:apply-templates select="ATOM"/>
</xsl:template>

<xsl:template match="ATOM">
  <xsl:value-of select="."/>
</xsl:template>
```

The `select="."` in the second template tells the formatter to take the value of the matched element, `ATOM` in this example.

The second option is `xsl:for-each`. The `xsl:for-each` element processes each element chosen by its `select` attribute in turn. However, no additional template is required. For example:

```
<xsl:template match="PERIODIC_TABLE">
  <xsl:for-each select="ATOM">
    <xsl:value-of select="."/>
  </xsl:for-each>
</xsl:template>
```

If the `select` attribute is omitted, then all children of the source node (`PERIODIC_TABLE` in this example) are processed.

```
<xsl:template match="PERIODIC_TABLE">
  <xsl:for-each>
    <xsl:value-of select="ATOM"/>
  </xsl:for-each>
</xsl:template>
```

Patterns for Matching Nodes

The match attribute of the xsl:template element supports a complex syntax that allows you to express exactly which nodes you do and do not want to match. The select attribute of xsl:apply-templates, xsl:value-of, xsl:for-each, xsl:copy-of, and xsl:sort supports an even more powerful superset of this syntax that allows you to express exactly which nodes you do and do not want to select. Various patterns for matching and selecting nodes are discussed below.

Matching the Root Node

In order that the output document be well-formed, the first thing output from an XSL transformation should be the output document's root element. Consequently, XSL style sheets generally start with a rule that applies to the root node. To specify the root node in a rule, you give its match attribute the value "/". For example:

```
<xsl:template match="/">
  <html>
    <xsl:apply-templates/>
  </html>
</xsl:template>
```

This rule applies to the root node and only the root node of the input tree. When the root node is read, the tag <html> is output, the children of the root node are processed, then the </html> tag is output. This rule overrides the default rule for the root node. Listing 14-6 shows a style sheet with a single rule that applies to the root node.

Listing 14-6: An XSL style sheet with one rule for the root node

```
<?xml version="1.0"?>
<xsl:stylesheet
  xmlns:xsl="http://www.w3.org/XSL/Transform/1.0">

    <xsl:template match="/">
      <html>
        <head>
          <title>Atomic Number vs. Atomic Weight</title>
        </head>
        <body>
          <table>
            Atom data will go here
```

Continued

Listing 14-6 *(continued)*

```
            </table>
          </body>

        </html>
      </xsl:template>

  </xsl:stylesheet>
```

Since this style sheet only provides a rule for the root node, and since that rule's template does not specify any further processing of child nodes, only literal output, what you see in the template is all that will be inserted in the result document. In other words, the result of applying the style sheet in Listing 14-6 to Listing 14-1 (or any other well-formed XML document) is this:

```
<html><head><title>Atomic Number vs. Atomic
Weight</title></head><body><table>
            Atom data will go here
          </table></body></html>
```

Matching Element Names

As previously mentioned, the most basic pattern contains a single element name which matches all elements with that name. For example, this template matches `ATOM` elements and marks their `ATOMIC_NUMBER` children bold:

```
<xsl:template match="ATOM">
  <b><xsl:value-of select="ATOMIC_NUMBER"/><b>
</xsl:template>
```

Listing 14-7 demonstrates a style sheet that expands on Listing 14-6. First, an `xsl:apply-templates` element is included in the template of the rule for the root node. This rule uses a `select` attribute to ensure that only `PERIODIC_TABLE` elements get processed.

Secondly, a rule that only applies to `PERIODIC_TABLE` elements is created using `match="PERIODIC_TABLE"`. This rule sets up the header for the table, then applies templates to form the body of the table from `ATOM` elements.

Finally, the `ATOM` rule specifically selects the `ATOM` element's NAME, ATOMIC_NUMBER, and ATOMIC_WEIGHT child elements with `<xsl:apply-templates select="NAME"/>`, `<xsl:apply-templates select="ATOMIC_NUMBER"/>`, and `<xsl:apply-templates select="ATOMIC_WEIGHT"/>`. These are wrapped up inside HTML's `tr` and `td` elements so that the end result is a table of atomic numbers matched to atomic weights. Figure 14-4 shows the output of applying the style sheet in Listing 14-7 to the complete periodic table document.

One thing you may wish to note about this style sheet: the exact order of the NAME, ATOMIC_NUMBER, and ATOMIC_WEIGHT elements in the input document is irrelevant. They appear in the output in the order they were selected; that is, first number, then weight. Conversely, the individual atoms are sorted in alphabetical order as they appear in the input document. Later, you'll see how to use an xsl:sort element to change that so you can arrange the atoms in the more conventional atomic number order.

Listing 14-7: Templates applied to specific classes of element with select

```xml
<?xml version="1.0"?>
<xsl:stylesheet
xmlns:xsl="http://www.w3.org/XSL/Transform/1.0">

    <xsl:template match="/">
      <html>
        <head>
          <title>Atomic Number vs. Atomic Weight</title>
        </head>
        <body>
          <xsl:apply-templates select="PERIODIC_TABLE"/>
        </body>
      </html>
    </xsl:template>

    <xsl:template match="PERIODIC_TABLE">
      <h1>Atomic Number vs. Atomic Weight</h1>
      <table>
        <th>Element</th>
        <th>Atomic Number</th>
        <th>Atomic Weight</th>
          <xsl:apply-templates select="ATOM"/>
      </table>
    </xsl:template>

    <xsl:template match="ATOM">
      <tr>
        <td><xsl:value-of select="NAME"/></td>
        <td><xsl:value-of select="ATOMIC_NUMBER"/></td>
        <td><xsl:value-of select="ATOMIC_WEIGHT"/></td>
      </tr>
    </xsl:template>

</xsl:stylesheet>
```

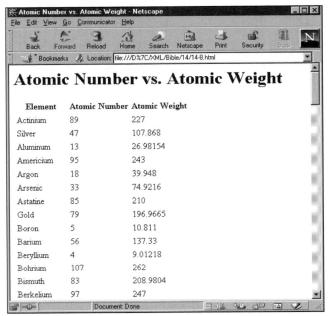

Figure 14-4: A table showing atomic number vs. atomic weight in Netscape Navigator 4.5

Matching Children with /

You're not limited to the children of the current node in `match` attributes. You can use the / symbol to match specified hierarchies of elements. Used alone, the / symbol refers to the root node. However, you can use it between two names to indicate that the second is the child of the first. For example, `ATOM/NAME` refers to `NAME` elements that are children of `ATOM` elements.

In `xsl:template` elements this enables you to match only some of the elements of a given kind. For example, this template rule marks `SYMBOL` elements that are children of `ATOM` elements strong. It does nothing to `SYMBOL` elements that are not direct children of `ATOM` elements.

```
<xsl:template match="ATOM/SYMBOL">
  <strong><xsl:value-of select="."/></strong>
</xsl:template>
```

Caution

Remember that this rule selects `SYMBOL` elements that are children of `ATOM` elements, not `ATOM` elements that have `SYMBOL` children. In other words, the . in `<xsl:value-of select="."/>` refers to the `SYMBOL` and not to the `ATOM`.

You can specify deeper matches by stringing patterns together. For example, PERIODIC_TABLE/ATOM/NAME selects NAME elements whose parent is an ATOM element, whose parent is a PERIODIC_TABLE element.

You can also use the * wild card to substitute for an arbitrary element name in a hierarchy. For example, this template rule applies to all SYMBOL elements that are grandchildren of a PERIODIC_TABLE element.

```
<xsl:template match="PERIODIC_TABLE/*/SYMBOL">
  <strong><xsl:value-of select="."/></strong>
</xsl:template>
```

Finally, as you saw above, a / by itself selects the root node of the document. For example, this rule applies to all PERIODIC_TABLE elements that are root elements of the document:

```
<xsl:template match="/PERIODIC_TABLE">
  <html><xsl:apply-templates/></html>
</xsl:template>
```

While / refers to the root node, /* refers to the root element, whatever it is. For example,

```
<xsl:template match="/*">
  <html>
    <head>
      <title>Atomic Number vs. Atomic Weight</title>
    </head>
    <body>
      <xsl:apply-templates/>
    </body>
  </html>
</xsl:template>
```

Matching Descendants with //

Sometimes, especially with an uneven hierarchy, you may find it easier to bypass intermediate nodes and simply select all the elements of a given type whether they're immediate children, grandchildren, great-grandchildren, or what have you. The double slash, //, refers to a descendant element at an arbitrary level. For example, this template rule applies to all NAME descendants of PERIODIC_TABLE, no matter how deep:

```
<xsl:template match="PERIODIC_TABLE//NAME">
  <i><xsl:value-of select="."/></i>
</xsl:template>
```

The periodic table example is fairly shallow, but this trick becomes more important in deeper hierarchies, especially when an element can contain other elements of its type (for example, an ATOM contains an ATOM).

The // operator at the beginning of a pattern selects any descendant of the root node. For example, this template rule processes all ATOMIC_NUMBER elements while completely ignoring their location:

```
<xsl:template match="//ATOMIC_NUMBER">
  <i><xsl:value-of select="."/></i>
</xsl:template>
```

Matching by ID

You may want to apply a particular style to a particular single element without changing all other elements of that type. The simplest way to do that in XSL is to attach a style to the element's ID attribute. This is done with the id() selector which contains the ID value in single quotes. For example, this rule makes the element with the ID e47 bold:

```
<xsl:template match="id('e47')">
  <b><xsl:value-of select="."/></b>
</xsl:template>
```

This assumes of course that the elements you want to select in this fashion have an attribute declared as type ID in the source document's DTD. Usually this isn't the case, however. For one thing, many documents do not have DTDs. They're merely well-formed, not valid. And even if they have a DTD, there's no guarantee that any element has an ID type attribute. You can use the xsl:key element in the style sheet to declare that particular attributes in the input document should be treated as IDs.

Matching Attributes with @

As you already saw back in Chapter 5, the @ sign matches against attributes and selects nodes according to attribute names. Simply prefix the attribute you want to select with the @ sign. For example, Listing 14-8 shows a style sheet that outputs a table of atomic number vs. melting point. Not only is the value of the MELTING_POINT element written out, but also the value of its UNITS attribute. This is selected by <xsl:value-of select="@UNITS"/>.

Listing 14-8: An XSL style sheet that selects the UNITS attribute with @

```
<?xml version="1.0"?>
<xsl:stylesheet
  xmlns:xsl="http://www.w3.org/XSL/Transform/1.0">

  <xsl:template match="/PERIODIC_TABLE">
    <html>
      <body>
```

```
            <h1>Atomic Number vs. Melting Point</h1>
            <table>
              <th>Element</th>
              <th>Atomic Number</th>
              <th>Melting Point</th>
              <xsl:apply-templates/>
            </table>
          </body>
        </html>
      </xsl:template>

      <xsl:template match="ATOM">
        <tr>
          <td><xsl:value-of select="NAME"/></td>
          <td><xsl:value-of select="ATOMIC_NUMBER"/></td>
          <td><xsl:apply-templates select="MELTING_POINT"/></td>
        </tr>
      </xsl:template>

      <xsl:template match="MELTING_POINT">
        <xsl:value-of select="."/>
        <xsl:value-of select="@UNITS"/>
      </xsl:template>

    </xsl:stylesheet>
```

Recall that the value of an attribute node is simply the string value of the attribute. Once you apply the style sheet in Listing 14-8, ATOM elements come out formatted like this:

```
<tr><td>Hydrogen</td><td>1</td><td>13.81Kelvin</td></tr>

<tr><td>Helium</td><td>2</td><td>0.95Kelvin</td></tr>
```

You can combine attributes with elements using the various hierarchy operators. For example, BOILING_POINT/@UNITS refers to the UNITS attribute of a BOILING_POINT element. ATOM/*/@UNITS matches any UNITS attribute of a child element of an ATOM element. This is especially helpful when matching against attributes in template rules. You must remember that what's being matched is the attribute node, not the element that contains it. It's a very common mistake to implicitly confuse the attribute node with the element node that contains it. For example, consider this rule, which attempts to apply templates to all child elements that have UNITS attributes:

```
<xsl:template match="ATOM">
  <xsl:apply-templates select="@UNITS"/>
</xsl:template>
```

What it actually does is apply templates to the non-existent UNITS attributes of ATOM elements.

You can also use the * to select all attributes of an element, for example BOILING_POINT/@* to select all attributes of BOILING_POINT elements.

Matching Comments with comment()

Most of the time you should simply ignore comments in XML documents. Making comments an essential part of a document is a very bad idea. Nonetheless, XSL does provide a means to select a comment if you absolutely have to.

To select a comment, use the pattern comment(). Although this pattern has function-like parentheses, it never actually takes any arguments. You cannot easily distinguish between different comments. For example, recall that a DENSITY element looks like this:

```
<DENSITY UNITS="grams/cubic centimeter"><!— At 300K —>
  6.51
</DENSITY>
```

This template rule not only outputs the value of the density and the units; it also prints the conditions under whichthe density is measured:

```
<xsl:template match="DENSITY">
  <xsl:value-of select="."/>
  <xsl:value-of select="@UNITS"/>
  <xsl:apply-templates select="comment()"/>
</xsl:template>
```

The only reason Listing 14-1 uses a comment to specify conditions instead of an attribute or element is precisely for this example. In practice, you should never put important information in comments. The only real reason XSL ever allows you to select comments is so a style sheet can transform from one markup language to another while leaving the comments intact. Any other use indicates a poorly designed original document. The following rule matches all comments, and copies them back out again using the xsl:comment element.

```
<xsl:template match="comment()">
  <xsl:comment><xsl:value-of select="."/></xsl:comment>
</xsl:template>
```

Note, however, that the default rules used to apply templates do not apply to comments. Thus, if you want this rule to be activated when a comment is encountered, you'll need to include an xsl:apply-templates element that selects comments wherever comments may be found.

You can use the hierarchy operators to select particular comments. For example, this rule matches comments that occur inside DENSITY elements:

```
<xsl:template match="DENSITY/comment()">
    <xsl:comment><xsl:value-of select="."/></xsl:comment>
</xsl:template>
```

Matching Processing Instructions with pi()

When it comes to writing structured, intelligible, maintainable XML, processing instructions aren't much better than comments. However, there are some necessary uses for them including attaching style sheets to documents.

The pi() function selects processing instructions. The argument to pi() is a quoted string giving the name of the processing instruction to select. If you do not include an argument, the first processing instruction child of the current node is matched. However, you can use hierarchy operators. For example, this rule matches the first processing instruction child of the root node (most likely the xml-stylesheet processing instruction). The xsl:pi element inserts a processing instruction with the specified name and value in the output document.

```
<xsl:template match="/pi()">
  <xsl:pi name="xml-stylesheet">
    type="text/xsl" value="auto.xsl"
  </xsl:pi>
</xsl:template/>
```

This rule also matches the xml-stylesheet processing instruction, but by its name:

```
<xsl:template match="pi('xml-stylesheet')">
  <xsl:pi name="xml-stylesheet">
    <xsl:value-of select="."/>
  </xsl:pi>
</xsl:template/>
```

In fact, one of the main reasons for distinguishing between the root element and the root node is so that processing instructions from the prolog can be read and processed. Although the xml-stylesheet processing instruction uses a name=value syntax, XSL does not consider these to be attributes because processing instructions are not elements. The value of a processing instruction is simply everything between the whitespace following its name and the closing ?>.

The default rules used to apply templates do not match processing instructions. Thus, if you want this rule to be activated when the xml-stylesheet processing instruction is encountered, you'll need to include an xsl:apply-templates element that matches it in the appropriate place. For example, this template rule for the root node does apply templates to processing instructions:

```
<xsl:template match="/">
  <xsl:apply-templates select="pi()"/>
  <xsl:apply-templates select="*"/>
</xsl:template>
```

Matching Text Nodes with text()

Text nodes generally get ignored as nodes, though their values are included as part of the value of a selected element. However, the text() operator does enable you to specifically select the text child of an element. Despite the parentheses, this operator takes no arguments. For example:

```
<xsl:template match="SYMBOL">
  <xsl:value-of select="text()"/>
</xsl:template>
```

The main reason this operator exists is for the default rules. XSL processors must provide the following default rule whether the author specifies it or not:

```
<xsl:template match="text()">
  <xsl:value-of select="."/>
</xsl:template>
```

This means that whenever a template is applied to a text node, the text of the node is output. If you do not want the default behavior, you can override it. For example, including the following empty template rule in your style sheet will prevent text nodes from being output unless specifically matched by another rule.

```
<xsl:template match="text()">
</xsl:template>
```

Using the Or Operator |

The vertical bar (|) allows a template rule to match multiple patterns. If a node matches one pattern or the other, it will activate the template. For example, this template rule matches both ATOMIC_NUMBER and ATOMIC_WEIGHT elements:

```
<xsl:template match="ATOMIC_NUMBER|ATOMIC_WEIGHT">
  <B><xsl:apply-templates/></B>
</xsl:template>
```

You can include whitespace around the | if that makes the code clearer. For example,

```
<xsl:template match="ATOMIC_NUMBER | ATOMIC_WEIGHT">
  <B><xsl:apply-templates/></B>
</xsl:template>
```

You can also use more than two patterns in sequence. For example, this template rule applies to ATOMIC_NUMBER, ATOMIC_WEIGHT, and SYMBOL elements (that is, it matches ATOMIC_NUMBER, ATOMIC_WEIGHT and SYMBOL elements):

```
<xsl:template match="ATOMIC_NUMBER | ATOMIC_WEIGHT | SYMBOL">
  <B><xsl:apply-templates/></B>
</xsl:template>
```

The / operator is evaluated before the | operator. Thus, the following template rule selects an ATOMIC_NUMBER child of an ATOM, or an ATOMIC_WEIGHT of unspecified parentage, not an ATOMIC_NUMBER child of an ATOM or an ATOMIC_WEIGHT child of an ATOM.

```
<xsl:template match="ATOM/ATOMIC_NUMBER|ATOMIC_WEIGHT">
  <B><xsl:apply-templates/></B>
</xsl:template>
```

Testing with []

So far, we've merely tested for the presence of various nodes. However, you can test for more details about the nodes that match a pattern using []. You can perform many different tests including:

✦ Whether an element contains a given child, attribute, or other node

✦ Whether the value of an attribute is a given string

✦ Whether the value of an element matches a string

✦ What position a given node occupies in the hierarchy

For example, seaborgium, element 106, has only been created in microscopic quantities. Even its most long-lived isotope has a half-life of only 20 seconds. With such a hard-to-create, short-lived element, it's virtually impossible to measure the density, melting point, or other bulk properties. Consequently, the periodic table document omits the elements describing the bulk properties of seaborgium and similar atoms as a result of unavailable data. If you want to create a table of atomic number vs. melting point, you should omit those elements with unknown melting points. To do this, you can specify a match against ATOM elements that have MELTING_POINT children like this:

```
<xsl:template match="ATOM[MELTING_POINT]">
  <tr>
    <td><xsl:value-of select="NAME"/></td>
    <td><xsl:value-of select="MELTING_POINT"/></td>
  </tr>
</xsl:template>
```

Note here, that it is the ATOM element being matched, not the MELTING_POINT element as in the case of ATOM/MELTING_POINT.

The test brackets can contain more than simply a child element name. In fact, they can contain any select expression. (Select expressions are a superset of match patterns that will be discussed in the next section.) If the specified element has a child matching that expression, it is considered to match the total pattern. For example, this template rule matches ATOM elements with NAME or SYMBOL children.

```
<xsl:template match="ATOM[NAME | SYMBOL]">
</xsl:template>
```

This template rule uses a * to match any element that contains a NAME child:

```
<xsl:template match="*[NAME]">
</xsl:template>
```

This template rule matches ATOM elements with a DENSITY child that has a UNITS attribute:

```
<xsl:template match="ATOM[DENSITY/@UNITS]">
</xsl:template>
```

To revisit an earlier example, to correctly find all child elements that have UNITS attributes, use * to find all elements and [@UNITS] to winnow those down to the ones with UNITS attributes, like this:

```
<xsl:template match="ATOM">
  <xsl:apply-templates select="*[@UNITS]"/>
</xsl:template>
```

One type of pattern testing that proves especially useful is string equality. An equals sign (=) can test whether the value of a node identically matches a given string. For example, this template finds the ATOM element that contains an ATOMIC_NUMBER element whose contents include the string 10 (Neon).

```
<xsl:template match="ATOM[ATOMIC_NUMBER='10']">
  This is Neon!
</xsl:template>
```

Testing against element content may seem extremely tricky because of the need to get the value exactly right, including whitespace. You may find it easier to test against attribute values since those are less likely to contain insignificant whitespace. For example, the style sheet in Listing 14-9 applies templates only to those ATOM elements whose STATE attribute value is the three letters GAS.

Listing 14-9: An XSL style sheet that selects only those ATOM elements whose STATE attribute has the value GAS

```
<?xml version="1.0"?>
<xsl:stylesheet
xmlns:xsl="http://www.w3.org/XSL/Transform/1.0">

  <xsl:template match="PERIODIC_TABLE">
    <html>
      <head><title>Gases</title></head>
      <body>
        <xsl:apply-templates select="ATOM[@STATESTATE='GAS']"/>
      </body>
    </html>
```

```
    </xsl:template>

    <xsl:template match="ATOM">
        <P><xsl:value-of select="."/></P>
    </xsl:template>

</xsl:stylesheet>
```

You can use other XSL expressions (discussed in the next section) for more complex matches. For example, you can select all elements whose names begin with "A" or all elements with an atomic number less than 100.

Expressions for Selecting Nodes

The `select` attribute is used in `xsl:apply-templates`, `xsl:value-of`, `xsl:for-each`, `xsl:copy-of`, and `xsl:sort` to specify exactly which nodes are operated on. The value of this attribute is an *expression*. Expressions are a superset of the match patterns discussed in the last section. That is, all match patterns are select expressions, but not all select expressions are match patterns. Recall that match patterns enable you to match nodes by element name, child elements, descendants, and attributes, as well by making simple tests on these items. Select expressions allow you to select nodes through all these criteria but also by referring to parent elements, sibling elements, and making much more complicated tests. Furthermore, expressions aren't limited to producing merely a list of nodes, but can also produce booleans, numbers, and strings.

Node Axes

Expressions are not limited to specifying the children and descendants of the current node. XSL provides a number of axes you can use to select from different parts of the tree relative to the current node (generally the node that the template matches). Table 14-2 summarizes these axes and their meanings.

Table 14-2 Expression Axes	
Axis	**Selects From**
`from-ancestors()`	the parent of the current node, the parent of the parent of the current node, the parent of the parent of the parent of the current node, and so forth back to the root node

Continued

Table 14-2 *(continued)*

Axis	Selects From
`from-ancestors-or-self()`	the ancestors of the current node and the current node itself
`from-attributes()`	the attributes of the current node
`from-children()`	the immediate children of the current node
`from-descendants()`	the children of the current node, the children of the children of the current node, and so forth
`from-descendants-or-self()`	the current node itself and its descendants
`from-following()`	all nodes that start after the end of the current node
`from-following-siblings()`	all nodes that start after the end of the current node and have the same parent as the current node
`from-parent()`	the single parent node of the current node
`from-preceding()`	all nodes that start before the start of the current node
`from-preceding-siblings()`	all nodes that start before the start of the current node and have the same parent as the current node
`from-self()`	the current node

Caution   The `from-following` and `from-preceding` axes are on the questionable side. They may not be included in the final release of XSL. If they are included, their exact meaning may change.

These axes serve as functions that select from the set of nodes indicated in the second column of Table 14-2. The parentheses contain a select expression to further winnow down this node list. For example, they may contain the name of the element to be selected as in the following template rule:

```
<xsl:template match="ATOM">
  <tr>
    <td>
      <xsl:value-of select="from-children(NAME)"/>
    </td>
    <td>
      <xsl:value-of select="from-children(ATOMIC_NUMBER)"/>
    </td>
    <td>
      <xsl:value-of select="from-children(ATOMIC_WEIGHT)"/>
    </td>
  </tr>
</xsl:template>
```

The template rule matches ATOM elements. When an ATOM element is matched, a NAME element, an ATOMIC_NUMBER element, and an ATOMIC_WEIGHT element are all selected from the children of that matched ATOM element and output as table cells. (If there's one more than one of these desired elements — for example, three NAME elements — then only the first one is selected.)

The from-children() axis doesn't let you do anything you can't do with element names alone. In fact select="ATOMIC_WEIGHT" is just an abbreviated form of select="from-children(ATOMIC_WEIGHT)". However, the other axes are a little more interesting.

Referring to the parent element is illegal in match patterns, but not in select expressions. To refer to the parent, you use the from-parent() axis. For example, this rule outputs the value of atoms that have a BOILING_POINT child:

```
<xsl:template match="ATOM/BOILING_POINT">
  <P><xsl:value-of select="from-parent(ATOM)"/></P>
</xsl:template>
```

Here the BOILING_POINT child element is matched, but the ATOM parent element is output.

Some radioactive atoms like polonium have half-lives so short that bulk properties like the boiling point and melting point can't be measured. Therefore, not all ATOM elements will necessarily have BOILING_POINT child elements. The above rule would allow you to only output those elements that actually have boiling points. Expanding on this example, Listing 14-10 matches the MELTING_POINT elements but actually outputs the parent ATOM element using from-parent(ATOM).

> **Listing 14-10: A style sheet that outputs only those elements with known melting points**

```
<?xml version="1.0"?>
<xsl:stylesheet
xmlns:xsl="http://www.w3.org/XSL/Transform/1.0">

    <xsl:template match="/">
      <html>
        <body>
          <xsl:apply-templates select="PERIODIC_TABLE"/>
        </body>
      </html>
    </xsl:template>

    <xsl:template match="PERIODIC_TABLE">
      <h1>Elements with known Melting Points</h1>
```

Continued

Listing 14-10 *(continued)*

```
        <xsl:apply-templates select="//MELTING_POINT"/>
    </xsl:template>

    <xsl:template match="MELTING_POINT">
      <p>
        <xsl:value-of select="from-parent(ATOM)"/>
      </p>
    </xsl:template>

</xsl:stylesheet>
```

Once in awhile, you may need to select the nearest ancestor of an element with a given type. The `from-ancestors()` function does this. For example, this rule inserts the value of the nearest `PERIODIC_TABLE` element that contains the matched `SYMBOL` element.

```
<xsl:template match="SYMBOL">
  <xsl:value-of select="from-ancestors(PERIODIC_TABLE)"/>
</xsl:template>
```

The `from-ancestors-or-self()` function behaves like the `from-ancestors()` function except that if the current node matches the type of the argument, then it will be returned instead of the actual ancestor. For example, this rule matches all elements. If the matched element is a `PERIODIC_TABLE`, then that very `PERIODIC_TABLE` is selected in `xsl:value-of`.

```
<xsl:template match="*">
<xsl:value-of select="from-ancestors-or-self(PERIODIC_TABLE)"/>
</xsl:template>
```

Node Types

As well as the name of a node and the wild card, the arguments to a `from-axis()` function may be one of these four node-type functions:

✦ `comment()`

✦ `text()`

✦ `pi()`

✦ `node()`

The `comment()` node type selects a comment node. The `text()` node type selects a text node. The `pi()` node type selects a processing instruction node, and the `node()` node type selects any type of node. (The * wild card only selects element nodes.) The `pi()` node type can also contain an optional argument specifying the name of the processing instruction to select.

For example, this rule wraps the value of a matched ATOM element in a P element using `from-self()` with the `node()` node type:

```
<xsl:template match="ATOM">
  <P><xsl:value-of select="from-self(node())"/></P>
</xsl:template>
```

Here, selecting `from-self(node())` is not the same as selecting ATOM. The next rule tries to take the value of the ATOM child of an ATOM element. This is not the value of the matched ATOM element, but rather the value of a different ATOM element that's a child of the matched ATOM element:

```
<xsl:template match="ATOM">
  <P><xsl:value-of select="ATOM"/></P>
</xsl:template>
```

Hierarchy Operators

You can use the / and // operators to string select expressions together. For example, Listing 14-11 prints a table of element names, atomic numbers, and melting points for only those elements that have melting points. It does this by selecting the parent of the MELTING_POINT element, then finding that parent's NAME and ATOMIC_NUMBER children with `select="from-parent(*)/from-children(NAME)"`.

Listing 14-11: A table of melting point versus atomic number

```
<?xml version="1.0"?>
<xsl:stylesheet
  xmlns:xsl="http://www.w3.org/XSL/Transform/1.0">

  <xsl:template match="/PERIODIC_TABLE">
    <html>
      <body>
        <h1>Atomic Number vs. Melting Point</h1>
        <table>
          <th>Element</th>
          <th>Atomic Number</th>
          <th>Melting Point</th>
          <xsl:apply-templates select="from-children(ATOM)"/>
        </table>
      </body>
    </html>
  </xsl:template>

  <xsl:template match="ATOM">
```

Continued

Listing 14-11 *(continued)*

```
        <xsl:apply-templates
         select="from-children(MELTING_POINT)"/>
      </xsl:template>

      <xsl:template match="MELTING_POINT">
         <tr>
          <td>
            <xsl:value-of
             select="from-parent(*)/from-children(NAME)"/>
          </td>
          <td>
            <xsl:value-of
           select="from-parent(*)/from-children(ATOMIC_NUMBER)"/>
          </td>
          <td>
            <xsl:value-of select="from-self(*)"/>
            <xsl:value-of select="from-attributes(UNITS)"/>
          </td>
         </tr>
      </xsl:template>

</xsl:stylesheet>
```

This is not the only way to solve the problem. Another possibility would be to use the `from-preceding-siblings()` and `from-following-siblings()` axes or both if the relative location (preceding or following) is uncertain. The necessary template rule for the `MELTING_POINT` element would look like this:

```
    <xsl:template match="MELTING_POINT">
      <tr>
       <td>
         <xsl:value-of
          select="from-preceding-siblings(NAME)
                | from-following-siblings(NAME)"/>
       </td>
       <td>
         <xsl:value-of
          select="from-preceding-siblings(ATOMIC_NUMBER)
                | from-following-siblings(ATOMIC_NUMBER)"/>
       </td>
       <td>
         <xsl:value-of select="from-self(*)"/>
         <xsl:value-of select="from-attributes(UNITS)"/>
       </td>
      </tr>
    </xsl:template>
```

Abbreviated Syntax

The various `from-axis()` functions in Table 14-2 are a bit too wordy for comfortable typing. XSL also defines an abbreviated syntax that can substitute for the most common of these axes and is more used in practice. Table 14-3 shows the full and abbreviated equivalents.

Table 14-3
Abbreviated Syntax for Select Expressions

Abbreviation	Full
.	`from-self(node())`
..	`from-parent(node())`
name	`from-children(name)`
@*name*	`from-attributes(name)`
//	`/from-descendants-or-self(node())/`

Listing 14-12 demonstrates by rewriting Listing 14-11 using the abbreviated syntax. The output produced by the two style sheets is exactly the same, however.

Listing 14-12: **A table of melting point versus atomic number using the abbreviated syntax**

```
<?xml version="1.0"?>
<xsl:stylesheet
  xmlns:xsl="http://www.w3.org/XSL/Transform/1.0">

    <xsl:template match="/PERIODIC_TABLE">
      <html>
        <body>
          <h1>Atomic Number vs. Melting Point</h1>
          <table>
            <th>Element</th>
            <th>Atomic Number</th>
            <th>Melting Point</th>
            <xsl:apply-templates select="ATOM"/>
          </table>
        </body>
      </html>
    </xsl:template>
```

Continued

Listing 14-12 *(continued)*

```
<xsl:template match="ATOM">
  <xsl:apply-templates
    select="MELTING_POINT"/>
</xsl:template>

<xsl:template match="MELTING_POINT">
    <tr>
     <td>
       <xsl:value-of
         select="../NAME"/>
     </td>
     <td>
       <xsl:value-of
       select="../ATOMIC_NUMBER"/>
     </td>
     <td>
       <xsl:value-of select="."/>
       <xsl:value-of select="@UNITS"/>
     </td>
    </tr>
  </xsl:template>

</xsl:stylesheet>
```

Match patterns can only use the abbreviated syntax (and not all of that). The full syntax using the `from-axis()` functions of Table 14-2 is restricted to select expressions.

Expression Types

Every expression evaluates to a single value. For example, the expression $3 + 2$ evaluates to the value 5. The expressions used above all evaluated to node sets. However, there are five types of expressions in XSL. These are:

✦ Node-sets

✦ Booleans

✦ Numbers

✦ Strings

✦ Result tree fragments

Node Sets

A node set is a list of nodes from the input document. The from-*axis*() functions in Table 14-2 all return a node set containing the node they match. Which nodes are in the node set one of these functions returns depends on the current node (also known as the context node), the argument to the function, and of course, which function it is.

Tip

Programmers accustomed to object-oriented languages like Java and C++ can think of the current node as the object which invokes the function; that is, in a.doSomething(b, c) the current node is a. However, in XSL the current node is always implicit; that is, it's written more like doSomething(b, c) as might be done in the file where a's class is defined.

For example, the expression select="from-children(ATOM)" returns a node set that contains both ATOM elements in that document when the current node is the PERIODIC_TABLE element of Example 14-1. The expression select="from-children(ATOM)/from-children(NAME)" returns a node set containing the two element nodes <NAME>Hydrogen</NAME> and <NAME>Helium</NAME> when the context node is the PERIODIC_TABLE element of Example 14-1.

The context node is a member of the *context node list*. The context node list is that group of elements that all match the same rule at the same time, generally as a result of one xsl:apply-templates or xsl:for-each call. For instance, when Listing 14-12 is applied to Listing 14-1, the ATOM template is invoked twice, first for the hydrogen atom, second for the helium atom. The first time it's invoked, the context node is the hydrogen ATOM element. The second time it's invoked, the context node is the helium ATOM element. However, both times the context node list is the set containing both the helium and hydrogen ATOM elements.

Table 14-4 lists a number of functions that operate on node-sets, either as arguments or as the context node.

Table 14-4
Functions That Operate on Node Sets

Function	Return Type	Returns
position()	number	The position of the context node in the context node list. The first node in the list has position 1.
last()	number	The number of nodes in the context node set.
count(*node-set*)	number	The number of nodes in *node-set*.

Continued

Table 14-4 *(continued)*

Function	Return Type	Returns
`id(string)`	node set	A node set containing the single element anywhere in the same document whose ID is `string`; or the empty set if no element has the specified ID.
`idref(node-set)`	node set	A node set containing all of the elements in the document whose ID is one of the tokens (separated by whitespace) in the values of the nodes in the argument `node-set`.
`key(string name, string value)`	node set	A node set containing all nodes in this document that have a key with the specified value. Keys are set with the top-level `xsl:key` element.
`keyref(string name, node set values)`	node set	A node set containing all nodes in this document that have a key whose value is the same as the value of one of the nodes in the second argument.
`doc(string URI)`	node set	A node set in the document or portion referred to by the URI; the nodes are chosen from the named anchor or XPointer used by the URI. If there is no named anchor or Xpointer, then the root element of the named document is in the node set. Relative URIs are relative to the current node in the input document.
`docref(node set)`	node set	A node set containing all the nodes (in one or more documents) referred to by the URIs that are the value of the `node set` argument.
`local-part(node set)`	string	The local part (everything after the namespace prefix) of the first node in the `node set` argument; can be used without any arguments to get the local part of the context node.
`namespace(node set)`	string	The URI of the namespace of the first node in the node set; can be used without any arguments to get the URI of the namespace of the context node; returns an empty string if the node is in the default namespace.
`qname(node set)`	string	The qualified name (both prefix and local part) of the first node in the `node set` argument; can be used without any argument to get the qualified name of the context node.
`generate-id(node set)`	string	A unique identifier for the first node in the argument `node set`; can be used without any argument to generate an ID for the context node.

Cross-Reference Chapter 18, *Namespaces*, discusses namespace URIs, prefixes, and local parts.

Caution The doc() and docref() functions are a little hazy, especially if their URIs refer to only fragments of a node or data that is not well-formed XML. The details remain to be cleaned up in a future version of the XSL specification.

If an argument of the wrong type is passed to one of these functions, then XSL will attempt to convert that argument to the correct type; for instance, by converting the number 12 to the string "12". However, no arguments may be converted to node sets.

The position() function can be used to count elements. Listing 14-13 is a style sheet that prefixes the name of each atom's name with its position in the document using <xsl:value-of select="position()"/>.

Listing 14-13: A style sheet that numbers the atoms in the order they appear in the document

```
<?xml version="1.0"?>
<xsl:stylesheet
xmlns:xsl="http://www.w3.org/XSL/Transform/1.0">

  <xsl:template match="/PERIODIC_TABLE">
    <HTML>
      <HEAD><TITLE>The Elements</TITLE></HEAD>
      <BODY>
        <xsl:apply-templates select="ATOM"/>
      </BODY>
    </HTML>
  </xsl:template>

  <xsl:template match="ATOM">
    <P>
      <xsl:value-of select="position()"/>.
      <xsl:value-of select="NAME"/>
    </P>
  </xsl:template>

</xsl:stylesheet>
```

When this style sheet is applied to Listing 14-1, the output is this:

```
<HTML><HEAD><TITLE>The Elements</TITLE></HEAD><BODY><P>1.
    Hydrogen</P><P>2.
    Helium</P></BODY></HTML>
```

Booleans

A Boolean has one of two values, true or false. XSL allows any kind of data to be transformed into a Boolean. This is often done implicitly when a string or a number or a node set is used where a Boolean is expected, as in the test attribute of an xsl:if element. These conversions can also be performed by the boolean() function which converts an argument of any type (or the context node if no argument is provided) to a Boolean according to these rules:

✦ a number is false if it's zero or NaN (a special symbol meaning "Not a Number", used for the result of dividing by zero and similar illegal operations), true otherwise

✦ an empty node set is false; all other node sets are true

✦ an empty result fragment is false; all other result fragments are true

✦ a zero length string is false; all other strings are true

Booleans are also produced as the result of expressions involving these operators:

=	equality
<	less-than (really <)
>	greater-than
<=	less-than or equal to (really <=)
>=	greater-than or equal to

Caution The < sign is illegal in attribute values. Consequently, it must be replaced by < even when used as the less-than operator.

These operators are most commonly used in predicate tests to determine whether a rule is invoked. A select expression can contain not only a pattern that selects certain nodes, but also a predicate that further filters the list of nodes selected. For example, from-children(ATOM) selects all the ATOM children of the current node. However, from-children(ATOM[position()=1]) selects only the first ATOM child of the current node. [position()=1] is a predicate on the node test ATOM that returns a Boolean result, true if the position of the current node is equal to one, false otherwise. Each node test can have any number of predicates. However, more than one is unusual.

For example, this template rule applies to the first ATOM element in the periodic table, but not to subsequent ones, by testing whether or not the position of the element equals 1.

```
<xsl:template match="PERIODIC_TABLE/ATOM[position()=1]">
  <xsl:value-of select="."/>
</xsl:template>
```

This template rule applies to all ATOM elements that are not the first child element of the PERIODIC_TABLE by testing whether the position is greater than 1:

```
<xsl:template match="PERIODIC_TABLE/ATOM[position()>1]">
  <xsl:value-of select="."/>
</xsl:template>
```

The keywords and and or logically combine two Boolean expressions according to the normal rules of logic. For example, suppose you want to apply a template to an ATOMIC_NUMBER element that is both the first and last child of its parent element; that is; it is the only element of its parent. This template rule uses and to accomplish that:

```
<xsl:template
 match="ATOMIC_NUMBER[position()=1 and position()=last()]">
  <xsl:value-of select="."/>
</xsl:template>
```

This template rule applies to both the first and last ATOM elements in their parent by matching when the position is 1 or when the position is last:

```
<xsl:template match="ATOM[position()=1 or position()=last()]">
  <xsl:value-of select="."/>
</xsl:template>
```

This is logical or, so it will also match if both conditions are true. That is, it will match an ATOM that is both the first and last child of its parent.

There is no not keyword in XSL, but there is a not() function. You can reverse the sense of an operation by enclosing it in not(). For example, this template rule selects all ATOM elements that are not the first child of their parents:

```
<xsl:template match="ATOM[not(position()=1)]">
  <xsl:value-of select="."/>
</xsl:template>
```

This template rule selects all ATOM elements that are neither the first nor last ATOM child of their parent:

```
<xsl:template match =
 "ATOM[not(position()=1 or position()=last())]">
  <xsl:value-of select="."/>
</xsl:template>
```

There is no exclusive or operator. However, one can be formed by judicious use of not(), and, and or. For example, this rule selects those ATOM elements that are either the first or last child, but not both.

```
<xsl:template
 match="ATOM[(position()=1 or position()=last())
             and not(position()=1 and position()=last())]">
```

```
   <xsl:value-of select="."/>
</xsl:template>
```

There are three remaining functions that return Booleans:

✦ `true()` always returns true

✦ `false()` always returns false

✦ `lang(code)` returns true if the current node has the same language (as given by the `xml:lang` attribute) as the *code* argument.

Numbers

XSL numbers are 64-bit IEEE floating-point doubles. Numbers like 42 or -7000 that look like integers are stored as doubles. Non-number values like strings and Booleans are converted to numbers as necessary, or by the `number()` function using these rules:

✦ Booleans are 1 if true; 0 if false.

✦ A string is trimmed of leading and trailing whitespace; then converted to a number in the fashion you would expect; for example, the string "12" is converted to the number 12. If the string cannot be interpreted as a number, then it is converted to 0.

✦ Node sets and result fragments are converted to strings; then the string is converted to a number.

For example, this rule only outputs the non-naturally occurring trans-uranium elements; those with atomic numbers greater than 92, which is the atomic number of uranium. The node set produced by ATOMIC_NUMBER is implicitly converted to the string value of the current ATOMIC_NUMBER node. This string is then converted into a number.

```
<xsl:template match="/PERIODIC_TABLE">
  <HTML>
    <HEAD><TITLE>The TransUranium Elements</TITLE></HEAD>
    <BODY>
      <xsl:apply-templates select="ATOM[ATOMIC_NUMBER>92]"/>
    </BODY>
  </HTML>
</xsl:template>
```

XSL provides the standard four arithmetic operators:

✦ + for addition

✦ - for subtraction

✦ * for multiplication

✦ `div` for division (the more common / is already used for other purposes in XSL)

For example, `<xsl:value-of select="2+2"/>` inserts the string "4" into the output document. These operations are more commonly used as part of a test. For example, this rule selects those elements whose atomic weight is more than twice the atomic number:

```
<xsl:template match="/PERIODIC_TABLE">
  <HTML>
    <BODY>
      <H1>High Atomic Weight to Atomic Number Ratios</H1>
      <xsl:apply-templates
        select="ATOM[ATOMIC_WEIGHT > 2 * ATOMIC_NUMBER]"/>
    </BODY>
  </HTML>
</xsl:template>
```

This template actually prints the ratio of atomic weight to atomic number:

```
<xsl:template match="ATOM">
  <p>
    <xsl:value-of select="NAME"/>
    <xsl:value-of select="ATOMIC_WEIGHT div ATOMIC_NUMBER"/>
  </p>
</xsl:template>
```

XSL also provides two less-familiar binary operators:

✦ mod for taking the remainder of two numbers

✦ quo for dividing two numbers, then truncating the fractional part to produce an integer

XSL also includes four functions that operate on numbers:

floor() returns the greatest integer smaller than the number

ceiling() returns the smallest integer greater than the number

round() rounds the number to the nearest integer

sum() returns the sum of its arguments

For example, this template rule estimates the number of neutrons in an atom by subtracting the atomic number (the number of protons) from the atomic weight (the weighted average over the natural distribution of isotopes of the of number of neutrons plus the number of protons) and rounding to the nearest integer:

```
<xsl:template match="ATOM">
  <p>
    <xsl:value-of select="NAME"/>
    <xsl:value-of
     select="round(ATOMIC_WEIGHT - ATOMIC_NUMBER)"/>
  </p>
</xsl:template>
```

This rule calculates the average atomic weight of all the atoms in the table by adding all the atomic weights, and then dividing by the number of atoms:

```
<xsl:template match="/PERIODIC_TABLE">
  <HTML>
    <BODY>
    <H1>Average Atomic Weight</H1>
      <xsl:value-of
        select="sum(from-descendants(ATOMIC_WEIGHT))
                div count(from-descendants(ATOMIC_WEIGHT))"/>
    </BODY>
  </HTML>
</xsl:template>
```

Strings

A string is a sequence of Unicode characters. Other data types can be converted to strings using the `string()` function according to these rules:

✦ Node sets are converted by concatenating the values of the nodes in the set. The values of the nodes in the set are calculated as by the `xsl:value-of` element according to the rules given in Table 14-1.

✦ Result tree fragments are converted by acting as if they're contained in a single element, and then taking the value of that imaginary element. Again, the value of this element is calculated as by the `xsl:value-of` element according to the rules given in Table 14-1. That is, all the result tree fragment's text (but not markup) is concatenated.

✦ A number is converted to a European-style number string like "-12" or "3.1415292".

✦ Boolean false is converted to the English word "false". Boolean true is converted to the English word "true".

Besides `string()`, XSL contains seven functions that operate on strings. These are summarized in Table 14-5.

Table 14-5
Functions That Operate on Strings

Function	Return Type	Returns
`starts-with(main_string, prefix_string)`	Boolean	true if *main_string* starts with *prefix_string*, false otherwise.
`contains(containing_string, contained_string)`	Boolean	true if the *contained_string* is part of the *containing_string*; false otherwise

Function	Return Type	Returns
substring-before(*string*, *marker-string*)	string	the part of the *string* from the beginning of the string up to (but not including) the first occurrence of *marker-string*
substring-after(*string*, *marker-string*)	string	the part of the *string* from the end of the first occurrence of *marker-string* to the end of *string*
normalize(*string*)	string	the *string* after leading and trailing whitespace is stripped and runs of whitespace are replaced with a single space; if the argument is omitted the string value of the context node is normalized
translate(*string*, *replaced_text*, *replacement_text*)	string	returns *string* with occurrences of characters in *replaced_text* replaced by the corresponding characters from *replacement_text*
concat(*string1*, *string2*, ...)	string	returns the concatenation of as many strings as are passed as arguments in the order they were passed
format-number(*number*, *format-string*, *locale-string*)	string	returns the string form of *number* formatted according to the specified *format-string* in the locale specified by *locale-string* as if by Java 1.1's java.text.DecimalFormat class (see http://java.sun.com/products/jdk/1.1/docs/api/java.text.DecimalFormat.html)

Result Tree Fragments

A result tree fragment is a portion of an XML document that is not a complete node or set of nodes. For instance, using the doc() function with a URI that points into the middle of an element might produce a result tree fragment. Result tree fragments may also be returned by some extension functions (functions unique to a particular XSL implementation or installation).

Since result tree fragments aren't well-formed XML, you can't do much with them. In fact, the only allowed operations are to convert them to a string or a Boolean using string() and boolean() respectively.

The Default Template Rules

Having to carefully map the hierarchy of an XML document in an XSL style sheet may be inconvenient. This is especially true if the document does not follow a stable, predictable order like the periodic table but rather throws elements together willy-nilly like many Web pages. In those cases, you should have general rules that can find an element and apply templates to it regardless of where it appears in the source document.

To make this process easier, XSL defines two default template rules implicitly included in all style sheets. The first default rule recursively descends the element tree, applying templates to the children of all elements. This guarantees that all template rules that apply to elements will be instantiated. The second default rule applies to text nodes, copying their value onto the output stream. Together these two rules mean that even a blank XSL style sheet with no elements will still produce the raw character data of the input XML document as output.

The Default Rule for Elements

The first default rule applies to element nodes of any type or the root node:

```
<xsl:template match="*|/">
  <xsl:apply-templates/>
</xsl:template>
```

`*|/` is XSL shorthand for "any element node or the root node". The purpose of this rule is to ensure that all elements are recursively processed even if they aren't reached by following the explicit rules. That is, unless another rule overrides this one (especially for the root element) all element nodes will be processed.

However, once an explicit rule for any parent of an element is present, this rule will not be activated for the child elements unless the template rule for the parent has an `xsl:apply-templates` child. For instance, you can stop all processing by matching the root element and neither applying templates nor using `xsl:for-each` to process the children like this:

```
<xsl:template match="/">
</xsl:template>
```

The Default Rule for Text Nodes

Exceptionally observant readers may have noted several of the examples seem to have output the contents of some elements without actually taking the value of the element they were outputting! These contents were provided by XSL's default rule for text nodes that occur as element content. This rule is:

```
<xsl:template match="text()">
  <xsl:value-of select="."/>
</xsl:template>
```

This rule matches all text nodes (`match="text()"`) and outputs the value of the text node (`<xsl:value-of select="."/>`). In other words, it copies the text from the input to the output.

This rule ensures that at the very least an element's text is output, even if no rule specifically matches it. Another rule can override this one for specific elements where you want either more or less than the text content of an element.

Implication of the Two Default Rules

Together, the two default rules imply that applying an empty style sheet with only an `xsl:stylesheet` element but no children (such as Listing 14-14) to an XML document will copy all the #PCDATA out of the elements in the input to the output. However, this method produces no markup. These are, however, extremely low priority rules. Consequently, any other matches take precedence over these two.

Listing 14-14: **An empty XML style sheet**

```
<?xml version="1.0"?>
<xsl:stylesheet
xmlns:xsl="http://www.w3.org/XSL/Transform/1.0">

</xsl:stylesheet>
```

Caution   One of the most common sources of confusion about XSL in Internet Explorer 5.0 is that it does not provide either of these default rules. You have to make sure that you explicitly match any node whose contents (including descendants) you want to output.

Deciding What Output to Include

It's often necessary to defer decisions about what markup to emit until the input document has been read. For instance, you may want to change the contents of a FILENAME element into the HREF attribute of an A element, or replace one element type in the input with several different element types in the output depending on the value of one of its attributes. This is accomplished by using of `xsl:element`, `xsl:attribute`, `xsl:pi`, `xsl:comment`, and `xsl:text` elements. XSL instructions are used in the contents of these elements and attribute value templates are used in the attribute values of these elements to vary their output.

Using Attribute Value Templates

Attribute value templates copy data from element content in the input to attribute values in the style sheet. From there, it can be written to the output. For example, suppose you want to convert the periodic table into empty ATOM elements with this attribute-based form:

```
<ATOM NAME="Vanadium"
  ATOMIC_WEIGHT="50.9415"
  ATOMIC_NUMBER="23"
  OXIDATION_STATES="5, 4, 3, 2"
  BOILING_POINT="3650K"
  MELTING_POINT="2163K"
  SYMBOL="V"
  DENSITY="6.11 grams/cubic centimeter"
/>
```

To do this, you'll need to extract the contents of elements in the input document and place those in attribute values in the output document. The first thing you're likely to attempt is something like this:

```
<xsl:template match="ATOM">
    <ATOM NAME="<xsl:value-of select='NAME'/>"
    ATOMIC_WEIGHT="<xsl:value-of select='ATOMIC_WEIGHT'/>"
    ATOMIC_NUMBER="<xsl:value-of select='ATOMIC_NUMBER'/>"
    />
```

</xsl:template>But this is malformed XML. You can't use the < character inside an attribute value. Furthermore, it's extremely difficult to write software that can parse this in its most general case.

Instead, inside attribute values, data enclosed in curly braces { } takes the place of the xsl:value-of element. The correct way to write the above is like this:

```
<xsl:template match="ATOM">
  <ATOM NAME="{NAME}/>"
    ATOMIC_WEIGHT="{ATOMIC_WEIGHT}/>"
    ATOMIC_NUMBER="{ATOMIC_NUMBER}/>"
  />
</xsl:template>
```

In the output, {NAME} is replaced by the value of the NAME child element of the current node. {ATOMIC_WEIGHT} is replaced by the value of the ATOMIC_WEIGHT child element of the current node. {ATOMIC_NUMBER} is replaced by the value of the ATOMIC_NUMBER child element, and so on.

Attribute value templates can have more complicated patterns than merely an element name. In fact, you can use any of the string expressions discussed earlier in an attribute value template. For example, this template rule selects `DENSITY` elements in the form used in Listing 14-1.

```
<xsl:template match="DENSITY">
  <BULK_PROPERTY
    NAME="DENSITY"
    ATOM="{../NAME}"
    VALUE="{.}"
    UNITS="{@UNITS}"
  />
</xsl:template>
```

It converts them into `BULK_PROPERTY` elements that look like this:

```
<BULK_PROPERTY NAME="DENSITY" ATOM="Helium" VALUE="
    0.1785
  " UNITS="grams/cubic centimeter"/>
```

Attribute values are not limited to a single attribute value template. You can combine an attribute value template with literal data or with other attribute value templates. For example, this template rule matches `ATOM` elements and replaces them with their name formatted as a link to a file in the format H.html, He.html, and so on. The file name is derived from the attribute value template `{SYMBOL}` while the literal data provides the period and extension.

```
<xsl:template match="ATOM">
  <A HREF="{SYMBOL}.html">
    <xsl:value-of select="NAME"/>
  </A>
</xsl:template>
```

More than one attribute value template can be included in an attribute value. For example, this template rule includes the density units as part of the `VALUE` attribute rather than making them a separate attribute:

```
<xsl:template match="DENSITY">
  <BULK_PROPERTY
    NAME="DENSITY"
    ATOM="{../NAME}"
    VALUE="{.} {@UNITS}"
  />
</xsl:template>
```

You can use attribute value templates in the value of most attributes in an XSL style sheet. This is particularly important in `xsl:element`, `xsl:attribute`, and `xsl:pi` elements where attribute value templates allow the designer to defer the decision about exactly what element, attribute, or processing instruction appears in the output until the input document is read. You cannot use attribute value templates as the value of a `select` or `match` attribute, an `xmlns` attribute, an attribute that provides the name of another XSL instruction element, or an attribute of a top-level element (one that's an immediate child of `xsl:stylesheet`).

Cross-Reference   Chapter 18, *Namespaces*, discusses `xmlns` attributes.

Inserting Elements into the Output with xsl:element

Elements usually get inserted into the output document simply by using the literal elements themselves. For instance, to insert a P element you merely type `<P>` and `</P>` at the appropriate points in the style sheet. However, occasionally you need to use details from the input to determine which element to place in the output. This might happen, for example, when making a transformation from a source vocabulary that uses attributes for information to an output vocabulary that uses elements for the same information.

The `xsl:element` element inserts an element into the output document. The name of the element is given by an attribute value template in the `name` attribute of `xsl:element`. The contents of the element derive from the contents of the `xsl:element` element which may include `xsl:attribute`, `xsl:pi`, and `xsl:comment` instructions (all discussed below) to insert these items.

For example, suppose you want to replace the ATOM elements with GAS, LIQUID, and SOLID elements, depending on the value of the STATE attribute. Using `xsl:element`, a single rule can do this by converting the value of the STATE attribute to an element name. This is how it works:

```
<xsl:template match="ATOM">
  <xsl:element name="{@STATE}">
    <NAME><xsl:value-of select="NAME"/></NAME>
    <!— rules for other children —>
  </xsl:element>
</xsl:template>
```

By using more complicated attribute value templates, you can perform most calculations you might need.

Inserting Attributes into the Output with xsl:attribute

You can include attributes in the output document simply by using the literal attributes themselves. For instance, to insert a DIV element with an ALIGN attribute bearing the value CENTER, you merely type `<DIV ALIGN="CENTER">` and `</DIV>` at the appropriate points in the style sheet. However, you frequently have to rely on data you read from the input to determine an attribute value and sometimes even to determine the attribute name.

For example, suppose you want a style sheet that selects atom names and formats them as links to files named H.html, He.html, Li.html, and so forth like this:

```
<LI><A HREF="H.html">Hydrogen</A></LI>
<LI><A HREF="He.html">Helium</A></LI>
<LI><A HREF="Li.html">Lithium</A></LI>
```

Each different element in the input will have a different value for the HREF attribute. The xsl:attribute element calculates an attribute name and value and inserts it into the output. Each xsl:attribute element is a child of either an xsl:element element or a literal element. The attribute calculated by xsl:attribute will be attached to the element calculated by its parent in the output. The name of the attribute is specified by the name attribute of the xsl:attribute element. The value of the attribute is given by the contents of the xsl:attribute element. For example, this template rule produces the output shown above:

```
<xsl:template match="ATOM">
  <LI><A>
    <xsl:attribute name="HREF">
      <xsl:value-of select="SYMBOL"/>.html
    </xsl:attribute>
    <xsl:value-of select="NAME"/>
  </A></LI>
</xsl:template>
```

All xsl:attribute elements must come before any other content of their parent element. You can't add an attribute to an element after you've already started writing out its contents. For example, this template is illegal:

```
<xsl:template match="ATOM">
  <LI><A>
    <xsl:value-of select="NAME"/>
    <xsl:attribute name="HREF">
      <xsl:value-of select="SYMBOL"/>.html
    </xsl:attribute>
  </A></LI>
</xsl:template>
```

Defining Attribute Sets

You often need to apply the same group of attributes to many different elements, of either the same or different classes. For instance, you might want to apply a style attribute to each cell in an HTML table. To make this simpler, you can define one or more attributes as members of an attribute set at the top level of the style sheet with xsl:attribute-set, then include that attribute set in an element with xsl:use.

For example, this `xsl:attribute-set` element defines an element named `cellstyle` with a `font-family` attribute of `New York, Times New Roman, Times, serif` and a `font-size` attribute of `12pt`.

```
<xsl:attribute-set name="cellstyle">
  <xsl:attribute name="font-family">
    New York, Times New Roman, Times, serif
  </xsl:attribute>
  <xsl:attribute name="font-size">12pt</xsl:attribute>
</xsl:attribute-set>
```

This template rule then applies those attributes to `td` elements in the output. As with `xsl:attribute`, the `xsl:use` element that inserts the attribute set must come before any content that's to be added as a child of `td`.

```
<xsl:template match="ATOM">
  <tr>
    <td>
      <xsl:use attribute-set="cellstyle"/>
      <xsl:value-of select="NAME"/>
    </td>
    <td>
      <xsl:use attribute-set="cellstyle"/>
      <xsl:value-of select="ATOMIC_NUMBER"/>
    </td>
  </tr>
</xsl:template>
```

If an element uses more than one attribute set, then all attributes from all the sets are applied to the element. If more than one attribute set defines the same attribute with different values, then the one from the more important set is used. A style sheet in which multiple attribute sets of the same importance define the same attribute is in error.

Generating Processing Instructions with xsl:pi

The `xsl:pi` element places a processing instruction in the output document. The target of the processing instruction is specified by a required `name` attribute. The contents of the `xsl:pi` element become the contents of the processing instruction. For example, this rule replaces `PROGRAM` elements with a gcc processing instruction:

```
<xsl:template select="PROGRAM">
  <xsl:pi name="gcc"> -O4</xsl:pi>
</xsl:template>
```

`PROGRAM` elements in the input are replaced by this processing instruction in the output:

```
<?gcc -O4?>
```

The contents of the `xsl:pi` element can include `xsl:value-of` elements and `xsl:apply-templates` elements provided the result of these instructions is pure text. For example,

```
<xsl:template select="PROGRAM">
  <xsl:pi name="gcc">-O4 <xsl:value-of select="NAME"/></xsl:pi>
</xsl:template>
```

One common use for `xsl:pi` is to insert the XML declaration when generating XML from XML (even though the XML declaration is technically not a processing instruction). For example:

```
<xsl:pi name="xml">version="1.0" standalone="yes"</xsl:pi>
```

The `xsl:pi` element may not contain `xsl:element` and other instructions that produce elements and attributes in the result. Furthermore, `xsl:pi` may not include any instructions or literal text that inserts a `?>` in the output since that would prematurely end the processing instruction.

Generating Comments with xsl:comment

The `xsl:comment` element inserts a comment in the output document. It has no attributes. Its contents are the text of the comment. For example,

```
<xsl:template select="ATOM">
  <xsl:comment>There was an atom here once.</xsl:comment>
</xsl:template>
```

This rule replaces `ATOM` nodes with this output:

```
<!—There was an atom here once.—>
```

The contents of the `xsl:comment` element can include `xsl:value-of` elements and `xsl:apply-templates` elements provided the result of these instructions is pure text. It may not contain `xsl:element` and other instructions that produce elements and attributes in the result. Furthermore, `xsl:comment` may not include any instructions or literal text that inserts a double hyphen in the comment. This would result in a malformed comment in the output, which is forbidden.

Generating Text with xsl:text

The `xsl:text` element inserts its contents into the output document as literal text. For example, this rule replaces each ATOM element with the string "There was an atom here once."

```
<xsl:template select="ATOM">
  <xsl:text>There was an atom here once.</xsl:text>
</xsl:template>
```

The `xsl:text` element isn't much used because most of the time it's easier to simply type the text. However, `xsl:text` does have one advantage. It preserves whitespace exactly. This is useful when dealing with poetry, computer source code, or other information where whitespace is significant.

Copying the Current Node with xsl:copy

The `xsl:copy` element copies the source node into the output. Child elements, attributes, and other content are not automatically copied. However, the contents of the `xsl:copy` element are an `xsl:template` element that can select these things to be copied as well. This is often useful when transforming a document from one markup vocabulary to the same or a closely related markup vocabulary. For example, this template rule strips the attributes and child elements off an atom and replaces it with the value of its contents:

```
<xsl:template match="ATOM">
  <xsl:copy>
    <xsl:apply-templates/>
  </xsl:copy>
</xsl:template>
```

One useful template `xsl:copy` makes possible is the identity transformation; that is, a transformation from a document into itself. Such a transformation looks like this:

```
<xsl:template match="*|@*|comment()|pi()|text()">
  <xsl:copy>
    <xsl:apply-templates select="*|@*|comment()|pi()|text()"/>
  </xsl:copy>
</xsl:template>
```

You can adjust the identity transformation a little to produce similar documents. For example, Listing 14-15 is a style sheet that strips comments from a document, leaving the document otherwise untouched. It resulted from leaving the `comment()` node out of the `match` and `select` attribute values in the identity transformation.

Listing 14-15: An XSL style sheet that strips comments from a document

```
<?xml version="1.0"?>
<xsl:stylesheet
xmlns:xsl="http://www.w3.org/XSL/Transform/1.0">

  <xsl:template match="*|@*|pi()|text()">
    <xsl:copy>
```

```
        <xsl:apply-templates select="*|@*|pi()|text()"/>
      </xsl:copy>
    </xsl:template>

</xsl:stylesheet>
```

xsl:copy only copies the source node. You can copy other nodes, possibly more than one of them, using xsl:copy-of. The select attribute of xsl:copy-of chooses the nodes to be copied. For example, Listing 14-16 is a stylesheet that uses xsl:copy-of to strip out elements without melting points from the periodic table by copying only ATOM elements that have MELTING_POINT children.

Listing 14-16: A stylesheet that copies only ATOM elements that have MELTING_POINT children

```
<?xml version="1.0"?>
<xsl:stylesheet
  xmlns:xsl="http://www.w3.org/XSL/Transform/1.0">

    <xsl:template match="/PERIODIC_TABLE">
      <PERIODIC_TABLE>
        <xsl:apply-templates select="ATOM"/>
      </PERIODIC_TABLE>
    </xsl:template>

    <xsl:template match="ATOM">
      <xsl:apply-templates
        select="MELTING_POINT"/>
    </xsl:template>

   <xsl:template match="MELTING_POINT">
     <xsl:copy-of select="..">
        <xsl:apply-templates select="*|@*|pi()|text()"/>
     </xsl:copy-of>
    </xsl:template>

    <xsl:template match="*|@*|pi()|text()">
      <xsl:copy>
        <xsl:apply-templates select="*|@*|pi()|text()"/>
      </xsl:copy>
    </xsl:template>

</xsl:stylesheet>
```

Note   This is an example of an XSL transformation from a source vocabulary to the same vocabulary. Unlike most of the examples in this chapter, it does not transform to well-formed HTML.

Counting Nodes with xsl:number

The xsl:number element inserts a formatted integer into the output document. The value of the integer is given by rounding the number calculated by the expr attribute to the nearest integer, then formatting it according to the value of the format attribute. Reasonable defaults are provided for both these attributes. For example, consider the style sheet for the ATOM elements in Listing 14-17.

Listing 14-17: An XSL style sheet that counts atoms

```
<?xml version="1.0"?>
<xsl:stylesheet
xmlns:xsl="http://www.w3.org/XSL/Transform/1.0">

    <xsl:template match="PERIODIC_TABLE">
      <html>
        <head><title>The Elements</title></head>
        <body>
          <table>
            <xsl:apply-templates select="ATOM"/>
          </table>
        </body>
      </html>
    </xsl:template>

    <xsl:template match="ATOM">
      <tr>
        <td><xsl:number expr="position()"/></td>
        <td><xsl:value-of select="NAME"/></td>
      </tr>
    </xsl:template>

</xsl:stylesheet>
```

When this style sheet is applied to Listing 14-1, the output appears like this:

```
<html><head><title>The
Elements</title></head><body><table><tr><td>1</td><td>Hydrogen<
/td></tr>
```

```
<tr><td>2</td><td>Helium</td></tr>
</table></body></html>
```

Hydrogen gets number 1 because it is the first ATOM element in its parent. Helium gets number 2 because it is the second ATOM element in its parent. (That these are the atomic numbers of hydrogen and helium is a side effect of Listing 14-1 being arranged in order of atomic number.)

Default Numbers

If you use the expr attribute to calculate the number, that's all you need. However, if the expr attribute is omitted, then the position of the current node in the source tree is used as the number. However, this default can be adjusted using these three attributes:

✦ level

✦ count

✦ from

Caution   These three attributes are a holdover from previous drafts of XSL that did not support the more complex expressions now possible. If they seem at all confusing to you, I recommend that you ignore them and use expr instead.

The level Attribute

By default, with no expr attribute, xsl:number counts sibling nodes of the source node. For instance, if the ATOMIC_NUMBER elements were numbered instead of ATOM elements, none would have a number higher than 1 because an ATOM never has more than one ATOMIC_NUMBER child. Although the document contains more than one ATOMIC_NUMBER element, these are not siblings.

Setting the level attribute of xsl:number to any counts all of the elements of the same kind as the current node in the document. This includes not just the ones that may match the current rule, but all elements of the right type. Even if you select only the atomic numbers of the gases, for example, the solids and liquids would still count, even if they weren't output. Consider, these rules:

```
<xsl:template match="ATOM">
  <xsl:apply-templates select="NAME"/>
</xsl:template>

<xsl:template match="NAME">
  <td><xsl:number level="any"/></td>
  <td><xsl:value-of select="."/></td>
</xsl:template>
```

Since level is set to any, they produce output that doesn't start from 1 with each new NAME element like this:

```
<td>1</td><td>Hydrogen</td>

<td>2</td><td>Helium</td>
```

If you remove the level attribute or set it to its default value of single, then the output would look like this:

```
<td>1</td><td>Hydrogen</td>

<td>1</td><td>Helium</td>
```

A slightly less useful option sets the level attribute of xsl:number to multi to specify that both the siblings of the current node and its ancestors (but not their children that aren't siblings of the current node) should be counted.

The count Attribute

By default, with no expr attribute, only elements of the same type as the element of the current node get counted. However, you can set the count attribute of xsl: number to a select expression that specifies what to count. For instance, this rule applies numbers all the child elements of an ATOM:

```
<xsl:template match="ATOM/*">
  <td><xsl:number count="*"/></td>
  <td><xsl:value-of select="."/></td>
</xsl:template>
```

The output from applying this rule looks like this:

```
<td>1</td><td>Helium</td>
<td>2</td><td>He</td>
<td>3</td><td>2</td>
<td>4</td><td>4.0026</td>
<td>5</td><td>1</td>
<td>6</td><td>4.216</td>
<td>7</td><td>0.95</td>
<td>8</td><td>
  0.1785
</td>
```

The from Attribute

The from attribute contains a select expression that specifies which element the counting begins with in the input tree. However, the counting still begins from one, not two or ten or some other number. The from attribute only changes which element is considered to be the first element.

Number to String Conversion

Until now, I've implicitly assumed that numbers looked like 1, 2, 3, and so on; that is, a European numeral starting from 1 and counting by 1. However, that's not the only possibility. For instance, the pages of the preface and other front matter of books often appear in small Roman numerals like i, ii, iii, iv, and so on. And different countries use different conventions to group the digits, separate the integer and fractional parts of a real number, and represent the symbols for the various digits. These are all adjustable through five attributes of xsl:number:

+ format
+ letter-value
+ digit-group-sep
+ n-digits-per-group
+ sequence-src

The format Attribute

You can adjust the numbering style used by xsl:number using the format attribute. This attribute generally has one of the following values:

+ i: produces the sequence of lowercase Roman numerals i, ii. iii, iv, v, vi, ...

+ I: produces the sequence of uppercase Roman numerals I, II, III, IV, V, VI, ...

+ a: produces the sequence of lowercase letters a, b, c, d, e, f, ...

+ A: produces the sequence of uppercase letters A, B, C, D, E, F, ...

For example, this rule numbers the atoms with capital Roman numerals:

```
<xsl:template match="ATOM">
  <P>
    <xsl:number expr="position()" format="I"/>
    <xsl:value-of select="."/>
  </P>
</xsl:template>
```

You can adjust the number (or letter) at which counting starts by changing the value of the format attribute. For example, to start numbering at 5, set format= "5". To start numbering at iii, set format="iii".

You can also specify decimal numbering with leading zeroes by including the number of leading zeroes you want in the format attribute. For instance, setting format="01", produces the sequence 01, 02, 03, 04, 05, 06, 07, 08, 09, 10, 11, 12, ... You might find this useful when lining numbers up in columns.

The letter-value Attribute

The letter-value attribute distinguishes between letters interpreted as numbers and letters interpreted as letters. For instance, if you want to use format="I" to start the sequence I, J, K, L, M, N, ... instead of I, II, III, IV, V, VI, ... you would set the letter-value attribute to the keyword alphabetic. The keyword other specifies a numeric sequence. For example,

```
<xsl:template match="ATOM">
  <P>
    <xsl:number expr="position()"
                format="I" letter-value="alphabetic"/>
    <xsl:value-of select="."/>
  </P>
</xsl:template>
```

Group Separator Attributes

In the United States, we tend to write large numbers with commas grouping every three digits like 4,567,302,000. However, in many languages and countries, a period or a space separates the groups instead; for instance, 4.567.302.000 or 4 567 302 000. Furthermore, in some countries it's customary to group large numbers every four digits instead of every three; for example, 4,5673,0000. If you're dealing with very long lists that may contain a thousand or more items, you need to worry about these issues.

The digit-group-sep attribute specifies the grouping separator used between groups of digits. The n-digits-per-group attribute specifies the number of digits used in a group. Generally, you'd make these attributes contingent on the language. For example,

```
<xsl:number digit-group-sep=" "/>
```

The sequence-src Attribute

Finally, if you want to use an unusual order (for example, a list of date strings like 1-1-1999, 1-2-1999, 1-3-1999, ... or a list that jumps by tens like 10, 20, 30, 40, ...) you can store this list (separated by whitespace) in a separate document. The sequence-src attribute has a value representing the relative or absolute URL of this document. For example,

```
<xsl:number sequence-src="1999.txt"/>
```

Sorting Output Elements

The xsl:sort element sorts the output elements into a different order than they appear in the input. An xsl:sort element appears as a child of an xsl:apply-templates element or xsl:for-each element. The select attribute of the xsl:sort element defines the key used to sort the elements' output by xsl:apply-templates or xsl:for-each.

By default, sorting is performed in alphabetical order of the keys. If more than one xsl:sort element is present in a given xsl:apply-templates or xsl:for-each element, then the output sorts first by the first key, then by the second key, and so on. If any elements still compare equally, they output in the order they appear in the source document.

For example, suppose you have a file full of ATOM elements arranged alphabetically. To sort by atomic number, you can use the style sheet in Listing 14-18.

Listing 14-18: **An XSL style sheet that sorts by atomic number**

```
<?xml version="1.0"?>
<xsl:stylesheet
xmlns:xsl="http://www.w3.org/XSL/Transform/1.0">

    <xsl:template match="PERIODIC_TABLE">
      <html>
        <head>
          <title>Atomic Number vs. Atomic Weight</title>
        </head>
        <body>
          <h1>Atomic Number vs. Atomic Weight</h1>
          <table>
            <th>Element</th>
            <th>Atomic Number</th>
            <th>Atomic Weight</th>
            <xsl:apply-templates>
               <xsl:sort select="ATOMIC_NUMBER"/>
            </xsl:apply-templates>
          </table>
        </body>
      </html>
    </xsl:template>

    <xsl:template match="ATOM">
      <tr>
        <td><xsl:apply-templates select="NAME"/></td>
        <td><xsl:apply-templates select="ATOMIC_NUMBER"/></td>
        <td><xsl:apply-templates select="ATOMIC_WEIGHT"/></td>
      </tr>
    </xsl:template>

</xsl:stylesheet>
```

Figure 14-5 shows the results that display the limits of alphabetical sorting. Hydrogen, atomic number 1, is the first element. However, the second element is not helium, atomic number 2, but rather neon, atomic number 10. Although 10 sorts after 9 numerically, alphabetically 10 falls before 2.

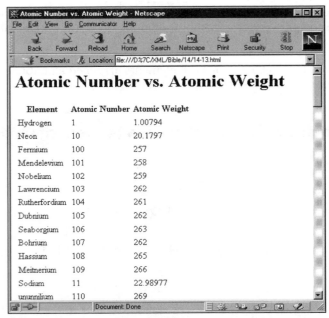

Figure 14-5: Atoms alphabetically sorted by atomic number

You can, however, adjust the order of the sort by setting the optional data-type attribute to the value number. For example,

```
<xsl:sort data-type="number" select="ATOMIC_NUMBER"/>
```

Figure 14-6 shows the elements sorted properly.

You can change the order of the sort from the default ascending order to descending by setting the order attribute to descending like this:

```
<xsl:sort order="descending"
          sort="number"
          select="ATOMIC_NUMBER"/>
```

This sorts the elements from the largest atomic number to the smallest so that hydrogen now appears last in the list.

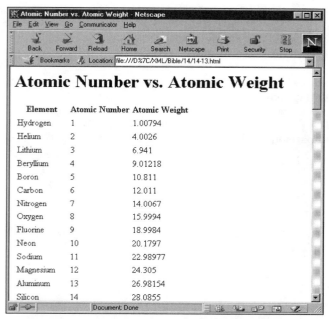

Figure 14-6: Atoms numerically sorted by atomic number

Alphabetical sorting naturally depends on the alphabet. The lang attribute can set the language of the keys. The value of this attribute should be an ISO 639 language code like en for English.

Cross-Reference These are the same values supported by the xml:lang attribute discussed in Chapter 10, *Attribute Declarations in DTDs*.

Finally, you can set the case-order attribute to one of the two values upper-first or lower-first to specify whether uppercase letters sort before lowercase letters or vice versa. The default depends on the language.

CDATA and < Signs

Standard XSL contains no means to insert raw, unescaped < characters that are not part of a tag into the output. Raw less-than signs make the output document mal-formed, something XSL does not allow. Instead, if you use a character reference like < or the entity reference < to insert the < character, the formatter will insert < or perhaps <.

This only really becomes important when you're embedding JavaScript into a page because JavaScript uses the < character to mean numerical less than rather than the start of the tag. Furthermore, JavaScript implementations do not allow the < character to be replaced with the HTML entity <.

You can insert raw, unescaped > and >= signs into the output, however. Consequently, if your output needs to contain JavaScript that makes numerical comparisons, you can rewrite a less-than comparison as a greater-than-or-equal-to comparison by reversing the order of the operands. You can rewrite a less-than-or-equal-to comparison as a greater-than comparison. For example, here's a few lines of JavaScript code I use in a lot of my Web pages:

```
if (location.host.tolowercase().indexof("sunsite") < 0) {
  location.href="http://metalab.unc.edu/xml/";
}
```

These lines are malformed because of the less-than sign in the first two lines. However, these lines are completely equivalent to these lines:

```
if (0 > location.host.tolowercase().indexof("sunsite")) {
  location.href="http://metalab.unc.edu/xml/";
}
```

If you have multiple tests combined with Boolean operators, you may need to change logical ands to logical ors as well. For example, these two lines of JavaScript effetively test whether the location of the page is not on metalab and not on sunsite:

```
if (location.host.toLowerCase().indexOf("metalab") < 0
 && location.host.tolowercase().indexof("sunsite") < 0) {
    location.href="http://metalab.unc.edu/xml/";
}
```

These lines are malformed because of the less-than signs in the first two lines. However, these lines which test whether the page is on metalab or sunsite are completely equivalent:

```
if (0 > location.host.toLowerCase().indexOf("metalab")
 || 0 > location.host.tolowercase().indexof("sunsite")) {
    location.href="http://metalab.unc.edu/xml/";
}
```

> **Tip** You can also place the offending JavaScript in a separate document, and link to it from the SCRIPT element's SRC attribute. However, this is unreliable prior to Internet Explorer 4 and Netscape Navigator 3.

CDATA sections are not allowed in output for reasons of simplicity. A CDATA section can always be replaced by an equivalent collection of character data with

Unicode escapes for problem characters like < and &. CDATA sections are purely a convenience for humans writing XML files by hand. Computer programs like XSL formatters don't need them.

Note The XSL formatter included in Internet Explorer 5.0 does support a non-standard `xsl:cdata` element for inserting CDATA sections into the output. However, it's unlikely that this will be added to standard XSL, and it may even be removed from later releases of Internet Explorer.

Modes

Sometimes you want to include the same content from the source document in the output document multiple times. That's easy to do by simply applying templates multiple times, once in each place where you want the data to appear. However, suppose you want the data to be formatted differently in different locations? That's a little trickier.

For example, suppose you want the output of processing the periodic table to be a series of 100 links to more detailed descriptions of the individual atoms. In this case, the output document would start like this:

```
<UL>
<LI><A HREF="#Ac">Actinium</A></LI>
<LI><A HREF="#Al">Aluminum</A></LI>
<LI><A HREF="#Am">Americium</A></LI>
<LI><A HREF="#Sb">Antimony</A></LI>
<LI><A HREF="#Ar">Argon</A></LI>
. . .
```

Later in the document, the actual atom description would appear, formatted like this:

```
<H3><A NAME="Al">Aluminum</A></H3><P>
    Aluminum
    26.98154
    13
    3
    2740
    933.5
    Al

     2.7

</P>
```

This sort of application is common anytime you automatically generate a hypertext table of contents or index. The NAME of the atom must be formatted differently in the table of contents than in the body of the document. You need two different rules that both apply to the ATOM element at different places in the document. The solution is to give each of the different rules a mode attribute. Then you can choose which template to apply by setting the mode attribute of the xsl:apply-templates element. Listing 14-19 demonstrates.

Listing 14-19: **An XSL stylesheet that uses modes to format the same data differently in two different places**

```
<?xml version="1.0"?>
<xsl:stylesheet
xmlns:xsl="http://www.w3.org/XSL/Transform/1.0">

  <xsl:template match="/PERIODIC_TABLE">
    <HTML>
      <HEAD><TITLE>The Elements</TITLE></HEAD>
      <BODY>

        <H2>Table of Contents</H2>
        <UL>
          <xsl:apply-templates select="ATOM" mode="toc"/>
        </UL>

        <H2>The Elements</H2>
        <xsl:apply-templates select="ATOM" mode="full"/>

      </BODY>
    </HTML>
  </xsl:template>

  <xsl:template match="ATOM" mode="toc">
    <LI><A>
      <xsl:attribute name="HREF">#<xsl:value-of
        select="SYMBOL"/></xsl:attribute>
      <xsl:value-of select="NAME"/>
    </A></LI>
  </xsl:template>

  <xsl:template match="ATOM" mode="full">
    <H3><A>
      <xsl:attribute name="NAME">
        <xsl:value-of select="SYMBOL"/>
      </xsl:attribute>
      <xsl:value-of select="NAME"/>
    </A></H3>
      <P>
        <xsl:value-of select="."/>
      </P>
```

```
  </xsl:template>

</xsl:stylesheet>
```

Defining Constants with xsl:variable

Named constants help clean up code. They can replace commonly used boiler-plate text with a simple name and reference. They can also make it easy to adjust boilerplate text that appears in multiple locations by simply changing the constant definition.

The `xsl:variable` element defines a named string for use elsewhere in the style sheet via an attribute value template. The `xsl:variable` element is an empty element that appears as a direct child of `xsl:stylesheet`. It has a single attribute, `name`, which provides a name by which the variable can be referred to. The contents of the `xsl:variable` element provides the replacement text. For example, this `xsl:variable` element defines a variable with the name `copy99` and the value `Copyright 1999 Elliotte Rusty Harold`:

```
<xsl:variable name="copy99">
  Copyright 1999 Elliotte Rusty Harold
</xsl:variable>
```

To access the value of this variable, you prefix a dollar sign to the name of the variable. To insert this in an attribute, use an attribute value template. For example:

```
<BLOCK COPYRIGHT="{$copy99}">
</BLOCK >
```

You can use `xsl:value-of` to insert the variable's replacement text into the output document as text:

```
<xsl:value-of select="$copy99"/>
```

The contents of the `xsl:variable` can contain markup including other XSL instructions. This means that you can calculate the value of a variable based on other information, including the value of other variables. However, a variable may not refer to itself recursively, either directly or indirectly. For instance, the following example is in error:

```
<xsl:variable name="GNU">
  <xsl:value-of select="$GNU"/>'s not Unix
</xsl:variable>
```

Similarly, two variables may not refer to each other in a circular fashion like this:

```
<xsl:variable name="Thing1">
  Thing1 loves <xsl:value-of select="$Thing2"/>
</xsl:variable>

<xsl:variable name="Thing2">
  Thing2 loves <xsl:value-of select="$Thing1"/>
</xsl:variable>
```

Named Templates

Variables are limited to basic text and markup. XSL provides a more powerful macro facility that can wrap standard markup and text around changing data. For example, suppose you want an atom's atomic number, atomic weight, and other key values format as a table cell in small, bold type Times in blue. In other words, you want the output to look like this:

```
<td>
  <font face="Times, serif" color="blue" size="2">
    <b>52</b>
  </font>
</td>
```

You can certainly include all that in a template rule like this:

```
<xsl:template match="ATOMIC_NUMBER">
  <td>
    <font face="Times, serif" color="blue" size="2">
      <b>
        <xsl:value-of select="."/>
      </b>
    </font>
  </td>
</xsl:template>
```

This markup can repeat as the template of other rules, or as a part of the template used in other rules. When the detailed markup grows more complex and when it appears in several different places in a style sheet, you may elect to turn it into a named template. Named templates resemble variables. However, they enable you to include data from the place where the template is applied, rather than merely inserting fixed text.

The xsl:template element can have a name attribute by which it can be explicitly invoked, even when it isn't applied indirectly. For example, this shows a sample named template for the above pattern:

```
<xsl:template name="ATOM_CELL">
  <td>
```

```
   <font face="Times, serif" color="blue" size="2">
     <b>
       <xsl:value-of select="."/>
     </b>
   </font>
  </td>
</xsl:template>
```

The `<xsl:value-of select="."/>` element in the middle of the macro will be replaced by the contents of the current node from which this template was called.

The `xsl:call-template` element appears in the contents of a template rule. It has a required `name` argument that names the template it will call. When processed, the `xsl:call-template` element is replaced by the contents of the `xsl:template` element it names. For example, we can now rewrite the ATOMIC_NUMBER rule like this using the `xsl:call-template` element to call the ATOM_CELL named template:

```
<xsl:template match="ATOMIC_NUMBER">
  <xsl:call-template name="ATOM_CELL"/>
</xsl:template>
```

This fairly simple example only saves a few lines of code, but the more complicated the template, and the more times it's reused, the greater the reduction in complexity of the style sheet. Named templates also have the advantage, like variables, of factoring out common patterns in the style sheet so you can edit them as one. For instance, if you decide to change the color of atomic number, atomic weight, and other key values from blue to red, you only need to change it once in the named template. You do not have to change it in each separate template rule. This facilitates greater consistency of style in the long run.

Parameters

Each separate invocation of a named template can pass parameters to the template to customize its output. In the `xsl:template` element, the parameters are represented as `xsl:param-variable` child elements. In the `xsl:call-template` element, parameters are represented as `xsl:param` child elements.

For example, suppose you want to also include a link to a particular file for each atom cell. The output should look something like this:

```
<td>
  <font face="Times, serif" color="blue" size="2">
    <b>
      <a href="atomic_number.html">52</a>
    </b>
  </font>
</td>
```

The trick is that the value of the href attribute has to be passed in from the point where the template is invoked because it changes for each separate invocation of the template. For example, atomic weights will have to be formatted like this:

```
<td>
  <font face="Times, serif" color="blue" size="2">
    <b>
      <a href="atomic_weight.html">4.0026</a>
    </b>
  </font>
</td>
```

The template that supports this looks like this:

```
<xsl:template name="ATOM_CELL">
  <xsl:param-variable name="file">
   index.html
  </xsl:param-variable>
  <td>
    <font face="Times, serif" color="blue" size="2">
      <b>
        <a href="{$file}"><xsl:value-of select="."/></a>
      </b>
    </font>
  </td>
</xsl:template>
```

The name attribute of the xsl:param-variable element gives the parameter a name (important if there are multiple arguments) and the contents of the xsl:param-variable element supplies a default value for this parameter to be used if the invocation doesn't provide a value. (This can also be given as a string expression using an expr attribute, exactly like xsl:variable.)

When this template is called, an xsl:param child of the xsl:call-template element provides the value of the parameter using its name attribute to identify the parameter and its contents to provide a value for the parameter. For example:

```
<xsl:template match="ATOMIC_NUMBER">
  <xsl:call-template macro="ATOM_CELL">
    <xsl:param name="file">atomic_number.html</xsl:param>
    <xsl:value-of select="."/>
  </xsl:call-template>
</xsl:template>
```

Again, this is a fairly simple example. However, much more complex named templates exist. For instance, you could define header and footer macros for pages on a Web site for importing by many different style sheets, each of which would only have to change a few parameters for the name of the page author, the title of the page, and the copyright date.

Stripping and Preserving Whitespace

You may have noticed that all the examples of output up till now have been formatted a little strangely. The reason the examples appeared strange is that the source document needed to break long lines across multiple lines to fit between the margins of this book. Unfortunately, the extra whitespace added to the input document carried over into the output document. For a computer, the details of insignificant whitespace aren't important, but for a person they can be distracting.

The default behavior for text nodes like the content of an ATOMIC_NUMBER or DENSITY element is to preserve all whitespace. A typical DENSITY element looks like this:

```
<DENSITY UNITS="grams/cubic centimeter"><!— At 300K —>
   7.9
</DENSITY>
```

When its value is taken the leading and trailing whitespace is included, like this, even though it's really only there to help fit on this printed page and isn't at all significant:

```
      7.9
```

However, there is one exception. If the text node contains only whitespace, no other text, then the space is considered insignificant and stripped. But there is one exception to the exception: if the text has an ancestor with an xml:space attribute with the value preserve, then it is not stripped unless a closer ancestor contains an xml: space attribute with the value default. (This is really simpler than it sounds. All this says is that you can ignore text nodes that contain only whitespace unless they're specifically set to have significant whitespace. Otherwise whitespace is preserved.)

If none of the elements in the document should preserve whitespace, then you can set the default-space attribute of the xsl:stylesheet element to strip and all leading and trailing whitespace will be removed from text nodes before they're output. This is the easiest solution for the periodic table problem. For example:

```
<xsl:stylesheet xmlns:xsl="http://www.w3.org/XSL/Transform/1.0"
                default-space="strip">
```

If you don't want to strip space from all elements, you can use xsl:strip-space elements to identify the specific elements in the input document whose whitespace should be considered insignificant and not copied to the output document. The element attribute identifies the element whose excess space should be trimmed.

For example, these rules could be added to the periodic table style sheet to avoid excess whitespace:

```
<xsl:strip-space element="DENSITY"/>
<xsl:strip-space element="BOILING_POINT"/>
<xsl:strip-space element="MELTING_POINT"/>
```

The `xsl:preserve-space` element is the opposite of the `xsl:strip-space` element. Its `element` attribute names an element whose whitespace should be preserved. For example:

```
<xsl:preserve-space element="ATOM"/>
```

Whitespace in the style sheet itself (as opposed to whitespace in the input XML document) is not considered significant and is reduced to a single space by default. You can avoid this behavior only by enclosing the literal whitespace in an `xsl:text` element. For example:

```
<xsl:template select="ATOM">
<xsl:text>     This is indented exactly five spaces.</xsl:text>
</xsl:template>
```

One final trick you can play with whitespace is to attach an indent-result attribute to the root `xsl:stylesheet` element. If this attribute has the value `yes`, then the processor is allowed to inset (but not remove) extra whitespace into the output to try to "pretty-print" the output. This may include indentation and line breaks. For example:

```
<?xml version="1.0"?>
<xsl:stylesheet xmlns:xsl="http://www.w3.org/XSL/Transform/1.0"
  indent-result="yes">
  <!- usual templates and such go here... ->
</xsl:stylesheet>
```

If you're generating HTML, specifying `indent-result="yes"` can only make the output more readable. The default value of `indent-result` is no because other, non-HTML output formats may consider whitespace more significant.

Making Choices

XSL provides two elements that allow you to change the output based on the input. The `xsl:if` element either does or does not output a given fragment of XML depending on what patterns are present in the input. The `xsl:choose` element picks one of several possible XML fragments depending on what patterns are present in the input. Most of what you can do with `xsl:if` and `xsl:choose` can also be done by suitable application of templates. However, sometimes the solution with `xsl:if` or `xsl:choose` is simpler and more obvious.

xsl:if

The `xsl:if` element provides a simple facility for changing the output based on a pattern. The `test` attribute of `xsl:if` contains a select expression that evaluates to a Boolean. If the expression is true, the contents of the `xsl:if` element are output. Otherwise, they're not. For example, this template writes out the names of all `ATOM` elements. A comma and a space is added after all except the last element in the list.

```
<xsl:template match="ATOM">
  <xsl:value-of select="NAME"/>
  <xsl:if test="not(position()=last())">, </xsl:if>
</xsl:template>
```

This ensures that the list looks like "Hydrogen, Helium" and not "Hydrogen, Helium,".

There are no `xsl:else` or `xsl:else-if` elements. The `xsl:choose` element provides this functionality.

xsl:choose

The `xsl:choose` element selects one of several possible outputs depending on several possible conditions. Each condition and its associated output template is provided by an `xsl:when` child element. The `test` attribute of the `xsl:when` element is a select expression with a Boolean value. If multiple conditions are true, only the first true one is instantiated. If none of the `xsl:when` elements are true, the contents of the `xsl:otherwise` child elements are instantiated. For example, this rule changes the color of the output based on whether the `STATE` attribute of the `ATOM` element is `SOLID`, `LIQUID`, or `GAS`:

```
<xsl:template match="ATOM">
  <xsl:choose>
    <xsl:when test="@STATE='SOLID'">
      <P style="color:black">
        <xsl:value-of select="."/>
      </P>
    </xsl:when>
    <xsl:when test="@STATE='LIQUID'">
      <P style="color:blue">
        <xsl:value-of select="."/>
      </P>
    </xsl:when>
    <xsl:when test="@STATE='GAS'">
      <P style="color:red">
        <xsl:value-of select="."/>
      </P>
    </xsl:when>
    <xsl:other>
      <P style="color:green">
        <xsl:value-of select="."/>
      </P>
```

```
        </xsl:other>
      </xsl:choose>
    </xsl:template>
```

Merging Multiple Style Sheets

A single XML document may use many different markup vocabularies described in many different DTDs. You may also wish to use different standard style sheets for those different vocabularies. However, you'll also want style rules for particular documents as well. The xsl:import and xsl:include elements enable you to merge multiple style sheets so that you can organize and reuse style sheets for different vocabularies and purposes.

Import with xsl:import

The xsl:import element is a top level element whose href attribute provides the URI of a style sheet to import. All xsl:import elements must appear before any other top level elements in the xsl:stylesheet root element. For example, these xsl:import elements import the style sheets genealogy.xsl and standards.xsl.

```
<xsl:stylesheet
xmlns:xsl="http://www.w3.org/XSL/Transform/1.0">
  <xsl:import href="genealogy.xsl"/>
  <xsl:import href="standards.xsl"/>
  <!— other child elements follow —>
</xsl:stylesheet>
```

Rules in the imported style sheets may conflict with rules in the importing style sheet. If so, rules in the importing style sheet take precedence. If two rules in different imported style sheets conflict, then the last one imported (standards.xsl above) takes precedence.

The xsl:apply-imports elements is a slight variant of xsl:apply-templates that only uses imported rules. It does not use any rules from the importing style sheet. This allows access to imported rules that would otherwise be overridden by rules in the importing style sheet. Other than the name, it has identical syntax to xsl:apply-templates. The only behavioral difference is that it only matches template rules in imported style sheets.

Inclusion with xsl:include

The xsl:include element is a top level element that copies another style sheet into the current style sheet at the point where it occurs. (More precisely, it copies the contents of the xsl-stylesheet element in the remote document into the current document.) Its href attribute provides the URI of the style sheet to include. An xsl:include element can occur anywhere at the top level after the last xsl:import element.

Unlike rules included by xsl:import elements, rules included by xsl:include elements have the same precedence in the including style sheet that they would have if they were copied and pasted from one stylesheet to the other. As far as the formatting engine is concerned, there is no difference between an included rule and a rule that's physically present.

Embed Style Sheets in Documents with xsl:stylesheet

You can directly include an XSL style sheet in the XML document it applies to. I don't recommend this in practice, and browsers and formatting engines are not required to support it. Nonetheless, a few might. To do this, the xsl:stylesheet element must appear as a child of the document element, rather than as a root element itself. It would have an id attribute giving it a unique name, and this id attribute would appear as the value of the href attribute in the xml-stylesheet processing instruction, following the anchor identifier #. Listing 14-20 demonstrates:

> **Listing 14-20: An XSL style sheet embedded in an XML document**

```
<?xml version="1.0"?>
<?xml-stylesheet type="text/xsl" href="#id(mystyle)"?>
<PERIODIC_TABLE>

  <xsl:stylesheet
    xmlns:xsl="http://www.w3.org/XSL/Transform/1.0"
    id="mystyle">

  <xsl:template match="/">
    <html>
      <xsl:apply-templates/>
    </html>
  </xsl:template>

  <xsl:template match="PERIODIC_TABLE">
      <xsl:apply-templates/>
  </xsl:template>

  <xsl:template match="ATOM">
    <P>
      <xsl:value-of select="."/>
    </P>
  </xsl:template>

  </xsl:stylesheet>
```

Continued

Listing 14-20 *(continued)*

```
<ATOM>
  <NAME>Actinium</NAME>
  <ATOMIC_WEIGHT>227</ATOMIC_WEIGHT>
  <ATOMIC_NUMBER>89</ATOMIC_NUMBER>
  <OXIDATION_STATES>3</OXIDATION_STATES>
  <BOILING_POINT UNITS="Kelvin">3470</BOILING_POINT>
  <MELTING_POINT UNITS="Kelvin">1324</MELTING_POINT>
  <SYMBOL>Ac</SYMBOL>
  <DENSITY UNITS="grams/cubic centimeter"><!— At 300K —>
    10.07
  </DENSITY>
  <ELECTRONEGATIVITY>1.1</ELECTRONEGATIVITY>
  <ATOMIC_RADIUS UNITS="Angstroms">1.88</ATOMIC_RADIUS>
</ATOM>

</PERIODIC_TABLE>
```

Summary

In this chapter, you learned about XSL transformations. In particular, you learned the following:

✦ The Extensible Style Language (XSL) comprises two separate XML applications for transforming and formatting XML documents.

✦ An XSL transformation applies rules to a tree read from an XML document to transform it into an output tree written as an XML document.

✦ An XSL template rule is an `xsl:template` element with a `match` attribute. Nodes in the input tree are compared against the patterns of the `match` attributes of the different template elements. When a match is found, the contents of the template are output.

✦ The value of a node is a pure text (no markup) string containing the contents of the node. This can be calculated by the `xsl:value-of` element.

✦ You can process multiple elements in two ways: the `xsl:apply_templates` element and the `xsl:for each` element.

✦ The value of the `match` attribute of the `xsl:template` element is a match pattern specifying which nodes the template matches.

✦ Select expressions are a superset of the match attribute used by the `select` attribute of `xsl:apply-templates`, `xsl:value-of`, `xsl:for-each`, `xsl:copy-of`, and `xsl:sort` and various other elements.

✦ Two default rules apply templates to element nodes and take the value of text nodes.

✦ The xsl:element, xsl:attribute, xsl:pi, xsl:comment, and xsl:text elements can output elements, attributes, processing instructions, comments, and text calculated from data in the input document.

✦ The xsl:attribute-set element defines a common group of attributes that can be applied to multiple elements in different templates with the xsl:use element.

✦ The xsl:copy element copies the current input node into the output.

✦ The xsl:number element inserts the number specified by its expr attribute into the output using a specified number format given by the format attribute.

✦ The xsl:sort element can reorder the input nodes before copying them to the output.

✦ XSL cannot output CDATA sections or unescaped < signs.

✦ Modes can apply different templates to the same element from different locations in the style sheet.

✦ The xsl:variable element defines named constants that can clarify your code.

✦ Named templates help you reuse common template code.

✦ Whitespace is maintained by default unless an xsl:strip-space element or xml:space attribute says otherwise.

✦ The xsl:if element produces output if, and only if, its test attribute is true.

✦ The xsl:choose element outputs the template of the first one of its xsl:when children whose test attribute is true, or the template of its xsl:default element if no xsl:when element has a true test attribute.

✦ The xsl:import and xsl:include elements merge rules from different style sheets.

In the next chapter, we'll take up the second half of XSL: the formatting objects vocabulary. Formatting objects are an extremely powerful way of specifying the precise layout you want your pages to have. XSL transformations are used to transform an XML document into an XSL formatting object document.

✦   ✦   ✦

XSL Formatting Objects

The second half of the Extensible Style Language (XSL) is the formatting language. This is an XML application used to describe how content should be rendered when presented to a reader. Generally, a style sheet uses the XSL transformation language to transform an XML document into a new XML document that uses the XSL formatting objects vocabulary. While many hope that Web browsers will one day know how to directly display data marked up with XSL formatting objects, for now an additional step is necessary in which the output document is further transformed into some other format such as PDF.

Overview of the XSL Formatting Language

XSL formatting objects provide a more sophisticated visual layout model than HTML+CSS (even CSS2). Formatting supported by XSL formatting objects but not supported by HTML+CSS includes non-Western layout, footnotes, margin notes, page numbers in cross references, and more. In particular, while CSS is primarily intended for use on the Web, XSL formatting objects are designed for more general use. You should, for instance, be able to write an XSL style sheet that uses formatting objects to lay out an entire printed book. A different style sheet should be able to transform the same XML document into a Web site.

A Word of Caution about the XSL Formatting Language

XSL is still under development. The XSL language has changed radically in the past, and will change again in the future. This chapter is based on the April 21, 1999 (fourth) draft of the XSL specification. By the time you are reading this book, this draft of XSL will probably have been superseded and the exact syntax of XSL will have changed. The formatting objects part of the specification is, if anything, even less complete than the transformation language specification. If you do encounter something that doesn't seem to work quite right, you should compare the examples in this book against the most current specification.

To make matters worse, no software implements all of the April 21, 1999 draft of the XSL specification, even just the formatting objects half. In fact, so far there's exactly one partial implementation of XSL formatting objects, James Tauber's FOP, which converts XML documents using the XSL formatting objects into PDF. There are no Web browsers that can display a document written with XSL formatting objects.

Eventually, of course, this should be straightened out as the standard evolves toward its final incarnation and more vendors implement XSL formatting objects. Until then, you're faced with a choice: You can either work out on the bleeding edge with XSL in its current, incomplete, unfinished state and try to work around all the bugs and omissions you'll encounter, or stick with a more established technology, such as CSS, until XSL is more solid.

Formatting Objects and Their Properties

There are exactly 51 XSL formatting object elements. Of the 51 elements, most signify various kinds of rectangular areas. Most of the rest are containers for rectangular areas and spaces. In alphabetical order, these formatting objects are:

- bidi-override
- block
- character
- display-graphic
- display-included-container
- display-rule
- display-sequence
- first-line-marker
- float
- flow
- footnote
- footnote-citation
- inline-graphic
- inline-included-container
- inline-rule
- inline-sequence
- layout-master-set
- list-block
- list-item
- list-item-body
- list-item-label
- multi-case
- multi-properties
- multi-property-set

- multi-switch
- multi-toggle
- page-number
- page-number-citation
- page-sequence
- region-after
- region-before
- region-body
- region-end
- region-start
- root
- sequence-specification
- sequence-specifier-alternating
- sequence-specifier-repeating
- sequence-specifier-single
- simple-link
- simple-page-master
- static-content
- table
- table-and-caption
- table-body
- table-caption
- table-cell
- table-column
- table-footer
- table-header
- table-row

The XSL formatting model is based on rectangular boxes called *areas* that can contain text, empty space, or other formatting objects. As with CSS boxes, each area has borders and padding on each of its sides, although CSS margins are replaced by XSL indents. An XSL formatter reads the formatting objects to determine which areas to place where on the page. Many formatting objects produce single areas (at least most of the time), but due to page breaks, word wrapping, hyphenation, and other aspects of fitting a potentially infinite amount of text into a finite area, some formatting objects do occasionally generate more than one area.

Note   A box that contains space is not the same as a box that contains whitespace characters. A box containing empty space refers to a physical blank area on the page or screen, for example the margins on the left and right sides of this page. This is not the same as the space characters between the words on this page.

The formatting objects differ primarily in what they contain. For example, the list-item-label formatting object is a box that contains a bullet, a number, or another indicator placed in front of a list item. A list-item-body formatting object is a box that contains the text, sans label, of the list item. And a list-item formatting object is a box that contains both the list-item-label and list-item formatting objects.

The formatting objects are further divided into four different kinds of rectangular areas:

1. area containers
2. block areas
3. line areas
4. inline-areas

These form a rough hierarchy. Area containers contain other smaller area containers and block areas. Block areas contain other block areas, line areas, and content. Line areas contain inline areas. Inline areas contain other inline areas and content. More specifically:

✦ An area container is the highest-level container in XSL. It can be positioned at precise coordinates inside the area that contains it. It can contain either other, smaller area containers or a sequence of block areas and display spaces. You can think of a page of this book as an area container that contains five other area containers: the header, the main body of the page, the footer, and the left and right margins. (In this example, the margin areas contain no content.) Formatting objects that produce area containers include `region-body`, `region-before`, `region-after`, `region-start`, and `region-end`.

✦ A block area represents a block-level element such as a paragraph or a list item. Although block areas may contain other block areas, there should always be a line break before the start and after the end of each block area. A block area, rather than being precisely positioned by coordinates, is placed sequentially in the area that contains it. As other block areas are added and deleted before it or within it, the block area's position shifts as necessary to make room. A block area may contain line areas, display spaces, and other block areas that are sequentially arranged in the containing block area. A block area also may contain a single graphic image. Formatting objects that produce block areas include `block`, `display-graphic`, `display-link`, `display-rule`, and `list-block`.

✦ A line area represents a line of text inside a block. For example, each separate line in this list item is a line area. Line areas can contain inline areas and inline spaces. There are no formatting objects that correspond to line areas. Instead, the formatting engine calculates the line areas as it decides how to wrap lines inside block areas.

✦ Inline areas are parts of a line such as a single character, a footnote reference, or a mathematical equation. Inline areas can contain other inline areas and inline spaces. Formatting objects that produce inline areas include `character`, `inline-graphic`, `inline-link`, `inline-rule`, `inline-sequence` and `page-number`.

The fo Namespace

XML elements for XSL formatting objects are placed in the `http://www.w3.org/XSL/Format/1.0` namespace with this declaration in an XSL stylesheet:

```
<xsl:stylesheet
  xmlns:xsl="http://www.w3.org/TR/WD-xsl"
  xmlns:fo="http://www.w3.org/XSL/Format/1.0"
  result-ns="fo">
```

About 99 times out of 100, the chosen prefix is `fo`. Consequently, you almost always see the following elements with the `fo` prefix in this form:

- `fo:bidi-override`
- `fo:block`
- `fo:character`
- `fo:display-graphic`
- `fo:display-included-container`
- `fo:display-rule`
- `fo:display-sequence`
- `fo:first-line-marker`
- `fo:float`
- `fo:flow`
- `fo:footnote`
- `fo:footnote-citation`
- `fo:inline-graphic`
- `fo:inline-included-container`
- `fo:inline-rule`
- `fo:inline-sequence`
- `fo:layout-master-set`
- `fo:list-block`
- `fo:list-item`
- `fo:list-item-body`
- `fo:list-item-label`
- `fo:multi-case`
- `fo:multi-properties`
- `fo:multi-property-set`

- `fo:multi-switch`
- `fo:multi-toggle`
- `fo:page-number`
- `fo:page-number-citation`
- `fo:page-sequence`
- `fo:region-after`
- `fo:region-before`
- `fo:region-body`
- `fo:region-end`
- `fo:region-start`
- `fo:root`
- `fo:sequence-specification`
- `fo:sequence-specifier-alternating`
- `fo:sequence-specifier-repeating`
- `fo:sequence-specifier-single`
- `fo:simple-link`
- `fo:simple-page-master`
- `fo:static-content`
- `fo:table`
- `fo:table-and-caption`
- `fo:table-body`
- `fo:table-caption`

- ✦ `fo:table-cell`
- ✦ `fo:table-column`
- ✦ `fo:table-footer`
- ✦ `fo:table-header`
- ✦ `fo:table-row`

In this chapter, I will use the `fo` prefix without further comment.

Cross-Reference Namespaces are discussed in Chapter 18, *Namespaces*. Until then, all you have to know is that the names of all XSL formatting object elements begin with `fo:`.

Formatting Properties

When taken as a whole, the various formatting objects in an XSL document specify the order in which content is to be placed on pages. However, all the details of formatting including but not limited to page size, element size, font, color, and a lot more are specified by XSL properties. These formatting properties are represented as attributes on the individual formatting object elements.

The details of many of these properties should be familiar from CSS. Work is ongoing to ensure that CSS and XSL use the same names to mean the same things. For example, the CSS property `font-family` means the same thing as the XSL `font-family` property; and although the syntax for assigning values to properties is different in CSS and XSL, the syntax of the values themselves is exactly the same. To indicate that the `fo:block` element is formatted in some approximation of Times, you might use this CSS rule:

```
fo:block {font-family: New York, Times New Roman, Times, serif}
```

The XSL equivalent is to include a `font-family` attribute in the `fo:block` start tag in this way:

```
<fo:block
   font-family="New York, Times New Roman, Times, serif">
```

Although this is superficially different, the style name (`font-family`) and the style value (`New York, Times New Roman, Times, serif`) are exactly the same. CSS's `font-family` property is specified as a list of font names, separated by commas, and in order from first choice to last choice. XSL's `font-family` property is specified as a list of font names, separated by commas, and in order from first choice to last choice. Both CSS and XSL understand the keyword `serif` to mean an arbitrary serif font.

Note As of the fourth draft of the XSL draft specification on which this chapter is based, complete synchronization between equivalent CSS and XSL properties isn't quite finished. This should be cleaned up in the next draft.

Of course, XSL formatting objects support many properties that have no CSS equivalent, such as `font-size-adjust`, `ligature`, `character`, and `hyphenation-keep`. You need to learn these to take full advantage of XSL. The standard XSL properties follow:

- `auto-restore`
- `azimuth`
- `background`
- `background-attachment`
- `background-color`
- `background-image`
- `background-position`
- `background-repeat`
- `border`
- `border-after-color`
- `border-after-style`
- `border-after-width`
- `border-before-color`
- `border-before-style`
- `border-before-width`
- `border-bottom`
- `border-bottom-color`
- `border-bottom-style`
- `border-bottom-width`
- `border-collapse`
- `border-color`
- `border-end-color`
- `border-end-style`
- `border-end-width`
- `border-left`
- `border-left-color`
- `border-left-style`
- `border-left-width`
- `border-right`
- `border-right-color`

- `border-right-style`
- `border-right-width`
- `border-spacing`
- `border-start-color`
- `border-start-style`
- `border-start-width`
- `border-style`
- `border-top`
- `border-top-color`
- `border-top-style`
- `border-top-width`
- `border-width`
- `bottom`
- `break-after`
- `break-before`
- `caption-side`
-
- `cell-height`
- `character`
- `clear`
- `clip`
- `color`
- `column-count`
- `column-gap`
- `column-number`
- `column-width`
- `country`
- `cue`
- `cue-after`
- `cue-before`

- ✦ digit-group-sep
- ✦ direction
- ✦ elevation
- ✦ empty-cells
- ✦ end-indent
- ✦ ends-row
- ✦ extent
- ✦ external-destination
- ✦ float
- ✦ flow-name
- ✦ font
- ✦ font-family
- ✦ font-height-override-after
- ✦ font-height-override-before
- ✦ font-size
- ✦ font-size-adjust
- ✦ font-stretch
- ✦ font-style
- ✦ font-variant
- ✦ font-weight
- ✦ format
- ✦ height
- ✦ href
- ✦ hyphenate
- ✦ hyphenation-char
- ✦ hyphenation-keep
- ✦ hyphenation-ladder-count
- ✦ hyphenation-push-char-count
- ✦ hyphenation-remain-char-count
- ✦ id
- ✦ indicate-destination
- ✦ inhibit-line-breaks
- ✦ initial
- ✦ initial-page-number
- ✦ internal-destination
- ✦ keep-with-next
- ✦ keep-with-previous
- ✦ language
- ✦ last-line-end-indent
- ✦ left
- ✦ length
- ✦ letter-spacing
- ✦ letter-value
- ✦ line-height
- ✦ line-height-shift-adjustment
- ✦ line-stacking-strategy
- ✦ margin
- ✦ margin-bottom
- ✦ margin-left
- ✦ margin-right
- ✦ margin-top
- ✦ max-height
- ✦ max-width
- ✦ may-break-after-row
- ✦ may-break-before-row
- ✦ min-height
- ✦ min-width
- ✦ name
- ✦ n-columns-repeated
- ✦ n-columns-spanned

- ✦ n-digits-per-group
- ✦ n-rows-spanned
- ✦ orphans
- ✦ overflow
- ✦ padding
- ✦ padding-after
- ✦ padding-before
- ✦ padding-bottom
- ✦ padding-end
- ✦ padding-left
- ✦ padding-right
- ✦ padding-start
- ✦ padding-top
- ✦ page-break-inside
- ✦ page-height
- ✦ page-master-blank-even
- ✦ page-master-even
- ✦ page-master-first
- ✦ page-master-last-even
- ✦ page-master-last-odd
- ✦ page-master-name
- ✦ page-master-odd
- ✦ page-master-repeating
- ✦ page-width
- ✦ pause
- ✦ pause-after
- ✦ pause-before
- ✦ pitch
- ✦ pitch-range
- ✦ play-during
- ✦ position
- ✦ precedence

- ✦ provisional-distance-between-starts
- ✦ provisional-label-separation
- ✦ reference-orientation
- ✦ ref-id
- ✦ richness
- ✦ right
- ✦ row-height
- ✦ rule-orientation
- ✦ rule-style
- ✦ rule-thickness
- ✦ scale
- ✦ score-spaces
- ✦ script
- ✦ sequence-src
- ✦ show-destination
- ✦ size
- ✦ space-above-destination-block
- ✦ space-above-destination-start
- ✦ space-after
- ✦ space-before
- ✦ space-between-list-rows
- ✦ space-end
- ✦ space-start
- ✦ span
- ✦ speak
- ✦ speak-header
- ✦ speak-numeral
- ✦ speak-punctuation
- ✦ speech-rate

- ✦ start-indent
- ✦ starts-row
- ✦ state
- ✦ stress
- ✦ switch-to
- ✦ table-height
- ✦ table-layout
- ✦ table-omit-middle-footer
- ✦ table-omit-middle-header
- ✦ table-width
- ✦ text-align
- ✦ text-align-last
- ✦ text-decoration
- ✦ text-indent

- ✦ text-shadow
- ✦ text-transform
- ✦ title
- ✦ top
- ✦ vertical-align
- ✦ visibility
- ✦ voice-family
- ✦ volume
- ✦ white-space-treatment
- ✦ widows
- ✦ width
- ✦ word-spacing
- ✦ wrap-option
- ✦ writing-mode
- ✦ z-index

Transforming to Formatting Objects

XSL formatting objects are a complete XML vocabulary used to arrange elements on a page. A document that uses XSL formatting objects is simply a well-formed XML document that uses this vocabulary. That means it has an XML declaration, a root element, child elements, and so forth. It must adhere to all the well-formedness rules of any XML document, or formatters will not accept it. By convention, a file that contains XSL formatting objects has the three-letter suffix .fob. However, it might have the suffix .xml because it also is a well-formed XML file.

Listing 15-1 is a simple document marked up using XSL formatting objects. The root of the document is fo:root. This element contains a fo:layout-master-set and a fo:page-sequence. The fo:layout-master-set element contains fo:simple-page-master child elements. Each fo:simple-page-master describes a kind of page on which content will be placed. Here there's only one very simple page, but more complex documents can have different master pages for first, right, and left, body pages, front matter, back matter, and more; each with a potentially different set of margins, page numbering, and other features.

Content is placed on copies of the master page using a `fo:page-sequence`. The `fo:page-sequence` contains a `fo:sequence-specification` specifying the order in which the different master pages should be used. Next, it contains a `fo:flow` child that holds the actual content to be placed on the master pages in the specified sequence. The content here is given as two The `fo:block` children each have a `font-size` property of 20 points and a `font-family` property of `serif`.

Listing 15-1: A simple document using the XSL formatting object vocabulary

```
<fo:root xmlns:fo="http://www.w3.org/XSL/Format/1.0">

  <fo:layout-master-set>
    <fo:simple-page-master page-master-name="only">
      <fo:region-body/>
    </fo:simple-page-master>
  </fo:layout-master-set>

  <fo:page-sequence>

    <fo:sequence-specification>
      <fo:sequence-specifier-single page-master-name="only"/>
    </fo:sequence-specification>

    <fo:flow>
      <fo:block font-size="20pt" font-family="serif">
        Hydrogen
      </fo:block>
      <fo:block font-size="20pt" font-family="serif">
        Helium
      </fo:block>
    </fo:flow>

  </fo:page-sequence>

</fo:root>
```

Although you could write a document such as the one in Listing 15-1 by hand, that would lose all the benefits of content-format independence achieved by XML. Normally you write an XSL style sheet that uses the XSL transformation vocabulary to transform the source document into the formatting object vocabulary. Listing 15-2 is the XSL style sheet that produced Listing 15-1 by transforming the previous chapter's Listing 14-1.

| Listing 15-2: **A transformation from a source vocabulary to XSL formatting objects** |

```xml
<?xml version="1.0"?>
<xsl:stylesheet
  xmlns:xsl="http://www.w3.org/XSL/Transform/1.0"
  xmlns:fo="http://www.w3.org/XSL/Format/1.0"
  result-ns="fo" indent-result="yes">

  <xsl:template match="/">
    <fo:root xmlns:fo="http://www.w3.org/XSL/Format/1.0">

      <fo:layout-master-set>
        <fo:simple-page-master page-master-name="only">
          <fo:region-body/>
        </fo:simple-page-master>
      </fo:layout-master-set>

      <fo:page-sequence>

        <fo:sequence-specification>
          <fo:sequence-specifier-single
              page-master-name="only"/>
        </fo:sequence-specification>

        <fo:flow>

         <xsl:apply-templates select="//ATOM"/>
        </fo:flow>

      </fo:page-sequence>

    </fo:root>
  </xsl:template>

  <xsl:template match="ATOM">
    <fo:block font-size="20pt" font-family="serif">
      <xsl:value-of select="NAME"/>
    </fo:block>
  </xsl:template>

</xsl:stylesheet>
```

Using FOP

At the time of this writing, no browser can directly display XML documents transformed into XSL formatting objects. There is only one piece of software that can work with a file marked up with XSL formatting objects, James Tauber's FOP. FOP is a free Java program that converts FO (formatting object) documents to

Adobe Acrobat PDF files. You can download the latest version of FOP at
`http://www.jtauber.com/fop/`.

At the time of this writing, the available version of FOP is 0.6.0, which incompletely
supports a subset of the formatting objects and properties in the fourth draft of
XSL. FOP is a Java program that should run on any platform with a reasonably
compatible Java 1.1 virtual machine. To install it, just place the fop.jar archive in
your CLASSPATH. The `com.jtauber.fop.FOP` class contains the `main()` method
for this program. Run it from the command line with arguments specifying the input
and output files. For example:

```
C:\XML\BIBLE\15>java com.jtauber.fop.FOP 15-1.fob 15-1.pdf
James Tauber's FOP 0.6.0
auto page-height: using 11in
auto page-width: using 8in
successfully read and parsed 15-1.fob
laying out page 1...
done page 1.
successfully wrote 15-1.pdf
```

Here 15-1.fob is the input XML file that uses the formatting object vocabulary.
15-1.pdf is the output PDF file that can be displayed and printed by Adobe Acrobat
or other programs that read PDF files.

Although PDF files are themselves ASCII text, this isn't a book about PostScript, so
there's nothing to be gained by showing you the exact output of the above
command. If you're curious, open the PDF file in any text editor. Instead, Figure 15-1
shows the rendered file displayed in Netscape Navigator using the Acrobat plug-in.

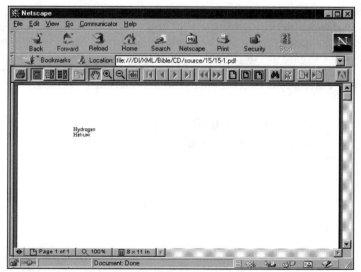

Figure 15-1: The PDF file displayed in Netscape Navigator

PDF files are not the only or even the primary eventual destination format for XML documents styled with XSL formatting objects. Certainly, one would hope that Web browsers will directly support XSL formatting objects in the not-too-distant future. For now, PDF files are the only available format, so that's what I show in this chapter. Eventually there should be more software that can read and display these files.

Page Layout

The root element of a formatting objects file is `fo:root`. This element contains one `fo:layout-master-set` element and zero or more `fo:page-sequence` elements. The `fo:root` element generally has an `xmlns:fo` attribute with the value `http://www.w3.org/XSL/Format/1.0` and may (though it generally does not) have an `id` attribute. The `fo:root` element exists just to declare the namespace and be the document root. It has no direct affect on page layout or formatting.

Master Pages

The `fo:layout-master-set` element is a container for all the different master pages used by the document. Simple page masters are similar in purpose to Quark XPress master pages or PowerPoint slide masters. Each defines a general layout for a page including its margins, the sizes of the header, footer, body area of the page, and so forth. Each actual page in the rendered document is based on one master page, and inherits certain properties like margins, page numbering, and layout from that master page.

Simple Page Masters

Each master page is represented by a `fo:simple-page-master` element. A `fo:layout-master-set` may contain one or more of these. A `fo:simple-page-master` element defines the layout of a page including the size of its before region, body region, after region, end region, and start region. Figure 15-2 shows the typical layout of these parts. The body is everything in the middle that's left over.

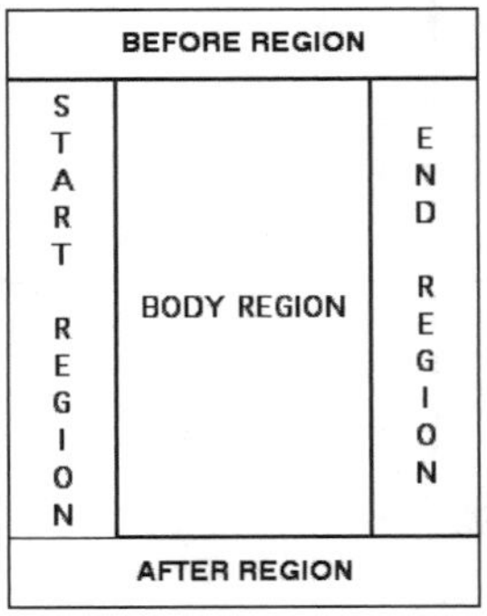

Figure 15-2: The layout of the parts of a simple page of English text

In normal English text, the end region is the right side of the page and the start region is the left side of the page. This is reversed in Hebrew or Arabic text, because these languages read from right to left. In almost all modern languages, the before region is the header and the after region is the footer, but this could be reversed in a language that wrote from bottom to top.

The designer sets the size of the body (center) region, header, footer, end region, and start region as well as the distances between them using the appropriate region child elements. These are:

✦ `fo:region-before`

✦ `fo:region-after`

✦ `fo:region-body`

✦ `fo:region-start`

✦ `fo:region-end`

Each of the five regions of a simple page master may be filled with content from a `fo:flow` or `fo:static-content` element.

The `simple-page-master` element generally has three main attributes:

1. `page-master-name`: the name of this page master that page sequences will use to select the master page a particular page will be based on

2. `page-height`: the height of the page

3. `page-width`: the width of the page

The `page-height` and `page-width` can be subsumed into a single shorthand `size` property. If they are not provided, then the formatter chooses a reasonable default based on the media being used (e.g. 8.5" by 11").

For example, here is a `fo:layout-master-set` containing two `fo:simple-page-master` elements, one for even (left) pages and one for odd (right) pages. Both specify an 8.5-by-11-inch page size. Both have top and bottom margins of 0.5 inches. Each has an inner margin of 0.5 inches and an outer margin of 1 inch, as is common for facing pages.

```
<fo:layout-master-set>
  <fo:simple-page-master page-master-name="even"
     height="8.5in"        width="11in"
     margin-top="0.5in"    margin-bottom="0.5in"
     margin-left="1.0in"   margin-right="0.5in">
    <fo:region-body/>
  </fo:simple-page-master>
```

```
<fo:simple-page-master page-master-name="odd"
    height="8.5in"          width="11in"
    margin-top="0.5in"      margin-bottom="0.5in"
    margin-left="0.5in"     margin-right="1.0in">
    <fo:region-body/>
  </fo:simple-page-master>
</fo:layout-master-set>
```

Other attributes commonly applied to page masters include:

✦ Attributes that affect the margins of the page: `margin-bottom`, `margin-left`, `margin-right`, `margin-top`, `margin`

✦ Attributes that affect the direction of the writing on the page: `writing-mode`, `reference-orientation`

Region Properties

The five regions (`before`, `after`, `body`, `start`, `end`) share the same basic properties. These include:

✦ Attributes that determine how content that overflows the borders of the region is handled: `clip`, `overflow`

✦ Attribute that determine how the content is wrapped in columns: `column-count`, which isthe number of columns in the region, and `column-gap`, which is the distance between columns

✦ Attributes that affect the background of the region: `background`, `background-attachment`, `background-color`, `background-image`, `background-repeat`, `background-position`

✦ Attributes that affect the border of the region: `border-before-color`, `border-before-style`, `border-before-width`, `border-after-color`, `border-after-style`, `border-after-width`, `border-start-color`, `border-start-style`, `border-start-width`, `border-end-color`, `border-end-style`, `border-end-width`, `border-top-color`, `border-top-style`, `border-top-width`, `border-bottom-color`, `border-bottom-style`, `border-bottom-width`, `border-left-color`, `border-left-style`, `border-left-width`, `border-right-color`, `border-right-style`, `border-right-width`, `border`, `border-top`, `border-bottom`, `border-left`, `border-right`, `border-color`, `border-style`, `border-width`

✦ Attributes that affect the padding of the region: `padding-bottom`, `padding-left`, `padding-right`, `padding-top`, `padding-bottom`, `padding-start`, `padding-end`, `padding-before`, `padding-after`, `padding`

✦ Attributes that affect the margins of the region: `margin-bottom`, `margin-left`, `margin-right`, `margin-top`, `margin`, `margin`, `space-before`, `space-after`, `start-indent`, `end-indent`

✦ Attributes that affect the direction of the writing in the region: `writing-mode`, `reference-orientation`

Most of these properties should be familiar from the CSS properties of the same name. Reasonable defaults are picked for all these values if they're not explicitly set. By adjusting them, you affect the overall layout of the page.

Additionally, the four outer regions (before, after, start, and end but not body) have an `extent` property that determines the size of the region. The size of the body is determined by whatever's left over in the middle after the other four regions are accounted for.

For example, here is a `fo:layout-master-set` that makes all outer regions one inch. Each region is given a two-pixel black border. Furthermore, the page itself has a half-inch margin on all sides.

```
<fo:layout-master-set>
  <fo:simple-page-master page-master-name="only"
      height="8.5in" width="11in"
      margin-top="0.5in"      margin-bottom="0.5in"
      margin-left="1.0in"     margin-right="0.5in">
    <fo:region-start extent="1.0in"
      border-color="black" border-width="2px"/>
    <fo:region-before extent="1.0in"
      border-color="black" border-width="2px"/>
    <fo:region-body
      border-color="black" border-width="2px"/>
    <fo:region-end  extent="1.0in"
      border-color="black" border-width="2px"/>
    <fo:region-after  extent="1.0in"
      border-color="black" border-width="2px"/>
  </fo:simple-page-master>
</fo:layout-master-set>
```

The body pages based on this page master will be 5.5 inches wide and 8 inches high. That's calculated by subtracting the size of everything else on the page from the size of the page.

Page Sequences

As well as a `fo:layout-master-set`, each formatting object document will generally contain one or more `fo:page-sequence` elements. Each page sequence contains three things in the following order:

✦ One `fo:sequence-specification` element defining the order in which the master pages are used

✦ Zero or more `fo:static-content` elements containing text to be placed on every page

✦ One `fo:flow` element containing data to be placed on each page in turn

The main difference between a `fo:flow` and a `fo:static-content` is that text from the flow isn't placed on more than one page, whereas the static content is. For example, the lines you're reading now are flow content that only appear on this page, whereas the part and chapter titles at the top of the page are static content that is repeated from page to page.

The `fo:sequence-specification` provides a list of the master pages for this sequence. Each page in the sequence has an associated page master that defines how the page will look. Listing 15-1 only used a single master page, but it is not uncommon to have more; for instance, one for the first page of a chapter, one for all the subsequent left-hand pages, and one for all the subsequent right-hand pages. For instance, there might be one simple page master for a table of contents, another for body text, and a third for the index. In this case, there is one page sequence each for the table of contents, the body text, and the index.

The `fo:flow` element contains, in order, the elements to be placed on the page. As each page fills up with elements from the flow, a new page is created with the next master layout in the sequence specification for the elements that remain in the flow.

The `fo:static-content` element contains information to be placed on each page. For instance, it may place the title of the book in the header of each page. Static content can be adjusted depending on the master page. For instance, the part title may be placed on left-hand pages, and the chapter title on right-hand pages. The `fo:static-content` element can also be used for items like page numbers that have to be calculated from page to page when the same calculation is repeated. In other words, what is static is not the text, but the calculation that produces the text.

Sequence Specifications

The `fo:sequence-specification` element lists the order in which particular master pages will be instantiated using one or more of these three child elements:

✦ fo:sequence-specifier-single

✦ fo:sequence-specifier-alternating

✦ fo:sequence-specifier-repeating

Each of these child elements has attributes that determine which master pages are used when. The simplest is `fo:sequence-specifier-single` whose `page-master-name` attribute identifies the master page to be instantiated. For example, this `fo:sequence-specification` element says that all content must be placed on a single instance of the master page named letter:

```
<fo:sequence-specification>
  <fo:sequence-specifier-single page-master-name="letter"/>
</fo:sequence-specification>
```

If there's more content than will fit on a single page, then the extra content is either truncated or scrolled, depending on the values of the clip and overflow attributes of the various regions where the content is placed. However, no more than one page will be created. Now consider this sequence specification:

```
<fo:sequence-specification>
  <fo:sequence-specifier-single page-master-name="letter"/>
  <fo:sequence-specifier-single page-master-name="letter"/>
</fo:sequence-specification>
```

This provides for up to pages, each based on the letter page master. If the first page fills up, a second will be created. If that page fills up, then content will be truncated or scrolled.

The same technique can be used to apply different master pages. For example, this sequence specification bases the first page on the master page named letter1 and the second on the master page named letter2:

```
<fo:sequence-specification>
  <fo:sequence-specifier-single page-master-name="letter1"/>
  <fo:sequence-specifier-single page-master-name="letter2"/>
</fo:sequence-specification>
```

Of course, most of the time you don't know in advance exactly how many pages there will be. The fo:sequence-specifier-alternating and fo:sequence-specifier-repeating elements let you specify that as many pages as necessary will be used to hold the content. The fo:sequence-specifier-repeating element specifies one master page for the first page and a second master page for all subsequent pages. The fo:sequence-specifier-alternating element specifies up to six different master pages for the first page, even pages with content, odd pages with content, blank even pages, last even pages, and last odd pages.

For example, this sequence specifier says that the first page output should use the master page named letter first, but that all subsequent pages should use the master page named letter:

```
<fo:sequence-specification>
  <fo:sequence-specifier-repeating
    page-master-first="letter_first"
    page-master-repeating="letter"
  />
</fo:sequence-specification>
```

If the total content overflows the first page, it will be placed on a second page. If it overflows the second page, a third page will be created. As many pages as needed to hold all the content will be constructed.

Tip

At the time of this writing, it has not yet been decided whether or not `page-master-first` and `page-master-repeating` are both required. However, if you only have a single master page, you can certainly reuse it as the value for both `page-master-first` and `page-master-repeating` like this:

```
<fo:sequence-specification>
<fo:sequence-specifier-repeating
  page-master-first="letter"
  page-master-repeating="letter"
/>
</fo:sequence-specification>
```

The `fo:sequence-specifier-alternating` element is designed more for a chapter of a printed book in which the first and last pages, as well as the even and odd pages, traditionally have different margins, headers, and footers. This element has attributes that allow you to specify master pages for all these different pages. For example:

```
<fo:sequence-specification>
<fo:sequence-specifier-repeating
  page-master-first="chapter_first"
  page-master-even="chapter_even"
  page-master-blank-even="chapter_blank"
  page-master-odd="chapter_odd"
  page-master-last-even="chapter_last_even"
  page-master-last-odd="chapter_last_odd"
  page-master-repeating="letter"
/>
</fo:sequence-specification>
```

Note

If the above attributes seem a little asymmetrical — for instance, there's no `page-master-blank-odd` attribute — that's because traditional publishing is asymmetrical. If you look carefully at the pages of this book, and indeed at almost any other book you own, you'll notice that the odd-numbered pages are always on the right, the even-numbered pages on the left, and that chapters always begin on a right-hand page. Chapters can end on either right-hand (odd) or left-hand (even) pages, but if they do end on an odd page, then a blank even page is inserted so the next chapter begins on an odd page.

Flows

The `fo:flow` object holds the actual content which will be placed on the instances of the master pages specified by the sequence specification. This content is composed of a sequence of `fo:block`, `fo:display-graphic`, `fo:display-link`, `fo:display-rule`, and other block-level elements. In this section, we'll stick to basic `fo:block` elements, which are roughly equivalent to HTML's `DIV` elements. Later in this chapter, we'll see a lot more block-level elements a flow can contain.

For example, here is a basic flow containing the names of several atoms, each in its own block:

```
<fo:flow name="xsl-body">
  <fo:block>Actinium</fo:block>
  <fo:block>Aluminum</fo:block>
  <fo:block>Americium</fo:block>
</fo:flow>
```

The name attribute of the fo:flow, here with the value xsl-body, specifies which of the five regions of the page this flow's content will be placed in. The allowed values are:

✦ xsl-body

✦ xsl-after

✦ xsl-before

✦ xsl-start

✦ xsl-end

For example, a flow for the header (in left-to-right, top-to-bottom English text) has a flow-name value of xsl-before. Here is a flow for a footer:

```
<fo:flow id="q2" flow-name="xsl-after">
  <fo:block>
     The XML Bible
     Chapter 15: XSL Formatting Objects
  </fo:block>
</fo:flow>
```

Static Content

Whereas each piece of the content of a fo:flow element appears on one page, each piece of the content of a fo:static-content element appears on every page; a header or a footer for example. You do not have to use fo:static-content elements, but if you do use them, they must appear before all the fo:flow elements in the page sequence.

fo:static-content elements have the same attributes and contents as a fo:flow. However, because a fo:static-content cannot break its contents across multiple pages, if necessary, it will generally have less content than a fo:flow. For example, here is a fo:static-content for a header:

```
<fo:static-content id="sc2" flow-name="xsl-before">
  <fo:block>
     The XML Bible
     Chapter 15: XSL Formatting Objects
  </fo:block>
</fo:static-content>
```

Page Numbering

Besides the usual `id` attribute that any formatting object element can have, `fo:page-sequence` element has six optional attributes that define page numbering for the sequence. These are:

- ✦ `initial-page-number`
- ✦ `format`
- ✦ `letter-value`
- ✦ `digit-group-sep`
- ✦ `n-digits-per-group`
- ✦ `sequence-src`

The `initial-page-number` attribute defines the number of the first page in this sequence. The most likely value for this attribute is 1, but it could be a larger number if the previous pages are in a different file. The remaining five attributes have exactly the same syntax and meaning as when used as attributes of the `xsl:number` element from the XSL transformation language.

The `xsl:number` element and the `format`, `letter-value`, `digit-group-sep`, `n-digits-per-group`, `sequence-src` attributes are discussed in the "Number to String Conversion" section in Chapter 14, *XSL Transformations*.

The `fo:page-number` formatting object is an empty inline element that inserts the number of the current page. The formatter is responsible for determining what that number is. This element has only a single attribute, `id`. Otherwise, you wrap `fo:page-number` in a `fo:inline-sequence`, `fo:block`, or similar element to apply font properties and the like to it. For example, this footer uses `fo:static-content` and `fo:page-number` to put the page number at the bottom of every page:

```
<fo:static-content id="sc2" flow-name="xsl-after">
  <fo:block>
     <fo:page-number/>
  </fo:block>
</fo:static-content>
```

This page sequence specifies that the page number uses small Roman numerals and begins counting from ten.

```
<fo:page-sequence initial-page-number="10" format="i">

  <!- sequence specification ->

  <fo:static-content flow-name="xsl-after">
    <fo:block text-align-last="centered" font-size="10pt">
      <fo:page-number/>
    </fo:block>
  </fo:static-content>
```

```
<!- flows ->

</fo:page-sequence>
```

Content

The content (as opposed to markup) of an XSL formatting objects document is mostly text. Additionally, external images can be linked to in a fashion similar to the IMG element of HTML. This content is stored in several kinds of elements including:

✦ Block-level formatting objects

✦ Inline formatting objects

✦ Table formatting objects

✦ Out-of-line formatting objects

All of these different kinds of elements will be descendants of either a fo:flow or a fo:static-content element. They are never placed directly on page masters or page sequences.

Block-level Formatting Objects

A block-level formatting object is drawn as a rectangular area separated by a line break and possibly extra whitespace from any content that precedes or follows it. Blocks may contain other blocks, in which case the contained blocks also are separated from the containing block by a line break and perhaps extra whitespace. Block-level formatting objects include:

✦ fo:block

✦ fo:display-graphic

✦ fo:display-rule

✦ fo:display-included-container

✦ fo:display-sequence

✦ fo:list

✦ fo:list-item

The fo:block element is the XSL equivalent of display: block in CSS or DIV in HTML. Blocks may be contained in fo:flow elements, other fo:block elements, and fo:static-content elements. fo:block elements may contain other fo:block elements, other block-level elements such as fo:display-graphic and fo:display-rule, and inline elements such as fo:inline-sequence and fo:page-number. They may also contain raw text. For example:

```
<fo:block>
   <fo:inline-sequence font-style="italic">
     The XML Bible
   </fo:inline-sequence>
   Page <fo:page-number/>
   <fo:inline-sequence>
      Chapter 15: XSL Formatting Objects
   </fo:inline-sequence>
</fo:block>
```

The fo:block elements generally have attributes for both area properties and text formatting properties. The text formatting properties are inherited by any child elements of the block unless overridden. Allowed properties include:

✦ **alignment properties:** text-align **and** text-align-last

✦ **aural properties:** azimuth, cue, cue-after, cue-before, elevation, pause, pause-after, pause-before, pitch, pitch-range, play-during, richness, speak, speak-header, speak-numeral, speak-punctuation, speech-rate, stress, voice-family, **and** volume

✦ **background properties:** background, background-attachment, background-color, background-image, background-position, **and** background-repeat

✦ **border properties:** border-before-color, border-before-style, border-before-width, border-after-color, border-after-style, border-after-width, border-start-color, border-start-style, border-start-width, border-end-color, border-end-style, border-end-width, border-top-color, border-top-style, border-top-width, border-bottom-color, border-bottom-style, border-bottom-width, border-left-color, border-left-style, border-left-width, border-right-color, border-right-style, border-right-width, border, border-top, border-bottom, border-left, border-right, border-color, border-style, **and** border-width

✦ **break properties:** page-break-inside, widows, orphans, **and** wrap-option

✦ **color properties:** color

✦ **column properties:** span

✦ **font properties:** font-family, system-font, font-size, font-size-adjust, font-stretch, font-style, font-variant, font-weight, **and** font

✦ **hyphenation properties:** country, hyphenate, hyphenation-char, hyphenation-push-char-count, hyphenation-remain-char-count, language, script, hyphenation-keep, **and** hyphenation-ladder-count

✦ **indentation properties:** text-indent **and** last-line-end-indent

✦ **layering property:** z-index

- ✦ **line-height properties:** `line-height`, `line-height-shift-adjustment` and, `line-stacking-strategy`
- ✦ **margin properties:** `margin-bottom`, `margin-left`, `margin-right`, `margin-top`, `margin`, `margin`, `space-before`, `space-after`, `start-indent`, **and** `end-indent`
- ✦ **padding properties:** `padding-top`, `padding-bottom`, `padding-left`, `padding-right`, `padding-before`, `padding-after`, `padding-start`, **and** `padding-end`
- ✦ **position properties:** `position`, `top`, `bottom`, `right`, **and** `left`
- ✦ **text direction properties:** `writing-mode`
- ✦ **visibility property:** `visibility`
- ✦ **whitespace properties:** `white-space-treatment`

Most of these are familiar from CSS. The rest will be discussed below. The other block-level elements have very similar property lists.

Inline Formatting Objects

An inline formatting object is drawn as a rectangular area that may contain text or other inline areas. Inline areas are most commonly arranged in lines running from left to right. When a line fills up, a new line is started below the previous one. However, the exact order in which inline elements are placed depends on the writing mode. For example, when working in Hebrew or Arabic, it makes sense to first place inline elements on the left and then fill to the right. Inline formatting objects include:

- ✦ `fo:bidi-override`
- ✦ `fo:character`
- ✦ `fo:first-line-marker`
- ✦ `fo:inline-graphic`
- ✦ `fo:inline-included-container`
- ✦ `fo:inline-rule`
- ✦ `fo:inline-sequence`
- ✦ `fo:list-item-body`
- ✦ `fo:list-item-label`
- ✦ `fo:page-number`
- ✦ `fo:page-number-citation`

Table-formatting Objects

The table formatting objects designed are the XSL equivalents of CSS2 table properties. However, tables do work somewhat more naturally in XSL than in CSS. For the most part, an individual table is a block-level object, while the parts of the table aren't really either inline or block level. However, an entire table can be turned into an inline object by wrapping it in a `fo:inline-included-container`.

There are nine XSL table-formatting objects:

- ✦ `fo:table-and-caption`
- ✦ `fo:table`
- ✦ `fo:table-caption`
- ✦ `fo:table-column`
- ✦ `fo:table-header`
- ✦ `fo:table-footer`
- ✦ `fo:table-body`
- ✦ `fo:table-row`
- ✦ `fo:table-cell`

The root of a table is not a `fo:table`, but rather a `fo:table-and-caption` which contains a `fo:table` and a `fo:caption`. The fo:table contains a `fo:table-header`, `fo:table-body`, and `fo:table-footer`. The table body contains `fo:table-row` elements which are divided up into `fo:table-cell` elements.

Out-of-line Formatting Objects

There are three out-of-line formatting objects:

- ✦ `fo:float`
- ✦ `fo:footnote`
- ✦ `fo:footnote-citation`

Out-of-line formatting objects "borrow" space from existing inline or block objects. On the page, they do not necessarily appear between the same elements they appeared between in the input formatting object XML tree.

Rules

A rule is a horizontal line inserted into text. XSL has two kinds of horizontal lines. The `fo:display-rule` formatting object is a block-level element that creates a horizontal line such as that produced by HTML's `<HR>` tag. The `fo:inline-rule` formatting object element is similar to the `fo:display-rule` element. However, as the name suggests, `fo:inline-rule` is an inline element instead of a block-level element. Thus, it may appear in the middle of a line of text and does not imply a line break. For example, this is a display rule:

However, this _____ is an inline rule.

Both the `fo:inline-rule` and `fo:display-rule` elements have six primary attributes that describe them:

1. `length:` the length of the line, such as `12pc` or `5in`

2. `rule-orientation:` escapement, horizontal, line-progression, or vertical

3. `rule-style:` exact values remain to be determined at the time of this writing

4. `rule-thickness:` the thickness of the line, such as `1px` or `0.1cm`

5. `vertical-align:` baseline, bottom, middle, sub, super, text-bottom, text-top, top, or a length or percentage of the line height

6. `color:` the color of the line, such as `pink` or `#FFCCCC`

For example, this is a green block-level rule that's 7.5 inches long and 2 points thick:

```
<fo:display-rule length="7.5in"
                 line-thickness="2pt" color="#00FF00"/>
```

Additionally, the `fo:display-rule` can have most of the usual attributes of a block-level element like those describing margins and padding, and a `fo:inline-rule` can have the usual attributes of an inline element like `line-height`. The exceptions are those attributes that are directly related to text, like font-family. Obviously, these attributes make no sense for a rule.

Graphics

XSL provides two means of embedding pictures in a rendered document. The `fo:display-graphic` element inserts a block-level graphic. The `fo:inline-graphic` element inserts an inline graphic. These two elements provide the equivalent of an HTML `IMG` tag. Six attributes describe the picture:

1. `href`: the URI of the image file
2. `min-height`: the minimum vertical height of the image
3. `min-width`: the minimum horizontal width of the image
4. `max-height`: the maximum vertical height of the image
5. `max-width`: the maximum horizontal width of the image
6. `scale`: with a value `max`, expand the graphic to the size of `max-height` and `max-width`; with the value `max-uniform`, expand the graphic by the same amount in the vertical and horizontal directions to either the `max-height` or `max-width`, whichever comes first; with the value a single real number, multiply both height and width by that number; with the value two real numbers, multiply width by the first and height by the second

For example, consider this standard HTML `IMG` element:

```
<IMG SRC="logo.gif" WIDTH="100" HEIGHT="100"
     ALIGN="right" ALT="alt text" BORDER="0">
```

The `fo:display-graphic` element equivalent looks like this:

```
<fo:display-graphic image="logo.gif"
                    height="100px" width="100px" />
```

Links

For online presentations only, XSL provides the `fo:simple-link` element. Assuming a Web browser-style user interface, clicking anywhere on the contents of a link element jumps to the link target. This element can act as either a block-level or inline link depending on what it contains. The link behavior is controlled by these six attributes:

✦ external-destination

✦ internal-destination

✦ indicate-destination

✦ show-destination

✦ space-above-destination-block

✦ space-above-destination-start

A link to a remote document target specifies the URI through the value of the external-destination attribute. The document at this URI should be loaded when the link is activated. In GUI environments, the link most likely is activated by clicking on the link contents. For example:

```
<fo:block> Be sure to visit the
    <fo:simple-link
      external-destination="http://metalab.unc.edu/xml/">
      Cafe con Leche Web site!
    </fo:simple-link>
</fo:block>
```

You can also link to another node in the same document by using the internal-destination attribute. The value of this attribute is not a URI, but rather the ID of the element you're linking to. You should not specify both the internal and external destination for one link.

The other four attributes affect the appearance and behavior of the link. The indicate-destination attribute has a Boolean value (true or false, false by default) that specifies whether, when the linked item is loaded it should somehow be distinguished from non-linked parts of the same document. For example, if you follow a link to one ATOM element in a table of 100 atoms, the specific atom you were connecting to might be in bold face while the other atoms would be in normal type. The exact details are system dependent.

The show-destination attribute has two possible values, replace (the default) and new. With a value of replace, when a link is followed it replaces the existing document in the same window. With a value of new, when a link is followed, the targeted document is opened in a new window.

When a browser follows an HTML link into the middle of a document, generally the specific linked element is positioned at the tippy-top of the window. The space-above-destination-start and space-above-destination-block attributes let you specify that the browser should position the linked element further down in the window by leaving a certain amount of space (not empty space, it will generally contain the content preceding the linked element) above the linked item.

In addition, the link may have an usual property such as color that will be inherited by the link's contents. This allows you to format content that's in a link differently from content that's not; for example, by underlining all links. However, XSL formatting objects do not provide a means to distinguish between visited, unvisited, and active links, unlike CSS and HTML which do.

Lists

The `fo:list-block` formatting object element describes a block-level list element. (There are no inline lists.) A list may or may not be bulleted, numbered, indented, or otherwise formatted. Each `fo:list-block` element contains either a series of `fo:list-item` elements or `fo:list-item-label` `fo:list-item-body` pairs. (It cannot contain both.) A `fo:list-item` must contain a `fo:list-item-label` and a `fo:list-item-body`. The `fo:list-item-label` contains the bullet, number, or other label for the list item. The `fo:list-item-body` contains the actual content of the list item. To summarize, a `fo:list-block` contains `fo:list-item` elements. Each `fo:list-item` contains a `fo:list-item-label` and `fo:list-item-body`. However, the `fo:list-item` elements can be omitted. For example:

```
<fo:list-block>
  <fo:list-item>
    <fo:list-item-label>*</fo:list-item-label>
    <fo:list-item-body>Actinium</fo:list-item-body>
  </fo:list-item>
  <fo:list-item>
    <fo:list-item-label>*</fo:list-item-label>
    <fo:list-item-body>Aluminum</fo:list-item-body>
  </fo:list-item>
</fo:list-block>
```

Or, with the `fo:list-item` tags removed:

```
<fo:list-block>
  <fo:list-item-label>*</fo:list-item-label>
  <fo:list-item-body>Actinium</fo:list-item-body>
  <fo:list-item-label>*</fo:list-item-label>
  <fo:list-item-body>Aluminum</fo:list-item-body>
</fo:list-block>
```

The `fo:list-block` element has three special attributes:

1. `provisional-label-separation`: the distance between the list item label and the list item body, given as a triplet of maximum;minimum;optimum, such as `2cm;0.5cm;1cm`.

2. `provisional-distance-between-starts`: the distance between the start edge of the list item label and the start edge of the list item body.

3. `space-between-list-rows`: vertical distance between successive list items, given as a triplet of maximum;minimum;optimum, such as `36pt;4pt;12pt`.

The `fo:list-item` element has the standard block-level properties for backgrounds, position, aural rendering, borders, padding, margins, line and page breaking.

Tables

The fundamental table element in XSL is a `fo:table-and-caption`. This is a block-level object. However, it can be turned into an inline object by wrapping it in a `fo:inline-included-container` or an out-of-line object by wrapping it in a `fo:float`. The table model is quite close to HTML's. Table 15-1 shows the equivalence between HTML 4.0 table elements and XSL formatting objects:

Table 15-1	
HTML Tables versus XSL Formatting Object Tables	
HTML Element	**XSL FO Element**
TABLE	fo:table-and-caption
no equivalent	fo:table
CAPTION	fo:table-caption
COL	fo:table-column
COLGROUP	no equivalent
THEAD	fo:table-header
TBODY	fo:table-body
TFOOT	fo:table-footer
TD	fo:table-cell
TR	fo:table-row

The `fo:table-and-caption` contains an optional `fo:caption` element and one `fo:table` element. The caption can contain any block-level elements you care to place in the caption. By default, captions are placed before the table, but this can be adjusted by setting the `caption-side` property of the `table-and-caption` element to one of these eight values:

- ✦ before
- ✦ after
- ✦ start
- ✦ end
- ✦ top
- ✦ bottom
- ✦ left
- ✦ right

For example, here's a table with a caption on the bottom:

```
<fo:table-and-caption caption-side="bottom">
  <fo:table-caption>
    <fo:block font-weight="bold"
            font-family="Helvetica, Arial, sans"
            font-size="12pt">
      Table 15-1: HTML Tables vs. XSL Formatting Object Tables
    </fo:block>
  </fo:table-caption>
  <fo:table>
    <!-- table contents go here -->
  </fo:table>
</fo:table-and-caption>
```

The `fo:table` element contains an optional `fo:table-column`, `fo:table-header`, an optional `fo:table-footer`, and one or more `fo:table-body` elements. The `fo:table-body` is divided into `fo:table-row` elements. Each `fo:table-row` is divided into `fo:table-cell` elements. The `fo:table-header` and `fo:table-footer` can either be divided into `fo:table-cell` or `fo:table-row` elements. For example, here's a simple table that matches the first three rows of Table 15-1:

```
<fo:table>
  <fo:table-header>
    <fo:table-cell>
      <fo:block font-family="Helvetica, Arial, sans"
              font-size="11pt" font-weight="bold">
        HTML Element
      </fo:block>
    </fo:table-cell>
    <fo:table-cell>
      <fo:block font-family="Helvetica, Arial, sans"
              font-size="11pt" font-weight="bold">
        XSL FO Element
      </fo:block>
    </fo:table-cell>
  </fo:table-header>
  <fo:table-body>
    <fo:table-row>
      <fo:table-cell>
        <fo:block font-family="Courier, monospace">
          TABLE
        </fo:block>
      </fo:table-cell>
      <fo:table-cell>
        <fo:block font-family="Courier, monospace">
          fo:table-and-caption
        </fo:block>
      </fo:table-cell>
    </fo:table-row>
    <fo:table-row>
      <fo:table-cell>
        <fo:block>no equivalent</fo:block>
```

```
          </fo:table-cell>
          <fo:table-cell>
            <fo:block font-family="Courier, monospace">
              fo:table
            </fo:block>
          </fo:table-cell>
        </fo:table-row>
      </fo:table-body>
    </fo:table>
```

Table cells can span multiple rows and columns by setting the `n-columns-spanned` and/or `n-rows-spanned` attributes to an integer giving the number of rows or columns to span. The optional `column-number` attribute can change which column the spanning begins in. The default is the current column.

Borders can be drawn around table parts using the normal border properties which we'll discuss later. The `empty-cells` attribute has the value `show` or `hide`, `show` if borders are to be drawn around cells with no content, `hide` if not. The default is `show`.

Most table parts do not use the standard width and height properties. Instead, they have equivalent attributes. Any or all of these may be omitted, in which case the formatter will simply size everything as it sees fit:

✦ `table`: `table-width`, `table-height`

✦ `table-caption`: `caption-width`, **height determined automatically by the formatter**

✦ `table-row`: `row-height`, **width determined by contents**

✦ `table-cell`: `cell-height`, `column-number`, **column-width**, `n-columns-spanned`, `n-rows-spanned`

The `fo:table-row` element has optional `may-break-after-row` and `may-break-before-row` attributes with the values `yes` or `no` that determine whether a page break is allowed before and after the row. The defaults are both `yes`.

When a long table extends across multiple pages, the header and footer are sometimes repeated on each page. You can specify this behavior with the `table-omit-middle-header` and `table-omit-middle-footer` attributes of the `fo:table` element. The value `yes` indicates that the header or footer is to be repeated from page to page. The value `no` indicates that it is not. The default is `no`.

The optional `fo:table-column` element is an empty element that specifies values for all cells in a particular column. The cells it applies to are identified by the `column-number` attribute. `fo:table-column` does not actually contain any cells. A `fo:table-column` can apply properties to more than one consecutive column by setting the `n-columns-spanned` property to an integer greater than one. The most common property to set in a `fo:table-column` is `column-width` (a signed length) but the standard border, padding, and background properties (discussed below) can also be set.

Characters

The `fo:character` formatting object replaces a particular character or string of characters in the input with a different character in the output. You might use this to translate between the American decimal point and the French decimal comma, for example. The `character` attribute specifies what replacement character to use. For example, this template rule substitutes * for the characters in a PASSWORD element:

```
<xsl:template match="PASSWORD">
  <fo:character character="*">
    <xsl:value-of select="."/>
  </fo:character>
</xsl:template>
```

However, this use is rare. The main purpose of the `fo:character` element is so that formatting engines can treat each character and glyph as its own element. If you're not writing a formatting engine, you probably can ignore this element.

Sequences

Sequences have no particular effect on the layout of either inline or block-level boxes. They're simply elements on which you can hang formatting attributes such as `font-style` or `text-indent` for application to the sequence's children.

The `fo:display-sequence` formatting object element is a container that groups block-level objects together. In fact, it can only hold block-level elements such as `fo:display-graphic` and `fo:block`. It cannot contain inline elements or raw text.

The `fo:inline-sequence` formatting object element is a container that groups inline objects together. It cannot contain block-level elements. For example, you can use `inline-sequence` elements to add style to various parts of the footer, like this:

```
<fo:flow id="q2" flow-name="xsl-after">
  <fo:block font-style="bold" font-size="10pt"
            font-family="Arial, Helvetica, sans">
    <fo:inline-sequence font-style="italic"
                        text-align="start">
      The XML Bible
    </fo:inline-sequence>
    <fo:inline-sequence text-align="centered">
      Page <fo:page-number/>
    </fo:inline-sequence>
    <fo:inline-sequence text-align="right">
      Chapter 15: XSL Formatting Objects
    </fo:inline-sequence>
  </fo:block>
</fo:flow>
```

Footnotes

The `fo:footnote` element represents a footnote. The author places the `fo:footnote` element in the flow exactly where the footnote reference like [1] or [*] will occur. The `fo:footnote` element contains both a `fo:footnote-reference` and a block-level element containing the text of the footnote. However, only the footnote reference is inserted inline. The formatter places the note text in the after region (generally the footer) of the page.

For example, this footnote uses an asterisk as a footnote marker and refers to "*JavaBeans*, Elliotte Rusty Harold (IDG Books, Foster City, 1998), p. 147". Standard XSL properties like `font-size` and `vertical-align` are used to format both the note marker and the text in the customary fashion.

```
<fo:footnote>
  <fo:footnote-reference
    font-size="smaller" vertical-align="super">
    *
  </fo:footnote-reference>
  <fo:block font-size="smaller">
    <fo:inline-sequence
      font-size="smaller" vertical-align="super">
      *
    </fo:inline-sequence>
    <fo:inline-sequence
      font-style="italic">JavaBeans</fo:inline-sequence>,
      Elliotte Rusty Harold
      (IDG Books, Foster City, 1998), p. 147
  </fo:block>
</fo:footnote>
```

Tip   The formatting objects vocabulary doesn't provide any means of automatically numbering and citing footnotes, but this can be done by judicious use of `xsl:number` in the transformation stylesheet. XSL transformations also make end notes easy as well.

Floats

A `fo:float` produces a floating box anchored to the top of the region where it occurs. A `fo:float` is most commonly used for graphics, charts, tables, or other out–of-line content that needs to appear somewhere on the page, but exactly where it appears in not particularly important. For example, here is a the code for a floating graphic with a caption embedded in the middle of a paragraph:

```
<fo:block>
  Although PDF files are themselves ASCII text,
  this isn't a book about PostScript, so there's
  nothing to be gained by showing you the exact
```

```
output of the above command. If you're curious,
open the PDF file in any text editor.
Instead, Figure 15-1
<fo:float>
  <fo:display-graphic
    image="3236-7fg1501.jpg"
    height="485px" width="623px" />
  <fo:block font-family="Helvetica, sans">
    <fo:inline-sequence font-weight="bold">
      Figure 15-1:
    </fo:inline-sequence>
    The PDF file displayed in Netscape Navigator
  </fo:block>
</fo:float>
shows the rendered file displayed in
Netscape Navigator using the Acrobat plug-in.
</fo:block>
```

The formatter makes a best effort to place the graphic somewhere on the same page where the content surrounding the fo:float appears, though this is not always possible, in which case it moves the object to the subsequent page. Within these limits, it's free to place it anywhere on that page.

XSL Formatting Properties

By themselves, formatting objects say relatively little about how content is formatted. They merely put content in abstract boxes, which are placed in particular parts of a page. Attributes on the various formatting objects determine how the content in those boxes is styled.

As already mentioned, there are about 200 separate formatting properties. Not all properties can be attached to all elements. For instance, there isn't much point to specifying the font-style of a fo:display-graphic. Most properties, however, can be applied to more than one kind of formatting object element. (The few that can't, such as href and provisional-label-separation, are discussed above with the formatting objects they apply to.) When a property is common to multiple formatting objects, it shares the same syntax and meaning across the objects. For example, you use identical code to format the fo:list-label in 14-point Times bold as you do to format a fo:block in 14-point Times bold.

Many of the XSL properties are similar to CSS properties. The value of a CSS font-family property is the same as the value of an XSL font-family attribute. If you've read about CSS in Chapters 12 and 13, you're already more than half finished learning XSL properties.

Units and Data Types

The value of an XSL formatting property may be a keyword such as `auto`, `italic`, or `transparent`; or it may be a literal value such as `true`, 5px, -5.0cm, or `http://www.w3.org/index.html`. Literal values in XSL are given as one of 24 data types, which are listed in Table 15-2.

Table 15-2
Formatting Property Data Types

Data Type	Definition	Examples
Name	An XML name token.	q1 copyright
ID	A unique XML name token.	q1 copyright
IDREF	A name token that matches the ID of an element in the document.	q1 copyright
Boolean	Either the string "true" or the string "false".	true false
Char	A single, non-whitespace Unicode character.	A —
Signed Integer	A sequence of digits, optionally prefixed by a plus or minus sign.	0 -28 +1000000000
Unsigned Integer	A sequence of digits.	0 28 1000000000
Positive Integer	A sequence of digits that includes at least one nonzero digit.	28 1000000000
Signed Real	A floating point number in the format sign-digits-period-digits. Exponential notation is not supported. The + is optional for positive numbers.	+0.879 -31.14 2.71828
Unsigned Real	A non-negative floating point number in the format digits-period-digits. Exponential notation is not supported.	0.0 31.14 2.71828
Positive Real	A positive floating point number in the format digits-period-digits. Exponential notation is not supported.	0.01 31.14 2.71828

Continued

Table 15-2 (*continued*)

Data Type	Definition	Examples
Signed Length	A signed integer or signed real followed by a unit.	`5px` `-0.5in`
Unsigned Length	An unsigned integer or unsigned real number followed by a unit.	`10px` `0.5cm`
Positive Length	A positive integer or positive real number followed by a unit.	`10px` `1pc`

Percent	A signed real number that must be divided by 100 to get its actual value.	`100.0`
		`-43.2`
		`0.0`

Space Specifier	Minimum length semicolon maximum length semicolon optimal length semicolon precedence semicolon conditionality.	`0px;72px;12px;` `force;discard`
Limit Specifier	Minimum length semicolon maximum length.	`0px;72px`
Color	A named color or a hexadecimal triple in the form #RRGGBB.	`white` `#FFFFFF`

URI	A Uniform Resource Identifier; in practice, a URL.	`http://www.w3`
		`.org/index.html`
		`/index.html`
		`/`
		`../index.html`

Language	An ISO 639 language code.	`en` `la`
Font Name	The name of a font, either actual or symbolic.	`Times New Roman` `serif`
Font List	Font names separated by commas and possibly whitespace.	`Times New Roman,` `Times,serif`

Enumeration	An XML enumeration.	`(airplane |`
		`train | car |`
		`horse)`

String	Any sequence of characters.	`Fred`
		`Lucy and Ethel`
		`Castles don't`
		`have phones.`

Informational Properties

There are two informational properties, which can be applied to any formatting object. However, neither has a direct affect on the formatting. In essence, these are non-formatting properties.

The id Property

The first such property is `id`. This is an XML ID-type attribute. The value of this property must, therefore, be an XML name that's unique within the style sheet and within the output formatting object document. The last requirement is a little tricky since it's possible that one template rule in the stylesheet may generate several hundred elements in the output document. The `generate-id()` function of XSL transformations can be useful here.

The language Property

The second such property is `language`. This specifies the language of the content contained in this element. Generally, the value of this property is an ISO 639 language code such as `en` (English) or `la` (Latin). It may also be the keyword `none` or `use-document`. The latter means to simply use the language of the input as specified by the `xml:lang` attribute. For example, consider the first verse of Caesar's *Gallic Wars*:

```
<fo:block id="verse1.1.1" language="la">
   Gallia est omnis divisa in partes tres,
   quarum unam incolunt Belgae, aliam Aquitani,
   tertiam qui ipsorum lingua Celtae, nostra Galli appellantur
</fo:block>
```

Although the `language` property has no direct effect on formatting, it may have an indirect effect if the formatter selects layout algorithms depending on the language. For instance, the formatter may use different default writing modes for Arabic and English text. This carries over into determination of the start and end regions, and the inline progression direction.

Paragraph Properties

Paragraph properties are styles that normally are thought of as applying to an entire block of text in a traditional word processor, though perhaps block-level text properties are more appropriate here. For example, indentation is a paragraph property, because you can indent a paragraph but you can't indent a single word separate from its enclosing paragraph.

Break Properties

The break properties specify where page breaks are and are not allowed. There are five loosely related break properties:

- ✦ keep-with-next
- ✦ keep-with-previous
- ✦ break-before
- ✦ break-after
- ✦ inhibit-line-breaks

The keep-with-next and keep-with-previous properties are Booleans that specify whether the formatting object should remain in the same parent-formatting object as the next and previous formatting objects, respectively. This has the effect of keeping two formatting objects on the same page, but it's more strict than that.

The break-before property inserts a break before the formatting object starts. Possible things to break include column, page, odd-page and even-page. The value may also be none or auto-page. The break-after property inserts a break after the formatting object finishes. The same values are used as for break-before. For example, this template rule ensures that each SONNET of sufficiently small size prints on a page of its own:

```
<xsl:template match="SONNET">
  <fo:block break-before="page" break-after="page">
    <xsl:apply-templates/>
  </fo:block>
</xsl:template>
```

Finally, the inhibit-line-breaks property is a Boolean that can be set to true to indicate that not even a line break is allowed, much less a page break.

Hyphenation Properties

The hyphenation properties determine whether hyphenation is allowed and how it should be used. This applies only to soft or "optional" hyphens such as the ones sometimes used to break long words at the end of a line. It does not apply to hard hyphens such as the ones in the word *mother-in-law*, though these hyphens may affect where soft hyphens are allowed. There are six hyphenation properties. They are:

- ✦ hyphenate: automatic hyphenation is allowed only if this Boolean property has the value true

- ✦ hyphenation-char: the Unicode character used to hyphenate words, such as - in English

- ✦ hyphenation-keep: one of the four keywords (column, none, page, spread) that specify whether hyphenation is allowed at the end of a facing page pair or column

✦ `hyphenation-ladder-count`: an unsigned integer that specifies the maximum number of hyphenated lines that may appear in a row

✦ `hyphenation-push-char-count`: an unsigned integer that specifies the minimum number of characters that must follow an automatically inserted hyphen. (Short syllables look bad in isolation.)

✦ `hyphenation-remain-char-count`: an unsigned integer specifying the minimum number of characters that must precede an automatically inserted hyphen

Hyphenation also depends on the language and script in use. Thus, the following three properties have particular impact here:

✦ `country`

✦ `language`

✦ `script`

For example:

```
<fo:block hyphenate=true
          hyphenation-char="-"
          hyphenation-keep="none"
          hyphenation-ladder-count="2"
          hyphenation-push-char-count="4"
          hyphenation-remain-char-count="4" >
  some content...
</fo:block>
```

XSL does not specify a syllable-breaking algorithm to determine where a soft hyphen may be applied. Even with these properties allowing hyphenation, it's still completely up to the formatter to figure out how to hyphenate individual words.

The vertical-align Property

The `vertical-align` property determines the vertical position of a formatting object on its line. It is identical in behavior to the CSS2 propety of the same name. There are eight possible keyword values for this property:

1. `baseline`: align the baseline of the box with the baseline of the line box

2. `sub`: align the baseline of the box with the baseline of subscripts inside the line box

3. `super`: raise the baseline of the box to the baseline of superscripts in the line box

4. `top`: align the top of box with the top of the line box

5. `middle`: align the midpoint of the box with the baseline of the line box, plus half the x-height of the line box

6. `bottom`: align the bottom of the box with the bottom of the line box

7. `text-top`: align the top of the box with the top of the font

8. `text-bottom`: align the bottom of the box with the bottom of the font

You can also set `vertical-align` to a signed length that raises or lowers the box by the specified distance from the baseline.

Indentation Properties

The four indent properties `start-indent`, `end-indent`, `text-indent` and `last-line-end-indent` specify how far lines are indented from the edge of the text. The `start-indent` property offsets all lines from the start edge (left edge in English). The `end-indent` property offsets all lines from the end edge (right edge in English). The `text-indent` property offsets only the first line from the start edge. The `last-line-end-indent` property offsets only the last line from the start edge. Values are given as a signed length. Using a positive value for `start-indent` and a negative value for `text-indent` creates hanging indents. For example, a standard paragraph with 0.5-inch, first-line indent might be formatted this way:

```
<fo:block text-indent="0.5in">
  The first line of this paragraph is indented
</fo:block>
```

A block quote with a 1-inch indent on all lines on both sides is formatted like this:

```
<fo:block start-indent="1.0in" end-indent="1.0in">
  This text is offset one inch from both edges.
</fo:block>
```

Character Properties

Character properties describe the qualities of individual characters, although they can apply to elements that contain characters such as `fo:block` and `fo:list-item-body` elements. These include color, font, style, weight, and similar properties.

The color Property

The `color` property sets the foreground color of the contents using the same syntax as the CSS `color` property. For example, this colors the text "Lions and tigers and bears, oh my!" pink:

```
<fo:inline-sequence color="#FFCCCC">
  Lions and tigers and bears, oh my!
</fo:inline-sequence>
```

Font Properties

Any formatting object that holds text can have a wide range of font properties. Most of these are familiar from CSS, including:

- ✦ font-family: a list of font names in order of preference
- ✦ font-size: a signed length
- ✦ font-size-adjust: the preferred ratio between the x-height and size of a font, specified as an unsigned real number or none
- ✦ font-stretch: the "width" of a font, given as one of the keywords condensed, expanded, extra-condensed, extra-expanded, narrower, normal, semi-condensed, semi-expanded, ultra-condensed, ultra-expanded, or wider
- ✦ font-style: the style of font specified as one of the keywords italic, normal, oblique, reverse-normal, or reverse-oblique
- ✦ font-variant: either normal or small-caps
- ✦ font-weight the thickness of the strokes that draw the font, given as one of the keywords 100, 200, 300, 400, 500, 600, 700, 800, 900, bold, bolder, lighter, normal

The text-transform Property

The text-transform property defines how text is capitalized, and is identical to the CSS property of the same name. The four possible values are:

- ✦ none: don't; change the case (the default)
- ✦ capitalize: make the first letter of each word uppercase and all subsequent letters lowercase
- ✦ uppercase: make all characters uppercase
- ✦ lowercase: make all characters lowercase

This property is somewhat language specific. (Chinese, for example, doesn't have separate upper and lower cases.) Formatters are free to ignore the case recommendations when they're applied to non-Latin-1 text.

The text-shadow Property

The text-shadow property applies a shadow to text. This is similar to a background color, but differs in that the shadow attaches to the text itself rather than the box containing the text. The value of text-shadow can be the keyword none or a named or RGB color. For example:

```
<fo:inline-seqence text-shadow="FFFF66">
  This sentence is yellow.
</fo:inline-sequence>
```

The text-decoration Property

The `text-decoration` property is identical to the CSS2 text-decoration property. It has these five possible values:

- ✦ none
- ✦ underline
- ✦ overline
- ✦ line-through
- ✦ blink

The default is none.

The score-space Property

Scoring is a catchall word for <u>underlining</u>, ~~line through~~, double strike-through, and so forth. The `score-space` property determines whether whitespace is scored. <u>For example, if</u> `score-spaces` <u>is</u> `true`<u>, an underlined sentence looks like this.</u> If `score-spaces` <u>is</u> `false`, <u>an underlined sentence looks like this.</u>

Sentence Properties

Sentence properties apply to groups of characters, that is, a property that makes sense only for more than one letter at a time, such as the space between letters or words.

Letter Spacing Properties

Kerning of text is a slippery measure of how much space separates two characters. It's not an absolute number. Most formatters adjust the space between letters based on local necessity, especially in justified text. Furthermore, high-quality fonts use different amounts of space between different glyphs. However, you can make text looser or tighter overall.

The `letter-spacing` property adds additional space between each pair of glyphs, beyond that provided by the kerning. It's given as a signed length specifying the desired amount of extra space to add. For example:

```
<fo:block letter-spacing="1.5px">
  This is fairly loose text
</fo:block>
```

You can make the length negative to tighten up the text. Formatters, however, will generally impose limits on how much extra space they allow to be added to, or removed from, the space between letters.

Word Spacing Properties

The `word-spacing` property adjusts the amount of space between words. Otherwise, it behaves much like the letter spacing properties. The value is a signed length giving the amount of extra space to add between two words. For example:

```
<fo:block word-spacing="0.3cm">
  This is pretty loose text.
</fo:block>
```

Line Spacing Properties

An XSL formatting engine divides block areas into line areas. You cannot create line areas directly from XSL. However, with these five properties you can affect how they're vertically spaced:

✦ `line-height`: the minimum height of a line

✦ `line-height-shift-adjustment`: `consider-shifts` if subscripts and superscripts should expand the height of a line, `disregard-shifts` if they shouldn't

✦ `line-stacking-strategy`: `line-height` (the CSS model and the default); `font-height` (make the line as tall as the font height after addition of `font-height-override-before` and `font-height-override-after`); or `max-height` (distance between the maximum ascender height and maximum descender depth)

✦ `font-height-override-after`: a signed length specifying additional vertical space added after each line; can also be the keyword `use-font-metrics` (the default) to indicate that this depends on the font

✦ `font-height-override-before`: a signed length specifying the minimum additional vertical space added before each line; can also be the keyword `use-font-metrics` (the default) to indicate that this depends on the font

The line height also depends to a large extent on the size of the font in which the line is drawn. Larger font sizes will naturally have taller lines. For example, the following opening paragraph from Mary Wollstonecraft's *Of the Rights of Woman* is effectively double-spaced:

```
<fo:block font-size="12pt" line-height="24pt">
  In the present state of society it appears necessary to go
  back to first principles in search of the most simple truths,
  and to dispute with some prevailing prejudice every inch of
  ground. To clear my way, I must be allowed to ask some plain
  questions, and the answers will probably appear as
  unequivocal as the axioms on which reasoning is built;
  though, when entangled with various motives of action, they
  are formally contradicted, either by the words or conduct
  of men.
</fo:block>
```

Text Alignment Properties

The text-align and text-align-last properties specify how the inline content is horizontally aligned within its box. The six possible values are:

1. start: left aligned in right-to-left scripts
2. centered: centered
3. end: right aligned in right-to-left scripts
4. justify: expanded with extra space as necessary to fill out the line
5. page-inside: align with the inside edge of the page, that is, the right edge on the left page of two facing pages or the left edge on the right page of two facing pages
6. page-outside: align with the outside edge of the page, that is, the left edge on the left page of two facing pages or the right edge on the right page of two facing pages

The text-align-last property enables you to specify a different value for the last line in a block. This is especially important for justified text, where the last line often doesn't have enough words to be attractively justified. The possible values are start, end, justified, and relative. The relative value uses the same value as the text-align property unless text-align is justified, in which case the last line will align with the start edge instead.

Whitespace Property

The whitespace-treatment property specifies what the formatting engine should do with whitespace that's still present after the original source document is transformed into formatting objects. There are three possible values:

1. preserve: leave the whitespace as it is
2. collapse: collapse all whitespace to a single space
3. ignore: throw away leading and trailing whitespace

My preference is to preserve all whitespace that's still left after transformation. If it's insignificant, it's easy for the transformation process to throw it away using xsl:strip-space.

The wrap-option Property

The wrap-option property determines how text that's too long to fit on a line is handled. This property has two possible keyword values:

1. wrap: soft wrap the text to the next line
2. no-wrap: do not wrap the text

Area Properties

Area properties are applied to boxes. These may be either block-level or inline boxes. Each of these boxes has:

✦ a background

✦ margins

✦ borders

✦ padding

✦ a size

Background Properties

The background properties are basically identical to the CSS1 background properties. There are five:

✦ The `background-color` property specifies the color of the box's background. Its value is either a color or the keyword `transparent`.

✦ The `background-image` property gives the URI of an image to be used as a background. The value can be the keyword `none`.

✦ The `background-attachment` property specifies whether the background image is attached to the window or the document. Its value is one of the two keywords `fixed` or `scroll`.

✦ The `background-position` property specifies how a background image is placed in the box. Possible values include `center`, `left`, `right`, `bottom`, `middle`, `top`, or a coordinate.

✦ The `background-repeat` property specifies how and whether a background image is tiled if it is smaller than its box. Possible values include `repeat`, `no-repeat`, `repeat-x`, and `repeat-y`.

The following block shows the use of the `background-image`, `background-position`, `background-repeat`, and `background-color` properties:

```
<fo:block background-image="/bg/paper.gif"
          background-position="0,0"
          background-repeat="repeat"
          background-color="white">
   Two strings walk into a bar...
</fo:block>
```

Border Properties

The border properties describe the appearance of a border around the box. They are mostly the same as the CSS border properties. However, as well as `border-XXX-bottom`, `border-XXX-top`, `border-XXX-left`, and `border-XXX-right` properties, the XSL versions also have `border-XXX-before`, `border-XXX-after`, `border-XXX-start`, and `border-XXX-end` versions. There are 31 border properties in all. These are:

✦ color: `border-color`, `border-before-color`, `border-after-color`, `border-start-color`, `border-end-color`, `border-top-color`, `border-bottom-color`, `border-left-color`, `border-right-color`. The default border color is black.

✦ width: `border-width`, `border-before-width`, `border-after-width`, `border-start-width`, `border-end-width`, `border-top-width`, `border-bottom-width`, `border-left-width`, `border-right-width`.

✦ style: `border-style`, `border-before-style`, `border-after-style`, `border-start-style`, `border-end-style`, `border-top-style`, `border-bottom-style`, `border-left-style`, `border-right-style`

✦ shorthand properties: `border`, `border-top`, `border-bottom`, `border-left`, `border-right`, `border-color`, `border-style`, `border-width`

For example, this draws a 2-pixel-wide blue box around a block:

```
<fo:block border-before-color="blue" border-before-width="2px"
          border-after-color="blue" border-after-width="2px"
          border-start-color="blue" border-start-width="2px"
          border-end-color="blue" border-end-width="2px">
  Two strings walk into a bar...
</fo:block>
```

Padding Properties

The padding properties specify the amount of space between the border of the box and the contents of the box. The border of the box, if shown, falls between the margin and the padding. The padding properties are mostly the same as the CSS padding properties. However, as well as `padding-bottom`, `padding-top`, `padding-left`, and `padding-right` properties the XSL versions also have `padding-before`, `padding-after`, `padding-start`, and `padding-end` versions. Thus, in total there are eight padding properties, each of which has a signed length for a value. These are:

✦ `padding-after`

✦ `padding-before`

✦ `padding-bottom`

✦ padding-end

✦ padding-left

✦ padding-start

✦ padding-right

✦ padding-top

For example, this block has 0.5 centimeters of padding on all sides:

```
<fo:block padding-before="0.5cm" padding-after="0.5cm"
          padding-start="0.5cm"  padding-end="0.5cm">
  Two strings walk into a bar...
</fo:block>
```

Margin Properties for Blocks

There are five margin properties , each of whose value is given as an unsigned length. These are:

✦ margin-top

✦ margin-bottom

✦ margin-left

✦ margin-right

✦ margin

However, these properties are only here for compatibility with CSS. In general it's recommended that you use the following properties instead, which fit better into the XSL formatting model:

✦ space-before

✦ space-after

✦ start-indent

✦ end-indent

The space-before and space-after properties are exactly equivalent to the margin-top and margin-bottom properties respectively. The start-indent property is equivalent to the sum of padding-left, border-left-width, and margin-left. The end-indent property is equivalent to the sum of padding-right, border-right-width, and margin-right. Figure 15-3 should make this clearer.

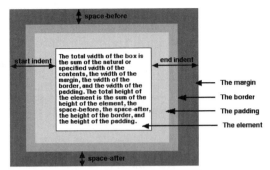

Figure 15-3: Padding, indents, borders, and space before and after an XSL box

For example, this block has 0.5 centimeters of margin at its start and end sides:

```
<fo:block start-indent="0.5cm" end-indent="0.5cm">
  Two strings walk into a bar...
</fo:block>
```

Margin Properties for Inline Boxes

There are two margin properties that apply only to inline elements. These are:

- ✦ space-end
- ✦ space-start

Their values are space specifiers that give a range of extra space to be added before and after the element. The actual spaces may be smaller or larger. Because the space is not part of the box itself, one box's end space can be part of the next box's start space.

A space specifier provides a range of values including a minimum, maximum, and optimum value. The formatter is free to pick from within this range to fit the constraints of the page. Furthermore, a space specifier includes values for precedence and conditionality. All five of these are separated by semicolons.

The precedence can either be an integer or the keyword force. The precedence determines what happens when the space-end of one inline area conflicts with the space-start of the next. The area with higher precedence wins. The default precedence is 0.

The conditionality is one of two keywords: discard or retain. These keywords determine what happens to extra space at the end of a line. The default is to discard it.

Contents Height and Width Properties

There are four properties that specify the height and width of the content area of a box as unsigned lengths. These are:

✦ height

✦ width

✦ max-height

✦ max-width

These do not specify the total width and height of the box, which also include the margins, padding, and borders. This is only the width and height of the content area. As well as an unsigned length, the height and width properties may be set to the keyword auto, which chooses the height and width based on the amount of content in the box. However, in no case are the height and width larger than the values specified by the max-height and max-width properties. For example:

```
<fo:block height="2in" width="2in">
  Two strings walk into a bar...
</fo:block>
```

The overflow Properties

The overflow property determines what happens if there's too much content to fit within a box of a specified size. This may be an explicit specification using the size properties or an implicit specification based on page size or other constraints. There are four possibilities, each represented by a keyword:

1. auto: use scrollbars if there is overflow; don't use them if there isn't

2. hidden: don't show any content that runs outside the box

3. scroll: attach scrollbars to the box so the reader can scroll to the additional content

4. visible: the complete contents are shown, if necessary, by overriding the size constraints on the box

The clip property specifies the shape of the clipping region if the overflow property does not have the value visible. The default clipping region is simply the box itself. However, you can change this by specifying a particular rectangle like this:

```
clip=rect(top_offset right_offset bottom_offset left_offset)
```

Here top_offset, right_offset, bottom_offset, and left_offset are signed lengths giving the offsets of the clipping region from the top, right, bottom, and left sides of the box. This allows you to make the clipping region smaller than the box itself.

The reference-orientation Property

The `reference-orientation` property enables you to specify that the content of a box is rotated in 90° increments relative to its normal orientation. The only valid values are 90° increments, which are measured counterclockwise, that is 0, 90, 180, and 270. You can also specify `-90`, `-180`, and `-270`. For example, here's a 90° rotation:

```
<fo:block reference-orientation="90">
  Bottom to Top
</fo:block>
```

Writing Mode Properties

The writing mode specifies the direction of text in the box. This has important implications for the ordering of formatting objects in the box. Most of the time, speakers of English and other Western languages assume a left-to-right, top-to-bottom writing mode, such as this:

```
A B C D E F G
H I J K L M N
O P Q R S T U
V W X Y Z
```

However, in the Hebrew- and Arabic-speaking worlds, a right-to-left, top-to-bottom ordering such as this one seems more natural:

```
G F E D C B A
N M L K J I H
U T S R Q P O
Z Y X W V
```

In Taiwan, a top-to-bottom, right-to-left order is most comfortable:

```
A E I M Q U Y
B F J N R V Z
C G K O S W
D H L P T X
```

In the XSL formatting language, the writing mode doesn't just affect text. It also affects how objects in a flow or sequence are laid out, how wrapping is performed, and more. You've already noticed that many properties are organized in start, end, before, and after variations instead of left, right, top, and bottom. Specifying style rules in terms of start, end, before, and after, instead of left, right, top, and bottom, produces more robust, localizable style sheets.

The `writing-mode` property specifies the writing mode for an area. This property can have one of the same 14 keyword values. These are:

1. `bt-lr`: bottom-to-top, left-to-right

2. `bt-rl`: bottom-to-top, right-to-left

3. `lr-alternating-rl-bt`: left-to-right lines alternating with right-to-left lines, bottom-to-top

4. `lr-alternating-rl-tb`: left-to-right lines alternating with right-to-left lines, top-to-bottom

5. `lr-bt`: left-to-right, bottom-to-top

6. `lr-inverting-rl-bt`: left to right, then move up to the next line and go right to left (that is, snake up the page like a backward S)

7. `lr-inverting-rl-tb`: left to right, then move down to the next line and go right to left (that is, snake down the page like a backward S)

8. `lr-tb`: left to right, top to bottom

9. `rl-bt`: right to left, bottom to top

10. `rl-tb`: right to left, top to bottom

11. `tb-lr`: top to bottom, left to right

12. `tb-rl`: top to bottom, right to left

13. `tb-rl-in-rl-pairs`: top to bottom, right to left

14. `use-page-writing-mode`: whatever writing mode the page on which this object appears uses; the default

Orphans and Widows

To a typesetter, an orphan is a single line of a paragraph at the bottom of a page. A widow is a single line of a paragraph at the top of a page. Good typesetters move an extra line from the previous page or to the next page as necessary to avoid orphans and widows. You can adjust the number of lines considered to be an orphan by setting the `orphans` property to an unsigned integer. You can adjust the number of lines considered to be a widow by setting the `widows` property to an unsigned integer. For instance, if you want to make sure that every partial paragraph at the end of a page has at least three lines, set the `orphans` property to 3. For example:

```
<fo:simple-page-master page-master-name="even"
    orphans="3" page-height="8.5in" page-width="11in"
/>
```

Aural Properties

XSL supports the full collection of CSS2 aural stylesheet properties including:

✦ `azimuth`

✦ `cue`

- ✦ cue-after
- ✦ cue-before
- ✦ elevation
- ✦ pause
- ✦ pause-after
- ✦ pause-before
- ✦ pitch
- ✦ pitch-range
- ✦ play-during
- ✦ richness
- ✦ speak
- ✦ speak-header
- ✦ speak-numeral
- ✦ speak-punctuation
- ✦ speech-rate
- ✦ stress
- ✦ voice-family
- ✦ volume

Cross-Reference The aural style sheet properties are discussed in the last section of Chapter 13, *Cascading Style Sheets Level 2*. They have exactly the same semantics and syntax in XSL formatting objects as they do in CSS2.

Summary

In this chapter, you learned about the XSL formatting language in detail. In particular, you learned:

- ✦ An XSL transformation is performed to turn an XML source document into a new XML document marked up in the XSL formatting object vocabulary.

- ✦ Most XSL formatting objects generate one or more rectangular areas. Page areas contain block areas. Block areas contain block areas and line areas. Line areas contain inline areas. Inline areas contain other inline areas and character areas.

- ✦ The root element of a formatting object document is fo:root. This contains fo:layout-master-set elements and fo:page-sequence elements.

✦ The `fo:layout-master-set` elements contain one or more `fo:simple-page-master` elements, each of which defines the layout of a particular kind of page by dividing it into five regions (before, after, start, end, and body), and assigning properties to each one.

✦ The `fo:page-sequence` elements contains one `fo:sequence-specifier` element, zero or more `fo:static-content` elements, and one `fo:flow` element. The contents of the `fo:flow` are copied onto instances of the master pages in the order specified by the `fo:sequence-specifier` element. The contents of the `fo:static-content` elements are copied onto every page that's created.

✦ The `fo:display-rule` element produces a block-level horizontal line. The `fo:inline-rule` element produces an inline horizontal line.

✦ The `fo:display-graphic` element loads an image from a URL and displays it in a block. The `fo:inline-graphic` element loads an image from a URL and displays it inline.

✦ The `fo:simple-link` element creates a hypertext link to a URL that's displayed in a block.

✦ A list is a block-level element created by a `fo:list-block` element. It contains block-level `fo:list-item` elements. Each `fo:list-item` contains a `fo:list-item-label` and `fo:list-item-body`.

✦ The `fo:page-number` element inserts the current page number.

✦ The `fo:character` element replaces a particular character or string of characters in the input with a different character in the output.

✦ The `fo:display-sequence` and `fo:inline-sequence` elements are containers used to attach properties to the text and areas they contain.

✦ The `fo:footnote` element inserts an out-of-line footnote and an inline footnote reference into the page.

✦ The `fo:float` element inserts an out-of-line block-level element like a figure or a pullquote onto the page.

✦ There are more than 200 separate XSL formatting properties, many of which are identical to CSS properties of the same name. These are attached to XSL formatting object elements as attributes.

The next chapter introduces XLinks, a more powerful linking syntax than the standard HTML A element hyperlinks or XSL's `fo:display-link` and `fo:inline-link`.

✦   ✦   ✦

Supplemental Technologies

XLinks

XLL (eXtensible Linking Language) is divided into two parts, XLinks and XPointers. XLink, the XML Linking Language, defines how one document links to another document. XPointer, the XML Pointer Language, defines how individual parts of a document are addressed. XLinks point to a URI (in practice, a URL) that specifies a particular resource. This URL may include an XPointer part that more specifically identifies the desired part or section of the targeted resource or document. This chapter explores XLinks. The next chapter explores XPointers.

XLinks versus HTML Links

The Web conquered the more established gopher protocol for one main reason: It was possible to embed hypertext links in documents. These links could embed images or let the user to jump from inside one document to another document or another part of the same document. To the extent that XML is rendered into other formats such as HTML for viewing, the same syntax HTML uses for linking can be used in XML documents. Alternate syntaxes can be converted into HTML syntax using XSL, as you saw in several examples in Chapter 14.

However, HTML linking has limits. For one thing, URLs are mostly limited to pointing out a single document. More granularity than that, such as linking to the third sentence of the 17th paragraph in a document, requires you to manually insert named anchors in the targeted file. It can't be done without write access to the document to which you're linking.

Furthermore, HTML links don't maintain any sense of history or relations between documents. Although browsers may track the path you've followed through a series of documents, such tracking isn't very reliable. From inside the HTML, there's no way to know from where a reader came. Links are purely one way. The linking document knows to whom it's linking, but not vice versa.

XLL is a proposal for more powerful links between documents. It's designed especially for use with XML documents, but some parts can be used with HTML files as well. XLL achieves everything possible with HTML's URL-based hyperlinks and anchors. Beyond this, however, it supports multidirectional links where the links run in more than one direction. Any element can become a link, not just the A element. Links do not even have to be stored in the same file as the documents they link. Furthermore, the XPointer part (described in the next chapter) allows links to arbitrary positions in an XML document. These features make XLL more suitable not only for new uses, but for things that can be done only with considerable effort in HTML, such as cross-references, footnotes, end notes, interlinked data, and more.

Caution   I should warn you that at the time of this writing (spring, 1999), XLL is still undergoing significant development and modification. Although it is beginning to stabilize, some bits and pieces likely will change by the time you read this.

Furthermore, there are no general-purpose applications that support arbitrary XLinks. That's because XLinks have a much broader base of applicability than HTML links. XLinks are not just used for hypertext connections and embedding images in documents. They can be used by any custom application that needs to establish connections between documents and parts of documents, for any reason. Thus, even when XLinks are fully implemented in browsers they may not always be blue underlined text that you click to jump to another page. They can be that, but they can also be both more and less, depending on your needs.

Simple Links

In HTML, a link is defined with the <A> tag. However, just as XML is more flexible with tags that describe elements, it is more flexible with tags that refer to external resources. In XML, almost any tag can be a link. Elements that include links are called *linking elements*.

Linking elements are identified by an xlink:form attribute with either the value simple or extended. Furthermore, each linking element contains an href attribute whose value is the URI of the resource being linked to. For example, these are three linking elements:

```
<FOOTNOTE xlink:form="simple" href="footnote7.xml">7</FOOTNOTE>
<COMPOSER xlink:form="simple" inline="true"
    href="http://www.users.interport.net/~beand/">
    Beth Anderson
</COMPOSER>
<IMAGE xlink:form="simple" href="logo.gif"/>
```

Notice that the elements have semantic names that describe the content they contain rather than how the elements behave. The information that these elements are links is included in the attributes of the tags.

These three examples are simple XLinks. Simple XLinks are similar to standard HTML links and are likely to be supported by application software before the more complex (and more powerful) extended links, so I'll begin with them. Extended links are discussed in the next section.

In the FOOTNOTE example above, the link target attribute's name is href. Its value is the relative URL footnote7.xml. The protocol, host, and directory of this document are taken from the protocol, host, and directory of the document in which this link appears.

In the COMPOSER example above, the link target attribute's name is href. The value of the href attribute is the absolute URL http://www.users.interport.net/~beand/In the third example above, which is IMAGE, the link target attribute's name is href. The value of the href attribute is the relative URL logo.gif. Again, the protocol, host, and directory of this document are taken from the protocol, host, and directory of the document in which this link appears.

If your document has a DTD, these attributes must be declared like any other. For example, DTD declarations of the FOOTNOTE, COMPOSER, and IMAGE elements might look like this:

```
<!ELEMENT FOOTNOTE (#PCDATA)>
<!ATTLIST FOOTNOTE
    xlink:form   CDATA     #FIXED "simple"
    href         CDATA     #REQUIRED
>
<!ELEMENT COMPOSER (#PCDATA)>
<!ATTLIST COMPOSER
    xlink:form   CDATA     #FIXED "simple"
    href         CDATA     #REQUIRED
>
<!ELEMENT IMAGE EMPTY>
<!ATTLIST IMAGE
    xlink:form   CDATA     #FIXED "simple"
    href         CDATA     #REQUIRED
>
```

With these declarations, the xlink:form attribute has a fixed value. Therefore it does not need to be included in the instances of the elements, which you may now write more compactly like this:

```
<FOOTNOTE href="footnote7.xml">7</FOOTNOTE>
<COMPOSER href="http://www.users.interport.net/~beand/">
  Beth Anderson
</COMPOSER>
<IMAGE href="logo.gif"/>
```

Making an element a link element doesn't impose any restriction on other attributes or contents of an element. A link element may contain arbitrary children or other attributes, always subject to the restrictions of the DTD, of course. For example, here's a more realistic declaration of the IMAGE element. Note that most of the attributes don't have anything to do with linking.

```
<!ELEMENT IMAGE EMPTY>
<!ATTLIST IMAGE
      xlink:form CDATA    #FIXED "simple"
      href       CDATA    #REQUIRED
      ALT        CDATA    #REQUIRED
      HEIGHT     CDATA    #REQUIRED
      WIDTH      CDATA    #REQUIRED
>
```

Descriptions of the Local Resource

A linking element may contain optional content-role and content-title elements that provide extra information and further describe the purpose of the link inside the document in which it appears. For example:

```
<AUTHOR href="http://www.macfaq.com/personal.html"
   content-title="author of the page"
   content-role="whom to contact for questions about this page">
      Elliotte Rusty Harold
</AUTHOR>
```

The content-role and content-title attributes describe the local resource — that is, the contents of the link element, which is Elliotte Rusty Harold in this example. These attributes, however, do not describe the remote resource, which is the document at http://www.macfaq.com/personal.html in this example. Thus, this example says that Elliotte Rusty Harold has the title "author of the page" and the role "whom to contact for questions about this page." This does not necessarily have any relation to the document that is found at http://www.macfaq.com/personal.html.

The content-title attribute is generally used by an application reading the XML to show a bit of extra information to the user, perhaps in the browser's status bar or via a tool tip, when the user moves the mouse over the linked element. However, the application is not required to show this information to the user. It simply may do so if it chooses.

The content-role attribute indicates the purpose of the linked element in the document. The content-role attribute is similar to a processing instruction in that it's intended to pass data to the application reading the XML. It has no real purpose as XML, though, and applications are free to ignore it.

Like all other attributes, content-title and content-role should be declared in the DTD for all elements to which they belong. For example, this is a reasonable declaration for the above AUTHOR element:

```
<!ELEMENT AUTHOR (#PCDATA)>
<!ATTLIST AUTHOR
     xlink:form       CDATA     #FIXED     "simple"
     href             CDATA     #REQUIRED
     content-title    CDATA     #IMPLIED
     content-role     CDATA     #IMPLIED
>
```

Descriptions of the Remote Resource

The link element may contain optional role and title attributes that describe the remote resource, that is, the document or other resource to which the link points. For example:

```
<AUTHOR href="http://www.macfaq.com/personal.html"
   title="Elliotte Rusty Harold's personal home page"
   role="further information about the author of this page"
   content-title="author of the page"
   content-role="whom to contact for questions about this page">
   Elliotte Rusty Harold
</AUTHOR>
```

The role and title attributes describe the remote resource, not the local element. The remote resource in the above example is the document at http://www.macfaq.com/personal.html. Thus, the above example says that the page at http://www.macfaq.com/personal.html has the title "Elliotte Rusty Harold's personal home page" and the role "further information about the author of this page." It is not uncommon, though it's not required, for the title to be the same as the contents of the TITLE element of the page to which you are linking.

The application reading the XML might use these two attributes to show extra information to the user. However, the application is not required to show this information to the user or do anything with it.

The role attribute indicates the purpose of the remote resource (the one to which it's linked) in the linking document (the one from which it's linked). For example, it might distinguish between footnotes, endnotes, and citations.

As with all other attributes, the title and role attributes should be declared in the DTD for all the elements to which they belong. For example, this is a reasonable declaration for the above author element:

```
<!ELEMENT AUTHOR (#PCDATA)>
<!ATTLIST AUTHOR
     xlink:form       CDATA     #FIXED "simple"
     href             CDATA     #REQUIRED
     content-title    CDATA     #IMPLIED
     content-role     CDATA     #IMPLIED
     title            CDATA     #IMPLIED
     role             CDATA     #IMPLIED
>
```

Link Behavior

Link elements can contain three more optional attributes that suggest to applications how the remote resource is associated with the current page. These are:

1. show
2. actuate
3. behavior

The show attribute suggests how the content should be displayed when the link is activated, for example, by opening a new window to hold the content. The actuate attribute suggests whether the link should be traversed automatically or whether a specific user request is required. The behavior attribute can provide detailed information to the application about exactly how the link is to be traversed, such as a time delay before the link is traversed. These are all application dependent, however, and applications are free to ignore the suggestions.

The show Attribute

The show attribute has three legal values: replace, new, and embed.

With a value of replace when the link is activated (generally by clicking on it, at least in GUI browsers), the target of the link replaces the current document in the same window. This is the default behavior of HTML links. For example:

```
<COMPOSER href="http://www.users.interport.net/~beand/"
          show="replace">
   Beth Anderson
</COMPOSER>
```

With a value of new, activating the link opens a new window in which the targeted resource is displayed. This is similar to the behavior of HTML links when the target attribute is set to _blank. For example:

```
<WEBSITE href="http://www.quackwatch.com/" show="new">
   Check this out, but don't leave our site completely!
</WEBSITE>
```

Caution

Readers do not expect a new window to open after clicking a link. They expect that when they click a link, the new page will load into the current window, unless they specifically ask for the link to open in a new window.

Some companies are so self-important that they find it impossible to believe that any user would ever want to leave their sites. Thus they "help" the readers by opening new windows. Most of the time this only serves to confuse and annoy. Don't change the behavior users expect without a very good reason. The thin hope that a reader might spend an additional two seconds on your site or view one more page and see one more ad is not a good reason.

With a value of embed, activating the link inserts the targeted resource into the existing document. Exactly what this means is application dependent. However, you can imagine it being used to provide client-side includes for Web pages. For example, this element, rather than directly including individual elements for the members of a family, copies them out of the separate files ThomasCorwinAnderson.xml, LeAnahDeMintEnglish.xml, JohnJayAnderson.xml, and SamuelEnglishAnderson.xml.

```
<FAMILY ID="f732">
  <HUSBAND href="ThomasCorwinAnderson.xml"   show="embed"/>
  <WIFE    href="LeAnahDeMintEnglish.xml"    show="embed"/>
  <CHILD   href="JohnJayAnderson.xml"        show="embed"/>
  <CHILD   href="SamuelEnglishAnderson.xml"  show="embed"/>
</FAMILY>
```

The result, after the links are traversed and their contents embedded in the FAMILY element, is something like this:

```
<FAMILY ID="f732">
  <PERSON ID="p1035" SEX="M">
    <NAME>
      <GIVEN>Thomas Corwin</GIVEN>
      <SURNAME>Anderson</SURNAME>
    </NAME>
    <BIRTH>
      <DATE>24 Aug 1845</DATE>
    </BIRTH>
    <DEATH>
      <PLACE>Mt. Sterling, KY</PLACE>
      <DATE>18 Sep 1889</DATE>
    </DEATH>
  </PERSON>
  <PERSON ID="p1098" SEX="F">
    <NAME>
      <GIVEN>LeAnah (Lee Anna, Annie) DeMint</GIVEN>
      <SURNAME>English</SURNAME>
    </NAME>
    <BIRTH>
      <PLACE>Louisville, KY</PLACE>
      <DATE>1 Mar 1843</DATE>
    </BIRTH>
    <DEATH>
      <PLACE>acute Bright's disease, 504 E. Broadway</PLACE>
      <DATE>31 Oct 1898</DATE>
    </DEATH>
  </PERSON>
  <PERSON ID="p1102" SEX="M">
    <NAME>
      <GIVEN>John Jay (Robin Adair )</GIVEN>
      <SURNAME>Anderson</SURNAME>
    </NAME>
    <BIRTH>
```

```
      <PLACE>Sideview</PLACE>
      <DATE>13 May 1873</DATE>
   </BIRTH>
   <DEATH>
      <DATE>18 Sep 1889 </DATE>
   </DEATH>
 </PERSON>
 <PERSON ID="p37" SEX="M">
   <NAME>
      <GIVEN>Samuel English</GIVEN>
      <SURNAME>Anderson</SURNAME>
   </NAME>
   <BIRTH>
      <PLACE>Sideview</PLACE>
      <DATE>25 Aug 1871</DATE>
   </BIRTH>
   <DEATH>
      <PLACE>Mt. Sterling, KY</PLACE>
      <DATE>10 Nov 1919</DATE>
   </DEATH>
 </PERSON>
</FAMILY>
```

Although each of these PERSON elements exists in a separate file, the complete
FAMILY element is treated as though it was in one file.

Like all attributes in valid documents, the show attribute must be declared in a
<!ATTLIST> declaration for the DTD's link element. For example:

```
<!ELEMENT WEBSITE (#PCDATA)>
<!ATTLIST WEBSITE
      xlink:form CDATA    #FIXED "simple"
      href       CDATA    #REQUIRED
      show       (new | replace | embed) "new"
>
```

The actuate Attribute

A link element's actuate attribute has two possible values: user and auto. The
value user, the default, specifies that the link is to be traversed only when and if
the user requests it. On the other hand, if the link element's actuate attribute is set
to auto, the link is traversed any time one of the other targeted resources of the
same link element is traversed. This is useful for link groups (discussed below).

Like all attributes in valid documents, the actuate attribute must be declared in
the DTD in a <!ATTLIST> declaration for the link elements in which it appears. For
example:

```
<!ELEMENT WEBSITE (#PCDATA)>
<!ATTLIST WEBSITE
      xlink:form CDATA    #FIXED "simple"
      href       CDATA    #REQUIRED
```

```
        show        (new | replace | embed) "new"
        actuate     (user | auto) "user"
>
```

The behavior Attribute

The `behavior` attribute is used to pass arbitrary data in an arbitrary format to the application reading the data. The application is expected to use this data to make additional determinations about how the link behaves. For example, if you want to specify that the sound file fanfare.au play when a link is traversed, you might write this:

```
<COMPOSER xlink:form="simple"
    href="http://www.users.interport.net/~beand/"
    behavior="sound: fanfare.au">
    Beth Anderson
</COMPOSER>
```

A Shortcut for the DTD

Because the attribute names and types are standardized, if you have more than one link element in a document, often it's convenient to make the attribute declarations a parameter entity reference and simply repeat that in the declaration of each linking element. For example:

```
<!ENTITY % link-attributes
    "xlink:form    CDATA    #FIXED 'simple'
    href          CDATA    #REQUIRED
    behavior      CDATA    #IMPLIED
    content-role  CDATA    #IMPLIED
    content-title CDATA    #IMPLIED
    role          CDATA    #IMPLIED
    title         CDATA    #IMPLIED
    show          (new | replace | embed) 'new'
    actuate       (user | auto) 'user'
    behavior      CDATA    #IMPLIED"
>
<!ELEMENT COMPOSER (#PCDATA)>
<!ATTLIST COMPOSER
    %link-attributes;
>
<!ELEMENT AUTHOR (#PCDATA)>
<!ATTLIST AUTHOR
    %link-attributes;
>
<!ELEMENT WEBSITE (#PCDATA)>
<!ATTLIST WEBSITE
    %link-attributes;
>
```

However, this requires that the application reading the XML file understand that a `behavior` attribute with the value `sound: fanfare.au` means the sound file fanfare.au should play when the link is traversed. Most, probably all, applications don't understand this. However, they may use the `behavior` attribute as a convenient place to store nonstandard information they do understand.

As with all attributes in valid documents, the `behavior` attribute must be declared in the DTD for the link elements in which it appears. For example, the above `COMPOSER` element could be declared this way:

```
<!ELEMENT COMPOSER (#PCDATA)>
<!ATTLIST COMPOSER
      xlink:form   CDATA     #FIXED "simple"
      href         CDATA     #REQUIRED
      behavior     CDATA     #IMPLIED
>
```

Extended Links

Simple links behave more or less like the standard links you're accustomed to from HTML. Each contains a single local resource and a reference to a single remote resource. The local resource is the link element's contents. The remote resource is the link's target.

Extended links, however, go substantially beyond what you can do with an HTML link to include multidirectional links between many documents and out-of-line links. Extended links are identified by an `xlink:form` attribute with the value `extended`, like this:

```
<WEBSITE xlink:form="extended">
```

The first capability of extended links is to point to more than one target. To allow this, extended links store the targets in child `locator` elements of the linking element rather than in a single `href` attribute of the linking element as simple links do. For example:

```
<WEBSITE xlink:form="extended">Cafe au Lait
  <locator href="http://metalab.unc.edu/javafaq/">
    North Carolina
  </locator>
  <locator
    href="http://sunsite.univie.ac.at/jcca/mirrors/javafaq/">
    Austria
  </locator>
  <locator href="http://sunsite.icm.edu.pl/java-corner/faq/">
    Poland
  </locator>
  <locator href="http://sunsite.uakom.sk/javafaq/">
```

```
      Slovakia
    </locator>
    <locator href="http://sunsite.cnlab-switch.ch/javafaq/">
      Switzerland
    </locator>
</WEBSITE>
```

Both the linking element itself, WEBSITE, in this example, and the individual locator children may have attributes. The linking element only has attributes that apply to the entire link andthe local resource, such as content-title and content-role. The locator elements have attributes that apply to the particular remote resource to which they link, such as role and title. For example:

```
<WEBSITE xlink:form="extended" content-title="Cafe au Lait"
        content-role="Java news">
  <locator href="http://metalab.unc.edu/javafaq/"
    title="Cafe au Lait" role=".us"/>
  <locator
    href="http://sunsite.univie.ac.at/jcca/mirrors/javafaq/"
    title="Cafe au Lait" role=".at"/>
  <locator href="http://sunsite.icm.edu.pl/java-corner/faq/"
    title="Cafe au Lait" role=".pl"/>
  <locator href="http://sunsite.uakom.sk/javafaq/"
    title="Cafe au Lait" role=".sk"/>
  <locator href="http://sunsite.cnlab-switch.ch/javafaq/"
    title="Cafe au Lait" role=".ch"/>
</WEBSITE>
```

The actuate, behavior, and show attributes, if present, belong to the individual locator elements.

In some cases, as in the above example, where the individual locators point to mirror copies of the same page, remote resource attributes for individual locator elements may be the same across the linking element. In this case, you can use remote resource attributes in the linking element itself. These attributes apply to each of the locator children that does not declare a conflicting value for the same attribute. For example:

```
<WEBSITE xlink:form="extended" content-title="Cafe au Lait"
    content-role="Java news" title="Cafe au Lait">
  <locator href="http://metalab.unc.edu/javafaq/" role=".us"/>
  <locator
    href="http://sunsite.univie.ac.at/jcca/mirrors/javafaq/"
    role=".at"/>
  <locator href="http://sunsite.icm.edu.pl/java-corner/faq/"
    role=".pl"/>
  <locator href="http://sunsite.uakom.sk/javafaq/" role=".sk"/>
  <locator href="http://sunsite.cnlab-switch.ch/javafaq/"
    role=".ch"/>
</WEBSITE>
```

Another Shortcut for the DTD

If you have many link and `locator` elements, it may be advantageous to define the common attributes in parameter entities in the DTD, which you can reuse in different elements. For example:

```
<!ENTITY % remote-resource-semantics.att
   "role          CDATA                    #IMPLIED
   title          CDATA                    #IMPLIED
   show           (embed|replace|new) #IMPLIED 'replace'
   actuate        (auto|user)              #IMPLIED 'user'
   behavior       CDATA                    #IMPLIED"
>


<!ENTITY % local-resource-semantics.att
   "content-title CDATA                    #IMPLIED
   content-role   CDATA                    #IMPLIED"
>


<!ENTITY % locator.att
   "href          CDATA                    #REQUIRED"
>


<!ENTITY % link-semantics.att
   "inline        (true|false)             'true'
   role           CDATA                    #IMPLIED"
>

<!ELEMENT WEBSITE (locator*) >
<!ATTLIST WEBSITE
   xlink:form     CDATA     #FIXED "extended"
   %local-resource-semantics.att;
>

<!ELEMENT locator EMPTY>
<!ATTLIST locator
   xlink:form     CDATA     #FIXED "locator"
   %locator.att;
   %link-semantics.att;
>
```

As always, in valid documents, the link elements and all their possible attributes must be declared in the DTD. For example, the following declares the WEBSITE and locator elements used in the above examples, as well as their attributes:

```
<!ELEMENT WEBSITE (locator*) >
<!ATTLIST WEBSITE
   xlink:form      CDATA     #FIXED "extended"
   content-title  CDATA     #IMPLIED
   content-role   CDATA     #IMPLIED
   title          CDATA     #IMPLIED
>
<!ELEMENT locator EMPTY>
<!ATTLIST locator
   xlink:form      CDATA     #FIXED "locator"
   href            CDATA     #REQUIRED
   role            CDATA     #IMPLIED
>
```

Out-of-Line Links

The links considered so far, both simple and extended, are inline links. Inline links, such as the familiar A element from HTML, use the contents of the link element as part of the document that contains the link. It is shown to the reader.

XLinks can also be out-of-line. An out-of-line link may not be present in any of the documents it connects. Instead, the links are stored in a separate linking document. For example, this might be useful to maintain a slide show where each slide requires next and previous links. By changing the order of the slides in the linking document, you can change the targets of the previous and next links on each page without having to edit the slides themselves.

To mark a link as out-of-line, provide an inline attribute with the value false. For example, the following simple, out-of-line link describes a Web site using an empty element. An empty element has no content; in the case of a link it has no local resource. Therefore, it should not have content-role or content-title attributes that describe the local resource. It may have, as in this example, role and title attributes that describe the remote resource.

```
<WEBSITE xlink:form="simple" inline="false"
        href="http://metalab.unc.edu/xml/"
        title = "Cafe con Leche" role="XML News"/>
```

Note   Because all the links you've seen until now were inline links, they implicitly had inline attributes with the value true, the default.

Simple out-of-line links, as in the above example, are relatively rare. Much more common and useful are out-of-line extended links, as shown below:

```
<WEBSITE xlink:form="extended" inline="false">
   <locator href="http://metalab.unc.edu/javafaq/" role=".us"/>
```

```
<locator
  href="http://sunsite.univie.ac.at/jcca/mirrors/javafaq/"
  role=".at"/>
<locator href="http://sunsite.icm.edu.pl/java-corner/faq/"
  role=".pl"/>
<locator href="http://sunsite.uakom.sk/javafaq/" role=".sk"/>
<locator href="http://sunsite.cnlab-switch.ch/javafaq/"
  role=".ch"/>
</WEBSITE>
```

Something such as this might be stored in a separate file on a Web server in a known location where browsers can find and query it to determine the nearest mirror of a page they're looking for. The out-of-line-ness, however, is that this element does not appear in the document from which the link is activated.

This expands the abstraction of style sheets into the linking domain. A style sheet is completely separate from the document it describes and yet provides rules that modify how the document is presented to the reader. A linking document containing out-of-line links is separated from the documents it connects, yet it provides the necessary links to the reader. This has several advantages, including keeping more presentation-oriented markup separate from the document and allowing the linking of read-only documents.

 Caution Style sheets are *much* farther along than out-of-line links. There currently is no general proposal for how you attach "link sheets" to XML documents, much less how you decide which individual elements in a document are associated with which links.

One obvious choice is to add an `<?xml-linksheet?>` processing instruction to a document's prolog to specify where the links are found. The link sheet itself could use something akin to XSL select patterns to map links to individual XML elements. The selectors could even become the value of the `locator` element's `role` attribute.

Extended Link Groups

An extended link group element contains a list of links that connect a particular group of documents. Each document in the group is targeted by means of an extended link document element. It is the application's responsibility to understand how to activate and understand the connections between the group members.

 Caution I feel compelled to note that application support for link groups is at best hypothetical at the time of this writing. Although I can show you how to write such links, their actual implementation and support likely is some time away. Some of the details remain to be defined and likely will be implemented in vendor-specific fashions, at least initially. Still, they hold the promise of enabling more sophisticated linking than can be achieved with HTML.

An Example

For example, I've put the notes for a Java course I teach on my Web site. Figure 16-1 shows the introductory page. This particular course consists of 13 classes, each of which contains between 30 and 60 individual pages of notes. A table of contents is then provided for each class. Each of the several hundred pages making up the entire site has links to the previous document, the next document, and the table of contents (Top link) for the week, as shown in Figure 16-2. Putting it all together, this amounts to more than a thousand interconnections among this set of documents.

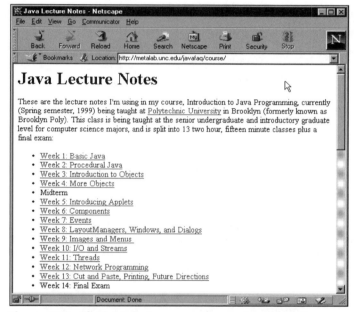

Figure 16-1: The introductory page for my class Web site shows 13 weeks of lecture notes

The possible interconnections grow exponentially with the number of documents. Every time a single document is moved, renamed, or divided into smaller pieces, the links need to be adjusted on that page, on the page before it and after it in the set, and on the table of contents for the week. Quite frankly, this is a lot more work than it should be, and it tends to discourage necessary modifications and updates to the course notes.

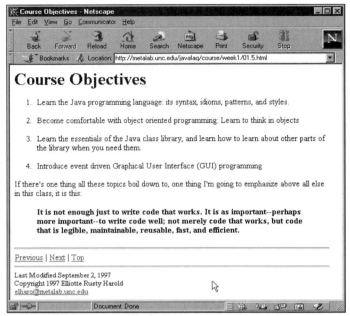

Figure 16-2: One page of lecture notes displaying the
Previous, Next, and Top links

The sensible thing to do, if HTML supported it, would be to store the connections
in a separate document. Reorganization of the pages then could be performed by
editing that one document. HTML links don't support this, but XLinks do. Instead
of storing the links inline in HTML files, they can be stored out-of-line in group
elements. For example:

```
<COURSE xlink:form="group">
  <CLASS xlink:form="document" href="week1/index.xml"/>
  <CLASS xlink:form="document" href="week2/index.xml"/>
  <CLASS xlink:form="document" href="week3/index.xml"/>
  <CLASS xlink:form="document" href="week4/index.xml"/>
  <CLASS xlink:form="document" href="week5/index.xml"/>
  <CLASS xlink:form="document" href="week6/index.xml"/>
  <CLASS xlink:form="document" href="week7/index.xml"/>
  <CLASS xlink:form="document" href="week8/index.xml"/>
  <CLASS xlink:form="document" href="week9/index.xml"/>
  <CLASS xlink:form="document" href="week10/index.xml"/>
  <CLASS xlink:form="document" href="week11/index.xml"/>
  <CLASS xlink:form="document" href="week12/index.xml"/>
  <CLASS xlink:form="document" href="week13/index.xml"/>
</COURSE>
```

This defines the COURSE element as an extended link group, which consists of 13
extended link document elements, the CLASS elements.

The steps Attribute

One thing an application may choose to do with a link group is preload all the documents in the link group. These documents may contain link groups of their own. For example, each of the CLASS elements above refers to one of the site's table of contents pages for a specific week, as shown in Figure 16-3. These documents could then load. For example, the file week6/index.xml could contain this link group:

```
<CLASS xlink:form="group">
  <SLIDE xlink:form="document" href="01.xml"/>
  <SLIDE xlink:form="document" href="02.html"/>
  <SLIDE xlink:form="document" href="06.html"/>
  <SLIDE xlink:form="document" href="12.html"/>
  <SLIDE xlink:form="document" href="13.html"/>
  <SLIDE xlink:form="document" href="16.html"/>
  <SLIDE xlink:form="document" href="17.html"/>
  <SLIDE xlink:form="document" href="19.html"/>
  <SLIDE xlink:form="document" href="21.html"/>
  <SLIDE xlink:form="document" href="22.html"/>
  <SLIDE xlink:form="document" href="24.html"/>
</CLASS >
```

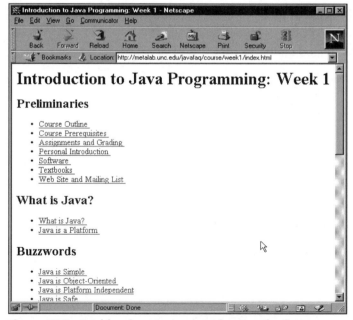

Figure 16-3: A table-of-contents page showing the first week's lecture notes

Now suppose one of these documents refers back to the original document. This might trigger an infinite regression, with the same documents repeatedly loading until the application runs out of memory. To prevent this, the group element may contain a `steps` attribute that specifies the number of levels to recursively follow link groups. For example, to specify that preloading shouldn't go deeper than three levels from the current document, write:

```
<group xlink:form="group" steps="3">
```

Note   To be honest, I'm not sure how important this is. It's not hard for an application to note when it's already followed a document and not process the document a second time. I suspect it is better to place the requirement for preventing recursion with the XML processor rather than the page author.

The `steps` attribute can be used to limit the amount of preloading that occurs. For instance, in the class notes example, it's unlikely that any person is going to read the entire set of course notes in one sitting, though perhaps he or she may want to print or copy all of them. In any case, by setting the `steps` attribute to 1, you can limit the depth of the traversal to simply the named pages rather than the several hundred pages in the course.

As always, these elements and their attributes must be declared in the DTD of any valid document in which they appear. In practice, the `xlink:form` attribute is fixed so that it need not be included in instances of the element. For example:

```
<!ELEMENT CLASS (document*)>
<!ATTLIST CLASS
    xlink:form   CDATA    #FIXED      "group"
    steps        CDATA    #IMPLIED
  >
<!ELEMENT SLIDE EMPTY>
<!ATTLIST SLIDE
    xlink:form   CDATA  #FIXED      "document"
    href         CDATA  #REQUIRED
>
```

Renaming XLink Attributes

XLinks are built around the ten attributes discussed in the previous sections. They are listed below.

```
xlink:form
href
steps
title
role
content-title
content-role
show
```

```
actuate
behavior
```

It is far from inconceivable that one or more of these attributes will already be used as an attribute name in a particular XML application. The `title` attribute seems particularly likely to be taken. The only one that really shouldn't be used for other purposes is `xlink:form`.

The XLink specification anticipates this problem and allows you to rename the XLink attributes to something more convenient using the `xml:attributes` attribute. This attribute is declared in an `<!ATTLIST>` declaration in the DTD as a fixed attribute with type `CDATA` and a value that's a whitespace-separated list of pairs of standard names and new names.

> **Note**   This is exactly the problem that namespaces (discussed in Chapter 18) were designed to solve. I would not be surprised to see this entire mechanism deleted in a future draft of XLL and replaced with a simple namespace prefix such as `xlink:`.

For example, the link elements shown in this chapter look a little funny because the standard names are all lowercase while this book's convention is all uppercase. It's easy enough to change the XLink attributes to uppercase with a declaration such as this:

```
<!ELEMENT WEBSITE (#PCDATA)>
<!ATTLIST WEBSITE
    xlink:form CDATA    #FIXED "simple"
    xml:attributes CDATA #FIXED
        "href HREF show SHOW actuate ACTUATE"
    HREF        CDATA       #REQUIRED
    SHOW        CDATA       (new | replace | embed) "new"
    ACTUATE     CDATA       (user | auto) user
>
```

Now you can rewrite the `WEBSITE` example in this more congruous form:

```
<WEBSITE HREF="http://www.microsoft.com/" SHOW="new">
  Check this out, but don't leave our site completely!
</WEBSITE>
```

The above `ATTLIST` declaration only changes the attributes of the `WEBSITE` element. If you want to change them the same way in multiple other examples, the easiest approach is to use a parameter entity:

```
<!ENTITY LINK_ATTS
  'xlink:form    CDATA     #FIXED "simple"
  xml:attributes CDATA #FIXED
        "href HREF show SHOW actuate ACTUATE"
  HREF        CDATA       #REQUIRED
  SHOW        CDATA       (new | replace | embed) "new"
  ACTUATE     CDATA       (user | auto) "user"'
```

```
>
<!ELEMENT WEBSITE (#PCDATA)>
<!ATTLIST WEBSITE %LINK_ATTS;>

<!ELEMENT COMPOSER (#PCDATA)>
<!ATTLIST COMPOSER %LINK_ATTS;>

<!ELEMENT FOOTNOTE (#PCDATA)>
<!ATTLIST FOOTNOTE %LINK_ATTS;>
```

Summary

In this chapter, you learned about XLinks. In particular you learned:

✦ XLinks can do everything HTML links can do and quite a bit more, but they aren't supported by current applications.

✦ Simple links behave much like HTML links, but they are not restricted to a single <A> tag.

✦ Link elements are identified by `xlink:form` and `href` attributes.

✦ Link elements can describe the local resource with `content-title` and `content-role` attributes.

✦ Link elements can describe the remote resource they're linking to with `title` and `role` attributes.

✦ Link elements can use the `show` attribute to tell the application how the content should be displayed when the link is activated, for example, by opening a new window.

✦ Link elements can use the `behavior` attribute to provide the application with detailed, application dependent information about exactly how the link is to be traversed.

✦ Link elements can use the `actuate` attribute to tell the application whether the link should be traversed without a specific user request.

✦ Extended links can include more than a single URI in a linking element. Currently, it's left to the application to decide how to choose between different alternatives.

✦ An extended link group element contains a list of links that connect a particular group of documents.

✦ You can use the `xml:attributes` attribute in the DTD to rename the standard XLink attributes such as `href` and `title`.

In the next chapter you see how XPointers can be used to link not only to remote documents, but to very specific elements in remote documents.

✦   ✦   ✦

XPointers

XPointer, the XML Pointer Language, defines an addressing scheme for individual parts of an XML document. XLinks point to a URI (in practice, a URL) that specifies a particular resource. The URI may include an XPointer part that more specifically identifies the desired part or element of the targeted resource or document. This chapter discusses XPointers.

 Caution This chapter is based on the March 3, 1998 working draft of the XPointer specification. The broad picture presented here is likely to be correct but the details are subject to change. You can find the latest working draft at `http://www.w3.org/TR/WD-xptr`.

Why Use XPointers?

URLs are simple and easy to use, but they're also quite limited. For one thing, a URL only points at a single, complete document. More granularity than that, such as linking to the third sentence of the 17th paragraph in a document, requires the author of the targeted document to manually insert named anchors at the targeted location. The author of the document doing the linking can't do this unless he or she also has write access to the document being linked to.Even if the author doing the linking can insert named anchors into the targeted document, it's almost always inconvenient.

It would be more useful to be able to link to a particular element or group of elements on a page without having to change the document you're linking to. For example, given a large page such as the complete baseball statistics of Chapters 4 and 5, you might want to link to only one team or one player. There are several parts to this problem. The first part is addressing the individual elements. This is the part that XPointers solve. XPointers allow you to target a given element by number, name, type, or relation to other elements in the document.

The second part of the problem is the protocol by which a browser asks a Web server to send only part of a document rather than the whole thing. This is an area of active research and speculation. More work is needed. XPointers do little to solve this problem, except for providing a foundation on which such systems can build. For instance, the best effort to date are the so-called "byte range extensions to HTTP" available in HTTP 1.1. So far these have not achieved widespread adoption, mostly because Web authors aren't comfortable specifying a byte range in a document. Furthermore, byte ranges are extremely fragile. Trivial edits to a document, even simple reformatting, can destroy byte range links. HTTP 1.1 does allow other range units besides raw bytes (for example, XML elements), but does not require Web servers or browsers to support such units. Much work remains to be done.

The third part of the problem is making sure that the retrieved document makes sense without the rest of the document to go along with it. In the context of XML, this effectively means the linked part is well-formed or perhaps valid. This is a tricky proposition, because most XML documents, especially ones with nontrivial prologs, don't decompose well. Again, XPointers don't address this. The W3C XML Fragment Working Group is addressing this issue, but the work is only just beginning.

For the moment, therefore, an XPointer can be used as an index into a complete document, the whole of which is loaded and then positioned at the location identified by the XPointer. In the long-term, extensions to both XML, XLink, HTTP, and other protocols may allow more sophisticated uses of XPointers. For instance, you might be able to quote a remote document by including only an XLink with an XPointer to the paragraph you want to quote, rather than retyping the text of the quote. You could include cross-references inside a document that automatically update themselves as the document is revised. These uses, however, will have to wait for the development of several next-generation technologies. For now, we must be content with precisely identifying the part of a document we want to jump to when following an XLink.

XPointer Examples

HTML links generally point to a particular document. Additional granularity, that is, pointing to a particular section, chapter, or paragraph of a particular document, isn't well-supported. Provided you control both the linking and the linked document, you can insert a named anchor into an HTML file at the position to which you want to link. For example:

```
<H2><A NAME="xpointers">XPointers</A></H2>
```

You can then link to this particular position in the file by adding a # and the name of the anchor into the link. For example, in a table of contents you might see:

```
<A HREF="#xpointers">XPointers</A>
```

In practice, this solution is kludgy. It's not always possible to modify the target document so the source can link to it. The target document may be on a different server controlled by someone other than the author of the source document. And the author of the target document may change or move it without notifying the author of the source.

Furthermore, named anchors violate the separation of markup from content. Placing a named anchor in a document says nothing about the document or its content. It's just a marker for other documents to refer to. It adds nothing to the document's own content.

XLinks allow much more sophisticated connections between documents through the use of XPointers. An XPointer can refer to a particular element of a document; to the first, second, or 17th such element; to the first element that's a child of a given element; and so on. XPointers provide extremely powerful connections between documents. They do not require the targeted document to contain additional markup just so its individual pieces can be linked to.

Furthermore, unlike HTML anchors, XPointers don't point to just a single point in a document. They can point to ranges or spans. Thus, you can use an XPointer to select a particular part of a document, perhaps so it can be copied or loaded into a program.

Here are a few examples of XPointers:

```
root()
id(dt-xmldecl)
descendant(2,termref)
following(,termdef,term,CDATA Section)
html(recent)
id(NT-extSubsetDecl)
```

Each of these selects a particular element in a document. The document is not specified in the XPointer; rather, the XLink specifies the document. The XLinks you saw in the previous chapter did not contain XPointers, but it isn't hard to add XPointers to them. Most of the time you simply append the XPointer to the URI separated by a #, just as you do with named anchors in HTML. For example, the above list of XPointers could be suffixed to URLs and come out looking like the following:

```
http://www.w3.org/TR/1998/REC-xml-19980210.xml#root()
http://www.w3.org/TR/1998/REC-xml-19980210.xml#id(dt-xmldecl)
http://www.w3.org/TR/1998/REC-xml-
19980210.xml#descendant(2,termref)
http://www.w3.org/TR/1998/REC-xml-
19980210.xml#following(,termdef,term,CDATA Section)
http://www.w3.org/TR/1998/REC-xml-19980210.xml#id(NT-
extSubsetDecl)
```

Normally these are used as values of the `href` attribute of a `locator` element. For example:

```
<locator
  href="http://www.w3.org/TR/1998/REC-xml-19980210.xml#root()">
  Extensible Markup Language (XML) 1.0
</locator>
```

You can use a vertical bar (`|`) instead of a `#` to indicate that you do not want the entire document. Instead, you want only the part of the document referenced by the XPointer. For example:

```
http://www.w3.org/TR/1998/REC-xml-19980210.xml|root()
http://www.w3.org/TR/1998/REC-xml-19980210.xml|id(dt-xmldecl)
http://www.w3.org/TR/1998/REC-xml-
19980210.xml|descendant(2,termref)
http://www.w3.org/TR/1998/REC-xml-
19980210.xml|following(.termdef,term,CDATA Section)
http://www.w3.org/TR/1998/REC-xml-19980210.xml|id(NT-
extSubsetDecl)
```

Whether the client is able to retrieve only a piece of the document is protocol dependent. Most current Web browsers and servers aren't able to handle the sophisticated requests that these XPointers imply. However, this can be useful for custom protocols that use XML as an underlying transport mechanism.

Absolute Location Terms

XPointers are built from *location terms*. Each location term specifies a point in the targeted document, generally relative to some other well-known point such as the start of the document or another location term. The type of location term is given by a keyword such as `id()`, `root()`, or `child()`.

Some location terms take arguments between the parentheses. To demonstrate the point, it's useful to have a concrete example in mind. Listing 17-1 is a simple, valid document that should be self-explanatory. It contains information about two related families and their members. The root element is `FAMILYTREE`. A `FAMILYTREE` can contain `PERSON` and `FAMILY` elements. Each `PERSON` and `FAMILY` element has a required `ID` attribute. Persons contain a name, birth date, and death date. Families contain a husband, a wife, and zero or more children. The individual persons are referred to from the family by reference to their IDs. Any child element may be omitted from any element.

 Cross-Reference   This XML application is revisited in Chapter 23, *Designing a New XML Application*.

Listing 17-1: **A family tree**

```xml
<?xml version="1.0"?>
<!DOCTYPE FAMILYTREE [

  <!ELEMENT FAMILYTREE (PERSON | FAMILY)*>

  <!— PERSON elements —>
  <!ELEMENT PERSON (NAME*, BORN*, DIED*, SPOUSE*)>
  <!ATTLIST PERSON
    ID      ID     #REQUIRED
    FATHER  CDATA  #IMPLIED
    MOTHER  CDATA  #IMPLIED
  >
  <!ELEMENT NAME (#PCDATA)>
  <!ELEMENT BORN (#PCDATA)>
  <!ELEMENT DIED  (#PCDATA)>
  <!ELEMENT SPOUSE EMPTY>
  <!ATTLIST SPOUSE IDREF IDREF #REQUIRED>

  <!—FAMILY—>
  <!ELEMENT FAMILY (HUSBAND?, WIFE?, CHILD*) >
  <!ATTLIST FAMILY ID ID #REQUIRED>

  <!ELEMENT HUSBAND EMPTY>
  <!ATTLIST HUSBAND IDREF IDREF #REQUIRED>
  <!ELEMENT WIFE EMPTY>
  <!ATTLIST WIFE IDREF IDREF #REQUIRED>
  <!ELEMENT CHILD EMPTY>
  <!ATTLIST CHILD IDREF IDREF #REQUIRED>

]>
<FAMILYTREE>

  <PERSON ID="p1">
    <NAME>Domeniquette Celeste Baudean</NAME>
    <BORN>11 Feb 1858</BORN>
    <DIED>12 Apr 1898</DIED>
    <SPOUSE IDREF="p2"/>
  </PERSON>

  <PERSON ID="p2">
    <NAME>Jean Francois Bellau</NAME>
    <SPOUSE IDREF="p1"/>
  </PERSON>

  <PERSON ID="p3" FATHER="p2" MOTHER="p1">
    <NAME>Elodie Bellau</NAME>
    <BORN>11 Feb 1858</BORN>
```

Continued

Listing 17-1 *(continued)*

```xml
    <DIED>12 Apr 1898</DIED>
    <SPOUSE IDREF="p4"/>
</PERSON>

<PERSON ID="p4" FATHER="p2" MOTHER="p1">
  <NAME>John P. Muller</NAME>
  <SPOUSE IDREF="p3"/>
</PERSON>

<PERSON ID="p7">
  <NAME>Adolf Eno</NAME>
  <SPOUSE IDREF="p6"/>
</PERSON>

<PERSON ID="p6" FATHER="p2" MOTHER="p1">
  <NAME>Maria Bellau</NAME>
  <SPOUSE IDREF="p7"/>
</PERSON>

<PERSON ID="p5" FATHER="p2" MOTHER="p1">
  <NAME>Eugene Bellau</NAME>
</PERSON>

<PERSON ID="p8" FATHER="p2" MOTHER="p1">
  <NAME>Louise Pauline Bellau</NAME>
  <BORN>29 Oct 1868</BORN>
  <DIED>11 May 1879</DIED>
  <SPOUSE IDREF="p9"/>
</PERSON>

<PERSON ID="p9">
  <NAME>Charles Walter Harold</NAME>
  <BORN>about 1861</BORN>
  <DIED>about 1938</DIED>
  <SPOUSE IDREF="p8"/>
</PERSON>

<PERSON ID="p10" FATHER="p2" MOTHER="p1">
  <NAME>Victor Joseph Bellau</NAME>
  <SPOUSE IDREF="p11"/>
</PERSON>

<PERSON ID="p11">
  <NAME>Ellen Gilmore</NAME>
  <SPOUSE IDREF="p10"/>
</PERSON>

<PERSON ID="p12" FATHER="p2" MOTHER="p1">
  <NAME>Honore Bellau</NAME>
</PERSON>
```

```
<FAMILY ID="f1">
  <HUSBAND IDREF="p2"/>
  <WIFE IDREF="p1"/>
  <CHILD IDREF="p3"/>
  <CHILD IDREF="p5"/>
  <CHILD IDREF="p6"/>
  <CHILD IDREF="p8"/>
  <CHILD IDREF="p10"/>
  <CHILD IDREF="p12"/>
</FAMILY>

<FAMILY ID="f2">
  <HUSBAND IDREF="p7"/>
  <WIFE IDREF="p6"/>
</FAMILY>

</FAMILYTREE>
```

In sections that follow, this document is assumed to be present at the URL
http://www.theharolds.com/genealogy.xml. This isn't a real URL, but the
emphasis here is on selecting individual parts of a document rather than a
document as a whole.

id()

The id() location term is one of the simplest and most useful location terms. It
selects the element in the document that has an ID type attribute with a specified
value. For example, consider the URI http://www.theharolds.com/genealogy.
xml#id(p12). If you look back at Listing 17-1, you find this element:

```
<PERSON ID="p12" FATHER="p2" MOTHER="p1">
  <NAME>Honore Bellau</NAME>
</PERSON>
```

Because ID type attributes are unique, you know there aren't other elements
that match this XPointer. Therefore, http://www.theharolds.com/genealogy.
xml#id(p12) must refer to Honore Bellau's PERSON element. Note that the XPointer
selects the entire element to which it refers, including all its children, not just the
start tag.

The disadvantage of the id() location term is that it requires assistance from the
targeted document. If the element you want to point to does not have an ID type
attribute, you're out of luck. If other elements in the document have ID type
attributes, you may be able to point to one of them and use a relative XPointer
(discussed in the next section) to point to the one you really want. Nonetheless,
ID type attributes are best when you control both the targeted document and the
linking document, so you can ensure that the IDs match the links even as the
documents evolve and change over time.

In some cases, such as a document without a DTD, a targeted document may not have any `ID` type attributes, although it may have attributes named `ID`. In this case, the application may (or may not) try to guess which element you were pointing at. Generally it selects the first element in the document with an attribute of any type and a name whose value matches the requested `ID`. On the other hand, the application is free not to select any element.

root()

The `root()` location term points to the root element of the document. It takes no arguments. For example, the root element of the XML 1.0 specification at `http://www.w3.org/TR/REC-xml` is `spec`. Thus, to select it you can use this URI:

```
http://www.w3.org/TR/REC-xml#root()
```

The `root()` location term is primarily useful in compound XPointers as a basis from which to start. In fact, if no absolute location term is included in a compound location term, `root()` is assumed. However, `root()` can also be used to select the entire document in a URI that uses | to indicate that only a part is normally loaded. For example:

```
http://www.w3.org/TR/1999/REC-xml-names-19990114/xml-
names.xml|root()
```

html()

The `html()` location term selects named anchors in HTML documents. It has a single argument, the name of the anchor to which it refers. For example, the following named anchor exists in the file `http://metalab.unc.edu/xml/`:

<a name="quote"><font color="#AA0000">Quote of the Day</font></a>

The XPointer that refers to this element is:

```
http://metalab.unc.edu/xml#html(quote)
```

The `html()` location term primarily exists for backwards compatibility, that is, to allow XLinks to refer to HTML documents. Named anchors may be used in XML documents, provided all attribute values are quoted, the A element and its attributes are declared in the DTD, and all other well-formedness criteria are met. In general, however, XML has better means than named anchors to identify locations.

Relative Location Terms

`id`, `root`, and `html` are absolute location terms. Absolute location terms can find a particular element in a document regardless of what else is in the document. However, more commonly you want to find the first element of a given type, the last element of a given type, the first child of a particular type, the next element of a given type, all elements of a given type, or something similar. These tasks are accomplished by attaching a relative location term to an absolute location term to form a *compound locator.*

The most general XPointer is a single absolute location term followed by any number of relative location terms. Each term in the list is relative to the one that precedes it, except for the first absolute location term. Terms in the list are separated by periods.

For example, look at the family tree document in Listing 17-1. This fragment selects the first NAME element of the sixth PERSON element in the root element:

```
http://www.theharolds.com/genealogy.xml#root().child(6,PERSON).
child(1,NAME)
```

In this example, that's `<NAME>Maria Bellau</NAME>`.

For another example, suppose you want to link to the NAME element of Domeniquette Celeste Baudean. The easiest way to do this is to identify her PERSON element by its ID, p1, then use the child() relative location term to refer to the first (and only) NAME child element, like this:

```
http://www.theharolds.com/genealogy.xml#id(p1).child(1,NAME)
```

This URI says to look at the document http://www.theharolds.com/genealogy.xml, find its root element, then find the element with the ID p1, then select its first NAME child.

Although geneaology.xml includes ID attributes for most elements, and although they are convenient, they are not required for linking into the document. You can select any element in the document simply by counting down from the root element. Because Maria Bellau's the first person in the document, you can count one PERSON down from the root, then count one NAME down from that. This URI accomplishes that:

```
http://www.theharolds.com/genealogy.xml#root().child(1,
PERSON).child(1,NAME)
```

This URI says to look at the document http://www.theharolds.com/genealogy.xml, find its root element, then find the first PERSON element that's an immediate child of the root element, and then find its first NAME element.

If no absolute location term is included in the XPointer, then root() is assumed. For instance, the previous example could have been written more compactly, like this:

```
http://www.theharolds.com/genealogy.xml#child(1,PERSON).child
(1,NAME)
```

You can compress this still further by omitting the second `child` location term (though not its arguments). For example:

```
http://www.theharolds.com/genealogy.xml#child(1,PERSON).(1,NAME)
```

When the term is omitted this way, it is assumed to be the same as the previous term. Because there's no term in front of `.(1, NAME)`, it's assumed to be the same as the previous one, `child`.

There are other powerful selection techniques, which are discussed below. In fact, including `child()`, there are seven relative location terms. These are listed in Table 17-1. Each serves to select a particular subset of the elements in the document. For instance, the `following` relative location term selects from elements that come after the source element. The `preceding` relative location term selects from elements that come before the source element.

Table 17-1
Relative Location Terms

Term	Meaning
child	Selects from the immediate children of the source element
descendant	Selects from any of the content or child elements of the source element
ancestor	Selects from elements that contain the source element
preceding	Selects from elements that precede the source element
following	Selects from elements that follow the source element
psibling	Selects from sibling elements that precede the source element
fsibling	Selects from sibling elements that follow the source element

Because the relative location term alone is generally not enough to uniquely specify which element is being pointed to, additional arguments are passed that further specify the targeted element by instance number, node type, and attribute. The possible arguments are the same for all seven relative location keywords. They are explored in more detail in the "Relative Location Term Argument" section below.

child

The `child` relative location term selects from only the *immediate* children of the source element. For example, consider this URI:

```
http://www.theharolds.com/genealogy.xml#root().child(6,NAME)
```

This points nowhere because there are no NAME elements in the document that are direct, immediate children of the root. There are a dozen NAME elements that are indirect children. If you'd like to refer to these, you should use the descendant relative locator element instead of child.

descendant

The descendant relative location term searches through all the descendants of the source, not just the immediate children. For example, root().descendant(3,BORN) selects the third BORN element encountered in a depth-first search of the document tree. (Depth first is the order you get if you simply read through the XML document from top to bottom.) In Listing 17-1, that selects Louise Pauline Bellau's birthday, <BORN>29 Oct 1868</BORN>.

ancestor

The ancestor relative location term searches through all the ancestors of the source, starting with the nearest, until it finds the requested element. For example, root().descendant(2,BORN).ancestor(1) selects the PERSON element, which contains the second BORN element. In this example, it selects Elodie Bellau's PERSON element.

preceding

The preceding relative location term searches through all elements that occur before the source element. The preceding locator element has no respect for hierarchy. The first time it encounters an element's start tag, end tag, or empty tag, it counts that element. For example, consider this rule:

```
root().descendant(3,BORN).preceding(5)
```

This says go to Louise Pauline Bellau's birthday, <BORN>29 Oct 1868</BORN>, and then move back five elements. This lands on Maria Bellau's PERSON element.

following

The following relative location term searches through all elements that occur after the source element in the document. Like preceding, following has no respect for hierarchy. The first time it encounters an element's start tag, end tag, or empty tag, it counts that element. For example, consider this rule:

```
root().descendant(2,BORN).following(5)
```

This says go to Elodie Bellau's birthday, `<BORN>11 Feb 1858</BORN>`, and then move forward five elements. This lands on John P. Muller's `NAME` element, `<NAME>John P. Muller</NAME>`, after passing through Elodie Bellau's `DIED` element, Elodie Bellau's `SPOUSE` element, Elodie Bellau's `PERSON` element, and John P. Muller's `PERSON` element, in this order.

psibling

The `psibling` relative location term selects the element that precedes the source element in the same parent element. For example, `root().descendant(2, BORN).psibling(1)` selects Elodie Bellau's `NAME` element, `<NAME>Elodie Bellau</NAME>`. `root().descendant(2, BORN).psibling(2)` doesn't point to anything because there's only one sibling of Elodie Bellau's `NAME` element before it.

fsibling

The `fsibling` relative location term selects the element that follows the source element in the same parent element. For example, `root().descendant(2,born).fsibling(1)` selects Elodie Bellau's `DIED` element, `<DIED>12 Apr 1898</DIED>`. `root().descendant(2,born).fsibling(3)` doesn't point to anything because there are only two sibling elements following Elodie Bellau's `NAME` element.

Relative Location Term Arguments

Each relative location term begins at a particular place in the document called the *location source*. Generally the location source is indicated by an absolute location term (or the root if no absolute term is specified). You then search forward or backward in the document for the first match that meets specified criteria.

Criteria are given as a list of arguments to the relative location term. These may include the number of elements to search forward or backward, the type of thing to search (element, comment, processing instruction, and so on), and/or the value of an attribute to search. These are given in this order:

1. number
2. type
3. attribute

The number is a positive or negative integer that counts forward or backward from the location source. The type is the kind of thing to count, and the attribute is a list of attribute names and values to match. A relative location term can have a number; a number and a type; or a number, a type, and an attribute list.

The arguments that are present are separated by commas and *no whitespace*. For example:

```
child(1,PERSON,FATHER,p2)
```

The no-whitespace requirement is unusual. It exists so that XPointers can easily be attached to the ends of URLs. For example:

```
http://www.theharolds.com/genealogy.xml#child(1,PERSON,FATHER,p2)
```

If whitespace were allowed, the URLs would have to be x-form-www-url-encoded, like this:

```
http://www.theharolds.com/genealogy.xml#child(1,%20PERSON,
%20FATHER,%20p2)
```

For the most part, the same syntax applies to all seven relative location terms.

Selection by Number

The simplest form of selection is by number. The first argument to a relative location term is the index of the node you're pointing at. Positive numbers count forward in the document. Negative numbers count backward. You also can use the `all` keyword to point to all nodes that match the condition.

Number Forward

For instance, in Listing 17-1 the `FAMILYTREE` element is the root. It has 14 immediate children, 12 `PERSON` elements, and two `FAMILY` elements. In order, they are:

```
http://www.theharolds.com/genealogy.xml#root().child(1)
http://www.theharolds.com/genealogy.xml#root().child(2)
http://www.theharolds.com/genealogy.xml#root().child(3)
http://www.theharolds.com/genealogy.xml#root().child(4)
http://www.theharolds.com/genealogy.xml#root().child(5)
http://www.theharolds.com/genealogy.xml#root().child(6)
http://www.theharolds.com/genealogy.xml#root().child(7)
http://www.theharolds.com/genealogy.xml#root().child(8)
http://www.theharolds.com/genealogy.xml#root().child(9)
http://www.theharolds.com/genealogy.xml#root().child(10)
http://www.theharolds.com/genealogy.xml#root().child(11)
http://www.theharolds.com/genealogy.xml#root().child(12)
http://www.theharolds.com/genealogy.xml#root().child(13)
http://www.theharolds.com/genealogy.xml#root().child(14)
```

Greater numbers, such as `http://www.theharolds.com/genealogy.xml#root().child(15)`, don't point anywhere. They're just dangling URLs.

To count all elements in the document, not just the immediate children of the root, you can use descendant instead of child. Table 17-2 shows the first four descendant XPointers for Listing 17-1, and what they point to. Note especially that root().descendant(1) points to the entire first PERSON element, including its children, and not just the PERSON start tag.

Table 17-2 The First Four Descendants of the Root	
XPointer	**Points To**

root().descendant(1)	`<PERSON ID="p1">`
	
	`    <NAME>Domeniquette Celeste`
	`    Baudean</NAME>`
	
	`    <BORN>11 Feb 1858</BORN>`
	
	`    <DIED>12 Apr 1898</DIED>`
	
	`    <SPOUSE IDREF="p2"/>`
	
	`</PERSON>`

root().descendant(2)	`<NAME>Domeniquette Celeste Baudean</NAME>`
root().descendant(3)	`<BORN>11 Feb 1858</BORN>`
root().descendant(4)	`<DIED>12 Apr 1898</DIED>`

Number Backward

Negative numbers enable you to move backward from the current element to the item you're pointing at. In the case of child and descendant, they count backward from the end tag of the element rather than forward from the start tag. For example, this XPointer selects the element that immediately precedes the element with the ID f1:

```
http://www.theharolds.com/genealogy.xml#id(f1).following(-1)
```

In this example, that's the PERSON element for Honore Bellau. In general, however, your links will be clearer if you avoid negative numbers when possible and use an alternate selector. For example, this selects the same element:

```
http://www.theharolds.com/genealogy.xml#id(f1).preceding(1)
```

In tree-oriented selectors such as child and descendant, negative numbers indicate that you should count from the end of the parent rather than the beginning. For example, this points at the last PERSON element in the document:

```
http://www.theharolds.com/genealogy.xml#root().child(-1,person)
```

This points at the penultimate PERSON element in the document:

```
http://www.theharolds.com/genealogy.xml#root().child(-2,person)
```

Table 17-3 shows the last four descendant XPointers for Listing 17-1, and what they point to. Note that the order in which the elements are entered is now established by the end tags rather than the start tags.

Table 17-3 The Last Four Descendants of the Root	
XPointer	**Points To**

root().descendant(1)	`<FAMILY ID="f2">`
	`    <HUSBAND IDREF="p7"/>`
	`    <WIFE IDREF="p6"/>`
	`</FAMILY>`

root().descendant(2)	`<WIFE IDREF="p6"/>`
root().descendant(3)	`<HUSBAND IDREF="p7"/>`

root().descendant(4)	`<FAMILY ID="f1">`
	`    <HUSBAND IDREF="p2"/>`
	`    <WIFE IDREF="p1"/>`
	`    <CHILD IDREF="p3"/>`
	`    <CHILD IDREF="p5"/>`
	`    <CHILD IDREF="p6"/>`
	`    <CHILD IDREF="p8"/>`
	`    <CHILD IDREF="p10"/>`
	`    <CHILD IDREF="p12"/>`
	`</FAMILY>`

all

As well as specifying a number to select, you can use the keyword all. This points to all nodes that match a condition. For example, this rule refers to all children of the element with ID f1:

```
http://www.theharolds.com/genealogy.xml#id(f1).child(all)
```

In other words, this points to:

```
<HUSBAND IDREF="p2"/>
<WIFE IDREF="p1"/>
<CHILD IDREF="p3"/>
<CHILD IDREF="p5"/>
<CHILD IDREF="p6"/>
<CHILD IDREF="p8"/>
<CHILD IDREF="p10"/>
<CHILD IDREF="p12"/>
```

Selection by Node Type

The above rules chose particular elements in the document. However, sometimes you want to select the fifth WIFE or the third PERSON while ignoring elements of other types. Selecting these by instance number alone is prone to error if the document changes. The addition or deletion of a single element in the wrong place can misalign all links that rely only on instance numbers.

Occasionally you may want to select processing instructions, comments, CDATA sections, or particular raw text in a document. You can accomplish this by adding a second argument to the relative location term — after the number — that specifies which nodes you're counting and (implicitly) which you're ignoring. This can be the name of the element you want to point to or one of six keywords listed in Table 17-4.

Table 17-4
Possible Second Arguments for Relative Location Terms

Type	Match
#element	Any element
#pi	Any processing instruction
#comment	Any comment
#text	Any nonmarkup character data
#cdata	CDATA sections
#all	All of the above
Name	Elements with the specified name

Most selection rules include the type of the element sought. You've already seen examples where root().child(6, PERSON) selects the sixth PERSON child of root. This may refer to the wrong individual if a PERSON element is added or deleted, but at least it is a PERSON element instead of something else like a FAMILY.

You can also specify just a type and omit the instance number (though not the comma). For example, this URI selects all PERSON elements in the document regardless of position:

```
http://www.theharolds.com/genealogy.xml#root().child(,PERSON)
```

Pay special attention to the orphaned comma in front of PERSON. It is required by the BNF grammar in the current version of the XPointer specification. Its presence makes it slightly easier for programs to parse the XPointer, even if it makes it harder for humans to read the XPointer.

Exactly what the application does when all PERSON elements are targeted is up to the application. In general, something more complex than merely loading the document and positioning it at the targeted element is suggested, since there is more than one targeted element. If the application uses this fragment to decide which parts of a document to load, then it loads all the elements of the specified type.

However, this is unusual. Most of the time, selection by type is only used to further restrict the elements selected until only a single one remains targeted.

Name

The most common use for the second argument to a relative location term is to provide a name for the element type. For instance, suppose you want to point to the first FAMILY element that's a child of the root element, but you don't know how it's intermixed with PERSON elements. This rule accomplishes that:

```
http://www.theharolds.com/genealogy.xml#root().child(1,FAMILY)
```

This is particularly powerful when you chain selection rules. For example, this points to the second CHILD element of the first FAMILY element:

```
http://www.theharolds.com/genealogy.xml#root().child(1,FAMILY).
child(2,CHILD)
```

In fact, it's more common to specify the type of the element you're selecting than not to specify it. This is especially true for relative location terms that don't respect hierarchy such as following and preceding.

#element

If no second argument is specified, then elements are matched, but processing instructions, comments, CDATA sections, character data, and so forth are not matched. You can replicate this behavior with the keyword #element as the second argument. For example, these two URIs are the same:

```
http://www.theharolds.com/genealogy.xml#id(f2).preceding(1)
http://www.theharolds.com/genealogy.xml#id(f2).preceding
(1,#element)
```

The main reason to use #element is so you can then use a third argument to match against attributes.

#text

The #text argument selects raw text inside an element. It's most commonly used with mixed content. For example, consider this CITATION element from Listing 12-3 in Chapter 12:

```
<CITATION CLASS="TURING" ID="C2">
  <AUTHOR>Turing, Alan M.</AUTHOR>
  "<TITLE>On Computable Numbers,
    With an Application to the Entscheidungs-problem</TITLE>"
  <JOURNAL>
    Proceedings of the London Mathematical Society</JOURNAL>,
  <SERIES>Series 2</SERIES>,
  <VOLUME>42</VOLUME>
  (<YEAR>1936</YEAR>):
  <PAGES>230-65</PAGES>.
</CITATION>
```

The following XPointer refers to the quotation mark before the TITLE element.

```
id(C2).child(2,#text)
```

The first text node in this fragment is the whitespace between <CITATION CLASS="TURING" ID="C2"> and <AUTHOR>. Technically, this XPointer refers to all text between </AUTHOR> and <TITLE>, including the whitespace and not just the quotation mark.

Caution XPointers that point to text nodes are tricky. I recommend you avoid them if possible, just as you should avoid mixed content. Of course, you may not always be able to, especially if you need to point to parts of documents written by other authors who don't follow this best practice.

Because character data does not contain child elements, further relative location terms may not be attached to an XPointer that follows one that selects a text node. Since character data does not have attributes, attribute arguments may not be used after #text.

#cdata

The #cdata argument specifies that a CDATA section (more properly, the text of a CDATA section) is to be selected. For example, this XPointer refers to the second CDATA section in a document:

```
root().following(2,#cdata)
```

Because CDATA sections cannot have children, further relative location terms may not be attached to an XPointer that follows one that selects a CDATA section. Since CDATA sections do not have attributes, attribute arguments may not be used after #cdata.

#pi

On rare occasions you may want to select a processing instruction rather than an element. In this case, you can use #pi as the second argument to the location term. For example, this XPointer selects the second processing instruction in the document's third BEAN element:

```
root().descendant(3,BEAN).child(2,#pi)
```

Because processing instructions do not contain attributes or elements, you cannot add an additional relative location term after the first term that selects a processing instruction. However, you can use a string() location term to select part of the text of the processing instruction.

#comment

XPointers point to comments in much the same way they point to processing instructions. The literal #comment is used as the second argument to the location term. For example, this XPointer points to the third comment in Listing 17-1:

```
http://www.theharolds.com/genealogy.xml#descendant(3,#comment)
```

Because comments do not contain attributes or elements, you cannot add an additional relative location term after the first term that selects a processing instruction. You can use a string() location term to select part of the text of the processing instruction.

#all

On very rare occasions, you may wish to select a particular node in a document regardless of whether it's an element, raw character data, a processing instruction, a CDATA section, or a comment. The only reason I can think of to do this is if you're iterating through all nodes in the document or element. By using #all as the second argument to a relative location term, you can ignore the type of the thing you're matching. For example, consider this fragment from Listing 12-3 in Chapter 12:

```
<CITATION CLASS="TURING" ID="C3">
  <AUTHOR>Turing, Alan M.</AUTHOR>
  "<TITLE>Computing Machinery &amp; Intelligence</TITLE>"
  <JOURNAL>Mind</JOURNAL>
  <VOLUME>59</VOLUME>
  (<MONTH>October</MONTH>
  <YEAR>1950</YEAR>):
  <PAGES>433-60</PAGES>
</CITATION>
```

Table 17-5 lists four XPointers that simply count nodes down from the `CITATION` element. It also lists what is pointed to by the XPointers.

Table 17-5	
The First Four XPointer Nodes of the CITATION Element	

XPointer	Points To
`id(C3).following(1,#all)`	the whitespace between `<CITATION CLASS="TURING" ID="C3">` and `<AUTHOR>`
`id(C3).following(2,#all)`	`<AUTHOR>Turing, Alan M.</AUTHOR>`
`id(C3).following(3,#all)`	`Turing, Alan M.`
`id(C3).following(4,#all)`	`"`

Selection by Attribute

You can add third and fourth arguments to relative location terms to point to elements by attributes. The third argument is the attribute name. The fourth argument is the attribute value. For example, to find the first `PERSON` element in the document `http://www.theharolds.com/genealogy.xml` whose `FATHER` attribute is Jean Francois Bellau (ID `p2`), you could write:

```
root().child(1,PERSON,FATHER,p2)
```

If you include a third argument, you must include a fourth argument. You can't match against an attribute name without also matching against an attribute value. However, you can use an asterisk for either the name or the value to indicate that anything matches. Setting the third argument to an asterisk (*) indicates that any attribute name is allowed. For example, this XPointer selects all elements that have an attribute value of p2 for any attribute:

```
root().child(all,#element,*,p2)
```

This rule selects the first `PERSON` element in the document that has an attribute value of p2, regardless of whether that attribute appears as a `FATHER`, a `MOTHER`, an `ID`, or something else.

```
root().child(1,PERSON,*,p2)
```

In Listing 17-1, this is Jean Francois Bellau's `PERSON` element.

Setting the fourth argument to an asterisk (*) indicates that any value is allowed, including a default value read from the `ATTLIST` declaration in the DTD. For example, this rule selects the first element in the document that has a FATHER attribute:

```
root().child(1,#element,FATHER,*)
```

In Listing 17-1, this is Elodie Bellau's PERSON element.

You can use #IMPLIED as the fourth argument to match against attributes that don't have a value, either directly specified or defaulted. For instance, this rule finds the first PERSON element that doesn't have a FATHER attribute:

```
root().child(1,PERSON,FATHER,#IMPLIED)
```

In Listing 17-1, this is Domeniquette Celeste Baudean's PERSON element.

Attribute arguments only work on relative location terms that select an element. You cannot use them when the second argument is #text, #cdata, #pi, or #comment because these nodes do not have attributes.

String Location Terms

Selecting a particular element is almost always good enough for pointing into well-formed XML documents. However, on occasion you need to point into non-XML data or XML data in which large chunks of non-XML text is embedded via CDATA sections, comments, processing instructions, or some other means. In these cases you may need to refer to particular ranges of text in the document that don't map onto any particular markup element. You can use a string location term to do this.

A string location term points to an occurrence of a specified string. Unlike most other location terms, a string location term can point to locations inside comments, CDATA, and the like. For example, this fragment finds the first occurrence of the string "Harold" in Listing 17-1:

```
http://www.theharolds.com/genealogy.xml#string(1,"Harold")
```

This targets the position immediately preceding the *H* in Harold in Charles Walter Harold's NAME element. This is not the same as pointing at the entire NAME element as an element-based selector would do.

You can add an optional third position argument to specify how many characters to target to the right of the beginning of the matched string. For example, this targets whatever immediately follows the first occurrence of the string "Harold" because *Harold* has six letters:

```
http://www.theharolds.com/genealogy.xml#string(1,"Harold",6)
```

An optional fourth argument specifies the number of characters to select. For example, this URI selects the first occurrence of the entire string "Harold" in Listing 17-1:

```
http://www.theharolds.com/genealogy.xml#string(1,"Harold",1,6)
```

Use the empty string (" ") in a string location term to specify particular characters in the document. For example, the following URI targets the 256th character in the document. (To be precise, it targets the position between the 255th and 256th element in the document.)

```
http://www.theharolds.com/genealogy.xml#string(256, "")
```

When matching strings, case and whitespace are considered. Markup characters are ignored.

Instead of requesting a particular instance of a particular string match, you can ask for all of them by using the keyword `all` as the first argument. For example, this rule selects all occurrences of the string "Bellau" in the document:

```
http://www.theharolds.com/genealogy.xml#string(all,"Bellau")
```

This can result in a noncontiguous selection, which many applications may not understand, so use this technique with caution.

The origin Absolute Location Term

The fourth absolute location term is `origin`. However, it's only useful when used in conjunction with one or more relative location terms. In intradocument links, that is, links from one point in a document to another point in the same document, it's often necessary to refer to "the next element after this one," or "the parent element of this element." The `origin` absolute location term refers to the current element so that such references are possible.

Consider Listing 17-2, a simple slide show. In this example, `origin().following (1,SLIDE)` refers to the next slide in the show. `origin().preceding(1,SLIDE)` refers to the previous slide in the show. Presumably this would be used in conjunction with a style sheet that showed one slide at a time.

Listing 17-2: **A slide show**

```
<?xml version="1.0"?>
<SLIDESHOW>
  <SLIDE>
    <H1>Welcome to the slide show!</H1>
    <BUTTON xml:link="simple"
```

```
                  href="origin().following(1,SLIDE)">
      Next
    </BUTTON>
  </SLIDE>
  <SLIDE>
    <H1>This is the second slide</H1>
    <BUTTON xml:link="simple"
            href="origin().preceding(1,SLIDE)">
      Previous
    </BUTTON>
    <BUTTON xml:link="simple"
            href="origin().following(1,SLIDE)">
      Next
    </BUTTON>
  </SLIDE>
  <SLIDE>
    <H1>This is the second slide</H1>
    <BUTTON xml:link="simple"
            href="origin().preceding(1,SLIDE)">
      Previous
    </BUTTON>
    <BUTTON xml:link="simple"
            href="origin().following(1,SLIDE)">
      Next
    </BUTTON>
  </SLIDE>
  <SLIDE>
    <H1>This is the third slide</H1>
    <BUTTON xml:link="simple"
            href="origin().preceding(1,SLIDE)">
      Previous
    </BUTTON>
    <BUTTON xml:link="simple"
            href="origin().following(1,SLIDE)">
      Next
    </BUTTON>
  </SLIDE>
  ...
  <SLIDE>
    <H1>This is the last slide</H1>
    <BUTTON xml:link="simple"
            href="origin().preceding(1,SLIDE)">
      Previous
    </BUTTON>
  </SLIDE>

</SLIDESHOW>
```

Generally, the `origin()` location term is only used in fully relative URIs in XLinks. If any URI part is included, it must be the same as the URI of the current document.

Spanning a Range of Text

In some applications it may be important to specify a range of text rather than a particular point in a document. This can be accomplished via a *span*. A span begins at one XPointer and continues until another XPointer.

A span is indicated by the keyword span() used as a location term. However, the arguments to span() are two location terms separated by a comma identifying the beginning and end of the span. If these are relative location terms, then the term preceding the span is the source for both terms.

For example, suppose you want to select everything between the first PERSON element and the last PERSON element in genealogy.xml. This XPointer accomplishes that:

```
root().span(child(1,PERSON),child(-1,PERSON))
```

Summary

In this chapter you learned about XPointers. In particular you learned:

✦ XPointers refer to particular parts of or locations in XML documents.

✦ The id absolute location term points to an element with a specified value for an ID type attribute.

✦ The root absolute location term points to the root element of an XML document.

✦ The html absolute location term points to a named anchor in an HTML document.

✦ Relative location terms can be chained to make more sophisticated compound selectors. The term to which a term is relative is called the location source.

✦ The child relative location term points to an immediate child of the location source.

✦ The descendant relative location term points to any element contained in the location source.

✦ The ancestor relative location term points to an element that contains the location source.

✦ The preceding relative location term points to any element that comes before the location source.

✦ The following relative location term points to any element following the location source.

✦ The `psibling` relative location term selects from sibling elements that precede the target element.

✦ The `fsibling` relative location term selects from sibling elements that follow the target element.

✦ Each relative location term has between one and four arguments: a number, a type, an attribute name, and an attribute value.

✦ The first argument to a relative location term is a number determining the relative position of the targeted node or the keyword `all`.

✦ The second argument to a relative location term determines the type of the targeted node and may be the name of the element or one of the keywords `#element`, `#pi`, `#comment`, `#text`, `#cdata`, `#all`.

✦ The third argument to a relative location term determines the name of the attribute possessed by the targeted node.

✦ The fourth argument to a relative location term determines the value of an attribute of the targeted node.

✦ The `string` location term points to a specified block of text in the location source.

✦ The `origin` absolute location term points to the current element.

✦ Spans refer to a range of text instead of merely one particular element.

The next chapter explores namespaces. Namespaces use URIs as a means of sorting out the elements in a document that's formed from multiple XML applications. For example, namespaces allow you to simultaneously use two different XML vocabularies that define the same elements in incompatible ways.

✦   ✦   ✦

Namespaces

No XML is an island. While you might find it useful to write documents that use a single markup vocabulary, (witness the baseball examples of Chapters 4 and 5) it's even more useful to mix and match tags from different XML applications. For example, you may want to include a BIOGRAPHY element in each PLAYER element. Since the biography consists basically of free-form, formatted text, it's convenient to write it in well-formed HTML without reinventing all the tags for paragraphs, line breaks, list items, bold elements, and so forth from scratch.

The problem, however, is that when mixing and matching tags from different XML applications, you're likely to find the same tag used for two different things. Is a TITLE the title of a page or the title of a book? Is an ADDRESS the mailing address of a company or the email address of a Webmaster? Namespaces disambiguate these instances by associating a URI with each tag set, and attaching a prefix to each elementto indicate which tag set it belongs to. Thus, you can have both BOOK:TITLE and HTML:TITLE elements or POSTAL:ADDRESS and HTML:ADDRESS elements instead of just one kind of TITLE. or ADDRESS. This chapter shows you how to use namespaces.

What Is a Namespace?

XML enables developers to create their own markup languages for their own projects. These languages can be shared with individuals working on similar projects all over the world. One specific example of this is XSL. XSL is itself an XML application for styling XML documents. The XSL transformation language must output arbitrary, well-formed XML, possibly including XSL itself. Thus, you need a clear-cut means of distinguishing between those XML elements that are XSL transformation instructions and output XML elements, *even if they have the same names*!

Namespaces are the solution. They allow each element and attribute in a document to be placed in a different namespace. The XML elements that comprise XSL transformation instructions are placed in the `http://www.w3.org/XSL/Transform/1.0` namespace. The XML elements that are part of the output can reside in some other convenient namespace like `http://www.w3.org/TR/REC-html40` or `http://www.w3.org/XSL/Format/1.0`. The exact namespace isn't even important as long as it's different.

Caution If you're familiar with the concept of namespaces as used in C++ and other programming languages, you need to put aside your preconceptions before reading further. XML namespaces are similar to, but not quite the same as the namespaces used in programming. In particular, XML namespaces do not necessarily form a set (a collection with no duplicates).

Listing 15-2, a transformation from a source vocabulary to XSL formatting objects, initially appeared in Chapter 15, *XSL Formatting Objects*. It displays an XSL style sheet that converts from input XML to XSL formatting objects. The formatting engine distinguishes between elements that are XSL instructions and literal data for the output by using namespaces. Any element in the `http://www.w3.org/XSL/Transform/1.0` namespace represents a transformation instruction. Any element in the `http://www.w3.org/XSL/Format/1.0` namespace comprises part of the output.

```
<?xml version="1.0"?>
<xsl:stylesheet
  xmlns:xsl="http://www.w3.org/XSL/Transform/1.0"
  xmlns:fo="http://www.w3.org/XSL/Format/1.0"
  result-ns="fo" indent-result="yes">

<xsl:template match="/">
  <fo:root xmlns:fo="http://www.w3.org/XSL/Format/1.0">

    <fo:layout-master-set>
      <fo:simple-page-master page-master-name="only">
        <fo:region-body/>
      </fo:simple-page-master>
    </fo:layout-master-set>

    <fo:page-sequence>

     <fo:sequence-specification>
      <fo:sequence-specifier-single page-master-name="only"/>
     </fo:sequence-specification>

      <fo:flow>
        <xsl:apply-templates select="//ATOM"/>
      </fo:flow>

    </fo:page-sequence>

  </fo:root>
</xsl:template>
```

```
<xsl:template match="ATOM">
  <fo:block font-size="20pt" font-family="serif">
    <xsl:value-of select="NAME"/>
  </fo:block>
</xsl:template>

</xsl:stylesheet>
```

More specifically, these elements exist in the `http://www.w3.org/XSL/Transform/ 1.0` namespace and are XSL instructions:

- `stylesheet`
- `template`
- `apply-templates`
- `value-of`

These elements, in the `http://www.w3.org/XSL/Format/1.0` namespace, are XSL formatting objects and part of the output:

- `root`
- `layout-master-set`
- `simple-page-master`
- `region-body`
- `sequence-specification`
- `sequence-specifier-single`
- `page-sequence`
- `block`

The four elements with the `xsl` prefix have the *qualified names* beginning with the prefix:

- `xsl:stylesheet`
- `xsl:template`
- `xsl:apply-templates`
- `xsl:value-of`

However, their full names use the URL rather than the prefix:

- `http://www.w3.org/XSL/Transform/1.0:stylesheet`
- `http://www.w3.org/XSL/Transform/1.0:template`
- `http://www.w3.org/XSL/Transform/1.0:apply-templates`
- `http://www.w3.org/XSL/Transform/1.0:value-of`

In essence, the shorter qualified names are nicknames that are used only within the document because URLs often contain characters like ~, %, and / that aren't legal in XML names. However, qualified names do make documents a little easier to type and read.

Caution *Namespaces in an XML* is an official W3C recommendation. The W3C considers it complete, aside from possible minor errors and elucidations. Nonetheless, of all the XML specifications from the W3C, this one is the most controversial. Many people feel very strongly that this standard contains fundamental flaws. The main objection argues that namespaces are, in practice, incompatible with DTDs and validation. While I don't have a strong opinion on this one way or the other, I do question the wisdom of publishing a standard when nothing approaching a consensus has been reached. Namespaces are a crucial part of many XML related specifications such as XSL and XHTML, so you need to understand them. Nonetheless, a lot of developers and authors have chosen to ignore this specification for their own work.

Namespace Syntax

Namespaces have been crafted to layer on top of the XML 1.0 specification. An XML 1.0 processor that knows nothing about namespaces can still read a document that uses namespaces, and will not find any errors. Documents that use namespaces do not break existing XML parsers (at least ones that don't check for validity); and users don't have to wait for notoriously unpunctual software companies to release expensive upgrades before using namespaces.

Definition of Namespaces

Namespaces are defined using an `xmlns:prefix` attribute on the applicable elements they apply to. `prefix` is replaced by the actual prefix used for the namespace. The value of the attribute is the URI of the namespace. For example, this `xsl:stylesheet` tag associates the prefix `xsl` with the URI `http://www.w3.org/XSL/Transform/1.0`.

```
<xsl:stylesheet
xmlns:xsl="http://www.w3.org/XSL/Transform/1.0">
```

The `xsl` prefix can then be attached to the local element and attribute names within the `xsl:stylesheet` element to identify them as belonging to the `http://www.w3.org/XSL/Transform/1.0` namespace. The prefix is separated from the local name by a colon. Listing 14-2, a basic XSL style sheet for the periodic table, which was first shown in Chapter 14, *XSL Transformations*, demonstrates by using the `xsl` prefix on the `stylesheet`, `template`, and `apply-templates` elements.

```
<?xml version="1.0"?>
<xsl:stylesheet xmlns:xsl="http://www.w3.org/XSL/Transform/1.0">
```

```
<xsl:template match="PERIODIC_TABLE">
  <html>
    <xsl:apply-templates/>
  </html>
</xsl:template>

<xsl:template match="ATOM">
  <P>
    <xsl:apply-templates/>
  </P>
</xsl:template>

</xsl:stylesheet>
```

The URI that defines a namespace is purely formal. Its only purpose is to group and disambiguate element and attribute names in the document. It does not necessarily point to anything. In particular, there is no guarantee that the document at the URI describes the syntax used in the document; or, for that matter, that any document exists at the URI. Having said that, if there is a canonical URI for a particular XML application, then that URI is a good choice for the namespace definition.

A namespace prefix can be any legal XML name that does not contain a colon. Recall from Chapter 6, *Well-Formed XML Documents*, that a legal XML name must begin with a letter or an underscore (_). Subsequent letters in the name may include letters, digits, underscores, hyphens, and periods. They may not include whitespace.

Note

There are two prefixes that are specifically disallowed, xml and xmlns. The xml prefix is defined to refer to http://www.w3.org/XML/1998/namespace. The xmlns prefix is used to bind elements to namespaces, and is therefore not available as a prefix to be bound to.

Other than disallowing the colon character in XML names (aside from its use in separating prefixes and local names) namespaces have no direct effect on standard XML syntax. A document that uses namespaces must still be well-formed when read by a processor that knows nothing about namespaces. If the document is to be validated, then it must be validated without specifically considering the namespaces. To an XML processor, a document that uses namespaces is just a funny-looking document in which some of the element and attribute names may have a single colon.

Caution

Namespaces do present problems for validation. If a DTD was written without namespace prefixes, then it must be rewritten using the namespace prefixes before it can be used to validate documents that use the prefixes. For example, consider this element declaration:

```
<!ELEMENT DIVISION (DIVISION_NAME, TEAM+)>
```

You have to rewrite it like this if the elements are all given the bb namespace prefix:

```
<!ELEMENT bb:DIVISION (bb:DIVISION_NAME, bb:TEAM+)>
```

This means that you cannot use the same DTD for both documents with namespaces and documents without, even if they use essentially the same vocabulary. In fact, you can't even use the same DTD for documents that use the same tag sets and namespaces, but different prefixes, because DTDs are tied to the actual prefixes rather than the URIs of the namespaces.

Multiple Namespaces

Listing 14-2 did not actually place the HTML elements in a namespace, but that's not hard to do. Listing 18-1 demonstrates. Just as xsl is the conventional prefix for XSL transformation instructions, html is the conventional prefix for HTML elements. In this example, the xsl:stylesheet element declares two different namespaces, one for XSL and one for HTML.

Listing 18-1: An XSL stylesheet that uses the http://www.w3. org/TR/REC-html40 namespace for output

```
<?xml version="1.0"?>
<xsl:stylesheet xmlns:xsl="http://www.w3.org/XSL/Transform/1.0"
                xmlns:html="http://www.w3.org/TR/REC-html40">

  <xsl:template match="PERIODIC_TABLE">
    <html:html>
      <xsl:apply-templates/>
    </html:html>
  </xsl:template>

  <xsl:template match="ATOM">
    <html:p>
      <xsl:apply-templates/>
    </html:p>
  </xsl:template>

</xsl:stylesheet>
```

While it's customary, and generally useful to place the xmlns attribute on the root element, it can appear on other elements as well. In this case, the namespace prefix is understood only within the element where it's declared. Consider Listing 18-2. The html prefix is legal only in the xsl:template element where it's declared. It can't be applied in other template rules, unless they separately declare the html namespace.

Listing 18-2: An XSL style sheet with the http://www.w3.org/ TR/REC-html40 namespace declared in the template rules

```
<?xml version="1.0"?>
<xsl:stylesheet
xmlns:xsl="http://www.w3.org/XSL/Transform/1.0">

  <xsl:template match="PERIODIC_TABLE"
                xmlns:html="http://www.w3.org/TR/REC-html40">
    <html:html>
      <xsl:apply-templates/>
    </html:html>
  </xsl:template>

  <xsl:template match="ATOM">
    <p>
      <xsl:apply-templates/>
    <p>
  </xsl:template>

</xsl:stylesheet>
```

You can redefine a namespace in a child element. For example, consider the XSL style sheet in Listing 18-3. Here, the xsl prefix appears in different elements to refer to http://www.w3.org/XSL/Transform/1.0 and http://www.w3.org/XSL/Format/1.0 alternately. Although every element has the prefix xsl, the XSL transformation instructions and the XSL formatting objects still reside in different namespaces because the meaning of the xsl prefix changes from element to element.

Listing 18-3: Redefining the xsl prefix

```
<?xml version="1.0"?>
<xsl:stylesheet
  xmlns:xsl="http://www.w3.org/XSL/Transform/1.0">

  <xsl:template match="/">
    <xsl:root xmlns:xsl="http://www.w3.org/XSL/Format/1.0">

      <xsl:layout-master-set>
        <xsl:simple-page-master page-master-name="only">
          <xsl:region-body/>
        </xsl:simple-page-master>
```

Continued

Listing 18-3 *(continued)*

```
      </xsl:layout-master-set>

      <xsl:page-sequence>

      <xsl:sequence-specification>
       <xsl:sequence-specifier-single page-master-name="only"/>
      </xsl:sequence-specification>

        <xsl:flow>
          <xsl:apply-templates select="//ATOM"/
            xmlns:xsl="http://www.w3.org/XSL/Transform/1.0"/>
        </xsl:flow>

      </xsl:page-sequence>

    </xsl:root>
  </xsl:template>

  <xsl:template match="ATOM">
    <xsl:block font-size="20pt" font-family="serif"
       xmlns:xsl="http://www.w3.org/XSL/Format/1.0">
    <xsl:value-of select="NAME"
       xmlns:xsl="http://www.w3.org/XSL/Transform/1.0"/>
    </xsl:block>
  </xsl:template>

</xsl:stylesheet>
```

This is, however, needlessly confusing and I strongly recommend that you avoid it. There are more than enough prefixes to go around, and almost no need to reuse them within the same document. The main importance of this is if two different documents from different authors that happen to reuse a similar prefix are being combined. This is a good reason to avoid short prefixes like a, m, and x that are likely to be reused for different purposes.

Attributes

Since attributes belong to particular elements, they're more easily disambiguated from similarly named attributes without namespaces. Consequently, it's not nearly as essential to add namespaces to attributes as to elements. For example, the April 21, 1999 working draft of the XSL specification requires that all XSL transformation elements fall in the http://www.w3.org/XSL/Transform/1.0 namespace. However, it does not require that the attributes of these elements be in any particular namespace. (In fact, it requires that they not be in any namespace.) Nonetheless, you can attach namespace prefixes to attributes if necessary. For example, this PLAYER element and all its attributes live in the `http://metalab.unc.edu/xml/baseball` namespace.

```
<bb:PLAYER xmlns:bb="http://metalab.unc.edu/xml/baseball"
 bb:GIVEN_NAME="Tom" bb:SURNAME="Glavine"
 bb:POSITION="Starting Pitcher" bb:GAMES="33"
 bb:GAMES_STARTED="33" bb:WINS="20" bb:LOSSES="6" bb:SAVES="0"
 bb:COMPLETE_GAMES="4" bb:SHUT_OUTS="3" bb:ERA="2.47"
 bb:INNINGS="229.1" bb:HOME_RUNS_AGAINST="13"
 bb:RUNS_AGAINST="67" bb:EARNED_RUNS="63" bb:HIT_BATTER="2"
 bb:WILD_PITCHES="3" bb:BALK="0" bb:WALKED_BATTER="74"
 bb:STRUCK_OUT_BATTER="157"/>
```

This might occasionally prove useful if you need to combine attributes from two different XML applications on the same element.

It is possible (though mostly pointless) to associate the same namespace URI with two different prefixes. There's really no reason to do this. The only reason I bring it up here is simply to warn you that it is the full name of the attribute that must satisfy XML's rules for an element not having more than one attribute with the same name. For example, this is illegal because `bb:GIVEN_NAME` and `baseball:GIVEN_NAME` are the same:

```
<bb:PLAYER xmlns:bb="http://metalab.unc.edu/xml"
           xmlns:baseball="http://metalab.unc.edu/xml"
 bb:GIVEN_NAME="Hank" bb:SURNAME="Aaron"
 baseball:GIVEN_NAME="Henry" />
```

On the other hand, the URI does not actually get checked to see what it points to. The URIs `http://metalab.unc.edu/xml/` and `http://www.metalab.unc.edu/xml/` point to the same page. However, this is legal:

```
<bb:PLAYER xmlns:bb="http://metalab.unc.edu/xml"
           xmlns:baseball="http://www.metalab.unc.edu/xml"
 bb:GIVEN_NAME="Hank" bb:SURNAME="Aaron"
 baseball:GIVEN_NAME="Henry" />
```

Default Namespaces

In long documents with a lot of markup, all in the same namespace, you might find it inconvenient to add a prefix to each element name. You can attach a default namespace to an element and its child elements using an `xmlns` attribute with no prefix. The element itself, as well as all its children, are considered to be in the defined namespace unless they possess an explicit prefix. For example, Listing 18-4 shows an XSL style sheet that does not prefix XSL transformation elements with `xsl` as is customary.

Note   Attributes are never in a default namespace. They must be explicitly prefixed.

Listing 18-4: An XSL stylesheet that uses default namespaces

```xml
<?xml version="1.0"?>
<stylesheet
  xmlns="http://www.w3.org/XSL/Transform/1.0"
  xmlns:fo="http://www.w3.org/XSL/Format/1.0"
  result-ns="fo">

  <template match="/">
    <fo:root xmlns:fo="http://www.w3.org/XSL/Format/1.0">

      <fo:layout-master-set>
        <fo:simple-page-master page-master-name="only">
          <fo:region-body/>
        </fo:simple-page-master>
      </fo:layout-master-set>

      <fo:page-sequence>

       <fo:sequence-specification>
        <fo:sequence-specifier-single page-master-name="only"/>
       </fo:sequence-specification>

        <fo:flow>
          <apply-templates select="//ATOM"/>
        </fo:flow>

      </fo:page-sequence>

    </fo:root>
  </template>

  <template match="ATOM">
    <fo:block font-size="20pt" font-family="serif">
      <value-of select="NAME"/>
    </fo:block>
  </template>

</stylesheet>
```

Perhaps the best use of default namespaces attaches a namespace to every element in an existing document to which you're now going to add tags from a different language. For instance, if you place some MathML in an HTML document, you only have to add prefixes to the MathML elements. You could put all the HTML elements in the `http://www.w3.org/TR/REC-html40` namespace simply by replacing the `<html>` start tag with this tag:

```
<html xmlns="http://www.w3.org/TR/REC-html40">
```

You do not need to edit the rest of the file! The MathML tags you insert still need to be in a separate namespace. However, as long as they aren't mixed up with a lot of HTML markup, you can simply declare an xmlns attribute on the root element of the MathML. This defines a default namespace for the MathML elements that override the default namespace of the document containing the MathML. Listing 18-5 demonstrates.

Listing 18-5: A MathML math element embedded in a well-formed HTML document that uses namespaces

```
<?xml version="1.0"?>
<html xmlns="http://www.w3.org/TR/REC-html40">
  <head>
    <title>Fiat Lux</title>
    <meta name="GENERATOR" content="amaya V1.3b" />
  </head>
  <body>

    <P>And God said,</P>

    <math xmlns="http://www.w3.org/TR/REC-MathML/">
      <mrow>
        <msub>
          <mi>&#x3B4;</mi>
          <mi>&#x3B1;</mi>
        </msub>
        <msup>
          <mi>F</mi>
          <mi>&#x3B1;&#x3B2;</mi>
        </msup>
        <mi></mi>
        <mo>=</mo>
        <mi></mi>
        <mfrac>
          <mrow>
            <mn>4</mn>
            <mi>&#x3C0;</mi>
          </mrow>
          <mi>c</mi>
        </mfrac>
        <mi></mi>
        <msup>
          <mi>J</mi>
          <mrow>
            <mi>&#x3B2;</mi>
            <mo></mo>
          </mrow>
        </msup>
```

Continued

Listing 18-5 *(continued)*

```
        </mrow>
    </math>

    <P>and there was light</P>

    </body>
</html>
```

Here, math, mrow, msub, mo, mi, mfrac, mn, and msup are all in the http://www.w3.org/TR/REC-MathML/ namespace, even though the document that contains them uses the http://www.w3.org/TR/REC-html40 namespace.

Namespaces in DTDs

Namespaces do not get any special exemptions from the normal rules of well-formedness and validity. For a document that uses namespaces to be valid, the xmlns attributes must be declared in the DTD for those elements to which they're attached. Furthermore, you must declare the elements and attributes using the prefixes they use in the document. For instance, if a document uses a math:subset element, then the DTD must declare a math:subset element, not merely a subset element. (Of course, these rules do not apply to the merely well-formed documents discussed thus far.) For example:

```
<!ELEMENT math:subset EMPTY>
```

Default attribute values and #IMPLIED attributes can help here. For example, this ATTLIST declaration places every math:subset element in the http://www.w3.org/TR/REC-MathML/ namespace unless specified otherwise in the document.

```
<!ATTLIST math:subset
        xmlns:math "http://www.w3.org/TR/REC-MathML/" #IMPLIED>
```

When working with valid documents, default namespaces prove especially useful since they don't require you to add prefixes to all the elements. Adding prefixes to elements from an XML application whose DTD doesn't use prefixes will break validity.

There are, however, clear limits to how far default namespaces will take you. In particular, they are not sufficient to differentiate between two elements that use an element name in incompatible ways. For example, if one DTD defines a HEAD as containing a TITLE and a META element, and another DTD defines a HEAD as containing #PCDATA, then you will have to use prefixes in the DTD and the document to distinguish the two different HEAD elements.

Two different development efforts are underway that may (or may not) eventually solve the problem of merging incompatible DTDs from different domains. XML schemas may provide a more robust replacement for DTDs. XML fragments may enable different documents to be combined with more distinction between which parts come from where. However, neither of these is even close to finished. Consequently, for now, merging incompatible DTDs will probably require you to rewrite the DTD and your documents to use prefixes.

Tip If you have a question about whether a document that uses namespaces is well-formed or valid, forget everything you know about namespaces. Simply treat the document as a normal XML document that happens to have some element and attribute names that contain colons. The document is as well-formed and valid as it is when you don't consider namespaces.

Summary

This chapter explained how to work with namespaces. In particular, you learned:

✦ Namespaces distinguish between elements and attributes of the same name from different XML applications.

✦ Namespaces are declared by an xmlns attribute whose value is the URI of the namespace. The document referred to by this URI need not exist.

✦ The prefix associated with a namespace is the part of the name of the xmlns attribute that follows the colon; for example xmlns:prefix.

✦ Prefixes are attached to all element and attribute names that belong to the namespace identified by the prefix.

✦ If an xmlns attribute has no prefix, it establishes a default namespace for that element and its child elements (but not for any attributes).

✦ DTDs must be written in such a fashion that a processor that knows nothing about namespaces can still parse and validate the document.

The next chapter explores the Resource Description Framework, RDF, an XML application for encoding meta-data and information structures.

✦　　✦　　✦

The Resource Description Framework

The Resource Description Framework (RDF) is an XML application for encoding metadata. In particular, it's well-suited for describing Web sites and pages so that search engines can not only index them, but also understand what they're indexing. Once RDF and standard RDF vocabularies become prevalent on the Web, searching can become finding. This chapter discusses the RDF statements about resources, basic and abbreviated RDF syntax, the use of containers to group property values together, and RDF schemas.

What Is RDF?

Metadata is data about data, information about information. For example, the text of a book is its data. The name of the author, address of the publisher, copyright date, and so forth is metadata about the book. Metadata has many uses on the Web, including organizing, searching, filtering, and personalizing Web sites. Accurate metadata should make it much easier to find the Web sites you want while ignoring the Web sites you don't want.

In order for metadata to have these benefits, however, Web sites, search engines, and directories must agree to use a standard format for metadata. The Resource Description Framework is a W3C-recommended XML application for encoding, exchanging, and reusing structured metadata. RDF vocabularies can describe rating systems, site maps, privacy preferences, collaborative services, licensing restrictions, and more.

In general, metadata vocabularies must be customized for each individual knowledge domain. However, RDF strives to create a convention that controls how the semantics, syntax, and structure of metadata are formulated in the separate domains, so that metadata formats developed for one domain can be merged with formats developed for a second domain and used in a third domain without losing any of the clarity of the original statements. RDF is designed to make it easy for software to understand enough about a Web site so that it can discover resources on a site, catalog the site's content, rate that content, figure out who owns the content and under what terms and at what cost it may be used, and do other things a Web spider or intelligent agent might want to do.

RDF Statements

An RDF document or element makes statements about resources. A statement says that a certain resource has one or more properties. Each property has a type (that is, a name) and a value. The value of a property may be a literal such as a string, number, or date, or it may be another resource.

A statement can be thought of as a triple composed of three items: resource, property type, and property value. For example, an RDF statement might say, "The book *The XML Bible* (ISBN: 0-7645-3236-7) has the author Elliotte Rusty Harold." Here the resource is "The book *The XML Bible* (ISBN: 0-7645-3236-7)," and the author property of this resource has the value "Elliotte Rusty Harold." Figure 19-1 demonstrates a common way of pictorially describing this RDF statement.

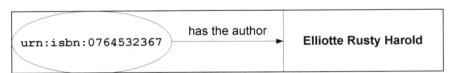

Figure 19-1: An RDF statement described in a picture

A resource can be anything that can have a Uniform Resource Identifier (URI). URIs are a superset of the more common Uniform Resource Locators (URLs), but they can also identify books, elements on a page, television shows, individual people, and more. In the above example, an ISBN is used as a URI for a book. Thus, a resource might be an entire Web site (`http://www.norml.org/`), a single Web page (`http://www.mozilla.org/rdf/doc/index.html`), a specific HTML or XML element on a Web page identified with an XPointer (`http://metalab.unc.edu/xml/mailinglists.html#root().child(1,dt)`), a book (`urn:isbn:0764532367`), a person (`mailto:elharo@metalab.unc.edu`), or just about anything—as long as a URI can be constructed for it. The only requirement for being a resource is a unique URI. This URI does not have to be a URL; it can be something else, such as an ISBN.

Resources are described with properties. A property is a specific characteristic, attribute, or relationship of a resource. Each property has a specific meaning that can be identified by the property's name and the associated schema. The schema should be found at the URI used for the property's namespace. The schema identifies the values, or value ranges, that are permitted for the property, and the types of resources it can describe.

Caution Schemas are still in the development stages, so don't be too surprised if you don't actually find a schema where one is supposed to be. Also note that a namespace URI pointing to a schema is an RDF requirement, not a requirement of namespaces in general. In fact, the namespaces specification specifically denies any such requirement.

RDF only defines an XML syntax for encoding these resource-property type-property value triples in XML. It does not define the actual vocabularies used for describing resources and properties. Eventually this need will need to be addressed as well, at least if RDF is to be useful beyond a local intranet. Efforts are underway to produce standard vocabularies for content rating (PICS 2.0), personal information (P3P), and digital library catalogs (Dublin Core). Others can be invented as needed.

An RDF statement combines a specific resource with a named property and its value. These three parts of the statement are called, respectively, the subject, the predicate, and the object. The resource being described is the subject. The property used to describe the resource is the predicate. And the value of the property is the statement's object.

Here's a normal, human-readable statement:

> *Elliotte Rusty Harold is the creator of the Web site at the URL http://metalab.unc.edu/xml/.*

This same statement can be written in several other ways in English. For example:

> *The Web site at the URL http://metalab.unc.edu/xml/ has the creator Elliotte Rusty Harold.*

> *The Web site at the URL http://metalab.unc.edu/xml/ was created by Elliotte Rusty Harold.*

> *The creator of the Web site at the URL http://metalab.unc.edu/xml/ is Elliotte Rusty Harold.*

> *Elliotte Rusty Harold created the Web site at the URL http://metalab.unc.edu/xml/.*

However, all five versions mean exactly the same thing. In each version, the subject is the Web site at the URL `http://metalab.unc.edu/xml/`. The predicate is the creator property. The object is the value of the creator property, Elliotte Rusty Harold. Figure 19-2 diagrams this statement as RDF understands it.

Figure 19-2: The statement in diagram form

 Note The RDF subject, object, and predicate do not correspond to the common use of those terms in English grammar. Indeed, part of the purpose of RDF is to separate the meaning of subject, object, predicate in an idea from their roles in any given sentence since the same idea can be expressed in multiple sentences, in each of which the grammatical subject, object, and predicate change places.

Basic RDF Syntax

The purpose of RDF is to take a meaningful statement such as "Elliotte Rusty Harold is the creator of the Web site at the URL `http://metalab.unc.edu/xml/`" and write it in a standard XML format that computers can parse.

The root Element

The root element of an RDF document is `RDF`. This and all other RDF elements are normally placed in the `http://www.w3.org/1999/02/22-rdf-syntax-ns#` namespace. (As strange as it looks, the # is not a typo. It's there so that when the element name is concatenated with the namespace, the result is a correct URL.) This namespace is either given the prefix `rdf` or set as the default namespace. For example, with an explicit prefix, an empty `RDF` element looks like this:

```
<rdf:RDF
  xmlns:rdf="http://www.w3.org/1999/02/22-rdf-syntax-ns#">
  <!— rdf:Description elements will go here —>
</rdf:RDF>
```

With the default namespace, it looks like this:

```
<RDF xmlns="http://www.w3.org/1999/02/22-rdf-syntax-ns#">
  <!— rdf:Description elements will go here —>
</RDF>
```

The Description Element

A RDF statement is serialized into XML encoded as a `Description` element. Each property of the resource being described is a child element of the `Description` element. The content of the child element is the value of the property. For example,

Listing 19-1 translates the statement "Elliotte Rusty Harold created the Web site at the URL `http://metalab.unc.edu/xml/`" into RDF.

Listing 19-1: **The statement translated into RDF**

```
<rdf:RDF
  xmlns:rdf="http://www.w3.org/1999/02/22-rdf-syntax-ns#">
  <rdf:Description about="http://metalab.unc.edu/xml/">
    <Creator>Elliotte Rusty Harold</Creator>
  </rdf:Description>
</rdf:RDF>
```

This `rdf:RDF` element contains a single statement. The statement is encoded as an `rdf:Description` element. The resource this statement is about (the subject) is `http://metalab.unc.edu/xml/`. The predicate of this statement is the content of the `rdf:Description` element, `<Creator>Elliotte Rusty Harold</Creator>`. The object of this statement is the content of the `Creator` element, `Elliotte Rusty Harold`. In short, the statement says that the resource at `http://metalab.unc.edu/xml/` has a `Creator` property whose value is the literal string `Elliotte Rusty Harold`.

Namespaces

Namespaces are used to distinguish between RDF elements and elements in property types and values. The `http://www.w3.org/1999/02/22-rdf-syntax-ns#` namespace is often used for RDF elements, generally with an `rdf` prefix. In the example above, the `Creator` element is in the default namespace. However, the descriptions may (and should) come from a different, nondefault namespace. For instance, the `RDF` element in Listing 19-2 uses the Dublin Core vocabulary and the `http://purl.org/DC/` namespace.

Listing 19-2: **Elements from the Dublin Core vocabulary are in the namespace**

```
<rdf:RDF
  xmlns:rdf="http://www.w3.org/1999/02/22-rdf-syntax-ns#"
  xmlns:dc="http://purl.org/DC/">
  <rdf:Description about="http://metalab.unc.edu/xml/">
    <dc:CREATOR>Elliotte Rusty Harold</dc:CREATOR>
  </rdf:Description>
</rdf:RDF>
```

The Dublin Core

The Dublin Core (`http://purl.org/dc/`) is a collection of elements designed to help researchers find electronic resources in a manner similar to using a library card catalog. Dublin Core elements include basic cataloging information, in particular:

✦ TITLE: The name given to the resource.

✦ CREATOR: The person or organization that created most of the resource (the author of a novel or the photographer who took a picture).

✦ SUBJECT: The topic of the resource.

✦ DESCRIPTION: A brief description of the resource, such as an abstract.

✦ PUBLISHER: The person or organization making the resource available (for example, IDG Books, Claremont University, or Apple Computer).

✦ CONTRIBUTOR: A non-CREATOR who contributed to the resource (the illustrator or editor of a novel).

✦ DATE: The date the resource was made available in its present form, generally in the format YYYY-MM-DD, such as 1999-12-31.

✦ TYPE: The category of the resource for example Web page, short story, poem, article, or photograph. Work is ongoing to produce a definitive list of acceptable resource types.

✦ FORMAT: The format of the resource, such as PDF, HTML, or JPEG. Work is ongoing to produce a definitive list of acceptable resource formats.

✦ IDENTIFIER: A unique string or number for the resource (as with a URL, a social security number, or an ISBN).

✦ SOURCE: A string or number that uniquely identifies the work from which the resource was derived. For instance, a Web page with the text of Jerome K. Jerome's 19th century novel *Three Men in a Boat* might use this to specify the specific edition from which text was scanned.

✦ LANGUAGE: The primary language in which the resource is written as ISO 639 language code.

✦ RIGHTS: Copyright and other intellectual property notices specifying the conditions under which the resource may or may not be used.

Several other possible Dublin Core elements are in the experimental stage including RELATION and COVERAGE. The Dublin Core is used throughout the examples in this chapter. However, you are by no means limited to using only these elements. You are free to use different vocabularies and namespaces for properties as long as you put them in a namespace.

Multiple Properties and Statements

A single Description element can state more than one property about a resource. For instance, what's missing from the previous statement is the name of the site, Cafe con Leche. A statement that includes this is, "Elliotte Rusty Harold is the author of the Cafe con Leche Web site at the URL http://metalab.unc.edu/xml/." Rewritten in more stilted, RDF-like syntax, this becomes "The Web site at the URL http://metalab.unc.edu/xml/ has the name Cafe con Leche and was created by Elliotte Rusty Harold." Figure 19-3 diagrams this statement. Listing 19-3 shows how to add the property name to the RDF serialization in a natural way as simply one more child of rdf:Description, dc:TITLE.

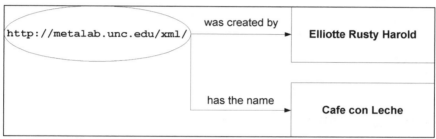

Figure 19-3: A statement with multiple properties in diagram form

Listing 19-3: **A statement with multiple properties in RDF serialization form**

```
<rdf:RDF
  xmlns:rdf="http://www.w3.org/1999/02/22-rdf-syntax-ns#"
  xmlns:dc="http://purl.org/DC/>

  <rdf:Description about="http://metalab.unc.edu/xml/>
    <dc:CREATOR>Elliotte Rusty Harold</dc:CREATOR>
    <dc:TITLE>Cafe con Leche</dc:TITLE>
  </rdf:Description>

</rdf:RDF>
```

A single RDF element can contain any number of Description elements, allowing it to make any number of statements. For example, suppose you want to make the two separate statements "Elliotte Rusty Harold is the author of the Cafe con Leche Web site at the URL http://metalab.unc.edu/xml/" and "Elliotte Rusty Harold is the author of the Cafe au Lait Web site at the URL http://metalab.unc.edu/javafaq/." These are two statements about two different resources. Listing 19-4 shows how these are encoded in RDF.

Listing 19-4 **Two separate statements encoded in RDF**

```
<rdf:RDF
  xmlns:rdf="http://www.w3.org/1999/02/22-rdf-syntax-ns#"
  xmlns:dc="http://purl.org/DC/">

  <rdf:Description about="http://metalab.unc.edu/xml/">
    <dc:CREATOR>Elliotte Rusty Harold</dc:CREATOR>
    <dc:TITLE>Cafe con Leche</dc:TITLE>
  </rdf:Description>

  <rdf:Description about="http://metalab.unc.edu/javafaq/">
    <dc:CREATOR>Elliotte Rusty Harold</dc:CREATOR>
    <dc:TITLE>Cafe au Lait</dc:TITLE>
  </rdf:Description>

</rdf:RDF>
```

Resource Valued Properties

A slightly more complicated example is the statement "The Cafe con Leche Web site at the URL `http://metalab.unc.edu/xml/` has the creator Elliotte Rusty Harold, whose email address is `elharo@metalab.unc.edu`." The email address is the key. It provides a unique identifier for an individual, specifically the URL `mailto:elharo@metalab.unc.edu`. Thus, the individual becomes a resource rather than simply a literal. This resource is the value of the "created by" property of the `http://metalab.unc.edu/xml/` resource. Figure 19-4 diagrams this statement.

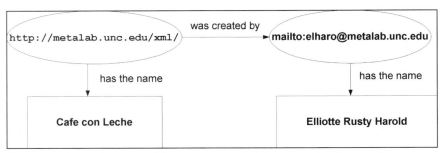

Figure 19-4: A statement with a resource valued property in diagram form

Encoding this statement in RDF is straightforward. Simply give the `Creator` element a `Description` child that describes the `mailto:elharo@metalab.unc.edu` resource, as in Listing 19-5.

Listing 19-5: A statement encoded in RDF with nested Description elements

```
<RDF xmlns="http://www.w3.org/1999/02/22-rdf-syntax-ns#""
     xmlns:dc="http://www.purl.org/DC/">

  <Description about="http://metalab.unc.edu/xml/">
    <dc:TITLE>Cafe con Leche</dc:TITLE>
    <dc:CREATOR/>
      <Description about="mailto:elharo@metalab.unc.edu">
        <dc:TITLE>Elliotte Rusty Harold</dc:TITLE>
      </Description>
    </dc:CREATOR>
  </Description>
</RDF>
```

There's no limit to the depth to which descriptions can be nested, nor is there any limit to the number of properties that can be applied to a Description element, nested or unnested.

RDF also provides an alternate syntax in which Description elements are not nested inside each other. Instead, the resource being described contains a resource attribute that points to the URI of the Description element. For example, Listing 19-6 is an equivalent serialization of the statement "The Cafe con Leche Web site at the URL http://metalab.unc.edu/xml/ has the creator Elliotte Rusty Harold, whose email address is elharo@metalab.unc.edu."

Listing 19-6: Descriptions by reference using the resource attribute

```
<rdf:RDF
  xmlns:rdf=http://www.w3.org/1999/02/22-rdf-syntax-ns#"
  xmlns:dc="http://www.purl.org/DC/>

  <rdf:Description about="http://metalab.unc.edu/xml/">
    <dc:TITLE>Cafe con Leche</dc:TITLE>
    <dc:CREATOR rdf:resource="mailto:elharo@metalab.unc.edu"/>
  </rdf:Description>

  <rdf:Description about=""mailto:elharo@metalab.unc.edu">
    <dc:TITLE>Elliotte Rusty Harold</dc:TITLE>
  </rdf:Description>

</rdf:RDF>
```

Although this syntax is harder for a human reader to parse, it doesn't present any significant difficulties to a computer program. The primary advantage is that it allows the same property to be attached to multiple resources. For example, consider the statement "Elliotte Rusty Harold, whose email address is `elharo@metalab.unc.edu`, created both the Cafe con Leche Web site at the URL `http://metalab.unc.edu/xml/` and the Cafe au Lait Web site at the URL `http://metalab.unc.edu/javafaq/`," which is diagrammed in Figure 19-5. This is easily serialized, as shown in Listing 19-7. The description of the resource `mailto:elharo@metalab.unc.edu` does not have to be repeated.

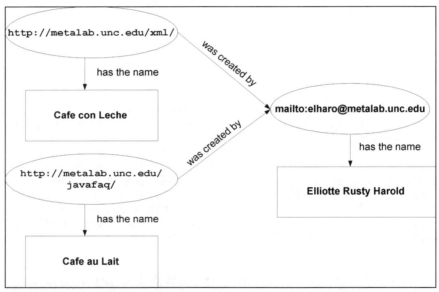

Figure 19-5: The statement in diagram form

Listing 19-7: A statement with the same property attached to multiple resources

```
<rdf:RDF
  xmlns:rdf="http://www.w3.org/1999/02/22-rdf-syntax-ns#"
  xmlns:dc="http://www.purl.org/DC/">

  <rdf:Description about="http://metalab.unc.edu/xml/">
    <dc:TITLE>Cafe con Leche</dc:TITLE>
```

```
        <dc:CREATOR rdf:resource="mailto:elharo@metalab.unc.edu"/>
      </rdf:Description>

      <rdf:Description about="http://metalab.unc.edu/javafaq/">
        <dc:TITLE>Cafe au Lait</dc:TITLE>
        <dc:CREATOR rdf:resource="mailto:elharo@metalab.unc.edu"/>
      </rdf:Description>

      <rdf:Description about="mailto:elharo@metalab.unc.edu">
        <dc:TITLE>Elliotte Rusty Harold</dc:TITLE>
      </rdf:Description>

  </rdf:RDF>
```

XML Valued Properties

Property values are most commonly either pure text or resources. However, they may also contain well-formed XML markup that is not itself RDF markup. In this case, the property element must have a `parseType` attribute with the value `Literal`, as shown in Listing 19-8.

Listing 19-8: **A literal property value that uses XML markup**

```
<rdf:RDF
  xmlns:rdf="http://www.w3.org/1999/02/22-rdf-syntax-ns#"
  xmlns:dc="http://www.purl.org/DC/"
  xmlns:nm="http://www.metalab.unc.edu/xml/names/">

  <rdf:Description about="http://metalab.unc.edu/xml/">
    <dc:CREATOR parseType="Literal">
      <nm:FirstName>Elliotte</nm:FirstName>
      <nm:MiddleName>Rusty</nm:MiddleName>
      <nm:LastName>Harold</nm:LastName>
    </dc:CREATOR>
  </rdf:Description>

</rdf:RDF>
```

Without `parseType="Literal"`, the value of a property must be a resource or parsed character data only. It must not contain any embedded markup.

Abbreviated RDF Syntax

As well as the basic syntax used above, RDF also defines an abbreviated syntax that uses attributes instead of parsed character data content. This is convenient when RDF data is embedded in an HTML page, because a Web browser can simply ignore the RDF tags without any affect on the rendered page. The two syntaxes are completely equivalent from the perspective of an RDF (as opposed to HTML) parser.

In abbreviated syntax, each property becomes an attribute of the `Description` element. The name of the property is the name of the attribute. If the property has a literal value, the value of the property is the value of the attribute. If the property has a resource value, the value of the property is the URI of the resource, and a separate `Description` element describes the resource. Because the `Description` element no longer has a variety of child elements, it does not need a closing tag and is written using normal empty element syntax.

The simple statement "Elliotte Rusty Harold created the Web site `http://metalab.unc.edu/xml/`" is written in abbreviated form, like this:

```
<RDF xmlns="http://www.w3.org/1999/02/22-rdf-syntax-ns#"
    xmlns:dc="http://purl.org/DC/">
  <Description about="http://metalab.unc.edu/xml/"
    dc:CREATOR="Elliotte Rusty Harold" />
</RDF>
```

The statement "Elliotte Rusty Harold created the Cafe con Leche Web site `http://metalab.unc.edu/xml/`" is written in abbreviated form, like this:

```
<RDF xmlns="http://www.w3.org/1999/02/22-rdf-syntax-ns#"
    xmlns:dc="http://purl.org/DC/">
  <Description about="http://metalab.unc.edu/xml/
    dc:CREATOR="Elliotte Rusty Harold"
    dc:TITLE="Cafe con Leche" />
</RDF>
```

Resource valued properties are trickier to abbreviate. The statement "The Cafe con Leche Web site at the URL `http://metalab.unc.edu/xml/` has the creator Elliotte Rusty Harold, whose email address is `elharo@metalab.unc.edu`" can be abbreviated like this:

```
<rdf:RDF
  xmlns:rdf="http://www.w3.org/1999/02/22-rdf-syntax-ns#"
  xmlns:dc="http://purl.org/DC/">
  <rdf:Description about="http://metalab.unc.edu/xml/"
```

```
      dc:TITLE="Cafe con Leche>
       <dc:CREATOR rdf:resource="mailto:elharo@metalab.unc.edu"
        dc:TITLE="Elliotte Rusty Harold" />
     </rdf:Description>
   </rdf:RDF>
```

Here the Description element is nonempty because it has a Creator child. However, it still doesn't contain any character data except white space.

Containers

When an RDF element describes a resource with multiple properties of the same type, for example to say that a document was written by multiple people or to list mirror sites where a Web page can be found, a container can group the property values. Every item in the group is a property value of the same type (property name). This allows you to describe the group as a whole rather than merely describe individual items in the container. RDF defines three types of container objects:

1. Bag: a group of unordered properties
2. Seq: a sequence (ordered list) of properties
3. Alt: a list of alternative properties from which a single one is chosen

The Bag container

A bag is a list of property values (resources and literals), in no particular order, all of which share the same property name (type). This allows you to declare a property that has more than one value, such as the authors of a book or the members of a committee. A bag may contain duplicate values.

A bag of properties is represented by a Bag element. Each item in the bag is a li child element of the Bag. The Bag itself is a child of the Description to which it applies.

For example, consider the statement "The Cafe con Leche Web site at http://metalab.unc.edu/xml/ was created by Elliotte Rusty Harold to provide XML news, XML mailing lists, XML conferences, and XML books." This is diagrammed in Figure 19-6. The four main subjects of the site can be collected in a Bag, as shown in Listing 19-9.

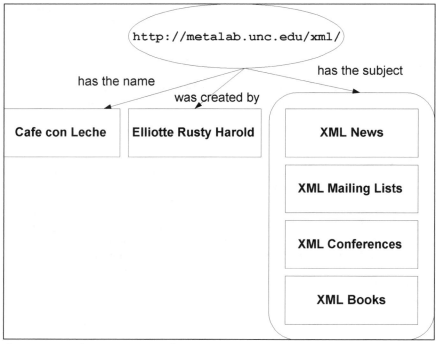

Figure 19-6: The statement in diagram form

Listing 19-9: **A bag with four members**

```
<rdf:RDF
  xmlns:rdf="http://www.w3.org/1999/02/22-rdf-syntax-ns#"
  xmlns:dc="http://www.purl.org/DC#">

  <rdf:Description about="http://metalab.unc.edu/xml/">
    <dc:TITLE>Cafe con Leche</dc:TITLE>
    <dc:CREATOR>Elliotte Rusty Harold</dc:CREATOR>
    <dc:SUBJECT>
      <rdf:Bag>
        <rdf:li>XML News</rdf:li>
        <rdf:li>XML Mailing lists</rdf:li>
        <rdf:li>XML Conferences</rdf:li>
        <rdf:li>XML Books</rdf:li>
      </rdf:Bag>
    </dc:SUBJECT>
  </rdf:Description>

</rdf:RDF>
```

If the members of the bag are resources rather than literals, they're identified with a `resource` attribute. For example, Listing 19-10 provides a simple site map for Cafe con Leche.

Listing 19-10: A simple site map for Cafe con Leche in a Bag

```
<rdf:RDF
  xmlns:rdf="http://www.w3.org/1999/02/22-rdf-syntax-ns#"
  xmlns:dc="http://www.purl.org/DC#">

  <rdf:Description about="http://metalab.unc.edu/xml/">
    <dc:TITLE>Cafe con Leche</dc:TITLE>
    <dc:CREATOR>Elliotte Rusty Harold</dc:CREATOR>
    <dc:SUBJECT>
      <rdf:Bag>
        <rdf:li
          resource="http://metalab.unc.edu/xml/news1999.html"/>
        <rdf:li
        resource="http://metalab.unc.edu/xml/mailinglists.html/>
        <rdf:li
          resource="http://metalab.unc.edu/xml/news1999.html"/>
        <rdf:li
        resource="http://metalab.unc.edu/xml/tradeshows.html"/>
      </rdf:Bag>
    </dc:SUBJECT>
  </rdf:Description>

  <rdf:Description
    about="http://metalab.unc.edu/xml/news1999.html">
    <dc:TITLE>XML News from 1999</dc:TITLE>
  </rdf:Description>

  <rdf:Description
    about="http://metalab.unc.edu/xml/books.html">
    <dc:TITLE>XML Books</dc:TITLE>
  </rdf:Description>

  <rdf:Description
    about="http://metalab.unc.edu/xml/mailinglists.html">
    <dc:TITLE>XML Mailing Lists</dc:TITLE>
  </rdf:Description>

  <rdf:Description
    about="http://metalab.unc.edu/xml/tradeshows.html">
    <dc:TITLE>XML Trade Shows and Conferences</dc:TITLE>
  </rdf:Description>

</rdf:RDF>
```

The Seq Container

A sequence container is similar to a bag container. However, it guarantees that the order of the contents is maintained. Sequences are written exactly like bags, except that the Seq element replaces the Bag element. For example, this sequence guarantees that when the Subject is read out by an RDF parser, it comes out in the order "XML News, XML Mailing Lists, XML Conferences, XML Books" and not some other order such as "XML Books, XML Conferences, XML Mailing Lists, XML News."

```
<dc:SUBJECT>
  <rdf:Seq>
    <rdf:li>XML News</rdf:li>
    <rdf:li>XML Mailing lists</rdf:li>
    <rdf:li>XML Conferences</rdf:li>
    <rdf:li>XML Books</rdf:li>
  </rdf:Seq>
</dc:SUBJECT>
```

In practice, maintaining the order of properties in a container is rarely important, so sequences aren't used as much as bags and alternatives.

The Alt Container

The Alt container includes one or more members from which a single one is picked. For example, this might be used to describe the mirrors of a Web site. Consider the statement "The Cafe au Lait Web site at http://metalab.unc.edu/javafaq/ created by Elliotte Rusty Harold is mirrored at Sunsite Austria (http://sunsite. univie.ac.at/jcca/mirrors/javafaq/), Sunsite Slovakia (http://sunsite. uakom.sk/javafaq/), Sunsite Sweden (http://sunsite.kth.se/javafaq/), and Sunsite Switzerland (http://sunsite.cnlab-switch.ch/javafaq/)." Because only one of these mirror sites is desired, they can be placed in an alternative list. Listing 19-11 shows the RDF serialization.

Listing 19-11: **Mirror sites of Cafe au Lait in a Seq**

```
<rdf:RDF
  xmlns:rdf="http://www.w3.org/1999/02/22-rdf-syntax-ns#"
  xmlns:dc="http://www.purl.org/DC#">

  <rdf:Description about="http://metalab.unc.edu/xml/">
    <dc:TITLE>Cafe con Leche</dc:TITLE>
    <dc:CREATOR>Elliotte Rusty Harold</dc:CREATOR>
    <dc:PUBLISHER>
      <rdf:Alt>
        <rdf:li resource =
```

```
          "http://sunsite.univie.ac.at/jcca/mirrors/javafaq/" />
        <rdf:li resource =
         "http://sunsite.kth.se/javafaq/" />
        <rdf:li resource =
         "http://sunsite.cnlab-switch.ch/javafaq/" />
        <rdf:li resource =
         "http://sunsite.uakom.sk/javafaq/" />
      </rdf:Alt>
    </dc:PUBLISHER>
  </rdf:Description>

  <rdf:Description
    about="http://sunsite.univie.ac.at/jcca/mirrors/javafaq/">
    <dc:PUBLISHER>Sunsite Austria</dc:PUBLISHER>
  </rdf:Description>

  <rdf:Description
    about="http://sunsite.uakom.sk/javafaq/">
    <dc:PUBLISHER>Sunsite Slovakia</dc:PUBLISHER>
  </rdf:Description>

  <rdf:Description
    about="http://sunsite.cnlab-switch.ch/javafaq/">
    <dc:PUBLISHER>Sunsite Switzerland</dc:PUBLISHER>
  </rdf:Description>

  <rdf:Description
    about="http://sunsite.kth.se/javafaq/">
    <dc:PUBLISHER>Sunsite Sweden</dc:PUBLISHER>
  </rdf:Description>

</rdf:RDF>
```

Statements about Containers

Statements can be made about a container as a whole, separate from statements about individual items in the container. You may want to say that a particular person developed a Web site without implying that he or she personally wrote each and every page on the site. Or perhaps you want to claim a copyright on a collection of links without claiming a copyright on the pages to which you're linking. (For example, the market values Yahoo's collection of links and descriptions at several hundred million dollars, even though Yahoo owns essentially none of the pages to which it links.) In fact, the individual members of the container might have different copyrights than the container itself. Figure 19-7 diagrams this.

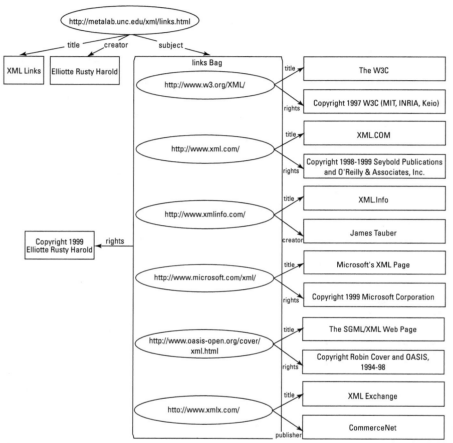

Figure 19-7: A bag whose rights information is different than the rights information of the individual members of the bag

To encode this in RDF, give the container (Bag, Seq, or Alt) an ID attribute. Description elements with about attributes, whose value is a relative URL pointing to the container ID, describe the container.

Listing 19-12: **A description of a container encoded in RDF**

```
<rdf:RDF
  xmlns:rdf="http://www.w3.org/1999/02/22-rdf-syntax-ns#"
  xmlns:dc="http://www.purl.org/DC#">

  <rdf:Description
    about="http://metalab.unc.edu/xml/links.html">
```

```
  <dc:TITLE>XML Links</dc:TITLE>
  <dc:CREATOR>Elliotte Rusty Harold</dc:CREATOR>
  <dc:SUBJECT>
    <rdf:Bag ID="links">
      <rdf:li resource="http://www.w3.org/XML/"/>
      <rdf:li resource="http://www.xml.com/"/>
      <rdf:li resource="http://www.xmlinfo.com/"/>
      <rdf:li resource="http://www.microsoft.com/xml//>
      <rdf:li
        resource="http://www.oasis-open.org/cover/xml.html"/>
      <rdf:li resource=http://www.xmlx.com//>
    </rdf:Bag>
  </dc:SUBJECT>
</rdf:Description>

<rdf:Description about="#links">
  <dc:RIGHTS>
    Copyright 1999 Elliotte Rusty Harold
  </dc:RIGHTS>
</rdf:Description>

<rdf:Description about="http://www.w3.org/XML/">
  <dc:TITLE>The W3C</dc:TITLE>
  <dc:RIGHTS>
    Copyright 1997 W3C (MIT, INRIA, Keio)
  </dc:RIGHTS>
</rdf:Description>

<rdf:Description about="http://www.xml.com/">
  <dc:TITLE>xml.com</dc:TITLE>
  <dc:RIGHTS>
    Copyright 1998-1999 Seybold Publications
    and O'Reilly &amp; Associates, Inc.
  </dc:RIGHTS>
</rdf:Description>

<rdf:Description about="http://www.xmlinfo.com/">
  <dc:TITLE>XML Info</dc:TITLE>
  <dc:CREATOR>James Tauber</dc:CREATOR>
</rdf:Description>

<rdf:Description about="http://www.microsoft.com/xml/">
  <dc:TITLE>Microsoft's XML Page</dc:TITLE>
  <dc:RIGHTS>Copyright 1999 Microsoft Corporation</dc:RIGHTS>
</rdf:Description>

<rdf:Description
  about="http://www.oasis-open.org/cover/xml.html">
  <dc:TITLE>Robin Cover's XML Web Page</dc:TITLE>
  <dc:RIGHTS>
    Copyright Robin Cover and OASIS, 1994-98
```

Continued

Listing 19-12 *(continued)*

```
    </dc:RIGHTS>
  </rdf:Description>

  <rdf:Description about="http://www.xmlx.com/">
    <dc:TITLE>XML Exchange</dc:TITLE>
    <dc:PUBLISHER>CommerceNet</dc:PUBLISHER>
  </rdf:Description>

</rdf:RDF>
```

Statements about Container Members

Sometimes you do want to make a statement about each member of a container, but you don't want to repeat the same description three or four times. For example, you may want to specify that the title and creator of each of the mirror sites is Cafe au Lait and Elliotte Rusty Harold, respectively, as shown in Figure 19-8.

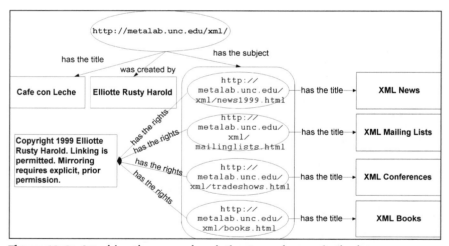

Figure 19-8: Attaching the same description to each page in the bag

You can include an `aboutEach` attribute in the `Bag`, `Seq`, or `Alt` element whose value is a name by which descriptions can be applied to all the members of the container. For example, suppose you want to apply a copyright notice to each page in a `Bag`. Listing 19-13 accomplishes this.

Listing 19-13: A description of each element in a Bag container

```
<rdf:RDF
  xmlns:rdf="http://www.w3.org/1999/02/22-rdf-syntax-ns#"
  xmlns:dc="http://www.purl.org/DC#">

  <rdf:Description about=""http://metalab.unc.edu/xml/">
    <dc:TITLE>Cafe con Leche</dc:TITLE>
    <dc:CREATOR>Elliotte Rusty Harold</dc:CREATOR>
    <dc:SUBJECT>
      <rdf:Bag aboutEach="pages">
        <rdf:li
          resource="http://metalab.unc.edu/xml/news1999.html"/>
        <rdf:li
      resource="http://metalab.unc.edu/xml/mailinglists.html"/>
        <rdf:li
          resource="http://metalab.unc.edu/xml/news1999.html"/>
        <rdf:li
          resource="http://metalab.unc.edu/xml/tradeshows.html"/>
      </rdf:Bag>
    </dc:SUBJECT>
  </rdf:Description>

  <rdf:Description aboutEach="#pages">
    <dc:RIGHTS>
      Copyright 1999 Elliotte Rusty Harold
      Linking is permitted.
      Mirroring requires explicit, prior permission.
    </dc:RIGHTS>
  </rdf:Description>

  <rdf:Description
    about="http://metalab.unc.edu/xml/news1999.html>
    <dc:TITLE>XML News from 1999</dc:TITLE>
  </rdf:Description>

  <rdf:Description
    about="http://metalab.unc.edu/xml/books.html">
    <dc:TITLE>XML Books</dc:TITLE>
  </rdf:Description>

  <rdf:Description
    about="http://metalab.unc.edu/xml/mailinglists.html">
    <dc:TITLE>XML Mailing Lists</dc:TITLE>
  </rdf:Description>

  <rdf:Description
    about="http://metalab.unc.edu/xml/tradeshows.html">
    <dc:TITLE>XML Trade Shows and Conferences</dc:TITLE>
  </rdf:Description>

</rdf:RDF>
```

Statements about Implied Bags

Sometimes you want to make a statement about a group of resources that may or may not be members of the same container. For example, suppose you want to specify that every page on the Web site `http://www.macfaq.com` is "Copyright 1999 Elliotte Rusty Harold." You can do this with a `Description` element that applies to all resources whose URI begins with the string "`http://www.macfaq. com`". This `Description` element must have an `aboutEachPrefix` attribute whose value is the URI prefix of the resources to which the description applies. For example:

```
<rdf:Description aboutEachPrefix="#http://www.macfaq.com">
    <dc:RIGHTS>Copyright 1999 Elliotte Rusty Harold</dc:RIGHTS>
</rdf:Description>
```

This `Description` element creates an implicit bag whose members are the resources matching the prefix. These resources may or may not be members of other containers in the RDF file, and they may or may not be sibling elements. The members of this implied bag are gathered from wherever they reside.

URI prefixes can be used to select only a subtree of a Web site. For example, this description claims that all pages at metalab.unc.edu in the /xml hierarchy are "Copyright 1999 Elliotte Rusty Harold". However, it does not apply to other pages outside that hierarchy such as `http://metalab.unc.edu/id/asiasylum` or `http://metalab.unc.edu/stats/`.

```
<rdf:Description
  aboutEachPrefix="#http://metalab.unc.edu/xml/">
  <dc:RIGHTS>Copyright 1999 Elliotte Rusty Harold</dc:RIGHTS>
</rdf:Description>
```

For another example, take ISBNs assigned by publishers. All books from IDG Books have an ISBN that begins 07645. Thus, this `Description` element creates an implicit `Bag` containing only books published by IDG Books and assigns a `Publisher` property to each member:

```
<rdf:Description aboutEachPrefix="#urn:isbn:07645">
  <dc:PUBLISHER>IDG Books</dc:PUBLISHER>
</rdf:Description>
```

RDF Schemas

Although there's no guarantee that a generic XML namespace URI points to anything in particular, RDF is stricter than that. Any namespace URI used in RDF should point to a schema for the vocabulary. The schema describes the semantics and allowed syntax of a particular element. For instance, the schema may say that the contents of a DATE element must be in the form 1999-12-31 and not in the form December 31, 1999. A schema may also make DTD-like statements, such as that each BOOK element must contain one or more AUTHOR child elements.

Exactly how a schema makes statements such as this is a subject of debate. In practice, current RDF schemas are mostly written in prose that human beings read. For example, part of the Dublin Core "schema" is shown in Figure 19-9. (In the long run, a more formal and complete schema for the Dublin Core is likely to be developed.)

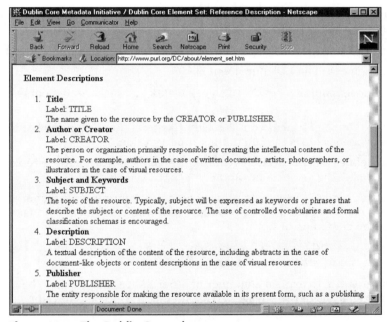

Figure 19-9: The Dublin Core schema

Eventually schemas will be written in a more formal syntax that computers can understand. In particular, the W3C RDF Schema Working Group is attempting to develop an RDF schema specification that writes RDF schema in RDF. This will enable an RDF processor to validate a particular RDF document against the schemas it uses. However, this work is far from finished as of spring, 1999. If you're curious about this work, you can retrieve the current draft of the RDF schema specification from http://www.w3.org/TR/1998/WD-rdf-schema/.

Summary

This chapter covered RDF. In particular, you learned:

✦ The Resource Description Framework (RDF) is an XML application for structured metadata. Metadata is information about information.

✦ An RDF document or element makes statements about resources.

✦ Each statement specifies a resource, a property of that resource, and the value of that property.

✦ A resource is anything that has a Uniform Resource Identifier (URI). URLs of Web pages are just one form of URI.

✦ The value of a property may be plain text, another resource, or XML markup.

✦ The root element of an RDF document is RDF.

✦ An RDF element contains Description elements that make statements about resources.

✦ Each Description element contains either a literal property or a resource attribute whose value is the URI of the property value.

✦ RDF also defines an abbreviated syntax in which properties may be replaced by attributes of the same name on the Description element.

✦ The Bag, Seq, and Alt elements provide containers for multiple resources. Properties can be applied to the container as a whole, to the individual elements of the container, or both.

✦ The namespace URI for each vocabulary used in an RDF document should point to a schema for the vocabulary.

The next chapter starts to explain a number of other XML applications. It begins with an in-depth analysis of the Voyager HTML-in-XML DTD to help develop your skills at reading DTDs written by others.

✦   ✦   ✦

XML
Applications

Reading Document Type Definitions

In an ideal world, every markup language created with XML would come with copious documentation and examples showing you the exact meaning and use of every element and attribute. In practice, most DTD authors, like most programmers, consider documentation an unpleasant and unnecessary chore, one best left to tech writers if it's to be done at all. Not surprisingly, therefore, the DTD that contains sufficient documentation is the exception, not the rule. Consequently, it's important to learn to read raw DTDs written by others.

There's a second good reason for learning to read DTDs. When you read good DTDs, you can often learn tricks and techniques that you can use in your own DTDs. For example, no matter how much theory I may mumble about the proper use of parameter entities for common attribute lists in DTDs, nothing proves quite as effective for learning that as really digging into a DTD that uses the technique. Reading other designers' DTDs teaches you by example how you can design your own.

In this chapter, we'll pick apart the modularized DTD for XHTML from the W3C. This DTD is quite complex and relatively well written. By studying it closely, you can pick up a lot of good techniques for developing your own DTDs. We'll see what its designers did right, and a few things they did wrong (IMHO). We'll explore some different ways the same thing could have been accomplished, and the advantages and disadvantages of each. We will also look at some common tricks in XML DTDs and techniques for developing your own DTDs.

The Importance of Reading DTDs

Some XML applications are very precisely defined by standards documents. MathML is one such application. It's been the subject of several person-years of work by a dedicated committee with representatives from across the computer math industry. It's been through several levels of peer review, and the committee's been quite responsive to problems discovered both in the language and in the documentation of that language. Consequently, a full DTD is available accompanied by an extensive informal specification.

Other XML applications are not as well documented. Microsoft, more or less, completely created CDF, discussed in Chapter 21. CDF is documented informally on Microsoft's Site Builder Network in a set of poorly organized Web pages, but no current DTD is available. Microsoft will probably update and add to CDF, but exactly what the updates will be is more or less a mystery to everyone else in the industry.

CML, the Chemical Markup Language invented by Peter Murray-Rust, is hardly documented at all. It contains a DTD, but it leaves a lot to the imagination. For instance, CML contains a `bondArray` element, but the only information about the `bondArray` element is that it contains `CDATA`. There's no further description of what sort of data should appear in a `bondArray` element.

Other times, there may be both a DTD and a prose specification. Microsoft and Marimba's Open Software Description (OSD format) is one example. However, the problem with prose specifications is that they leave pieces out. For instance, the spec for OSD generally neglects to say how many of a given child element may appear in a parent element or in what order. The DTD makes that clear. Conversely, the DTD can't really say that a `SIZE` attribute is given in the format KB-number. That's left to the prose part of the specification.

Note   Actually, this sort of information could and should appear in a comment in the DTD. The XML processor alone can't validate against this restriction. That has to be left to a higher layer of processing. In any case, simple comments can make the DTD more intelligible for humans, if nothing else. Currently, OSD does not have a solid DTD.

These are all examples of more or less public XML applications. However, many corporations, government agencies, Web sites, and other organizations have internal, private XML applications they use for their own documents. These are even less likely to be well documented and well written than the public XML applications. As an XML specialist, you may well find yourself trying to reverse engineer a DTD originally written by someone long gone and grown primarily through accretion of new elements over several years.

Clearly, the more documentation you have for an XML application, and the better the documentation is written, the easier it will be to learn and use that application. However it's an unfortunate fact of life that documentation is often an afterthought. Often, the only thing you have to work with is a DTD. You're reduced to reading the DTD, trying to understand what it says, and writing test documents to validate to try to figure out what is and isn't permissible. Consequently, it's important to be able to read DTDs and transform them in your head to examples of permissible markup.

In this chapter, you'll explore the XHTML DTD from the W3C. This is actually one of the better documented DTDs I've seen. However, in this chapter I'm going to pretend that it isn't. Instead of reading the prose specification, read the actual DTD files. We'll explore the techniques you can use to understand those DTDs, even in the absence of a prose specification.

What Is XHTML?

XHTML is the W3C's effort to rewrite HTML as strict XML. This requires tightening up a lot of the looseness commonly associated with HTML. End tags are required for elements that normally omit them like p and dt. Empty elements like hr must end in /> instead of just >. Attribute values must be quoted. The names of all HTML elements and attributes are standardized in lowercase.

XHTML goes one step further than merely requiring HTML documents to be well-formed XML like that discussed in Chapter 6. It actually provides a DTD for HTML you can use to validate your HTML documents. In fact, it provides three:

✦ The XHTML strict DTD for new HTML documents

✦ The XHTML loose DTD for converted old HTML documents that still use deprecated tags like applet

✦ The XHTML frameset DTD for documents that use frames

You can use the one that best fits your site.

Why Validate HTML?

Valid documents aren't absolutely required for HTML, but they do make it much easier for browsers to properly understand and display documents. A valid HTML document is far more likely to render correctly and predictably across many different browsers than an invalid one.

Until recently, too much of the competition among browser vendors revolved around just how much broken HTML they could make sense of. For instance, Internet Explorer fills in a missing </table> end tag whereas Netscape Navigator does not. Consequently, many pages on Microsoft's Web site (which were only tested in Internet Explorer) contained missing `</table>` tags and could not be viewed in Netscape Navigator. (I'll leave it to the reader to decide whether or not this was deliberate sabotage.) In any case, if Microsoft had required valid HTML on its Web site, this would not have happened.

It is extremely difficult for even the largest Web shops to test their pages against even a small fraction of the browsers that people actually use. Even testing the latest versions of both Netscape Navigator and Internet Explorer is more than some designers manage. While I won't argue that you shouldn't test your pages in as many versions of as many browsers as possible in an ideal world, the reality is that time and resources are finite. Validating HTML goes a long way toward ensuring that your pages render reasonably in a broad spectrum of browsers.

Modularization of XHTML Working Draft

This chapter covers the April 6, 1999 working draft of the Modularized XHTML specification, which is subject to change. The status of this version is, as given by the W3C:

> This document is a working draft of the W3C's HTML Working Group. This working draft may be updated, replaced or rendered obsolete by other W3C documents at any time. It is inappropriate to use W3C Working Drafts as reference material or to cite them as other than "work in progress." This is work in progress and does not imply endorsement by the W3C membership.
>
> This document has been produced as part of the W3C HTML Activity. The goals of the HTML Working Group (*members only*) are discussed in the HTML Working Group charter (*members only*).

Currently, the latest draft is from April 6, 1999. You can download this particular version from `http://www.w3.org/TR/1999/xhtml-modularization-19990406`. That document contains many more details about XHTML and rewriting Web pages in XML-compliant HTML. The most recent version is available on the Web at `http://www.w3.org/TR/xhtml-modularization`. This chapter focuses on reading the DTD for XHTML. The files I reproduce and discuss below are subject to the W3C Document Notice, reproduced in the sidebar.

The Structure of the XHTML DTDs

HTML is a fairly complex XML application. As noted above, XHTML documents can choose one of three DTDs. The three separate HTML DTDs discussed here are divided into about 40 different files and over 2,000 lines of code. These files are connected through parameter entities. By splitting the DTD into these different files, it's easier to understand the individual pieces. Furthermore, common pieces can be shared among the three different versions of the XHTML DTD: strict, loose, and frameset.

Document Notice

The three DTDs that can be used by your HTML in XML documents are listed below:

1. The XHTML strict DTD for new HTML documents.

2. The XHTML loose DTD for converted old HTML documents that still use deprecated tags like `applet`.

3. The XHTML frameset DTD for documents that use frames.

All three of these DTDs have this basic format:

1. Comment with title, copyright, namespace, formal public identifier, and other information for people who use this DTD.

2. Revised parameter entity declarations that will override parameter entities declared in the modules.

3. External parameter entity references to import the modules and entity sets.

XHTML Strict DTD

The XHTML strict DTD (XHTML1-s.dtd), shown in Listing 20-1, is for new HTML documents that can easily conform to the most stringent requirements for XML compatibility, and that do not need to use some of the older, less-well thought out and deprecated elements from HTML like `applet` and `basefont`. It does not support frames, and omits support for all presentational elements like `font` and `center`.

Listing 20-1: **XHTML1-s.dtd: the XHTML strict DTD**

```
<!- ............................................. ->
<!- XHTML 1.0 Strict DTD ............................ ->
<!- file: XHTML1-s.dtd
->

<!-  XHTML 1.0 Strict DTD

        This is XHTML 1.0, an XML reformulation of HTML 4.0.

Copyright 1998-1999 World Wide Web Consortium
(Massachusetts Institute of Technology, Institut National de
Recherche en Informatique et en Automatique, Keio University).
All Rights Reserved.

    Permission to use, copy, modify and distribute the XHTML
    1.0 DTD and its accompanying documentation for any purpose
    and without fee is hereby granted in perpetuity, provided
    that the above copyright notice and this paragraph appear
    in all copies. The copyright holders make no representation
```

about the suitability of the DTD for any purpose.

It is provided "as is" without expressed or implied warranty.

    Author: Murray M. Altheim <altheim@eng.sun.com>
    Revision: @(#)XHTML1-s.dtd 1.14 99/04/01 SMI

The XHTML 1.0 DTD is an XML variant based on the W3C HTML 4.0 DTD:

    Draft: $Date: 1999/04/02 14:27:27 $

    Authors: Dave Raggett <dsr@w3.org>
                Arnaud Le Hors <lehors@w3.org>
                Ian Jacobs <ij@w3.org>
—>
<!— This is the driver file for version 1.0 of the XHTML Strict DTD.

Please use this formal public identifier to identify it:

    "-//W3C//DTD XHTML 1.0 Strict//EN"

Please use this URI to identify the default namespace:

    "http://www.w3.org/TR/1999/REC-html-in-xml"

For example, if you are using XHTML 1.0 directly, use the FPI in the DOCTYPE declaration, with the xmlns attribute on the document element to identify the default namespace:

```
<?xml version="1.0" ?>
<!DOCTYPE html PUBLIC "-//W3C//DTD XHTML 1.0 Strict//EN"
                      "XHTML1-s.dtd" >
<html xmlns="http://www.w3.org/TR/1999/REC-html-in-xml"
      xml:lang="en" lang="en" >
...
</html>
```
—>

<!— The version attribute has historically been a container
     for the DTD's public identifier (an FPI), but is unused
     in Strict: —>
<!ENTITY % HTML.version "" >
<!ENTITY % Version.attrib "" >

<!— The xmlns attribute on <html> identifies the
     default namespace to namespace-aware applications: —>
<!ENTITY % XHTML.ns "http://www.w3.org/TR/1999/REC-html-in-xml" >

Continued

Listing 20-1 *(continued)*

```
<!- reserved for future use with document profiles ->
<!ENTITY % XHTML.profile  "" >

<!- used to ignore Transitional features within modules ->
<!ENTITY % XHTML.Transitional   "IGNORE" >


<!- XHTML Base Architecture Module (optional) ......... ->
<!ENTITY % XHTML1-arch.module "IGNORE" >
<![%XHTML1-arch.module;[
<!ENTITY % XHTML1-arch.mod
     PUBLIC "-//W3C//ELEMENTS XHTML 1.0 Base Architecture//EN"
            "XHTML1-arch.mod" >
%XHTML1-arch.mod;
]]>

<!- Common Names Module ............................. ->
<!ENTITY % XHTML1-names.module "INCLUDE" >
<![%XHTML1-names.module;[
<!ENTITY % XHTML1-names.mod
     PUBLIC "-//W3C//ENTITIES XHTML 1.0 Common Names//EN"
            "XHTML1-names.mod" >
%XHTML1-names.mod;
]]>

<!- Character Entities Module ......................... ->
<!ENTITY % XHTML1-charent.module "INCLUDE" >
<![%XHTML1-charent.module;[
<!ENTITY % XHTML1-charent.mod
     PUBLIC "-//W3C//ENTITIES XHTML 1.0 Character Entities//EN"
            "XHTML1-charent.mod" >
%XHTML1-charent.mod;
]]>

<!- Intrinsic Events Module ......................... ->
<!ENTITY % XHTML1-events.module "INCLUDE" >
<![%XHTML1-events.module;[
<!ENTITY % XHTML1-events.mod
     PUBLIC "-//W3C//ENTITIES XHTML 1.0 Intrinsic Events//EN"
            "XHTML1-events.mod" >
%XHTML1-events.mod;
]]>

<!- Common Attributes Module ......................... ->
<!ENTITY % XHTML1-attribs.module "INCLUDE" >
<![%XHTML1-attribs.module;[
<!ENTITY % align "" >
<!ENTITY % XHTML1-attribs.mod
     PUBLIC "-//W3C//ENTITIES XHTML 1.0 Common Attributes//EN"
            "XHTML1-attribs.mod" >
```

```
%XHTML1-attribs.mod;
]]>

<!-- Document Model Module ........................... -->
<!ENTITY % XHTML1-model.module "INCLUDE" >
<![%XHTML1-model.module;[
<!ENTITY % XHTML1-model.mod
     PUBLIC "-//W3C//ELEMENTS XHTML 1.0 Document Model//EN"
            "XHTML1-model.mod" >
%XHTML1-model.mod;
]]>

<!-- Inline Structural Module ........................ -->
<!ENTITY % XHTML1-inlstruct.module "INCLUDE" >
<![%XHTML1-inlstruct.module;[
<!ENTITY % XHTML1-inlstruct.mod
     PUBLIC "-//W3C//ELEMENTS XHTML 1.0 Inline Structural//EN"
            "XHTML1-inlstruct.mod" >
%XHTML1-inlstruct.mod;
]]>

<!-- Inline Presentational Module .................... -->
<!ENTITY % XHTML1-inlpres.module "INCLUDE" >
<![%XHTML1-inlpres.module;[
<!ENTITY % XHTML1-inlpres.mod
  PUBLIC "-//W3C//ELEMENTS XHTML 1.0 Inline Presentational//EN"
         "XHTML1-inlpres.mod" >
%XHTML1-inlpres.mod;
]]>

<!-- Inline Phrasal Module ........................... -->
<!ENTITY % XHTML1-inlphras.module "INCLUDE" >
<![%XHTML1-inlphras.module;[
<!ENTITY % XHTML1-inlphras.mod
     PUBLIC "-//W3C//ELEMENTS XHTML 1.0 Inline Phrasal//EN"
            "XHTML1-inlphras.mod" >
%XHTML1-inlphras.mod;
]]>

<!-- Block Structural Module ......................... -->
<!ENTITY % XHTML1-blkstruct.module "INCLUDE" >
<![%XHTML1-blkstruct.module;[
<!ENTITY % XHTML1-blkstruct.mod
     PUBLIC "-//W3C//ELEMENTS XHTML 1.0 Block Structural//EN"
            "XHTML1-blkstruct.mod" >
%XHTML1-blkstruct.mod;
]]>

<!-- Block Presentational Module ..................... -->
<!ENTITY % XHTML1-blkpres.module "INCLUDE" >
<![%XHTML1-blkpres.module;[
<!ENTITY % XHTML1-blkpres.mod
```

Continued

Listing 20-1 *(continued)*

```
      PUBLIC "-//W3C//ELEMENTS XHTML 1.0 Block
Presentational//EN"
            "XHTML1-blkpres.mod" >
%XHTML1-blkpres.mod;
]]>

<!- Block Phrasal Module ............................. ->
<!ENTITY % XHTML1-blkphras.module "INCLUDE" >
<![%XHTML1-blkphras.module;[
<!ENTITY % XHTML1-blkphras.mod
      PUBLIC "-//W3C//ELEMENTS XHTML 1.0 Block Phrasal//EN"
            "XHTML1-blkphras.mod" >
%XHTML1-blkphras.mod;
]]>

<!- Scripting Module ............................... ->
<!ENTITY % XHTML1-script.module "INCLUDE" >
<![%XHTML1-script.module;[
<!ENTITY % XHTML1-script.mod
      PUBLIC "-//W3C//ELEMENTS XHTML 1.0 Scripting//EN"
            "XHTML1-script.mod" >
%XHTML1-script.mod;
]]>

<!- Stylesheets Module ............................. ->
<!ENTITY % XHTML1-style.module "INCLUDE" >
<![%XHTML1-style.module;[
<!ENTITY % XHTML1-style.mod
      PUBLIC "-//W3C//ELEMENTS XHTML 1.0 Stylesheets//EN"
            "XHTML1-style.mod" >
%XHTML1-style.mod;
]]>

<!- Image Module ................................... ->
<!ENTITY % XHTML1-image.module "INCLUDE" >
<![%XHTML1-image.module;[
<!ENTITY % XHTML1-image.mod
      PUBLIC "-//W3C//ELEMENTS XHTML 1.0 Images//EN"
            "XHTML1-image.mod" >
%XHTML1-image.mod;
]]>

<!- Frames Module ................................... ->
<!ENTITY % XHTML1-frames.module  "IGNORE" >
<![%XHTML1-frames.module;[
<!ENTITY % XHTML1-frames.mod
      PUBLIC "-//W3C//ELEMENTS XHTML 1.0 Frames//EN"
            "XHTML1-frames.mod" >
%XHTML1-frames.mod;
]]>
```

```
<!- Linking Module .................................. ->
<!ENTITY % XHTML1-linking.module "INCLUDE" >
<![%XHTML1-linking.module;[
<!ENTITY % XHTML1-linking.mod
     PUBLIC "-//W3C//ELEMENTS XHTML 1.0 Linking//EN"
            "XHTML1-linking.mod" >
%XHTML1-linking.mod;
]]>

<!- Client-side Image Map Module ..................... ->
<!ENTITY % XHTML1-csismap.module "INCLUDE" >
<![%XHTML1-csismap.module;[
<!ENTITY % XHTML1-csismap.mod
   PUBLIC "-//W3C//ELEMENTS XHTML 1.0 Client-side Image Map//EN"
          "XHTML1-csismap.mod" >
%XHTML1-csismap.mod;
]]>

<!- Object Element Module ............................ ->
<!ENTITY % XHTML1-object.module "INCLUDE" >
<![%XHTML1-object.module;[
<!ENTITY % XHTML1-object.mod
     PUBLIC "-//W3C//ELEMENTS XHTML 1.0 Object Element//EN"
            "XHTML1-object.mod" >
%XHTML1-object.mod;
]]>

<!- Lists Module ................................. ->
<!ENTITY % XHTML1-list.module "INCLUDE" >
<![%XHTML1-list.module;[
<!ENTITY % XHTML1-list.mod
     PUBLIC "-//W3C//ELEMENTS XHTML 1.0 Lists//EN"
            "XHTML1-list.mod" >
%XHTML1-list.mod;
]]>

<!- Forms Module ................................. ->
<!ENTITY % XHTML1-form.module "INCLUDE" >
<![%XHTML1-form.module;[
<!ENTITY % XHTML1-form.mod
     PUBLIC "-//W3C//ELEMENTS XHTML 1.0 Forms//EN"
            "XHTML1-form.mod" >
%XHTML1-form.mod;
]]>

<!- Tables Module ................................. ->
<!ENTITY % XHTML1-table.module "INCLUDE" >
<![%XHTML1-table.module;[
<!ENTITY % XHTML1-table.mod
     PUBLIC "-//W3C//ELEMENTS XHTML 1.0 Tables//EN"
            "XHTML1-table.mod" >
%XHTML1-table.mod;
```

Continued

Listing 20-1 *(continued)*

```
]]>

<!— Document Metainformation Module .................. —>
<!ENTITY % XHTML1-meta.module "INCLUDE" >
<![%XHTML1-meta.module;[
<!ENTITY % XHTML1-meta.mod
     PUBLIC "-//W3C//ELEMENTS XHTML 1.0 Metainformation//EN"
            "XHTML1-meta.mod" >
%XHTML1-meta.mod;
]]>

<!— Document Structure Module ...................... —>
<!ENTITY % XHTML1-struct.module "INCLUDE" >
<![%XHTML1-struct.module;[
<!ENTITY % XHTML1-struct.mod
     PUBLIC "-//W3C//ELEMENTS XHTML 1.0 Document Structure//EN"
            "XHTML1-struct.mod" >
%XHTML1-struct.mod;
]]>

<!— end of XHTML 1.0 Strict DTD  ........................ —>
<!— ............................................ —>
```

The file begins with a comment identifying which file this is, and a basic copyright statement. That's followed by these very important words:

> Permission to use, copy, modify, and distribute the XHTML 1.0 DTD and its accompanying documentation for any purpose and without fee is hereby granted in perpetuity, provided that the above copyright notice and this paragraph appear in all copies. The copyright holders make no representation about the suitability of the DTD for any purpose.

A statement like this is *very* important for any DTD that you want to be broadly adopted. In order for people outside your organization to use your DTD, they must be allowed to copy it, put it on their Web servers, send it to other people with their own documents, and do a variety of other things normally prohibited by copyright. A simple statement like "Copyright 1999 XYZ Corp." with no further elucidation prevents many people from using your DTD.

Next comes a comment containing detailed information about how this DTD should be used including its formal public identifier and preferred name. Also provided are the preferred namespace and an example of how to begin a file that uses this DTD. All of this is very useful to an author.

Cross-Reference

Formal public identifiers are discussed in Chapter 8, *Document Type Definitions and Validity*.

Next come several entity definitions that are mostly for compatibility with old or future versions of this DTD. Finally, we get to the meat of the DTD: 24 external parameter entity definitions and references that import the modules used to form the complete DTD. Here's the last one in the file:

```
<!- Document Structure Module ....................... ->
<!ENTITY % XHTML1-struct.module "INCLUDE" >
<![%XHTML1-struct.module;[
<!ENTITY % XHTML1-struct.mod
     PUBLIC "-//W3C//ELEMENTS XHTML 1.0 Document Structure//EN"
            "XHTML1-struct.mod" >
%XHTML1-struct.mod;
]]>
```

All 24 follow the same basic structure:

1. A comment identifying the module to be imported.

2. A parameter entity declaration whose name is the name of the module to be imported suffixed with `.module` and whose replacement text is either `INCLUDE` or `IGNORE`.

3. An `INCLUDE` or `IGNORE` block; which one is determined by the value of the parameter entity reference in the previous step.

4. An external parameter entity declaration for the module to be imported suffixed with `.mod`, followed by an external parameter entity reference that actually imports the module.

Removing the module-specific material, the structure looks like this:

```
<!- Module Name Module ....................... ->
<!ENTITY % XHTML1-module_abbreviation.module "INCLUDE" >
<![%XHTML1-module_abbreviation.module;[
<!ENTITY % XHTML1-module_abbreviation.mod
     PUBLIC "-//W3C//ELEMENTS XHTML 1.0 Module Name//EN"
            "XHTML1-module_abbreviation.mod" >
%XHTML1-module_abbreviation.mod;
]]>
```

The way this is organized it is very easy to change, whether or not a particular module is loaded simply by changing the value of one internal parameter entity from `INCLUDE` to `IGNORE` or vice versa. The `.module` parameter entities act as switches that turn particular declarations on or off.

XHTML Transitional DTD

The XHTML transitional DTD (XHTML1-t.dtd), also known as the loose DTD and shown in Listing 20-2, is appropriate for HTML documents that have not fully made the transition to HTML 4.0. These documents depend on now deprecated elements like `applet` and `center`. It also adds support for presentational attributes like color and bullet styles for list items replaced with CSS style sheets in strict HTML 4.0.

Listing 20-2: **XHTML1-t.dtd: the XHTML transitional DTD**

```
<!- .............................................. ->
<!- XHTML 1.0 Transitional DTD
............................................ ->
<!- file: XHTML1-t.dtd
->

<!-   XHTML 1.0 Transitional DTD

        This is XHTML 1.0, an XML reformulation of HTML 4.0.

        Copyright 1998-1999 World Wide Web Consortium
            (Massachusetts Institute of Technology, Institut
            National de Recherche en Informatique et en
            Automatique, Keio University). All Rights Reserved.

        Permission to use, copy, modify and distribute the XHTML
        1.0 DTD and its accompanying documentation for any
        purpose and without fee is hereby granted in perpetuity,
        provided that the above copyright notice and this
        paragraph appear in all copies.  The copyright holders
        make no representation about the suitability of the DTD
        for any purpose.

        It is provided "as is" without expressed or implied
        warranty.

            Author:     Murray M. Altheim <altheim@eng.sun.com>
            Revision:   @(#)XHTML1-t.dtd 1.14 99/04/01 SMI

        The XHTML 1.0 DTD is an XML variant based on the
        W3C HTML 4.0 DTD:

            Draft:      $Date: 1999/04/02 14:27:27 $

            Authors:    Dave Raggett <dsr@w3.org>
                        Arnaud Le Hors <lehors@w3.org>
                        Ian Jacobs <ij@w3.org>

->
<!-   This is the driver file for version 1.0 of the
        XHTML Transitional DTD.

        Please use this formal public identifier to identify it:

            "-//W3C//DTD XHTML 1.0 Transitional//EN"

        Please use this URI to identify the default namespace:

            "http://www.w3.org/TR/1999/REC-html-in-xml"

        For example, if you are using XHTML 1.0 directly,
```

```
              use the FPI in the DOCTYPE declaration, with the
              xmlns attribute on the
              document element to identify the default namespace:

  <?xml version="1.0" ?>
  <!DOCTYPE html PUBLIC "-//W3C//DTD XHTML 1.0 Transitional//EN"
                  "XHTML1-t.dtd" >
   <html xmlns="http://www.w3.org/TR/1999/REC-html-in-xml"
        xml:lang="en" lang="en" >
        ...
  </html>
-->

<!-- The version attribute has historically been a container
     for the DTD's public identifier (an FPI):  -->
<!ENTITY % HTML.version  "-//W3C//DTD XHTML 1.0
Transitional//EN" >

<!-- The xmlns attribute on <html> identifies the
     default namespace to namespace-aware applications:  -->
<!ENTITY % XHTML.ns  "http://www.w3.org/TR/1999/REC-html-in-
xml" >

<!-- reserved for future use with document profiles -->
<!ENTITY % XHTML.profile  "" >

<!ENTITY % XHTML1-frames.module  "IGNORE" >
<!ENTITY % XHTML.Transitional    "INCLUDE" >


<!-- XHTML Base Architecture Module (optional) ........ -->
<!ENTITY % XHTML1-arch.module "IGNORE" >
<![%XHTML1-arch.module;[
<!ENTITY % XHTML1-arch.mod
     PUBLIC "-//W3C//ELEMENTS XHTML 1.0 Base Architecture//EN"
            "XHTML1-arch.mod" >
%XHTML1-arch.mod;
]]>

<!-- Common Names Module ............................. -->
<!ENTITY % XHTML1-names.module "INCLUDE" >
<![%XHTML1-names.module;[
<!ENTITY % XHTML1-names.mod
     PUBLIC "-//W3C//ENTITIES XHTML 1.0 Common Names//EN"
            "XHTML1-names.mod" >
%XHTML1-names.mod;
]]>

<!-- Character Entities Module ........................ -->
<!ENTITY % XHTML1-charent.module "INCLUDE" >
<![%XHTML1-charent.module;[
<!ENTITY % XHTML1-charent.mod
```

Continued

Listing 20-2 *(continued)*

```
       PUBLIC "-//W3C//ENTITIES XHTML 1.0 Character Entities//EN"
             "XHTML1-charent.mod" >
%XHTML1-charent.mod;
]]>

<!- Intrinsic Events Module .......................... ->
<!ENTITY % XHTML1-events.module "INCLUDE" >
<![%XHTML1-events.module;[
<!ENTITY % XHTML1-events.mod
     PUBLIC "-//W3C//ENTITIES XHTML 1.0 Intrinsic Events//EN"
             "XHTML1-events.mod" >
%XHTML1-events.mod;
]]>

<!- Transitional Attributes Module ................... ->
<!ENTITY % XHTML1-attribs-t.module "INCLUDE" >
<![%XHTML1-attribs-t.module;[
<!ENTITY % XHTML1-attribs-t.mod
PUBLIC "-//W3C//ENTITIES XHTML 1.0 Transitional Attributes//EN"
       "XHTML1-attribs-t.mod" >
%XHTML1-attribs-t.mod;
]]>

<!- Transitional Document Model Module ............... ->
<!ENTITY % XHTML1-model-t.module "INCLUDE" >
<![%XHTML1-model-t.module;[
<!ENTITY % XHTML1-model-t.mod
     PUBLIC "-//W3C//ELEMENTS XHTML 1.0 Transitional Document
Model//EN"
             "XHTML1-model-t.mod" >
%XHTML1-model-t.mod;
]]>

<!- Inline Structural Module ........................ ->
<!ENTITY % XHTML1-inlstruct.module "INCLUDE" >
<![%XHTML1-inlstruct.module;[
<!ENTITY % XHTML1-inlstruct.mod
     PUBLIC "-//W3C//ELEMENTS XHTML 1.0 Inline Structural//EN"
             "XHTML1-inlstruct.mod" >
%XHTML1-inlstruct.mod;
]]>

<!- Inline Presentational Module .................... ->
<!ENTITY % XHTML1-inlpres.module "INCLUDE" >
<![%XHTML1-inlpres.module;[
<!ENTITY % XHTML1-inlpres.mod
  PUBLIC "-//W3C//ELEMENTS XHTML 1.0 Inline Presentational//EN"
  "XHTML1-inlpres.mod" >
%XHTML1-inlpres.mod;
]]>
```

```
<!— Inline Phrasal Module ........................... —>
<!ENTITY % XHTML1-inlphras.module "INCLUDE" >
<![%XHTML1-inlphras.module;[
<!ENTITY % XHTML1-inlphras.mod
     PUBLIC "-//W3C//ELEMENTS XHTML 1.0 Inline Phrasal//EN"
            "XHTML1-inlphras.mod" >
%XHTML1-inlphras.mod;
]]>


<!— Block Structural Module ......................... —>
<!ENTITY % XHTML1-blkstruct.module "INCLUDE" >
<![%XHTML1-blkstruct.module;[
<!ENTITY % XHTML1-blkstruct.mod
     PUBLIC "-//W3C//ELEMENTS XHTML 1.0 Block Structural//EN"
            "XHTML1-blkstruct.mod" >
%XHTML1-blkstruct.mod;
]]>


<!— Block Presentational Module ..................... —>
<!ENTITY % XHTML1-blkpres.module "INCLUDE" >
<![%XHTML1-blkpres.module;[
<!ENTITY % XHTML1-blkpres.mod
   PUBLIC "-//W3C//ELEMENTS XHTML 1.0 Block Presentational//EN"
          "XHTML1-blkpres.mod" >
%XHTML1-blkpres.mod;
]]>


<!— Block Phrasal Module ............................ —>
<!ENTITY % XHTML1-blkphras.module "INCLUDE" >
<![%XHTML1-blkphras.module;[
<!ENTITY % XHTML1-blkphras.mod
     PUBLIC "-//W3C//ELEMENTS XHTML 1.0 Block Phrasal//EN"
            "XHTML1-blkphras.mod" >
%XHTML1-blkphras.mod;
]]>


<!— Scripting Module ................................ —>
<!ENTITY % XHTML1-script.module "INCLUDE" >
<![%XHTML1-script.module;[
<!ENTITY % XHTML1-script.mod
     PUBLIC "-//W3C//ELEMENTS XHTML 1.0 Scripting//EN"
            "XHTML1-script.mod" >
%XHTML1-script.mod;
]]>


<!— Stylesheets Module .............................. —>
<!ENTITY % XHTML1-style.module "INCLUDE" >
<![%XHTML1-style.module;[
<!ENTITY % XHTML1-style.mod
     PUBLIC "-//W3C//ELEMENTS XHTML 1.0 Stylesheets//EN"
            "XHTML1-style.mod" >
%XHTML1-style.mod;
```

Continued

Listing 20-2 *(continued)*

```
]]>

<!-- Image Module .................................. -->
<!ENTITY % XHTML1-image.module "INCLUDE" >
<![%XHTML1-image.module;[
<!ENTITY % XHTML1-image.mod
     PUBLIC "-//W3C//ELEMENTS XHTML 1.0 Images//EN"
            "XHTML1-image.mod" >
%XHTML1-image.mod;
]]>

<!-- Frames Module ................................. -->
<![%XHTML1-frames.module;[
<!ENTITY % XHTML1-frames.mod
     PUBLIC "-//W3C//ELEMENTS XHTML 1.0 Frames//EN"
            "XHTML1-frames.mod" >
%XHTML1-frames.mod;
]]>

<!-- Linking Module ................................ -->
<!ENTITY % XHTML1-linking.module "INCLUDE" >
<![%XHTML1-linking.module;[
<!ENTITY % XHTML1-linking.mod
     PUBLIC "-//W3C//ELEMENTS XHTML 1.0 Linking//EN"
            "XHTML1-linking.mod" >
%XHTML1-linking.mod;
]]>

<!-- Client-side Image Map Module .................... -->
<!ENTITY % XHTML1-csismap.module "INCLUDE" >
<![%XHTML1-csismap.module;[
<!ENTITY % XHTML1-csismap.mod
  PUBLIC "-//W3C//ELEMENTS XHTML 1.0 Client-side Image Map//EN"
         "XHTML1-csismap.mod" >
%XHTML1-csismap.mod;
]]>

<!-- Object Element Module ........................... -->
<!ENTITY % XHTML1-object.module "INCLUDE" >
<![%XHTML1-object.module;[
<!ENTITY % XHTML1-object.mod
     PUBLIC "-//W3C//ELEMENTS XHTML 1.0 Object Element//EN"
            "XHTML1-object.mod" >
%XHTML1-object.mod;
]]>

<!-- Java Applet Element Module ...................... -->
<!ENTITY % XHTML1-applet.module "INCLUDE" >
<![%XHTML1-applet.module;[
<!ENTITY % XHTML1-applet.mod
     PUBLIC "-//W3C//ELEMENTS XHTML 1.0 Java Applets//EN"
```

```
                  "XHTML1-applet.mod" >
%XHTML1-applet.mod;
]]>

<!- Lists Module ...................................... ->
<!ENTITY % XHTML1-list.module "INCLUDE" >
<![%XHTML1-list.module;[
<!ENTITY % XHTML1-list.mod
     PUBLIC "-//W3C//ELEMENTS XHTML 1.0 Lists//EN"
            "XHTML1-list.mod" >
%XHTML1-list.mod;
]]>

<!- Forms Module ...................................... ->
<!ENTITY % XHTML1-form.module "INCLUDE" >
<![%XHTML1-form.module;[
<!ENTITY % XHTML1-form.mod
     PUBLIC "-//W3C//ELEMENTS XHTML 1.0 Forms//EN"
            "XHTML1-form.mod" >
%XHTML1-form.mod;
]]>

<!- Tables Module ...................................... ->
<!ENTITY % XHTML1-table.module "INCLUDE" >
<![%XHTML1-table.module;[
<!ENTITY % XHTML1-table.mod
     PUBLIC "-//W3C//ELEMENTS XHTML 1.0 Tables//EN"
            "XHTML1-table.mod" >
%XHTML1-table.mod;
]]>

<!- Document Metainformation Module ................... ->
<!ENTITY % XHTML1-meta.module "INCLUDE" >
<![%XHTML1-meta.module;[
<!ENTITY % XHTML1-meta.mod
     PUBLIC "-//W3C//ELEMENTS XHTML 1.0 Metainformation//EN"
            "XHTML1-meta.mod" >
%XHTML1-meta.mod;
]]>

<!- Document Structure Module ......................... ->
<!ENTITY % XHTML1-struct.module "INCLUDE" >
<![%XHTML1-struct.module;[
<!ENTITY % XHTML1-struct.mod
     PUBLIC "-//W3C//ELEMENTS XHTML 1.0 Document Structure//EN"
            "XHTML1-struct.mod" >
%XHTML1-struct.mod;
]]>

<!- end of XHTML 1.0 Transitional DTD
................................. ->
<!- .............................................. ->
```

This DTD is organized along the same lines as the strict DTD. First, comments tell you how to use this DTD. Next come entity declarations that are important for the imported modules, particularly XHTML.Transitional which is defined here as INCLUDE. In the strict DTD this was defined as IGNORE. Thus, the individual modules can use this to provide features that will only apply when the transitional DTD is being used. Finally, the various modules are imported. The difference between the strict and transitional DTDs lies in which modules are imported and how the parameter entities are overridden. The transitional DTD supports a superset of the strict DTD.

The XHTML Frameset DTD

The XHTML frameset DTD (XHTMl1-f.dtd), shown in Listing 20-3, is a superset of the transitional DTD that adds support for frames.

Listing 20-3: XHTMl1-f.dtd: the Voyager loose DTD for documents with frames

```
<!- ............................................................ ->
<!- XHTML 1.0 Frameset DTD
............................................... ->
<!- file: XHTMl1-f.dtd
->

<!-  XHTML 1.0 Frameset DTD

        This is XHTML 1.0, an XML reformulation of HTML 4.0.

        Copyright 1998-1999 World Wide Web Consortium
            (Massachusetts Institute of Technology, Institut
            National de Recherche en Informatique et en
            Automatique, Keio University). All Rights Reserved.

        Permission to use, copy, modify and distribute the XHTML
        1.0 DTD and its accompanying documentation for any
        purpose and without fee is hereby granted in perpetuity,
        provided that the above copyright notice and this
        paragraph appear in all copies.  The copyright holders
        make no representation about the suitability of the DTD
        for any purpose.

        It is provided "as is" without expressed or implied
        warranty.

          Author:    Murray M. Altheim <altheim@eng.sun.com>
          Revision:  @(#)XHTML1-f.dtd 1.17 99/04/01 SMI

        The XHTML 1.0 DTD is an XML variant based on
        the W3C HTML 4.0 DTD:
```

```
          Draft:        $Date: 1999/04/02 14:27:26 $

          Authors:      Dave Raggett <dsr@w3.org>
                        Arnaud Le Hors <lehors@w3.org>
                        Ian Jacobs <ij@w3.org>
  ->
  <!-  This is the driver file for version 1.0 of
       the XHTML Frameset DTD.

       Please use this formal public identifier to identify it:

            "-//W3C//DTD XHTML 1.0 Frameset//EN"

       Please use this URI to identify the default namespace:

            "http://www.w3.org/TR/1999/REC-html-in-xml"

       For example, if you are using XHTML 1.0 directly, use the
       FPI in the DOCTYPE declaration, with the xmlns attribute
       on the document element to identify the default
       namespace:

     <?xml version="1.0" ?>
     <!DOCTYPE html PUBLIC "-//W3C//DTD XHTML 1.0 Frameset//EN"
                        "XHTML1-f.dtd" >
     <html xmlns="http://www.w3.org/TR/1999/REC-html-in-xml"
           xml:lang="en" lang="en" >
     ...
     </html>
  ->

  <!- The version attribute has historically been a container
      for the DTD's public identifier (an FPI):  ->
  <!ENTITY % HTML.version  "-//W3C//DTD XHTML 1.0 Frameset//EN" >

  <!- The xmlns attribute on <html> identifies the
      default namespace to namespace-aware applications:  ->
  <!ENTITY % XHTML.ns
    "http://www.w3.org/TR/1999/REC-html-in-xml" >

  <!- reserved for future use with document profiles ->
  <!ENTITY % XHTML.profile   "" >

  <!ENTITY % XHTML1-frames.module   "INCLUDE" >
  <!ENTITY % XHTML.Transitional     "INCLUDE" >


  <!- declare and instantiate the XHTML Transitional DTD  ->
  <!ENTITY % XHTML1-t.dtd
      PUBLIC "-//W3C//DTD XHTML 1.0 Transitional//EN"
```

Continued

Listing 20-3 *(continued)*

```
        "XHTML1-t.dtd" >
%XHTML1-t.dtd;

<!- end of XHTML 1.0 Frameset DTD
...................................... ->
<!- .................................................... ->
```

This DTD is organized differently than the previous two DTDs. Instead of repeating all the definitions already in the transitional DTD, it simply imports that DTD using the XHTML1-t.dtd external parameter entity. Before doing this, however, it defines XHTML1-frames.module as INCLUDE. This entity was defined in the transitional DTD as IGNORE. However, the definition given here takes precedence. This DTD changes the meaning of the DTD it imports.

You could make a strict DTD that uses frames by importing the strict DTD instead of the transitional DTD like this:

```
<!- declare and instantiate the XHTML Strict DTD  ->
<!ENTITY % XHTML1-s.dtd
    PUBLIC "-//W3C//DTD XHTML 1.0 Strict//EN"
           "XHTML1-s.dtd" >
%XHTML1-s.dtd;
```

Other DTDsAlthough, XHTML1-s.dtd, XHTML1-t.dtd and XHTML1-f.dtd are the three main document types you can create with XHTML several other possibilities exist. One is documented in XHTML1-m.dtd, a DTD that includes both HTML and MathML (with a couple of changes needed to make MathML fully compatible with HTML).

There are also flat versions of the three main DTDs that use a single DTD file rather than many separate modules. They don't define different XML applications, and they're not as easy to follow as the modularized DTDs discussed here, but they are easier to place on Web sites. These include:

✦ XHTML1-s-flat.dtd: a strict XHTML DTD in a single file

✦ XHTML1-t-flat.dtd: a transitional XHTML DTD in a single file

✦ XHTML1-f-flat.dtd: a transitional XHTML DTD with frame support in a single file

In addition, as you'll learn below, it's possible to form your own DTDs that mix and match pieces of standard HTML. You can include the parts you need and leave out those you don't. You can even mix these parts with DTDs of your own devising. But before you can do this, you'll need to take a closer look at the modules that are available for use.

The XHTML Modules

XHTML divides HTML into 28 different modules. Each module is a DTD for a particular related subset of HTML elements. Each module can be used independently of the other modules. For example, you can add basic table support to your own XML application by importing the table module into your DTD and providing definitions for a few parameter entities like `Inline` and `Flow` that include the elements of your vocabulary. The available modules include:

1. XHTML1-applet.mod
2. XHTML1-arch.mod
3. XHTML1-attribs-t.mod
4. XHTML1-attribs.mod
5. XHTML1-blkphras.mod
6. XHTML1-blkpres.mod
7. XHTML1-blkstruct.mod
8. XHTML1-charent.mod
9. XHTML1-csismap.mod
10. XHTML1-events.mod
11. XHTML1-form.mod
12. XHTML1-frames.mod
13. XHTML1-image.mod
14. XHTML1-inlphras.mod
15. XHTML1-inlpres.mod
16. XHTML1-inlstruct.mod
17. XHTML1-linking.mod
18. XHTML1-list.mod
19. XHTML1-tables.mod
20. XHTML1-meta.mod
21. XHTML1-model-t.mod
22. XHTML1-model.mod
23. XHTML1-names.mod

24. XHTML1-object.mod

25. XHTML1-script.mod

26. XHTML1-struct.mod

27. XHTML1-style.mod

28. XHTML1-table.mod

The frameset DTD uses all 28 modules. The transitional DTD uses most of these except the XHTML1-frames module, the XHTML1-arch module, the XHTML1-attribs module, and the XHTML1-model module. The strict DTD only uses 22, omitting the XHTML1-arch module, the XHTML1-attribs-t module, the XHTML1-frames module, the XHTML1-applet module, and the XHTML1-model-t module.

The Common Names Module

The first module all three entities import is XHTML1-names.mod, the common names module, shown in Listing 20-4.

Listing 20-4: XHTML1-names.mod: the XHTML module that defines commonly used names

```
<!— ........................................................ —>
<!— XHTML 1.0 Document Common Names Module  .............. —>
<!— file: XHTML1-names.mod

        This is XHTML 1.0, an XML reformulation of HTML 4.0.
        Copyright 1998-1999 W3C (MIT, INRIA, Keio), All Rights
        Reserved. Revision: @(#)XHTML1-names.mod 1.16 99/04/01 SMI

        This DTD module is identified by the PUBLIC and SYSTEM
        identifiers:

        PUBLIC "-//W3C//ENTITIES XHTML 1.0 Common Names//EN"
        SYSTEM "XHTML1-names.mod"

        Revisions:
# 1999-01-31  added URIs PE for multiple URI attribute values
        ......................................................... —>

<!— i. Common Names

        defines the following common names, many of these imported
        from other specifications and standards.
—>

<!— .... Imported Names  .... —>
```

```
<!- media type, as per [RFC2045] ->
<!ENTITY % ContentType "CDATA" >

<!- comma-separated list of media types, as per [RFC2045] ->
<!ENTITY % ContentTypes "CDATA" >

<!- a character encoding, as per [RFC2045] ->
<!ENTITY % Charset "CDATA" >

<!- a space separated list of character encodings,
     as per [RFC2045] ->
<!ENTITY % Charsets "CDATA" >

<!- date and time information. ISO date format ->
<!ENTITY % Datetime "CDATA" >

<!- a single character from [ISO10646] ->
<!ENTITY % Character "CDATA" >

<!- a language code, as per [RFC1766] ->
<!ENTITY % LanguageCode "NMTOKEN" >

<!- space-separated list of link types ->
<!ENTITY % LinkTypes "NMTOKENS" >

<!- single or comma-separated list of media descriptors ->
<!ENTITY % MediaDesc "CDATA" >

<!- one or more digits (NUMBER) ->
<!ENTITY % Number "CDATA" >

<!- a Uniform Resource Identifier, see [URI] ->
<!ENTITY % URI "CDATA" >

<!- a space-separated list of Uniform Resource Identifiers, see
[URI] ->
<!ENTITY % URIs "CDATA" >

<!- script expression ->
<!ENTITY % Script "CDATA" >

<!- style sheet data ->
<!ENTITY % StyleSheet "CDATA" >

<!ENTITY % Text "CDATA" >

<!-Length defined in strict DTD for cellpadding/cellspacing->

<!- nn for pixels or nn% for percentage length ->
<!ENTITY % Length "CDATA" >

<!- pixel, percentage, or relative ->
```

Continued

Listing 20-4 *(continued)*

```
<!ENTITY % MultiLength "CDATA" >

<!— comma-separated list of MultiLength —>
<!ENTITY % MultiLengths "CDATA" >

<!— integer representing length in pixels —>
<!ENTITY % Pixels "CDATA" >

<!— render in this frame —>
<!ENTITY % FrameTarget "CDATA" >

<!— a color using sRGB: #RRGGBB as Hex values —>
<!ENTITY % Color "CDATA" >

<!— end of XHTML1-names.mod —>
```

DTDs aren't optimized for human legibility, even when relatively well written like this one—even less so when thrown together as is all too often the case. One of the first things you can do to understand a DTD is to reorganize it in a less formal but more legible fashion. Table 20-1 sorts the Imported Names section into a three-column table corresponding to the parameter entity name, the parameter entity value, and the comment associated with each parameter entity. This table form makes it clearer that the primary responsibility of this module is to provide parameter entities for use as element content models.

Table 20-1
Summary of Imported Names Section

Parameter Entity Name	Parameter Entity Value	Comment Associated with Parameter Entity
ContentType	CDATA	Media type, as per [RFC2045]
ContentTypes	CDATA	Comma-separated list of media types, as per [RFC2045]
Charset	CDATA	A character encoding, as per [RFC2045]
Charsets	CDATA	A space-separated list of character encodings, as per [RFC2045]
Datetime	CDATA	Date and time information. ISO date format

Parameter Entity Name	*Parameter Entity Value*	*Comment Associated with Parameter Entity*
Character	CDATA	A single character from a single character from [ISO10646]
LanguageCode	CDATA	A language code, as per [RFC1766]
LinkTypes	NMTOKENS	Space-separated list of link types
MediaDesc	CDATA	Single or comma-separated list of media descriptors
Number	CDATA	One or more digits (NUMBER)
URI	CDATA	A Uniform Resource Identifier, see [URI]
URIs	CDATA	A space-separated list of Uniform Resource Identifiers, see [URI]
Script	CDATA	Script expression
StyleSheet	CDATA	Style sheet data
Text	CDATA	
Length	CDATA	nn for pixels or nn% for percentage length
MultiLength	CDATA	Pixel, percentage, or relative
MultiLengths	CDATA	Comma-separated list of MultiLength
Pixels	CDATA	Integer representing length in pixels
FrameTarget	CDATA	Render in this frame
Color	CDATA	A color using sRGB: #RRGGBB as Hex values

What really stands out in this summary table is the number of synonyms for CDATA. In fact, all but one of these parameter entities is just a different synonym for CDATA. Why is that? It's certainly no easier to type %MultiLengths; than CDATA, even ignoring the issue of how much time it takes to remember all of these different parameter entities.

The answer is that although each of these parameter entity references resolves to simply CDATA, the use of the more descriptive parameter entity names like

Datetime, FrameTarget, or Length makes it more obvious to the reader of the DTD exactly what should go in a particular element or attribute value. Furthermore, the author of the DTD may look forward to a time when a schema language enables more detailed requirements to impose on attribute values. It may, at some point in the future, be possible to write declarations like this:

```
<!ATTLIST img
  src        URI       #REQUIRED
  alt        String    #REQUIRED
  longdesc   URI       #IMPLIED
  height     Integer   #IMPLIED
  width      Integer   #IMPLIED
  usemap     URI       #IMPLIED
  ismap      (ismap)   #IMPLIED
  author     CDATA     #IMPLIED
  copyright  CDATA     #IMPLIED
>
```

In this case, rather than having to find and replace all the places in this rather long DTD where CDATA is used as a length, a string, a URI, or an integer, the author can simply change the declaration of the %Length;, %URI; and %Text; entity references like this:

```
<!ENTITY % Length  "Integer">
<!ENTITY % URI     "URI">
<!ENTITY % Text    "String">
```

Almost certainly, whatever schema is eventually adopted for data-typing attributes in XML will not look exactly like the one I mocked up here. But it will likely be able to be integrated into the XHTML DTD very quickly, simply by adjusting a few of the entity declarations in the main DTD without painstakingly editing 28 modules.

The Character Entities Module

The second module all three DTDs import is XHTML1-charent.mod, shown in Listing 20-5. This module imports the DTDs that define entity sets for the standard HTML entities like ©, , and α for hard-to-type characters. These sets are:

- ✦ XHTML1-lat1.ent, characters 160 through 255 of Latin-1, Listing 20-30.

- ✦ XHTML1-symbol.ent, assorted useful characters and punctuation marks from outside the Latin-1 set such as the Euro sign and the em dash, Listing 20-31.

- ✦ XHTML1-special.ent, the Greek alphabet and assorted symbols commonly used for math like ∞ and ∫, Listing 20-32.

Listing 20-5: **XHTML1-charent.mod: the XHTML module that defines commonly used entities**

```
<!- ..................................................... ->
<!- XHTML 1.0 Character Entities Module
.............................. ->
<!- file: XHTML1-charent.mod

    This is XHTML 1.0, an XML reformulation of HTML 4.0.
    Copyright 1998-1999 W3C (MIT, INRIA, Keio), All Rights
    Reserved. Revision: @(#)XHTML1-charent.mod 1.16 99/04/01
    SMI

    This DTD module is identified by the PUBLIC and SYSTEM
    identifiers:

    PUBLIC "-//W3C//ENTITIES XHTML 1.0 Character Entities//EN"
    SYSTEM "XHTML1-charent.mod"

    Revisions: (none)
    ................................................. ->

<!- v. Character Entities for XHTML

    declares the set of character entities for XHTML,
    including Latin 1, symbol and special characters.
->

<!- to exclude character entity declarations from a normalized
    DTD, declare %XHTML1.ents; as "IGNORE" in the internal
    subset of the dummy XHTML file used for normalization.
->
<!ENTITY % XHTML1.ents "INCLUDE" >

<![%XHTML1.ents;[
<!ENTITY % XHTML1-lat1
    PUBLIC "-//W3C//ENTITIES Latin 1//EN//XML"
           "XHTML1-lat1.ent" >
%XHTML1-lat1;

<!ENTITY % XHTML1-symbol
    PUBLIC "-//W3C//ENTITIES Symbols//EN//XML"
           "XHTML1-symbol.ent" >
%XHTML1-symbol;

<!ENTITY % XHTML1-special
    PUBLIC "-//W3C//ENTITIES Special//EN//XML"
           "XHTML1-special.ent" >
%XHTML1-special;
]]>
```

Continued

```
<!- end of XHTML1-charent.mod ->
Notice that a PUBLIC ID tries to load these entity sets. In
this case, the public ID may simply be understood by a Web
browser as referring to its standard HTML entity set. If not,
then the relative URL giving the name of the entity set can
find the necessary declarations.
```

The Intrinsic Events Module

The third module all three DTDs import is the intrinsic events module. This module defines the attributes for different events that can occur to different elements, and that can be scripted through JavaScript. It defines both a generic set of events that will be used for most elements (the Events.attrib entity) and more specific event attributes for particular elements like form, button, label, and input.

Listing 20-6: XHTML1-events.mod: the intrinsic events module

```
<!- ............................................... ->
<!- XHTML 1.0 Intrinsic Events Module  ................. ->
<!- file: XHTML1-events.mod

    This is XHTML 1.0, an XML reformulation of HTML 4.0.
    Copyright 1998-1999 W3C (MIT, INRIA, Keio), All Rights
    Reserved. Revision: @(#)XHTML1-events.mod 1.16 99/04/01
    SMI

    This DTD module is identified by the PUBLIC and SYSTEM
    identifiers:

    PUBLIC "-//W3C//ENTITIES XHTML 1.0 Intrinsic Events//EN"
    SYSTEM "XHTML1-events.mod"

        Revisions:
#1999-01-14  transferred onfocus and onblur ATTLIST for 'a'
from link module
#1999-04-01  transferred remaining events attributes from other
modules

............................................... ->

<!- iv. Intrinsic Event Attributes

    These are the event attributes defined in HTML 4.0,
    Section 18.2.3 "Intrinsic Events"
```

```
     "Note: Authors of HTML documents are advised that changes
      are likely to occur in the realm of intrinsic events
      (e.g., how scripts are bound to events). Research in this
      realm is carried on by members of the W3C Document Object
      Model Working Group (see the W3C Web site at
      http://www.w3.org/ for more information)."
 -->

 <!ENTITY % Events.attrib
      "onclick       %Script;              #IMPLIED
       ondblclick    %Script;              #IMPLIED
       onmousedown   %Script;              #IMPLIED
       onmouseup     %Script;              #IMPLIED
       onmouseover   %Script;              #IMPLIED
       onmousemove   %Script;              #IMPLIED
       onmouseout    %Script;              #IMPLIED
       onkeypress    %Script;              #IMPLIED
       onkeydown     %Script;              #IMPLIED
       onkeyup       %Script;              #IMPLIED"
 >

 <!-- additional attributes on anchor element -->

 <!ATTLIST a
      onfocus       %Script;              #IMPLIED
      onblur        %Script;              #IMPLIED
 >

 <!-- additional attributes on form element -->

 <!ATTLIST form
      onsubmit      %Script;              #IMPLIED
      onreset       %Script;              #IMPLIED
 >

 <!-- additional attributes on label element -->

 <!ATTLIST label
      onfocus       %Script;              #IMPLIED
      onblur        %Script;              #IMPLIED
 >

 <!-- additional attributes on input element -->

 <!ATTLIST input
      onfocus       %Script;              #IMPLIED
      onblur        %Script;              #IMPLIED
      onselect      %Script;              #IMPLIED
      onchange      %Script;              #IMPLIED
 >
```

Continued

Listing 20-6 *(continued)*

```
<!- additional attributes on select element ->

<!ATTLIST select
     onfocus        %Script;                     #IMPLIED
     onblur         %Script;                     #IMPLIED
     onchange       %Script;                     #IMPLIED
>

<!- additional attributes on textarea element ->

<!ATTLIST textarea
     onfocus        %Script;                     #IMPLIED
     onblur         %Script;                     #IMPLIED
     onselect       %Script;                     #IMPLIED
     onchange       %Script;                     #IMPLIED
>

<!- additional attributes on button element ->

<!ATTLIST button
     onfocus        %Script;                     #IMPLIED
     onblur         %Script;                     #IMPLIED
>

<!- additional attributes on body element ->

<!ATTLIST body
     onload         %Script;                     #IMPLIED
     onunload       %Script;                     #IMPLIED
>

<!- additional attributes on area element ->

<!ATTLIST area
     onfocus        %Script;                     #IMPLIED
     onblur         %Script;                     #IMPLIED
>

<!ENTITY % XHTML1-frames.module "IGNORE" >
<![%XHTML1-frames.module;[
<!- additional attributes on frameset element ->

<!ATTLIST frameset
     onload         %Script;                     #IMPLIED
     onunload       %Script;                     #IMPLIED
>
]]>

<!- end of XHTML1-events.mod ->
```

The values of the various attributes are all given as %Script;. This is a parameter entity reference that was defined back in XHTML1-names.mod as being equivalent to CDATA.

None of these elements have actually been defined yet. They will be declared in modules that are yet to be imported

The Common Attributes Modules

The next module imported declares the attributes common to most elements like id, class, style, and title. However, there are two different sets of these: one for the strict DTD and one for the transitional DTD that also provides an align attribute. XHTML1-s.dtd imports XHTML1-attribs.mod, shown in Listing 20-7. XHTML1-t.dtd imports XHTML1-attribs-t.mod, shown in Listing 20-8. The .t stands for "transitional".

Listing 20-7: XHTML1-attribs.mod: the XHTML strict common attributes module

```
<!- ............................................... ->
<!- XHTML 1.0 Common Attributes Module  ................. ->
<!- file: XHTML1-attribs.mod

    This is XHTML 1.0, an XML reformulation of HTML 4.0.
    Copyright 1998-1999 W3C (MIT, INRIA, Keio), All Rights
    Reserved. Revision: @(#)XHTML1-attribs.mod 1.14 99/04/01
    SMI

    This DTD module is identified by the PUBLIC and SYSTEM
    identifiers:

    PUBLIC "-//W3C//ENTITIES XHTML 1.0 Common Attributes//EN"
    SYSTEM "XHTML1-attribs.mod"

    Revisions:
# 1999-02-24  changed PE names for attribute classes to
*.attrib;

............................................... ->

<!- ii. Common Attributes

    This modules declares many of the common attributes for
    the Strict DTD.
->

<!ENTITY % Core.attrib
```

Continued

Listing 20-7 *(continued)*

```
     "id            ID                        #IMPLIED
      class         CDATA                     #IMPLIED
      style         %StyleSheet;              #IMPLIED
      title         %Text;                    #IMPLIED"
>

<!ENTITY % I18n.attrib
    "lang           %LanguageCode;            #IMPLIED
     xml:lang       %LanguageCode;            #IMPLIED
     dir            (ltr|rtl)                 #IMPLIED"
>

<!- HTML intrinsic event attributes declared previously ->
<!ENTITY % Events.attrib "" >

<!ENTITY % Common.attrib
    "%Core.attrib;
     %I18n.attrib;
     %Events.attrib;" >

<!ENTITY % Align.attrib "" >

<!ENTITY % XLink.attribs  "INCLUDE" >
<![%XLink.attribs;[
<!- XLink attributes for a simple 'a' style link ->

<!ENTITY % Alink.attrib
    "xml:link       CDATA                     #FIXED    'simple'
     role           CDATA                     #IMPLIED
     inline         CDATA                     #FIXED    'true'
     content-role CDATA                       #IMPLIED
     content-title CDATA                      #IMPLIED
     show           CDATA                     #FIXED    'replace'
     activate       CDATA                     #FIXED    'user'
     behavior       CDATA                     #IMPLIED"
>
]]>
<!ENTITY % Alink.attrib  "" >

<!- end of XHTML1-attribs.mod ->
```

Listing 20-8: XHTML1-attribs-t.mod: the XHTML transitional common attributes module

```
<!- ............................................ ->
<!- XHTML 1.0 Transitional Attributes Module  .......... ->
<!- file: XHTML1-attribs-t.mod
```

```
     This is XHTML 1.0, an XML reformulation of HTML 4.0.
     Copyright 1998-1999 W3C (MIT, INRIA, Keio), All Rights
     Reserved. Revision: @(#)XHTML1-attribs-t.mod 1.14 99/04/01
     SMI

     This DTD module is identified by the PUBLIC and SYSTEM
     identifiers:

 PUBLIC "-//W3C//ELEMENTS XHTML 1.0 Transitional
Attributes//EN"
 SYSTEM "XHTML1-attribs-t.mod"

     Revisions:
# 1999-01-24  changed PE names for attribute classes to
*.attrib;
     .................................................. ->

<!- ii(t). Common Transitional Attributes

     This modules declares the same set of common attributes as
     the Strict version, but additionally includes ATTLIST
     declarations for the additional attribute specifications
     found in the Transitional DTD.
->

<!ENTITY % Core.attrib
     "id            ID                 #IMPLIED
      class         CDATA              #IMPLIED
      style         %StyleSheet;       #IMPLIED
      title         %Text;             #IMPLIED"
>


<!ENTITY % I18n.attrib
     "lang          %LanguageCode;     #IMPLIED
      xml:lang      %LanguageCode;     #IMPLIED
      dir           (ltr|rtl)          #IMPLIED"
>

<!- HTML intrinsic event attributes declared previously ->

<!ENTITY % Common.attrib
     "%Core.attrib;
      %I18n.attrib;
      %Events.attrib;"
>

<!- horizontal text alignment ->
<!ENTITY % Align.attrib
     "align  (left|center|right|justify)   #IMPLIED"
>
```

Continued

Listing 20-8 *(continued)*

```
<!- horizontal and vertical alignment ->
<!ENTITY % IAlign.attrib
     "align   (top|middle|bottom|left|right) #IMPLIED"
>

<!ENTITY % XLink.attribs  "INCLUDE" >
<![%XLink.attribs;[
<!- XLink attributes for a simple anchor link ->

<!ENTITY % Alink.attrib
     "xml:link    CDATA                 #FIXED   'simple'
      role        CDATA                 #IMPLIED
      inline      CDATA                 #FIXED   'true'
      content-role CDATA                #IMPLIED
      content-title CDATA               #IMPLIED
      show        CDATA                 #FIXED   'replace'
      activate    CDATA                 #FIXED   'user'
      behavior    CDATA                 #IMPLIED"
>
]]>
<!ENTITY % Alink.attrib  "" >

<!- end of XHTML1-attribs-t.mod ->
```

Aside from the `align` attributes (which are only included by the transitional DTD), these two modules are very similar. They define parameter entities for attributes (and groups of attributes) that can apply to any (or almost any) HTML element. These parameter entities are used inside `ATTLIST` declarations in other modules.

To grasp this section, let's use a different trick. Pretend we're cheating on one of those fast food restaurant menu mazes, and work backwards from the goal rather than forwards from the start. Consider the `Common.attrib` entity:

```
<!ENTITY % Common.attrib
     "%Core.attrib;
      %I18n.attrib;
      %Events.attrib;"
>
```

This entity sums up those attributes that apply to almost any element and will serve as the first part of most `ATTLIST` declarations in the individual modules. For example:

```
<!ATTLIST address
     %Common.attrib;
>
```

The last item in the declaration of Common.attrib is %Events.attrib;. This is defined as an empty string in XHTML1-attribs.mod.

```
<!— HTML intrinsic event attributes declared previously —>
<!ENTITY % Events.attrib "" >
```

However, as the comment indicates, this can be overridden in the base DTD to add attributes to the ones normally present. In particular, it was overridden in Listing 20-6 like this:

```
<!ENTITY % Events.attrib
    "onclick        %Script;                #IMPLIED
     ondblclick     %Script;                #IMPLIED
     onmousedown    %Script;                #IMPLIED
     onmouseup      %Script;                #IMPLIED
     onmouseover    %Script;                #IMPLIED
     onmousemove    %Script;                #IMPLIED
     onmouseout     %Script;                #IMPLIED
     onkeypress     %Script;                #IMPLIED
     onkeydown      %Script;                #IMPLIED
     onkeyup        %Script;                #IMPLIED"
>
```

The %Script; parameter entity reference was defined in Listing 20-4, XHTML1-names.mod as CDATA. Thus the replacement text of Common.attrib looks like this:

```
     %Core.attrib;
     %I18n.attrib;
     onclick        CDATA                   #IMPLIED
     ondblclick     CDATA                   #IMPLIED
     onmousedown    CDATA                   #IMPLIED
     onmouseup      CDATA                   #IMPLIED
     onmouseover    CDATA                   #IMPLIED
     onmousemove    CDATA                   #IMPLIED
     onmouseout     CDATA                   #IMPLIED
     onkeypress     CDATA                   #IMPLIED
     onkeydown      CDATA                   #IMPLIED
     onkeyup        CDATA                   #IMPLIED
```

The second to last item in the declaration of Common.attrib is %I18n.attrib;. This is defined in the same module with this declaration:

```
<!ENTITY % I18n.attrib
    "lang           %LanguageCode;          #IMPLIED
     xml:lang       %LanguageCode;          #IMPLIED
     dir            (ltr|rtl)               #IMPLIED"
>
```

The %LanguageCode;. parameter entity reference was also defined in XHTML1-names.mod as an alias for CDATA. Including these, %Common.attrib; now expands to:

```
%Core.attrib;
lang          CDATA; #IMPLIED
xml:lang      CDATA     #IMPLIED
dir           (ltr|rtl) #IMPLIED
onclick       CDATA     #IMPLIED
ondblclick    CDATA     #IMPLIED
onmousedown   CDATA     #IMPLIED
onmouseup     CDATA     #IMPLIED
onmouseover   CDATA     #IMPLIED
onmousemove   CDATA     #IMPLIED
onmouseout    CDATA     #IMPLIED
onkeypress    CDATA     #IMPLIED
onkeydown     CDATA     #IMPLIED
onkeyup       CDATA     #IMPLIED
```

The last remaining parameter entity reference to expand is %Core.attrib;. This is also declared in XHTML1-attribs.mod as:

```
<!ENTITY % Core.attrib
      "id         ID                 #IMPLIED
       class      CDATA              #IMPLIED
       style      %StyleSheet;       #IMPLIED
       title      %Text;             #IMPLIED"
>
```

This declaration includes two more parameter entity references: %StyleSheet; and %Text;. Each of these expands to CDATA., again from previous declarations in XHTML1-names.mod. Thus, the final expansion of %Common.attrib; is:

```
id            ID        #IMPLIED
class         CDATA     #IMPLIED
style         CDATA     #IMPLIED
title         CDATA     #IMPLIED
lang          CDATA     #IMPLIED
xml:lang      CDATA     #IMPLIED
dir           (ltr|rtl) #IMPLIED
onclick       CDATA     #IMPLIED
ondblclick    CDATA     #IMPLIED
onmousedown   CDATA     #IMPLIED
onmouseup     CDATA     #IMPLIED
onmouseover   CDATA     #IMPLIED
onmousemove   CDATA     #IMPLIED
onmouseout    CDATA     #IMPLIED
onkeypress    CDATA     #IMPLIED
onkeydown     CDATA     #IMPLIED
onkeyup       CDATA     #IMPLIED
```

Note   I've been a little cavalier with whitespace in this example. The true expansion of %Common.attrib; isn't so nicely formatted. However, whitespace is insignificant in declarations so this isn't really important, and you should feel free to manually adjust whitespace to line columns up or insert line breaks when manually expanding a parameter entity reference to see what it says.

Thus, %Common.attrib; has subsumed most of the other material in this section. You won't see %Core.attrib; or %I18N.attrib; or %Events.attrib; often again in later modules. They're just like private methods in C++ that could be inlined but aren't solely for the sake of efficiency.

The XLink attributes are not subsumed into %Common.attrib;. That's because although many elements can possess the link attributes, many cannot. Thus, when the XLink attributes are added to an element, you must use a separate parameter entity reference, %Alink.attrib;.

The Document Model Module

The XHTML DTDs next import a module that declares entities for all the text flow elements like p, div, and blockquote. These are the elements that form the basic tree structure of a well-formed HTML document. Again, two separate modules are provided; one for the strict DTD (Listing 20-9, XHTML1-model.mod) and one for the transitional DTD (Listing 20-10, XHTML1-model-t.mod).

Listing 20-9: **XHTML1-model.mod: the strict document model module**

```
<!- .............................................. ->
<!- XHTML 1.0 Document Model Module  ................... ->
<!- file: XHTML1-model.mod

    This is XHTML 1.0, an XML reformulation of HTML 4.0.
    Copyright 1998-1999 W3C (MIT, INRIA, Keio), All Rights
    Reserved. Revision: @(#)XHTML1-model.mod 1.12 99/04/01 SMI

    This DTD module is identified by the PUBLIC and SYSTEM
    identifiers:

    PUBLIC "-//W3C//ELEMENTS XHTML 1.0 Document Model//EN"
    SYSTEM "XHTML1-model.mod"

    Revisions:
    (none)
    .............................................. ->

<!- iii. Document Model
```

Continued

Listing 20-9 *(continued)*

```
      This modules declares entities describing all text flow
      elements, excluding Transitional elements. This module
      describes the groupings of elements that make up HTML's
      document model.

      HTML has two basic content models:

           %Inline.mix;   character-level elements
           %Block.mix;    block-like elements, eg., paragraphs and
lists

      The reserved word '#PCDATA' (indicating a text string) is
      now included explicitly with each element declaration, as
      XML requires that the reserved word occur first in a
      content model specification..
-->

<!- ................ Miscellaneous Elements ........ -->

<!- These elements are neither block nor inline, and can
      essentially be used anywhere in the document body -->

<!ENTITY % Misc.class
      "ins | del | script | noscript" >

<!- ................... Inline Elements ............. -->

<!ENTITY % Inlstruct.class
      "bdo | br | span" >

<!ENTITY % Inlpres.class   "tt | i | b | big | small | sub |
sup" >

<!ENTITY % Inlphras.class
      "em | strong | dfn | code | samp | kbd | var | cite | abbr
| acronym | q" >

<!ENTITY % Inlspecial.class   "a | img | object | map" >

<!ENTITY % Formctrl.class   "input | select | textarea | label |
button" >

<!- %Inline.class; includes all inline elements, used as a
component in mixes -->

<!ENTITY % Inline.class
      "%Inlstruct.class;
      | %Inlpres.class;
      | %Inlphras.class;
      | %Inlspecial.class;
```

```
        | %Formctrl.class;"
>

<!- %Inline.mix; includes all inline elements, including
%Misc.class; ->

<!ENTITY % Inline.mix
    "%Inline.class;
    | %Misc.class;"
>

<!- %Inline-noa.class; includes all non-anchor inlines,
    used as a component in mixes ->

<!ENTITY % Inline-noa.class
    "%Inlstruct.class;
    | %Inlpres.class;
    | %Inlphras.class;
    | img | object | map
    | %Formctrl.class;"
>

<!- %Inline-noa.mix; includes all non-anchor inlines ->

<!ENTITY % Inline-noa.mix
    "%Inline-noa.class;
    | %Misc.class;"
>

<!- .................... Block Elements  ......... ->

<!- In the HTML 4.0 DTD, heading and list elements were
    included in the %block; parameter entity. The
    %Heading.class; and %List.class; parameter entities must
    now be included explicitly on element declarations where
    desired.
->

<!-  There are six levels of headings from H1 (the most
    important) to H6 (the least important).
  ->
<!ENTITY % Heading.class  "h1 | h2 | h3 | h4 | h5 | h6" >

<!ENTITY % List.class "ul | ol | dl" >

<!ENTITY % Blkstruct.class  "p | div" >

<!ENTITY % Blkpres.class "hr" >

<!ENTITY % Blkphras.class  "pre | blockquote | address" >

<!ENTITY % Blkform.class  "form | fieldset" >
```

Continued

Listing 20-9 *(continued)*

```
<!ENTITY % Blkspecial.class  "table" >

<!— %Block.class; includes all block elements,
     used as an component in mixes —>

<!ENTITY % Block.class
     "%Blkstruct.class;
      | %Blkpres.class;
      | %Blkphras.class;
      | %Blkform.class;
      | %Blkspecial.class;"
>

<!— %Block.mix; includes all block elements plus %Misc.class;
—>

<!ENTITY % Block.mix
     "%Block.class;
      | %Misc.class;"
>

<!— %Block-noform.class; includes all non-form block elements,
     used as a component in mixes —>

<!ENTITY % Block-noform.class
     "%Blkstruct.class;
      | %Blkpres.class;
      | %Blkphras.class;
      | %Blkspecial.class;"
>

<!— %Block-noform.mix; includes all non-form block elements,
     plus %Misc.class; —>

<!ENTITY % Block-noform.mix
     "%Block-noform.class;
      | %Misc.class;"
>

<!— ............... All Content Elements ......... —>

<!— %Flow.mix; includes all text content, block and inline —>

<!ENTITY % Flow.mix
      "%Heading.class;
      | %List.class;
      | %Block.class;
```

```
    |  %Inline.class;
    |  %Misc.class;"
>

<!— end of XHTML1-model.mod —>
```

Listing 20-10: **XHTML1-model-t.mod: the transitional document model module**

```
<!— .................................................. —>
<!— XHTML 1.0 Transitional Text Markup Module ......... —>
<!— file: XHTML1-model-t.mod

    This is XHTML 1.0, an XML reformulation of HTML 4.0.
    Copyright 1998-1999 W3C (MIT, INRIA, Keio), All Rights
    Reserved. Revision: @(#)XHTML1-model-t.mod 1.14 99/04/01
    SMI

    This DTD module is identified by the PUBLIC and SYSTEM
    identifiers:

    PUBLIC "-//W3C//ELEMENTS XHTML 1.0 Transitional Document
    Model//EN" SYSTEM "XHTML1-model-t.mod"

    Revisions:
#1999-01-14  rearranged forms and frames PEs, adding
%Blkform.class;
    .................................................. —>

<!— iii(t). Transitional Document Model

    This modules declares entities describing all text flow
    elements, including Transitional elements. This module
    describes the groupings of elements that make up HTML's
    document model.

    HTML has two basic content models:

        %Inline.mix;   character-level elements
        %Block.mix;    block-like elements, eg., paragraphs and
lists

    The reserved word '#PCDATA' (indicating a text string) is
    now included explicitly with each element declaration, as
    XML requires that the reserved word occur first in a
```

Continued

Listing 20-10 *(continued)*

```
      content model specification..
—>

<!— ................ Miscellaneous Elements ...............
—>

<!— These elements are neither block nor inline, and can
     essentially be used anywhere in the document body —>

<!ENTITY % Misc.class
      "ins | del | script | noscript" >

<!— .................. Inline Elements ............. —>

<!ENTITY % Inlstruct.class
      "bdo | br | span" >

<!ENTITY % Inlpres.class
"tt | i | b | u | s | strike | big | small | font | basefont
    | sub | sup" >

<!ENTITY % Inlphras.class
      "em | strong | dfn | code | samp | kbd | var | cite
      | abbr | acronym | q" >

<![%XHTML1-frames.module;[
<!— %Inlspecial.class; includes iframe in Frameset DTD version
—>

<!ENTITY % Inlspecial.class  "a | img | applet | object | map
                              | iframe">
]]>

<!ENTITY % Inlspecial.class  "a | img | applet | object | map">

<!ENTITY % Formctrl.class  "input | select | textarea | label
                            | button">

<!— %Inline.class; includes all inline elements, used
                 as a component in mixes —>

<!ENTITY % Inline.class
     "%Inlstruct.class;
      | %Inlpres.class;
      | %Inlphras.class;
      | %Inlspecial.class;
      | %Formctrl.class;"
>

<!— %Inline.mix; includes all inline elements,
                 including %Misc.class; —>
```

```
<!ENTITY % Inline.mix
     "%Inline.class;
      | %Misc.class;"
>

<!-- %Inline-noa.class; includes all non-anchor inlines,
     used as a component in mixes -->

<!ENTITY % Inline-noa.class
     "%Inlstruct.class;
      | %Inlpres.class;
      | %Inlphras.class;
      | img | applet | object | map
      | %Formctrl.class;"
>

<!-- %Inline-noa.mix; includes all non-anchor inlines -->

<!ENTITY % Inline-noa.mix
     "%Inline-noa.class;
      | %Misc.class;"
>

<!-- .................... Block Elements  .......... -->

<!-- In the HTML 4.0 DTD, heading and list elements were
     included in the %block; parameter entity. The
     %Heading.class; and %List.class; parameter entities must
     now be included explicitly on element declarations where
     desired.
-->

<!-- There are six levels of headings from h1 (the most
important)
     to h6 (the least important).
-->
<!ENTITY % Heading.class  "h1 | h2 | h3 | h4 | h5 | h6">

<!ENTITY % List.class  "ul | ol | dl | menu | dir" >

<!ENTITY % Blkstruct.class  "p | div" >

<!ENTITY % Blkpres.class  "center | hr" >

<!ENTITY % Blkphras.class  "pre | blockquote | address" >

<!ENTITY % Blkform.class  "form | fieldset" >

<![%XHTML1-frames.module;[
<!-- Blkspecial.class includes noframes in Frameset DTD version
-->
```

Continued

Listing 20-10 *(continued)*

```
<!ENTITY % Blkspecial.class  "noframes | table" >
]]>

<!ENTITY % Blkspecial.class  "table" >

<!— %Block.class; includes all block elements,
    used as an component in mixes —>
<!ENTITY % Block.class
    "%Blkstruct.class;
    | %Blkpres.class;
    | %Blkphras.class;
    | %Blkform.class;
    | %Blkspecial.class;"
>

<!— %Block.mix; includes all block elements plus %Misc.class; —
>
<!ENTITY % Block.mix
    "%Block.class;
    | %Misc.class;"
>

<!— %Block-noform.class; includes all non-form block elements,
    used as a component in mixes —>
<!ENTITY % Block-noform.class
    "%Blkstruct.class;
    | %Blkpres.class;
    | %Blkphras.class;
    | %Blkspecial.class;"
>

<!— %Block-noform.mix; includes all non-form block elements,
    plus %Misc.class; —>
<!ENTITY % Block-noform.mix
    "%Block-noform.class;
    | %Misc.class;"
>

<!— ............... All Content Elements ............ —>

<!— %Flow.mix; includes all text content, block and inline —>
<!ENTITY % Flow.mix
    "%Heading.class;
    | %List.class;
    | %Block.class;
```

```
    |   %Inline.class;
    |   %Misc.class;"
>

<!- end of XHTML1-model-t.mod ->
```

The elements themselves are notwhat's declared in these two modules, but rather entities that can be used in content models for these elements and the elements that contain them. The actual element declarations come later.

These modules are divided into logical sections denoted by comments. The first is the Miscellaneous Elements section. This defines the `Misc.class` parameter entity for four elements that may appear as either inline or block elements:

```
<!ENTITY % Misc.class
    "ins | del | script | noscript" >
```

Next, the Inline Elements section defines the inline elements of HTML, those elements that may not contain block level elements. Here the transitional and strict DTDs differ in exactly which elements they include. However, they both divide the inline elements into structural (`Inlstruct.class`), presentational (`Inlpres.class`), phrasal (`Inlphras.class`), special (`Inlspecial.class`), and form (`Formctrl.class`) classes. These intermediate parameter entities are combined to form the `Inline.class` parameter entity which lists all the elements that may appear as inline elements. Then `%Inline.class;` is combined with the previously defined `%Misc.class;` parameter entity reference to create the `Inline.mix` parameter entity that includes both inline and miscellaneous elements.

```
<!ENTITY % Inline.mix
    "%Inline.class;
    |   %Misc.class;"
>
```

A similar parameter entity called `Inline-noa.class` is also defined. Here `noa` stands for "no a element". This one element is left out because it will be needed elsewhere when the block-level entities are defined next. Including it here has the potential to lead to ambiguous content models; not a major disaster but something to be avoided if possible.

The Block Elements section lists the different kinds of block-level elements, and defines parameter entities for each. This builds up in steps to the final `%Block.class;` parameter entity reference, which lists all block-level elements and `%Flow.mix;` which lists all block and inline elements.

Parameter entities are defined for headings h1 through h6 (Heading.class) and lists (List.class). Block-level parameter entities include structural blocks p and div (Blkstruct.class), presentational blocks, particularly hr, (Blkpres.class), forms and fieldsets (Blkform.class), and tables (Blkspecial.class). These are all combined in the Block.class parameter entity. This is merged with the Misc. class parameter entity to form the Block.mix parameter entity that contains both block-level and miscellaneous elements. Finally, Block-noform.class and a Block-noform.mix entities are defined to be used when all block-level elements ,except forms, are desired.

The final Content Elements section defines Flow.mix, which pulls together all of the above: block, inline, heading, list, and miscellaneous.

```
<!ENTITY % Flow.mix
      "%Heading.class;
    | %List.class;
    | %Block.class;
    | %Inline.class;
    | %Misc.class;"
>
```

The Inline Structural Module

The next module, XHTML1-inlstruct.mod, shown in Listing 20-11, is used by both the transitional and the strict DTDs to define the inline structural elements bdo, br, del, ins, and span.

Listing 20-11: **XHTML1-inlstruct.mod: the inline structural module**

```
<!- ........................................................ ->
<!- XHTML 1.0 Inline Phrasal Module  .................... ->
<!- file: XHTML1-inlstruct.mod

    This is XHTML 1.0, an XML reformulation of HTML 4.0.
    Copyright 1998-1999 W3C (MIT, INRIA, Keio), All Rights
    Reserved. Revision: @(#)XHTML1-inlstruct.mod 1.10 99/04/01
    SMI

    This DTD module is identified by the PUBLIC and SYSTEM
    identifiers:

    PUBLIC "-//W3C//ELEMENTS XHTML 1.0 Inline Structural//EN"
    SYSTEM "XHTML1-inlstruct.mod"

    Revisions:
    (none)
    ................................................................ -
>
```

```
<!- c1. Inline Structural

        bdo, br, del, ins, span
->

<!ENTITY % Bdo.content   "( #PCDATA | %Inline.mix; )*" >
<!ELEMENT bdo  %Bdo.content; >
<!ATTLIST bdo
     %Core.attrib;
     lang             %LanguageCode;           #IMPLIED
     dir              (ltr|rtl)                #REQUIRED
>

<!ENTITY % Br.content   "EMPTY" >
<!ELEMENT br  %Br.content; >
<!ATTLIST br
     %Core.attrib;
>

<!ENTITY % Del.content   "( #PCDATA | %Flow.mix; )*" >
<!ELEMENT del  %Del.content; >
<!ATTLIST del
     %Common.attrib;
     cite             %URI;                    #IMPLIED
     datetime         %Datetime;               #IMPLIED
>

<!ENTITY % Ins.content   "( #PCDATA | %Flow.mix; )*" >
<!ELEMENT ins  %Ins.content; >
<!ATTLIST ins
     %Common.attrib;
     cite             %URI;                    #IMPLIED
     datetime         %Datetime;               #IMPLIED
>

<!ENTITY % Span.content   "( #PCDATA | %Inline.mix; )*" >
<!ELEMENT span  %Span.content; >
<!ATTLIST span
     %Common.attrib;
>

<!- end of XHTML1-inlstruct.mod ->
```

This module actually begins to use the parameter entities the last several modules have defined. In particular, it defines the attributes of del, ins, and span as %Common.attrib; and those of bdo and br as %Core.attrib. It also uses several of the CDATA aliases from XHTML1-names.mod; specifically, %LanguageCode;, %URI; and %Datetime;.

Also note that the content models for elements are given as locally declared entities. For example:

```
<!ENTITY % Span.content  "( #PCDATA | %Inline.mix; )*" >
<!ELEMENT span  %Span.content; >
```

Why not simply declare them without the extra parameter entity reference like the following?

```
<!ELEMENT span ( #PCDATA | %Inline.mix; )* >
```

The reason is simple: using the parameter entity reference allows other modules to override this content model. These aren't necessarily the modules used here, but modules from completely different XML applications that may be merged with the XHTML modules.

Inline Presentational Module

The next module, XHTML1-inlpres.mod, shown in Listing 20-12, is used by both the transitional and the strict DTDs to define the inline presentational elements b, big, i, small, sub, sup, and tt.

Listing 20-12: **XHTML1-inlpres.mod: the inline presentational module**

```
<!- ............................................... ->
<!- XHTML 1.0 Inline Presentational Module ............. ->
<!- file: XHTML1-inlpres.mod

        This is XHTML 1.0, an XML reformulation of HTML 4.0.
        Copyright 1998-1999 W3C (MIT, INRIA, Keio), All Rights
        Reserved. Revision: @(#)XHTML1-inlpres.mod 1.13 99/04/01
        SMI

        This DTD module is identified by the PUBLIC and SYSTEM
        identifiers:

        PUBLIC "-//W3C//ELEMENTS XHTML 1.0 Inline
        Presentational//EN" SYSTEM "XHTML1-inlpres.mod"

        Revisions:
        (none)
        ............................................... ->

<!- c3. Inline Presentational
```

```
          b, big, i, small, sub, sup, tt

     A conditional section includes additional declarations for
     the Transitional DTD

          basefont, font, s, strike, u
-->

<!ENTITY % B.content   "( #PCDATA | %Inline.mix; )*" >
<!ELEMENT b  %B.content; >
<!ATTLIST b
     %Common.attrib;
>

<!ENTITY % Big.content   "( #PCDATA | %Inline.mix; )*" >
<!ELEMENT big  %Big.content; >
<!ATTLIST big
     %Common.attrib;
>

<!ENTITY % I.content   "( #PCDATA | %Inline.mix; )*" >
<!ELEMENT i  %I.content; >
<!ATTLIST i
     %Common.attrib;
>

<!ENTITY % Small.content   "( #PCDATA | %Inline.mix; )*" >
<!ELEMENT small  %Small.content; >
<!ATTLIST small
     %Common.attrib;
>

<!ENTITY % Sub.content   "( #PCDATA | %Inline.mix; )*" >
<!ELEMENT sub  %Sub.content; >
<!ATTLIST sub
     %Common.attrib;
>

<!ENTITY % Sup.content   "( #PCDATA | %Inline.mix; )*" >
<!ELEMENT sup  %Sup.content; >
<!ATTLIST sup
     %Common.attrib;
>

<!ENTITY % Tt.content   "( #PCDATA | %Inline.mix; )*" >
<!ELEMENT tt     %Tt.content; >
<!ATTLIST tt
     %Common.attrib;
>

<![%XHTML.Transitional;[
```

Continued

Listing 20-12 *(continued)*

```
<!ENTITY % Basefont.content  "EMPTY" >
<!ELEMENT basefont  %Basefont.content; >
<!ATTLIST basefont
     id              ID                       #IMPLIED
     size            CDATA                    #REQUIRED
     color           %Color;                  #IMPLIED
     face            CDATA                    #IMPLIED
>

<!ENTITY % Font.content  "( #PCDATA | %Inline.mix; )*" >
<!ELEMENT font  %Font.content; >
<!ATTLIST font
     %Core.attrib;
     %I18n.attrib;
     size            CDATA                    #IMPLIED
     color           %Color;                  #IMPLIED
     face            CDATA                    #IMPLIED
>

<!ENTITY % S.content  "( #PCDATA | %Inline.mix; )*" >
<!ELEMENT s  %S.content; >
<!ATTLIST s
     %Common.attrib;
>

<!ENTITY % Strike.content  "( #PCDATA | %Inline.mix; )*" >
<!ELEMENT strike  %Strike.content; >
<!ATTLIST strike
     %Common.attrib;
>

<!ENTITY % U.content  "( #PCDATA | %Inline.mix; )*" >
<!ELEMENT u  %U.content; >
<!ATTLIST u
     %Common.attrib;
>

]]>

<!- end of XHTML1-inlpres.mod ->
```

There's a neat trick in this file that defines the deprecated basefont, font, s, strike, and u elements for the transitional DTD but not for the strict DTD. The declarations for these elements and their attributes are all wrapped in this construct:

```
<![%XHTML.Transitional;[
    <!— basefont, font, s, strike, and u declarations —>
]]>
```

Recall that XHTML-t.dtd defined the parameter entity `XHTML.Transitional` as `INCLUDE` but the XHTML-s.dtd defined it as `IGNORE`. Thus these declarations are included by the transitional DTD and ignored by the strict one.

Inline Phrasal Module

The next module, XHTML1-inlphras.mod, shown in Listing 20-13, is used by both the transitional and the strict DTDs to define the inline phrasal elements: `abbr`, `acronym`, `cite`, `code`, `dfn`, `em`, `kbd`, `q`, `samp`, `strong`, and `var`.

Listing 20-13: XHTML1-inlphras.mod: the inline phrasal module

```
<!— .............................................. —>
<!— XHTML 1.0 Inline Phrasal Module ..................... —>
<!— file: XHTML1-inlphras.mod

    This is XHTML 1.0, an XML reformulation of HTML 4.0.
    Copyright 1998-1999 W3C (MIT, INRIA, Keio), All Rights
    Reserved. Revision: @(#)XHTML1-inlphras.mod 1.14 99/04/01
    SMI

    This DTD module is identified by the PUBLIC and SYSTEM
    identifiers:

    PUBLIC "-//W3C//ELEMENTS XHTML 1.0 Inline Phrasal//EN"
    SYSTEM "XHTML1-inlphras.mod"

    Revisions:
#1999-01-29  moved bdo, br, del, ins, span to inline
            structural module
    .............................................. —>

<!— c2. Inline Phrasal

        abbr, acronym, cite, code, dfn, em, kbd, q, samp,
strong, var
—>

<!ENTITY % Abbr.content  "( #PCDATA | %Inline.mix; )*" >
```

Continued

Listing 20-13 *(continued)*

```
<!ELEMENT abbr  %Abbr.content; >
<!ATTLIST abbr
     %Common.attrib;
>

<!ENTITY % Acronym.content  "( #PCDATA | %Inline.mix; )*" >
<!ELEMENT acronym  %Acronym.content; >
<!ATTLIST acronym
     %Common.attrib;
>

<!ENTITY % Cite.content  "( #PCDATA | %Inline.mix; )*" >
<!ELEMENT cite  %Cite.content; >
<!ATTLIST cite
     %Common.attrib;
>

<!ENTITY % Code.content  "( #PCDATA | %Inline.mix; )*" >
<!ELEMENT code  %Code.content; >
<!ATTLIST code
     %Common.attrib;
>

<!ENTITY % Dfn.content  "( #PCDATA | %Inline.mix; )*" >
<!ELEMENT dfn  %Dfn.content; >
<!ATTLIST dfn
     %Common.attrib;
>

<!ENTITY % Em.content  "( #PCDATA | %Inline.mix; )*" >
<!ELEMENT em  %Em.content; >
<!ATTLIST em
     %Common.attrib;
>

<!ENTITY % Kbd.content  "( #PCDATA | %Inline.mix; )*" >
<!ELEMENT kbd  %Kbd.content; >
<!ATTLIST kbd
     %Common.attrib;
>

<!ENTITY % Q.content  "( #PCDATA | %Inline.mix; )*" >
<!ELEMENT q  %Q.content; >
<!ATTLIST q
     %Common.attrib;
     cite          %URI;                       #IMPLIED
>

<!ENTITY % Samp.content  "( #PCDATA | %Inline.mix; )*" >
<!ELEMENT samp  %Samp.content; >
<!ATTLIST samp
```

```
        %Common.attrib;
>

<!ENTITY % Strong.content  "( #PCDATA | %Inline.mix; )*" >
<!ELEMENT strong  %Strong.content; >
<!ATTLIST strong
        %Common.attrib;
>

<!ENTITY % Var.content  "( #PCDATA | %Inline.mix; )*" >
<!ELEMENT var  %Var.content; >
<!ATTLIST var
        %Common.attrib;
>

<!- end of XHTML1-inlphras.mod ->
```

With the exception of q, all these inline elements in this module have identical content models and identical attribute lists. They may all contain #PCDATA | %Inline.mix; and they all have %Common.attrib; attributes. The q element can have all of these, too. However, it may also have one additional optional attribute, cite, which should contain a URI pointing to the source of the quotation.

This example demonstrates the power of the parameter entity approach particularly well. Without parameter entity references, this module would appear several times longer and several times less easy to grasp as a whole.

Block Structural Module

The next module, XHTML1-blkstruct.mod, shown in Listing 20-14, is a very simple module used by both the transitional and the strict DTDs to define the p and the div block-level structural elements.

Listing 20-14: **XHTML1-blkstruct.mod: the inline phrasal module**

```
<!- ............................................. ->
<!- XHTML 1.0 Block Structural Module ................. ->
<!- file: XHTML1-blkstruct.mod

     This is XHTML 1.0, an XML reformulation of HTML 4.0.
     Copyright 1998-1999 W3C (MIT, INRIA, Keio), All Rights
     Reserved. Revision: @(#)XHTML1-blkstruct.mod 1.10 99/04/01
     SMI
```

Continued

Listing 20-14 *(continued)*

```
     This DTD module is identified by the PUBLIC and SYSTEM
     identifiers:

     PUBLIC "-//W3C//ELEMENTS XHTML 1.0 Block Structural//EN"
     SYSTEM "XHTML1-blkstruct.mod"

     Revisions:
     (none)
     ....................................................... ->

<!- b1. Block Structural

     div, p
->

<!ENTITY % Div.content  "( #PCDATA | %Flow.mix; )*" >
<!ELEMENT div  %Div.content; >
<!ATTLIST div
     %Common.attrib;
     %Align.attrib;
>

<!ENTITY % P.content  "( #PCDATA | %Inline.mix; )*" >
<!ELEMENT p  %P.content; >
<!ATTLIST p
     %Common.attrib;
>

<!- end of XHTML1-blkstruct.mod ->
```

Block-Presentational Module

The next module, XHTML1-blkpres.mod, shown in Listing 20-15, defines the hr
and the center block-level structural elements for both the transitional and the
strict DTDs.

**Listing 20-15: XHTML1-blkpres.mod: the inline presentational
module**

```
<!- ....................................................... ->
<!- XHTML 1.0 Block Presentational Module ............... ->
<!- file: XHTML1-blkpres.mod

     This is XHTML 1.0, an XML reformulation of HTML 4.0.
     Copyright 1998-1999 W3C (MIT, INRIA, Keio), All Rights
```

Reserved. Revision: @(#)XHTML1-blkpres.mod 1.15 99/04/01 SMI

This DTD module is identified by the PUBLIC and SYSTEM identifiers:

PUBLIC "-//W3C//ELEMENTS XHTML 1.0 Block Presentational//EN" SYSTEM "XHTML1-blkpres.mod"

Revisions:
1999-01-31 added I18n.attrib to hr (errata)
.... ->

```
<!- b3. Block Presentational

       hr

    A conditional section includes additional declarations
    for the Transitional DTD

       center
->
<!ENTITY % Hr.content  "EMPTY" >
<!ELEMENT hr  %Hr.content; >
<!ATTLIST hr
     %Core.attrib;
     %I18n.attrib;
     %Events.attrib;
>

<![%XHTML.Transitional;[
<!ENTITY % Center.content  "( #PCDATA | %Flow.mix; )*" >
<!ELEMENT center  %Center.content; >
<!ATTLIST center
     %Common.attrib;
>

<!- additional attributes on hr ->
<!ATTLIST hr
     align          (left|center|right)     #IMPLIED
     noshade        (noshade)               #IMPLIED
     size           %Pixels;                #IMPLIED
     width          %Length;                #IMPLIED
>
]]>

<!- end of XHTML1-blkpres.mod ->
```

The center element is deprecated in HTML 4.0 so it's placed in the <![%XHTML.Transitional;[ ]]> region that will be included by the transitional DTD and ignored by the strict DTD. The hr element is included by both. However, some (but not all) of its attributes are deprecated in HTML 4.0. Consequently, it has two ATTLIST declarations, one for the undeprecated attributes and one for the deprecated attributes. The ATTLIST for the deprecated attributes is placed in the <![%XHTML.Transitional;[ ]]> region so it will be ignored by the strict DTD.

Block-Phrasal Module

The next module, XHTML1-blkphras.mod, shown in Listing 20-16, is a very simple module used by both the transitional and the strict DTDs to define the address, blockquote, pre, h1, h2, h3, h4, h5, and h6 block-level phrasal elements.

Listing 20-16: XHTML1-blkphras.mod: the block-phrasal module

```
<!- ............................................ ->
<!- XHTML 1.0 Block Phrasal Module ................... ->
<!- file: XHTML1-blkphras.mod

      This is XHTML 1.0, an XML reformulation of HTML 4.0.
      Copyright 1998-1999 W3C (MIT, INRIA, Keio), All Rights
      Reserved. Revision: @(#)XHTML1-blkphras.mod 1.13 99/04/01
      SMI

      This DTD module is identified by the PUBLIC and SYSTEM
      identifiers:

      PUBLIC "-//W3C//ELEMENTS XHTML 1.0 Block Phrasal//EN"
      SYSTEM "XHTML1-blkphras.mod"

      Revisions:
# 1998-11-10  removed pre exclusions - content model
              changed to mimic HTML 4.0
# 1999-01-29  moved div and p to block structural module
      ............................................ ->

<!- b2. Block Phrasal

      address, blockquote, pre, h1, h2, h3, h4, h5, h6
->

<!ENTITY % Address.content  "( #PCDATA | %Inline.mix; )*" >
<!ELEMENT address  %Address.content; >
<!ATTLIST address
      %Common.attrib;
>
```

```
<![%XHTML.Transitional;[
<!ENTITY % Blockquote.content  "( %Flow.mix; )*" >
]]>
<!ENTITY % Blockquote.content
    "( %Heading.class;
     | %List.class;
     | %Block.mix; )+"
>

<!ELEMENT blockquote  %Blockquote.content; >
<!ATTLIST blockquote
    %Common.attrib;
    cite           %URI;                      #IMPLIED
>

<!ENTITY % Pre.content
    "( #PCDATA | tt | i | b
     | %Inlstruct.class; | %Inlphras.class;
     | a | script | map
     | %Formctrl.class; )*"
>

<!ELEMENT pre  %Pre.content; >
<!ATTLIST pre
    %Common.attrib;
    xml:space      CDATA                      #FIXED "preserve"
>

<!- .................. Heading Elements .............. ->

<!ENTITY % Heading.content  "( #PCDATA | %Inline.mix; )*" >

<!ELEMENT h1  %Heading.content; >
<!ATTLIST h1
    %Common.attrib;
    %Align.attrib;
>

<!ELEMENT h2  %Heading.content; >
<!ATTLIST h2
    %Common.attrib;
    %Align.attrib;
>

<!ELEMENT h3  %Heading.content; >
<!ATTLIST h3
    %Common.attrib;
    %Align.attrib;
>

<!ELEMENT h4  %Heading.content; >
<!ATTLIST h4
```

Continued

Listing 20-16 *(continued)*

```
        %Common.attrib;
        %Align.attrib;
>

<!ELEMENT h5   %Heading.content; >
<!ATTLIST h5
        %Common.attrib;
        %Align.attrib;
>

<!ELEMENT h6   %Heading.content; >
<!ATTLIST h6
        %Common.attrib;
        %Align.attrib;
>

<!- end of XHTML1-blkphras.mod ->
```

Once again, the `<![%XHTML.Transitional;[ ]]>` region separates the declarations for the strict DTD from those for the transitional DTD. Here it's the content model of the `blockquote` element that's adjusted depending on which DTD is being used in these lines:

```
<![%XHTML.Transitional;[
<!ENTITY % Blockquote.content   "( %Flow.mix; )*" >
]]>
<!ENTITY % Blockquote.content
     "( %Heading.class;
      | %List.class;
      | %Block.mix; )+"
>
```

The first definition of `Blockquote.content` is used only with the transitional DTD. If it is included, it takes precedence over the second redefinition. However, with the strict DTD, only the second definition is ever seen or used.

The Scripting Module

The next module, XHTML1-script.mod, shown in Listing 20-17, is a very simple module used by both the transitional and the strict DTDs to define the `script` and `noscript` elements.

Listing 20-17: **XHTML1-script.mod: the scripting module**

```
<!- ...................................................... ->
<!- XHTML 1.0 Document Scripting Module  ................ ->
<!- file: XHTML1-script.mod

     This is XHTML 1.0, an XML reformulation of HTML 4.0.
     Copyright 1998-1999 W3C (MIT, INRIA, Keio), All Rights
     Reserved.
     Revision: @(#)XHTML1-script.mod 1.13 99/04/01 SMI

     This DTD module is identified by the PUBLIC
     and SYSTEM identifiers:

     PUBLIC "-//W3C//ELEMENTS XHTML 1.0 Scripting//EN"
     SYSTEM "XHTML1-script.mod"

     Revisions:
# 1999-01-30  added xml:space to script
# 1999-02-01  removed for and event attributes from script
     .................................................... ->

<!- d4. Scripting

       script, noscript
->

<!ENTITY % Script.content   "( #PCDATA )" >
<!ELEMENT script  %Script.content; >
<!ATTLIST script
      charset       %Charset;               #IMPLIED
      type          %ContentType;           #REQUIRED
      src           %URI;                   #IMPLIED
      defer         (defer)                 #IMPLIED
      xml:space     CDATA                   #FIXED 'preserve'
>

<!ENTITY % Noscript.content
      "( %Heading.class;
       | %List.class;
       | %Block.mix; )+"
>
<!ELEMENT noscript  %Noscript.content; >
<!ATTLIST noscript
      %Common.attrib;
>

<!- end of XHTML1-script.mod ->
```

The Stylesheets Module

The next module, XHTML1-style.mod, shown in Listing 20-18, is a particularly simple module used by both the transitional and the strict DTDs to define a single element, style.

Listing 20-18: XHTML1-style.mod: the stylesheets module

```
<!- ...................................... ->
<!- XHTML 1.0 Document Stylesheet Module  ................ ->
<!- file: XHTML1-style.mod

     This is XHTML 1.0, an XML reformulation of HTML 4.0.
     Copyright 1998-1999 W3C (MIT, INRIA, Keio), All Rights
     Reserved.
     Revision: @(#)XHTML1-style.mod 1.13 99/04/01 SMI

     This DTD module is identified by the PUBLIC and SYSTEM
     identifiers:

     PUBLIC "-//W3C//DTD XHTML 1.0 Stylesheets//EN"
     SYSTEM "XHTML1-style.mod"

     Revisions:
# 1999-01-30  added xml:space to style

...................................... ->

<!- d5. Stylesheets

        style
->

<!ENTITY % Style.content   "( #PCDATA )" >
<!ELEMENT style  %Style.content; >
<!ATTLIST style
     %I18n.attrib;
     type         %ContentType;          #REQUIRED
     media        %MediaDesc;            #IMPLIED
     title        %Text;                 #IMPLIED
     xml:space    CDATA                  #FIXED 'preserve'
>

<!- end of XHTML1-style.mod ->
```

The Image Module

The next module, XHTML1-image.mod, shown in Listing 20-19, is another particularly simple module used by both the transitional and the strict DTDs to define a single element, img.

Listing 20-19: **XHTML1-image.mod: the image module**

```
<!— ............................................... —>
<!— XHTML 1.0 Images Module  ........................... —>
<!— file: XHTML1-image.mod

     This is XHTML 1.0, an XML reformulation of HTML 4.0.
     Copyright 1998-1999 W3C (MIT, INRIA, Keio), All Rights
     Reserved.
     Revision: @(#)XHTML1-image.mod 1.15 99/04/01 SMI

     This DTD module is identified by the PUBLIC and SYSTEM
     identifiers:

     PUBLIC "-//W3C//ELEMENTS XHTML 1.0 Images//EN"
     SYSTEM "XHTML1-image.mod"

     Revisions:
# 1999-01-31  corrected transitional attributes (errata)
     ............................................... —>

<!— d3.1. Images

       img
—>

<!— To avoid problems with text-only UAs as well as
       to make image content understandable and navigable
       to users of non-visual UAs, you need to provide
       a description with ALT, and avoid server-side image maps
—>

<!ENTITY % Img.content   "EMPTY" >
<!ELEMENT img  %Img.content; >
<!ATTLIST img
     %Common.attrib;
     src            %URI;                #REQUIRED
     alt            %Text;               #REQUIRED
     longdesc       %URI;                #IMPLIED
     height         %Length;             #IMPLIED
     width          %Length;             #IMPLIED
     usemap         %URI;                #IMPLIED
     ismap          (ismap)              #IMPLIED
```

Continued

Listing 20-19 *(continued)*

```
>

<!— USEMAP points to a MAP element which may be in this
     document or an external document, although the latter is
     not widely supported
—>

<![%XHTML.Transitional;[
<!— additional Transitional attributes —>
<!ATTLIST img
     %IAlign.attrib;
     border        %Pixels;                    #IMPLIED
     hspace        %Pixels;                    #IMPLIED
     vspace        %Pixels;                    #IMPLIED
>
]]>

<!— end of XHTML1-image.mod —>
```

Note that the `alt` attribute is required on `img`. Omitting it produces a validity error.

The Frames Module

Next, both the strict and transitional DTDs conditionally import the frames module, XHTML1-frames.mod shown in Listing 20-20. This module defines those elements and attributes used on Web pages with frames. Specifically, it defines the `frameset`, `frame`, `noframes`, and `iframe` elements and their associated attribute lists.

However, this import is wrapped in:

```
<![%XHTML1-frames.module;[
  <!— frames declarations —>
]]>
```

Consequently, these imports only take place if `%XHTML1-frames.module;` parameter entity reference evaluates to `INCLUDE` which it does only if the frameset DTD is in use.

Listing 20-20: XHTML1-image.mod: the frames module

```
<!— ................................................... —>
<!— XHTML 1.0 Frames Module  ......................... —>
<!— file: XHTML1-frames.mod
```

```
      This is XHTML 1.0, an XML reformulation of HTML 4.0.
      Copyright 1998-1999 W3C (MIT, INRIA, Keio), All Rights
      Reserved.
      Revision: @(#)XHTML1-frames.mod 1.15 99/04/01 SMI

      This DTD module is identified by the PUBLIC and SYSTEM
      identifiers:

      PUBLIC "-//W3C//ELEMENTS XHTML 1.0 Frames//EN"
      SYSTEM "XHTML1-frames.mod"

      Revisions:
#1999-01-14  transferred 'target' attribute on 'a' from linking
module
      ................................................ ->

<!- a2. Frames

      frame, frameset, iframe, noframes
   ->

<!- The content model for HTML documents depends on whether
      the HEAD is followed by a FRAMESET or BODY element. The
      widespread omission of the BODY start tag makes it
      impractical to define the content model without the use of
      a conditional section.
   ->

<!ENTITY % Frameset.content  "(( frameset | frame )+, noframes?
)" >
<!ELEMENT frameset  %Frameset.content; >
<!ATTLIST frameset
      %Core.attrib;
      rows          %MultiLengths;          #IMPLIED
      cols          %MultiLengths;          #IMPLIED
>

<!- reserved frame names start with "_" otherwise starts with
letter ->

<!ENTITY % Frame.content  "EMPTY" >
<!ELEMENT frame %Frame.content; >
<!ATTLIST frame
      %Core.attrib;
      longdesc     %URI;          #IMPLIED
      name         CDATA          #IMPLIED
      src          %URI;          #IMPLIED
      frameborder  (1|0)          '1'
      marginwidth  %Pixels;       #IMPLIED
      marginheight %Pixels;       #IMPLIED
      noresize     (noresize)     #IMPLIED
      scrolling    (yes|no|auto)  'auto'
```

Continued

Listing 20-20 *(continued)*

```
>

<!— Inline Frames ......................... —>

<!ENTITY % Iframe.content   "( %Flow.mix; )*" >
<!ELEMENT iframe  %Iframe.content; >
<!ATTLIST iframe
     %Core.attrib;
     longdesc    %URI;                   #IMPLIED
     name        CDATA                   #IMPLIED
     src         %URI;                   #IMPLIED
     frameborder (1|0)                   '1'
     marginwidth %Pixels;                #IMPLIED
     marginheight %Pixels;               #IMPLIED
     scrolling   (yes|no|auto)           'auto'
     %IAlign.attrib;
     height      %Length;                #IMPLIED
     width       %Length;                #IMPLIED
>

<!— changes to other declarations ................... —>

<!— redefine content model for html element,
     substituting frameset for body —>
<!ENTITY % Html.content "( head, frameset )" >

<!— alternate content container for non frame-based rendering
—>

<!ENTITY % Noframes.content "( body )">
<!— in HTML 4.0 was "( body ) -( noframes )"
     exclusion on body —>
<!ELEMENT noframes  %Noframes.content; >
<!ATTLIST noframes
     %Common.attrib;
>

<!— add 'target' attribute to 'a' element —>
<!ATTLIST a
     target       %FrameTarget;          #IMPLIED
>

<!— end of XHTML1-frames.mod —>
```

There's not a lot to say about these declarations. There are no particularly interesting tricks here you haven't seen before, and adding frames to the DTD doesn't require overriding any previous parameter entities, at least not here. The most unusual aspect of this particular module is that the name attribute of both frame and iframe appears as CDATA rather than as some parameter entity reference. The reason is that there aren't any significant restrictions on frame names other than that they be CDATA. An eventual schema language can't add anything to raw CDATA in this case.

The Linking Module

The next module imported by both strict and transitional DTDs, XHTML1-image.mod, shown in Listing 20-21, is another simple module that defines the linking elements a, base, and link.

Listing 20-21: **XHTML1-image.mod: the linking module**

```
<!- ..................................................... ->
<!- XHTML 1.0 Linking Module  ........................... ->
<!- file: XHTML1-linking.mod

     This is XHTML 1.0, an XML reformulation of HTML 4.0.
     Copyright 1998-1999 W3C (MIT, INRIA, Keio), All Rights
     Reserved.
     Revision: @(#)XHTML1-linking.mod 1.13 99/04/01 SMI

     This DTD module is identified by the PUBLIC
     and SYSTEM identifiers:

     PUBLIC "-//W3C//ELEMENTS XHTML 1.0 Linking//EN"
     SYSTEM "XHTML1-linking.mod"

     Revisions:
# 1998-10-27  exclusion on 'a' within 'a' removed for XML
# 1998-11-15  moved shape and coords attributes on 'a' to
             csismap module
# 1999-01-14  moved onfocus and onblur attributes on 'a' to
             events module
     .............................. ->

<!- d2. Linking

      a, base, link
->

<!- ........... Anchor Element  ........... ->

<!ENTITY % Shape "(rect|circle|poly|default)">
```

Continued

Listing 20-21 *(continued)*

```
<!ENTITY % Coords "CDATA" >

<!ENTITY % A.content  "( #PCDATA | %Inline-noa.mix; )*" >
<!ELEMENT a  %A.content; >
<!ATTLIST a
     %Common.attrib;
     name          CDATA                    #IMPLIED
     href          %URI;                    #IMPLIED
     %Alink.attrib;
     charset       %Charset;                #IMPLIED
     type          %ContentType;            #IMPLIED
     hreflang      %LanguageCode;           #IMPLIED
     rel           %LinkTypes;              #IMPLIED
     rev           %LinkTypes;              #IMPLIED
     accesskey     %Character;              #IMPLIED
     tabindex      %Number;                 #IMPLIED
>

<!- ........... Base Element ............ ->

<!ENTITY % Base.content  "EMPTY" >
<!ELEMENT base  %Base.content; >
<!ATTLIST base
     href          %URI;                    #REQUIRED
>

<!- ........... Link Element ............ ->

<!- Relationship values can be used in principle:

   a) for document specific toolbars/menus when used
      with the LINK element in document head e.g.
      start, contents, previous, next, index, end, help
   b) to link to a separate style sheet (rel=stylesheet)
   c) to make a link to a script (rel=script)
   d) by stylesheets to control how collections of
      html nodes are rendered into printed documents
   e) to make a link to a printable version of this document
      e.g. a postscript or pdf version
      (rel=alternate media=print)
->

<!ENTITY % Link.content  "EMPTY" >
<!ELEMENT link  %Link.content; >
<!ATTLIST link
     %Common.attrib;
     charset       %Charset;                #IMPLIED
     href          %URI;                    #IMPLIED
     hreflang      %LanguageCode;           #IMPLIED
     type          %ContentType;            #IMPLIED
     rel           %LinkTypes;              #IMPLIED
```

```
        rev             %LinkTypes;            #IMPLIED
        media           %MediaDesc;            #IMPLIED
>

<!- end of XHTML1-linking.mod -->
```

The Client-side Image Map Module

The next module imported by both strict and transitional DTDs, XHTML1-csismap.mod, shown in Listing 20-22, is another simple module that defines the client-side image map elements map and area. The map element provides a client-side image map and must contain one or more block-level elements, miscellaneous elements, or area elements. The area element has an unusual, non-standard set of attributes. This should not surprise you, though, because the area element is unlike most other HTML elements. It's the only HTML element that acts like a vector graphic.

Listing 20-22: XHTML1-csismap.mod: the client-side image map module

```
<!- ................................................. -->
<!- XHTML 1.0 Client-side Image Map Module
............................ -->
<!- file: XHTML1-csismap.mod

    This is XHTML 1.0, an XML reformulation of HTML 4.0.
    Copyright 1998-1999 W3C (MIT, INRIA, Keio), All Rights
    Reserved.
    Revision: @(#)XHTML1-csismap.mod 1.15 99/04/01 SMI

    This DTD module is identified by the
    PUBLIC and SYSTEM identifiers:

 PUBLIC "-//W3C//ELEMENTS XHTML 1.0 Client-side Image Maps//EN"
 SYSTEM "XHTML1-csismap.mod"

    Revisions:
# 1999-01-31   fixed map content model (errata)
    ............................................... -->

<!- d3.2. Client-side Image Maps

      area, map
-->
```

Continued

Listing 20-22 *(continued)*

```
<!— These can be placed in the same document or grouped in a
      separate document although this isn't widely supported —>

<!ENTITY % Map.content
  "(( %Heading.class; | %List.class; | %Block.mix; ) | area)+">
<!ELEMENT map  %Map.content; >
<!ATTLIST map
      %Common.attrib;
      name          CDATA                   #REQUIRED
>

<!ENTITY % Area.content  "EMPTY" >
<!ELEMENT area  %Area.content; >
<!ATTLIST area
      %Common.attrib;
      href          %URI;                   #IMPLIED
      shape         %Shape;                 'rect'
      coords        %Coords;                #IMPLIED
      nohref        (nohref)                #IMPLIED
      alt           %Text;                  #REQUIRED
      tabindex      %Number;                #IMPLIED
      accesskey     %Character;             #IMPLIED
>

<!— modify anchor (<a>) attribute definition list to
     allow for client-side image maps —>

<!ATTLIST a
      shape         %Shape;                 'rect'
      coords        %Coords;                #IMPLIED
>

<!— end of XHTML1-csismap.mod —>
```

The Object Element Module

The next module imported by both strict and transitional DTDs, XHTML1-object.mod, shown in Listing 20-23, is another simple module that defines the `object` and `param` elements used to embed non-HTML content such as Java applets, ActiveX controls, and so forth in Web pages.

Listing 20-23: XHTML1-object.mod: the object module

```
<!— .............................................. —>
<!— XHTML 1.0 External Inclusion Module
.............................. —>
```

```
<!— file: XHTML1-object.mod

    This is XHTML 1.0, an XML reformulation of HTML 4.0.
    Copyright 1998-1999 W3C (MIT, INRIA, Keio), All Rights
    Reserved.
    Revision: @(#)XHTML1-object.mod 1.16 99/04/01 SMI

    This DTD module is identified by the
    PUBLIC and SYSTEM identifiers:

    PUBLIC "-//W3C//ELEMENTS XHTML 1.0 Object Element//EN"
    SYSTEM "XHTML1-object.mod"

    Revisions:
# 1999-01-31  changed object's archive attr
              to allow for multiple URIs
# 1999-01-31  corrected transitional attributes (errata)
    .................................................. —>

<!— d3.3. Objects

      object, param

    object is used to embed objects as part of HTML pages;
    param elements should precede other content.
—>

<!ENTITY % Object.content  "( %Flow.mix; | param )*" >
<!ELEMENT object  %Object.content; >
<!ATTLIST object
    %Common.attrib;
    declare       (declare)              #IMPLIED
    classid       %URI;                  #IMPLIED
    codebase      %URI;                  #IMPLIED
    data          %URI;                  #IMPLIED
    type          %ContentType;          #IMPLIED
    codetype      %ContentType;          #IMPLIED
    archive       %URIs;                 #IMPLIED
    standby       %Text;                 #IMPLIED
    height        %Length;               #IMPLIED
    width         %Length;               #IMPLIED
    usemap        %URI;                  #IMPLIED
    name          CDATA                  #IMPLIED
    tabindex      %Number;               #IMPLIED
>

<![%XHTML.Transitional;[
<!— additional Transitional attributes —>
<!ATTLIST object
    %IAlign.attrib;
    border        %Pixels;               #IMPLIED
    hspace        %Pixels;               #IMPLIED
```

Continued

Listing 20-23 *(continued)*

```
        vspace          %Pixels;                    #IMPLIED
>
]]>

<!ENTITY % Param.content   "EMPTY" >
<!ELEMENT param  %Param.content; >
<!ATTLIST param
        id              ID                          #IMPLIED
        name            CDATA                       #REQUIRED
        value           CDATA                       #IMPLIED
        valuetype       (data|ref|object)           'data'
        type            %ContentType;               #IMPLIED
>

<!- end of XHTML1-object.mod ->
```

Only two elements are declared; object and param. The content model for object is spelled out using the Flow.mix and param entities. Also, note that the mixed-content model of the object element requires a stricter declaration than is actually provided. That's the purpose of the comment "param elements should precede other content". However, a DTD can't specify that param elements should precede other content since mixed content requires that #PCDATA come first, and that a choice be used instead of a sequence.

The Java Applet Element Module

The applet element was originally invented by Sun to embed Java applets in Web pages. The next module imported only by the transitional DTD — XHTML1-applet.mod, shown in Listing 20-24 — is another simple module that defines the applet element. However, HTML 4.0 deprecates the applet element in favor of the more generic object element which can embed not only applets, but also ActiveX controls, images, Shockwave animations, QuickTime movies, and other forms of active and multimedia content. Consequently, only the transitional XHTML DTD uses the applet module.

Listing 20-24: XHTML1-applet.mod: the applet module

```
<!- ............................................. ->
<!- XHTML 1.0 Draft Document Java Applet Module
...................... ->
<!- file: XHTML1-applet.mod

     This is XHTML 1.0, an XML reformulation of HTML 4.0.
     Copyright 1998-1999 W3C (MIT, INRIA, Keio), All Rights
```

```
      Reserved.
      Revision: @(#)XHTML1-applet.mod 1.14 99/04/01 SMI

      This DTD module is identified by the
      PUBLIC and SYSTEM identifiers:

      PUBLIC "-//W3C//ELEMENTS XHTML V1.0 Java Applets//EN"
      SYSTEM "XHTML1-applet.mod"

      Revisions:
      (none)
      ...................................... ->

<!- d4. Scripting

        applet
->

<!- One of code or object attributes must be present.
      Place param elements before other content.
->

<!ENTITY % Applet.content  "( param | %Flow.mix; )*">
<!ELEMENT applet  %Applet.content; >
<!ATTLIST applet
      %Core.attrib;
      codebase        %URI;                   #IMPLIED
      archive         CDATA                   #IMPLIED
      code            CDATA                   #IMPLIED
      object          CDATA                   #IMPLIED
      alt             %Text;                  #IMPLIED
      name            CDATA                   #IMPLIED
      width           %Length;                #REQUIRED
      height          %Length;                #REQUIRED
      %IAlign.attrib;
      hspace          %Pixels;                #IMPLIED
      vspace          %Pixels;                #IMPLIED
>

<!- If the Object module that supplies the param element
      declarations is not used, redeclare %Param.local.module;
      as 'INCLUDE':  ->
<!ENTITY % Param.local.module  "IGNORE" >
<![%Param.local.module;[
<!ENTITY % Param.content  "EMPTY">
<!ELEMENT param  %Param.content; >
<!ATTLIST param
      id              ID                      #IMPLIED
      name            CDATA                   #REQUIRED
      value           CDATA                   #IMPLIED
      valuetype       (data|ref|object)       'data'
      type            %ContentType;           #IMPLIED
```

Continued

Listing 20-24 *(continued)*

```
>
]]>

<!- end of XHTML1-applet.mod ->
```

The content model and attribute list for applet essentially resembles object. The param element that's used to pass parameters to applets is declared in Listing 22-3, XHTML1-object.mod. However, if for some reason that's not imported as well, then the Param.local.module entity can be redefined to INCLUDE instead of IGNORE, and this DTD will declare param.

The Lists Module

The XHTML1-list.mod module, shown in Listing 20-25, operates in both DTDs and defines the elements used in ordered, unordered, and definition lists.

Listing 20-25: XHTML1-list.mod: the Voyager module for lists

```
<!- ............................................. ->
<!- XHTML 1.0 Lists Module
............................................. ->
<!- file: XHTML1-list.mod

     This is XHTML 1.0, an XML reformulation of HTML 4.0.
     Copyright 1998-1999 W3C (MIT, INRIA, Keio), All Rights
     Reserved.
     Revision: @(#)XHTML1-list.mod 1.13 99/04/01 SMI

     This DTD module is identified by the PUBLIC and SYSTEM
     identifiers:

     PUBLIC "-//W3C//ELEMENTS XHTML 1.0 Lists//EN"
     SYSTEM "XHTML1-list.mod"

     Revisions:
     (none)
     ............................................. ->

<!- a3. Lists

        dl, dt, dd, ol, ul, li

     A conditional section includes additional declarations for
     the Transitional DTD
```

```
        dir, menu
—>

<!— definition lists - DT for term, DD for its definition —>

<!ENTITY % Dl.content   "( dt | dd )+" >
<!ELEMENT dl   %Dl.content; >
<!ATTLIST dl
     %Common.attrib;
>

<!ENTITY % Dt.content   "( #PCDATA | %Inline.mix; )*" >
<!ELEMENT dt   %Dt.content; >
<!ATTLIST dt
     %Common.attrib;
>

<!ENTITY % Dd.content   "( #PCDATA | %Flow.mix; )*" >
<!ELEMENT dd   %Dd.content; >
<!ATTLIST dd
     %Common.attrib;
>

<!— Ordered Lists (ol) numbered styles —>

<!ENTITY % Ol.content   "( li )+" >
<!ELEMENT ol   %Ol.content; >
<!ATTLIST ol
     %Common.attrib;
>

<!— Unordered Lists (ul) bullet styles —>

<!ENTITY % Ul.content   "( li )+" >
<!ELEMENT ul   %Ul.content; >
<!ATTLIST ul
     %Common.attrib;
>

<!ENTITY % Li.content   "( #PCDATA | %Flow.mix; )*" >
<!ELEMENT li   %Li.content; >
<!ATTLIST li
     %Common.attrib;
>

<![%XHTML.Transitional;[
<!— Ordered lists (ol) Numbering style

     1    arabic numbers     1, 2, 3, ...
     a    lower alpha        a, b, c, ...
     A    upper alpha        A, B, C, ...
     i    lower roman        i, ii, iii, ...
```

Continued

Listing 20-25 *(continued)*

```
    I    upper roman            I, II, III, ...

    The style is applied to the sequence number which by
    default is reset to 1 for the first list item in
    an ordered list.
-->

<!ENTITY % OlStyle "CDATA" >

<!ATTLIST ol
        type            %OlStyle;                #IMPLIED
        compact         (compact)                #IMPLIED
        start           %Number;                 #IMPLIED
>

<!-- Unordered Lists (ul) bullet styles -->
<!ENTITY % UlStyle "(disc|square|circle)" >

<!ATTLIST ul
        type            %UlStyle;                #IMPLIED
        compact         (compact)                #IMPLIED
>

<!ENTITY % Dir.content   "( li )+" >
<!ELEMENT dir  %Dir.content; >
<!ATTLIST dir
        %Common.attrib;
        compact         (compact)                #IMPLIED
>

<!ENTITY % Menu.content   "( li )+" >
<!ELEMENT menu  %Menu.content; >
<!ATTLIST menu
        %Common.attrib;
        compact         (compact)                #IMPLIED
>
]]>

<!-- end of XHTML1-list.mod -->
```

You can define ordered and unordered lists much the same way. Each contains one list element (ol or ul) which may contain one or more list items (li). Both ol and ul elements may have the standard %Common.attrib; attributes of any HTML element. The definition list resembles this except that dl dt pairs are used instead of li list items.

The Forms Module

The XHTML1-form.mod module — shown in Listing 20-26 and used in both DTDs — covers the standard HTML form elements form, label, input, select, optgroup, option, textarea, fieldset, legend, and button. This is a relatively complicated module, reflecting the complexity of HTML forms.

Listing 20-26: **XHTML1-form.mod: the XHTML forms module**

```
<!- .............................................. ->
<!- XHTML 1.0 Forms Module
.......................................... ->
<!- file: XHTML1-form.mod

    This is XHTML 1.0, an XML reformulation of HTML 4.0.
    Copyright 1998-1999 W3C (MIT, INRIA, Keio), All Rights
    Reserved.
    Revision: @(#)XHTML1-form.mod 1.18 99/04/01 SMI

    This DTD module is identified by the PUBLIC and SYSTEM
    identifiers:

    PUBLIC "-//W3C//ELEMENTS XHTML 1.0 Forms//EN"
    SYSTEM "XHTML1-form.mod"

    Revisions:
# 1998-10-27  exclusion on form within form removed for XML
# 1998-11-10  changed button content model to mirror exclusions
# 1999-01-31  added 'accept' attribute on form (errata)
    .............................................. ->

<!- d7. Forms

        form, label, input, select, optgroup, option, textarea,
        fieldset, legend, button
->

<![%XHTML.Transitional;[
<!ENTITY % Form.content
    "( %Heading.class;
     | %List.class;
     | %Inline.class;
     | %Block-noform.mix;
     | fieldset )*"
>
]]>
<!ENTITY % Form.content
    "( %Heading.class;
     | %List.class;
```

Continued

Listing 20-26 *(continued)*

```
          |   %Block-noform.mix;
          |   fieldset )+"
>

<!ELEMENT form   %Form.content; >
<!ATTLIST form
%Common.attrib;
action          %URI;              #REQUIRED
method          (get|post)         'get'
enctype         %ContentType;      'application/x-www-form-urlencoded'
accept-charset  %Charsets;         #IMPLIED
accept          %ContentTypes;     #IMPLIED
>

<!-- Each label must not contain more than ONE field -->

<!ENTITY % Label.content
     "( #PCDATA
        |   %Inlstruct.class;
        |   %Inlpres.class;
        |   %Inlphras.class;
        |   %Inlspecial.class;
        |   input | select | textarea | button
        |   %Misc.class; )*"
>
<!ELEMENT label   %Label.content; >
<!ATTLIST label
     %Common.attrib;
     for             IDREF                     #IMPLIED
     accesskey       %Character;               #IMPLIED
>

<!ENTITY % InputType.class
     "( text | password | checkbox | radio | submit
      | reset | file | hidden | image | button )"
>

<!-- attribute name required for all but submit & reset -->

<!ENTITY % Input.content   "EMPTY" >
<!ELEMENT input   %Input.content; >
<!ATTLIST input
     %Common.attrib;
     type            %InputType.class;         'text'
     name            CDATA                     #IMPLIED
     value           CDATA                     #IMPLIED
     checked         (checked)                 #IMPLIED
     disabled        (disabled)                #IMPLIED
     readonly        (readonly)                #IMPLIED
     size            CDATA                     #IMPLIED
     maxlength       %Number;                  #IMPLIED
```

```
              src          %URI;                    #IMPLIED
              alt          CDATA                    #IMPLIED
              usemap       %URI;                    #IMPLIED
              tabindex     %Number;                 #IMPLIED
              accesskey    %Character;              #IMPLIED
              accept       %ContentTypes;           #IMPLIED
>

<!ENTITY % Select.content  "( optgroup | option )+" >
<!ELEMENT select  %Select.content; >
<!ATTLIST select
      %Common.attrib;
      name         CDATA                    #IMPLIED
      size         %Number;                 #IMPLIED
      multiple     (multiple)               #IMPLIED
      disabled     (disabled)               #IMPLIED
      tabindex     %Number;                 #IMPLIED
>

<!ENTITY % Optgroup.content  "( option )+" >
<!ELEMENT optgroup  %Optgroup.content; >
<!ATTLIST optgroup
      %Common.attrib;
      disabled     (disabled)               #IMPLIED
      label        %Text;                   #REQUIRED
>

<!ENTITY % Option.content   "( #PCDATA )" >
<!ELEMENT option  %Option.content; >
<!ATTLIST option
      %Common.attrib;
      selected     (selected)               #IMPLIED
      disabled     (disabled)               #IMPLIED
      label        %Text;                   #IMPLIED
      value        CDATA                    #IMPLIED
>

<!ENTITY % Textarea.content   "( #PCDATA )" >
<!ELEMENT textarea  %Textarea.content; >
<!ATTLIST textarea
      %Common.attrib;
      name         CDATA                    #IMPLIED
      rows         %Number;                 #REQUIRED
      cols         %Number;                 #REQUIRED
      disabled     (disabled)               #IMPLIED
      readonly     (readonly)               #IMPLIED
      tabindex     %Number;                 #IMPLIED
      accesskey    %Character;              #IMPLIED
>

<!— #PCDATA is to solve the mixed content problem, per
     specification only whitespace is allowed there!
```

Continued

Listing 20-26 *(continued)*

```
 ->

<!ENTITY % Fieldset.content
    "( #PCDATA | legend | %Flow.mix; )*" >
<!ELEMENT fieldset  %Fieldset.content; >
<!ATTLIST fieldset
    %Common.attrib;
>

<![%XHTML.Transitional;[
<!ENTITY % LegendAlign.attrib
    "align          (top|bottom|left|right)  #IMPLIED" >
]]>
<!ENTITY % LegendAlign.attrib  "" >

<!ENTITY % Legend.content  "( #PCDATA | %Inline.mix; )*" >
<!ELEMENT legend  %Legend.content; >
<!ATTLIST legend
    %Common.attrib;
    accesskey    %Character;                #IMPLIED
    %LegendAlign.attrib;
>

<!ENTITY % Button.content
    "( #PCDATA
      | %Heading.class;
      | %List.class;
      | %Inlpres.class;
      | %Inlphras.class;
      | %Block-noform.mix;
      | img | object | map )*"
>
<!ELEMENT button  %Button.content; >
<!ATTLIST button
    %Common.attrib;
    name         CDATA                     #IMPLIED
    value        CDATA                     #IMPLIED
    type         (button|submit|reset)     'submit'
    disabled     (disabled)                #IMPLIED
    tabindex     %Number;                  #IMPLIED
    accesskey    %Character;               #IMPLIED
>

<!- end of forms.mod ->
```

This module is starting to come close to the limits of DTDs. Several times you see comments specifying restrictions that are difficult to impossible to include in the declarations. For example, the comment that "attribute name required for all but submit & reset" for input elements. You can specify that all input elements must have a name attribute, or you can specify that all input elements may or may not have a name attribute, but you cannot specify that some must have it while others do not have to have it.

You might argue that this points more toward a deficiency in HTML forms than a deficiency in DTDs, and perhaps you'd be right. After all, submit and reset buttons certainly don't have to be input elements. Still, you can witness several other places in this module where the DTD begins to creak under its own weight. Perhaps what's really being demonstrated here is that XML and DTDs were designed for display of static documents, not for heavy interactive use.

The Table Module

The XHTML1-table.mod module, shown in Listing 20-15 and used by both DTDs, defines the elements used to lay out tables in HTML; specifically caption, col, colgroup, table, tbody, td, tfoot, th, thead, and tr. Like form elements, most of these elements should only appear inside a table element and consequently this module runs somewhat longer since it can't rely on elements defined previously, and since many elements defined here don't appear anywhere else.

Listing 20-27: **XHTML1-table.mod: the XHTML tables module**

```
<!- ........................................... ->
<!- XHTML 1.0 Table Module
.................................... ->
<!- file: XHTML1-table.mod

    This is XHTML 1.0, an XML reformulation of HTML 4.0.
    Copyright 1998-1999 W3C (MIT, INRIA, Keio), All Rights
    Reserved.
    Revision: @(#)XHTML1-table.mod 1.15 99/04/01 SMI

    This DTD module is identified by the
    PUBLIC and SYSTEM identifiers:

    PUBLIC "-//W3C//ELEMENTS XHTML 1.0 Tables//EN"
    SYSTEM "XHTML1-table.mod"

    Revisions:
    (none)
    ...................................... ->

<!- d6. HTML 4.0 Tables
```

Continued

Listing 20-27 *(continued)*

```
           caption, col, colgroup, table, tbody,
           td, tfoot, th, thead, tr

     A conditional section includes additional
     declarations for the Transitional DTD
->

<!- IETF HTML table standard, see [RFC1942] ->

<!- The border attribute sets the thickness of the frame
       around the table. The default units are screen pixels.

     The frame attribute specifies which parts of the frame
     around the table should be rendered. The values are not
     the same as CALS to avoid a name clash with the valign
     attribute.

     The value "border" is included for backwards compatibility
     with <table border> which yields frame=border and
     border=implied For <table border="1"> you get border="1"
     and frame="implied". In this case, it is appropriate to
     treat this as frame=border for backwards compatibility
     with deployed browsers.
->

<!ENTITY % TFrame
"(void|above|below|hsides|lhs|rhs|vsides|box|border)">

<!- The rules attribute defines which rules to draw between
cells:

     If rules is absent then assume:

     "none" if border is absent or border="0" otherwise "all"
->

<!ENTITY % TRules "(none | groups | rows | cols | all)">

<!- horizontal placement of table relative to document ->
<!ENTITY % TAlign "(left|center|right)">

<!- horizontal alignment attributes for cell contents ->
<!ENTITY % CellHAlign.attrib
     "align          (left|center|right|justify|char) #IMPLIED
      char           %Character;             #IMPLIED
      charoff        %Length;                #IMPLIED"
>

<!- vertical alignment attributes for cell contents ->
<!ENTITY % CellVAlign.attrib
```

```
      "valign          (top|middle|bottom|baseline) #IMPLIED"
>

<!ENTITY % CaptionAlign "(top|bottom|left|right)">

<!— Scope is simpler than axes attribute for common tables —>

<!ENTITY % Scope "(row|col|rowgroup|colgroup)" >

<!ENTITY % Table.content
     "( caption?, ( col* | colgroup* ),
       (( thead?, tfoot?, tbody+ ) | ( tr+ )))"
>
<!ELEMENT table  %Table.content; >
<!ATTLIST table
     %Common.attrib;
     summary       %Text;                 #IMPLIED
     width         %Length;               #IMPLIED
     border        %Pixels;               #IMPLIED
     frame         %TFrame;               #IMPLIED
     rules         %TRules;               #IMPLIED
     cellspacing   %Length;               #IMPLIED
     cellpadding   %Length;               #IMPLIED
     datapagesize CDATA                   #IMPLIED
>

<!ENTITY % Caption.content  "( #PCDATA | %Inline.mix; )*" >
<!ELEMENT caption  %Caption.content; >
<!ATTLIST caption
     %Common.attrib;
>

<!ENTITY % Thead.content  "( tr )+" >
<!ELEMENT thead  %Thead.content; >
<!— Use thead to duplicate headers when breaking table
     across page boundaries, or for static headers when
     TBODY sections are rendered in scrolling panel.

     Use tfoot to duplicate footers when breaking table
     across page boundaries, or for static footers when
     TBODY sections are rendered in scrolling panel.

     Use multiple tbody sections when rules are needed
     between groups of table rows.
—>
<!ATTLIST thead
     %Common.attrib;
     %CellHAlign.attrib;
     %CellVAlign.attrib;
>

<!ENTITY % Tfoot.content  "( tr )+" >
```

Continued

Listing 20-27 *(continued)*

```
<!ELEMENT tfoot  %Tfoot.content; >
<!ATTLIST tfoot
    %Common.attrib;
    %CellHAlign.attrib;
    %CellVAlign.attrib;
>

<!ENTITY % Tbody.content  "( tr )+" >
<!ELEMENT tbody  %Tbody.content; >
<!ATTLIST tbody
    %Common.attrib;
    %CellHAlign.attrib;
    %CellVAlign.attrib;
>

<!ENTITY % Colgroup.content  "( col )*" >
<!ELEMENT colgroup  %Colgroup.content; >
<!- colgroup groups a set of col elements. It allows you to
    group several semantically related columns together.
-->
<!ATTLIST colgroup
    %Common.attrib;
    span          %Number;                 '1'
    width         %MultiLength;            #IMPLIED
    %CellHAlign.attrib;
    %CellVAlign.attrib;
>

<!ENTITY % Col.content  "EMPTY" >
<!ELEMENT col  %Col.content; >
<!- col elements define the alignment properties for cells in
    one or more columns.

   The width attribute specifies the width of the columns, e.g.

       width="64"          width in screen pixels
       width="0.5*"        relative width of 0.5

   The span attribute causes the attributes of one
   col element to apply to more than one column.
  -->
<!ATTLIST col
    %Common.attrib;
    span          %Number;                 '1'
    width         %MultiLength;            #IMPLIED
    %CellHAlign.attrib;
    %CellVAlign.attrib;
>

<!ENTITY % Tr.content  "( th | td )+" >
<!ELEMENT tr  %Tr.content; >
```

```
<!ATTLIST tr
     %Common.attrib;
     %CellHAlign.attrib;
     %CellVAlign.attrib;
>

<!— th is for headers, td for data, but for cells
     acting as both use td —>

<!ENTITY % Th.content  "( #PCDATA | %Flow.mix; )*" >
<!ELEMENT th  %Th.content; >
<!ATTLIST th
     %Common.attrib;
     abbr          %Text;                 #IMPLIED
     axis          CDATA                  #IMPLIED
     headers       IDREFS                 #IMPLIED
     scope         %Scope;                #IMPLIED
     rowspan       %Number;               '1'
     colspan       %Number;               '1'
     %CellHAlign.attrib;
     %CellVAlign.attrib;
>

<!ENTITY % Td.content  "( #PCDATA | %Flow.mix; )*" >
<!ELEMENT td  %Td.content; >
<!ATTLIST td
     %Common.attrib;
     abbr          %Text;                 #IMPLIED
     axis          CDATA                  #IMPLIED
     headers       IDREFS                 #IMPLIED
     scope         %Scope;                #IMPLIED
     rowspan       %Number;               '1'
     colspan       %Number;               '1'
     %CellHAlign.attrib;
     %CellVAlign.attrib;
>

<![%XHTML.Transitional;[
<!— additional Transitional attributes for XHTML tables:
     (in XML, multiple ATTLIST declarations are merged)
—>

<!ATTLIST table
     align         %TAlign;               #IMPLIED
     bgcolor       %Color;                #IMPLIED
>

<!ATTLIST caption
     align         %CaptionAlign;         #IMPLIED
>

<!ATTLIST tr
```

Continued

Listing 20-27 *(continued)*

```
        bgcolor     %Color;                        #IMPLIED
>

<!ATTLIST th
        nowrap      (nowrap)                       #IMPLIED
        bgcolor     %Color;                        #IMPLIED
        width       %Pixels;                       #IMPLIED
        height      %Pixels;                       #IMPLIED
>

<!ATTLIST td
        nowrap      (nowrap)                       #IMPLIED
        bgcolor     %Color;                        #IMPLIED
        width       %Pixels;                       #IMPLIED
        height      %Pixels;                       #IMPLIED
>
]]>

<!- end of XHTML1-table.mod ->
```

The Meta Module

The next module is imported by both strict and transitional DTDs. XHTML1-meta.mod, shown in Listing 20-28, gets its name by defining the meta element placed in HTML head elements to provide keyword, authorship, abstract, and other indexing information that's mostly useful to Web robots. This module also defines the title element Although the title is meta-information in some sense, I suspect XHTML1-head.mod might be a better name here, except that the head element isn't defined here.

Listing 20-28: XHTML1-meta.mod: the XHTML meta module

```
<!- .............................................. ->
<!- XHTML 1.0 Document Metainformation Module
    ........................... ->
<!- file: XHTML1-meta.mod

    This is XHTML 1.0, an XML reformulation of HTML 4.0.
    Copyright 1998-1999 W3C (MIT, INRIA, Keio), All Rights
    Reserved.
    Revision: @(#)XHTML1-meta.mod 1.14 99/04/01 SMI
```

```
        This DTD module is identified by the PUBLIC and SYSTEM
        identifiers:

        PUBLIC "-//W3C//ELEMENTS XHTML 1.0 Metainformation//EN"
        SYSTEM "XHTML1-meta.mod"

        Revisions:
# 1998-11-11  title content model changed
             - exclusions no longer necessary
# 1999-02-01  removed isindex
        ............................................ ->

<!- d1. Meta Information

        meta, title
->

<!- The title element is not considered part of the flow of
     text. It should be displayed, for example as the page
     header or window title. Exactly one title is required per
     document.
->

<!ENTITY % Title.content  "( #PCDATA )" >
<!ELEMENT title  %Title.content; >
<!ATTLIST title
     %I18n.attrib;
>

<!ENTITY % Meta.content  "EMPTY" >
<!ELEMENT meta  %Meta.content; >
<!ATTLIST meta
     %I18n.attrib;
     http-equiv    NMTOKEN                 #IMPLIED
     name          NMTOKEN                 #IMPLIED
     content       CDATA                   #REQUIRED
     scheme        CDATA                   #IMPLIED
>

<!- end of XHTML1-meta.mod ->
```

The Structure Module

The final standard module takes all the previously defined elements, attributes, and entities and puts them together in an HTML document. This is XHTML1-struct.mod, shown in Listing 20-29. Specifically, it defines the html, head, and body elements.

Listing 20-29: **XHTML1-struct.mod: the XHTML structure module**

```
<!- ............................................. ->
<!- XHTML 1.0 Structure Module
........................................ ->
<!- file: XHTML1-struct.mod

    This is XHTML 1.0, an XML reformulation of HTML 4.0.
    Copyright 1998-1999 W3C (MIT, INRIA, Keio),
    All Rights Reserved.
    Revision: @(#)XHTML1-struct.mod 1.15 99/04/01 SMI

    This DTD module is identified by the PUBLIC and SYSTEM
    identifiers:

    PUBLIC "-//W3C//ELEMENTS XHTML 1.0 Document Structure//EN"
    SYSTEM "XHTML1-struct.mod"

    Revisions:
# 1998-10-27  content model on head changed to
              exclude multiple title or base
# 1998-11-11  ins and del inclusions on body removed,
              added to indiv. elements
# 1998-11-15  added head element version attribute
              (restoring from HTML 3.2)
# 1999-03-24  %Profile.attrib; unused,
              but reserved for future use
    ............................................... ->

<!- a1. Document Structure

      body, head, html
->

<!ENTITY % Head-opts.mix  "( script | style | meta | link |
object )*" >

<!ENTITY % Head.content "( title, base?, %Head-opts.mix; )" >

<!- reserved for future use with document profiles ->
<!ENTITY % Profile.attrib
    "profile       %URI;                      #FIXED
'%XHTML.profile;'" >

<!ELEMENT head  %Head.content; >
<!ATTLIST head
      %I18n.attrib;
      profile       %URI;                      #IMPLIED
>

<![%XHTML.Transitional;[
```

```
<!— in Transitional, allow #PCDATA and inlines directly within
body —>

<!ENTITY % Body.content  "( #PCDATA | %Flow.mix; )*" >
]]>
<!ENTITY % Body.content
    "( %Heading.class;
     | %List.class;
     | %Block.class;
     | %Misc.class; )+"
>

<!ELEMENT body  %Body.content; >
<!ATTLIST body
      %Common.attrib;
>

<![%XHTML.Transitional;[
<!— .... additional Transitional attributes on body .... —>

<!— There are also 16 widely known color names with their sRGB
values:

Black =#000000 Maroon =#800000 Green  = #008000 Navy = #000080
Silver=#C0C0C0 Red    =#FF0000 Lime   = #00FF00 Blue = #0000FF
Gray  =#808080 Purple =#800080 Olive  = #808000 Teal = #008080
White =#FFFFFF Fuchsia=#FF00FF Yellow = #FFFF00 Aqua = #00FFFF
—>

<!ATTLIST body
     bgcolor        %Color;                    #IMPLIED
     text           %Color;                    #IMPLIED
     link           %Color;                    #IMPLIED
     vlink          %Color;                    #IMPLIED
     alink          %Color;                    #IMPLIED
     background     %URI;                      #IMPLIED
>
]]>

<!ENTITY % Html.content  "( head, body )" >

<!—version and namespace attribute values defined in driver—>
<!ENTITY % Version.attrib
     "version        CDATA         #FIXED '%HTML.version;'" >
<!ENTITY % Ns.attrib
     "xmlns          %URI;         #FIXED '%XHTML.ns;'" >

<!ELEMENT html  %Html.content; >
<!ATTLIST html
     %I18n.attrib;
     %Version.attrib;
     %Ns.attrib;
```

Continued

Listing 20-29 *(continued)*

```
>

<!— end of XHTML1-struct.mod —>
```

Non-Standard modules

There are a number of non-standard modules included in the XHTML distribution that aren't used as part of the main XHTML application and won't be discussed here, but may be useful as parts of your custom program. These include:

✦ XHTML1-form32.mod: HTML 3.2 forms (as opposed to the HTML 4.0 forms used by XHTML)

✦ XHTML1-table32.mod: HTML 3.2 tables (as opposed to the HTML 4.0 tables used by XHTML)

✦ XHTML1-math.mod: MathML with slight revisions to make it fully compatible with XHTML

The XHTML Entity Sets

XML requires all entities to be declared (with the possible exception of the five standard entity references <, >, ', ", &).The XHTML DTD defines three entity sets declaring all entities commonly used in HTML:

1. XHTML1-lat1.ent, characters 160 through 255 of Latin-1, Listing 20-30.

2. XHTML1-symbol.ent, assorted useful characters and punctuation marks from outside the Latin-1 set such as the Euro sign and the em dash, Listing 20-31.

3. XHTML1-special.ent, the Greek alphabet and assorted symbols commonly used for math like ∞ and ∫, Listing 20-32.

Each of these entity sets is included in all versions of the XHTML DTD through the XHTML1-chars.mod module. Each of these entity sets has the same basic format:

1. A comment containing basic title, usage, and copyright information.

2. Lots of general internal entity declarations. The value of each general entity is given as a character reference to a Unicode character. Since no one can be expected to remember the all 40,000 Unicode characters by number, a brief textual description of the referenced character is given in a comment following each entity declaration.

The XHTML Latin-1 Entities

The XHTML1-lat1.ent file shown in Listing 20-30 declares entity references for the upper half of the ISO 8859-1, Latin-1 character set.

Listing 20-30: XHTML1-lat1.ent: the XHTML entity set for the upper half of ISO 8859-1, Latin-1

```
<!— XML-compatible ISO Latin 1 Character Entity Set for XHTML
1.0

    Typical invocation:

      <!ENTITY % XHTML1-lat1
          PUBLIC "-//W3C//ENTITIES Latin 1//EN//XML"
              "XHTML1-lat1.ent">
      %XHTML1-lat1;

    Revision:  @(#)XHTML1-lat1.ent 1.13 99/04/01 SMI

    Portions (C) International Organization for
    Standardization 1986 Permission to copy in any form is
    granted for use with conforming SGML systems and
    applications as defined in ISO 8879, provided this notice
    is included in all copies.
—>
<!ENTITY nbsp  " " ><!— no-break space=non-breaking space,
                                U+00A0 ISOnum —>
<!ENTITY iexcl  "&#161;" ><!— inverted exclamation mark,
                                U+00A1 ISOnum —>
<!ENTITY cent   "&#162;" ><!— cent sign,
                                U+00A2 ISOnum —>
<!ENTITY pound  "&#163;" ><!— pound sign,
                                U+00A3 ISOnum —>
<!ENTITY curren "&#164;" ><!— currency sign,
                                U+00A4 ISOnum —>
<!ENTITY yen    "&#165;" ><!— yen sign = yuan sign,
                                U+00A5 ISOnum —>
<!ENTITY brvbar "&#166;" ><!— broken bar =broken vertical bar,
                                U+00A6 ISOnum —>
<!ENTITY sect   "&#167;" ><!— section sign,
                                U+00A7 ISOnum —>
<!ENTITY uml    "&#168;" ><!— diaeresis = spacing diaeresis,
                                U+00A8 ISOdia —>
<!ENTITY copy   "&#169;" ><!— copyright sign,
                                U+00A9 ISOnum —>
<!ENTITY ordf   "&#170;" ><!— feminine ordinal indicator,
                                U+00AA ISOnum —>
<!ENTITY laquo  "&#171;" ><!— left-pointing double angle
```

Continued

Listing 20-30 *(continued)*

```
                        quotation mark = left pointing guillemet,
                        U+00AB ISOnum —>
<!ENTITY not     "&#172;" ><!— not sign,
                        U+00AC ISOnum —>
<!ENTITY shy "&#173;" ><!— soft hyphen = discretionary hyphen,
                        U+00AD ISOnum —>
<!ENTITY reg     "&#174;" ><!— registered sign
                        = registered trade mark sign,
                        U+00AE ISOnum —>
<!ENTITY macr    "&#175;" ><!— macron = spacing macron
                        = overline = APL overbar,
                        U+00AF ISOdia —>
<!ENTITY deg     "&#176;" ><!— degree sign,
                        U+00B0 ISOnum —>
<!ENTITY plusmn "&#177;" ><!— plus-minus sign
                        = plus-or-minus sign,
                        U+00B1 ISOnum —>
<!ENTITY sup2    "&#178;" ><!— superscript two
                        = superscript digit two = squared,
                        U+00B2 ISOnum —>
<!ENTITY sup3    "&#179;" ><!— superscript three
                        = superscript digit three = cubed,
                        U+00B3 ISOnum —>
<!ENTITY acute   "&#180;" ><!— acute accent = spacing acute,
                        U+00B4 ISOdia —>
<!ENTITY micro   "&#181;" ><!— micro sign,
                        U+00B5 ISOnum —>
<!ENTITY para    "&#182;" ><!— pilcrow sign = paragraph sign,
                        U+00B6 ISOnum —>
<!ENTITY middot "&#183;" ><!— middle dot = Georgian comma
                        = Greek middle dot,
                        U+00B7 ISOnum —>
<!ENTITY cedil   "&#184;" ><!— cedilla = spacing cedilla,
                        U+00B8 ISOdia —>
<!ENTITY sup1    "&#185;" ><!— superscript one
                        = superscript digit one,
                        U+00B9 ISOnum —>
<!ENTITY ordm    "&#186;" ><!— masculine ordinal indicator,
                        U+00BA ISOnum —>
<!ENTITY raquo   "&#187;" ><!— right-pointing
    double angle quotation mark = right pointing guillemet,
                        U+00BB ISOnum —>
<!ENTITY frac14 "&#188;" ><!— vulgar fraction one quarter
                        = fraction one quarter,
                        U+00BC ISOnum —>
<!ENTITY frac12 "&#189;" ><!— vulgar fraction one half
                        = fraction one half,
                        U+00BD ISOnum —>
<!ENTITY frac34 "&#190;" ><!— vulgar fraction three quarters
                        = fraction three quarters,
                        U+00BE ISOnum —>
```

```
<!ENTITY iquest "&#191;" ><!- inverted question mark
                                = turned question mark,
                                U+00BF ISOnum ->
<!ENTITY Agrave "&#192;" ><!-latin capital letter A with grave
                            = latin capital letter A grave,
                                U+00C0 ISOlat1 ->
<!ENTITY Aacute "&#193;"><!-latin capital letter A with acute,
                                U+00C1 ISOlat1 ->
<!ENTITY Acirc  "&#194;" ><!- latin capital letter A
                            with circumflex,
                                U+00C2 ISOlat1 ->
<!ENTITY Atilde "&#195;"><!-latin capital letter A with tilde,
                                U+00C3 ISOlat1 ->
<!ENTITY Auml   "&#196;" ><!- latin capital letter A
                            with diaeresis,
                                U+00C4 ISOlat1 ->
<!ENTITY Aring  "&#197;" ><!- latin capital letter A
                            with ring above
                            = latin capital letter A ring,
                                U+00C5 ISOlat1 ->
<!ENTITY AElig  "&#198;" ><!- latin capital letter AE
                                = latin capital ligature AE,
                                U+00C6 ISOlat1 ->
<!ENTITY Ccedil "&#199;" ><!- latin capital letter C
                            with cedilla,
                                U+00C7 ISOlat1 ->
<!ENTITY Egrave "&#200;"><!-latin capital letter E with grave,
                                U+00C8 ISOlat1 ->
<!ENTITY Eacute "&#201;"><!-latin capital letter E with acute,
                                U+00C9 ISOlat1 ->
<!ENTITY Ecirc  "&#202;" ><!- latin capital letter E
                            with circumflex,
                                U+00CA ISOlat1 ->
<!ENTITY Euml   "&#203;" ><!- latin capital letter E with
diaeresis,
                                U+00CB ISOlat1 ->
<!ENTITY Igrave "&#204;"><!-latin capital letter I with grave,
                                U+00CC ISOlat1 ->
<!ENTITY Iacute "&#205;"><!-latin capital letter I with acute,
                                U+00CD ISOlat1 ->
<!ENTITY Icirc  "&#206;" ><!- latin capital letter I
                            with circumflex,
                                U+00CE ISOlat1 ->
<!ENTITY Iuml   "&#207;" ><!- latin capital letter I
                            with diaeresis,
                                U+00CF ISOlat1 ->
<!ENTITY ETH    "&#208;" ><!- latin capital letter ETH,
                                U+00D0 ISOlat1 ->
<!ENTITY Ntilde "&#209;"><!-latin capital letter N with tilde,
                                U+00D1 ISOlat1 ->
<!ENTITY Ograve "&#210;"><!-latin capital letter O with grave,
                                U+00D2 ISOlat1 ->
```

Continued

Listing 20-30 *(continued)*

```
<!ENTITY Oacute "&#211;"><!—latin capital letter O with acute,
                                U+00D3 ISOlat1 —>
<!ENTITY Ocirc  "&#212;" ><!— latin capital letter O
                            with circumflex,
                                U+00D4 ISOlat1 —>
<!ENTITY Otilde "&#213;"><!—latin capital letter O with tilde,
                                U+00D5 ISOlat1 —>
<!ENTITY Ouml   "&#214;" ><!— latin capital letter O
                            with diaeresis,
                                U+00D6 ISOlat1 —>
<!ENTITY times  "&#215;" ><!— multiplication sign,
                                U+00D7 ISOnum —>
<!ENTITY Oslash "&#216;"><!—latin capital letter O with stroke
                        = latin capital letter O slash,
                                U+00D8 ISOlat1 —>
<!ENTITY Ugrave "&#217;"><!—latin capital letter U with grave,
                                U+00D9 ISOlat1 —>
<!ENTITY Uacute "&#218;"><!—latin capital letter U with acute,
                                U+00DA ISOlat1 —>
<!ENTITY Ucirc  "&#219;" ><!— latin capital letter U
                            with circumflex,
                                U+00DB ISOlat1 —>
<!ENTITY Uuml   "&#220;" ><!— latin capital letter U
                            with diaeresis,
                                U+00DC ISOlat1 —>
<!ENTITY Yacute "&#221;"><!—latin capital letter Y with acute,
                                U+00DD ISOlat1 —>
<!ENTITY THORN  "&#222;" ><!— latin capital letter THORN,
                                U+00DE ISOlat1 —>
<!ENTITY szlig  "&#223;" ><!— latin small letter sharp s
                            = ess-zed,
                                U+00DF ISOlat1 —>
<!ENTITY agrave "&#224;" ><!— latin small letter a with grave
                        = latin small letter a grave,
                                U+00E0 ISOlat1 —>
<!ENTITY aacute "&#225;" ><!— latin small letter a with acute,
                                U+00E1 ISOlat1 —>
<!ENTITY acirc  "&#226;" ><!— latin small letter a
                            with circumflex,
                                U+00E2 ISOlat1 —>
<!ENTITY atilde "&#227;" ><!— latin small letter a with tilde,
                                U+00E3 ISOlat1 —>
<!ENTITY auml   "&#228;" ><!— latin small letter a
                            with diaeresis,
                                U+00E4 ISOlat1 —>
<!ENTITY aring  "&#229;" ><!— latin small letter a
                            with ring above
                        = latin small letter a ring,
                                U+00E5 ISOlat1 —>
<!ENTITY aelig  "&#230;" ><!— latin small letter ae
                            = latin small ligature ae,
```

```
                                          U+00E6 ISOlat1 —>
<!ENTITY ccedil "&#231;" ><!— latin small letter c
                                   with cedilla,
                                          U+00E7 ISOlat1 —>
<!ENTITY egrave "&#232;" ><!— latin small letter e with grave,
                                          U+00E8 ISOlat1 —>
<!ENTITY eacute "&#233;" ><!— latin small letter e with acute,
                                          U+00E9 ISOlat1 —>
<!ENTITY ecirc  "&#234;" ><!— latin small letter e
                                   with circumflex,
                                          U+00EA ISOlat1 —>
<!ENTITY euml   "&#235;" ><!— latin small letter e
                                   with diaeresis,
                                          U+00EB ISOlat1 —>
<!ENTITY igrave "&#236;" ><!— latin small letter i with grave,
                                          U+00EC ISOlat1 —>
<!ENTITY iacute "&#237;" ><!— latin small letter i with acute,
                                          U+00ED ISOlat1 —>
<!ENTITY icirc  "&#238;" ><!— latin small letter i
                                   with circumflex,
                                          U+00EE ISOlat1 —>
<!ENTITY iuml   "&#239;" ><!— latin small letter I
                                   with diaeresis,
                                          U+00EF ISOlat1 —>
<!ENTITY eth    "&#240;" ><!— latin small letter eth,
                                          U+00F0 ISOlat1 —>
<!ENTITY ntilde "&#241;" ><!— latin small letter n with tilde,
                                          U+00F1 ISOlat1 —>
<!ENTITY ograve "&#242;" ><!— latin small letter o with grave,
                                          U+00F2 ISOlat1 —>
<!ENTITY oacute "&#243;" ><!— latin small letter o with acute,
                                          U+00F3 ISOlat1 —>
<!ENTITY ocirc  "&#244;" ><!— latin small letter o
                                   with circumflex,
                                          U+00F4 ISOlat1 —>
<!ENTITY otilde "&#245;" ><!— latin small letter o with tilde,
                                          U+00F5 ISOlat1 —>
<!ENTITY ouml   "&#246;" ><!— latin small letter o
                                   with diaeresis,
                                          U+00F6 ISOlat1 —>
<!ENTITY divide "&#247;" ><!— division sign,
                                          U+00F7 ISOnum —>
<!ENTITY oslash "&#248;" ><!—latin small letter o with stroke,
                                = latin small letter o slash,
                                          U+00F8 ISOlat1 —>
<!ENTITY ugrave "&#249;" ><!— latin small letter u with grave,
                                          U+00F9 ISOlat1 —>
<!ENTITY uacute "&#250;" ><!— latin small letter u with acute,
                                          U+00FA ISOlat1 —>
<!ENTITY ucirc  "&#251;" ><!— latin small letter u
                                   with circumflex,
```

Continued

Listing 20-30 *(continued)*

```
                                        U+00FB ISOlat1 —>
<!ENTITY uuml   "&#252;" ><!— latin small letter u
                                with diaeresis,
                                        U+00FC ISOlat1 —>
<!ENTITY yacute "&#253;" ><!— latin small letter y with acute,
                                        U+00FD ISOlat1 —>
<!ENTITY thorn  "&#254;" ><!— latin small letter thorn with,
                                        U+00FE ISOlat1 —>
<!ENTITY yuml   "&#255;" ><!— latin small letter y
                                with diaeresis,
                                        U+00FF ISOlat1 —>
```

The XHTML Special Character Entities

XHTML1-special.ent, shown in Listing 20-31, defines the general entities for an assortment of characters not in Latin-1, but present in Unicode.

Listing 20-31: XHTML1-special.ent: the XHTML definitions for a few character entities that don't really fit anywhere else

```
<!—
   XML-compatible ISO Special Character Entity Set for XHTML 1.0

     Typical invocation:

        <!ENTITY % XHTML1-special
            PUBLIC "-//W3C//ENTITIES Special//EN//XML"
                   "XHTML1-special.ent">
        %XHTML1-special;

     Revision:  @(#)XHTML1-special.ent 1.13 99/04/01 SMI

     Portions (C) International Organization for
     Standardization 1986: Permission to copy in any form is
     granted for use with conforming SGML systems and
     applications as defined in ISO 8879, provided this notice
     is included in all copies.
—>

<!— Relevant ISO entity set is given unless names are newly
      introduced. New names (i.e., not in ISO 8879 list) do not
      clash with any existing ISO 8879 entity names. ISO 10646
      character numbers are given for each character, in hex.
```

CDATA values are decimal conversions of the ISO 10646
values and refer to the document character set. Names are
Unicode 2.0 names.
-->

<!-- C0 Controls and Basic Latin -->
<!ENTITY quot """> <!-- quotation mark = APL quote,
                              U+0022 ISOnum -->
<!ENTITY amp   "&"> <!-- ampersand, U+0026 ISOnum -->
<!ENTITY lt   "<"> <!-- less-than sign, U+003C ISOnum-->
<!ENTITY gt   ">"> <!-- greater-than sign, U+003E ISOnum-->

<!-- Latin Extended-A -->
<!ENTITY OElig   "Œ"> <!-- latin capital ligature OE,
                              U+0152 ISOlat2 -->
<!ENTITY oelig   "œ"> <!-- latin small ligature oe,
                              U+0153 ISOlat2 -->
<!-- ligature is a misnomer, this is a separate character
     in some languages -->
<!ENTITY Scaron "Š"> <!-- latin capital letter S
                                with caron,
                                U+0160 ISOlat2 -->
<!ENTITY scaron "š"> <!-- latin small letter s
                                with caron,
                                U+0161 ISOlat2 -->
<!ENTITY Yuml   "Ÿ"> <!-- latin capital letter Y
                                with diaeresis,
                                U+0178 ISOlat2 -->

<!-- Spacing Modifier Letters -->
<!ENTITY circ   "ˆ"> <!-- modifier letter
                                circumflex accent,
                                U+02C6 ISOpub -->
<!ENTITY tilde   "˜"> <!-- small tilde, U+02DC ISOdia -->

<!-- General Punctuation -->
<!ENTITY ensp   " "> <!-- en space, U+2002 ISOpub -->
<!ENTITY emsp   " "> <!-- em space, U+2003 ISOpub -->
<!ENTITY thinsp " "> <!-- thin space, U+2009 ISOpub -->
<!ENTITY zwnj   "‌"> <!-- zero width non-joiner,
                                U+200C NEW RFC 2070 -->
<!ENTITY zwj   "‍"> <!-- zero width joiner,
                                U+200D NEW RFC 2070 -->
<!ENTITY lrm   "‎"> <!-- left-to-right mark,
                                U+200E NEW RFC 2070 -->
<!ENTITY rlm   "‏"> <!-- right-to-left mark,
                                U+200F NEW RFC 2070 -->
<!ENTITY ndash   "–"> <!-- en dash, U+2013 ISOpub -->
<!ENTITY mdash   "—"> <!-- em dash, U+2014 ISOpub -->
<!ENTITY lsquo   "‘"> <!-- left single quotation mark,
                                U+2018 ISOnum -->

Continued

Listing 20-31 *(continued)*

```
<!ENTITY rsquo    "&#8217;"> <!- right single quotation mark,
                                    U+2019 ISOnum ->
<!ENTITY sbquo    "&#8218;"> <!- single low-9 quotation mark,
                                    U+201A NEW ->
<!ENTITY ldquo    "&#8220;"> <!- left double quotation mark,
                                    U+201C ISOnum ->
<!ENTITY rdquo    "&#8221;"> <!- right double quotation mark,
                                    U+201D ISOnum ->
<!ENTITY bdquo    "&#8222;"> <!- double low-9 quotation mark,
                                    U+201E NEW ->
<!ENTITY dagger   "&#8224;"> <!- dagger, U+2020 ISOpub ->
<!ENTITY Dagger   "&#8225;"> <!- double dagger,
                                    U+2021 ISOpub ->
<!ENTITY permil   "&#8240;"> <!- per mille sign,
                                    U+2030 ISOtech ->
<!ENTITY lsaquo   "&#8249;"> <!- single left-pointing angle
                                    quotation mark,
                                    U+2039 ISO proposed ->
<!- lsaquo is proposed but not yet ISO standardized ->
<!ENTITY rsaquo   "&#8250;"> <!- single right-pointing
                                    angle quotation mark,
                                    U+203A ISO proposed ->
<!- rsaquo is proposed but not yet ISO standardized ->
<!ENTITY euro     "&#8364;"> <!-  euro sign, U+20AC NEW ->
```

The XHTML Symbol Entities

XHTML1-symbol.ent, shown in Listing 20-32, defines the general entities for the
Greek alphabet and various mathematical symbols like the integral and square root
signs.

Listing 20-32: **XHTML1-symbol.ent: the Voyager entity set for
mathematical symbols, including the Greek
alphabet**

```
<!- XML-compatible ISO Mathematical, Greek and Symbolic
    Character Entity Set for XHTML 1.0

    Typical invocation:

      <!ENTITY % XHTML1-symbol
          PUBLIC "-//W3C//ENTITIES Symbols//EN//XML"
                 "XHTML1-symbol.ent">
      %XHTML1-symbol;
```

```
             Revision:  @(#)XHTML1-symbol.ent 1.13 99/04/01 SMI

             Portions (C) International Organization for
             Standardization 1986: Permission to copy in any form is
             granted for use with conforming SGML systems and
             applications as defined in ISO 8879, provided this notice
             is included in all copies.
    ->

    <!- Relevant ISO entity set is given unless names are newly
        introduced. New names (i.e., not in ISO 8879 list) do not
        clash with any existing ISO 8879 entity names. ISO 10646
        character numbers are given for each character, in hex.
        CDATA values are decimal conversions of the ISO 10646
        values and refer to the document character set. Names are
        Unicode 2.0 names.
    ->

    <!- Latin Extended-B ->
    <!ENTITY fnof      "&#402;"> <!- latin small f with hook
                                    = function
                                    = florin, U+0192 ISOtech>

    <!- Greek ->
    <!ENTITY Alpha     "&#913;" ><!- greek capital letter alpha,
                                    U+0391 ->
    <!ENTITY Beta      "&#914;" ><!- greek capital letter beta,
                                    U+0392 ->
    <!ENTITY Gamma     "&#915;" ><!- greek capital letter gamma,
                                    U+0393 ISOgrk3 ->
    <!ENTITY Delta     "&#916;" ><!- greek capital letter delta,
                                    U+0394 ISOgrk3 ->
    <!ENTITY Epsilon   "&#917;" ><!- greek capital letter epsilon,
                                    U+0395 ->
    <!ENTITY Zeta      "&#918;" ><!- greek capital letter zeta,
                                    U+0396 ->
    <!ENTITY Eta       "&#919;" ><!- greek capital letter eta,
                                    U+0397 ->
    <!ENTITY Theta     "&#920;" ><!- greek capital letter theta,
                                    U+0398 ISOgrk3 ->
    <!ENTITY Iota      "&#921;" ><!- greek capital letter iota,
                                    U+0399 ->
    <!ENTITY Kappa     "&#922;" ><!- greek capital letter kappa,
                                    U+039A ->
    <!ENTITY Lambda    "&#923;" ><!- greek capital letter lambda,
                                    U+039B ISOgrk3 ->
    <!ENTITY Mu        "&#924;" ><!- greek capital letter mu,
                                    U+039C ->
    <!ENTITY Nu        "&#925;" ><!- greek capital letter nu,
                                    U+039D ->
```

Continued

Listing 20-32 *(continued)*

```
<!ENTITY Xi        "&#926;" ><!- greek capital letter xi,
                                 U+039E ISOgrk3 ->
<!ENTITY Omicron   "&#927;" ><!- greek capital letter omicron,
                                 U+039F ->
<!ENTITY Pi        "&#928;" ><!- greek capital letter pi,
                                 U+03A0 ISOgrk3 ->
<!ENTITY Rho       "&#929;" ><!- greek capital letter rho,
                                 U+03A1 ->
<!- there is no Sigmaf, and no U+03A2 character either ->
<!ENTITY Sigma     "&#931;" ><!- greek capital letter sigma,
                                 U+03A3 ISOgrk3 ->
<!ENTITY Tau       "&#932;" ><!- greek capital letter tau,
                                 U+03A4 ->
<!ENTITY Upsilon   "&#933;" ><!- greek capital letter upsilon,
                                 U+03A5 ISOgrk3 ->
<!ENTITY Phi       "&#934;" ><!- greek capital letter phi,
                                 U+03A6 ISOgrk3 ->
<!ENTITY Chi       "&#935;" ><!- greek capital letter chi,
                                 U+03A7 ->
<!ENTITY Psi       "&#936;" ><!- greek capital letter psi,
                                 U+03A8 ISOgrk3 ->
<!ENTITY Omega     "&#937;" ><!- greek capital letter omega,
                                 U+03A9 ISOgrk3 ->
<!ENTITY alpha     "&#945;" ><!- greek small letter alpha,
                                 U+03B1 ISOgrk3 ->
<!ENTITY beta      "&#946;" ><!- greek small letter beta,
                                 U+03B2 ISOgrk3 ->
<!ENTITY gamma     "&#947;" ><!- greek small letter gamma,
                                 U+03B3 ISOgrk3 ->
<!ENTITY delta     "&#948;" ><!- greek small letter delta,
                                 U+03B4 ISOgrk3 ->
<!ENTITY epsilon   "&#949;" ><!- greek small letter epsilon,
                                 U+03B5 ISOgrk3 ->
<!ENTITY zeta      "&#950;" ><!- greek small letter zeta,
                                 U+03B6 ISOgrk3 ->
<!ENTITY eta       "&#951;" ><!- greek small letter eta, U+03B7
                                 ISOgrk3 ->
<!ENTITY theta     "&#952;" ><!- greek small letter theta,
                                 U+03B8 ISOgrk3 ->
<!ENTITY iota      "&#953;" ><!- greek small letter iota,
                                 U+03B9 ISOgrk3 ->
<!ENTITY kappa     "&#954;" ><!- greek small letter kappa,
                                 U+03BA ISOgrk3 ->
<!ENTITY lambda    "&#955;" ><!- greek small letter lambda,
                                 U+03BB ISOgrk3 ->
<!ENTITY mu        "&#956;" ><!- greek small letter mu, U+03BC
                                 ISOgrk3 ->
<!ENTITY nu        "&#957;" ><!- greek small letter nu, U+03BD
                                 ISOgrk3 ->
<!ENTITY xi        "&#958;" ><!- greek small letter xi, U+03BE
                                 ISOgrk3 ->
```

```
<!ENTITY omicron  "&#959;" ><!— greek small letter omicron,
                                 U+03BF NEW —>
<!ENTITY pi       "&#960;" ><!— greek small letter pi,
                                 U+03C0 ISOgrk3 —>
<!ENTITY rho      "&#961;" ><!— greek small letter rho,
                                 U+03C1 ISOgrk3 —>
<!ENTITY sigmaf   "&#962;" ><!— greek small letter final
                                 sigma, U+03C2 ISOgrk3 —>
<!ENTITY sigma    "&#963;" ><!— greek small letter sigma,
                                 U+03C3 ISOgrk3 —>
<!ENTITY tau      "&#964;" ><!— greek small letter tau,
                                 U+03C4 ISOgrk3 —>
<!ENTITY upsilon  "&#965;" ><!— greek small letter upsilon,
                                 U+03C5 ISOgrk3 —>
<!ENTITY phi      "&#966;" ><!— greek small letter phi,
                                 U+03C6 ISOgrk3 —>
<!ENTITY chi      "&#967;" ><!— greek small letter chi,
                                 U+03C7 ISOgrk3 —>
<!ENTITY psi      "&#968;" ><!— greek small letter psi,
                                 U+03C8 ISOgrk3 —>
<!ENTITY omega    "&#969;" ><!— greek small letter omega,
                                 U+03C9 ISOgrk3 —>
<!ENTITY thetasym "&#977;" ><!— greek small letter theta
                                 symbol, U+03D1 NEW —>
<!ENTITY upsih    "&#978;" ><!— greek upsilon with hook
                                 symbol, U+03D2 NEW —>
<!ENTITY piv      "&#982;" ><!— greek pi symbol,
                                 U+03D6 ISOgrk3 —>

<!— General Punctuation —>
<!ENTITY bull     "&#8226;" ><!— bullet = black small circle,
                                 U+2022 ISOpub  —>
<!— bullet is NOT the same as bullet operator, U+2219 —>
<!ENTITY hellip   "&#8230;" ><!— horizontal ellipsis
                        = three dot leader, U+2026 ISOpub —>
<!ENTITY prime    "&#8242;" ><!— prime = minutes = feet,
                                 U+2032 ISOtech —>
<!ENTITY Prime    "&#8243;" ><!— double prime = seconds
                             = inches, U+2033 ISOtech —>
<!ENTITY oline    "&#8254;" ><!— overline = spacing overscore,
                                 U+203E NEW —>
<!ENTITY frasl    "&#8260;" ><!— fraction slash, U+2044 NEW—>

<!— Letterlike Symbols —>
<!ENTITY weierp   "&#8472;" ><!— script capital P = power set
                        = Weierstrass p, U+2118 ISOamso —>
<!ENTITY image    "&#8465;" ><!— blackletter capital I
                        = imaginary part, U+2111 ISOamso —>
<!ENTITY real     "&#8476;" ><!— blackletter capital R
                        = real part symbol, U+211C ISOamso —>
<!ENTITY trade    "&#8482;" ><!— trade mark sign,
                                 U+2122 ISOnum —>
```

Continued

Listing 20-32 *(continued)*

```
<!ENTITY alefsym  "&#8501;" ><!- alef symbol
                    = first transfinite cardinal, U+2135 NEW ->
<!- alef symbol is NOT the same as hebrew letter alef,
    U+05D0 although the same glyph could be used to depict
    both characters ->

<!- Arrows ->
<!ENTITY larr    "&#8592;" ><!- leftwards arrow,
                    U+2190 ISOnum ->
<!ENTITY uarr    "&#8593;" ><!-upwards arrow, U+2191 ISOnum->
<!ENTITY rarr    "&#8594;" ><!- rightwards arrow,
                    U+2192 ISOnum ->
<!ENTITY darr    "&#8595;" ><!- downwards arrow,
                    U+2193 ISOnum ->
<!ENTITY harr    "&#8596;" ><!- left right arrow,
                    U+2194 ISOamsa ->
<!ENTITY crarr   "&#8629;" ><!- downwards arrow with corner
                    leftwards = carriage return, U+21B5 NEW ->
<!ENTITY lArr    "&#8656;" ><!- leftwards double arrow,
                    U+21D0 ISOtech ->
<!- Unicode does not say that lArr is the same as the
    'is implied by' arrow but also does not have any other
    character for that function. So ? lArr can
    be used for 'is implied by' as ISOtech suggests ->
<!ENTITY uArr    "&#8657;" ><!- upwards double arrow,
                    U+21D1 ISOamsa ->
<!ENTITY rArr    "&#8658;" ><!- rightwards double arrow,
                    U+21D2 ISOtech ->
<!- Unicode does not say this is the 'implies' character
    but does not have  another character with this function
    so ? rArr can be used for 'implies' as ISOtech suggests ->
<!ENTITY dArr    "&#8659;" ><!- downwards double arrow,
                    U+21D3 ISOamsa ->
<!ENTITY hArr    "&#8660;" ><!- left right double arrow,
                    U+21D4 ISOamsa ->

<!- Mathematical Operators ->
<!ENTITY forall  "&#8704;" ><!- for all, U+2200 ISOtech ->
<!ENTITY part    "&#8706;" ><!- partial differential,
                    U+2202 ISOtech  ->
<!ENTITY exist   "&#8707;"><!-there exists, U+2203 ISOtech->
<!ENTITY empty   "&#8709;" ><!- empty set = null set
                    = diameter, U+2205 ISOamso ->
<!ENTITY nabla   "&#8711;" ><!- nabla = backward difference,
                    U+2207 ISOtech ->
<!ENTITY isin    "&#8712;" ><!- element of, U+2208 ISOtech->
<!ENTITY notin   "&#8713;" ><!- not an element of,
                    U+2209 ISOtech ->
<!ENTITY ni      "&#8715;" ><!- contains as member,
                    U+220B ISOtech ->
<!- should there be a more memorable name than 'ni'? ->
```

```
<!ENTITY prod      "&#8719;" ><!- n-ary product = product sign,
                                U+220F ISOamsb ->
<!- prod is NOT the same character as U+03A0 'greek capital
      letter pi' though the same glyph might be used for both->
<!ENTITY sum       "&#8721;" ><!- n-ary sumation,
                                U+2211 ISOamsb ->
<!- sum is NOT the same character as U+03A3
      'greek capital letter sigma' though the same glyph
      might be used for both ->
<!ENTITY minus     "&#8722;" ><!- minus sign, U+2212 ISOtech->
<!ENTITY lowast    "&#8727;" ><!- asterisk operator,
                                U+2217 ISOtech ->
<!ENTITY radic     "&#8730;" ><!- square root = radical sign,
                                U+221A ISOtech ->
<!ENTITY prop      "&#8733;" ><!- proportional to,
                                U+221D ISOtech ->
<!ENTITY infin     "&#8734;" ><!- infinity, U+221E ISOtech ->
<!ENTITY ang       "&#8736;" ><!- angle, U+2220 ISOamso ->
<!ENTITY and       "&#8743;" ><!- logical and = wedge,
                                U+2227 ISOtech ->
<!ENTITY or        "&#8744;" ><!- logical or = vee,
                                U+2228 ISOtech ->
<!ENTITY cap       "&#8745;" ><!- intersection = cap,
                                U+2229 ISOtech ->
<!ENTITY cup       "&#8746;" ><!-union = cup, U+222A ISOtech->
<!ENTITY int       "&#8747;" ><!- integral, U+222B ISOtech ->
<!ENTITY there4    "&#8756;" ><!- therefore, U+2234 ISOtech ->
<!ENTITY sim       "&#8764;" ><!- tilde operator
                  = varies with = similar to, U+223C ISOtech ->
<!- tilde operator is NOT the same character as the tilde,
      U+007E, although the same glyph might be used to
      represent both  ->
<!ENTITY cong      "&#8773;" ><!- approximately equal to, U+2245
ISOtech ->
<!ENTITY asymp     "&#8776;" ><!- almost equal to
                  = asymptotic to, U+2248 ISOamsr ->
<!ENTITY ne        "&#8800;" ><!- not equal to,
                                U+2260 ISOtech ->
<!ENTITY equiv     "&#8801;" ><!- identical to,
                                U+2261 ISOtech ->
<!ENTITY le        "&#8804;" ><!- less-than or equal to,
                                U+2264 ISOtech ->
<!ENTITY ge        "&#8805;" ><!- greater-than or equal to,
                                U+2265 ISOtech ->
<!ENTITY sub       "&#8834;" ><!- subset of, U+2282 ISOtech ->
<!ENTITY sup       "&#8835;" ><!-superset of, U+2283 ISOtech->
<!- note that nsup, 'not a superset of, U+2283' is not covered
      by the Symbol font encoding and is not included. Should it
      be, for symmetry? It is in ISOamsn  ->
<!ENTITY nsub      "&#8836;" ><!- not a subset of,
                                U+2284 ISOamsn ->
```

Continued

Listing 20-32 *(continued)*

```
<!ENTITY sube      "&#8838;" ><!- subset of or equal to,
                                 U+2286 ISOtech ->
<!ENTITY supe      "&#8839;" ><!- superset of or equal to,
                                 U+2287 ISOtech ->
<!ENTITY oplus     "&#8853;" ><!- circled plus = direct sum,
                                 U+2295 ISOamsb ->
<!ENTITY otimes    "&#8855;" ><!- circled times
                              = vector product, U+2297 ISOamsb ->
<!ENTITY perp      "&#8869;" ><!- up tack = orthogonal to
                              = perpendicular, U+22A5 ISOtech ->
<!ENTITY sdot      "&#8901;" ><!- dot operator,
                                 U+22C5 ISOamsb ->
<!- dot operator is NOT the same character as
    U+00B7 middle dot ->

<!- Miscellaneous Technical ->
<!ENTITY lceil     "&#8968;" ><!- left ceiling = apl upstile,
                                 U+2308 ISOamsc  ->
<!ENTITY rceil     "&#8969;" ><!- right ceiling,
                                 U+2309 ISOamsc ->
<!ENTITY lfloor    "&#8970;" ><!- left floor = apl downstile,
                                 U+230A ISOamsc  ->
<!ENTITY rfloor    "&#8971;" ><!- right floor,
                                 U+230B ISOamsc  ->
<!ENTITY lang      "&#9001;" ><!- left-pointing angle bracket
                              = bra, U+2329 ISOtech ->
<!- lang is NOT the same character as U+003C 'less than'
    or U+2039 'single left-pointing angle quotation mark' ->
<!ENTITY rang      "&#9002;" ><!- right-pointing angle bracket
                              = ket, U+232A ISOtech ->
<!- rang is NOT the same character as U+003E 'greater than'
    or U+203A 'single right-pointing angle quotation mark' ->

<!- Geometric Shapes ->
<!ENTITY loz       "&#9674;" ><!- lozenge, U+25CA ISOpub ->

<!- Miscellaneous Symbols ->
<!ENTITY spades    "&#9824;" ><!- black spade suit,
                                 U+2660 ISOpub ->
<!- black here seems to mean filled as opposed to hollow ->
<!ENTITY clubs     "&#9827;" ><!- black club suit = shamrock,
                                 U+2663 ISOpub ->
<!ENTITY hearts    "&#9829;" ><!- black heart suit = valentine,
                                 U+2665 ISOpub ->
<!ENTITY diams     "&#9830;" ><!- black diamond suit,
                                 U+2666 ISOpub ->
```

Simplified Subset DTDs

Not all HTML-based systems need every piece of HTML. Depending on your needs, you may well be able to omit forms, applets, images, image maps, and other advanced, interactive features of HTML. For instance, returning to the baseball examples of Part I, if you were to give each PLAYER a BIO element, you could use simple HTML to include basic text with each player.

The key modules that you'll probably want to include in any application you design using XHTML are:

- ✦ XHTML1-attribs.mod
- ✦ XHTML1-blkphras.mod
- ✦ XHTML1-blkpres.mod
- ✦ XHTML1-blkstruct.mod
- ✦ XHTML1-charent.mod
- ✦ XHTML1-inlphras.mod
- ✦ XHTML1-inlpres.mod
- ✦ XHTML1-inlstruct.mod
- ✦ XHTML1-model.mod
- ✦ XHTML1-names.mod

In addition, it's easy to mix in other modules to this basic set. For instance, XHTML1-image for images or XHTML1-linking for hypertext. While you can link these into your own DTDs using external parameter entity references (as you'll see an example of in Chapter 23), the simplest way to choose the parts you do and don't want is to copy either the transitional or strict DTD and IGNORE the parts you don't want. Listing 20-33 is a copy of the strict DTD (Listing 20-1) in which only the modules listed above are included:

Listing 20-33: **A core DTD that supports basic HTML**

```
<!- .............................................. ->
<!- Basic HTML for Player BIOs, based on XHTML 1.0 strict ->
<!- file: XHTML1-bb.dtd
->

<!-  This derived from
      XHTML 1.0, an XML reformulation of HTML 4.0.

 Copyright 1998-1999 World Wide Web Consortium
```

Continued

Listing 20-33 *(continued)*

```
(Massachusetts Institute of Technology, Institut National de
Recherche en Informatique et en Automatique, Keio University).
All Rights Reserved.

   Permission to use, copy, modify and distribute the XHTML
   1.0 DTD and its accompanying documentation for any purpose
   and without fee is hereby granted in perpetuity, provided
   that the above copyright notice and this paragraph appear
   in all copies. The copyright holders make no representation
   about the suitability of the DTD for any purpose.

   It is provided "as is" without expressed or implied
   warranty.

   Original Author:    Murray M. Altheim <altheim@eng.sun.com>
   Original Revision:  @(#)XHTML1-s.dtd 1.14 99/04/01 SMI

   The DTD is an XML variant based on the
   W3C HTML 4.0 DTD:

      Draft:        $Date: 1999/04/02 14:27:27 $

      Authors:      Dave Raggett <dsr@w3.org>
                    Arnaud Le Hors <lehors@w3.org>
                    Ian Jacobs <ij@w3.org>

-->

<!-- The version attribute has historically been a container
     for the DTD's public identifier (an FPI), but is unused
     in Strict:  -->
<!ENTITY % HTML.version   "" >
<!ENTITY % Version.attrib "" >

<!-- The xmlns attribute on <html> identifies the
     default namespace to namespace-aware applications:  -->
<!ENTITY % XHTML.ns   "http://www.w3.org/TR/1999/REC-html-in-
xml" >

<!-- reserved for future use with document profiles -->
<!ENTITY % XHTML.profile   "" >

<!-- used to ignore Transitional features within modules -->
<!ENTITY % XHTML.Transitional    "IGNORE" >


<!-- XHTML Base Architecture Module (optional) ......... -->
<!ENTITY % XHTML1-arch.module "IGNORE" >
<![%XHTML1-arch.module;[
<!ENTITY % XHTML1-arch.mod
     PUBLIC "-//W3C//ELEMENTS XHTML 1.0 Base Architecture//EN"
```

```
                    "XHTML1-arch.mod" >
%XHTML1-arch.mod;
]]>

<!— Common Names Module ............................. —>
<!ENTITY % XHTML1-names.module "INCLUDE" >
<![%XHTML1-names.module;[
<!ENTITY % XHTML1-names.mod
     PUBLIC "-//W3C//ENTITIES XHTML 1.0 Common Names//EN"
            "XHTML1-names.mod" >
%XHTML1-names.mod;
]]>

<!— Character Entities Module ........................ —>
<!ENTITY % XHTML1-charent.module "INCLUDE" >
<![%XHTML1-charent.module;[
<!ENTITY % XHTML1-charent.mod
     PUBLIC "-//W3C//ENTITIES XHTML 1.0 Character Entities//EN"
            "XHTML1-charent.mod" >
%XHTML1-charent.mod;
]]>

<!— Intrinsic Events Module ......................... —>
<!ENTITY % XHTML1-events.module "IGNORE" >
<![%XHTML1-events.module;[
<!ENTITY % XHTML1-events.mod
     PUBLIC "-//W3C//ENTITIES XHTML 1.0 Intrinsic Events//EN"
            "XHTML1-events.mod" >
%XHTML1-events.mod;
]]>

<!— Common Attributes Module ........................ —>
<!ENTITY % XHTML1-attribs.module "INCLUDE" >
<![%XHTML1-attribs.module;[
<!ENTITY % align "" >
<!ENTITY % XHTML1-attribs.mod
     PUBLIC "-//W3C//ENTITIES XHTML 1.0 Common Attributes//EN"
            "XHTML1-attribs.mod" >
%XHTML1-attribs.mod;
]]>

<!— Document Model Module ........................... —>
<!ENTITY % XHTML1-model.module "INCLUDE" >
<![%XHTML1-model.module;[
<!ENTITY % XHTML1-model.mod
     PUBLIC "-//W3C//ELEMENTS XHTML 1.0 Document Model//EN"
            "XHTML1-model.mod" >
%XHTML1-model.mod;
]]>

<!— Inline Structural Module ........................ —>
<!ENTITY % XHTML1-inlstruct.module "INCLUDE" >
```

Continued

Listing 20-33 *(continued)*

```
<![%XHTML1-inlstruct.module;[
<!ENTITY % XHTML1-inlstruct.mod
     PUBLIC "-//W3C//ELEMENTS XHTML 1.0 Inline Structural//EN"
            "XHTML1-inlstruct.mod" >
%XHTML1-inlstruct.mod;
]]>

<!- Inline Presentational Module ..................... ->
<!ENTITY % XHTML1-inlpres.module "INCLUDE" >
<![%XHTML1-inlpres.module;[
<!ENTITY % XHTML1-inlpres.mod
  PUBLIC "-//W3C//ELEMENTS XHTML 1.0 Inline Presentational//EN"
         "XHTML1-inlpres.mod" >
%XHTML1-inlpres.mod;
]]>

<!- Inline Phrasal Module ............................ ->
<!ENTITY % XHTML1-inlphras.module "INCLUDE" >
<![%XHTML1-inlphras.module;[
<!ENTITY % XHTML1-inlphras.mod
     PUBLIC "-//W3C//ELEMENTS XHTML 1.0 Inline Phrasal//EN"
            "XHTML1-inlphras.mod" >
%XHTML1-inlphras.mod;
]]>

<!- Block Structural Module ........................... ->
<!ENTITY % XHTML1-blkstruct.module "INCLUDE" >
<![%XHTML1-blkstruct.module;[
<!ENTITY % XHTML1-blkstruct.mod
     PUBLIC "-//W3C//ELEMENTS XHTML 1.0 Block Structural//EN"
            "XHTML1-blkstruct.mod" >
%XHTML1-blkstruct.mod;
]]>

<!- Block Presentational Module ...................... ->
<!ENTITY % XHTML1-blkpres.module "INCLUDE" >
<![%XHTML1-blkpres.module;[
<!ENTITY % XHTML1-blkpres.mod
     PUBLIC "-//W3C//ELEMENTS XHTML 1.0 Block
Presentational//EN"
            "XHTML1-blkpres.mod" >
%XHTML1-blkpres.mod;
]]>

<!- Block Phrasal Module ............................ ->
<!ENTITY % XHTML1-blkphras.module "INCLUDE" >
<![%XHTML1-blkphras.module;[
<!ENTITY % XHTML1-blkphras.mod
```

```
         PUBLIC "-//W3C//ELEMENTS XHTML 1.0 Block Phrasal//EN"
               "XHTML1-blkphras.mod" >
%XHTML1-blkphras.mod;
]]>

<!— Scripting Module ................................ —>
<!ENTITY % XHTML1-script.module "IGNORE" >
<![%XHTML1-script.module;[
<!ENTITY % XHTML1-script.mod
      PUBLIC "-//W3C//ELEMENTS XHTML 1.0 Scripting//EN"
               "XHTML1-script.mod" >
%XHTML1-script.mod;
]]>

<!— Stylesheets Module ................................ —>
<!ENTITY % XHTML1-style.module "IGNORE" >
<![%XHTML1-style.module;[
<!ENTITY % XHTML1-style.mod
      PUBLIC "-//W3C//ELEMENTS XHTML 1.0 Stylesheets//EN"
               "XHTML1-style.mod" >
%XHTML1-style.mod;
]]>

<!— Image Module ................................ —>
<!ENTITY % XHTML1-image.module "IGNORE" >
<![%XHTML1-image.module;[
<!ENTITY % XHTML1-image.mod
      PUBLIC "-//W3C//ELEMENTS XHTML 1.0 Images//EN"
               "XHTML1-image.mod" >
%XHTML1-image.mod;
]]>

<!— Frames Module ................................ —>
<!ENTITY % XHTML1-frames.module  "IGNORE" >
<![%XHTML1-frames.module;[
<!ENTITY % XHTML1-frames.mod
      PUBLIC "-//W3C//ELEMENTS XHTML 1.0 Frames//EN"
               "XHTML1-frames.mod" >
%XHTML1-frames.mod;
]]>

<!— Linking Module ................................ —>
<!ENTITY % XHTML1-linking.module "IGNORE" >
<![%XHTML1-linking.module;[
<!ENTITY % XHTML1-linking.mod
      PUBLIC "-//W3C//ELEMENTS XHTML 1.0 Linking//EN"
               "XHTML1-linking.mod" >
%XHTML1-linking.mod;
]]>
```

Continued

Listing 20-33 *(continued)*

```
<!— Client-side Image Map Module ..................... —>
<!ENTITY % XHTML1-csismap.module "IGNORE" >
<![%XHTML1-csismap.module;[
<!ENTITY % XHTML1-csismap.mod
   PUBLIC "-//W3C//ELEMENTS XHTML 1.0 Client-side Image Map//EN"
         "XHTML1-csismap.mod" >
%XHTML1-csismap.mod;
]]>

<!— Object Element Module ........................... —>
<!ENTITY % XHTML1-object.module "IGNORE" >
<![%XHTML1-object.module;[
<!ENTITY % XHTML1-object.mod
     PUBLIC "-//W3C//ELEMENTS XHTML 1.0 Object Element//EN"
             "XHTML1-object.mod" >
%XHTML1-object.mod;
]]>

<!— Lists Module ................................... —>
<!ENTITY % XHTML1-list.module "IGNORE" >
<![%XHTML1-list.module;[
<!ENTITY % XHTML1-list.mod
     PUBLIC "-//W3C//ELEMENTS XHTML 1.0 Lists//EN"
             "XHTML1-list.mod" >
%XHTML1-list.mod;
]]>

<!— Forms Module ................................... —>
<!ENTITY % XHTML1-form.module "IGNORE" >
<![%XHTML1-form.module;[
<!ENTITY % XHTML1-form.mod
     PUBLIC "-//W3C//ELEMENTS XHTML 1.0 Forms//EN"
             "XHTML1-form.mod" >
%XHTML1-form.mod;
]]>

<!— Tables Module .................................. —>
<!ENTITY % XHTML1-table.module "IGNORE" >
<![%XHTML1-table.module;[
<!ENTITY % XHTML1-table.mod
     PUBLIC "-//W3C//ELEMENTS XHTML 1.0 Tables//EN"
             "XHTML1-table.mod" >
%XHTML1-table.mod;
]]>

<!— Document Metainformation Module .................. —>
<!ENTITY % XHTML1-meta.module "IGNORE" >
<![%XHTML1-meta.module;[
```

```
<!ENTITY % XHTML1-meta.mod
     PUBLIC "-//W3C//ELEMENTS XHTML 1.0 Metainformation//EN"
            "XHTML1-meta.mod" >
%XHTML1-meta.mod;
]]>

<!— Document Structure Module ........................ —>
<!ENTITY % XHTML1-struct.module "IGNORE" >
<![%XHTML1-struct.module;[
<!ENTITY % XHTML1-struct.mod
     PUBLIC "-//W3C//ELEMENTS XHTML 1.0 Document Structure//EN"
            "XHTML1-struct.mod" >
%XHTML1-struct.mod;
]]>

<!— end of XHTML 1.0 Strict DTD  ........................ —>
<!— ................................................ —>
```

Aside from some changes to the comments at the top to indicate that this is a derived version of the XHTML strict DTD, the only changes are the replacement of INCLUDE by IGNORE in several parameter entity references like XHTML1-struct.module.

It would also be possible to simply delete the unnecessary sections completely, rather than simply ignoring them. However, this approach makes it very easy to include them quickly if a need for them is discovered in the future.

You can't call the resulting application HTML, but it does provide a neat way to add basic hypertext structure to a more domain-specific DTD without going overboard and pulling in the full multimedia smorgasbord that is HTML 4.0.

For example, by adding Listing 20-33 to the DTD for baseball players from Chapter 10, I could give each player a BIOGRAPHY element that contains basic HTML. The declarations would look like this:

```
<!ENTITY % XHTML1-bb.dtd SYSTEM "XHTML1-bb.dtd">

%XHTML1-bb.dtd;
<!ENTITY % BIOGRAPHY.content  "( #PCDATA | %Flow.mix; )*" >
<ELEMENT BIOGRAPHY %BIOGRAPHY.content;>
```

This says that a BIOGRAPHY can contain anything an HTML block can contain as defined by the XHTML modules used here. If you prefer, you can use any of the other elements or content model entity references from the XHTML modules.

Copyright Notices in DTDs

Techniques to Imitate

Pablo Picasso is often quoted as saying, "Good artists copy. Great artists steal." As you've already seen, part of the reason the XHTML DTD is so modular — broken up into so many parts — is precisely so that you can steal from it. If you need basic hypertext formatting as part of an XML application you're developing, you really don't need to invent your own. You can simply import the necessary modules. This has the added advantage that document authors who have to use your XML application are likely already familiar with this markup from HTML. Nonetheless, let's go ahead and look at some techniques you can borrow from the XHTML DTD for your own DTDs without out-and-out stealing the DTDs themselves.

Comments

The XHTML DTDs are profusely commented. Every single file has a comment that gives a title, the relevant copyright notice, and an abstract of what's in the file, before there's even one single declaration. Every section of the file is separated off by a new comment that specifies the purpose of the section. And almost every declaration features a comment discussing what that declaration means. This all makes the file *much* easier to read and understand.

This still isn't perfect, however. Many of the attribute declarations are not sufficiently commented. For example, consider this declaration from XHTM1-applet.mod:

```
<!ATTLIST applet
    %Core.attrib;
    codebase        %URI;                   #IMPLIED
    archive         CDATA                   #IMPLIED
    code            CDATA                   #IMPLIED
    object          CDATA                   #IMPLIED
    alt             %Text;                  #IMPLIED
    name            CDATA                   #IMPLIED
    width           %Length;                #REQUIRED
    height          %Length;                #REQUIRED
    %IAlign.attrib;
    hspace          %Pixels;                #IMPLIED
    vspace          %Pixels;                #IMPLIED
>
```

There's no indication of what the value of all these attributes should be. An additional comment like this would be helpful:

```
<!- ATTLIST applet
    codebase    the URI where of the directory from which the
                applet is downloaded; defaults to the URI of the
                document containing the applet tag
    archive     the name of the JAR file that contains the applet;
                omitted if the applet isn't stored in a JAR
                archive
    code        the name of the main class of the applet
    object      the name of the serialized object that contains
                the main applet class; must match the name of the
                class in the applet attribute
    alt         text displayed if the applet cannot be located
    name        the name of the applet
    width       width of the applet in pixels
    height      height of the applet in pixels
    align       bottom, middle, top, left, or right
                meaning the bottom, middle, or top of the applet
                is aligned with the baseline or that the
                applet floats to the left or the right
    hspace      number of pixels with which
                to pad the left and right sides of the applet
    vspace      number of pixels with which
                to pad the top and bottom of the applet
    ->
```

Of course all this could be found out by reading the specification for HTML 4.0. However, many times when complete documentation is left to a later, prose document, that prose document never gets written. It certainly doesn't hurt to include extra commentary when you're actually writing the DTD for the first time.

Part of the problem is that restrictions on attribute values are not well expressed in DTDs; for instance that the height and width must be integers. In the future, this shortcoming may be addressed by a schema language layered on top of standard XML syntax.

In cases of complicated attribute and element declarations, it's also often useful to provide an example in a comment. For instance:

```
<!--

<applet width="500" height="500"
        codebase="http://www.site.com/directory/subdirectory/"
        archive="MyApplet.jar"
        code="MyApplet.class"
        object="MyApplet.ser"
        name="FirstInstance"
        align="top"
        hspace="5"
        vspace="5"
>
    <param name="name1" value="value1"/>
    <param name="name2" value="value2"/>
    Some text for browsers that don't understand the
    applet tag
</applet>

-->
```

Parameter Entities

The XHTML DTD makes extremely heavy use of both internal and external parameter entities. Your DTDs can, too. There are many uses for parameter entities that were demonstrated in the XHTML DTD. In summary, you can use them to:

✦ Break up long content models and attribute lists into manageable, related pieces

✦ Standardize common sets of elements and attributes

✦ Enable different DTDs to change content models and attribute lists

✦ Better document content models

✦ Compress the DTD by reusing common sequences of text

✦ Split the DTD into individual, related modules

Break Up Long Content Models and Attribute Lists into Manageable, Related Pieces

A typical HTML element like p can easily have 30 or more possible attributes and dozens of potential children. Listing them all in a content model or attribute list will simply overwhelm anyone trying to read a DTD. To the extent that related elements and attributes can be grouped, it's better to separate them into several parameter entities. For example, here's XHTML's element declaration for p:

```
<!ELEMENT p  %P.content; >
```

It uses only a single parameter entity reference, rather than the many separate element names that the reference resolves into.

Here's XHTML's attribute list for p:

```
<!ATTLIST p
      %Common.attrib;
>
```

It uses only one-parameter entities rather than the many separate attribute names and content types they resolve into.

Standardize Common Sets of Elements and Attributes

When you're dealing with 30 or more items in a list, it's easy to miss one if you have to keep repeating the list. For instance, almost all HTML elements can have these attributes:

```
id class style title lang xml:lang dir onclick ondblclick
onmousedown onmouseup onmousemove onmouseout onkeypress
onkeydown onkeyup onclick ondblclick onmousedown onmouseup
onmouseover onmousemove onmouseout onkeypress onkeydown onkeyup
```

By combining them all into one %Common.attrib; parameter entity reference, you avoid the chance of omitting or mis-typing one of them in an attribute list. If at any point in the future, you want to add an attribute to this list, you can add it just by adding it to the declaration of Common.attrib. You don't have to add it to each of a hundred or more element declarations.

Enable Different DTDs to Change Content Models and Attribute Lists

One of the neatest tricks with parameter entity references in XHTML is how they're used to customize three different DTDs from the same basic modules. The key is that each customizable item, whether a content model or an attribute list, is given as a parameter entity reference. Each DTD can then redefine the content model or attribute list by redefining the parameter entity reference. This allows particular DTDs to both add and remove items from content models and attribute lists.

For example, in the XHTML1-table module, the `caption` element is defined like this:

```
<!ENTITY % Caption.content   "( #PCDATA | %Inline.mix; )*" >
<!ELEMENT caption   %Caption.content; >
<!ATTLIST caption
     %Common.attrib;
>
```

Suppose your DTD requires that captions only contain unmarked-up PCDATA. Then it is easy to place this entity definition in the file that imports XHTML1-table.mod:

```
<!ENTITY % Caption.content   "( #PCDATA )" >
```

This will override the declaration in XHTML1-table.mod so that captions adhering to your DTD can only include text and no mark up.

Better Document Content Models

One of the most unusual tricks the XHTML DTD plays with parameter entity references is using them to replace the `CDATA` attribute type. Although `%ContentType;`, `%ContentTypes;`, `%Charset;`, `%Charsets;`, `%LanguageCode;`, `%Character;`, `%Number;`, `%LinkTypes;`, `%MediaDesc;`, and `%URI;`, are on one level just synonyms for `CDATA`, on another level they make the attribute types a lot more specific. `CDATA` can really mean almost anything. Using parameter entities in this way goes a long way toward narrowing down and documenting the actual meaning in a particular context. While such parameter entities can't enforce their meanings, simply documenting them is no small achievement.

Compress the DTD by Reusing Common Sequences of Text

The XHTML DTD occupies just about 80 kilobytes. That's not a huge amount, especially for applications that reside on a local drive or network, but it is non-trivial for Internet applications. It would probably be three to five times larger if all the parameter entity references were fully expanded.

Even more significant than the file size saving achieved by parameter entity references are the savings in legibility. Short files are easier to read and comprehend. A 600-kilobyte DTD, even broken up into 60-kilobyte chunks, would be too much to ask document authors to read, especially given the turgid, non-English code that makes up DTDs. (Let me put it this way: Of the much smaller modules in this chapter, how many of them did you actually read from start to finish and how many did you just skip over until the example was done? Any code module that's longer than a page is likely to thwart all but the most determined and conscientious readers.)

Split the DTD into Individual, Related Modules

On a related note, splitting the DTD into several related modules makes it easier to grasp overall. All the forms material is conveniently gathered in one place, as is all the tables material, all the applet material, and so forth. Furthermore, this makes the DTD easier to understand because you can take it one bite-sized piece at a time.

On the other hand, the interconnections between some of the modules do make this a little more confusing than perhaps it needs to be. In order to truly understand any one of the modules, you must understand the XHTML1-names.mod and XHTML1-attribs.mod because these provide crucial definitions for entities used in all the other modules. Furthermore, a module can only really be understood in the context of either the strict, loose, or frameset DTD. So there are four files you need to grasp before you can really start to get a handle on any one. Still, the clean separation between modules is impressive, and recommends itself for imitation.

Summary

In this chapter, you learned:

- ✦ All writers learn by reading other writers' work. XML writers should read other XML writers' work.

- ✦ The XHTML DTD is an XMLized version of HTML that comes in three flavors: strict, loose, and frameset.

- ✦ The XHTML DTD divides HTML into 29 different modules and three entity sets.

- ✦ You can never have too many comments in your DTDs, which make the file much easier to read.

- ✦ Parameter entities are extremely powerful tools for building complex yet manageable DTDs.

In the next chapter, we'll explore another XML application, the Channel Definition Format (CDF), used to push content to subscribers. Whereas we've concentrated almost completely on the XHTML DTD in this chapter, CDF does not actually have a published DTD, so we'll take a very different approach to understanding it.

✦   ✦   ✦

Pushing Web Sites with CDF

This chapter covers Microsoft's Channel Definition Format (CDF), which is an XML application for defining channels. A channel is a set of Web pages that can be pushed to a subscriber automatically. A CDF document lists the pages to be pushed, the means by and the frequency with which they're pushed, and similar information. Readers can subscribe to channels using Internet Explorer 4.0 and later. As well as Web pages, channels can use Dynamic HTML, Java, and JavaScript to create interactive, continually updated stock tickers, sports score boxes, and the like. Subject to security restrictions, channels can even push software updates to registered users and install them automatically.

What Is CDF?

The Channel Definition Format (CDF) is an XML application developed at Microsoft for defining channels. Channels enable Web sites to automatically notify readers of changes to critical information. This method is sometimes called *Webcasting* or *push*. Currently, Internet Explorer is the only major browser that implements CDF and broader adoption seems unlikely. The W3C has not done more than formally acknowledge receipt of the CDF specification, and they seem unlikely to do more in the future.

A CDF file is an XML document, separate from, but linked to, the HTML documents on a site. The CDF document defines the parameters for a connection between the readers and the content on the site. The data can be transferred through *push* — sending notifications, or even entire Web sites to registered readers — or through *pull*-readers choose to load the page in their Web browser and get the update information.

You do not need to rewrite your site to take advantage of CDF. The CDF file is simply an addition to the site. A link to a CDF file, generally found on a site's home page downloads a copy of the channel index to the reader's machine. This places an icon on the reader's channel bar, which can be clicked to access the current contents of the channel.

How Channels Are Created

To establish a channel, follow these three steps:

1. Decide what content to include in the channel.

2. Write the channel definition file that identifies this content.

3. Link from the home page of the Web site to the channel-definition file.

Determining Channel Content

Before you get bogged down in the nitty-gritty technical details of creating a channel with CDF, you first have to decide what content belongs in the channel and how it should be delivered.

Your first consideration when converting existing sites to channels is how many and which pages to include. Human interface factors suggest that no channel should have more than eight items for readers to choose from. Otherwise, readers will become confused and have trouble finding what they need. However, channels can be arranged hierarchically. Additional levels of content can be added as sub-channels. For example, a newspaper channel might have sections for business, science, entertainment, international news, national news, and local news. The entertainment section might be divided into sub-channels for television, movies, books, music, and art.

The organization and hierarchy you choose may or may not match the organization and hierarchy of your existing Web site, just as the organization and hierarchy of your Web site does not necessarily match the organization and hierarchy of the files on the server hard drive. However, matching the hierarchy of the channel to the hierarchy of the Web site will make the channel easier to maintain. Nonetheless, you can certainly select particular pages out of the site and arrange them in a hierarchy specific to the channel if it seems logical.

Your second consideration is the way new content will be delivered to subscribers. When subscribing to a channel, readers are offered a choice from three options:

1. The channel can be added to the channel bar and subscribers can check in when they feel like it.

2. Subscribers can be notified of new content via email and then load the channel when they feel like it.

3. The browser can periodically check the site for updates and download the changed content automatically.

Your content should be designed to work well with whichever of these three options the reader chooses.

Creating CDF Files and Documents

Once you've decided what content will be in your channel, and how that content will be organized and delivered, you're ready to write the CDF document that implements these decisions. A CDF document contains identifying information about the contents, schedule, and logos for the channel. All of this information is marked up using a particular set of XML tags. The resulting document is a well-formed XML file. This document will be placed on the Web server where clients can download it.

Note While it would be almost trivial to design a DTD for CDF, and while I suspect Microsoft has one internally, they have not yet published it for the current version of CDF. A DTD for a much earlier and obsolete version of CDF can be found in a W3C note at `http://www.w3.org/TR/NOTE-CDFsubmit.html`. However, this really doesn't come close to describing the current version of CDF. Consequently, CDF documents can be at most well-formed, but not valid.

A CDF document begins with an XML declaration because a CDF document is an XML document and follows the same rules as all XML documents. The root and only required element of a CDF document is `CHANNEL`. The `CHANNEL` element must have an `HREF` attribute that specifies the page being monitored for changes. The root `CHANNEL` element usually identifies the key page in the channel. Listing 21-1 is a simple CDF document that points to a page that is updated more or less daily.

Listing 21-1: **The simplest possible CDF document for a page**

```xml
<?xml version="1.0"?>
<CHANNEL HREF="http://metalab.unc.edu/xml/index.html">
</CHANNEL>
```

Note Most Microsoft documentation for CDF is based on a pre-release of the XML specification that used the uppercase `<?XML version="1.0"?>` instead of the now current lowercase `<?xml version="1.0"?>`. However, both case conventions seem to work with Internet Explorer, so in this chapter I'll use the lowercase `xml` that conforms to standard XML usage.

As well as the main page, most channels contain a collection of other pages identified by ITEM children. Each ITEM has an HREF attribute pointing to the page. Listing 21-2 demonstrates a channel that contains a main page (http://metalab.unc.edu/xml/index.html) with three individual sub-pages in ITEM elements. Channels are often shown in a collapsible outline view that allows the user to show or hide the individual items in the channel as they choose. Figure 21-1 shows this channel expanded in Internet Explorer 5.0's Favorites bar.

Listing 21-2: A CDF channel with ITEM children

```xml
<?xml version="1.0"?>
<CHANNEL HREF="http://metalab.unc.edu/xml/index.html">
  <ITEM HREF="http://metalab.unc.edu/xml/books.html">
  </ITEM>
  <ITEM HREF="http://metalab.unc.edu/xml/tradeshows.html">
  </ITEM>
  <ITEM HREF="http://metalab.unc.edu/xml/mailinglists.html">
  </ITEM>
</CHANNEL>
```

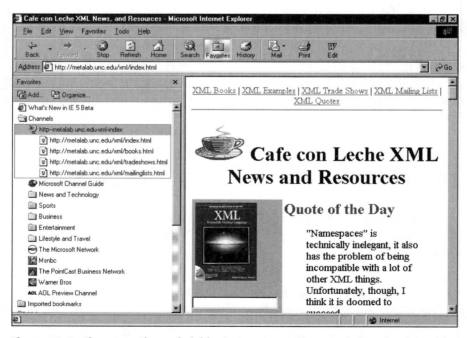

Figure 21-1: The open Channels folder in Internet Explorer 5.0's favorites bar with three sub-pages displayed

Linking the Web Page to the Channel

The third and final step is to make the CDF file available to the reader. To do this, you provide a link from the Web page to the CDF file. The simplest way to accomplish this is with a standard HTML A element that readers click to activate. Generally, the contents of this element will be some text or an image asking the reader to subscribe to the channel. For example:

```
<A HREF="cafeconleche.cdf">Subscribe to Cafe con Leche</A>
```

When the reader activates this link in a CDF-enabled browser (which is just a fancy way of saying Internet Explorer 4.0 and later), the browser downloads the CDF file named in the HREF attribute and adds the channel to its list of subscriptions. Other browsers that don't support CDF will probably ask the user to save the document as shown in Figure 21-2.

Once the CDF file has been downloaded, the browser will ask the user how they wish to be notified of future changes to the channel as shown in Figure 21-3. The user has three choices:

1. The channel can be added to the browser and active desktop channel bars. The subscriber must manually select the channel to get the update. This isn't all that different from a bookmark, except that when the user opens the "channel mark," all pages in the channel are refreshed rather than just one.

2. The browser periodically checks the channel for updates and notifies the subscriber of any changes via email. The user must still choose to download the new content.

3. The browser periodically checks the channel for updates and notifies the subscriber of any changes via email. However, when a change is detected, the browser automatically downloads and caches the new content so it's immediately available for the user to view, even if they aren't connected to the Internet when they check the channel site.

Listing 21-2 only makes the first choice available because this particular channel doesn't provide a schedule for update, but we'll add that soon.

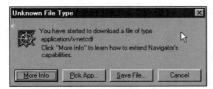

Figure 21-2: Netscape Navigator 5.0 does not support CDF nor understand CDF files.

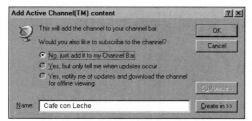

Figure 21-3: Internet Explorer 4.0 asks the user to choose how they wish to be notified of changes at the site.

Description of the Channel

The channel itself and each item in the channel can have a title, an abstract, and up to three logos of different sizes. These are established by giving the CHANNEL and ITEM elements TITLE, ABSTRACT, and LOGO children.

Title

The title of the channel is not the same as the title of the Web page. Rather, the channel title appears in the channel guide, the channel list, and the channel bar, as shown in Figure 21-1 where the title is http—metalab.unc.edu-xml-index (though the subscriber did have the option to customize it by typing a different title as shown in Figure 21-3). You can provide a more descriptive default title for each CHANNEL and ITEM element by giving it a TITLE child. Each TITLE element can contain only character data, no markup. Listing 21-3 adds titles to the individual pages in the Cafe con Leche channel as well as to the channel itself. Figure 21-4 shows how this affects the individual items in the channel list.

Listing 21-3: **A CDF channel with titles**

```xml
<?xml version="1.0"?>
<CHANNEL HREF="http://metalab.unc.edu/xml/index.html">
  <TITLE>Cafe con Leche</TITLE>
  <ITEM HREF="http://metalab.unc.edu/xml/books.html">
    <TITLE>Books about XML</TITLE>
  </ITEM>
  <ITEM HREF="http://metalab.unc.edu/xml/tradeshows.html">
    <TITLE>Trade shows and conferences about XML</TITLE>
  </ITEM>
  <ITEM HREF="http://metalab.unc.edu/xml/mailinglists.html">
    <TITLE>Mailing Lists dedicated to XML</TITLE>
  </ITEM>
</CHANNEL>
```

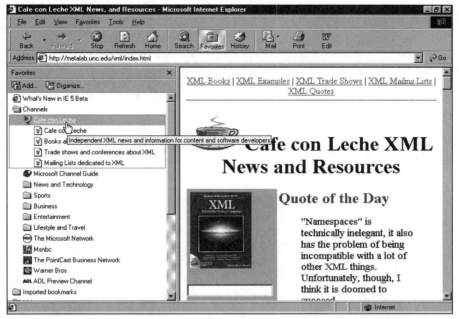

Figure 21-4: Titles are shown in the channels bar and abstracts are shown in tool tips.

Abstract

Titles may be sufficient for a channel with a well-established brand like Disney or MSNBC, but for the rest of us lesser lights in the news firmament it probably doesn't hurt to tell subscribers a little more about what they can expect to find at a given site. To this end, each CHANNEL and ITEM element can contain a single ABSTRACT child element. The ABSTRACT element should contain a short (200 characters or less) block of text describing the item or channel. Generally, this description will appear in a tool-tip window as shown in Figure 21-4, which is based on Listing 21-4.

Listing 21-4: **A CDF channel with titles and abstracts**

```
<?xml version="1.0"?>
<CHANNEL HREF="http://metalab.unc.edu/xml/index.html">
  <TITLE>Cafe con Leche</TITLE>
  <ABSTRACT>
    Independent XML news and information for content
    and software developers
  </ABSTRACT>
```

Continued

Listing 21-4 *(continued)*

```
<ITEM HREF="http://metalab.unc.edu/xml/books.html">
  <TITLE>Books about XML</TITLE>
  <ABSTRACT>
    A comprehensive list of books about XML
    with capsule reviews and ratings
  </ABSTRACT>
</ITEM>

<ITEM HREF="http://metalab.unc.edu/xml/tradeshows.html">
  <TITLE>Trade shows and conferences about XML</TITLE>
  <ABSTRACT>
    Upcoming conferences and shows with an XML focus
  </ABSTRACT>
</ITEM>

<ITEM HREF="http://metalab.unc.edu/xml/mailinglists.html">
  <TITLE>Mailing Lists dedicated to XML</TITLE>
  <ABSTRACT>
    Mailing lists where you can discuss XML
  </ABSTRACT>
</ITEM>
</CHANNEL>
```

Logos

CDF documents can specify logos for channels. These logos appear on the reader's machine; either on the desktop or in the browser's channel list. Logos can be used in a number of different ways within the channel: icons on the desktop, icons in the program launcher, and logos in the channel guide and channel bar. Each CHANNEL and ITEM element can have up to three logos: one for the desktop, one for the program launcher, and one for the channel bar.

A particular logo is attached to a channel with the LOGO element. This element is a child of the CHANNEL it represents. The HREF attribute of the LOGO element is an absolute or relative URL where the graphic file containing the logo is found. Internet Explorer supports GIF, JPEG, and ICO format images for logos — but not animated GIFs. Because logos may appear against a whole range of colors and patterns on the desktop, GIFs with a transparent background that limit themselves to the Windows halftone palette work best.

The LOGO element also has a required STYLE attribute that specifies the size of the image. The value of the STYLE attribute must be one of the three keywords ICON, IMAGE, or IMAGE-WIDE. These are different sizes of images, as given in Table 21-1. Figure 21-5 shows the logos used for Cafe con Leche in the three different sizes.

Table 21-1
Values for the STYLE Attribute of the LOGO Element

Image Size Value	Description
ICON	A 16-pixel-wide by 16-pixel-high icon displayed in the file list and in the channel bar next to the child elements in a hierarchy, as shown in Figure 21-2.
IMAGE	An 80-pixel-wide by 32-pixel-high image displayed in the desktop channel bar.
IMAGE-WIDE	A 194-pixel-wide by 32-pixel-high image displayed in the browser's channel bar. If a hierarchy of channels is nested underneath, they appear when the reader clicks this logo, as shown in Figure 21-3.

Figure 21-5: The Cafe con Leche channel icons in three different sizes

When the content in the channel changes, the browser places a highlight gleam in the upper-left corner of the logo image. This gleam hides anything in that corner. Also, if a reader stretches the window width beyond the recommended 194 pixels, the browser uses the top-right pixel to fill the expanded logo. Consequently you need to pay special attention to the upper-left and right corners of the logo.

Information Update Schedules

The CHANNEL, TITLE, ABSTRACT, and LOGO elements are enough to build a working channel, but all they provide is a visible connection that readers can use to pilot themselves quickly to your site. However, you don't have any means to push content to the readers. Passive channels — that is, channels like Listings 21-1 through 21-5 that don't have an explicit push schedule — don't do very much.

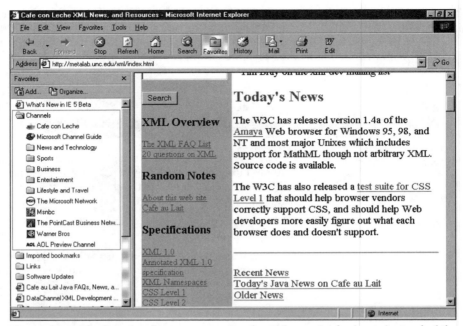

Figure 21-6: The favorites bar now contains the Cafe con Leche icons instead of the generic channel icon.

Listing 21-5 is a CDF document that provides various sizes of logos. Figure 21-6 shows the Internet Explorer 5.0 favorites bar with the new Cafe con Leche logo.

Listing 21-5: **A CDF channel with various sizes of logos**

```
<?xml version="1.0"?>
<CHANNEL HREF="http://metalab.unc.edu/xml/index.html">
  <TITLE>Cafe con Leche</TITLE>
  <ABSTRACT>
    Independent XML news and information for content
    and software developers
  </ABSTRACT>
  <LOGO HREF="cup_ICON.gif"      STYLE="ICON"/>
  <LOGO HREF="cup_IMAGE.gif"     STYLE="IMAGE"/>
  <LOGO HREF="cup_IMAGE-WIDE.gif" STYLE="IMAGE-WIDE"/>
  <ITEM HREF="http://metalab.unc.edu/xml/books.html">
    <TITLE>Books about XML</TITLE>
    <ABSTRACT>
      A comprehensive list of books about XML
      with capsule reviews and ratings
    </ABSTRACT>
  </ITEM>
```

```
<ITEM HREF="http://metalab.unc.edu/xml/tradeshows.html">
   <TITLE>Trade shows and conferences about XML</TITLE>
   <ABSTRACT>
     Upcoming conferences and shows with an XML focus
   </ABSTRACT>
</ITEM>

<ITEM HREF="http://metalab.unc.edu/xml/mailinglists.html">
   <TITLE>Mailing Lists dedicated to XML</TITLE>
   <ABSTRACT>
     Mailing lists where you can discuss XML
   </ABSTRACT>
</ITEM>
</CHANNEL>
```

To actually push the contents to subscribers, you have to include scheduling information for updates. You can schedule the entire channel as one or schedule individual items in the channel separately. This is accomplished by adding a SCHEDULE child element to the channel. For example:

```
<SCHEDULE STARTDATE="1998-03-29" STOPDATE="1999-03-29"
   TIMEZONE="-0500">
   <INTERVALTIME DAY="7"/>
   <EARLIESTTIME DAY="1" HOUR="0" MIN="0"/>
   <LATESTTIME DAY="2" HOUR="12" MIN="0"/>
</SCHEDULE>
```

The SCHEDULE element has three attributes: STARTDATE, STOPDATE, and TIMEZONE. The STARTDATE indicates when the schedule begins and STOPDATE indicates when it ends. Target the period between your usual site overhauls. If you change the structure of your Web site on a regular interval, use that interval. STARTDATE and STOPDATE use the same date format: full numeric year, two-digit numeric month, and two-digit day of month; for example 1999-12-31.

The TIMEZONE attribute shows the difference in hours between the server's time zone and Greenwich Mean Time. If the tag does not include the TIMEZONE attribute, the scheduled update occurs according to the reader's time zone — not the server's. In the continental U.S., Eastern Standard Time is -0500, Central Standard Time is -0600, Mountain Standard Time is -0700, and Pacific Standard Time is -0800. Hawaii and Alaska are -1000.

SCHEDULE can have between one and three child elements. INTERVALTIME is a required, empty element that specifies how often the browser should check the channel for updates (assuming the user has asked the browser to do so). INTERVALTIME has DAY, HOUR, and MIN attributes. The DAY, HOUR, and MIN attributes are added to calculate the amount of time that is allowed to elapse between updates. As long as one is present, the other two can be omitted.

EARLIESTTIME and LATESTTIME are optional elements that specify times between which the browser should check for updates. The updates and resulting server load are distributed over the interval between the earliest and latest times. If you don't specify these, the browser simply checks in at its convenience. EARLIESTTIME and LATESTTIME have DAY and HOUR attributes used to specify when updates take place. DAY ranges from 1 (Sunday) to 7 (Saturday). HOUR ranges from 0 (midnight) to 23 (11:00 P.M.). For instance, the above example says that the browser should update the channel once a week (INTERVALTIME DAY="7") between Sunday midnight (EARLIESTTIME DAY="1" HOUR="0") and noon Monday (LATESTTIME DAY="2" HOUR="12").

EARLIESTTIME and LATESTTIME may also have a TIMEZONE attribute that specifies the time zone in which the earliest and latest times are calculated. If a time zone isn't specified, the reader's time zone is used to determine the earliest and latest times. To force the update to a particular time zone, include the optional TIMEZONE attribute in the EARLIESTTIME and LATESTTIME tags. For example:

```
<EARLIESTTIME DAY="1" HOUR="0" TIMEZONE="-0500"/>
<LATESTTIME DAY="2" HOUR="12" TIMEZONE="-0500"/>
```

To push an update across a LAN, you can choose the day of the week (for example, Sunday) and the time span (midnight to five in the morning). All browsers update during that five-hour period. If you update across Internet connections, your readers have to be connected to the Internet for the browser to update the channel.

Listing 21-6 expands the Cafe con Leche channel to include scheduled updates. Since content is updated almost daily INTERVALTIME is set to one day. Most days the update takes place between 7:00 a.m. and 12:00 noon Eastern time. Consequently, it sets EARLIESTTIME to 10:00 a.m. EST and LATESTTIME to 12:00 noon EST. There's no particular start or end date for the changes to this content, so the STARTDATE and STOPDATE attributes are omitted from the schedule.

Listing 21-6: **A CDF channel with scheduled updates**

```
<?xml version="1.0"?>
<CHANNEL HREF="http://metalab.unc.edu/xml/index.html">

  <TITLE>Cafe con Leche</TITLE>
  <ABSTRACT>
    Independent XML news and information for content
    and software developers
  </ABSTRACT>
  <LOGO HREF="cup_ICON.gif" STYLE="ICON"/>
  <LOGO HREF="cup_IMAGE.gif" STYLE="IMAGE"/>
  <LOGO HREF="cup_IMAGE-WIDE.gif" STYLE="IMAGE-WIDE"/>

  <SCHEDULE TIMEZONE="-0500">
```

```
      <INTERVALTIME DAY="1"/>
      <EARLIESTTIME HOUR="10" TIMEZONE="-0500"/>
      <LATESTTIME HOUR="12" TIMEZONE="-0500"/>
   </SCHEDULE>

   <ITEM HREF="http://metalab.unc.edu/xml/books.html">
      <TITLE>Books about XML</TITLE>
      <ABSTRACT>
         A comprehensive list of books about XML
         with capsule reviews and ratings
      </ABSTRACT>
   </ITEM>

   <ITEM HREF="http://metalab.unc.edu/xml/tradeshows.html">
      <TITLE>Trade shows and conferences about XML</TITLE>
      <ABSTRACT>
         Upcoming conferences and shows with an XML focus
      </ABSTRACT>
   </ITEM>

   <ITEM HREF="http://metalab.unc.edu/xml/mailinglists.html">
      <TITLE>Mailing Lists dedicated to XML</TITLE>
      <ABSTRACT>
         Mailing lists where you can discuss XML
      </ABSTRACT>
   </ITEM>
</CHANNEL>
```

Precaching and Web Crawling

If the subscriber has chosen to download the channel's contents automatically when they change, then the site owner has the option of allowing subscribers to view the pages offline and even to download more than merely those pages identified in the CDF document. In particular, you can allow the browser to spider through your site, downloading additional pages between one and three levels deep from the specified pages.

Precaching

By default, browsers precache the pages listed in a channel for offline browsing if the user has requested that they do so. However, the author can prevent a page from being precached by including a PRECACHE attribute in the CHANNEL or ITEM element with the value NO. For example:

```
<CHANNEL PRECACHE="NO"
         HREF="http://metalab.unc.edu/xml/index.html">
...
</CHANNEL>
```

If the value of PRECACHE is NO, then the content will not be precached regardless of user settings. If the value of PRECACHE is YES (or there is no explicit PRECACHE attribute) *and* the user requested precaching when they subscribed, then the content will be downloaded automatically. However, if the user has not requested precaching, then the site channel will not be precached regardless of the value of the PRECACHE attribute.

When you design a channel, you must keep in mind that some readers will view content offline almost exclusively. As a result, any links in the channel contents are effectively dead. If you are pushing documents across an intranet, the cache option doesn't make a lot of sense, as you'll be duplicating the same files on disks across the corporation. If you are delivering content to readers who pay for online time, you may want to organize it so that it can be cached and easily browsed offline.

Web Crawling

Browsers are not limited to loading only the Web pages specified in CHANNEL and ITEM elements. If a CHANNEL or ITEM element has a LEVEL attribute with a value higher than zero, the browser will Web crawl during updates. Web crawling lets the browser collect more pages than are listed in the channel. For example, if the page listed in a channel contains a number of links to related topics, it may be easier to let the browser load them all rather than list them in individual ITEM elements. If the site has a fairly even hierarchy, you can safely add a LEVEL attribute to the top-most channel tag and allow the Web crawl to include all of the pages at the subsequent levels. LEVEL can range from zero (the default) to three, which indicates how far down into the link hierarchy you want the browser to dig when caching the content. The hierarchy is the abstract hierarchy defined by the document links, not the hierarchy defined by the directory structure of files on the Web server. Framed pages are considered to be at the same level as the frameset page, even though an additional link is required for the former. The LEVEL attribute really only has meaning if precaching is enabled.

Listing 21-7 sets the LEVEL of the Cafe con Leche channel to 3. This goes deep enough to reach every page on the site. Since the pages previously referenced in ITEM children are only one level down from the main page, there's not as much need to list them separately. However, Web-crawling this deep may not be such a good idea. Most of the pages on the site don't change daily. Nonetheless, they'll still be checked each and every update.

Listing 21-7: **A CDF channel that precaches three levels deep**

```
<?xml version="1.0"?>
<CHANNEL LEVEL="3"
        HREF="http://metalab.unc.edu/xml/index.html">
```

```
<TITLE>Cafe con Leche</TITLE>
<ABSTRACT>
   Independent XML news and information for content
   and software developers
</ABSTRACT>
<LOGO HREF="logo_icon.gif" STYLE="ICON"/>
<LOGO HREF="corp_logo_regular.gif" STYLE="IMAGE"/>
<LOGO HREF="corp_logo_wide.gif" STYLE="IMAGE-WIDE"/>

<SCHEDULE TIMEZONE="-0500">
   <INTERVALTIME DAY="1"/>
   <EARLIESTTIME HOUR="10" TIMEZONE="-0500"/>
   <LATESTTIME HOUR="12" TIMEZONE="-0500"/>
</SCHEDULE>

</CHANNEL>
```

Reader Access Log

One disadvantage to channels compared to traditional Web surfing is that the server does not necessarily know which pages the surfer actually saw. This can be important for tracking advertisements, among other things. Internet Explorer can track the reader's passage through a site cached offline, and report it back to the Web server. However, the user always has the option to disable this behavior if they feel it's a privacy violation.

To collect statistics about the offline browsing of a site, you add LOG and LOGTARGET child elements to the CHANNEL element. During a channel update, the server sends the new channel contents to the browser while the browser sends the log file to the server. The LOG element always has this form, though other possible values of the VALUE attribute may be added in the future:

```
<LOG VALUE="document:view"/>
```

The LOGTARGET element has an HREF attribute that identifies the URL it will be sent to, a METHOD attribute that identifies the HTTP method like POST or PUT that will be used to upload the log file, and a SCOPE attribute that has one of the three values: ALL, ONLINE, or OFFLINE indicating which page views should be counted. The LOGTARGET element may have a PURGETIME child with an HOUR attribute that specifies the number of hours for which the logging information is considered valid. It may also have any number of HTTP-EQUIV children used to set particular key-value pairs in the HTTP MIME header. Listing 21-8 demonstrates a channel with a reader-access log.

Listing 21-8: **A CDF channel with log reporting**

```
<?xml version="1.0"?>
<CHANNEL HREF="http://metalab.unc.edu/xml/index.html">

  <TITLE>Cafe con Leche</TITLE>
  <ABSTRACT>
    Independent XML news and information for content
    and software developers
  </ABSTRACT>
  <LOGO HREF="logo_icon.gif" STYLE="ICON"/>
  <LOGO HREF="corp_logo_regular.gif" STYLE="IMAGE"/>
  <LOGO HREF="corp_logo_wide.gif" STYLE="IMAGE-WIDE"/>

  <LOG VALUE="document:view"/>
  <LOGTARGET METHOD="POST" SCOPE="ALL"
   HREF="http://metalab.unc.edu/xml/cgi-bin/getstats.pl" >
    <PURGETIME HOUR="12"/>
    <HTTP-EQUIV NAME="ENCODING-TYPE" VALUE="text"/>
  </LOGTARGET>

  <SCHEDULE TIMEZONE="-0500">
    <INTERVALTIME DAY="1"/>
    <EARLIESTTIME HOUR="10" TIMEZONE="-0500"/>
    <LATESTTIME HOUR="12" TIMEZONE="-0500"/>
  </SCHEDULE>

  <ITEM HREF="http://metalab.unc.edu/xml/books.html">
    <TITLE>Books about XML</TITLE>
    <ABSTRACT>
      A comprehensive list of books about XML
      with capsule reviews and ratings
    </ABSTRACT>
    <LOG VALUE="document:view"/>
  </ITEM>

  <ITEM HREF="http://metalab.unc.edu/xml/tradeshows.html">
    <TITLE>Trade shows and conferences about XML</TITLE>
    <ABSTRACT>
      Upcoming conferences and shows with an XML focus
    </ABSTRACT>
    <LOG VALUE="document:view"/>
  </ITEM>

  <ITEM HREF="http://metalab.unc.edu/xml/mailinglists.html">
    <TITLE>Mailing Lists dedicated to XML</TITLE>
    <ABSTRACT>
      Mailing lists where you can discuss XML
    </ABSTRACT>
  </ITEM>
</CHANNEL>
```

Only elements with `LOG` children will be noted in the log file. For instance, in Listing 21-8, hits to `http://metalab.unc.edu/xml/index.html`, `http://metalab.unc.edu/xml/books.html`, and `http://metalab.unc.edu/xml/tradeshows.html` will be logged. However hits to `http://metalab.unc.edu/xml/mailinglists.html` will not be.

The CDF logging information is stored in the Extended File Log format used by most modern Web servers. However, the Web server must be configured, most commonly through a CGI program, to accept the log file the client sends and merge it into the main server log.

The `LOGTARGET` element should appear as a child of the top-level `CHANNEL` tag, and describes log file handling for all items it contains. However, each `CHANNEL` and `ITEM` element that you want included in the log must include its own `LOG` child.

The BASE Attribute

The previous examples have all used absolute URLs for `CHANNEL` and `ITEM` elements. However, absolute URLs are inconvenient. For one thing, they're often long and easy to mistype. For another, they make site maintenance difficult when pages are moved from one directory to another, or from one site to another. You can use relative URLs instead if you include a `BASE` attribute in the `CHANNEL` element.

The value of the `BASE` attribute is a URL to which relative URLs in the channel can be relative. For instance, if the `BASE` is set to `"http://metalab.unc.edu/xml/`", then an `HREF` attribute can simply be "`books.html`" instead of "`http://metalab.unc.edu/xml/books.html`". Listing 21-9 demonstrates.

Listing 21-9: A CDF channel with a BASE attribute

```
<?xml version="1.0"?>
<CHANNEL BASE="http://metalab.unc.edu/xml/">
  <TITLE>Cafe con Leche</TITLE>
  <ABSTRACT>
    Independent XML news and information for content
    and software developers
  </ABSTRACT>
  <LOGO HREF="cup_ICON.gif" STYLE="ICON"/>
  <LOGO HREF="cup_IMAGE.gif" STYLE="IMAGE"/>
  <LOGO HREF="cup_IMAGE-WIDE.gif" STYLE="IMAGE-WIDE"/>
  <ITEM HREF="books.html">
    <TITLE>Books about XML</TITLE>
    <ABSTRACT>
      A comprehensive list of books about XML
```

Continued

Listing 21-9 *(continued)*

```
      with capsule reviews and ratings
    </ABSTRACT>
  </ITEM>

  <ITEM HREF="tradeshows.html">
    <TITLE>Trade shows and conferences about XML</TITLE>
    <ABSTRACT>
      Upcoming conferences and shows with an XML focus
    </ABSTRACT>
  </ITEM>

  <ITEM HREF="mailinglists.html">
    <TITLE>Mailing Lists dedicated to XML</TITLE>
    <ABSTRACT>
      Mailing lists where you can discuss XML
    </ABSTRACT>
  </ITEM>
</CHANNEL>
```

Whichever location you use for the link to the content, you can use a relative URL in the child elements if you specify a BASE attribute in the parent CHANNEL element. The BASE attribute also changes the hierarchy display in Internet Explorer. The base page will display in the browser window when child elements are not associated with a page.

The LASTMOD Attribute

When a browser makes a request of a Web server, the server sends a MIME header along with the requested file. This header includes various pieces of information like the MIME type of the file, the length of the file, the current date and time, and the time the file was last modified. For example:

```
HTTP/1.1 200 OK
Date: Wed, 27 Jun 1999 21:42:31 GMT
Server: Stronghold/2.4.1 Apache/1.3.3 C2NetEU/2409 (Unix)
Last-Modified: Tue, 20 Oct 1998 13:15:36 GMT
ETag: "4b94d-c70-362c8cf8"
Accept-Ranges: bytes
Content-Length: 3184
Connection: close
Content-Type: text/html
```

If a browser sends a HEAD request instead of the more common GET request, only the header is returned. The browser can then inspect the Last-Modified header to determine whether a previously loaded file from the channel needs to be reloaded or not. However, although HEAD requests are quicker than GET requests, a lot of them still eat up server resources.

To cut down on the load that frequent channel updates place on your server, you can add LASTMOD attributes to all CHANNEL and ITEM tags. The browser will only have to check back with the server for modification times for those items and channels that don't provide LASTMOD attributes.

The value of the LASTMOD attribute is a date and time in a *year-month-day*T*hour: minutes* form like 2000-05-23T21:42 when the page referenced by the HREF attribute was last changed. The browser detects and compares the LASTMOD date given in the CDF file with the last modified date provided by the Web server. When the content on the Web server has changed, the cache is updated with the current content. This way the browser only needs to check one file, the CDF document, for modification times rather than every file that's part of the channel. Listing 21-10 demonstrates.

Listing 21-10: **A CDF channel with LASTMOD attributes**

```
<?xml version="1.0"?>
<CHANNEL BASE="http://metalab.unc.edu/xml/"
         LASTMOD="1999-01-27T12:16" >
  <TITLE>Cafe con Leche</TITLE>
  <ABSTRACT>
    Independent XML news and information for content
    and software developers
  </ABSTRACT>
  <LOGO HREF="cup_ICON.gif" STYLE="ICON"/>
  <LOGO HREF="cup_IMAGE.gif" STYLE="IMAGE"/>
  <LOGO HREF="cup_IMAGE-WIDE.gif" STYLE="IMAGE-WIDE"/>
  <ITEM HREF="books.html" LASTMOD="1999-01-03T16:25">
    <TITLE>Books about XML</TITLE>
    <ABSTRACT>
      A comprehensive list of books about XML
      with capsule reviews and ratings
    </ABSTRACT>
  </ITEM>

  <ITEM HREF="tradeshows.html" LASTMOD="1999-01-10T11:40">
    <TITLE>Trade shows and conferences about XML</TITLE>
    <ABSTRACT>
      Upcoming conferences and shows with an XML focus
```

Continued

Listing 21-10 *(continued)*

```
      </ABSTRACT>
    </ITEM>

    <ITEM HREF="mailinglists.html" LASTMOD="1999-01-06T10:50">
      <TITLE>Mailing Lists dedicated to XML</TITLE>
      <ABSTRACT>
         Mailing lists where you can discuss XML
      </ABSTRACT>
    </ITEM>
  </CHANNEL>
```

In practice, this is way too much trouble to do manually, especially for frequently changed documents (and the whole point of channels and push is that they provide information that changes frequently). However, you might be able to write the CDF document as a file full of server-side includes that automatically incorporate LASTMOD values in the appropriate format or devise some other programmatic solution rather than manually adjusting the LASTMOD attribute every time you edit a file.

The USAGE Element

A CHANNEL or ITEM element may contain an optional USAGE child element that extends the presence of the channel on the subscriber's desktop. The meaning of the USAGE element is determined by its VALUE attribute. Possible values for the VALUE attribute are:

✦ Channel

✦ DesktopComponent

✦ Email

✦ NONE

✦ ScreenSaver

✦ SoftwareUpdate

Most of the time USAGE is an empty element. For example:

```
<USAGE VALUE="ScreenSaver" />
```

The default value for USAGE is Channel. Items with channel usage appear in the browser channel bar. All the CHANNEL and ITEM elements you've seen until now have had Channel usage, even though they didn't have an explicit usage element. Other values for USAGE allow different user interfaces to the channel content.

DesktopComponent Value

Desktop components are small Web pages or images that are displayed directly on the user's desktop. Since a Web page can contain a Java applet, fancy DHTML, or an ActiveX control, a desktop component can actually be a program (assuming the subscriber has abandoned all semblance of caution and installed Active Desktop).

The desktop component is installed on the subscriber's desktop with a separate CDF document containing an ITEM element that points to the document to be displayed on the user's desktop. As well as the usual child elements, this ITEM must contain a non-empty USAGE element whose VALUE is DesktopComponent. This USAGE element may contain OPENAS, HEIGHT, WIDTH, and CANRESIZE children.

The VALUE attribute of the OPENAS element specifies the type of file at the location in the ITEM element's HREF attribute. This should either be HTML or Image. If no OPENAS element is present, Internet Explorer assumes it is an HTML file.

The VALUE attributes of the HEIGHT and WIDTH elements specify the number of pixels the item occupies on the desktop.

The VALUE attribute of the CANRESIZE element indicates whether the reader can change the height and width of the component on the fly. Its possible values are Yes and No. Yes is the default. You can also allow or disallow horizontal or vertical resizing independently with CANRESIZEX and CANRESIZEY elements.

Listing 21-11 is a simple desktop component that displays a real time image of the Sun as provided by the friendly folks at the National Solar Observatory in Sunspot, New Mexico (http://vtt.sunspot.noao.edu/gifs/video/sunnow.jpg). The image is 640 pixels high, 480 pixels wide, but resizable. The image is refreshed every minute between 6:00 a.m. MST and 7:00 p.m. MST. (There's no point refreshing the image at night.)

Listing 21-11: **A DesktopComponent channel**

```
<?xml version="1.0"?>
<CHANNEL HREF="http://vtt.sunspot.noao.edu/sunpic.html">
  <TITLE>
    Hydrogen Alpha Image of the Sun Desktop Component
  </TITLE>
  <ABSTRACT>
```

Continued

Listing 21-11 *(continued)*

```
   This desktop component shows a picture of the Sun
   as it appears this very minute from the top of
   Sacramento Peak in New Mexico. The picture is taken
   in a single color at the wavelength of the Hydrogen
   alpha light (6563 Angstroms) using a monochrome
   camera which produces a greyscale image in
   which the red light of Hydrogen alpha appears white.
   </ABSTRACT>

   <ITEM
     HREF="http://vtt.sunspot.noao.edu/gifs/video/sunnow.jpg">
     <TITLE>Hydrogen Alpha Image of the Sun</TITLE>

     <SCHEDULE TIMEZONE="-0700">
       <INTERVALTIME MIN="1"/>
       <EARLIESTTIME HOUR="6"/>
       <LATESTTIME HOUR="19"/>
     </SCHEDULE>

     <USAGE VALUE="DesktopComponent">
       <WIDTH VALUE="640"/>
       <HEIGHT VALUE="480"/>
       <CANRESIZE VALUE="Yes"/>
       <OPENAS VALUE="Image"/>
     </USAGE>
   </ITEM>
</CHANNEL>
```

Email Value

Normally, when a browser notifies a subscriber of a change to channel content by sending them email, it sends along the main page of the channel as the text of the email message. However, you can specify that a different email message be sent by including an ITEM in the channel whose USAGE element has the value email.

Listing 21-12 specifies that the file at http://metalab.unc.edu/xml/what-snew.html will be used to notify subscribers of content changes. If the first ITEM were not present, then http://metalab.unc.edu/xml/ from the CHANNEL HREF attribute would be used instead. This gives you an opportunity to send a briefer message specifying what has changed, rather than sending the entire changed page. Often "What's new" information is easier for readers to digest than the entire page.

Listing 21-12: A channel that emails a separate notification

```xml
<?xml version="1.0"?>
<CHANNEL BASE="http://metalab.unc.edu/xml/">
  <TITLE>Cafe con Leche</TITLE>
  <ABSTRACT>
    Independent XML news and information for content
    and software developers
  </ABSTRACT>
  <LOGO HREF="cup_ICON.gif" STYLE="ICON"/>
  <LOGO HREF="cup_IMAGE.gif" STYLE="IMAGE"/>
  <LOGO HREF="cup_IMAGE-WIDE.gif" STYLE="IMAGE-WIDE"/>

  <ITEM HREF="whatsnews.html">
    <USAGE VALUE="Email"/>
  </ITEM>

  <ITEM HREF="books.html">
    <TITLE>Books about XML</TITLE>
    <ABSTRACT>
      A comprehensive list of books about XML
      with capsule reviews and ratings
    </ABSTRACT>
  </ITEM>

  <ITEM HREF="tradeshows.html">
    <TITLE>Trade shows and conferences about XML</TITLE>
    <ABSTRACT>
      Upcoming conferences and shows with an XML focus
    </ABSTRACT>
  </ITEM>

  <ITEM HREF="mailinglists.html">
    <TITLE>Mailing Lists dedicated to XML</TITLE>
    <ABSTRACT>
      Mailing lists where you can discuss XML
    </ABSTRACT>
  </ITEM>
</CHANNEL>
```

NONE Value

Items whose USAGE value is NONE don't appear anywhere; not in the channel bar, not on the Active Desktop, not on the favorites menu, nowhere. However, such items are precached and are thus more quickly available for applets and HTML pages that refer to them later.

Precaching channel content is useful for including items — such as sound and video clips — that you want to move to the reader's machine for use by channel pages. You can precache a single item or a series of items by defining a channel that includes the set of precached items, as is demonstrated in this example:

```
<ITEM HREF="welcome.wav">   <USAGE="NONE"/> </ITEM>
<ITEM HREF="spacemusic.au"> <USAGE="NONE"/> </ITEM>
```

This example includes two sound files used at the site when the browser downloads the channel contents for offline viewing. These two files won't be displayed in the channel bar, but if a file in the channel bar does use one of these sound files, then it will be immediately available, already loaded when the page is viewed offline. The reader won't have to wait for them to be downloaded from a remote Web site, an important consideration when dealing with relatively large multimedia files.

ScreenSaver Value

Items whose USAGE value is ScreenSaver point to an HTML page to replace the normal desktop after a user-specified period of inactivity. Generally, a screen saver will be written as a completely separate CDF document from the normal channel, and will require a separate download and install link. For example:

```
<A HREF="ccl_screensaver.cdf">
  Download and install the Cafe con Leche Screen Saver!
</A>
```

Unless the subscriber has already selected the Channel Screen Saver as the system screen saver in the Display control panel as shown in Figure 21-7, the browser will ask the user whether they want to use the Channel Screen Saver or the currently selected screen saver. Assuming they choose the Channel Screen Saver, the next time the screen is saved, the document referenced in the screen saver channel will be loaded and displayed. If the user has subscribed to more than one screen saver channel, the browser will rotate through the subscribed screen saver channels every 30 seconds. The user can change this interval and a few other options (whether screen savers play sounds, for instance) using the screen saver settings in the Display control panel.

Listing 21-13 is a simple screen saver channel. The actual document displayed when the screen is saved is pointed to by the ITEM elements HREF attribute. This page will generally make heavy use of DHTML, JavaScript, and other tricks to animate the screen. A static screen saver page is a bad idea.

Listing 21-13: **A screen saver channel**

```xml
<?xml version="1.0"?>
<CHANNEL BASE="http://metalab.unc.edu/xml/">

  <ITEM HREF="http://metalab.unc.edu/screensaver.html">
    <USAGE VALUE="ScreenSaver"/>
  </ITEM>

</CHANNEL>
```

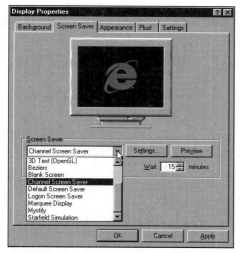

Figure 21-7: The Screen Saver tab of the Display Properties control panel in Windows NT 4.0

Two things you should keep in mind when designing screen savers:

1. Presumably the user is doing something else when the screen is saved. After all, inactivity activates the screen saver. Therefore, don't go overboard or expect a lot of user attention or interaction with your screen saver.

2. Although almost no modern display really needs its screen saved, screen savers should save the screen nonetheless. Thus most of the screen should be dark most of the time, and no pixel on the screen should ever be continuously on. Most importantly, no pixel should continuously be one non-black color, especially white.

SoftwareUpdate Value

The final possible value of the USAGE element is SoftwareUpdate. Channels aren't limited to delivering news and Web pages. They can send software updates too. Software update channels can both notify users of updates to software and deliver the product across the Internet. Given a sufficiently trusting (perhaps insufficiently paranoid is more accurate) user, they can even automatically install the software.

To create a software push channel, write a CDF file with a root CHANNEL element whose USAGE element has the value SoftwareUpdate. This channel can have a title, abstract, logos, and schedule, just like any other channel. Listing 21-14 is a fake software update channel.

Listing 21-14: **A software update channel**

```
<?xml version="1.0"?>
<CHANNEL HREF="http://www.whizzywriter.com/updates/2001.html">
  <TITLE>WhizzyWriter 2001 Update</TITLE>
  <ABSTRACT>
    WhizzyWriter 2001 offers the same kitchen sink approach
    to word processing that WhizzyWriter 2000 was infamous for,
    but now with tint control! plus many more six-legged
    friends to delight and amuse!  Don't worry though. All the
    old arthropods you've learned to love and adore in the
    last 2000 versions are still here!
  </ABSTRACT>

  <USAGE VALUE="SoftwareUpdate"/>
  <SOFTPKG NAME="WhizzyWriter 2001 with tint control 2.1EA3"
    HREF="http://www.whizzywriter.com/updates/2001.cab"
    VERSION="2001,0,d,3245" STYLE="ActiveSetup">

    <!— other OSD elements can go here —>

  </SOFTPKG>

</CHANNEL>
```

Besides the VALUE of the USAGE element, the key to a software update channel is its SOFTPKG child element. The HREF attribute of the SOFTPKG element provides a URL from which the software can be downloaded and installed. The URL should point to a compressed archive of the software in Microsoft's cabinet (CAB) format. This archive must carry a digital signature from a certificate authority. Furthermore, it must also contain an OSD file describing the software update. OSD, the

Open Software Description format, is an XML application for describing software updates invented by Microsoft and Marimba. The OSD file structure and language is described on the Microsoft Web site at `http://www.microsoft.com/standards/osd/`.

 OSD is covered briefly in Chapter 2, *An Introduction to XML Applications.*

The SOFTPKG element must also have a NAME attribute that contains up to 260 characters describing the application. For example, "WhizzyWriter 2100 with tint control 2.1EA3".

The SOFTPKG element must also have a STYLE attribute with one of two values — ActiveSetup or MSICD (Microsoft Internet Component Download) which determines how the software is downloaded and installed.

There are several optional attributes to SOFTPKG as well. The SOFTPKG element may have a PRECACHE attribute with either the value Yes or No. This has the same meaning as other PRECACHE attributes; that is, determining whether the package will be downloaded before the user decides whether they want it. The VERSION attribute is a comma-separated list of major, minor, custom, and build version numbers such as "6,2,3,3124". Finally, setting the AUTOINSTALL attribute to Yes tells the browser to download the software package automatically as soon as the CDF document is loaded. The value No instructs the browser to wait for a specific user request and is the default if the AUTOINSTALL attribute is not included.

These child elements can go inside the SOFTPKG element:

✦ TITLE

✦ ABSTRACT

✦ LANGUAGE

✦ DEPENDENCY

✦ NATIVECODE

✦ IMPLEMENTATION

However these elements are not part of CDF. Rather they're part of OSD. (Technically SOFTPKG is too.) Consequently, I'll only summarize them here:

✦ The TITLE element of the SOFTPKG uses the same options as the standard CDF TITLE.

✦ The ABSTRACT element describes the software and is essentially the same as the CDF ABSTRACT element.

✦ The LANGUAGE element defines the language supported by this update using a VALUE attribute whose value is an ISO 639/RFC 1766 two-letter language code such as EN for English. If multiple languages are supported, they're separated by semicolons.

✦ The DEPENDENCY element is empty with a single attribute, ACTION which may take on one of two values — Assert or Install. Assert is the default and means that the update will only be installed if the necessary CAB file is already on the local computer. With a value of Install, the necessary files will be downloaded from the server.

✦ The NATIVECODE element holds CODE child elements. Each CODE child element points to the distribution files for a particular architecture such as Windows 98 on X86 or Windows NT on alpha.

✦ The IMPLEMENTATION element describes the configuration required for the software package. If the requirements described in the implementation tag are not found on the reader's machine, the download and installation do not proceed. The IMPLEMENTATION element is an optional element with child elements CODEBASE, LANGUAGE, OS, and PROCESSOR.

The CODEBASE element has FILENAME and HREF attributes that say where the files for the update can be found.

The LANGUAGE element is the same as the LANGUAGE element above.

The OS element has a VALUE attribute whose value is Mac, Win95, or Winnt, thereby identifying the operating system required for the software. This element can have an empty child element called OSVERSION with a VALUE attribute that identifies the required release.

The PROCESSOR element is an empty element whose VALUE attribute can have the value Alpha, MIPS, PPC, or x86. This describes the CPU architecture the software supports.

For more details about OSD, you can see the reference at http://www.micro-soft.com/workshop/delivery/osd/reference/reference.asp, or the specification at http://www.microsoft.com/standards/osd/default.asp.

Summary

In this chapter, you learned:

✦ The Channel Definition Format (CDF) is an XML application used to describe data pushed from Web sites to Web browsers.

✦ CDF files are XML files, although they customarily have the file name extension .cdf instead of .xml. The root element of a CDF file is CHANNEL.

✦ Each CHANNEL element must contain an HREF attribute identifying the pushed page.

✦ A CHANNEL element may contain additional ITEM child elements whose HREF attributes contain URLs of additional pages to be pushed.

✦ Each CHANNEL and ITEM element may contain TITLE, ABSTRACT, and LOGO children that describe the content of the page the element references.

✦ The SCHEDULE element specifies when and how often the browser should check the server for updates.

✦ The LOG element identifies items whose viewing is reported back to the Web server, though the subscriber can disable this reporting.

✦ The LOGTARGET element defines how logging information from a channel is reported back to the server.

✦ The BASE attribute provides a starting point from which relative URLs in child element HREF attributes can be calculated.

✦ The LASTMOD attribute specifies the last time a page was changed so the browser can tell whether or not it needs to be downloaded.

✦ The USAGE attribute allows you to use Web pages as channels, precached content, Active Desktop components, screen savers, and software updates.

The next chapter explores a completely different application of XML to vector graphics — the Vector Markup Language (VML for short).

✦　　✦　　✦

The Vector Markup Language

The Vector Markup Language (VML), the subject of this chapter, is an XML application that combines vector information with CSS markup to describe vector graphics that can be embedded in Web pages in place of the bitmapped GIF and JPEG images loaded by HTML's IMG element. Vector graphics take up less space and thus display much faster over slow network connections than traditional GIF and JPEG bitmap images. VML is supported by the various components of Microsoft Office 2000 (Word, PowerPoint, Excel) as well as by Internet Explorer 5.0. When you save a Word 2000, PowerPoint 2000, or Excel 2000 document as HTML, graphics created in those programs are converted to VML.

What Is VML?

VML elements represent shapes: rectangles, ovals, circles, triangles, clouds, trapezoids, and so forth. Each shape is described as a path formed from a series of connected lines and curves. VML uses elements and attributes to describe the outline, fill, position, and other properties of each shape. Standard CSS properties can be applied to VML elements to set their positions.

Listing 22-1 is an HTML document. Embedded in this HTML file is the VML code to draw a five-pointed blue star and a red circle. Figure 22-1 shows the document displayed in Internet Explorer 5.0.

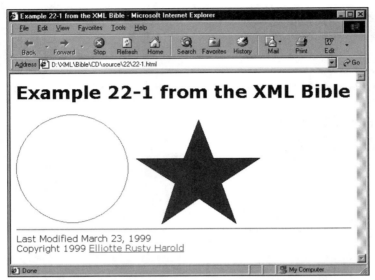

Figure 22-1: An HTML document with embedded VML elements

Listing 22-1: An HTML document with VML code that draws a five-pointed blue star and a red circle.

```
<html xmlns:vml="urn:schemas-microsoft-com:vml">

  <head>
    <title>Example 22-1 from the XML Bible</title>
    <object id="VMLRender"
      classid="CLSID:10072CEC-8CC1-11D1-986E-00A0C955B42E">
    </object>
    <style>
      vml\:* { behavior: url(#VMLRender) }
    </style>
  </head>

  <body>
    <h1>Example 22-1 from the XML Bible</h1>

    <div>
      <vml:oval
        style="width:200px; height: 200px"
        stroke="true"
        strokecolor="red"
        strokeweight="2">
```

```
        </vml:oval>

        <vml:polyline
          style="width: 250px; height: 250px"
          stroke="false"
          fill="true"
          fillcolor="blue"
          points="8pt, 65pt, 72pt, 65pt, 92pt, 11pt, 112pt, 65pt,
                 174pt, 65pt, 122pt, 100pt, 142pt, 155pt, 92pt,
                 121pt, 42pt, 155pt, 60pt, 100pt">
        </vml:polyline>
      </div>
      <hr></hr>
      Last Modified March 23, 1999<br />
      Copyright 1999
      <a href="http://www.macfaq.com/personal.html">
        Elliotte Rusty Harold
      </a>
    </body>

</html>
```

Listing 22-1 obviously isn't an ordinary HTML document, even though it contains some standard HTML elements. First of all, the `html` root element declares the namespace prefix `vml` as shorthand for `urn:schemas-microsoft-com:vml`. The `head` element contains an `object` child with the `id` VMLRender. (VMLRender is a program installed with IE5.) And there's a CSS style rule that specifies that all elements in the `vml` namespace (that is, all elements that begin with `vml:`) should have the `behavior` property `url(#VMLRender)`. This is a relative URL that happens to point to the aforementioned `object` element. This tells the Web browser to pass all elements that begin with `vml:` (the backslash in `vml\:` is used to ensure that the `:` is treated as part of the element name rather than a selector separator) to the object with the ID VMLRender for display.

The `body` element contains several of the usual HTML elements including `div`, `h1`, `hr`, and `a`. However, it also contains `vml:oval` and `vml:polyline` elements. The `vml:oval` element is set to have a red border (stroke) 2 pixels wide. Furthermore, the `style` attribute sets the CSS `width` and `height` properties of this oval to 200 pixels each. These also set the width and height of the implicit rectangular box that holds the oval. The `vml:polyline` element is set to be filled in blue. The CSS `width` and `height` properties of this oval are set to 250 pixels each. A five-pointed star has ten vertices. The `points` attribute provides 10 pairs of x-y coordinates, one for each vertex.

Drawing with a Keyboard

Drawing pictures with a keyboard is like hammering a nail into wood with a sponge. Writing VML pictures by typing raw XML code in a text editor is not easy. I suggest you start any attempts to program vector images with some graph paper, and draw the images with a pencil the way you wish to see them on the screen. You can then use the images from the graph paper to determine coordinates for various VML elements like shape, oval, and polyline.

The shape Element

The fundamental VML element is shape. This describes an arbitrary closed curve in two dimensions. Most shapes have a path that defines the outline of the shape. The outline may or may not have a stroke with a particular color and width - that is, the outline may or may not be visible. The shape may or may not be filled with a particular color. For example, in Figure 22-1 the circle has a black stroke but no fill, whereas the star has a blue fill but no stroke.

Most properties of a shape element can be defined by various attributes. Table 22-1 lists these. For example, here's a shape element that draws an isosceles triangle. The id attribute gives the shape a unique name. The coordsize attribute defines the size of the local coordinate system. The style attribute uses CSS width and height properties to specify the absolute width and height of the box that contains the triangle. The path attribute provides data to the formulas child element that calculates the exact outline of this particular triangle. And the fillcolor attribute makes the entire triangle blue.

```
<vml:shape id="_x0000_t5" coordsize="21600,21600"
  style="width:200px; height: 200px" adj="10800"
  path="m@0,0l0,21600,21600,21600xe" fillcolor="blue">
  <vml:formulas>
    <vml:f eqn="val #0"/>
    <vml:f eqn="prod #0 1 2"/>
    <vml:f eqn="sum @1 10800 0"/>
  </vml:formulas>
</vml:shape>
```

Don't worry if it isn't obvious to you that this is an isosceles triangle. In fact, I'd be surprised if it were even obvious that this is a triangle. Most VML elements (including this one) are drawn using a GUI, and only saved into VML form. Consequently, you don't need to know the detailed syntax of each and every VML element and attribute. However, if you know a little, you can sometimes do some surprising tricks with the VML file that may prove impossible with a graphical editor. For example, you can search for all the blue elements, and change them to red.

Table 22-1
Attributes of the Shape Element

Attribute	Default Value	Description
id	none	a unique XML name for the element (same as any other XML ID type attribute)
adj	none	input parameters for formulas child elements that define the shape's path
alt	none	alternate text shown if the shape can't be drawn for any reason; like the ALT attribute of HTML's IMG element
chromakey	none	a transparent background color for the shape which anything behind the shape will show through; for example, red or #66FF33
class	none	the CSS class of the shape
coordorigin	0 0	local coordinate corner of the upper left-hand corner of the shape's box
coordsize	1000 1000	width and height of the shape's box in the local coordinate space
fill	true	whether the shape is filled
fillcolor	white	color the shape is filled with; for example, red or #66FF33
href	none	URL to jump to when the shape is clicked
opacity	1.0	transparency of shape as a floating point number between 0.0 (invisible) and 1.0 (fully opaque)
path	none	commands that define the shape's path
print	true	whether the shape should be printed when the page is printed
stroke	true	whether the path (outline) of the shape should be drawn
strokecolor	black	color used to draw the shape's path
strokeweight	0.75pt	width of the line used to draw the shape's path
style	none	CSS properties applied to this shape
target	none	the name of the frame loaded when a frameset page loads
title	none	name of the shape
type	none	a reference to the id of a shapetype element
v	none	command defining the path of shape
wrapcoords	none	specifies how tightly text wraps around a shape

Some properties of shapes are more convenient to set with child elements rather than attributes. Furthermore, using child elements allows for more detailed control of some aspects of a shape. For instance, the above isosceles triangle required three formulas to describe its path. Each of these was encapsulated in an `vml:f` child element. By using attributes, only a single formula could have easily been included. Table 22-2 lists the possible child elements of a shape. If a child element conflicts with an attribute, then the value specified by the child element is used.

Table 22-2
Shape Child Elements

Element	Description
path	the edge of the shape
formulas	formulas that specify the outline of the shape
handles	visual controls used to alter the shape
fill	how the path should be filled
stroke	how to draw the path, if the artist wants something more elaborate than a straight line and solid color
shadow	the shadow effect for the shape
textbox	the text that should appear inside of the shape
textpath	the vector path used by the text
imagedata	a picture rendered on top of the shape
line	a straight line path
polyline	a path defined by connecting the dots between specified points
curve	a path defined by a cubic Bezier curve
rect	a path defined by a rectangle of a specific height and width
roundrect	a path defined by a rectangle with rounded corners of a specific size
oval	a path defined by an oval enclosed in a rectangle of a specific height and width
arc	a path defined by the arc of an angle between two points
image	a bitmapped image loaded from an external source

Each of these child elements itself has a variety of attributes and child elements used to define its appearance. For instance, `line`, one of the simplest, has `from` and `to` attributes that define the starting and ending points of the line. The value of each of these attributes is a 2-D coordinate in the local coordinate space like 0 5 or

32 10. You can read about the details in the Vector Markup Language submission to the W3C or on the Microsoft Web site at `http://www.microsoft.com/standards/vml/`.

Caution Treat the VML specification with a pinch of salt. It contains a number of really obvious and quite a few not-so-obvious mistakes.

Note The `line`, `polyline`, `curve`, `rect`, `roundrect`, `oval`, `arc`, and `image` elements do not have to be children of `shape`. They can stand on their own.

The shapetype Element

The `shapetype` element defines a shape that can be reused multiple times, by referencing it at a later point within a document using a `shape` element. The `shapetype` element is identical in all ways to the `shape` element except that it cannot be used to reference another `shapetype` element. This element is always hidden. The `shape` element refers to the `shapetype` element using a `type` attribute whose value is a relative URL pointing to the `id` of the `shapetype` element.

For example, Listing 22-2 includes a `shapetype` element that defines a blue right triangle. It also includes three shape elements that merely reference this `shapetype`. Thus there are three right triangles in Figure 22-2, even though it's only defined once. Each of these triangles has a different size as set in the individual `shape` elements even though they're all calculated from the same formulas.

Listing 22-2: Multiple shape elements copy a single shapetype

```
<html xmlns:vml="urn:schemas-microsoft-com:vml">

  <head>
    <title>Example 22-2 from the XML Bible</title>
    <object id="VMLRender"
      classid="CLSID:10072CEC-8CC1-11D1-986E-00A0C955B42E">
    </object>
    <style>
      vml\:* { behavior: url(#VMLRender) }
    </style>
  </head>

  <body>
    <h1>Example 22-2 from the XML Bible</h1>

    <vml:shapetype id="fred"
```

Continued

Listing 22-2 *(continued)*

```
      coordsize="21600,21600"
      fillcolor="blue"
      path="m@0,0l0,21600,21600,21600xe">
   <vml:formulas>
     <vml:f eqn="val #0"/>
     <vml:f eqn="prod #0 1 2"/>
     <vml:f eqn="sum @1 10800 0"/>
   </vml:formulas>
 </vml:shapetype>

 <vml:shape type="#fred" style="width:50px; height:50px" />
 <vml:shape type="#fred" style="width:100px; height:100px"/>
 <vml:shape type="#fred" style="width:150px; height:150px"/>

 <hr></hr>
 Last Modified March 23, 1999<br />
 Copyright 1999
 <a href="http://www.macfaq.com/personal.html">
   Elliotte Rusty Harold
 </a>
</body>

</html>
```

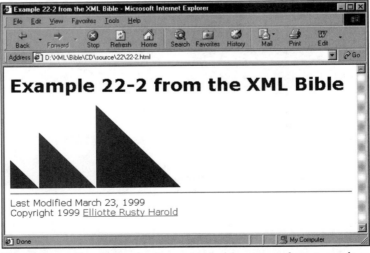

Figure 22-2: Three triangle shapes copied from one shapetype element

When a shape element references a shapetype element, shape may duplicate some of the attributes applied to the shapetype element. In this case, the values associated with shape will override those of shapetype.

The group Element

The group top-level element combines shapes and other top-level elements. The group has its own local coordinate space in which its child shapes are placed. This entire collection of shapes can then be moved and positioned as a unit. The only attributes the group can have are the core attributes that a shape can have (for example, id, class, style, title, href, target, alt, coordorigin, and coordsize). For example, suppose you need a shape that is a star inside a circle. You can create it by combining an oval with a polyline in a group element like this:

```
<vml:group style="width:6cm; height: 6cm"
  coordorigin="0 0" coordsize="250 250">
  <vml:oval style =
 "position:absolute; top: 15; left: 15; width:200; height: 200"
    stroke="true" strokecolor="black" strokeweight="2"
    fill="true" fillcolor="red">
  </vml:oval>

  <vml:polyline style =
   "position:absolute; top:25; left: 25; width:200; height:200"
    stroke="true" strokecolor="black" strokeweight="5"
    fill="true" fillcolor="blue"
    points="8, 65, 72, 65, 92, 11, 112, 65, 174, 65, 122,
            100, 142, 155, 92, 121, 42, 155, 60, 100">
  </vml:polyline>
</vml:group>
```

The coordsize and coordorigin attributes define the local coordinate system of the elements contained in the group. The coordsize attribute defines how many units there are along the width of the containing block. The coordorigin attribute defines the coordinate of the top left corner of the containing block.

This is an abstract system, not one based in any sort of physical units like inches, pixels, or ems. The conversion between the local units and the global units depends on the height and the width of the group. For example, in the above example the group's actual height and width is 6cm by 6cm, and its coordsize is 250 250. Thus, each local unit is 0.024cm (6cm/250). As the height and width of the group change, the sizes of the contents of the group scale proportionately.

Inside a group, all the CSS properties used to position VML like left and width are given as non-dimensional numbers in the local coordinate space. In other words, unlike normal CSS properties, they do not use units, and are only pure numbers, not real lengths. For example, consider this group:

```
<vml:group style="width: 400px; height: 400px"
```

```
coordsize="100,100"
coordorigin="-50,-50">
```

The containing block is 400 pixels wide by 400 pixels high. The `coordsize` property specifies that there are 100 units both horizontally and vertically within this `group`. Each of the local units is four pixels long. The coordinate system inside the containing block ranges from –50.0 to 50.0 along the x-axis and –50.0 to 50.0 along the y-axis with 0.0, 0.0 right in the center of the rectangle. Shapes positioned outside this region will not be truncated, but they are likely to fall on top of or beneath other elements on the page. All children of the `group` are positioned and sized according to the local coordinate system.

Positioning VML Shapes with Cascading Style Sheet Properties

VML elements fit directly into the CSS Level 2 visual rendering model, exactly like HTML elements. This means that each VML element is contained in an implicit box, which positions at a certain point on the page. The following standard CSS properties place the box at particular absolute or relative positions on the page:

- ✦ `display`
- ✦ `position`
- ✦ `float`
- ✦ `clear`
- ✦ `height`
- ✦ `width`
- ✦ `top`
- ✦ `bottom`
- ✦ `left`
- ✦ `right`
- ✦ `border`
- ✦ `margin`
- ✦ `visibility`
- ✦ `z-index`

Cross-Reference

Chapter 12, *Cascading Stylesheets Level 1*, and Chapter 13, *Cascading Style Sheets Level 2,* discuss CSS.

In addition to supporting the standard CSS2 visual-rendering model, VML adds four new properties so shapes can be rotated, flipped, and positioned. These are:

✦ rotation

✦ flip

✦ center-x

✦ center-y

Note

Personally, I think adding non-standard CSS properties to the style attribute is a very bad idea. I would much prefer that these properties simply be additional attributes on the various VML shape elements. The center-x and center-y properties are particularly annoying because they do nothing the left and right properties don't already do.

VML elements use a style attribute to set these properties, just like HTML elements. This has the same syntax as the HTML style attribute. For example, this VML oval uses its style attribute to set its position, border, and margin properties:

```
<vml:oval style="top: 15; left: 15; width:200; height: 100;
    margin:10; border-style:solid; border-right-width: 2;
    border-left-width: 2; border-top-width: 1.5;
    border-bottom-width: 1.5"
    stroke="false" fill="true" fillcolor="green">
</vml:oval>
```

VML shapes are positioned on the page using the CSS position, left, right, width, and height properties. If the position property has the value absolute, the invisible rectangular box that contains the shape is placed at particular coordinates relative to the window that displays the shape, regardless of what else appears on the page. This means that different shapes and HTML elements can overlap. VML uses the z-index CSS property to layer the first (lowest) to the last (highest) layer, with the latest elements obscuring the earlier elements. This allows you to stack elements on top of each other to build intricate images for your Web pages. If elements don't have z-index properties, then elements that come later in the document are placed on top of elements that come earlier in the document.

Listing 22-3 uses absolute positioning to place the blue star on top of the red circle, which is itself on top of the h1 header and the signature block. Figure 22-3 shows the result.

The default value of the position property is static, which simply means that both HTML elements and VML shapes are laid out one after the other, each taking as much space as it needs, but none laying on top of each other.

The position property can also be set to relative, which begins by placing the box where it would normally be, and then offsetting it from that position by the amount specified in the top, bottom, left, and right properties.

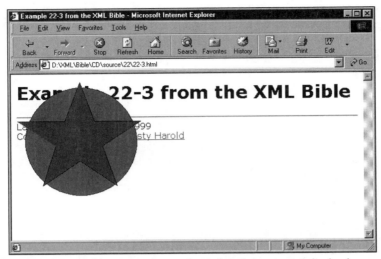

Figure 22-3: A blue star on top of a red circle on top of the body of the page

Listing 22-3: VML code that draws a five-pointed blue star on top of a red circle

```
<html xmlns:vml="urn:schemas-microsoft-com:vml">

  <head>
    <title>Example 22-3 from the XML Bible</title>
    <object id="VMLRender"
      classid="CLSID:10072CEC-8CC1-11D1-986E-00A0C955B42E">
    </object>
    <style>
      vml\:* { behavior: url(#VMLRender) }
    </style>
  </head>

  <body>
    <h1>Example 22-3 from the XML Bible</h1>

    <div>
      <vml:polyline
        style="position:absolute; top:0px; left:0px;
               width: 250px; height: 250px; z-index: 1"
        stroke="false"
        fill="true"
        fillcolor="blue"
```

```
      points="8pt, 65pt, 72pt, 65pt, 92pt, 11pt, 112pt, 65pt,
              174pt, 65pt, 122pt, 100pt, 142pt, 155pt, 92pt,
              121pt, 42pt, 155pt, 60pt, 100pt">
  </vml:polyline>

  <vml:oval style="position:absolute; top:25px; left:25px;
                   width:200px; height: 200px; z-index: 0"
        stroke="false"
        fill="true"
        fillcolor="red">
  </vml:oval>

  </div>
  <hr></hr>
  Last Modified March 23, 1999<br />
  Copyright 1999
  <a href="http://www.macfaq.com/personal.html">
    Elliotte Rusty Harold
  </a>
</body>

</html>
```

The rotation Property

The rotation property does not exist in standard CSS, but it can be used as a CSS property of VML shapes. The value of the rotation property represents the number of degrees a shape is rotated in a clockwise direction, about the center of the shape. If a negative number is given, the object is rotated counterclockwise. Degree values are specified in the format 45deg, 90deg, -30deg, and so forth. Listing 22-4 rotates Listing 22-1's star by 120 degrees. Figure 22-4 shows the result.

The flip Property

The flip property does not exist in standard CSS, but it can be used as a CSS property of VML shapes. It flips a shape around either its x- or y-axis, or both. This is given as a CSS property on the style attribute of a VML shape element. To flip the y coordinates about the x-axis, set flip to y. To flip the x coordinates about the y-axis, set flip to x. Listing 22-5 flips the shape about its x-axis. Figure 22-5 shows the result.

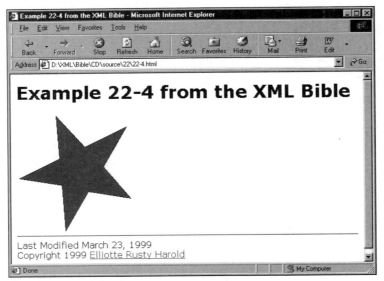

Figure 22-4: A star rotated by 120 degrees

Listing 22-4: **A star rotated by 120 degrees**

```
<html xmlns:vml="urn:schemas-microsoft-com:vml">

  <head>
    <title>Example 22-4 from the XML Bible</title>
    <object id="VMLRender"
      classid="CLSID:10072CEC-8CC1-11D1-986E-00A0C955B42E">
    </object>
    <style>
      vml\:* { behavior: url(#VMLRender) }
    </style>
  </head>

  <body>
    <h1>Example 22-4 from the XML Bible</h1>

    <div>

      <vml:polyline
        style="width: 250px; height: 250px; rotation: 120deg"
        stroke="true"
        strokecolor="black"
        strokeweight="5"
```

```
                  fill="true"
                  fillcolor="blue"
                  points="8pt, 65pt, 72pt, 65pt, 92pt,11pt, 112pt, 65pt,
                          174pt, 65pt, 122pt,100pt, 142pt, 155pt, 92pt,
                          121pt, 42pt, 155pt, 60pt, 100pt, 8pt, 65pt">
            </vml:polyline>
        </div>
        <hr></hr>
        Last Modified March 23, 1999<br />
        Copyright 1999
        <a href="http://www.macfaq.com/personal.html">
          Elliotte Rusty Harold
        </a>
      </body>

    </html>
```

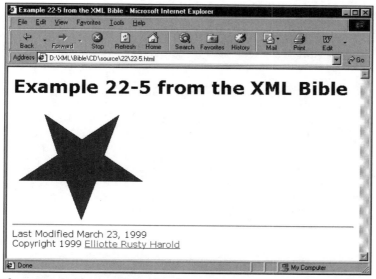

Figure 22-5: The star flipped on its x-axis

Listing 22-5: A star flipped about its *x*-axis

```
<html xmlns:vml="urn:schemas-microsoft-com:vml">

  <head>
    <title>Example 22-5 from the XML Bible</title>
    <object id="VMLRender"
      classid="CLSID:10072CEC-8CC1-11D1-986E-00A0C955B42E">
    </object>
    <style>
      vml\:* { behavior: url(#VMLRender) }
    </style>
  </head>

  <body>
    <h1>Example 22-5 from the XML Bible</h1>

    <div>

      <vml:polyline
        style="width: 250px; height: 250px; flip: y"
        stroke="true"
        strokecolor="black"
        strokeweight="5"
        fill="true"
        fillcolor="blue"
        points="8pt, 65pt, 72pt, 65pt, 92pt,11pt, 112pt, 65pt,
                174pt, 65pt, 122pt,100pt, 142pt, 155pt, 92pt,
                121pt, 42pt, 155pt, 60pt, 100pt, 8pt, 65pt">
      </vml:polyline>
    </div>
    <hr></hr>
    Last Modified March 23, 1999<br />
    Copyright 1999
    <a href="http://www.macfaq.com/personal.html">
      Elliotte Rusty Harold
    </a>
  </body>

</html>
```

The center-x and center-y Properties

The center-x and center-y properties locate the center of the block box that contains the shape. These properties offer alternatives to the left and right CSS properties and ultimately convey the same information. Because center-x and left are alternatives for each other as are center-y and right, you should not specify them both. If you employ both, then the value associated with center-x and center-y is used.

VML in Office 2000

Microsoft Word, Excel, and PowerPoint support VML by converting graphics drawn in these programs, into VML markup on HTML pages. In order to do this, you have to set up the Office products correctly.

Settings

The settings are in essentially the same location in each of the Office components that can create VML. To set VML as the default graphics type, you must perform the following steps:

1. From within Microsoft PowerPoint/Word/Excel, open the Tools menu and select Options.

2. Select the General tab.

3. Click the Web Options button.

4. Select the Pictures tab from the Web Options dialog window.

5. Check the option that reads: "Rely on VML for displaying graphics in browsers," as shown in Figures 22-6 (PowerPoint), 22-7 (Word), and 22-8 (Excel).

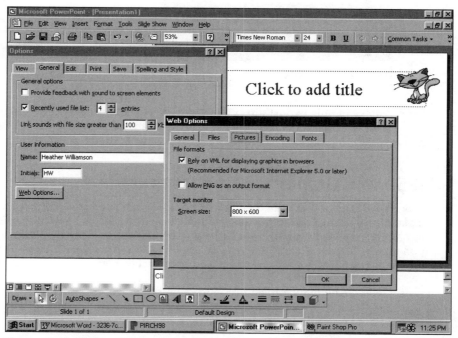

Figure 22-6: Setting VML as the default graphic type in PowerPoint

6. Click the OK button on the Web Options window, then OK again on the main program Options window, as shown in Figures 22-6, 22-7, and 22-8. PowerPoint/Word/Excel is now configured to use VML graphics whenever you save a presentation in Web format.

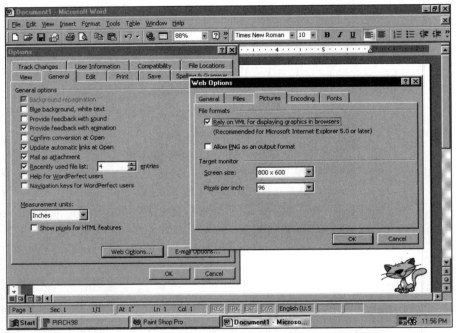

Figure 22-7: Setting VML as the default graphic type in Microsoft Word

Office 2000 will only export into VML those images you drew in their documents using their drawing tools. This means that you cannot use PowerPoint or Word as a conversion utility for other graphics that you have embedded in Office documents.

A Simple Graphics Demonstration of a House

Office 2000 may not have all the power of Adobe Illustrator or Corel Draw, but it does make drawing simple graphics easy—much easier than drawing with the key-board as shown previously. PowerPoint is the most graphically oriented of the Office components, so let's demonstrate by using PowerPoint to draw a little house. By employing the following steps, it's as simple as drawing a few squares, circles, and triangles:

1. Open a new blank presentation from within PowerPoint using the File menu, New option.

2. Select Blank Presentation, and then click OK.

3. In the New Slide window, select the slide with only a title bar at the top, as shown in Figure 22-9, then click OK.

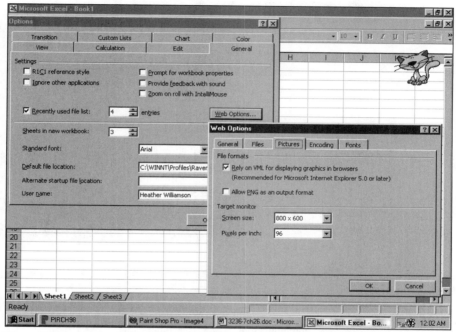

Figure 22-8: Setting VML as the default graphic type in Microsoft Excel

4. Click in the Title bar area, and give your slide a name, for example "My VML House".

5. On the drawing toolbar at the bottom of the window, click the Rectangle tool. Use this tool to draw the foundation for the VML House.

6. On the drawing toolbar, click the AutoShapes button, select the Basic Shapes option, and then the Isosceles triangle.

7. Draw a roof over the house.

8. Use the Oval and Rectangle tools to draw windows and doors on your house, until your image looks something like the one shown in Figure 22-10.

9. Open the File menu, and select Save As Web Page. Type the name of the page, for example "VMLHouse.html" then click the Save button.

10. Close PowerPoint, and open the file you just created using Internet Explorer 5.0, or select Preview Web Page Preview from the File menu.

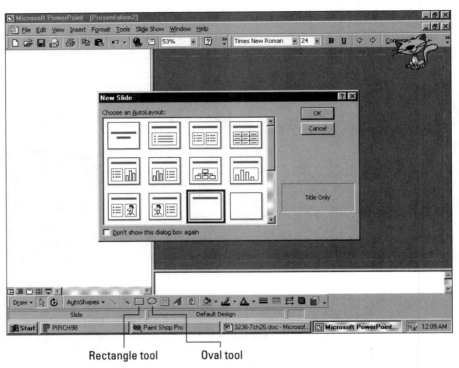

Rectangle tool   Oval tool

Figure 22-9: Selecting a template for our slide

Figure 22-11 shows the resulting Web page. The HTML and VML code created by PowerPoint to display this slide is shown in Listing 22-6. As well as a lot of standard HTML and VML code, you also see a number of elements in the `urn:schemas-microsoft-com:office:office` and `urn:schemas-microsoft-com:office:powerpoint` namespaces. These contain information that most Web browsers won't use, but that PowerPoint will if the HTML file is opened in PowerPoint. The purpose of these elements is to allow a document to make a round trip from PowerPoint to HTML and back again without losing anything along the way.

Note   The VML house will only be shown in Internet Explorer 5.0 or later. Netscape browsers will only see the embedded images, not the VML.

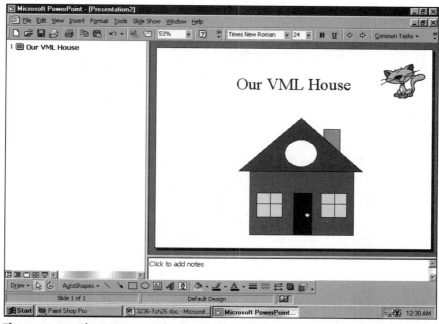

Figure 22-10: The VML House in PowerPoint 2000, ready for conversion into VML text

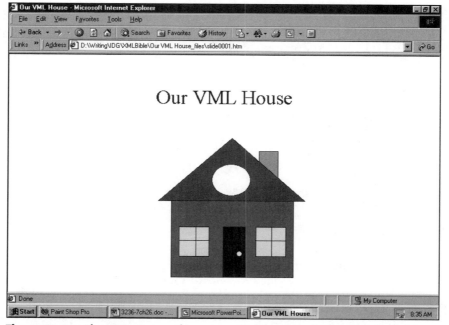

Figure 22-11: The VML House, shown as a Web page, in Internet Explorer 5.0

Listing 22-6: The "Our VML House" PowerPoint slide converts to an HTML file with embedded VML for use on the Web

```html
<html xmlns:v="urn:schemas-microsoft-com:vml"
      xmlns:o="urn:schemas-microsoft-com:office:office"
      xmlns:p="urn:schemas-microsoft-com:office:powerpoint"
      xmlns="-//W3C//DTD HTML 4.0//EN">

<head>
  <meta http-equiv=Content-Type content="text/html;
        charset=windows-1252">
  <meta name=ProgId content=PowerPoint.Slide>
  <meta name=Generator content="Microsoft PowerPoint 9">
  <link id=Main-File rel=Main-File
        href="../Our%20VML%20House.htm">
  <link rel=Preview href=preview.wmf>

  <!--[if !mso]>
   <style>
     v\:* {behavior:url(#default#VML);}
     o\:* {behavior:url(#default#VML);}
     p\:* {behavior:url(#default#VML);}
     shape {behavior:url(#default#VML);}
     v\:textbox {display:none;}
   </style>
  <![endif]-->
  <title>Our VML House</title>
  <meta name=Description content="8-Mar-99: Our VML House">
  <link rel=Stylesheet href="master03_stylesheet.css">

  <![if !ppt]>
    <style media=print>
    <!--.sld
      {left:0px !important;
      width:6.0in !important;
      height:4.5in !important;
      font-size:103% !important;}
    -->
    </style>
    <script src=script.js>
    </script>
    <!--[if vml]>
      <script>
       g_vml = 1;
      </script>
    <![endif]-->
    <script for=window event=onload>
      <!--LoadSld( gId );
      MakeSldVis(0);
      //-->
    </script>
  <![endif]>
```

```
    <o:shapelayout v:ext="edit">
      <o:idmap v:ext="edit" data="2"/>
    </o:shapelayout>
</head>

<body lang=EN-US style='margin:0px;background-color:white'
      onresize="_RSW()">
    <div id=SlideObj class=sld
        style='position:absolute;top:0px;left:0px;
               width:554px;height:415px;font-size:16px;
               background-color:white;clip:
               rect(0%, 101%, 101%, 0%);
               visibility:hidden'>
    <p:slide coordsize="720,540"
      colors="#FFFFFF,#000000,#808080,#000000,#00CC99,#3333CC,
              #CCCCFF,#B2B2B2"
      masterhref="master03.xml">
    <p:shaperange href="master03.xml#_x0000_s1025"/>
    <![if !ppt]>
      <p:shaperange href="master03.xml#_x0000_s1028"/>
      <![if !vml]>
      <img border=0
           v:shapes="_x0000_s1028"
           src="master03_image002.gif"
           style='position:absolute;top:91.08%;left:7.58%;
                  width:21.11%;height:6.98%'>
      <![endif]>
      <p:shaperange href="master03.xml#_x0000_s1029"/>
      <![if !vml]>
        <img border=0
             v:shapes="_x0000_s1029"
             src="master03_image003.gif"
             style='position:absolute;top:91.08%;left:34.11%;
                    width:31.94%;height:6.98%'>
      <![endif]>
    <![endif]>
    <v:rect id="_x0000_s2063"
            style='position:absolute;left:438pt;top:3in;
                   width:42pt; height:78pt;mso-wrap-style:
                   none;v-text-anchor:middle'
            fillcolor="#0c9 [4]"
            strokecolor="black [1]">
    <v:fill color2="white [0]"/>
    <v:shadow color="gray [2]"/>
    </v:rect>
    <p:shaperange href="master03.xml#_x0000_m1026"/>
    <v:shape id="_x0000_s2050"
             type="#_x0000_m1026"
             style='position:absolute;left:54pt;top:48pt;
                    width:612pt; height:90pt'>
    <v:fill o:detectmouseclick="f"/>
    <v:stroke o:forcedash="f"/>
```

Continued

Listing 22-6 *(continued)*

```
        <o:lock v:ext="edit" text="f"/>
        <p:placeholder type="title"/>
</v:shape>
<v:rect id="_x0000_s2051"
        style='position:absolute; left:246pt;top:330pt;
                width:270pt;height:174pt;mso-wrap-style:none;
                v-text-anchor:middle'
        fillcolor="red"
        strokecolor="black [1]">
    <v:shadow color="gray [2]"/>
</v:rect>
<v:shapetype id="_x0000_t5"
                coordsize="21600,21600"
                o:spt="5"
                adj="10800"
                path="m@0,0l0,21600,21600,21600xe">
    <v:stroke joinstyle="miter"/>
    <v:formulas>
      <v:f eqn="val #0"/>
      <v:f eqn="prod #0 1 2"/>
      <v:f eqn="sum @1 10800 0"/>
    </v:formulas>
    <v:path gradientshapeok="t"
            o:connecttype="custom"
            o:connectlocs="@0,0;@1,10800;0,21600;10800,21600;
                            21600,21600;@2,10800"
            textboxrect="0,10800,10800,18000;
                          5400,10800,16200,18000;
                          10800,10800,21600,18000;
                          0,7200,7200,21600;
                          7200,7200,14400,21600;
                          14400,7200,21600,21600"/>
    <v:handles>
      <v:h position="#0,topLeft" xrange="0,21600"/>
    </v:handles>
</v:shapetype>
<v:shape id="_x0000_s2053"
        type="#_x0000_t5"
        style='position:absolute;left:3in;top:186pt;
                width:324pt;height:2in;mso-wrap-style:none;
                v-text-anchor:middle'
        fillcolor="#33c [5]"
        strokecolor="black [1]">
    <v:shadow color="gray [2]"/>
</v:shape>
<v:oval id="_x0000_s2054"
        style='position:absolute;left:336pt;top:246pt;
        width:84pt;height:1in;mso-wrap-style:none;
                v-text-anchor:middle'
        fillcolor="white [0]"
        strokecolor="black [1]">
```

```
    <v:shadow color="gray [2]"/>
</v:oval>
<v:rect id="_x0000_s2055"
        style='position:absolute;left:264pt;top:390pt;
            width:66pt;height:66pt;mso-wrap-style:none;
            v-text-anchor:middle'
        fillcolor="#6ff"
        strokecolor="black [1]">
  <v:shadow color="gray [2]"/>
</v:rect>
<v:rect id="_x0000_s2056"
        style='position:absolute;left:5in;top:390pt;
            width:48pt;height:114pt;mso-wrap-style:none;
            v-text-anchor:middle'
        fillcolor="black [1]"
        strokecolor="black [1]">
  <v:shadow color="gray [2]"/>
</v:rect>
<v:rect id="_x0000_s2057"
        style='position:absolute;left:6in;top:390pt;
            width:66pt;height:66pt;mso-wrap-style:none;
            v-text-anchor:middle'
        fillcolor="#6ff"
        strokecolor="black [1]">
  <v:shadow color="gray [2]"/>
</v:rect>
<v:line id="_x0000_s2058"
        style='position:absolute'
        from="300pt,390pt"
        to="300pt,456pt"
        coordsize="21600,21600"
        strokecolor="black [1]">
  <v:shadow color="gray [2]"/>
</v:line>
<v:line id="_x0000_s2059"
        style='position:absolute'
        from="264pt,420pt"
        to="330pt,420pt"
        coordsize="21600,21600"
        strokecolor="black [1]">
  <v:shadow color="gray [2]"/>
</v:line>
<v:line id="_x0000_s2060"
        style='position:absolute'
        from="468pt,390pt"
        to="468pt,456pt"
        coordsize="21600,21600"
        strokecolor="black [1]">
  <v:shadow color="gray [2]"/>
</v:line>
<v:line id="_x0000_s2061"
        style='position:absolute'
```

Continued

Listing 22-6 *(continued)*

```
                from="6in,420pt"
                to="498pt,420pt"
                coordsize="21600,21600"
                strokecolor="black [1]">
    <v:shadow color="gray [2]"/>
  </v:line>
  <v:oval id="_x0000_s2062"
          style='position:absolute;left:390pt;top:444pt;
                  width:12pt;height:12pt;mso-wrap-style:none;
                  v-text-anchor:middle'
          fillcolor="yellow"
          strokecolor="black [1]">
    <v:shadow color="gray [2]"/>
  </v:oval>
  <![if !vml]>
    <img border=0
          v:shapes="_x0000_s2063,_x0000_s2050,_x0000_s2051,
                    _x0000_s2053,_x0000_s2054,_x0000_s2055,
                    _x0000_s2056,_x0000_s2057,_x0000_s2058,
                    _x0000_s2059,_x0000_s2060,_x0000_s2061,
                    _x0000_s2062"
          src="slide0001_image004.gif"
          style='position:absolute;top:8.91%;left:7.58%;
                  width:85.37%;height:84.81%'>
  <![endif]>
  <div v:shape="_x0000_s2050" class=T
       style='position:absolute;top:13.01%;
       left:8.48%;width:83.21%;height:9.15%'>
    Our VML House
  </div>
  </p:slide>
  </div>
</body>
</html>
```

A Quick Look at SVG

Let's be honest about something here. VML may well be another Microsoft technology that follows in the footsteps of ActiveX and Bob; that is, a technology, which will be implemented by Microsoft and no one else. VML is not supported by Netscape Navigator nor is it likely to be.

The W3C has received four different proposals for vector graphics in XML from a wide variety of vendors. It's formed the Scaleable Vector Graphics (SVG) working group composed of representatives from all these vendors to develop a single specification for an XML representation of Scalable Vector Graphics. When SVG is complete it should provide everything VML provides plus a lot more including animation, interactive elements, filters, clipping, masking, compositing, and pattern fills. However, both a full SVG specification and software that implements the specification is some time away. VML is here today.

The World Wide Web Consortium released the first working draft of SVG in February of 1999, and revised that draft in April 1999. Compared to other working drafts, however, it is woefully incomplete. It's really not much more than an outline of graphics elements that need to be included, without any details about how exactly those elements will be encoded in XML. I wouldn't be surprised if this draft got pushed out the door a little early to head off adoption of competing efforts like VML.

Microsoft has stated publicly that they intend to ignore any Web graphics efforts except VML. However, they are represented on the SVG working group. Whether its representatives actually participate or whether Microsoft's name is only on the masthead as a political gesture is unknown. In either case, SVG is a development that we are all going to have to watch for the next few development cycles to see where it is going, who is following, and who is leading.

Summary

In this chapter, we looked at developing VML graphics for use with Internet Explorer 5.0. In addition to the general overview of VML, we specifically looked at:

✦ What VML can do for Web graphics.

✦ The various elements and attributes associated with VML shapes, and how to use them to create the visual images that you need.

✦ How to configure Microsoft Office 2000 applications to use VML when creating graphics for Web documents and presentations.

✦ How to draw VML figures using PowerPoint 2000.

✦ How SVG may affect Web graphics, and what could happen to VML as a result.

The last few chapters, this one included, have looked at a variety of XML applications designed by third parties. In the next chapter, we will design a new XML application from scratch that covers genealogy.

✦   ✦   ✦

Designing a New XML Application

The last several chapters discussed XML applications that were already written by other people and showed you how to use them. This chapter shows you how to develop an XML application from scratch. In this chapter you see the gradual development of an XML application and associated DTDs for genealogical data.

Organization of the Data

When developing an XML application from scratch, you need to organize, either in your head or on paper, the data you're describing. There are three basic steps in this process:

1. List the elements.
2. Identify the fundamental elements.
3. Relate the elements.

One of the easiest ways to start the process is to explore the forms and reports that are already available from other formats that describe this data. Genealogy is a fairly well-established discipline, and genealogists have a fairly good idea of what information is and is not useful and how it should be arranged. This is often included in a family group sheet, a sample of which is shown in Figure 23-1.

You'll need to duplicate and organize the fields from the standard reports in your DTD to the extent that they match what you want to do. You can of course supplement or modify them to fit your specific needs.

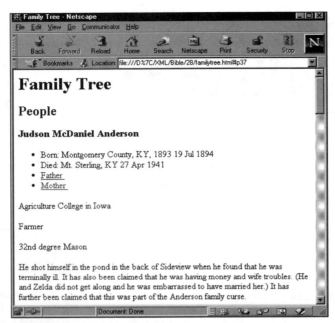

Figure 23-1: A family group sheet

Note Object-oriented programmers will note many similarities between what's described in this section and the techniques they gather user requirements. This is partly the result of my own experience and prejudices as an object-oriented programmer, but more of it is due to the similarity of the tasks involved. Gathering user requirements for software is not that different from gathering user requirements for markup languages. Database designers may also notice a lot of similarity between what's done here and what they do when designing a new database.

Listing the Elements

The first step in developing DTDs for a domain is to decide what the elements are. This isn't hard. It mostly consists of brainstorming to determine what may appear in the domain. As an exercise, write down everything you can think of that may be genealogical information. To keep the problem manageable, include only genealogical data. Assume you can use the XHTML DTD from Chapter 20 for standard text information such as paragraphs, page titles, and so forth. Again, include only elements that specifically apply to genealogy.

Don't be shy. It's easy to remove information later if there's too much or something doesn't prove useful. At this stage, expect to have redundant elements or elements you'll throw away after further thought.

Here's the list I came up with. Your list will almost certainly be at least a little different. And of course you may have used different names for the same things. That's okay. There's no one right answer (which is not to say that all answers are created equal or that some answers aren't better than others).

father	family
parent	birthday
baptism	burial
note	surname
aunt	grandmother
mother	son
child	death date
adoption	grandfather
grave site	given name
niece	uncle
person	daughter
baby	marriage
gender	date
source	middle name
grandparent	nephew

Identifying the Fundamental Elements

The list in the last section has effective duplicates and some elements that aren't really necessary. It is probably missing a few elements too, which you'll discover as you continue. This is normal. Developing an XML application is an iterative process that takes some time before you feel comfortable with the result.

What you really need to do at this stage is determine the fundamental elements of the domain. These are likely to be those elements that appear as immediate children of the root, rather than contained in some other element. There are two real possibilities here: family and person. Most of the other items in the list are either characteristics of a person or family (occupation, birthday, marriage) or they're a kind of family or person (uncle, parent, baby).

At this stage, most people's instinct is to say that family is the only fundamental element, and that families contain people. This is certainly consistent with the usage of the terms *parent* and *child* to describe the relationships of XML elements (a usage I eschew in this chapter to avoid confusion with the human parents and children we're modeling). For example, you might imagine that a family looks like this:

```
<FAMILY>
  <HUSBAND>Samuel English Anderson</HUSBAND>
  <WIFE>Cora Rucker McDaniel</WIFE>
  <CHILD>Judson McDaniel Anderson</CHILD>
  <CHILD>Thomas Corwin Anderson</CHILD>
  <CHILD>Rodger French Anderson</CHILD>
  <CHILD>Mary English Anderson</CHILD>
</FAMILY>
```

However, there's a problem with this approach. A single person likely belongs to more than one family. I am both the child of my parents and the husband of my wife. That's two different families. Perhaps you can think of this as one extended family, but how far back does this go? Are my grandparents part of the same family? My great-grandparents? My in-laws? Genealogists generally agree that for the purposes of keeping records, a family is a mother, a father, and their children.

Of course, the real world isn't even that simple. Some people have both adoptive and biological parents. Many people have more than one spouse over a lifetime. My father-in-law, Sidney Hart Anderson, was married 15 separate times to 12 different women. Admittedly, Sidney is an extreme case. When he died, he was only four marriages away from tying the world record for serial marriage. (Since then, former Baptist minister Glynn Wolfe pushed the record to 28 consecutive marriages.) Nonetheless, you do need to account for the likelihood that the same people belong to different families.

The standard family group sheets used by the Mormons, a variation of which was shown in Figure 23-1, account for this by repeating the same people and data on different sheets. But for computer applications it's better not to store the same information more than once. Among other things, this avoids problems where data stored in one place is updated while data stored in another is not. Instead, you can make connections between different elements by using ID and IDREF attributes.

Thus it is not enough to have only a single fundamental family element. There must be at least one other fundamental element, the person. Each person is unique. Each has a single birthday, a single death date, most of the time (though not always) a single name, and various other data. Families are composed of different collections of persons. By defining the persons who make up a family, as well as their roles inside the family, you define the family.

Note

We often think of our family as an extended family including grandparents, daughters-in-law, uncles, aunts, and cousins, and perhaps biologically unrelated individuals who happen to live in the same house. However, in the context of genealogy, a family is a single pair of parents and their children. In some cases the names of these people may be unknown, and in many cases there may be no children or no husband or wife (a single individual qualifies as a family of one). However, a family does not include more distant relationships. A large part of genealogy is the establishment of the actual biological or adoptive relationships between people. It's not uncommon to discover in the course of one's research that the "Cousin Puss" or "Aunt Moot" referred to in old letters was in fact no relation at all! Such people should certainly be included in your records, but failure to keep their actual connections straight can only lead to confusion farther down the road.

There's one more key element that may or may not be a direct child of the root. That's the source for information. A source is like a bibliographical footnote, specifying where each piece of information came from. The source may be a magazine article such as "Blaise Pradel, Man At Arms, May/June 1987, p. 26–31"; a book like "*A Sesquicentennial History of Kentucky*" by Frederik A. Wallis & Hambleon Tapp, 1945, The Historical Record Association, Hopkinsville, KY"; a family bible such as "English-Demint Anderson Bible, currently held by Beth Anderson in Brooklyn"; or simply word of mouth such as "Anne Sandusky, interview, 6-12-1995".

Tracking the source for a particular datum is important because different sources often disagree. It's not uncommon to see birth and death dates that differ by a day or a year, plus or minus. Less common but still too frequent are confusions between parents and grandparents, aunts and cousins, names of particular people, and more. When you uncover information that disputes information you've already collected, it's important to make a reasonable judgement about whether the new information is more reliable than the old. Not all sources are reliable. In my own research I've found a document claiming to trace my wife's lineage back to Adam and Eve through various English royalty from the Middle Ages, and assorted biblical figures. Needless to say, I don't take this particular source very seriously.

I can think of plausible reasons to make the source a child of the individual elements it documents, but ultimately I think the source is not part of a person or a family in the same way that a birth date or marriage date belongs to a particular person. Rather, it is associated information that should be stored separately and referenced through an ID. The main reason is that a single source such as an old family bible may well contain data about many different elements. In keeping with principles of data normalization, I'd prefer not to repeat the information about the source more than once in the document. If you like, think of this as akin to using end notes rather than footnotes.

Establishing Relationships Among the Elements

The third and final step before the actual writing of the DTD is to identify how the different pieces of information you want to track are connected. You've determined that the three fundamental elements are the person, the family, and the source. Now you must decide what you want to include in these fundamental elements.

FAMILY

A family is generally composed of a husband, a wife, and zero or more children. Either the husband or the wife is optional. If you wish to account for same-sex marriages (something most genealogy software couldn't do until recently), simply require one or two parents or spouses without specifying gender. Gender may then be included as an attribute of a person, which is where it probably belongs anyway.

Is there other information associated with a family, as opposed to individuals in the family? I can think of one thing that is important to genealogists: marriage information. The date and place a couple was married (if any) and the date and place a couple was divorced (again, if any), are important information. Although you could include such dates as part of each married individual, it really makes sense to make it part of the family. Given that, a family looks something like this:

```
<FAMILY>
  <MARRIAGE>
    <DATE>...</DATE>
    <PLACE>...</PLACE>
  </MARRIAGE>
  <DIVORCE>
    <DATE>...</DATE>
    <PLACE>...</PLACE>
  </DIVORCE>
  <HUSBAND>...</HUSBAND>
  <WIFE>...</WIFE>
  <CHILD>...</CHILD>
  <CHILD>...</CHILD>
  <CHILD>...</CHILD>
</FAMILY>
```

Information can be omitted if it isn't relevant (such as a couple never divorced) or if you don't have it.

PERSON

The PERSON element is likely to be more complex. Let's review the standard information you'd want to store about a person:

✦ name

✦ birth

- ✦ baptism
- ✦ death
- ✦ burial
- ✦ father
- ✦ mother

Of these, name, birth, death, and burial are likely to be elements contained inside a person. Father and mother are likely to be attributes of the person that refer back to the person elements for those people. Furthermore, a person needs an ID attribute so he or she can be referred to by family and other person elements.

Caution   Father and mother seem to be borderline cases where you might get away with using attributes, but there is the potential to run into trouble. Although everyone has exactly one biological mother and one biological father, many people have adoptive parents that may also need to be connected to the person.

Names are generally divided into family name and given name. This allows you to do things like write a style sheet that boldfaces all people with the last name "Harold".

Birth, death, burial (and possibly baptism, sometimes a baptismal record is all that's available for an individual) can all be divided into a date (possibly including a time) and a place. Again, the place may simply be CDATA or it can even be a full address element. However, in practice, full street addresses a post office could deliver to are not available. Much more common are partial names like "Mount Sterling, Kentucky" or the name of an old family farm.

Dates can either be stored as CDATA or broken up into day, month, and year. In general, it's easier to break them into day, month, and year than to stick to a common format for dates. On the other hand, allowing arbitrary text inside a date element also allows for imprecise dates like "1919-20", "before 1753", or "about 1800".

That may seem like everything, but we've left out one of the most interesting and important pieces of all—notes. A note about a person may contain simple data like "first Eagle Scout in Louisiana" or it may contain a complete story, like how Sam Anderson was killed in the field. This may be personal information like religious affiliation, or it may be medical information like which ancestors died of stomach cancer. If you've got a special interest in particular information like religion or medical history, you can make that a separate element of its own, but you should still include some element that can hold arbitrary information of interest that you dig up during your research.

There are other things you could include in a PERSON element, photographs for instance, but for now I'll stop here so this chapter is manageable. Let's move on to the SOURCE element.

SOURCE

The third and final top-level element is SOURCE. A source is bibliographic information that says where you learned a particular fact. It can be a standard citation to a published article or book such as "Collin's History of Kentucky, Volume II, p. 325, 1840, 1875". Sources like this have a lot of internal structure that could be captured with elements like BOOK, AUTHOR, VOLUME, PAGE_RANGE, YEAR, and so forth. Several efforts are currently underway to produce DTDs for generic bibliographies.

However, sources in genealogy tend to be lot messier than in the typical term paper. For instance, one of the most important sources in genealogy can be the family bible with records of births, dates, and marriages. In such a case, it's not the edition, translation, or the publisher of the bible that's important; it's the individual copy that resides in Aunt Doodie's house. For another example, consider exactly how you cite an obituary you found in a 50-year-old newspaper clipping in a deceased relative's purse. Chances are the information in the obituary is close to accurate, but it's not easy to figure out exactly what page of what newspaper on what date it came from.

Since developing an XML application for bibliographies could easily be more than a chapter of its own, and is a task best left to professional librarians, I will satisfy myself with making the SOURCE element contain only character data. It will also have an ID attribute in the form s1, s2, s3, and so forth, so that each source can be referred to by different elements. Let's move on to writing the DTD that documents this XML application.

The Person DTD

By using external entity references, it's possible to store individual people in separate files, then pull them together into families and family trees later. So let's begin with a DTD that works for a single person. We'll merge this into a DTD for families and family trees in the next section.

To develop a DTD, it's often useful to work backwards — that is, first write out the XML markup you'd like to see using a real example or two, then write the DTD that matches the data. I'm going to use my great-grandfather-in-law Samuel English Anderson as an example, because I have enough information about him to serve as a good example, and also because he's been dead long enough that no one should get upset over anything I say about him. (You'd be amazed at the scandals and gossip you dig up when doing genealogical research.) Here's the information I have about Samuel English Anderson:

Name: Samuel English Anderson[29, 43]

Birth: 25 Aug 1871   Sideview

Death: 10 Nov 1919   Mt. Sterling, KY

Father: Thomas Corwin Anderson (1845-1889)

Mother: LeAnah (Lee Anna, Annie) DeMint English (1843-1898)

Misc. Notes219

Samuel English Anderson was known in Montgomery County for his red hair and the temper that went with it. He did once *kill a man*, but the court found that it was in self defense.

He was shot by a farm worker whom he had fired the day before for smoking in a tobacco barn. Hamp says this may have been self-defense, because he threatened to kill the workers for smoking in the barn. He also claims that old-time rumors say they mashed his head with a fence post. Beth heard he was cut to death with machetes in the field, but Hamp says they wouldn't be cutting tobacco in November, only stripping it in the barn.

Now let's reformat this into XML as shown in Listing 23-1:

Listing 23-1: **An XML document for Samuel English Anderson**

```
<?xml version="1.0"?>
<!DOCTYPE PERSON SYSTEM "person.dtd">
<PERSON ID="p37" SEX="M">
  <REFERENCE SOURCE="s29"/>
  <REFERENCE SOURCE="s43"/>
  <NAME>
    <GIVEN>Samuel English</GIVEN>
    <SURNAME>Anderson</SURNAME>
  </NAME>
  <BIRTH>
    <PLACE>Sideview</PLACE>
    <DATE>25 Aug 1871</DATE>
  </BIRTH>
  <DEATH>
    <PLACE>Mt. Sterling, KY</PLACE>
    <DATE>10 Nov 1919</DATE>
  </DEATH>
  <SPOUSE PERSON="p1099"/>
  <SPOUSE PERSON="p2660"/>
  <FATHER PERSON="p1035"/>
  <MOTHER PERSON="p1098"/>
  <NOTE>
    <REFERENCE SOURCE="s219"/>
    <body>
      <p>
        Samuel English Anderson was known in Montgomery County
        for his red hair and the temper that went with it. He
        did once <strong>kill a man</strong>, but the court
        found that it was in self-defense.
```

Continued

Listing 23-1 *(continued)*

```
      </p>

      <p>
        He was shot by a farm worker whom he had
        fired the day before for smoking in a tobacco barn.
        Hamp says this may have been self-defense, because he
        threatened to kill the workers for smoking in the barn.
        He also says old-time rumors say they mashed his head
        with a fence post. Beth heard he was cut to death with
        machetes in the field, but Hamp says they wouldn't be
        cutting tobacco in November, only stripping it in the
        barn.
      </p>
    </body>
  </NOTE>
</PERSON>
```

The information about other people has been removed and replaced with references to them. The ID numbers are provided by the database I use to store this information (Reunion 5.0 for the Mac from Leister Productions). The end note numbers become SOURCE attributes of REFERENCE elements. HTML-like tags are used to mark up the note.

Now let's see what a DTD for this would look like. The first element is PERSON. This element may contain names, references, births, deaths, burials, baptisms, notes, spouses, fathers, and mothers. I'm going to allow zero or more of each in any order.

```
<!ELEMENT PERSON (NAME | REFERENCE | BIRTH | DEATH | BURIAL
    | BAPTISM | NOTE | SPOUSE | FATHER | MOTHER )*>
```

At first glance it may seem strange not to require a BIRTH or some of the other elements. After all, everybody has exactly one birthday. However, keep in mind that what's being described here is more our knowledge of the person than the person him or herself. You often know about a person without knowing the exact day or even year they were born. Similarly, you may sometimes have conflicting sources that give different values for birthdays or other information. Therefore, it may be necessary to include extra data.

The PERSON element has two attributes, an ID, which we'll require, and a SEX which we'll make optional. (Old records often contain children of unspecified gender, sometimes named, sometimes not. Even photographs don't always reveal gender, especially when children who died very young are involved.)

```
<!ATTLIST PERSON
    ID   ID      #REQUIRED
    SEX (M | F) #IMPLIED>
```

Next the child elements must be declared. Four of them—BIRTH, DEATH, BURIAL, and BAPTISM—consist of a place and a date, and are otherwise the same. This is a good place for a parameter entity reference:

```
<!ENTITY % event    "(REFERENCE*, PLACE?, DATE?)*">
<!ELEMENT  BIRTH   %event;>
<!ELEMENT  BAPTISM %event;>
<!ELEMENT  DEATH   %event;>
<!ELEMENT  BURIAL  %event;>
```

I've also added one or more optional REFERENCE element at the start, even though this example doesn't have a SOURCE for any event information. Sometimes, you'll have different sources for different pieces of information about a person. In fact I'll add REFERENCE elements as potential children of almost every element in the DTD. I declare REFERENCE like this, along with a comment in case it isn't obvious from glancing over the DTD exactly what's supposed to be found in the reference:

```
<!- The ID number of a REFERENCE element
     that documents this entry ->
<!ELEMENT   REFERENCE  EMPTY>
<!ATTLIST   REFERENCE SOURCE NMTOKEN #REQUIRED>
```

Here the SOURCE attribute merely contains the number of the corresponding source. When actual SOURCE elements are added to the DTD below, this can become the ID of the SOURCE element.

A PLACE contains only text. A DATE contains a date string. I decided against requiring a separate year, date, and month to allow for less-certain dates that are common in genealogy like "about 1876" or "sometime before 1920".

```
<!ELEMENT   PLACE  (#PCDATA)>
<!ELEMENT   DATE   (#PCDATA)>
```

The SPOUSE, FATHER, and MOTHER attributes each contain a link to the ID of a PERSON element via a PERSON attribute. Again, this is a good opportunity to use a parameter entity reference:

```
<!ENTITY % personref "PERSON NMTOKEN #REQUIRED">
<!ELEMENT   SPOUSE  EMPTY>
<!ATTLIST   SPOUSE  %personref;>
<!ELEMENT   FATHER  EMPTY>
<!ATTLIST   FATHER  %personref;>
<!ELEMENT   MOTHER  EMPTY>
<!ATTLIST   MOTHER  %personref;>
```

Ideally, the PERSON attribute would have type IDREF. However, as long as the person being identified may reside in another file, the best you can do is require a name token type.

The NAME element may contain any number of REFERENCE elements and zero or one SURNAME and GIVEN elements. Each of these may contain text.

```
<!ELEMENT NAME    (REFERENCE*, GIVEN?, SURNAME?)>
<!ELEMENT GIVEN   (#PCDATA)>
<!ELEMENT SURNAME (#PCDATA)>
The NOTE element may contain an arbitrary amount of text. Some
standard markup would be useful here. The easiest solution is
to adopt the XHTML DTD introduced in Chapter 20, Reading
Document Type Definitions. It's not necessary to rewrite it
all. Simply use a parameter reference entity to import it.
We'll allow each NOTE to contain zero or more REFERENCE
elements and a single body element.<!ENTITY % xhtml SYSTEM
"xhtml/XHTML1-s.dtd">
%xhtml;
<!ELEMENT NOTE    (REFERENCE*, body)>
```

Those three little lines get you the entire HTML 4.0 markup set. There's no need to invent your own. You can use the already familiar and well-supported HTML tag set. I have left out the header, though that would be easy to include — just by replacing body with html in the above. (I left it out because doing so also requires you to include head and title elements, which seemed superfluous here.) This does assume that the file XHTML1-s.dtd can be found at the relative URL xhtml/XHTML1-s.dtd, though that's easy to adjust if you want to put it somewhere else. You could even use the absolute URL at the W3C Web site, http://www.w3.org/TR/xhtml-modularization/DTD/XHTML1-s.dtd, though I prefer not to make my files dependent on the availability of a Web site I don't control. Listing 23-2 shows the complete DTD.

Listing 23-2: **person.dtd: The complete PERSON DTD**

```
<!ELEMENT PERSON ( NAME | REFERENCE | BIRTH | DEATH | BURIAL
                 | BAPTISM | NOTE | FATHER | MOTHER | SPOUSE )* >
<!ATTLIST PERSON ID  ID #REQUIRED>

<!—M means male, F means female —>
<!ATTLIST PERSON SEX (M | F) #IMPLIED>

<!— The ID number of a SOURCE element that documents
    this entry —>
<!ELEMENT REFERENCE  EMPTY>
<!ENTITY % sourceref "SOURCE NMTOKEN #REQUIRED">
<!ATTLIST  REFERENCE %sourceref;>

<!ENTITY % event    "(REFERENCE*, PLACE?, DATE?)">
<!ELEMENT BIRTH    %event;>
<!ELEMENT BAPTISM %event;>
<!ELEMENT DEATH    %event;>
```

```
<!ELEMENT    BURIAL    %event;>

<!ELEMENT    PLACE     (#PCDATA)>
<!ELEMENT    DATE      (#PCDATA)>

<!ENTITY % personref "PERSON NMTOKEN #REQUIRED">
<!ELEMENT    SPOUSE    EMPTY>
<!ATTLIST    SPOUSE    %personref;>
<!ELEMENT    FATHER    EMPTY>
<!ATTLIST    FATHER    %personref;>
<!ELEMENT    MOTHER    EMPTY>
<!ATTLIST    MOTHER    %personref;>

<!ELEMENT    NAME      (GIVEN?, SURNAME?)>
<!ELEMENT    GIVEN     (#PCDATA)>
<!ELEMENT    SURNAME   (#PCDATA)>

<!ENTITY % xhtml SYSTEM "xhtml/XHTML1-s.dtd">
%xhtml;
<!ELEMENT    NOTE      (REFERENCE*, body)>
```

The Family DTD

The next step is to write a DTD for a family. Let's begin with a sample family XML document, as shown in Listing 23-3:

Listing 23-3: An XML document for Samuel English Anderson's family

```
<?xml version="1.0" standalone="no"?>
<!DOCTYPE FAMILY SYSTEM "family.dtd">
<FAMILY>
  <HUSBAND PERSON="p37"/>
  <WIFE    PERSON="p1099"/>
  <CHILD   PERSON="p23"/>
  <CHILD   PERSON="p36"/>
  <CHILD   PERSON="p1033"/>
  <CHILD   PERSON="p1034"/>
  <MARRIAGE>
    <PLACE>Cincinatti, OH</PLACE>
    <DATE>15 Jul 1892</DATE>
  </MARRIAGE>
</FAMILY>
```

All that's needed here are references to the members of the family, not the actual family members themselves. The reference PERSON IDs are once again provided from the database where this information is stored. Their exact values aren't important as long as they're reliably unique and stable.

Now that you've got a sample family, you have to prepare the DTD for all families, like the one shown in Listing 23-4. Don't forget to include items that are needed for some families — even if not for this example — like a divorce. A parameter entity reference will pull in the declarations from the person DTD of Listing 23-2.

Listing 23-4: **family.dtd: A DTD that describes a family**

```
<!ENTITY % person SYSTEM "person.dtd">
%person;

<!ELEMENT FAMILY (REFERENCE*, HUSBAND?, WIFE?, CHILD*,
                  MARRIAGE*, DIVORCE*, NOTE*)>

<!ELEMENT  HUSBAND  EMPTY>
<!ATTLIST  HUSBAND  %personref;>
<!ELEMENT  WIFE     EMPTY>
<!ATTLIST  WIFE     %personref;>
<!ELEMENT  CHILD    EMPTY>
<!ATTLIST  CHILD    %personref;>
<!ELEMENT  DIVORCE  %event;>
<!ELEMENT  MARRIAGE %event;>
```

I'm assuming no more than one HUSBAND or WIFE per FAMILY element. This is a fairly standard assumption in genealogy, even in cultures where plural marriages are common, because it helps to keep the children sorted out. When documenting genealogy in a polygamous society, the same HUSBAND may appear in multiple FAMILY elements. When documenting genealogy in a polyandrous society, the same WIFE may appear in multiple FAMILY elements. Aside from overlapping dates, this is essentially the same procedure that's followed when documenting serial marriages. And of course there's nothing in the DTD that actually requires people to be married in order to have children (any more than there is anything in biology that requires it).

Overall, this scheme is very flexible, much more so than if a FAMILY element had to contain individual PERSON elements rather than merely pointers to them. That would almost certainly require duplication of data across many different elements and files. The only thing this DTD doesn't handle well are same-sex marriages, and that could easily be fixed by changing the FAMILY declaration to the following:

```
<!ELEMENT FAMILY (((HUSBAND, WIFE) | (HUSBAND, HUSBAND?)
                | (WIFE, WIFE?)), MARRIAGE*, DIVORCE*, CHILD*)>
```

Allowing multiple marriages and divorces in a single family may seem a little strange, but it does happen. My mother-in-law married and divorced my father-in-law three separate times. Remarriages to the same person aren't common, but they do happen.

The Source DTD

The third and final top-level element is SOURCE. I'm using a watered-down SOURCE element with little internal structure. However, by storing the DTD in a separate file, it would be easy to add structure to it later. Some typical SOURCE elements look like this:

```
<SOURCE ID="s218">Hamp Hoskins interview, 11-28-1996</SOURCE>
<SOURCE ID="s29">English-Demint Anderson Bible</SOURCE>
<SOURCE ID="s43">Anderson Bible</SOURCE>
<SOURCE ID="s43">
   Letter from R. Foster Adams to Beth Anderson, 1972
</SOURCE>
<SOURCE ID="s66">
   Collin's History of Kentucky, Volume II, p.325, 1840, 1875
</SOURCE>
```

A SOURCE element probably has a lot of internal structure. Work is ongoing in several places to produce a generic DTD for bibliographic information with elements for articles, authors, pages, publication dates, and more. However, this is quite a complex topic when considered in its full generality, and as previously mentioned, it doesn't work quite the same for genealogy as it does for most fields. The individual copy of a family bible or newspaper clipping with handwritten annotations may be more significant than the more generic, standard author, title, publisher data used in most bibliographies.

Because developing an XML application for bibliographies could easily be more than a chapter of its own, and is a task best left to professional librarians, I will satisfy myself with making the SOURCE element contain only character data. It will also have an ID attribute in the form s1, s2, s3, and so forth, so that each source can be referred to by different elements. Listing 23-5 shows the extremely simple DTD for sources.

Listing 23-5: **source.dtd: A simple SOURCE DTD**

```
<!ELEMENT   SOURCE   (#PCDATA)>
<!ATTLIST   SOURCE ID   ID #REQUIRED>
```

The Family Tree DTD

It's now possible to combine the various families, people, and sources into a single grouping that includes everyone. I'll call the root element of this document FAMILY_TREE. It will include PERSON, FAMILY and SOURCE elements in no particular order:

```
<!ELEMENT FAMILY_TREE (PERSON | FAMILY | SOURCE)*>
```

It's not necessary to re-declare the PERSON, FAMILY and SOURCE elements and their children. Instead, these can be imported by importing the family and source DTDs with external parameter entity references. The family DTD then imports the person DTD:

```
<!ENTITY % family SYSTEM "family.dtd">
%family;
<!ENTITY % source SYSTEM "source.dtd">
%source;
```

One thing you want to do at this point is switch from using NMTOKEN types for spouses, parents, and references to actual ID types. This is because a FAMILY element that's part of a FAMILY_TREE should include all necessary PERSON elements. You can do that by overriding the personref and sourceref parameter entity declarations in the DTD for the family tree:

```
<!ENTITY % personref "PERSON IDREF #REQUIRED">
<!ENTITY % sourceref "SOURCE IDREF #REQUIRED">
```

That's all you need. Everything else is contained in the imported person and family DTDs. Listing 23-6 shows the family-tree DTD. Listing 23-7 shows a complete family tree document that includes 11 people, three families, and seven sources.

Listing 23-6: **familytree.dtd: The family-tree DTD**

```
<!ENTITY % personref "PERSON IDREF #REQUIRED">
<!ENTITY % sourceref "SOURCE IDREF #REQUIRED">

<!ENTITY % family SYSTEM "family.dtd">
%family;

<!ENTITY % source SYSTEM "source.dtd">
%source;

<!ELEMENT FAMILY_TREE (SOURCE | PERSON | FAMILY )*>
```

Listing 23-7: An XML document of a complete family tree

```
<?xml version="1.0" standalone="no"?>
<!DOCTYPE FAMILY_TREE SYSTEM "familytree.dtd">
<FAMILY_TREE>

  <PERSON ID="p23" SEX="M">
    <REFERENCE SOURCE="s44"/>
    <FATHER PERSON="p37"/>
    <MOTHER PERSON="p1099"/>
    <NAME>
      <GIVEN>Judson McDaniel</GIVEN>
      <SURNAME>Anderson</SURNAME>
    </NAME>
    <BIRTH>
      <PLACE>Montgomery County, KY, 1893</PLACE>
      <DATE>19 Jul 1894</DATE>
    </BIRTH>
    <DEATH>
      <PLACE>Mt. Sterling, KY</PLACE>
      <DATE>27 Apr 1941</DATE>
    </DEATH>
    <NOTE><body>
      <p>Agriculture College in Iowa</p>
      <p>Farmer</p>
      <p>32nd degree Mason</p>
      <p>
        He shot himself in the pond in the back of Sideview
        when he found that he was terminally ill. It has also
        been claimed that he was having money and wife
        troubles. (He and Zelda did not get along and he was
        embarrassed to have  married her.) It has further been
        claimed that this was part of the Anderson family
        curse.
      </p>
    </body></NOTE>
  </PERSON>

  <PERSON ID="p36" SEX="F">
    <REFERENCE SOURCE="s43"/>
    <FATHER PERSON="p37"/>
    <MOTHER PERSON="p1099"/>
    <NAME>
      <GIVEN>Mary English</GIVEN>
      <SURNAME>Anderson</SURNAME>
    </NAME>
    <BIRTH>
      <PLACE>August 4, 1902?, Sideview, KY</PLACE>
      <DATE>8 Apr 1902</DATE>
    </BIRTH>
    <DEATH>
```

Continued

Listing 23-7 *(continued)*

```
        <PLACE>Mt. Sterling, KY</PLACE>
        <DATE>19 Dec 1972</DATE>
      </DEATH>
  </PERSON>

  <PERSON ID="p37" SEX="M">
    <REFERENCE SOURCE="s29"/>
    <REFERENCE SOURCE="s43"/>
    <FATHER PERSON="p1035"/>
    <MOTHER PERSON="p1098"/>
    <NAME>
      <GIVEN>Samuel English</GIVEN>
      <SURNAME>Anderson</SURNAME>
    </NAME>
    <BIRTH>
      <PLACE>Sideview</PLACE>
      <DATE>25 Aug 1871</DATE>
    </BIRTH>
    <DEATH>
      <PLACE>Mt. Sterling, KY</PLACE>
      <DATE>10 Nov 1919</DATE>
    </DEATH>
    <NOTE>
      <body>
        <p>
          Samuel English Anderson was known in Montgomery
          County for his red hair and the temper that went
          with it. He did once <strong>kill a man</strong>,
          but the court found that it was in self-defense.
        </p>

        <p>
          He was shot by a farm worker whom he had
          fired the day before for smoking in a tobacco barn.
          Hamp says this may have been self-defense, because he
          threatened to kill the workers for smoking in the
          barn. He also says old-time rumors say they mashed
          his head with  a fence post. Beth heard he was cut to
          death with machetes in the field, but Hamp says they
          wouldn't be cutting tobacco in November, only
          stripping it in the barn.
        </p>
      </body>
    </NOTE>

  </PERSON>

  <PERSON ID="p1033" SEX="M">
    <REFERENCE SOURCE="s43"/>
    <FATHER PERSON="p37"/>
    <MOTHER PERSON="p1099"/>
```

```
<NAME>
  <GIVEN>Thomas Corwin</GIVEN>
  <SURNAME>Anderson</SURNAME>
</NAME>
<BIRTH>
  <DATE>16 Jan 1898</DATE>
</BIRTH>
<DEATH>
  <PLACE>Probably Australia</PLACE>
</DEATH>
<NOTE>
  <body><p>
    Corwin fought with his father and then left home.
    His last letter was from Australia.
  </p></body>
</NOTE>
</PERSON>

<PERSON ID="p1034" SEX="M">
  <REFERENCE SOURCE="s43"/>
  <FATHER PERSON="p37"/>
  <MOTHER PERSON="p1099"/>
  <NAME>
    <GIVEN>Rodger French</GIVEN>
    <SURNAME>Anderson</SURNAME>
  </NAME>
  <BIRTH>
    <DATE>26 Nov 1899</DATE>
  </BIRTH>
  <DEATH>
    <PLACE>Birmingham, AL</PLACE>
  </DEATH>
  <NOTE>
    <body><p>
      Killed when the car he was driving hit a pig in the
      road; Despite the many suicides in the family, this is
      the only known sowicide.
    </p></body>
  </NOTE>
</PERSON>

<PERSON ID="p1035" SEX="M">
  <NAME>
    <GIVEN>Thomas Corwin</GIVEN>
    <SURNAME>Anderson</SURNAME>
  </NAME>
  <BIRTH>
    <DATE>24 Aug 1845</DATE>
  </BIRTH>
  <DEATH>
    <PLACE>Mt. Sterling, KY</PLACE>
    <DATE>18 Sep 1889</DATE>
```

Continued

Listing 23-7 *(continued)*

```
      </DEATH>
      <NOTE>
        <body>
          <p>Yale 1869 (did not graduate)</p>
          <p>Breeder of short horn cattle</p>
          <p>He was named after an Ohio senator. The name Corwin
             is from the Latin <i>corvinus</i> which means
        <i>raven</i> and is akin to <i>corbin</i>/<i>corbet</i>.
           In old French it was <i>cord</i> and in Middle English
           <i>Corse</i> which meant <i>raven</i> or <i>cow</i>.
        </p>
          <p>Attended Annapolis for one year, possibly to
             avoid service in the Civil War.</p>
          <p>He farmed the old Mitchell farm
             and became known as a leading short horn breeder.
             He suffered from asthma and wanted to move to
             Colorado in 1876 to avoid the Kentucky weather, but
             he didn't.
             </p>
        </body>
      </NOTE>
    </PERSON>

    <PERSON ID="p1098" SEX="F">
      <REFERENCE SOURCE="s29"/>
      <NAME>
        <GIVEN>LeAnah (Lee Anna, Annie) DeMint</GIVEN>
        <SURNAME>English</SURNAME>
      </NAME>
      <BIRTH>
        <PLACE>Louisville, KY</PLACE>
        <DATE>1 Mar 1843</DATE>
      </BIRTH>
      <DEATH>
        <REFERENCE SOURCE="s16"/>
        <PLACE>acute Bright's disease, 504 E. Broadway</PLACE>
        <DATE>31 Oct 1898</DATE>
      </DEATH>
      <NOTE>
        <body>
          <p>Writer (pseudonymously) for Louisville Herald</p>
          <p>Ann or Annie was from Louisville. She wrote under
             an assumed name for the Louisville Herald.</p>
        </body>
      </NOTE>
    </PERSON>

    <PERSON ID="p1099" SEX="F">
      <REFERENCE SOURCE="s39"/>
      <FATHER PERSON="p1100"/>
      <MOTHER PERSON="p1101"/>
```

```
<NAME>
  <GIVEN>Cora Rucker (Blevins?)</GIVEN>
  <SURNAME>McDaniel</SURNAME>
</NAME>
<BIRTH>
  <DATE>1 Aug 1873</DATE>
</BIRTH>
<DEATH>
  <REFERENCE SOURCE="s41"/>
  <REFERENCE SOURCE="s60"/>
  <PLACE>Sideview, bronchial trouble TB</PLACE>
  <DATE>21 Jul 1909</DATE>
</DEATH>
<NOTE>
  <body>
    <p>She was engaged to General Hood of the Confederacy,
    but she was seeing Mr. Anderson on the side. A servant
    was posted to keep Mr. Anderson away. However the girl
    fell asleep, and Cora eloped with Mr. Anderson.</p>
  </body>
</NOTE>
</PERSON>

<PERSON ID="p1100" SEX="M">
  <NAME>
    <GIVEN>Judson</GIVEN>
    <SURNAME>McDaniel</SURNAME>
  </NAME>
  <BIRTH>
    <DATE>21 Feb 1834</DATE>
  </BIRTH>
  <DEATH>
    <DATE>9 Dec 1905</DATE>
  </DEATH>
</PERSON>

<PERSON ID="p1101" SEX="F">
  <NAME>
    <GIVEN>Mary E.</GIVEN>
    <SURNAME>Blevins</SURNAME>
  </NAME>
  <BIRTH>
    <DATE>1847</DATE>
  </BIRTH>
  <DEATH>
    <DATE>1886</DATE>
  </DEATH>
  <BURIAL>
    <PLACE>Machpelah Cemetery, Mt. Sterling KY</PLACE>
  </BURIAL>
</PERSON>
```

Continued

Listing 23-7 *(continued)*

```xml
<PERSON ID="p1102" SEX="M">
  <REFERENCE SOURCE="s29"/>
  <NAME>
    <GIVEN>John Jay (Robin Adair )</GIVEN>
    <SURNAME>Anderson</SURNAME>
  </NAME>
  <BIRTH>
    <REFERENCE SOURCE="s43"/>
    <PLACE>Sideview</PLACE>
    <DATE>13 May 1873</DATE>
  </BIRTH>
  <DEATH>
    <DATE>18 Sep 1889        </DATE>
  </DEATH>
  <NOTE><body><p>
    Died of flux. Rumored to have been killed by his brother.
  </p></body></NOTE>
</PERSON>

<FAMILY ID="f25">
  <HUSBAND PERSON="p37"/>
  <WIFE PERSON="p1099"/>
  <CHILD PERSON="p23"/>
  <CHILD PERSON="p36"/>
  <CHILD PERSON="p1033"/>
  <CHILD PERSON="p1034"/>
</FAMILY>

<FAMILY ID="f732">
  <HUSBAND PERSON="p1035"/>
  <WIFE PERSON="p1098"/>
  <CHILD PERSON="p1102"/>
  <CHILD PERSON="p37"/>
</FAMILY>

<FAMILY ID="f779">
  <HUSBAND PERSON="p1102"/>
</FAMILY>

<SOURCE ID="s16">newspaper death notice in purse</SOURCE>
<SOURCE ID="s29">English-Demint Anderson Bible</SOURCE>
<SOURCE ID="s39">
  Judson McDaniel &amp; Mary E. Blevins Bible
</SOURCE>
<SOURCE ID="s41">
  Cora McDaniel obituary, clipping from unknown newspaper
</SOURCE>
<SOURCE ID="s43">Anderson Bible</SOURCE>
```

```
<SOURCE ID="s44">
  A Sesquicentenial History of Kentucky
  Frederik A. Wallis &amp; Hambleon Tapp, 1945,
  The Historical Record Association, Hopkinsville, KY
</SOURCE>
<SOURCE ID="s60">
  Interview with Ann Sandusky, May 1996
</SOURCE>

</FAMILY_TREE>
```

Designing a Style Sheet for Family Trees

The family tree document is organized as a data file rather than a narrative. To get a reasonably pleasing view of the document, you're going to need to reorder and reorganize the contents before displaying them. CSS really isn't powerful enough for this task. Consequently, an XSL style sheet is called for.

It's best to begin with the root node. Here the root node is merely replaced by the standard html, head and body elements. Templates are applied to the FAMILY_TREE root element to continue processing.

```
<xsl:template match="/">
  <html>
    <head>
      <title>Family Tree</title>
    </head>
    <body>
      <xsl:apply-templates select="FAMILY_TREE"/>
    </body>
  </html>
</xsl:template>
```

The template rule for the FAMILY_TREE element divides the document into three parts, one each for the families, people, and sources. Templates are applied to each separately:

```
<xsl:template match="FAMILY_TREE">

  <h1>Family Tree</h1>

  <h2>Families</h2>
  <xsl:apply-templates select="FAMILY"/>

  <h2>People</h2>
  <xsl:apply-templates select="PERSON"/>

  <h2>Sources</h2>
```

```
<ul>
 <xsl:apply-templates select="SOURCE"/>
</ul>

</xsl:template>
```

The SOURCE rule is quite simple. Each source is wrapped in a li element. Further-more, its ID is attached using the name attribute of the HTML a element. This allows for cross-references directly to the source, as shown below:

```
<xsl:template match="SOURCE">

<li>
  <xsl:element name="a">
    <xsl:attribute name="name">
      <xsl:value-of select="@ID"/>
    </xsl:attribute>
    <xsl:value-of select="."/>
  </xsl:element>
</li>

</xsl:template>
```

The PERSON element is much more complex so we'll break it up into several tem-plate rules. The PERSON template rule selects the individual parts, and formats those that aren't too complex. It applies templates to the rest. The name is placed in an h3 header. This is surrounded with an HTML anchor whose name is the person's ID. The BIRTH, DEATH, BAPTISM, and BURIAL elements are formatted as list items, as demonstrated below:

```
<xsl:template match="PERSON">

    <h3>
      <xsl:element name="a">
        <xsl:attribute name="name">
          <xsl:value-of select="@ID"/>
        </xsl:attribute>
      <xsl:value-of select="NAME"/>
      </xsl:element>
    </h3>

    <ul>
      <xsl:if test="BIRTH">
        <li>Born: <xsl:value-of select="BIRTH"/></li>
      </xsl:if>
      <xsl:if test="DEATH">
        <li>Died: <xsl:value-of select="DEATH"/></li>
      </xsl:if>
      <xsl:if test="BAPTISM">
```

```
        <li>Baptism: <xsl:value-of select="BAPTISM"/></li>
      </xsl:if>
      <xsl:if test="BURIAL">
        <li>Burial: <xsl:value-of select="BURIAL"/></li>
      </xsl:if>
      <xsl:apply-templates select="FATHER"/>
      <xsl:apply-templates select="MOTHER"/>
    </ul>

    <p>
      <xsl:apply-templates select="NOTE"/>
    </p>

  </xsl:template>
```

The FATHER and MOTHER elements are also list items, but they need to be linked to their respective people. These two template rules do that:

```
<xsl:template match="FATHER">
  <li>
    <xsl:element name="a">
      <xsl:attribute name="href">
        #<xsl:value-of select="@PERSON"/>
      </xsl:attribute>
      Father
    </xsl:element>
  </li>
</xsl:template>

<xsl:template match="MOTHER">
  <li>
    <xsl:element name="a">
      <xsl:attribute name="href">
        #<xsl:value-of select="@PERSON"/>
      </xsl:attribute>
      Mother
    </xsl:element>
  </li>
</xsl:template>
```

The final thing you need to do to format PERSON elements is to copy the contents of the NOTE into the finished document. Since the body of the NOTE uses standard HTML tags that don't need to be changed, an xsl:copy element is useful. The first of these rules copies the body element itself and its contents:

```
<xsl:template match="body | body//*">
  <xsl:copy>
    <xsl:apply-templates select="*|@*|comment()|pi()|text()"/>
  </xsl:copy>
</xsl:template>
```

The template rule for FAMILY elements will list the name and role of each member of the family as a list item in an unordered list. Each member will be linked to the description of that individual. The rules to do this look like the following:

```
<xsl:template match="FAMILY">
  <ul>
    <xsl:apply-templates select="HUSBAND"/>
    <xsl:apply-templates select="WIFE"/>
    <xsl:apply-templates select="CHILD"/>
  </ul>
</xsl:template>

<xsl:template match="HUSBAND">
  <li>Husband: <a href="#{@PERSON}">
    <xsl:value-of select="id(@PERSON)/NAME"/>
  </a></li>
</xsl:template>

<xsl:template match="WIFE">
  <li>Wife: <a href="#{@PERSON}">
    <xsl:value-of select="id(@PERSON)/NAME"/>
  </a></li>
</xsl:template>

<xsl:template match="CHILD">
  <li>Child: <a href="#{@PERSON}">
    <xsl:value-of select="id(@PERSON)/NAME"/>
  </a></li>
</xsl:template>
```

The trickiest thing about these rules is the insertion of data from one element (the PERSON) in a template for different elements (HUSBAND, WIFE, CHILD). The ID of the PERSON stored in the HUSBAND/WIFE/CHILD's PERSON attribute is used to locate the right PERSON element; then its NAME child is selected.

Listing 23-8 is the finished family tree style sheet. Figure 23-2 shows the document after it's been converted into HTML and loaded into Netscape Navigator.

Listing 23-8: **The complete family tree style sheet**

```
<?xml version="1.0"?>
<xsl:stylesheet
xmlns:xsl="http://www.w3.org/XSL/Transform/1.0">

  <xsl:template match="/">
    <html>
      <head>
        <title>Family Tree</title>
      </head>
      <body>
```

```
        <xsl:apply-templates select="FAMILY_TREE"/>
      </body>
  </html>
</xsl:template>

<xsl:template match="FAMILY_TREE">

  <h1>Family Tree</h1>

  <h2>Families</h2>
  <xsl:apply-templates select="FAMILY"/>

  <h2>People</h2>
  <xsl:apply-templates select="PERSON"/>

  <h2>Sources</h2>
  <ul>
   <xsl:apply-templates select="SOURCE"/>
  </ul>

</xsl:template>

<xsl:template match="PERSON">

  <h3>
    <xsl:element name="a">
      <xsl:attribute name="name">
        <xsl:value-of select="@ID"/>
      </xsl:attribute>
    <xsl:value-of select="NAME"/>
    </xsl:element>
  </h3>

  <ul>
    <xsl:if test="BIRTH">
      <li>Born: <xsl:value-of select="BIRTH"/></li>
    </xsl:if>
    <xsl:if test="DEATH">
      <li>Died: <xsl:value-of select="DEATH"/></li>
    </xsl:if>
    <xsl:if test="BAPTISM">
      <li>Baptism: <xsl:value-of select="BAPTISM"/></li>
    </xsl:if>
    <xsl:if test="BURIAL">
      <li>Burial: <xsl:value-of select="BURIAL"/></li>
    </xsl:if>
    <xsl:apply-templates select="FATHER"/>
    <xsl:apply-templates select="MOTHER"/>
  </ul>

  <p>
    <xsl:apply-templates select="NOTE"/>
```

Continued

Listing 23-8 *(continued)*

```
      </p>

  </xsl:template>

  <xsl:template match="FATHER">
    <li>
      <xsl:element name="a">
        <xsl:attribute name="href">
          #<xsl:value-of select="@PERSON"/>
        </xsl:attribute>
        Father
      </xsl:element>
    </li>
  </xsl:template>

  <xsl:template match="MOTHER">
    <li>
      <xsl:element name="a">
        <xsl:attribute name="href">
          #<xsl:value-of select="@PERSON"/>
        </xsl:attribute>
        Mother
      </xsl:element>
    </li>
  </xsl:template>

  <xsl:template match="body | body//*">
    <xsl:copy>
      <xsl:apply-templates
select="*|@*|comment()|pi()|text()"/>
    </xsl:copy>
  </xsl:template>

  <xsl:template match="SOURCE">

    <li>
      <xsl:element name="a">
        <xsl:attribute name="name">
          <xsl:value-of select="@ID"/>
        </xsl:attribute>
        <xsl:value-of select="."/>
      </xsl:element>
    </li>

  </xsl:template>

  <xsl:template match="FAMILY">
    <ul>
      <xsl:apply-templates select="HUSBAND"/>
      <xsl:apply-templates select="WIFE"/>
      <xsl:apply-templates select="CHILD"/>
```

```
      </ul>
    </xsl:template>

    <xsl:template match="HUSBAND">
      <li>Husband: <a href="#{@PERSON}">
        <xsl:value-of select="id(@PERSON)/NAME"/>
      </a></li>
    </xsl:template>

    <xsl:template match="WIFE">
      <li>Wife: <a href="#{@PERSON}">
        <xsl:value-of select="id(@PERSON)/NAME"/>
      </a></li>
    </xsl:template>

    <xsl:template match="CHILD">
      <li>Child: <a href="#{@PERSON}">
        <xsl:value-of select="id(@PERSON)/NAME"/>
      </a></li>
    </xsl:template>

</xsl:stylesheet>
```

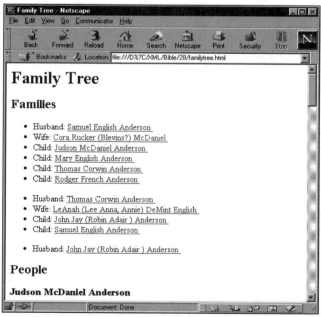

Figure 23-2: The family tree after conversion to HTML

Summary

In this chapter, you saw an XML application for genealogy developed from scratch.
Along the way you have learned:

   ◆ Always begin a new XML application by considering the domain you're
     describing.

   ◆ Try to identify the fundamental elements of the domain. Everything else is
     likely to either be contained in or be an attribute of one of these.

   ◆ Try to avoid including the same data in more than one place. Use ID and
     IDREF attributes to establish pointers from one element to another.

   ◆ Be sure to consider special cases. Don't base your entire design on the most
     obvious cases.

   ◆ Use parameter entities to merge the DTDs for each piece of the XML applica-
     tion into one complete DTD.

This concludes the main body of *XML Bible*. Go forth and write your own XML
applications! The next several parts provide a variety of useful reference
information and the official XML 1.0 Specification.

◆   ◆   ◆

XML Reference Material

This appendix contains XML reference material. It is divided into three main parts:

1. XML BNF Grammar
2. Well-Formedness Constraints
3. Validity Constraints

The XML BNF grammar reference section shows you how to read a BNF Grammar and includes the BNF rules for XML 1.0 and examples of the XML 1.0 productions. The well-formedness constraints reference section explains what a well-formedness constraint is and lists the productions associated with the well-formedness constraints. The validity constraints reference section explains what a validity constraint is and lists and explains all of the validity constraints in the XML 1.0 Standard.

XML BNF Grammar

According to the XML 1.0 specification, an XML document is well-formed if:

1. Taken as a whole it matches the production labeled document.

2. It meets all the well-formedness constraints given in this specification.

3. Each of the parsed entities which is referenced directly or indirectly within the document is well-formed.

This section is designed to help you understand the first of those requirements and more quickly determine whether your documents meet that requirement.

Reading a BNF Grammar

BNF is an abbreviation for Backus-Naur-Form. BNF grammars are an outgrowth of compiler theory. A BNF grammar defines what is and is not a syntactically correct program or, in the case of XML, a syntactically correct document. It is possible to compare a document to a BNF grammar and determine precisely whether it does or does not meet the conditions of that grammar. There are no borderline cases. BNF grammars, properly written, have the advantage of leaving no room for interpretation. The advantage of this should be obvious to anyone who's had to struggle with HTML documents that display in one browser but not in another.

Note   Technically, XML uses an Extended-Backus-Naur-Form grammar, which adds a few pieces not normally found in traditional, compiler-oriented BNF grammars.

Syntactical correctness is a necessary but not sufficient condition for XML documents. A document may strictly adhere to the BNF grammar, and yet fail to be well-formed or valid. For a document to be well-formed, it must also meet all the well-formedness constraints of the XML 1.0 specification. Well-formedness is the minimum level a document may achieve to be parsed. To be valid, a document must also meet all the validity constraints of the XML 1.0 specification. The well-formedness and validity constraints are discussed in the next two sections of this appendix, respectively.

BNF Grammar Parts

A BNF grammar has three parts:

1. A set of literal strings called *terminals*. For example, CDATA, </, <, >, #REQUIRED, and <!ENTITY are all terminals used in the XML 1.0 specification.

2. A set of *non-terminals* to ultimately be replaced by terminals.

3. A list of *productions* or rules that map non-terminals onto particular sequences of terminals and other non-terminals, including one specially identified as the *start* or *document* production.

If you're not a compiler theorist, that list probably could have been written in ancient Etruscan and made about as much sense. Let's see if we can make things clearer with a simple example, before we dive into the complexities of the XML 1.0 grammar.

Consider strings composed of non-negative integers added to or subtracted from each other, like these:

```
9+8+1+2+3
8-1-2-4-5
9+8-9-0+5+3
4
4+3
```

Notice a few things that are not in the list, and that we want to forbid in our grammar:

- ✦ Any character except the digits 0 through 9 and the plus and the minus signs
- ✦ Whitespace
- ✦ A string that begins with a + or a -
- ✦ Numbers less than 0 or greater than 9
- ✦ The empty string

Here's a BNF grammar that defines precisely those strings we want, and none of those we don't want:

```
[1] string ::= digit
[2] digit  ::= '0' | '1' | '2' | '3' | '4' | '5' | '6' | '7'
             | '8' | '9'
[3] string ::= string '+' digit
[3] string ::= string '-' digit
```

Suppose you want to determine whether the string "9+3-2" satisfies this grammar. You begin by looking at the first production. This says that a string is the nonterminal digit. So you move to Production [2] which defines digit. Indeed 9 is one of the terminals listed as a digit. Thus the string "9" is a legitimate string. Production [3] says that a string followed by the plus sign and another digit is also a legitimate string. Thus "9+3" satisfies the grammar. Furthermore, it itself is a string. Production [4] says that a string followed by the minus sign and another digit is a legitimate string. Thus "9+3-2" is a legitimate string and satisfies the grammar.

Now consider the string "-9+1". By Production [1] a string must begin with a digit. This string doesn't begin with a digit, so it's illegal.

The XML 1.0 grammar is much larger and more complicated than this simple grammar. The next section lists its 89 productions. The following section elaborates on each of these productions in detail.

BNF Symbols

In XML's EBNF grammar the following basic symbols are used on the right-hand sides of productions:

#xN	N is a hexadecimal integer, and #xN is the Unicode character with the number N
[a-zA-Z]	matches any character in the specified range
[#xN-#xN]	matches any character in the specified range where N is the hexadecimal value of a Unicode character

`[^a-z]`	matches any character not in the specified range
`[^#xN-#xN]`	matches any character not in the specified range where N is the hexadecimal value of a Unicode character
`[^abc]`	matches any character not in the list
`[^#xN#xN#xN]`	matches any character whose value is not in the list
`'string'`	matches the literal string inside the single quotes
`"string"`	matches the literal string inside the double quotes

These nine basic patterns may be grouped to match more complex expressions:

(*contents*)	the contents of the parentheses are treated as a unit
A?	matches zero or one occurrences of A
A B	matches A followed by B
A | B	matches A or B but not both
A - B	matches any string that matches A and does not match B
A+	matches one or more occurrences of A
A*	matches zero or more occurrences of A

The XML specification also uses three forms you probably won't encounter in non-XML-related specifications:

/* *text of comment* */	This is a comment, and any text inside the comment is ignored.
[WFC: *name*]	This names a well-formedness constraint associated with this production that documents must meet in order to qualify as well-formed. Well-formedness constraints will be found in the specification, but are not encapsulated in the BNF grammar.
[VC: *name*]	This names a validity constraint associated with this production that documents must meet in order to qualify as valid. Validity constraints will be found in the specification, but are not encapsulated in the BNF grammar.

The BNF Rules for XML 1.0

The complete BNF grammar for XML is given in the XML 1.0 specification, which you'll find in Appendix B of this book. However, if you're merely trying to match up your markup against productions in the grammar, it can be inconvenient to flip through the pages hunting for the necessary rules. For that purpose, the BNF rules and only the BNF rules for XML 1.0 are reproduced here.

Document
```
[1] document ::= prolog element Misc*
```

Character Range
```
[2] Char ::= #x9 | #xA | #xD | [#x20-#xD7FF] | [#xE000-#xFFFD]
             | [#x10000-#x10FFFF]
```

White Space
```
[3] S ::= (#x20 | #x9 | #xD | #xA)+
```

Names and Tokens
```
[4] NameChar ::= Letter | Digit | '.' | '-' | '_' | ':'
                 | CombiningChar | Extender
[5] Name     ::= (Letter | '_' | ':') (NameChar)*
[6] Names    ::= Name (S Name)*
[7] Nmtoken  ::= (NameChar)+
[8] Nmtokens ::= Nmtoken (S Nmtoken)*
```

Literals
```
[9]  EntityValue   ::= '"' ([^%&"] | PEReference | Reference)*
                       '"' | "'" ([^%&'] | PEReference
                       | Reference)* "'"
[10] AttValue      ::= '"' ([^<&"] | Reference)* '"'
                       | "'" ([^<&'] | Reference)* "'"
[11] SystemLiteral ::= ('"' [^"]* '"') | ("'" [^']* "'")
[12] PubidLiteral  ::= '"' PubidChar* '"'
                       | "'" (PubidChar - "'")* "'"
[13] PubidChar     ::= #x20 | #xD | #xA | [a-zA-Z0-9]
                       | [-'()+,./:=?;!*#@$_%]
```

Character Data
```
[14] CharData ::= [^<&]* - ([^<&]* ']]>' [^<&]*)
```

Comments
```
[15] Comment ::= '<!-' ((Char - '-')
                 | ('-' (Char - '-')))* '->'
```

Processing Instructions
```
[16] PI ::= '<?' PITarget
               (S (Char* - (Char* '?>' Char*)))? '?>'
[17] PITarget ::= Name - (('X' | 'x') ('M' | 'm') ('L' | 'l'))
```

CDATA Sections

```
[18] CDSect  ::= CDStart CData CDEnd
[19] CDStart ::= '<![CDATA['
[20] CData   ::= (Char* - (Char* ']]>' Char*))
[21] CDEnd   ::= ']]>'
```

Prolog

```
[22] prolog     ::= XMLDecl? Misc* (doctypedecl Misc*)?
[23] XMLDecl    ::= '<?xml' VersionInfo EncodingDecl? SDDecl?
                     S? '?>'
[24] VersionInfo ::= S 'version' Eq (' VersionNum '
                    | " VersionNum ")
[25] Eq         ::= S? '=' S?
[26] VersionNum ::= ([a-zA-Z0-9_.:] | '-')+
[27] Misc       ::= Comment | PI | S
```

Document Type Definition

```
[28] doctypedecl ::= '<!DOCTYPE' S Name (S ExternalID)?
                      S? ('[' (markupdecl | PEReference
                      | S)* ']' S?)? '>'
                      [ VC: Root Element Type ]
[29] markupdecl  ::= elementdecl | AttlistDecl
                     | EntityDecl | NotationDecl | PI
                     | Comment
                     [ VC: Proper Declaration/PE Nesting ]
                     [ WFC: PEs in Internal Subset ]
```

External Subset

```
[30] extSubset ::=    TextDecl? extSubsetDecl
[31] extSubsetDecl ::=   ( markupdecl | conditionalSect |
PEReference | S )*
```

Standalone Document Declaration

```
[32] SDDecl ::= S 'standalone' Eq (("'" ('yes' | 'no')
                "'") | ('"' ('yes' | 'no') '"'))
                [ VC: Standalone Document Declaration ]
```

Language Identification

```
[33] LanguageID ::= Langcode ('-' Subcode)*
[34] Langcode   ::= ISO639Code | IanaCode | UserCode
[35] ISO639Code ::= ([a-z] | [A-Z]) ([a-z] | [A-Z])
[36] IanaCode   ::= ('i' | 'I') '-' ([a-z] | [A-Z])+
[37] UserCode   ::= ('x' | 'X') '-' ([a-z] | [A-Z])+
[38] Subcode    ::= ([a-z] | [A-Z])+
```

Element

```
[39] element ::= EmptyElemTag | STag content ETag
                 [ WFC: Element Type Match ]
                 [ VC: Element Valid ]
```

Start tag

```
[40] STag ::= '<' Name (S Attribute)* S? '>'
              [ WFC: Unique Att Spec ]
[41] Attribute ::= Name Eq AttValue
              [ VC: Attribute Value Type ]
              [ WFC: No External Entity References ]
              [ WFC: No < in Attribute Values ]
```

End Tag

```
[42] ETag ::= '</' Name S? '>'
```

Content of Elements

```
[43] content ::= (element | CharData | Reference | CDSect
                  | PI | Comment)*
```

Tags for Empty Elements

```
[44] EmptyElemTag ::= '<' Name (S Attribute)* S? '/>'
                      [ WFC: Unique Att Spec ]
```

Element Type Declaration

```
[45] elementdecl ::= '<!ELEMENT' S Name S contentspec S? '>'
                     [ VC: Unique Element Type Declaration ]
[46] contentspec ::= 'EMPTY' | 'ANY' | Mixed | children
```

Element-content Models

```
[47] children ::= (choice | seq) ('?' | '*' | '+')?
[48] cp       ::= (Name | choice | seq) ('?' | '*' | '+')?
[49] choice   ::= '(' S? cp ( S? '|' S? cp )* S? ')'
                  [ VC: Proper Group/PE Nesting ]
[50] seq      ::=  '(' S? cp ( S? ',' S? cp )* S? ')'
                  [ VC: Proper Group/PE Nesting ]
```

Mixed-content Declaration

```
[51] Mixed ::= '(' S? '#PCDATA' (S? '|' S? Name)* S? ')*'
             | '(' S? '#PCDATA' S? ')'
        [ VC: Proper Group/PE Nesting ]
        [ VC: No Duplicate Types ]
```

Attribute-list Declaration

```
[52] AttlistDecl ::= '<!ATTLIST' S Name AttDef* S? '>'
[53] AttDef      ::= S Name S AttType S DefaultDecl
```

Attribute Types

```
[54] AttType ::= StringType | TokenizedType | EnumeratedType
[55] StringType ::= 'CDATA'
[56] TokenizedType ::= 'ID' | 'IDREF' | 'IDREFS' | 'ENTITY'
                     | 'ENTITIES' | 'NMTOKEN' | 'NMTOKENS'
            [ VC: ID ]
            [ VC: One ID per Element Type ]
            [ VC: ID Attribute Default ]
            [ VC: IDREF ]
            [ VC: Entity Name ]
            [ VC: Name Token ]
```

Enumerated Attribute Types

```
[57] EnumeratedType ::= NotationType | Enumeration
[58] NotationType   ::= 'NOTATION' S '(' S? Name (S? '|' S?
                        Name)* S? ')'
            [ VC: Notation Attributes ]
[59] Enumeration    ::= '(' S? Nmtoken (S? '|' S? Nmtoken)*
                        S? ')'
            [ VC: Enumeration ]
```

Attribute Defaults

```
[60] DefaultDecl ::= '#REQUIRED' | '#IMPLIED'
                   | (('#FIXED' S)? AttValue)
        [ VC: Required Attribute ]
        [ VC: Attribute Default Legal ]
        [ WFC: No < in Attribute Values ]
        [ VC: Fixed Attribute Default ]
```

Conditional Section

```
[61] conditionalSect    ::=  includeSect | ignoreSect
[62] includeSect        ::=  '<![' S? 'INCLUDE' S? '['
                             extSubsetDecl ']]>'
[63] ignoreSect         ::=  '<![' S? 'IGNORE' S? '['
                             ignoreSectContents* ']]>'
[64] ignoreSectContents ::=  Ignore ('<![' ignoreSectContents
                             ']]>' Ignore)*
[65] Ignore             ::=  Char* - (Char* ('<![' | ']]>') Char*)
```

Character Reference

```
[66] CharRef ::= '&#' [0-9]+ ';' | '&#x' [0-9a-fA-F]+ ';'
           [ WFC: Legal Character ]
```

Entity Reference

```
[67] Reference   ::= EntityRef | CharRef
[68] EntityRef   ::= '&' Name ';'
             [ WFC: Entity Declared ]
             [ VC: Entity Declared ]
             [ WFC: Parsed Entity ]
             [ WFC: No Recursion ]
[69] PEReference ::= '%' Name ';'
             [ VC: Entity Declared ]
             [ WFC: No Recursion ]
             [ WFC: In DTD ]
```

Entity Declaration

```
[70] EntityDecl ::= GEDecl | PEDecl
[71] GEDecl     ::= '<!ENTITY' S Name S EntityDef S? '>'
[72] PEDecl     ::= '<!ENTITY' S '%' S Name S PEDef S? '>'
[73] EntityDef  ::= EntityValue | (ExternalID NDataDecl?)
[74] PEDef      ::= EntityValue | ExternalID
```

External Entity Declaration

```
[75] ExternalID ::=   'SYSTEM' S SystemLiteral
                    | 'PUBLIC' S PubidLiteral S SystemLiteral
[76] NDataDecl  ::= S 'NDATA' S Name
             [ VC: Notation Declared ]
```

Text Declaration

```
[77] TextDecl ::= '<?xml' VersionInfo? EncodingDecl S? '?>'
```

Well-formed External Parsed Entity

```
[78] extParsedEnt ::= TextDecl? content
[79] extPE        ::= TextDecl? extSubsetDecl
```

Encoding Declaration

```
[80] EncodingDecl ::= S 'encoding' Eq ('"' EncName '"'
                      | "'" EncName "'" )
[81] EncName      ::= [A-Za-z] ([A-Za-z0-9._] | '-')*
```

Notation Declarations

```
[82] NotationDecl  ::= '<!NOTATION' S Name S (ExternalID
                       | PublicID) S? '>'
[83] PublicID      ::= 'PUBLIC' S PubidLiteral
```

Characters

```
[84] Letter   ::= BaseChar | Ideographic
[85] BaseChar ::= [#x0041-#x005A] | [#x0061-#x007A]
                | [#x00C0-#x00D6] | [#x00D8-#x00F6]
                | [#x00F8-#x00FF] | [#x0100-#x0131]
                | [#x0134-#x013E] | [#x0141-#x0148]
                | [#x014A-#x017E] | [#x0180-#x01C3]
                | [#x01CD-#x01F0] | [#x01F4-#x01F5]
                | [#x01FA-#x0217] | [#x0250-#x02A8]
                | [#x02BB-#x02C1] | #x0386 | [#x0388-#x038A]
                | #x038C | [#x038E-#x03A1] | [#x03A3-#x03CE]
                | [#x03D0-#x03D6] | #x03DA | #x03DC | #x03DE
                | #x03E0 | [#x03E2-#x03F3] | [#x0401-#x040C]
                | [#x040E-#x044F] | [#x0451-#x045C]
                | [#x045E-#x0481] | [#x0490-#x04C4]
                | [#x04C7-#x04C8] | [#x04CB-#x04CC]
                | [#x04D0-#x04EB] | [#x04EE-#x04F5]
                | [#x04F8-#x04F9] | [#x0531-#x0556] | #x0559
                | [#x0561-#x0586] | [#x05D0-#x05EA]
                | [#x05F0-#x05F2] | [#x0621-#x063A]
                | [#x0641-#x064A] | [#x0671-#x06B7]
                | [#x06BA-#x06BE] | [#x06C0-#x06CE]
                | [#x06D0-#x06D3] | #x06D5 | [#x06E5-#x06E6]
                | [#x0905-#x0939] | #x093D | [#x0958-#x0961]
                | [#x0985-#x098C] | [#x098F-#x0990]
                | [#x0993-#x09A8] | [#x09AA-#x09B0]
                | #x09B2 | [#x09B6-#x09B9] | [#x09DC-#x09DD]
                | [#x09DF-#x09E1] | [#x09F0-#x09F1]
                | [#x0A05-#x0A0A] | [#x0A0F-#x0A10]
```

```
[#x0A13-#x0A28]   |   [#x0A2A-#x0A30]
[#x0A32-#x0A33]   |   [#x0A35-#x0A36]
[#x0A38-#x0A39]   |   [#x0A59-#x0A5C]
#x0A5E  |  [#x0A72-#x0A74]  |  [#x0A85-#x0A8B]
#x0A8D  |  [#x0A8F-#x0A91]  |  [#x0A93-#x0AA8]
[#x0AAA-#x0AB0]   |   [#x0AB2-#x0AB3]
[#x0AB5-#x0AB9]   |   #x0ABD  |  #x0AE0
[#x0B05-#x0B0C]   |   [#x0B0F-#x0B10]
[#x0B13-#x0B28]   |   [#x0B2A-#x0B30]
[#x0B32-#x0B33]   |   [#x0B36-#x0B39]
#x0B3D  |  [#x0B5C-#x0B5D]  |  [#x0B5F-#x0B61]
[#x0B85-#x0B8A]   |   [#x0B8E-#x0B90]
[#x0B92-#x0B95]   |   [#x0B99-#x0B9A]  |  #x0B9C
[#x0B9E-#x0B9F]   |   [#x0BA3-#x0BA4]
[#x0BA8-#x0BAA]   |   [#x0BAE-#x0BB5]
[#x0BB7-#x0BB9]   |   [#x0C05-#x0C0C]
[#x0C0E-#x0C10]   |   [#x0C12-#x0C28]
[#x0C2A-#x0C33]   |   [#x0C35-#x0C39]
[#x0C60-#x0C61]   |   [#x0C85-#x0C8C]
[#x0C8E-#x0C90]   |   [#x0C92-#x0CA8]
[#x0CAA-#x0CB3]   |   [#x0CB5-#x0CB9]  |  #x0CDE
[#x0CE0-#x0CE1]   |   [#x0D05-#x0D0C]
[#x0D0E-#x0D10]   |   [#x0D12-#x0D28]
[#x0D2A-#x0D39]   |   [#x0D60-#x0D61]
[#x0E01-#x0E2E]   |   #x0E30  |  [#x0E32-#x0E33]
[#x0E40-#x0E45]   |   [#x0E81-#x0E82]  |  #x0E84
[#x0E87-#x0E88]   |   #x0E8A  |  #x0E8D
[#x0E94-#x0E97]   |   [#x0E99-#x0E9F]
[#x0EA1-#x0EA3]   |   #x0EA5  |  #x0EA7
[#x0EAA-#x0EAB]   |   [#x0EAD-#x0EAE]  |  #x0EB0
[#x0EB2-#x0EB3]   |   #x0EBD  |  [#x0EC0-#x0EC4]
[#x0F40-#x0F47]   |   [#x0F49-#x0F69]
[#x10A0-#x10C5]   |   [#x10D0-#x10F6]  |  #x1100
[#x1102-#x1103]   |   [#x1105-#x1107]  |  #x1109
[#x110B-#x110C]   |   [#x110E-#x1112]  |  #x113C
#x113E  |  #x1140   |   #x114C  |  #x114E  |  #x1150
[#x1154-#x1155]   |   #x1159  |  [#x115F-#x1161]
#x1163  |  #x1165   |   #x1167  |  #x1169
[#x116D-#x116E]   |   [#x1172-#x1173]  |  #x1175
#x119E  |  #x11A8   |   #x11AB  |  [#x11AE-#x11AF]
[#x11B7-#x11B8]   |   #x11BA  |  [#x11BC-#x11C2]
#x11EB  |  #x11F0   |   #x11F9  |  [#x1E00-#x1E9B]
[#x1EA0-#x1EF9]   |   [#x1F00-#x1F15]
[#x1F18-#x1F1D]   |   [#x1F20-#x1F45]
[#x1F48-#x1F4D]   |   [#x1F50-#x1F57]  |  #x1F59
#x1F5B  |  #x1F5D   |   [#x1F5F-#x1F7D]
[#x1F80-#x1FB4]   |   [#x1FB6-#x1FBC]  |  #x1FBE
[#x1FC2-#x1FC4]   |   [#x1FC6-#x1FCC]
[#x1FD0-#x1FD3]   |   [#x1FD6-#x1FDB]
[#x1FE0-#x1FEC]   |   [#x1FF2-#x1FF4]
[#x1FF6-#x1FFC]   |   #x2126  |  [#x212A-#x212B]
```

```
                         |  #x212E | [#x2180-#x2182] | [#x3041-#x3094]
                         |  [#x30A1-#x30FA] | [#x3105-#x312C]
                         |  [#xAC00-#xD7A3]
[86] Ideographic   ::= [#x4E00-#x9FA5] | #x3007
                     |  [#x3021-#x3029]
[87] CombiningChar ::= [#x0300-#x0345]  | [#x0360-#x0361]
                     |  [#x0483-#x0486]  | [#x0591-#x05A1]
                     |  [#x05A3-#x05B9]  | [#x05BB-#x05BD]
                     |  #x05BF | [#x05C1-#x05C2] | #x05C4
                     |  [#x064B-#x0652]  | #x0670
                     |  [#x06D6-#x06DC]  | [#x06DD-#x06DF]
                     |  [#x06E0-#x06E4]  | [#x06E7-#x06E8]
                     |  [#x06EA-#x06ED]  | [#x0901-#x0903]
                     |  #x093C | [#x093E-#x094C] | #x094D
                     |  [#x0951-#x0954]  | [#x0962-#x0963]
                     |  [#x0981-#x0983]  | #x09BC | #x09BE
                     |  #x09BF | [#x09C0-#x09C4]
                     |  [#x09C7-#x09C8]  | [#x09CB-#x09CD]
                     |  #x09D7 | [#x09E2-#x09E3] | #x0A02
                     |  #x0A3C | #x0A3E | #x0A3F
                     |  [#x0A40-#x0A42]  | [#x0A47-#x0A48]
                     |  [#x0A4B-#x0A4D]  | [#x0A70-#x0A71]
                     |  [#x0A81-#x0A83]  | #x0ABC
                     |  [#x0ABE-#x0AC5]  | [#x0AC7-#x0AC9]
                     |  [#x0ACB-#x0ACD]  | [#x0B01-#x0B03]
                     |  #x0B3C | [#x0B3E-#x0B43]
                     |  [#x0B47-#x0B48]  | [#x0B4B-#x0B4D]
                     |  [#x0B56-#x0B57]  | [#x0B82-#x0B83]
                     |  [#x0BBE-#x0BC2]  | [#x0BC6-#x0BC8]
                     |  [#x0BCA-#x0BCD]  | #x0BD7
                     |  [#x0C01-#x0C03]  | [#x0C3E-#x0C44]
                     |  [#x0C46-#x0C48]  | [#x0C4A-#x0C4D]
                     |  [#x0C55-#x0C56]  | [#x0C82-#x0C83]
                     |  [#x0CBE-#x0CC4]  | [#x0CC6-#x0CC8]
                     |  [#x0CCA-#x0CCD]  | [#x0CD5-#x0CD6]
                     |  [#x0D02-#x0D03]  | [#x0D3E-#x0D43]
                     |  [#x0D46-#x0D48]  | [#x0D4A-#x0D4D]
                     |  #x0D57 | #x0E31 | [#x0E34-#x0E3A]
                     |  [#x0E47-#x0E4E]  | #x0EB1
                     |  [#x0EB4-#x0EB9]  | [#x0EBB-#x0EBC]
                     |  [#x0EC8-#x0ECD]  | [#x0F18-#x0F19]
                     |  #x0F35 | #x0F37 | #x0F39 | #x0F3E
                     |  #x0F3F | [#x0F71-#x0F84]
                     |  [#x0F86-#x0F8B]  | [#x0F90-#x0F95]
                     |  #x0F97 | [#x0F99-#x0FAD]
                     |  [#x0FB1-#x0FB7]  | #x0FB9
                     |  [#x20D0-#x20DC]  | #x20E1
                     |  [#x302A-#x302F]  | #x3099 | #x309A
[88] Digit ::=          [#x0030-#x0039]  | [#x0660-#x0669]
                     |  [#x06F0-#x06F9]  | [#x0966-#x096F]
                     |  [#x09E6-#x09EF]  | [#x0A66-#x0A6F]
```

```
                            │ [#x0AE6-#x0AEF]  │ [#x0B66-#x0B6F]
                            │ [#x0BE7-#x0BEF]  │ [#x0C66-#x0C6F]
                            │ [#x0CE6-#x0CEF]  │ [#x0D66-#x0D6F]
                            │ [#x0E50-#x0E59]  │ [#x0ED0-#x0ED9]
                            │ [#x0F20-#x0F29]
   [89] Extender ::=        │ #x00B7  │  #x02D0  │ #x02D1  │  #x0387
                            │ #x0640  │  #x0E46  │ #x0EC6  │  #x3005
                            │ [#x3031-#x3035]  │ [#x309D-#x309E]
                            │ [#x30FC-#x30FE]
```

Examples of the XML 1.0 Productions

This section shows you some instances of the productions to give you a better idea
of what each one means.

Document

[1] document ::= prolog element Misc*

This rule says that an XML document is composed of a prolog (Production [22]),
followed by a single root element (Production [39]), followed by any number of
miscellaneous items (Production [27]). In other words, a typical structure looks like
this:

```
<?xml version="1.0"?>
<!− a DTD might go here −>
<ROOT_ELEMENT>
   Content
</ROOT_ELEMENT>
<!− comments can go here −>
<?Reader, processing instructions can also go here?>
```

In practice, it's rare for anything to follow the close of the root element.

Production [1] rules out documents with more than one element as a root. For
example,

```
<?xml version="1.0"?>
<ELEMENT1>
   Content
</ELEMENT1>
<ELEMENT2>
   Content
</ELEMENT2>
<ELEMENT1>
   Content
</ELEMENT1>
```

Character Range

[2] Char ::= #x9 | #xA | #xD | [#x20-#xD7FF] | [#xE000-#xFFFD] | [#x10000-#x10FFFF]

Production [2] defines the subset of Unicode characters which may appear in an XML document. The main items of interest here are the characters not included. Specifically, these are the non-printing ASCII control characters of which the most common are the bell, vertical tab, and formfeed; the surrogates block from #xD800 to #xDFFF, and the non-character #xFFFE. The control characters are not needed in XML and may cause problems in files displayed on old terminals or passed through old terminal servers and software.

The surrogates block will eventually be used to extend Unicode to support over one million different characters. However, none of these million plus are currently defined, and XML parsers are not allowed to support them.

The non-character #xFFFE is not defined in Unicode. Its appearance, especially at the start of a document, should indicate that you're reading the document with the wrong byte order; that is little endian instead of big endian or vice versa.

Whitespace

[3] S ::= (#x20 | #x9 | #xD | #xA)+

Production [3] defines whitespace as a run of one or more space characters (#x20), the horizontal tab (#x9), the carriage return (#xD), and the linefeed (#xA). Because of the +, 20 of these characters in a row are treated exactly the same as one.

Other ASCII whitespace characters like the vertical tab (#xB) are prohibited by production [2]. Other non-ASCII, Unicode whitespace characters like the non-breaking space (#A0) are not considered whitespace for the purposes of XML.

Names and Tokens

[4] NameChar ::= Letter | Digit | '.' | '-' | '_' | ':' | CombiningChar | Extender

Production [4] defines the characters that may appear in an XML name. XML names may only contain letters, digits, periods, hyphens, underscores, colons, combining characters, (Production [87]) and extenders (Production [89]).

[5] Name ::= (Letter | '_' | ':') (NameChar)*

Production [5] says an XML name must begin with a letter, an underscore, or a colon. It may not begin with a digit, a period, or a hyphen. Subsequent characters in an XML name may include any XML name character (Production [4]) including digits, periods, and hyphens. The following are acceptable XML names:

```
airplane
text.encoding
r
SEAT
Pilot
Pilot1
OscarWilde
BOOK_TITLE
:TITLE
_8ball
εινουζ
```

These are not acceptable XML names:

```
air plane
.encoding
-r
Wilde,Oscar
BOOK TITLE
8ball
AHA!
```

[6] Names ::= Name (S Name)*

Production [6] defines a group of names as one or more XML names (Production [5]) separated by whitespace. This is a valid group of XML names:

```
BOOK AUTHOR TITLE PAGE EDITOR CHAPTER
```

This is not a valid group of XML names:

```
BOOK, AUTHOR, TITLE, PAGE, EDITOR, CHAPTER
```

[7] Nmtoken ::= (NameChar)+

Production [7] defines a name token as any sequence of one or more name characters. Unlike an XML name, a name token has no restrictions on what the first character is as long as it is a valid name character (Production [4]). In other words, XML name tokens may begin with a digit, a period, or a hyphen while an XML name may not. All valid XML names are valid XML name tokens, but not all valid name tokens are valid XML names.

The following are acceptable name tokens:

```
airplane
text.encoding
r
SEAT
```

```
Pilot
Pilot1
OscarWilde
BOOK_TITLE
:TITLE
_8ball
ειvoυζ
.encoding
-r
8ball
```

The following are not acceptable name tokens:

```
air plane
Wilde,Oscar
BOOK TITLE
AHA!
```

[8] Nmtokens ::= Nmtoken (S Nmtoken)*

Production [8] says a group of name tokens is one or more XML name tokens (Production [7]) separated by whitespace. This is a valid group of XML name tokens:

```
1POTATO 2POTATO 3POTATO 4POTATO
```

This is not a valid group of XML name tokens:

```
1POTATO, 2POTATO, 3POTATO, 4POTATO
```

Literals
[9] EntityValue ::= "" ([^%&"] | PEReference | Reference)* "" | "" ([^%&'] | PEReference | Reference)* ""

Production [9] defines an entity value as any string of characters enclosed in double quotes or single quotes except for %, &, and the quote character (single or double) used to delimit the string. % and & may be used, however, if and only they're the start of a parameter entity reference (Production [69]), general entity reference (Production [67]) or character reference. If you really need to include % and & in your entity values, you can escape them with the character references % and &, respectively.

These are legal entity values:

```
"This is an entity value"
'This is an entity value'
"75&#37; off"
"Ben &amp; Jerry's New York Super Fudge Chunk Ice Cream"
```

These are not legal entity values:

```
"This is an entity value'
'This is an entity value"
"75% off"
"Ben & Jerry's New York Super Fudge Chunk Ice Cream"
'Ben &amp; Jerry's New York Su
```

[10] AttValue ::= "" ([^<&"] | Reference)* "" | "" ([^<&'] | Reference)* ""

Production [10] says that an attribute value may consist of any characters except, <, &, and " enclosed in double quotes or any characters except <, &, and ' enclosed in single quotes. The & may appear, however, only if it's used as the start of a reference (Production [67]) (either general or character).

These are legal attribute values:

```
"This is an attribute value"
'This is an attribute value'
'#FFCC33'
"75% off"
"Ben &amp; Jerry's New York Super Fudge Chunk Ice Cream"
"i &lt; j"
```

These are not legal attribute values:

```
"This is an attribute value'
'This is an attribute value"
"Ben & Jerry's New York Super Fudge Chunk Ice Cream"
'Ben &amp; Jerry's New York Super Fudge Chunk Ice Cream'
"i < j"
```

[11] SystemLiteral ::= ("" [^"]* "") | ("" [^']* "")

Production [11] defines a system literal as any string of text that does not contain the double quote mark enclosed in double quotes. Alternately, a system literal may be any string of text that does not contain the single quote mark enclosed in single quotes. These are grammatical system literals:

```
"test"
" Hello there! "
' Hello
  there!'
"Embedded markup is <OK/> in system literals"
```

These are ungrammatical system literals:

```
" He said, "Get out of here!""
'Bailey's Cove'
```

[12] PubidLiteral ::= "" PubidChar* "" | "" (PubidChar - "")* ""

Production [12] says that a public ID literal is either zero or more public ID characters (Production [13]) enclosed in double quotes or zero or more public ID characters except the single quote mark enclosed in single quotes.

These are grammatical public ID literals:

```
"-//IETF//NONSGML Media Type application/pdf//EN"
'-//IETF//NONSGML Media Type application/pdf//EN'
"-//W3C//DTD XHTML 1.0 Strict + Math//EN"
```

These are ungrammatical public ID literals:

```
"{-//IETF//NONSGML Media Type application/pdf//EN}"
"-//IETF//NONSGML Media Type application/▼__//GR}"
```

[13] PubidChar ::= #x20 | #xD | #xA | [a-zA-Z0-9] | [-'()+,./:=?;!*#@$_%]

Production [13] lists the permissible public ID characters, essentially, the ASCII space, carriage return, and linefeed, the letters *a* through *z* and *A* through *Z*, the digits *0* through *9*, and the punctuation characters -'()+,./:=?;!*#@$_%.

Character Data
[14] CharData ::= [^<&]* - ([^<&]* ']]>' [^<&]*)

Production [14] defines character data as any number of characters except for < and &. Furthermore the CDEnd string]]> may not appear as part of the character data. Character data may contain as few as zero characters.

Comments
[15] Comment ::= '<!—' ((Char - '-') | ('-' (Char - '-')))* '—>'

Production [15] defines a comment as any string of text enclosed between <!- and —> marks with the single exception of the double hyphen -. These are all valid comments:

```
<!—Hello—>
<!—Hello there!—>
<!- Hello there! —>
<!- Hello
     there! —>
<!—<Hello/> <there/>!—>
<!—<Hello/> </there>!—>
```

This is not a legal comment:

```
<!- Hello—there! —>
```

Processing Instructions

[16] PI ::= '<?' PITarget (S (Char* - (Char* '?>' Char*)))? '?>'

Production [16] says that a processing instruction starts with the literal <?, followed by the name of the processing instruction target (Production [17]), optionally followed by whitespace followed by any number of characters except ?>. Finally, the literal ?> closes the processing instruction.

These are all legal processing instructions:

```
<?gcc version="2.7.2" options="-04"?>
<?Terri Do you think this is a good example?>
```

These are not legal processing instructions:

```
<? I have to remember to fix this next part?>
<?Terri This is a good example!>
```

[17] PITarget ::= Name - (('X' | 'x') ('M' | 'm') ('L' | 'l'))

Production [17] says that a processing instruction target may be any XML name (Production [5]) except the string XML (in any combination of case). Thus, these are all acceptable processing instruction targets:

```
gcc
acrobat
Acrobat
Joshua
Acrobat_301
xml-stylesheet
XML_Whizzy_Writer_2000
```

These are not acceptable processing instruction targets:

```
xml
XML
xmL
```

CDATA Sections

[18] CDSect ::= CDStart CData CDEnd

Production [18] states that a CData section is composed of a CDStart (Production [19]), CData (Production [20]), and a CDEnd (Production [21]) in that order.

[19] CDStart ::= '<![CDATA['

Production [19] defines a CDStart as the literal string <![CDATA[and nothing else.

[20] CData ::= (Char* - (Char* ']]>' Char*))

Production [20] says that a CData section may contain absolutely any characters except the CDEnd string]]>.

[21] CDEnd ::= ']]>'

Production [21] defines a CDEnd as the literal string]]> and nothing else.

These are correct CDATA sections:

```
<![CDATA[ The < character starts a tag in XML ]]>
<![CDATA[ CDATA sections begin with the literal <![CDATA[ ]]>
```

This is not a legal CDATA section:

```
<![CDATA[
  The three characters ]]> terminate a CDATA section
]]>
```

Prolog

[22] prolog ::= XMLDecl? Misc* (doctypedecl Misc*)?

Production [22] says that a prolog consists of an optional XML declaration, followed by zero or more miscellaneous items (Production [27]), followed by an optional document type declaration (Production [28]), followed by zero or more miscellaneous items. For instance, this is a legal prolog:

```
<?xml version="1.0"?>
```

This is also a legal prolog:

```
<?xml version="1.0" standalone="yes"?>
<?xml:stylesheet type="text/css" href="greeting.css"?>
<!DOCTYPE greeting [
  <!ELEMENT greeting (#PCDATA)>
]>
```

This is also a legal prolog:

```
<!—This strange document really doesn't have anything
    in its prolog! —>
```

This is not a legal prolog because a comment precedes the XML declaration:

```
<!—This is from the example in Chapter 8 —>
<?xml version="1.0" standalone="yes"?>
```

```
<?xml:stylesheet type="text/css" href="greeting.css"?>
<!DOCTYPE greeting [
  <!ELEMENT greeting (#PCDATA)>
]>
```

[23] XMLDecl ::= '<?xml' VersionInfo EncodingDecl? SDDecl? S? '?>'

Production [23] defines an XML declaration as the literal string `<?xml` followed by a mandatory version info string (Production [24]), optionally followed by an encoding declaration (Production [80]), optionally followed by a standalone document declaration (Production [32]), optionally followed by whitespace, followed by the literal string `?>`. These are legal XML declarations:

```
<?xml version="1.0"?>
<?xml version="1.0" encoding="Big5"?>
<?xml version="1.0" encoding="ISO-8859-1" standalone="yes"?>
<?xml version="1.0" standalone="no"? >
<?xml version="1.0" encoding="ISO-8859-5"?>
```

These are not legal XML declarations:

```
<?xml?>
<?xml encoding="Big5"?>
<?xml version="1.0" standalone="yes"? encoding="ISO-8859-1" >
<?xml version="1.0" standalone="no"? styles="poems.css">
```

[24] VersionInfo ::= S 'version' Eq (' VersionNum ' | " VersionNum ")

Production [24] defines the version info string as whitespace followed by the literal string `version`, followed by an equals sign (Production [25]), followed by a version number enclosed in either single or double quotes. These are legal version info strings:

```
version="1.0"
version='1.0'
version = '1.0'
```

These are ungrammatical version info strings:

```
version='1.0"
"1.0"=version
```

[25] Eq ::= S? '=' S?

Production [25] defines the string `Eq` in the grammar as a stand-in for the equals sign (=) in documents. Whitespace (Production [3]) may or may not appear on either side of the equals sign.

[26] VersionNum ::= ([a-zA-Z0-9_.:] | '-')+

Production [26] says that a version number consists of one or more of the letters a through z, the capital letters A through Z, the underscore, the period, and the hyphen. The following are grammatically correct version numbers:

```
1.0
1.x
1.1.3
1.5EA2
v1.5
EA_B
```

The following are ungrammatical version numbers:

```
version 1.5
1,5
1!1
1 5 3
v 1.5
```

> **Note** The only version number currently used in XML documents is 1.0. This production might as well read:
>
> ```
> VersionNum ::= "1.0"
> ```

[27] Misc ::= Comment | PI | S

Production [27] defines miscellaneous items in an XML document include comments (Production [15]), processing instructions (Production [16]), and whitespace (Production [3]).

Document Type Definition

[28] doctypedecl ::= '<!DOCTYPE' S Name (S ExternalID)? S? ('[' (markupdecl | PEReference | S)* ']' S?)? '>'

Production [28] says that a document type declaration consists of the literal string <!DOCTYPE, followed by whitespace (Production [3]), followed by an XML name (Production [5]), optionally followed by whitespace and an external ID (Production [75]), optionally followed by more whitespace, followed by a left square bracket ([), followed by zero or more markup declarations (Production [29]), parameter entity references (Production [69]), and whitespace, followed by a right square bracket (]) and whitespace, followed by a closing angle bracket.

[29] markupdecl ::= elementdecl | AttlistDecl | EntityDecl | NotationDecl | PI | Comment

Production [29] says that a markup declaration may be either an element declaration (Production [45]), an attribute list declaration (Production [52]), an entity declaration (Production [70]), a notation declaration (Production [82]), a processing instruction (Production [16]), or a comment (Production [15]).

External Subset
[30] extSubset ::= TextDecl? extSubsetDecl

Production [30] says that an external subset consists of an optional text declaration (Production [77]), followed by an external subset declaration (Production [31]). Note that external subsets are merged into the document from the files they reside in before the syntax is checked against the BNF grammar.

[31] extSubsetDecl ::= (markupdecl | conditionalSect | PEReference | S)*

Production [31] says the external subset declaration contains any number of markup declarations (Production [29]), conditional sections (Production [61]), parameter entity references (Production [69]), and whitespace in any order. In essence, the external subset can contain anything the internal DTD can contain.

Standalone Document Declaration
[32] SDDecl ::= S 'standalone' Eq (("" ('yes' | 'no') "") | ('" ('yes' | 'no') '"))

Production [32] says that the standalone document declaration consists of the literal standalone, followed by an equals sign (which may be surrounded by whitespace), followed by one of the two values yes or no enclosed in single or double quotes. Legal standalone document declarations include:

```
standalone="yes"
standalone="no"
standalone='yes'
standalone='no'
standalone="yes"
standalone="no"
```

Language Identification
[33] LanguageID ::= Langcode ('-' Subcode)*

Production [33] defines a language ID as a language code (Production [34]), followed by zero or more hyphens and subcodes (Production [38]).

[34] Langcode ::= ISO639Code I IanaCode I UserCode

Production [34] defines a language code as either an ISO 639 code (Production [35]), an IANA code (Production [36]), or a user code (Production [37]).

[35] ISO639Code ::= ([a-z] I [A-Z]) ([a-z] I [A-Z])

Production [35] defines an ISO 639 code as exactly two small letters from the English alphabet. There are exactly 2704 (52 × 52) grammatical ISO 639 codes including:

```
en
fr
jp
EN
jP
Fr
```

There are an infinite number of strings that aren't grammatical ISO 639 codes including:

```
English
French
Japanese
рчсский
```

[36] IanaCode ::= ('i' I 'I') '-' ([a-z] I [A-Z])+

Production [36] defines an IANA code as the small or capital letter *I* followed by a hyphen, followed by one or more letters from the English alphabet. These are grammatical IANA codes:

```
i-no-bok
i-no-nyn
i-navajo
i-mingo
```

These are not grammatical IANA codes:

```
no-bok
no-nyn
navajo
mingo
i-рчсский
```

[37] UserCode ::= ('x' | 'X') '-' ([a-z] | [A-Z])+

Production [37] defines a user code as the small or capital letter *X* followed by a hyphen, followed by one or more letters from the English alphabet. These are grammatical user codes:

```
x-klingon
X-Elvish
```

These are not grammatical IANA codes:

```
Elvish
xklingon
x-русский
```

[38] Subcode ::= ([a-z] | [A-Z])+

Production [38] defines a subcode as one or more capital or small letters from the English alphabet. These are grammatical subcodes:

```
gb
GreatBritain
UK
uk
```

These are not grammatical subcodes:

```
Great Britain
россия
```

Element

[39] element ::= EmptyElemTag | STag content ETag

Production [39] defines an element as either an empty element tag (production [44]) or a start tag (production [40]), followed by content (production [43]), followed by an end tag (production [42]).

These are legal elements:

```
<P>Hello!</P>
<P/>
<P></P>
```

These are not legal elements:

```
<P>Hello!</p>
<P>
</Q>
```

Start Tag
[40] STag ::= '<' Name (S Attribute)* S? '>'

Production [40] says that a start tag begins with a < followed by an XML name (Production [5]), followed by any number of attributes (Production [41]) separated by whitespace, followed by a closing >. These are some legal start tags:

```
<DOCUMENT>
<докчмент>
<DOCUMENT  >
<DOCUMENT TITLE="The Red Badge of Courage" >
<DOCUMENT TITLE="The Red Badge of Courage" PAGES="129">
```

These are not legal start tags:

```
< DOCUMENT>
< >
<12091998>
```

[41] Attribute ::= Name Eq AttValue

Production [41] says that an attribute consists of an XML name (Production [5]), followed by an equals sign (which may be encased in whitespace) followed by an attribute value (Production [10]). Grammatical attributes include:

```
TITLE="The Red Badge of Courage"
PAGES="129"
TITLE = "The Red Badge of Courage"
PAGES = "129"
TITLE='The Red Badge of Courage'
PAGES='129'
SENTENCE='Jim said, "I didn&apos;t expect to see you here."'
```

Ungrammatical attributes include:

```
TITLE="The Red Badge of Courage'
PAGES=129
SENTENCE='Then Jim said, "I didn't expect to see you here."'
```

End Tag
[42] ETag ::= '</' Name S? '>'

Production [42] defines an end tag as the literal string </ immediately followed by an XML name, optionally followed by whitespace, followed by the > character. For example, these are grammatical XML end tags:

```
</PERSON>
</PERSON >
</AbrahamLincoln>
</докчмент>
```

These are not grammatical XML end tags:

```
</ PERSON>
</Abraham Lincoln>
</PERSON NAME="Abraham Lincoln">
</>
```

Content of Elements
[43] content ::= (element | CharData | Reference | CDSect | PI | Comment)*

Production [43] defines content as any number of elements (Production [39]), character data (Production [14]), references (Production [67]), CDATA sections (Production [18]), processing instructions (Production [16]), and comments (Production [15]) in any order. This production lists everything that can appear inside an element.

Tags for Empty Elements
[44] EmptyElemTag ::= '<' Name (S Attribute)* S? '/>'

Production [44] defines an empty element tag as the character <, followed by an XML name, followed by whitespace, followed by zero more attributes separated from each other by whitespace, optionally followed by whitespace, followed by the literal />. These are some grammatical empty tags:

```
<PERSON/>
<PERSON />
<Person/>
<person />
<AbrahamLincoln/>
<чепоВек/>
```

These are ungrammatical as empty tags:

```
< PERSON/>
<PERSON>
</Person>
</person/>
</>
```

(The second and third are grammatical start and end tags respectively.)

Element Type Declaration
[45] elementdecl ::= '<!ELEMENT' S Name S contentspec S? '>'

Production [45] says that an element declaration consists of the literal <!ELEMENT, followed by whitespace, followed by an XML name (Production [5]), followed by a content specification (Production [46]), optionally followed by whitespace, followed by the > character.

Grammatical element declarations include:

```
<!ELEMENT DOCUMENT ANY>
<!ELEMENT HR EMPTY>
<!ELEMENT DOCUMENT (#PCDATA | P | H)>
```

[46] contentspec ::= 'EMPTY' | 'ANY' | Mixed | children

Production [46] defines a content specification as either the literals EMPTY or ANY, a list of children (Production [47]) or mixed content (Production [51]).

Element-content Models
[47] children ::= (choice | seq) ('?' | '*' | '+')?

Production [47] says that a list of children consists of either a choice (Production [49]) or a sequence (Production [50]) optionally followed by one of the characters ?, *, or +.

[48] cp ::= (Name | choice | seq) ('?' | '*' | '+')?

Production [48] defines a content particle as an XML name (Production [5]), choice, (Production [49]), or sequence (Production [50], optionally suffixed with a ?, *, or +.

[49] choice ::= '(' S? cp (S? '|' S? cp)* S? ')'

Production [49] says that a choice is one or more content particles (Production [48]) enclosed in parentheses and separated from each other by vertical bars and optional whitespace. Grammatical choices include:

```
(P | UL | H1 | H2 | H3 | H4 | H5 | BLOCKQUOTE | PRE | HR | DIV)
(P|UL|H1|H2|H3|H4|H5|H6|BLOCKQUOTE|PRE|HR|DIV)
(SON | DAUGHTER)
( SON | DAUGHTER )
(ADDRESS | (NAME, STREET, APT, CITY, STATE, ZIP))
```

[50] seq ::=   '(' S? cp (S? ',' S? cp)* S? ')'

Production [50] says that a sequence is one or more content particles (Production [48]) enclosed in parentheses and separated from each other by commas and optional whitespace. Grammatical sequences include:

```
(NAME, STREET, APT, CITY, STATE, ZIP)
(NAME , STREET , APT , CITY , STATE , ZIP)
(NAME,STREET,APT,CITY,STATE,ZIP)
( NAME,STREET,APT, CITY,STATE,ZIP )
(NAME, (STREET|BOX), (APT|SUITE), CITY, STATE, ZIP, COUNTRY?)
(NAME)
```

Mixed-content Declaration

[51] Mixed ::= '(' S? '#PCDATA' (S? '|' S? Name)* S? ')*' | '(' S? '#PCDATA' S? ')'

Production [51] says that mixed content is either the literal (#PCDATA) (with allowances for optional whitespace) or a choice that includes the literal #PCDATA as its first content particle. These are some grammatical mixed-content models:

```
(#PCDATA)
( #PCDATA )
(#PCDATA | PERSON)
( #PCDATA | PERSON )
( #PCDATA | TITLE | JOURNAL | MONTH | YEAR | SERIES | VOLUME )
```

These are ungrammatical mixed content models:

```
(PERSON | #PCDATA)
(#PCDATA, TITLE, #PCDATA, JOURNAL, MONTH, YEAR, #PCDATA)
(#PCDATA | (NAME, STREET, APT, CITY, STATE, ZIP))
```

Attribute-list Declaration

[52] AttlistDecl ::= '<!ATTLIST' S Name AttDef* S? '>'

Production [52] says that an attribute list declaration consists of the literal <!ATTLIST, followed by whitespace, followed by an XML name (Production [5]), followed by zero or more attribute definitions (Production [53]), optionally followed by whitespace, followed by the > character.

Grammatical attribute list declarations include:

```
<!ATTLIST IMG ALT CDATA #REQUIRED>
<!ATTLIST AUTHOR EXTENSION CDATA #IMPLIED>
<!ATTLIST AUTHOR COMPANY   CDATA #FIXED "TIC">
<!ATTLIST P VISIBLE (TRUE | FALSE) "TRUE">
<!ATTLIST ADDRESS STATE NMTOKEN #REQUIRED>
<!ATTLIST ADDRESS STATES NMTOKENS #REQUIRED>
<!ATTLIST P PNUMBER ID #REQUIRED>
<!ATTLIST PERSON FATHER IDREF #IMPLIED>
<!ATTLIST SLIDESHOW SOURCES ENTITIES #REQUIRED>
<!ATTLIST SOUND PLAYER NOTATION (MP) #REQUIRED>
```

[53] AttDef ::= S Name S AttType S DefaultDecl

Production [53] defines an attribute definition as whitespace, an XML name
(Production [5]), more whitespace, an attribute type (Production [54]), more
whitespace, and a default declaration (Production [60]). Grammatical attribute
definitions include:

```
IMG ALT CDATA #REQUIRED
AUTHOR EXTENSION CDATA #IMPLIED
AUTHOR COMPANY   CDATA #FIXED "TIC"
P VISIBLE (TRUE | FALSE) "TRUE"
ADDRESS STATE NMTOKEN #REQUIRED
ADDRESS STATES NMTOKENS #REQUIRED
P PNUMBER ID #REQUIRED
PERSON FATHER IDREF #IMPLIED
SLIDESHOW SOURCES ENTITIES #REQUIRED
SOUND PLAYER NOTATION (MP) #REQUIRED
```

Attribute Types

[54] AttType ::= StringType | TokenizedType | EnumeratedType

Production [54] defines an attribute type as either a string type (Production [55]), a
tokenized type (Production [56]), or an enumerated type (Production [57]).

[55] StringType ::= 'CDATA'

Production [55] defines a string type as the literal CDATA.

[56] TokenizedType ::= 'ID' | 'IDREF' | 'IDREFS' | 'ENTITY' | 'ENTITIES' | 'NMTOKEN' | 'NMTOKENS'

Production [56] defines TokenizedType as any one of theses seven literals:

```
ID
IDREF
IDREFS
```

```
ENTITY
ENTITIES
NMTOKEN
NMTOKENS
```

Enumerated Attribute Types

[57] EnumeratedType ::= NotationType | Enumeration

Production [57] defines an enumerated type as either a notation type (Production [58]) or an enumeration (Production [59]).

[58] NotationType ::= 'NOTATION' S '(' S? Name (S? '|' S? Name)* S? ')'

Production [58] defines a notation type as the literal NOTATION, followed by whitespace, followed by one or more XML names (Production [5]), separated by vertical bars, and enclosed in parentheses. These are some grammatical notation types:

```
NOTATION (MP)
NOTATION (MP | PDF)
NOTATION (mp | gcc | xv)
NOTATION (A | B | C)
```

These are some ungrammatical notation types:

```
NOTATION ("MP")
NOTATION (MP PDF)
NOTATION (mp, gcc, xv)
NOTATION ("A" "B" "C")
```

[59] Enumeration ::= '(' S? Nmtoken (S? '|' S? Nmtoken)* S? ')'

Production [59] defines an enumeration as one or more XML name tokens (Production [7]) separated by vertical bars and enclosed in parentheses. These are some grammatical enumerations:

```
(airplane)
(airplane | train | car | horse)
( airplane | train | car | horse )
(cavalo | carro | trem |avi⁻o)
(A | B | C | D | E | F | G | H)
```

The following are not acceptable enumerations:

```
()
(airplane train car horse)
(A, B, C, D, E, F, G, H)
airplane | train | car | horse
```

Attribute Defaults

[60] DefaultDecl ::= '#REQUIRED' | '#IMPLIED' | (('#FIXED' S)? AttValue)

Production [60] defines the default declaration as one of these four things:

✦ the literal #REQUIRED

✦ the literal #IMPLIED

✦ the literal #FIXED followed by whitespace (Production [3]), followed by an attribute value (Production [10])

✦ an attribute value (Production [10])

Conditional Section

[61] conditionalSect ::= includeSect | ignoreSect

Production [61] defines a conditional section as either an include section (Production [62]) or an ignore section (Production [63]).

[62] includeSect ::= '<![' S? 'INCLUDE' S? '[' extSubsetDecl ']]>'

Production [62] defines an include section as an external subset declaration (Production [31]) sandwiched between <![INCLUDE[ ]]>, modulo whitespace. These are grammatical include sections:

```
<![ INCLUDE [ ]]>
<![INCLUDE[ ]]>
<![ INCLUDE[ ]]>
```

[63] ignoreSect ::= '<![' S? 'IGNORE' S? '[' ignoreSectContents* ']]>'

Production [63] defines an ignore section as ignore section contents (Production [64]) sandwiched between <![IGNORE[ ]]>, modulo whitespace. These are grammatical ignore sections:

```
<![ IGNORE [ ]]>
<![IGNORE[ ]]>
<![ IGNORE[ ]]>
```

[64] ignoreSectContents ::= Ignore ('<![' ignoreSectContents ']]>' Ignore)*

Production [64] defines an ignore section contents as an ignore block (Production [65]), optionally followed by a block of text sandwiched between <![and]]> literals, followed by more text. This may be repeated as many times as desired. This allows ignore sections to nest.

[65] Ignore ::= Char* - (Char* ('<![' | ']]>') Char*)

Production 65 defines an ignore block as any run of text that contains neither the <![or]]> literals. This prevents any possible confusion about where an ignore block ends.

Character Reference
[66] CharRef ::= '&#' [0-9]+ ';' | '&#x' [0-9a-fA-F]+ ';'

Production [66] defines two forms for character references. The first is the literal &# followed by one or more of the ASCII digits 0 through 9. The second form is the literal &#x followed by one or more of the hexadecimal digits 0 through F. The digits representing 10 through 16 (A through F) may be either lower- or uppercase.

Entity Reference
[67] Reference ::= EntityRef | CharRef

Production [67] defines a reference as either an entity reference (Production [68]) or a character reference (Production [66]).

[68] EntityRef ::= '&' Name ';'

Production [68] defines an entity reference as an XML name (Production [5]) sandwiched between the ampersand character and a semicolon. These are grammatical entity references:

```
&amp;
&agrave;
&my_abbreviation;
```

These are ungrammatical entity references:

```
&amp
& agrave ;
& my_abbreviation;
```

[69] PEReference ::= '%' Name ';'

Production [69] defines a parameter entity reference as an XML name (Production [5]) sandwiched between the percent character and a semicolon. These are grammatical parameter entity references:

```
%inlines;
%mathml;
%MyElements;
```

These are ungrammatical parameter entity references:

```
%inlines
% mathml ;
%my elements;
```

Entity Declaration

[70] EntityDecl ::= GEDecl | PEDecl

Production [70] defines an entity declaration as either a general entity declaration (Production [71]) or a parameter entity declaration (Production [71]).

[71] GEDecl ::= '<!ENTITY' S Name S EntityDef S? '>'

Production [71] defines a general entity declaration as the literal `<!ENTITY` followed by whitespace (Production [3]), followed by an XML name (Production [5]), followed by an entity definition (Production [73]), optionally followed by whitespace, followed by the `>` character. These are some grammatical general entity declarations:

```
<!ENTITY alpha "&#945;">
<!ENTITY Alpha "&#913;">
<!ENTITY SPACEMUSIC SYSTEM "/sounds/space.wav" NDATA MP >
<!ENTITY LOGO SYSTEM "logo.gif">
<!ENTITY COPY99 "Copyright 1999 %erh;">
```

These are some ungrammatical general entity declarations:

```
<!ENTITY alpha &#945;>
<!ENTITY Capital Greek Alpha "&#913;">
<!ENTITY LOGO SYSTEM logo.gif>
```

[72] PEDecl ::= '<!ENTITY' S '%' S Name S PEDef S? '>'

Production [72] defines a parameter entity declaration as the literal `<!ENTITY` followed by whitespace (Production [3]), followed by a percent sign and more whitespace, followed by an XML name (Production [5]), followed by an entity definition (Production [73]), optionally followed by whitespace, followed by the `>` character. In essence this says that parameter entity declarations are the same as general entity declarations except for the `%` between the `<!ENTITY` and the name. These are some grammatical parameter entity declarations:

```
<!ENTITY % fulldtd "IGNORE">
<!ENTITY % ERH "Elliotte Rusty Harold">
<!ENTITY % inlines
   "(person | degree | model | product | animal | ingredient)*">
```

These are some ungrammatical parameter entity declarations:

```
<!ENTITY %fulldtd; "IGNORE">
<!ENTITY % ERH  Elliotte Rusty Harold>
<!ENTITY % inlines
   "(person | degree | model | product | animal | ingredient)*'>
```

[73] EntityDef ::= EntityValue | (ExternalID NDataDecl?)

Production [73] says that an entity definition is either an entity value (Production [9]) or an external ID (Production [75]) followed by an NData declaration (Production [76]).

[74] PEDef ::= EntityValue | ExternalID

Production [74] says that the definition of a parameter entity may be either an entity value (Production [9]) or an external ID (Production [75]).

External Entity Declaration

[75] ExternalID ::= 'SYSTEM' S SystemLiteral | 'PUBLIC' S PubidLiteral S SystemLiteral

Production [75] defines an external ID as either the keyword SYSTEM followed by whitespace and a system literal (Production [11]) or the keyword PUBLIC followed by whitespace, a public ID literal (Production [12]), more whitespace, and a system literal (Production [11]). These are some grammatical external IDs:

```
SYSTEM "logo.gif"
SYSTEM "/images/logo.gif"
SYSTEM "http://www.idgbooks.com/logo.gif"
SYSTEM "../images/logo.gif"
PUBLIC "-//IETF//NONSGML Media Type image/gif//EN"
       "http://www.isi.edu/in-notes/iana/assignments/media-
types/image/gif"
```

These are some ungrammatical external IDs:

```
SYSTEM logo.gif
SYSTEM "/images/logo.gif'
SYSTEM http://www.idgbooks.com/logo.gif
PUBLIC "-//IETF//NONSGML Media Type image/gif//EN"
PUBLIC "http://www.isi.edu/in-notes/iana/assignments/media-
types/image/gif"
```

[76] NDataDecl ::= S 'NDATA' S Name

Production [76] defines an NData declaration as whitespace (Production [3]), followed by the NDATA literal, followed by whitespace, followed by an XML name (Production [5]). For example:

```
NDATA PDF
NDATA MIDI
```

Text Declaration

[77] TextDecl ::= '<?xml' VersionInfo? EncodingDecl S? '?>'

Production [77] says that a text declaration looks almost like an XML declaration (Production [23]) except that it may not have a standalone document declaration (Production [32]). These are grammatical text declarations:

```
<?xml version="1.0"?>
<?xml version="1.0" encoding="Big5"?>
<?xml version="1.0" encoding="ISO-8859-5"?>
```

These are not grammatical text declarations:

```
<?xml?>
<?xml encoding="Big5"?>
<?xml encoding="Big5" version="1.0" ?>
<?xml version="1.0" standalone="yes"? encoding="ISO-8859-1" >
<?xml version="1.0" styles="poems.css">
<?xml version="1.0" encoding="ISO-8859-1" standalone="yes"?>
<?xml version="1.0" standalone="no"? >
```

Well-formed External Parsed Entity

[78] extParsedEnt ::= TextDecl? content

Production [78] says that an external general parsed entity consists of an optional text declaration followed by content (Production [43]). The main point of this production is that the content may not include a DTD or any markup declarations.

[79] extPE ::= TextDecl? extSubsetDecl

Production [79] says that an external parameter entity consists of an optional text declaration followed by an external subset declaration (Production [31]).

Encoding Declaration

[80] EncodingDecl ::= S 'encoding' Eq ('"' EncName '"' | "'" EncName "'")

Production [80] defines an encoding declaration as whitespace (Production [3]), followed by the string "encoding" followed by an equals sign (Production [25]), followed by the name of the encoding (Production [81]) enclosed in either single or double quotes. These are all legal encoding declarations:

```
encoding="Big5"
encoding="ISO-8859-5"
encoding = "Big5"
encoding = "ISO-8859-5"
encoding= 'Big5'
encoding= 'ISO-8859-5'
```

These are not legal encoding declarations:

```
encoding "Big5"
encoding="ISO-8859-51'
encoding = "Big5
encoding = 'ISO-8859-5"
```

[81] EncName   ::= [A-Za-z] ([A-Za-z0-9._] | '-')*

Production [81] says the name of an encoding begins with one of the ASCII letters *A* through *Z* or *a* through *z*, followed by any number of ASCII letters, digits, periods, underscores, and hyphens. These are legal encoding names:

```
ISO-8859-1
Big5
GB2312
```

These are ungrammatical encoding names:

```
ISO 8859-1
Big5 Chinese
GB 2312
Eλor851
```

Notation Declarations

[82] NotationDecl ::= '<!NOTATION' S Name S (ExternalID | PublicID) S? '>'

Production [82] defines a notation declaration as the literal string "<!NOTATION", followed by whitespace (Production [3]), followed by an XML name (Production[5]) for the notation, followed by whitespace, followed by either an external ID (Production [75]) or a public ID (Production [83]), optionally followed by whitespace, followed by the literal string ">". These are grammatical notation declarations:

```
<!NOTATION GIF SYSTEM "image/gif">
<!NOTATION GIF SYSTEM "image/gif" >
<!NOTATION GIF PUBLIC
    "-//IETF//NONSGML Media Type image/gif//EN"
    "http://www.isi.edu/in-notes/iana/assignments/media-
types/image/gif">
```

These are not grammatical notation declarations:

```
<! NOTATION GIF SYSTEM "image/gif" >
< !NOTATION GIF SYSTEM "image/gif" >
<!NOTATION GIF "image/gif">
<!NOTATION GIF SYSTEM image/gif>
<!NOTATION GIF PUBLIC
   "http://www.isi.edu/in-notes/iana/assignments/media-
types/image/gif">
```

[83] PublicID ::= 'PUBLIC' S PubidLiteral

Production [83] defines a public ID as the literal string PUBLIC, followed by whitespace (Production [3]), followed by a public ID literal (Production [12]). These are grammatical public IDs:

```
PUBLIC "-//IETF//NONSGML Media Type image/gif//EN"
PUBLIC "ISO 8879:1986//ENTITIES Added Latin 1//EN//XML"
```

These are ungrammatical public IDs:

```
PUBLIC -//IETF//NONSGML Media Type image/gif//EN
PUBLIC 'ISO 8879:1986//ENTITIES Added Latin 1//EN//XML"
```

Characters

[84] Letter ::= BaseChar | Ideographic

Production [84] defines a letter as either a base character or an ideographic character.

[85] BaseChar ::= [#x0041-#x005A] | [#x0061-#x007A] | [#x00C0-#x00D6] | [#x00D8-#x00F6] | [#x00F8-#x00FF] | [#x0100-#x0131] | [#x0134-#x013E] | [#x0141-#x0148] | [#x014A-#x017E] | [#x0180-#x01C3] | [#x01CD-#x01F0] | [#x01F4-#x01F5] | [#x01FA-#x0217] | [#x0250-#x02A8] | [#x02BB-#x02C1] | #x0386 | [#x0388-#x038A] | #x038C | [#x038E-#x03A1] | [#x03A3-#x03CE] | [#x03D0-#x03D6] | #x03DA | #x03DC | #x03DE | #x03E0 | [#x03E2-#x03F3] | [#x0401-#x040C] | [#x040E-#x044F] | [#x0451-#x045C] | [#x045E-#x0481] | [#x0490-#x04C4] | [#x04C7-#x04C8] | [#x04CB-#x04CC] | [#x04D0-#x04EB] | [#x04EE-#x04F5] | [#x04F8-#x04F9] | [#x0531-#x0556] | #x0559 | [#x0561-#x0586] | [#x05D0-#x05EA] | [#x05F0-#x05F2] | [#x0621-#x063A] | [#x0641-#x064A] | [#x0671-#x06B7] | [#x06BA-#x06BE] | [#x06C0-#x06CE] | [#x06D0-#x06D3] | #x06D5 | [#x06E5-#x06E6] | [#x0905-#x0939] | #x093D | [#x0958-#x0961] | [#x0985-#x098C] | [#x098F-#x0990] | [#x0993-#x09A8] | [#x09AA-#x09B0] | #x09B2 | [#x09B6-#x09B9] | [#x09DC-#x09DD] | [#x09DF-#x09E1] | [#x09F0-#x09F1] | [#x0A05-#x0A0A] | [#x0A0F-#x0A10] | [#x0A13-#x0A28] | [#x0A2A-#x0A30] | [#x0A32-#x0A33] | [#x0A35-#x0A36] |

[#x0A38-#x0A39] | [#x0A59-#x0A5C] | #x0A5E | [#x0A72-#x0A74] | [#x0A85-#x0A8B] | #x0A8D | [#x0A8F-#x0A91] | [#x0A93-#x0AA8] | [#x0AAA-#x0AB0] | [#x0AB2-#x0AB3] | [#x0AB5-#x0AB9] | #x0ABD | #x0AE0 | [#x0B05-#x0B0C] | [#x0B0F-#x0B10] | [#x0B13-#x0B28] | [#x0B2A-#x0B30] | [#x0B32-#x0B33] | [#x0B36-#x0B39] | #x0B3D | [#x0B5C-#x0B5D] | [#x0B5F-#x0B61] | [#x0B85-#x0B8A] | [#x0B8E-#x0B90] | [#x0B92-#x0B95] | [#x0B99-#x0B9A] | #x0B9C | [#x0B9E-#x0B9F] | [#x0BA3-#x0BA4] | [#x0BA8-#x0BAA] | [#x0BAE-#x0BB5] | [#x0BB7-#x0BB9] | [#x0C05-#x0C0C] | [#x0C0E-#x0C10] | [#x0C12-#x0C28] | [#x0C2A-#x0C33] | [#x0C35-#x0C39] | [#x0C60-#x0C61] | [#x0C85-#x0C8C] | [#x0C8E-#x0C90] | [#x0C92-#x0CA8] | [#x0CAA-#x0CB3] | [#x0CB5-#x0CB9] | #x0CDE | [#x0CE0-#x0CE1] | [#x0D05-#x0D0C] | [#x0D0E-#x0D10] | [#x0D12-#x0D28] | [#x0D2A-#x0D39] | [#x0D60-#x0D61] | [#x0E01-#x0E2E] | #x0E30 | [#x0E32-#x0E33] | [#x0E40-#x0E45] | [#x0E81-#x0E82] | #x0E84 | [#x0E87-#x0E88] | #x0E8A | #x0E8D | [#x0E94-#x0E97] | [#x0E99-#x0E9F] | [#x0EA1-#x0EA3] | #x0EA5 | #x0EA7 | [#x0EAA-#x0EAB] | [#x0EAD-#x0EAE] | #x0EB0 | [#x0EB2-#x0EB3] | #x0EBD | [#x0EC0-#x0EC4] | [#x0F40-#x0F47] | [#x0F49-#x0F69] | [#x10A0-#x10C5] | [#x10D0-#x10F6] | #x1100 | [#x1102-#x1103] | [#x1105-#x1107] | #x1109 | [#x110B-#x110C] | [#x110E-#x1112] | #x113C | #x113E | #x1140 | #x114C | #x114E | #x1150 | [#x1154-#x1155] | #x1159 | [#x115F-#x1161] | #x1163 | #x1165 | #x1167 | #x1169 | [#x116D-#x116E] | [#x1172-#x1173] | #x1175 | #x119E | #x11A8 | #x11AB | [#x11AE-#x11AF] | [#x11B7-#x11B8] | #x11BA | [#x11BC-#x11C2] | #x11EB | #x11F0 | #x11F9 | [#x1E00-#x1E9B] | [#x1EA0-#x1EF9] | [#x1F00-#x1F15] | [#x1F18-#x1F1D] | [#x1F20-#x1F45] | [#x1F48-#x1F4D] | [#x1F50-#x1F57] | #x1F59 | #x1F5B | #x1F5D | [#x1F5F-#x1F7D] | [#x1F80-#x1FB4] | [#x1FB6-#x1FBC] | #x1FBE | [#x1FC2-#x1FC4] | [#x1FC6-#x1FCC] | [#x1FD0-#x1FD3] | [#x1FD6-#x1FDB] | [#x1FE0-#x1FEC] | [#x1FF2-#x1FF4] | [#x1FF6-#x1FFC] | #x2126 | [#x212A-#x212B] | #x212E | [#x2180-#x2182] | [#x3041-#x3094] | [#x30A1-#x30FA] | [#x3105-#x312C] | [#xAC00-#xD7A3]

Production [85] lists the base characters. These are the defined Unicode characters that are alphabetic but not punctuation marks or digits. For instance, A-Z and a-z are base characters but 0-9 and !, ", #, $, and so forth, are not. This list is so long because it contains characters from not only the English alphabet but also Greek, Hebrew, Arabic, Cyrillic, and all the other alphabetic scripts Unicode supports.

[86] Ideographic ::= [#x4E00-#x9FA5] | #x3007 | [#x3021-#x3029]

Production [86] lists the ideographic characters. #x4E00-#x9FA5 are Unicode's Chinese-Japanese-Korean unified ideographs. #x3007 is the ideographic number zero. Characters #x3021 through #x3029 are the Hangzhou style numerals.

[87] CombiningChar ::= [#x0300-#x0345] | [#x0360-#x0361] | [#x0483-#x0486] | [#x0591-#x05A1] | [#x05A3-#x05B9] | [#x05BB-#x05BD] | #x05BF | [#x05C1-#x05C2] | #x05C4 | [#x064B-#x0652] | #x0670 | [#x06D6-#x06DC] | [#x06DD-#x06DF] | [#x06E0-#x06E4] | [#x06E7-#x06E8] | [#x06EA-#x06ED] |

[#x0901-#x0903] | #x093C | [#x093E-#x094C] | #x094D | [#x0951-#x0954] | [#x0962-#x0963] | [#x0981-#x0983] | #x09BC | #x09BE | #x09BF | [#x09C0-#x09C4] | [#x09C7-#x09C8] | [#x09CB-#x09CD] | #x09D7 | [#x09E2-#x09E3] | #x0A02 | #x0A3C | #x0A3E | #x0A3F | [#x0A40-#x0A42] | [#x0A47-#x0A48] | [#x0A4B-#x0A4D] | [#x0A70-#x0A71] | [#x0A81-#x0A83] | #x0ABC | [#x0ABE-#x0AC5] | [#x0AC7-#x0AC9] | [#x0ACB-#x0ACD] | [#x0B01-#x0B03] | #x0B3C | [#x0B3E-#x0B43] | [#x0B47-#x0B48] | [#x0B4B-#x0B4D] | [#x0B56-#x0B57] | [#x0B82-#x0B83] | [#x0BBE-#x0BC2] | [#x0BC6-#x0BC8] | [#x0BCA-#x0BCD] | #x0BD7 | [#x0C01-#x0C03] | [#x0C3E-#x0C44] | [#x0C46-#x0C48] | [#x0C4A-#x0C4D] | [#x0C55-#x0C56] | [#x0C82-#x0C83] | [#x0CBE-#x0CC4] | [#x0CC6-#x0CC8] | [#x0CCA-#x0CCD] | [#x0CD5-#x0CD6] | [#x0D02-#x0D03] | [#x0D3E-#x0D43] | [#x0D46-#x0D48] | [#x0D4A-#x0D4D] | #x0D57 | #x0E31 | [#x0E34-#x0E3A] | [#x0E47-#x0E4E] | #x0EB1 | [#x0EB4-#x0EB9] | [#x0EBB-#x0EBC] | [#x0EC8-#x0ECD] | [#x0F18-#x0F19] | #x0F35 | #x0F37 | #x0F39 | #x0F3E | #x0F3F | [#x0F71-#x0F84] | [#x0F86-#x0F8B] | [#x0F90-#x0F95] | #x0F97 | [#x0F99-#x0FAD] | [#x0FB1-#x0FB7] | #x0FB9 | [#x20D0-#x20DC] | #x20E1 | [#x302A-#x302F] | #x3099 | #x309A

Production [87] lists the combining characters. These are characters that are generally combined with the preceding character to form the appearance of a single character. For example, character ̀ is the combining accent grave. The letter a (a) followed by a combining accent grave would generally be rendered as à and occupy only a single character width, even in a monospaced font.

[88] Digit ::= [#x0030-#x0039] | [#x0660-#x0669] | [#x06F0-#x06F9] | [#x0966-#x096F] | [#x09E6-#x09EF] | [#x0A66-#x0A6F] | [#x0AE6-#x0AEF] | [#x0B66-#x0B6F] | [#x0BE7-#x0BEF] | [#x0C66-#x0C6F] | [#x0CE6-#x0CEF] | [#x0D66-#x0D6F] | [#x0E50-#x0E59] | [#x0ED0-#x0ED9] | [#x0F20-#x0F29]

Production [88] lists the characters that are considered to be digits. These include not only the usual European numerals 0, 1, 2, 3, 4, 5, 6, 7, 8, and 9, but also the Arabic-Indic digits used primarily in Egyptian Arabic, the Eastern Arabic Indic digits used in Persian and Urdu, and many more.

[89] Extender ::= #x00B7 | #x02D0 | #x02D1 | #x0387 | #x0640 | #x0E46 | #x0EC6 | #x3005 | [#x3031-#x3035] | [#x309D-#x309E] | [#x30FC-#x30FE]

Production [89] lists the characters that are considered to be extenders. In order, these characters are the middle dot, the modifier letter triangular colon, the modifier letter half-triangular colon, the Greek middle dot, the Arabic tatweel, the Thai maiyamok, the Lao ko la, the ideographic iteration mark, five Japanese Kana repeat marks, the Japanese Hiragana iteration mark and voiced iteration mark, and the Japanese Katakana and Hiragana sound mark and prolonged sound mark. An extender is a character that's neither a letter nor a combining character, but that is nonetheless included in words as part of the word. The closest equivalent in English is perhaps the hyphen used in words like *mother-in-law* or *well-off*. However, the hyphen is not considered to be an extender in XML.

Note #x0387, the triangular colon, has been removed from the extender class in the latest Unicode errata sheet, but this has not yet trickled down into XML.

Well-formedness Constraints

According to the XML 1.0 specification, an XML document is well-formed if:

1. Taken as a whole it matches the production labeled document.

2. It meets all the well-formedness constraints given in this specification.

3. Each of the parsed entities which is referenced directly or indirectly within the document is well-formed.

This reference topic is designed to help you understand the second of those requirements and more quickly determine whether your documents meet that requirement.

What is a Well-formedness Constraint?

As you read the BNF grammar for XML 1.0, you should notice that some productions have associated well-formedness constraints, abbreviated WFC. For example, here's production [40]:

```
[40] STag ::= '<' Name (S Attribute)* S? '>'
              [ WFC: Unique Att Spec ]
```

What follows "WFC: " is the name of the well-formedness constraint, "Unique Att Spec" in this example. Generally, if you look a little below the production you'll find the constraint with the given name. For example, looking below Production [40] you'll find this:

Well-formedness Constraint: Unique Att Spec
No attribute name may appear more than once in the same start tag or empty-element tag.

This says that a given attribute may not appear more than once in a single element. For example, the following tag violates well-formedness:

```
<P COLOR="red" COLOR="blue">
```

Well-formedness constraints are used for requirements like this that are difficult or impossible to state in the form of a BNF grammar. As XML parsers read a document, they must not only check that the document matches the document production of the BNF grammar, they must also check that it satisfies all well-formedness constraints.

Note There are also validity constraints that must be satisfied by valid documents. XML processors are not required to check validity constraints if they do not wish to, however. Most validity constraints deal with declarations in the DTD. Validity constraints are covered later in this appendix.

Productions Associated with Well-formedness Constraints

This section lists the productions associated with well-formedness constraints and explains those constraints. Most productions don't have any well-formedness constraints; so most productions are not listed here. The complete list of productions is found in the BNF Grammar portion of this appendix.

[29] markupdecl ::= elementdecl | AttlistDecl | EntityDecl | NotationDecl | PI | Comment
[Well-formedness Constraint: PEs in Internal Subset]

This well-formedness constraint states that parameter entity references defined in the *internal* DTD subset cannot be used inside a markup declaration. For example, the following is illegal:

```
<!ENTITY % INLINES SYSTEM "(I | EM | B | STRONG | CODE)*">
<!ELEMENT P %INLINES; >
```

On the other hand, the above would be legal in the *external* DTD subset.

[39] element ::= EmptyElemTag | STag content ETag
[Well-Formedness Constraint: Element Type Match]

This well-formedness constraint simply says that the name of the start tag must match the name of the corresponding end tag. For instance, these elements are well-formed:

```
<TEST>content</TEST>
<test>content</test>
```

However, these are not:

```
<TEST>content</test>
<Fred>content</Ethel>
```

[40] STag ::= '<' Name (S Attribute)* S? '>'
[Well-formedness Constraint: Unique Att Spec]

This constraint says that a given attribute may not appear more than once in a single element. For example, the following tags violates well-formedness:

```
<P COLOR="red" COLOR="blue">
<P COLOR="red" COLOR="red">
```

The problem is that the COLOR attribute appears twice in the same tag. In the second case, it doesn't matter that the value is the same both times. It's still malformed. The following two tags are well-formed because the attributes have slightly different names:

```
<P COLOR1="red" COLOR2="blue">
<P COLOR1="red" COLOR2="red">
```

[41] Attribute ::= Name Eq AttValue
[Well-formedness Constraint: No External Entity References]

This constraint says that attribute values may not contain entity references that point to data in other documents. For example, consider this attribute:

```
<BOX COLOR="&RED;" />
```

Whether this is well-formed depends on how the entity RED is defined. If it's completely defined in the DTD, either in the internal or external subset, this tag is acceptable. For example:

```
<!ENTITY RED "#FF0000">
```

However, if the RED entity is defined as an external entity that refers to a separate file, then it's not well defined. In that case, the ENTITY declaration would look something like this:

```
<!ENTITY RED SYSTEM "red.txt" NDATA COLOR>
```

Note that this constraint applies to parsed entities. It does not apply to unparsed entities given as the value of an attribute of type ENTITY or ENTITIES. For example, the following is legal even though RED is an external entity used as an attribute value.

```
<?xml version="1.0"?>
<!DOCTYPE EXAMPLE [
  <!ELEMENT EXAMPLE ANY>
  <!NOTATION COLOR SYSTEM "x-color">
```

```
<!ENTITY RED SYSTEM "red.txt" NDATA COLOR>
<!ATTLIST EXAMPLE HUE ENTITY #REQUIRED>
]>
<EXAMPLE HUE="RED">
testing 1 2 3
</EXAMPLE>
```

[Well-formedness Constraint: No < in Attribute Values]

This constraint is very simple. The less-than sign (<) cannot be part of an attribute value. For example, the following tags are malformed:

```
<BOX COLOR="<6699FF>" />
<HALFPLANE REGION="X < 8" />
```

Technically, these tags are already forbidden by Production [10]. The real purpose of this constraint is to make sure that a < doesn't slip in via an external entity reference. The correct way to embed a < in an attribute value is to use the < entity reference like this:

```
<BOX COLOR="&lt;6699FF>" />
<HALFPLANE REGION="X &lt; 8" />
```

[44] EmptyElemTag ::= '<' Name (S Attribute)* S? '/>'
[Well-formedness Constraint: Unique Att Spec]

This constraint says that a given attribute may not appear more than once in a single empty element. For example, the following tags violate well-formedness:

```
<P COLOR="red" COLOR="blue" />
<P COLOR="red" COLOR="red" />
```

Take a look at the second example. Even the purely redundant attribute violates well-formedness.

[60] DefaultDecl ::= '#REQUIRED' | '#IMPLIED' | (('#FIXED' S)? AttValue)
[Well-formedness Constraint: No < in Attribute Values]

This is the same constraint seen in Production [41]. This merely states that you can't place a < in a default attribute value in a <!ATTLIST> declaration. For example, these are malformed attribute declarations:

```
<!ATTLIST RECTANGLE COLOR  CDATA "<330033>">
<!ATTLIST HALFPLANE REGION CDATA "X < 0" />
```

[66] CharRef ::= '&#' [0-9]+ ';' | '&#x' [0-9a-fA-F]+ ';'
[**Well-formedness Constraint: Legal Character**]

This constraint says that characters referred to by character references must be legal characters if they were simply typed in the document. Character references are convenience for inputting legal characters that are difficult to type on a particular system. They are not a means to input otherwise forbidden characters.

The definition of a legal character is given by Production [2]:

```
[2] Char ::= #x9 | #xA | #xD | [#x20-#xD7FF]
             | [#xE000-#xFFFD] | [#x10000-#x10FFFF]
```

The main items of interest here are the characters not included. Specifically, these are the non-printing ASCII control characters of which the most common are the bell, vertical tab, and formfeed; the surrogates block from #xD800 to #xDFFF, and the non-character #xFFFE.

[68] EntityRef ::= '&' Name ';'
[**Well-formedness Constraint: Entity Declared**]

The intent of this well-formedness constraint is to make sure that all entities used in the document are declared in the DTD using `<!ENTITY>`. However, there are two loopholes:

1. The five predefined entities: `&lt;`, `&apos;`, `&gt;`, `&quot;`, and `&amp;` are not required to be declared, although they may be.

2. A non-validating processor can allow undeclared entities if it's possible they may have been declared in the external DTD subset (which a non-validating processor is not required to read). Specifically, it's possible that entities were declared in an external DTD subset if:

   a. The standalone document declaration does not have `standalone="yes"`.

   b. The DTD contains at least one parameter entity reference.

If either of these conditions is violated, then undeclared entities (other than the five in loophole one) are not allowed.

This constraint also specifies that, if entities are declared, they must be declared before they're used.

[Well-formedness Constraint: Parsed Entity]

This constraint states that entity references may only contain the names of parsed entities. Unparsed entity names are only contained in attribute values of type ENTITY or ENTITIES. For example, this is a malformed document:

```
<?xml version="1.0" standalone="no"?>
<!DOCTYPE DOCUMENT [
  <!ELEMENT DOCUMENT ANY>
  <!ENTITY LOGO SYSTEM "http://metalab.unc.edu/xml/logo.gif"
    NDATA GIF>
<!NOTATION GIF SYSTEM "image/gif">
]>
<DOCUMENT>
  &LOGO;
</DOCUMENT>
```

This is the correct way to embed the unparsed entity LOGO in the document:

```
<?xml version="1.0" standalone="no"?>
<!DOCTYPE DOCUMENT [

  <!ELEMENT DOCUMENT ANY>
  <!ENTITY LOGO SYSTEM "http://metalab.unc.edu/xml/logo.gif"
    NDATA GIF>
  <!NOTATION GIF SYSTEM "image/gif">
  <!ELEMENT IMAGE EMPTY>
  <!ATTLIST IMAGE SOURCE ENTITY #REQUIRED>

]>
<DOCUMENT>
  <IMAGE SOURCE="LOGO" />
</DOCUMENT>
```

[Well-formedness Constraint: No Recursion]

This well-formedness constraint states that a parsed entity cannot refer to itself. For example, this open source classic is malformed:

```
<!ENTITY GNU "&GNU;'s not Unix!">
```

Circular references are a little trickier to spot, but are equally illegal:

```
<!ENTITY LEFT  "Left &RIGHT; Left!">
<!ENTITY RIGHT "Right &LEFT; Right!">
```

Note that it's only the recursion that's malformed, not the mere use of one entity reference inside another. The following is perfectly fine because although the

COPY99 entity depends on the ERH entity, the ERH entity does not depend on the COPY99 entity.

```
<!ENTITY ERH    "Elliotte Rusty Harold">
<!ENTITY COPY99 "Copyright 1999 &ERH;">
```

[69] PEReference ::= '%' Name ';'
[Well-formedness Constraint: No Recursion]

This is the same constraint that applies to Production [68]. Parameter entities can't recurse any more than general entities can. For example, this entity declaration is also malformed:

```
<!ENTITY % GNU "%GNU;'s not Unix!">
```

And this is still illegal:

```
<!ENTITY % LEFT  "Left  %RIGHT; Left!">
<!ENTITY % RIGHT "Right %LEFT; Right!">
```

[Well-formedness Constraint: In DTD]

This well-formedness constraint requires that parameter entity references can only appear in the DTD. They may not appear in the content of the document or anywhere else that's not the DTD.

Validity Constraints

This reference topic is designed to help you understand what is required in order for an XML document to be *valid*. Validity is often useful, but is not always required. You can do a lot with simply well-formed documents, and such documents are often easier to write because there are fewer rules to follow. For valid documents, you must follow the BNF grammar, the well-formedness constraints, *and* the validity constraints discussed in this section.

What Is a Validity Constraint?

A validity constraint is a rule that must be adhered to by a valid document. Not all XML documents are, or need to be, valid. It is not necessarily an error for a document to fail to satisfy a validity constraint. Validating processors have the option of reporting violations of these constraints as errors, but they do not have to. All syntax (BNF) errors and well-formedness violations must still be reported however.

Only documents with DTDs may be validated. Almost all the validity constraints deal with the relationships between the content of the document and the declarations in the DTD.

Validity Constraints in XML 1.0

This section lists and explains all of the validity constraints in the XML 1.0 standard. These are organized according to the BNF rule each applies to.

[28] doctypedecl ::= '<!DOCTYPE' S Name (S ExternalID)? S? ('[' (markupdecl | PEReference | S)* ']' S?)? '>'
Validity Constraint: Root Element Type

This constraint simply states that the name given in the DOCTYPE declaration must match the name of the root element. In other words, the bold parts below have to all be the same.

```
<?xml version="1.0"?>
<!DOCTYPE ROOTNAME [
  <!ELEMENT ROOTNAME ANY>
]>
<ROOTNAME>
  content
</ROOTNAME>
```

It's also true that the root element must be declared — that's done by the line in italic — however that declaration is required by a different validity constraint, not this one.

[29] markupdecl ::= elementdecl | AttlistDecl | EntityDecl | NotationDecl | PI | Comment
Validity Constraint: Proper Declaration/PE Nesting

This constraint requires that a markup declaration contain or be contained in one or more parameter entities, but that it may not be split across a parameter entity. For example, consider this element declaration:

```
<!ELEMENT PARENT ( FATHER | MOTHER )>
```

The parameter entity declared by the following entity declaration is a valid substitute for the content model, because the parameter entity contains both the < and the >:

```
<!ENTITY % PARENT_DECL "<!ELEMENT PARENT ( FATHER | MOTHER )>">
```

Given that entity, you can rewrite the element declaration like this:

```
%PARENT_DECL;
```

This is valid because the parameter entity contains both the ⟨ and the ⟩. Another option is to include only part of the element declaration in the parameter entity. For example, if you had many elements whose content model was (FATHER | MOTHER), then it might be useful to do something like this:

```
<!ENTITY % PARENT_TYPES "( FATHER | MOTHER )">
<!ELEMENT PARENT %PARENT_TYPES;>
```

Here, neither the ⟨ or ⟩ is included in the parameter entity. You cannot enclose one of the angle brackets in the parameter entity without including its mate. The following, for example, is invalid, even though it appears to expand into a legal element declaration:

```
<!ENTITY % PARENT_TYPES "( FATHER | MOTHER )>">
<!ELEMENT PARENT %PARENT_TYPES;
```

Note that the problem is *not* that the parameter entity's replacement text contains a ⟩ character. That's legal (unlike the use of a ⟨ character, which would be illegal in an internal parameter entity declaration). The problem is how the ⟩ character is used to terminate an element declaration that began in another entity.

[32] SDDecl ::= S 'standalone' Eq (("''" ('yes' | 'no') "''") | ("''" ('yes' | 'no') "''"))

Validity Constraint: Standalone Document Declaration

In short, this constraint says that a document must have a standalone document declaration with the value no (standalone="no") if any other files are required to process this file and determine its validity. Mostly this affects external DTD subsets linked in through parameter entities. This is the case if any of the following are true:

✦ An entity used in the document is declared in an external DTD subset.

✦ The external DTD subset provides default values for attributes that appear in the document without values.

✦ The external DTD subset changes how attribute values in the document may be normalized.

✦ The external DTD subset declares elements whose children are only elements (no character data or mixed content) when those children may themselves contain whitespace.

[39] element ::= EmptyElemTag | STag content ETag
Validity Constraint: Element Valid

This constraint simply states that this element matches an element declaration in the DTD. More precisely one of the following conditions must be true:

1. The element has no content and the element declaration declares the element EMPTY.

2. The element contains only child elements that match the regular expression in the element's content model.

3. The element is declared to have mixed content, and the element's content contains character data and child elements that are declared in the mixed-content declaration.

4. The element is declared ANY, and all child elements are declared.

[41] Attribute ::= Name Eq AttValue
Validity Constraint: Attribute Value Type

This constraint simply states that the attribute's name must have been declared in an ATTLIST declaration in the DTD. Furthermore, the attribute value must match the declared type in the ATTLIST declaration.

[45] elementdecl ::= '<!ELEMENT' S Name S contentspec S? '>'
Validity Constraint: Unique Element Type Declaration

An element cannot be declared more than once in the DTD, whether the declarations are compatible or not. For example, this is valid:

```
<!ELEMENT EM (#PCDATA)>
```

This, however, is not valid:

```
<!ELEMENT EM (#PCDATA)>
<!ELEMENT EM (#PCDATA | B)>
```

Neither is this valid:

```
<!ELEMENT EM (#PCDATA)>
<!ELEMENT EM (#PCDATA)>
```

This is most likely to cause problems when merging external DTD subsets from different sources that both declare some of the same elements. To a limited extent, namespaces can help resolve this.

[49] choice ::= '(' S? cp (S? '|' S? cp)* S? ')'
Validity Constraint: Proper Group/PE Nesting

This constraint states that a choice may contain or be contained in one or more parameter entities, but that it may not be split across a parameter entity. For example, consider this element declaration:

```
<!ELEMENT PARENT ( FATHER | MOTHER )>
```

The parameter entity declared by the following entity declaration is a valid substitute for the content model because the parameter entity contains both the (and the):

```
<!ENTITY % PARENT_TYPES "( FATHER | MOTHER )">
```

That is, you can rewrite the element declaration like this:

```
<!ELEMENT PARENT %PARENT_TYPES;>
```

This is valid because the parameter entity contains both the (and the). Another option is to include only the child elements, but leave out both parentheses. For example:

```
<!ENTITY % PARENT_TYPES " FATHER | MOTHER ">
<!ELEMENT PARENT ( %PARENT_TYPES; )>
```

The advantage here is that you can easily add additional elements not defined in the parameter entity. For example:

```
<!ELEMENT PARENT ( UNKNOWN | %PARENT_TYPES; ) >
```

What you cannot do, however, is enclose one of the parentheses in the parameter entity without including its mate. The following, for example, is invalid, even though it appears to expand into a legal element declaration.

```
<!ENTITY % FATHER " FATHER )">
<!ENTITY % MOTHER " ( MOTHER | ">
<!ELEMENT PARENT %FATHER; %MOTHER; ) >
```

The problem in this example is the ELEMENT declaration, not the ENTITY declarations. It is valid to declare the entities as done here. It's their use in the context of a choice that makes them invalid.

[50] seq ::= '(' S? cp (S? ',' S? cp)* S? ')'
Validity Constraint: Proper Group/PE Nesting

This is exactly the same constraint as above, except now it's applied to sequences rather than choices. It requires that a sequence may contain or be contained in one or more parameter entities, but it may not be split across a parameter entity. For example, consider this element declaration:

```
<!ELEMENT ADDRESS ( NAME, STREET, CITY, STATE, ZIP )>
```

The parameter entity declared by the following entity declaration is a valid substitute for the content model because the parameter entity contains both the (and the):

```
<!ENTITY % SIMPLE_ADDRESS "( NAME, STREET, CITY, STATE, ZIP )">
```

That is, you can rewrite the element declaration like this:

```
<!ELEMENT ADDRESS %SIMPLE_ADDRESS;>
```

This is valid because the parameter entity contains both the (and the). Another option is to include only the child elements, but leave out both parentheses. For example:

```
<!ENTITY % SIMPLE_ADDRESS " NAME, STREET, CITY, STATE, ZIP ">
<!ELEMENT ADDRESS( %SIMPLE_ADDRESS; )>
```

The advantage here is that you can easily add additional elements not defined in the parameter entity. For example:

```
<!ENTITY % INTERNATIONAL_ADDRESS " NAME, STREET, CITY,
   PROVINCE?, POSTAL_CODE?, COUNTRY ">
<!ELEMENT ADDRESS ( (%SIMPLE_ADDRESS;)
                  | (%INTERNATIONAL_ADDRESS;) ) >
```

What you cannot do, however, is enclose one of the parentheses in the parameter entity without including its mate. The following, for example, is invalid, even though it appears to expand into a legal element declaration:

```
<!ENTITY % SIMPLE_ADDRESS_1 "( NAME, STREET, ">
<!ENTITY % SIMPLE_ADDRESS_2 "CITY, STATE, ZIP)">
<!ELEMENT ADDRESS %SIMPLE_ADDRESS_1; %SIMPLE_ADDRESS_2; ) >
```

The problem in this example is the ELEMENT declaration, not the ENTITY declarations. It is valid to declare the entities like this. It's their use in the context of a sequence that makes them invalid.

[51] Mixed ::= '(' S? '#PCDATA' (S? '|' S? Name)* S? ')*' | '(' S? '#PCDATA' S? ')'
Validity Constraint: Proper Group/PE Nesting

This is exactly the same constraint as above, except now it's applied to mixed content rather than choices or sequences. It requires that a mixed-content model may contain or be contained in a parameter entity, but it may not be split across a parameter entity. For example, consider this element declaration:

```
<!ELEMENT P ( #PCDATA | I | EM | B | STRONG )>
```

The parameter entity declared by the following entity declaration is a valid substitute for the content model because the parameter entity contains both the (and the):

```
<!ENTITY % INLINES "( #PCDATA | I | EM | B | STRONG )">
```

That is, you can rewrite the element declaration like this:

```
<!ELEMENT P %INLINES;>
```

This is valid because the parameter entity contains both the (and the). Another option is to include only the content particles, but leave out both parentheses. For example:

```
<!ENTITY % INLINES " #PCDATA | I | EM | B | STRONG ">
<!ELEMENT P ( %INLINES; ) >
```

The advantage here is that you can easily add additional elements not defined in the parameter entity. For example:

```
<!ELEMENT QUOTE ( %INLINES; | SPEAKER ) >
```

What you cannot do, however, is enclose one of the parentheses in the parameter entity without including its mate. The following, for example, is invalid, even though it appears to expand into a legal element declaration:

```
<!ENTITY % INLINES1 " I | EM | B | STRONG )">
<!ENTITY % INLINES2 " ( #PCDATA | SPEAKER | ">
<!ELEMENT QUOTE %INLINES1; %INLINES2; ) >
```

The problem in this example is the ELEMENT declaration, not the ENTITY declarations. It is valid to declare the entities as is done here. It's their use in the context of a choice (or sequence) that makes them invalid.

Validity Constraint: No Duplicate Types

No element can be repeated in a mixed-content declaration. For example, the follwing is invalid:

```
( #PCDATA | I | EM | I | EM )
```

There's really no reason to write a mixed-content declaration like this, but at the same time, it's not obvious what the harm is. Interestingly, pure choices do allow content models like this:

```
( I | EM | I | EM )
```

It only becomes a problem when #PCDATA gets mixed in.

Caution This choice is ambiguous—that is, when the parser encounters an I or an EM, it doesn't know whether it matches the first or the second instance in the content model. So although legal, some parsers will report it as an error, and it should be avoided if possible.

[56] TokenizedType ::= 'ID' | 'IDREF' | 'IDREFS' | 'ENTITY' | 'ENTITIES' | 'NMTOKEN' | 'NMTOKENS'
Validity Constraint: ID

Attribute values of ID type must be valid XML names (Production [5]). Furthermore, a single name cannot be used more than once in the same document as the value of an ID type attribute. For example, this is invalid given that ID is declared to be ID:

```
<BOX ID="B1" WIDTH="50" HEIGHT="50" />
<BOX ID="B1" WIDTH="250" HEIGHT="250" />
```

This is also invalid because XML names cannot begin with numbers:

```
<BOX ID="1" WIDTH="50" HEIGHT="50" />
```

This is valid if NAME does not have type ID:

```
<BOX ID="B1" WIDTH="50" HEIGHT="50" />
<BOX NAME="B1" WIDTH="250" HEIGHT="250" />
```

On the other hand, that example is invalid if NAME does have type ID, even though the NAME attribute is different from the ID attribute. Furthermore, the following is invalid if NAME has type ID, even though two different elements are involved:

```
<BOX NAME="FRED" WIDTH="50" HEIGHT="50" />
<PERSON NAME="FRED" />
```

ID attribute values must be unique across all elements and ID attributes, not just a particular class of, or attributes of, a particular class of elements.

Validity Constraint: One ID per Element Type

Each element can have at most one attribute of type ID. For example, the following is invalid:

```
<!ELEMENT PERSON (ANY) >
<!ATTLIST PERSON SS_NUMBER   ID #REQUIRED>
<!ATTLIST PERSON EMPLOYEE_ID ID #REQUIRED>
```

Validity Constraint: ID Attribute Default

All attributes of ID type must be declared #IMPLIED or #REQUIRED. #FIXED is not allowed. For example, the following is invalid:

```
<!ATTLIST PERSON SS_NUMBER ID #FIXED "SS123-45-6789">
```

The problem is that if there's more than one PERSON element in the document, the ID validity constraint will automatically be violated.

Validity Constraint: IDREF

The IDREF validity constraint specifies that an attribute value of an IDREF type attribute must be the same as the value of an ID type attribute of an element in the document. Multiple IDREF attributes in the same or different elements may point to a single element. ID attribute values must be unique (at least among other ID attribute values in the same document), but IDREF attributes do not need to be.

Additionally, attribute values of type IDREFS must be a whitespace-separated list of ID attribute values from elements in the document.

Validity Constraint: Entity Name

The value of an attribute whose declared type is ENTITY must be the name of an unparsed general (non-parameter) entity declared in the DTD, whether in the internal or external subset.

The value of an attribute whose declared type is ENTITIES must be a whitespace-separated list of the names of unparsed general (non-parameter) entities declared in the DTD, whether in the internal or external subset.

Validity Constraint: Name Token

The value of an attribute whose declared type is NMTOKEN must match the NMTOKEN production of XML (Production [7]). That is, it must be composed of one or more name characters. It differs from an XML name in that it may start with a digit, a period, a hyphen, a combining character, or an extender.

The value of an attribute whose declared type is NMTOKENS must be a whitespace-separated list of name tokens. For example, this is a valid element with a COLORS attribute of type NMTOKENS:

```
<BOX WIDTH="50" HEIGHT="50" COLORS="red green blue" />
```

This is an invalid element with a COLORS attribute of type NMTOKENS:

```
<BOX WIDTH="50" HEIGHT="50" COLORS="red, green, blue" />
```

[58] NotationType ::= 'NOTATION' S '(' S? Name (S? '|' S? Name)* S? ')'
Validity Constraint: Notation Attributes

The value of an attribute whose declared type is NOTATION must be the name of a notation that's been declared in the DTD.

[59] Enumeration ::= '(' S? Nmtoken (S? '|' S? Nmtoken)* S? ')'
Validity Constraint: Enumeration

The value of an attribute whose declared type is ENUMERATION must be a whitespace-separated list of name tokens. These name tokens do not necessarily have to be the names of anything declared in the DTD or elsewhere. They simply have to match the NMTOKEN production (Production [7]). For example, this is an invalid enumeration because commas rather than whitespace are used to separate the name tokens:

```
( red, green, blue)
```

This is an invalid enumeration because the name tokens are enclosed in quote marks:

```
( "red" "green" "blue")
```

Neither commas nor quote marks are valid name characters so there's no possibility for these common mistakes to be misinterpreted as a whitespace-separated list of unusual name tokens.

[60] DefaultDecl ::= '#REQUIRED' | '#IMPLIED' | (('#FIXED' S)? AttValue)
Validity Constraint: Required Attribute

If an attribute of an element is declared to be #REQUIRED, then it is a validity error for any instance of the element not to provide a value for that attribute.

Validity Constraint: Attribute Default Legal

This common-sense validity constraint merely states that any default attribute value provided in an ATTLIST declaration must satisfy the constraints for an attribute of that type. For example, the following is invalid because the default value, UNKNOWN, is not one of the choices given by the content model.

```
<!ATTLIST CIRCLE VISIBLE (TRUE | FALSE) "UNKNOWN">
```

UNKNOWN would be invalid for this attribute whether it was provided as a default value or in an actual element like the following:

```
<CIRCLE VISIBLE="UNKNOWN" />
```

Validity Constraint: Fixed Attribute Default

This common-sense validity constraint merely states that if an attribute is declared #FIXED in its ATTLIST declaration, then that same ATTLIST declaration must also provide a default value. For example, the following is invalid:

```
<!ATTLIST AUTHOR COMPANY CDATA #FIXED>
```

Here's a corrected declaration:

```
<!ATTLIST AUTHOR COMPANY CDATA #FIXED "TIC">
```

[68] EntityRef ::= '&' Name ';'
Validity Constraint: Entity Declared

This constraint expands on the well-formedness constraint of the same name. In a valid document, all referenced entities must be defined by <!ENTITY> declarations in the DTD. Definitions must precede any use of the entity they define.

The loophole for standalone="no" documents that applies to merely well-formed documents is no longer available. The loophole for the five predefined entities: <, ', >, ", and & is still available. However, it is recommended that you declare them, even though you don't absolutely have to. Those declarations would look like this:

```
<!ENTITY lt   "&#38;#60;">
<!ENTITY gt   "&#62;">
<!ENTITY amp  "&#38;#38;">
<!ENTITY apos "&#39;">
<!ENTITY quot "&#34;">
```

[69] PEReference ::= '%' Name ';'
Validity Constraint: Entity Declared

This is the same constraint as the previous one, merely applied to parameter entity references instead of general entity references.

[76] NDataDecl ::= S 'NDATA' S Name
Validity Constraint: Notation Declared

The name used in a notation data declaration (which is in turn used in an entity definition for an unparsed entity) must be the name of a notation declared in the DTD. For example, the following document is valid. However, if you take away the line declaring the GIF notation (shown in bold) it becomes invalid.

```
<?xml version="1.0" standalone="no"?>
<!DOCTYPE DOCUMENT [
  <!ELEMENT DOCUMENT ANY>
  <!ENTITY LOGO SYSTEM "http://metalab.unc.edu/xml/logo.gif"
    NDATA gif>
  <!NOTATION GIF SYSTEM "image/gif">
]>
<DOCUMENT>
  &LOGO;
</DOCUMENT>
```

◆   ◆   ◆

The XML 1.0 Specification

This appendix has the complete, final XML 1.0 specification as published by the World Wide Web consortium. This document has been reviewed by W3C Members and other interested parties and has been endorsed by the Director as a W3C Recommendation. It is a stable document and may be used as reference material or cited as a normative reference from another document. If any changes to XML are required in the future (as they undoubtedly will be) a new version number will be applied.

This document isn't always easy reading. Precision is preferred over clarity. However, when you're banging your head against the wall, and trying to decide whether the problem is with your XML processor or with your XML code, this is the deciding document. Therefore, it's important to have at least a cursory familiarity with it, and be able to find things in it when you need to.

This document was primarily written by Tim Bray and C. M. Sperberg-McQueen with assistance from many others credited at the end of the document.

REC-xml-19980210

W3C Recommendation 10-February-1998

This version:

> http://www.w3.org/TR/1998/REC-xml-19980210
>
> http://www.w3.org/TR/1998/REC-xml-19980210.xml
>
> http://www.w3.org/TR/1998/REC-xml-19980210.html
>
> http://www.w3.org/TR/1998/REC-xml-19980210.pdf
>
> http://www.w3.org/TR/1998/REC-xml-19980210.ps

Latest version:

http://www.w3.org/TR/REC-xml

Previous version:

http://www.w3.org/TR/PR-xml-971208

Editors:

Tim Bray (Textuality and Netscape) <tbray@textuality.com>

Jean Paoli (Microsoft) <jeanpa@microsoft.com>

C. M. Sperberg-McQueen (University of Illinois at Chicago) <cmsmcq@uic.edu>

Abstract

The Extensible Markup Language (XML) is a subset of SGML that is completely described in this document. Its goal is to enable generic SGML to be served, received, and processed on the Web in the way that is now possible with HTML. XML has been designed for ease of implementation and for interoperability with both SGML and HTML.

Status of This Document

This document has been reviewed by W3C Members and other interested parties and has been endorsed by the Director as a W3C Recommendation. It is a stable document and may be used as reference material or cited as a normative reference from another document. W3C's role in making the Recommendation is to draw attention to the specification and to promote its widespread deployment. This enhances the functionality and interoperability of the Web.

This document specifies a syntax created by subsetting an existing, widely used international text processing standard (Standard Generalized Markup Language, ISO 8879:1986(E) as amended and corrected) for use on the World Wide Web. It is a product of the W3C XML Activity, details of which can be found at http://www.w3.org/XML. A list of current W3C Recommendations and other technical documents can be found at http://www.w3.org/TR.

This specification uses the term URI, which is defined by [Berners-Lee et al.], a work in progress expected to update [IETF RFC1738] and [IETF RFC1808].

The list of known errors in this specification is available at http://www.w3.org/XML/xml-19980210-errata.

Please report errors in this document to xml-editor@w3.org.

Extensible Markup Language (XML) 1.0

Table of Contents

E. Deterministic Content Models (Non-Normative)

F. Autodetection of Character Encodings (Non-Normative)

G. W3C XML Working Group (Non-Normative)

1. Introduction

Extensible Markup Language, abbreviated XML, describes a class of data objects called XML documents and partially describes the behavior of computer programs which process them. XML is an application profile or restricted form of SGML, the Standard Generalized Markup Language [ISO 8879]. By construction, XML documents are conforming SGML documents.

XML documents are made up of storage units called entities, which contain either parsed or unparsed data. Parsed data is made up of characters, some of which form character data, and some of which form markup. Markup encodes a description of the document's storage layout and logical structure. XML provides a mechanism to impose constraints on the storage layout and logical structure.

A software module called an **XML processor** is used to read XML documents and provide access to their content and structure. It is assumed that an XML processor is doing its work on behalf of another module, called the **application**. This specification describes the required behavior of an XML processor in terms of how it must read XML data and the information it must provide to the application.

1.1 Origin and Goals

XML was developed by an XML Working Group (originally known as the SGML Editorial Review Board) formed under the auspices of the World Wide Web Consortium (W3C) in 1996. It was chaired by Jon Bosak of Sun Microsystems with the active participation of an XML Special Interest Group (previously known as the SGML Working Group) also organized by the W3C. The membership of the XML Working Group is given in an appendix. Dan Connolly served as the WG's contact with the W3C.

The design goals for XML are:

1. XML shall be straightforwardly usable over the Internet.

2. XML shall support a wide variety of applications.

3. XML shall be compatible with SGML.

4. It shall be easy to write programs which process XML documents.

5. The number of optional features in XML is to be kept to the absolute minimum, ideally zero.

6. XML documents should be human-legible and reasonably clear.

7. The XML design should be prepared quickly.

8. The design of XML shall be formal and concise.

9. XML documents shall be easy to create.

10. Terseness in XML markup is of minimal importance.

This specification, together with associated standards (Unicode and ISO/IEC 10646 for characters, Internet RFC 1766 for language identification tags, ISO 639 for language name codes, and ISO 3166 for country name codes), provides all the information necessary to understand XML Version 1.0 and construct computer programs to process it.

This version of the XML specification may be distributed freely, as long as all text and legal notices remain intact.

1.2 Terminology

The terminology used to describe XML documents is defined in the body of this specification. The terms defined in the following list are used in building those definitions and in describing the actions of an XML processor:

may Conforming documents and XML processors are permitted to but need not behave as described.

must Conforming documents and XML processors are required to behave as described; otherwise they are in error.

error A violation of the rules of this specification; results are undefined. Conforming software may detect and report an error and may recover from it.

fatal error An error which a conforming XML processor must detect and report to the application. After encountering a fatal error, the processor may continue processing the data to search for further errors and may report such errors to the application. In order to support correction of errors, the processor may make unprocessed data from the document (with intermingled character data and markup) available to the application. Once a fatal error is detected, however, the processor must not continue normal processing (i.e., it must not continue to pass character data and information about the document's logical structure to the application in the normal way).

at user option Conforming software may or must (depending on the modal verb in the sentence) behave as described; if it does, it must provide users a means to enable or disable the behavior described.

validity constraint A rule which applies to all valid XML documents. Violations of validity constraints are errors; they must, at user option, be reported by validating XML processors.

well-formedness constraint A rule which applies to all well-formed XML documents. Violations of well-formedness constraints are fatal errors.

match (Of strings or names:) Two strings or names being compared must be identical. Characters with multiple possible representations in ISO/IEC 10646 (e.g. characters with both precomposed and base+diacritic forms) match only if they have the same representation in both strings. At user option, processors may normalize such characters to some canonical form. No case folding is performed. (Of strings and rules in the grammar:) A string matches a grammatical production if it belongs to the language generated by that production. (Of content and content models:) An element matches its declaration when it conforms in the fashion described in the constraint "Element Valid".

for compatibility A feature of XML included solely to ensure that XML remains compatible with SGML.

for interoperability A non-binding recommendation included to increase the chances that XML documents can be processed by the existing installed base of SGML processors which predate the WebSGML Adaptations Annex to ISO 8879.

2. Documents

A data object is an **XML document** if it is well-formed, as defined in this specification. A well-formed XML document may in addition be valid if it meets certain further constraints.

Each XML document has both a logical and a physical structure. Physically, the document is composed of units called entities. An entity may refer to other entities to cause their inclusion in the document. A document begins in a "root" or document entity. Logically, the document is composed of declarations, elements, comments, character references, and processing instructions, all of which are indicated in the document by explicit markup. The logical and physical structures must nest properly, as described in "4.3.2 Well-Formed Parsed Entities".

2.1 Well-Formed XML Documents

A textual object is a well-formed XML document if:

 ✦ Taken as a whole, it matches the production labeled document.

 ✦ It meets all the well-formedness constraints given in this specification.

Each of the parsed entities which is referenced directly or indirectly within the document is well-formed.

```
Document
[1] document ::= prolog element Misc*
```

Matching the document production implies that:

 ✦ It contains one or more elements.

✦ There is exactly one element, called the **root**, or document element, no part of which appears in the content of any other element. For all other elements, if the start-tag is in the content of another element, the end-tag is in the content of the same element. More simply stated, the elements, delimited by start- and end-tags, nest properly within each other.

✦ As a consequence of this, for each non-root element C in the document, there is one other element P in the document such that C is in the content of P, but is not in the content of any other element that is in the content of P. P is referred to as the **parent** of C, and C as a **child** of P.

2.2 Characters

A parsed entity contains **text**, a sequence of characters, which may represent markup or character data. A **character** is an atomic unit of text as specified by ISO/IEC 10646 [ISO/IEC 10646]. Legal characters are tab, carriage return, line feed, and the legal graphic characters of Unicode and ISO/IEC 10646. The use of "compatibility characters", as defined in section 6.8 of [Unicode], is discouraged.

```
Character Range
[2] Char ::= #x9 | #xA | #xD | [#x20-#xD7FF]    /* any Unicode
character,
          | [#xE000-#xFFFD]              excluding the surrogate
          | [#x10000-#x10FFFF]           blocks, FFFE, and FFFF.
*/
```

The mechanism for encoding character code points into bit patterns may vary from entity to entity. All XML processors must accept the UTF-8 and UTF-16 encodings of 10646; the mechanisms for signaling which of the two is in use, or for bringing other encodings into play, are discussed later, in "4.3.3 Character Encoding in Entities".

2.3 Common Syntactic Constructs

This section defines some symbols used widely in the grammar.

S (white space) consists of one or more space (#x20) characters, carriage returns, line feeds, or tabs.

```
White Space
[3] S ::= (#x20 | #x9 | #xD | #xA)+
```

Characters are classified for convenience as letters, digits, or other characters. Letters consist of an alphabetic or syllabic base character possibly followed by one or more combining characters, or of an ideographic character. Full definitions of the specific characters in each class are given in "B. Character Classes".

A **Name** is a token beginning with a letter or one of a few punctuation characters, and continuing with letters, digits, hyphens, underscores, colons, or full stops, together known as name characters. Names beginning with the string "xml", or any string which would match (('X'|'x') ('M'|'m') ('L'|'l')), are reserved for standardization in this or future versions of this specification.

Note: The colon character within XML names is reserved for experimentation with name spaces. Its meaning is expected to be standardized at some future point, at which point those documents using the colon for experimental purposes may need to be updated. (There is no guarantee that any name-space mechanism adopted for XML will in fact use the colon as a name-space delimiter.) In practice, this means that authors should not use the colon in XML names except as part of name-space experiments, but that XML processors should accept the colon as a name character.

An Nmtoken (name token) is any mixture of name characters.

Names and Tokens

```
[4] NameChar ::= Letter | Digit | '.' | '-' | '_' | ':'
                 | CombiningChar | Extender
[5] Name     ::= (Letter | '_' | ':') (NameChar)*
[6] Names    ::= Name (S Name)*
[7] Nmtoken  ::= (NameChar)+
[8] Nmtokens ::= Nmtoken (S Nmtoken)*
```

Literal data is any quoted string not containing the quotation mark used as a delimiter for that string. Literals are used for specifying the content of internal entities (EntityValue), the values of attributes (AttValue), and external identifiers (SystemLiteral). Note that a SystemLiteral can be parsed without scanning for markup.

Literals

```
[9]  EntityValue   ::= '"' ([^%&"] | PEReference | Reference)*
     '"'
                       | "'" ([^%&'] | PEReference |
     Reference)* "'"
[10] AttValue       ::= '"' ([^<&"] | Reference)* '"'
                       | "'" ([^<&'] | Reference)* "'"
[11] SystemLiteral  ::= ('"' [^"]* '"') | ("'" [^']* "'")
[12] PubidLiteral   ::= '"' PubidChar* '"'
                       | "'" (PubidChar - "'")* "'"
[13] PubidChar      ::= #x20 | #xD | #xA | [a-zA-Z0-9]
                       | [-'()+,./:=?;!*#@$_%]
```

2.4 Character Data and Markup

Text consists of intermingled character data and markup. **Markup** takes the form of start-tags, end-tags, empty-element tags, entity references, character references, comments, CDATA section delimiters, document type declarations, and processing instructions.

All text that is not markup constitutes the **character data** of the document.

The ampersand character (&) and the left angle bracket (<) may appear in their literal form *only* when used as markup delimiters, or within a comment, a processing instruction, or a CDATA section. They are also legal within the literal entity value of an internal entity declaration; see "4.3.2 Well-Formed Parsed Entities". If they are needed elsewhere, they must be escaped using either numeric character references or the strings "&" and "<" respectively. The right angle bracket (>) may be represented using the string ">", and must, for compatibility, be escaped using ">" or a character reference when it appears in the string "]]>" in content, when that string is not marking the end of a CDATA section.

In the content of elements, character data is any string of characters which does not contain the start-delimiter of any markup. In a CDATA section, character data is any string of characters not including the CDATA-section-close delimiter, "]]>".

To allow attribute values to contain both single and double quotes, the apostrophe or single-quote character (') may be represented as "'", and the double-quote character (") as """.

Character Data

```
[14] CharData ::= [^<&]* - ([^<&]* ']]>' [^<&]*)
```

2.5 Comments

Comments may appear anywhere in a document outside other markup; in addition, they may appear within the document type declaration at places allowed by the grammar. They are not part of the document's character data; an XML processor may, but need not, make it possible for an application to retrieve the text of comments. For compatibility, the string "—" (double-hyphen) must not occur within comments.

Comments

```
[15] Comment ::= '<!—' ((Char - '-') | ('-' (Char - '-')))* '—
>'
```

An example of a comment:

```
<!— declarations for <head> & <body> —>
```

2.6 Processing Instructions

Processing instructions (PIs) allow documents to contain instructions for applications.

```
Processing Instructions
[16] PI ::= '<?' PITarget
                (S (Char* - (Char* '?>' Char*)))? '?>'
[17] PITarget ::= Name - (('X' | 'x') ('M' | 'm') ('L' | 'l'))
```

PIs are not part of the document's character data, but must be passed through to the application. The PI begins with a target (PITarget) used to identify the application to which the instruction is directed. The target names "XML", "xml", and so on are reserved for standardization in this or future versions of this specification. The XML Notation mechanism may be used for formal declaration of PI targets.

2.7 CDATA Sections

CDATA sections may occur anywhere character data may occur; they are used to escape blocks of text containing characters which would otherwise be recognized as markup. CDATA sections begin with the string "<![CDATA[" and end with the string "]]>":

CDATA Sections

```
[18] CDSect  ::= CDStart CData CDEnd
[19] CDStart ::= '<![CDATA['
[20] CData   ::= (Char* - (Char* ']]>' Char*))
[21] CDEnd   ::= ']]>'
```

Within a CDATA section, only the CDEnd string is recognized as markup, so that left angle brackets and ampersands may occur in their literal form; they need not (and cannot) be escaped using "<" and "&". CDATA sections cannot nest.

An example of a CDATA section, in which "<greeting>" and "</greeting>" are recognized as character data, not markup:

```
<![CDATA[<greeting>Hello, world!</greeting>]]>
```

2.8 Prolog and Document Type Declaration

XML documents may, and should, begin with an **XML declaration** which specifies the version of XML being used. For example, the following is a complete XML document, well-formed but not valid:

```
<?xml version="1.0"?> <greeting>Hello, world!</greeting>
```

and so is this:

```
<greeting>Hello, world!</greeting>
```

The version number "1.0" should be used to indicate conformance to this version of this specification; it is an error for a document to use the value "1.0" if it does not conform to this version of this specification. It is the intent of the XML working group to give later versions of this specification numbers other than "1.0", but this intent does not indicate a commitment to produce any future versions of XML, nor if any are produced, to use any particular numbering scheme. Since future versions are not ruled out, this construct is provided as a means to allow the possibility of automatic version recognition, should it become necessary. Processors may signal an error if they receive documents labeled with versions they do not support.

The function of the markup in an XML document is to describe its storage and logical structure and to associate attribute-value pairs with its logical structures. XML provides a mechanism, the document type declaration, to define constraints on the logical structure and to support the use of predefined storage units. An XML document is **valid** if it has an associated document type declaration and if the document complies with the constraints expressed in it.

The document type declaration must appear before the first element in the document.

Prolog

```
[22] prolog      ::= XMLDecl? Misc* (doctypedecl Misc*)?
[23] XMLDecl   ::= '<?xml' VersionInfo EncodingDecl? SDDecl? S?
'?>'
[24] VersionInfo ::= S 'version' Eq (' VersionNum '
                      | " VersionNum ")
[25] Eq          ::= S? '=' S?
[26] VersionNum  ::= ([a-zA-Z0-9_.:] | '-')+
[27] Misc        ::= Comment | PI |  S
```

The XML **document type declaration** contains or points to markup declarations that provide a grammar for a class of documents. This grammar is known as a document type definition, or **DTD**. The document type declaration can point to an external subset (a special kind of external entity) containing markup declarations, or can contain the markup declarations directly in an internal subset, or can do both. The DTD for a document consists of both subsets taken together.

A **markup declaration** is an element type declaration, an attribute-list declaration, an entity declaration, or a notation declaration. These declarations may be contained in whole or in part within parameter entities, as described in the well-formedness and validity constraints below. For fuller information, see "4. Physical Structures".

Document Type Definition

```
[28] doctypedecl ::= '<!DOCTYPE' S Name (S ExternalID)?
                     S? ('[' (markupdecl | PEReference
                     | S)* ']' S?)? '>'
                     [ VC: Root Element Type ]
[29] markupdecl  ::= elementdecl | AttlistDecl
```

```
      | EntityDecl | NotationDecl | PI
      | Comment
      [ VC: Proper Declaration/PE Nesting ]
      [ WFC: PEs in Internal Subset ]
```

The markup declarations may be made up in whole or in part of the replacement text of parameter entities. The productions later in this specification for individual nonterminals (elementdecl, AttlistDecl, and so on) describe the declarations *after* all the parameter entities have been included.

Validity Constraint: Root Element Type: The Name in the document type declaration must match the element type of the root element.

Validity Constraint: Proper Declaration/PE Nesting: Parameter-entity replacement text must be properly nested with markup declarations. That is to say, if either the first character or the last character of a markup declaration (markupdecl above) is contained in the replacement text for a parameter-entity reference, both must be contained in the same replacement text.

Well-Formedness Constraint: PEs in Internal Subset: In the internal DTD subset, parameter-entity references can occur only where markup declarations can occur, not within markup declarations. (This does not apply to references that occur in external parameter entities or to the external subset.)

Like the internal subset, the external subset and any external parameter entities referred to in the DTD must consist of a series of complete markup declarations of the types allowed by the non-terminal symbol markupdecl, interspersed with white space or parameter-entity references. However, portions of the contents of the external subset or of external parameter entities may conditionally be ignored by using the conditional section construct; this is not allowed in the internal subset.

External Subset

```
[30] extSubset ::=    TextDecl? extSubsetDecl
[31] extSubsetDecl ::=    ( markupdecl | conditionalSect |
PEReference | S )*
```

The external subset and external parameter entities also differ from the internal subset in that in them, parameter-entity references are permitted *within* markup declarations, not only between markup declarations.

An example of an XML document with a document type declaration:

```
<?xml version="1.0"?>
<!DOCTYPE greeting SYSTEM "hello.dtd">
<greeting>Hello, world!</greeting>
```

The system identifier "hello.dtd" gives the URI of a DTD for the document.

The declarations can also be given locally, as in this example:

```
<?xml version="1.0" encoding="UTF-8" ?>
<!DOCTYPE greeting [
  <!ELEMENT greeting (#PCDATA)>
]>
<greeting>Hello, world!</greeting>
```

If both the external and internal subsets are used, the internal subset is considered to occur before the external subset. This has the effect that entity and attribute-list declarations in the internal subset take precedence over those in the external subset.

2.9 Standalone Document Declaration

Markup declarations can affect the content of the document, as passed from an XML processor to an application; examples are attribute defaults and entity declarations. The standalone document declaration, which may appear as a component of the XML declaration, signals whether or not there are such declarations which appear external to the document entity.

Standalone Document Declaration

```
[32] SDDecl ::= S 'standalone' Eq (("'" ('yes' | 'no')
               "'") | ('"' ('yes' | 'no') '"'))
              [ VC: Standalone Document Declaration ]
```

In a standalone document declaration, the value "yes" indicates that there are no markup declarations external to the document entity (either in the DTD external subset, or in an external parameter entity referenced from the internal subset) which affect the information passed from the XML processor to the application. The value "no" indicates that there are or may be such external markup declarations. Note that the standalone document declaration only denotes the presence of external declarations; the presence, in a document, of references to external *entities*, when those entities are internally declared, does not change its standalone status.

If there are no external markup declarations, the standalone document declaration has no meaning. If there are external markup declarations but there is no standalone document declaration, the value "no" is assumed.

Any XML document for which standalone="no" holds can be converted algorithmically to a standalone document, which may be desirable for some network delivery applications.

Validity Constraint: Standalone Document Declaration: The standalone document declaration must have the value "no" if any external markup declarations contain declarations of:

✦ attributes with default values, if elements to which these attributes apply appear in the document without specifications of values for these attributes, or

✦ entities (other than amp, lt, gt, apos, quot), if references to those entities appear in the document, or

✦ attributes with values subject to normalization, where the attribute appears in the document with a value which will change as a result of normalization, or

✦ element types with element content, if white space occurs directly within any instance of those types.

An example XML declaration with a standalone document declaration:

```
<?xml version="1.0" standalone='yes'?>
```

2.10 White Space Handling

In editing XML documents, it is often convenient to use "white space" (spaces, tabs, and blank lines, denoted by the nonterminal S in this specification) to set apart the markup for greater readability. Such white space is typically not intended for inclusion in the delivered version of the document. On the other hand, "significant" white space that should be preserved in the delivered version is common, for example in poetry and source code.

An XML processor must always pass all characters in a document that are not markup through to the application. A validating XML processor must also inform the application which of these characters constitute white space appearing in element content.

A special attribute named xml:space may be attached to an element to signal an intention that in that element, white space should be preserved by applications. In valid documents, this attribute, like any other, must be declared if it is used. When declared, it must be given as an enumerated type whose only possible values are "default" and "preserve". For example:

```
<!ATTLIST poem    xml:space (default|preserve) 'preserve'>
```

The value "default" signals that applications' default white-space processing modes are acceptable for this element; the value "preserve" indicates the intent that applications preserve all the white space. This declared intent is considered to apply to all elements within the content of the element where it is specified, unless overridden with another instance of the xml:space attribute.

The root element of any document is considered to have signaled no intentions as regards application space handling, unless it provides a value for this attribute or the attribute is declared with a default value.

2.11 End-of-Line Handling

XML parsed entities are often stored in computer files which, for editing convenience, are organized into lines. These lines are typically separated by some combination of the characters carriage-return (#xD) and line-feed (#xA).

To simplify the tasks of applications, wherever an external parsed entity or the literal entity value of an internal parsed entity contains either the literal two-character sequence "#xD#xA" or a standalone literal #xD, an XML processor must pass to the application the single character #xA. (This behavior can conveniently be produced by normalizing all line breaks to #xA on input, before parsing.)

2.12 Language Identification

In document processing, it is often useful to identify the natural or formal language in which the content is written. A special attribute named xml:lang may be inserted in documents to specify the language used in the contents and attribute values of any element in an XML document. In valid documents, this attribute, like any other, must be declared if it is used. The values of the attribute are language identifiers as defined by [IETF RFC 1766], "Tags for the Identification of Languages":

Language Identification

```
[33] LanguageID ::= Langcode ('-' Subcode)*
[34] Langcode   ::= ISO639Code | IanaCode | UserCode
[35] ISO639Code ::= ([a-z] | [A-Z]) ([a-z] | [A-Z])
[36] IanaCode   ::= ('i' | 'I') '-' ([a-z] | [A-Z])+
[37] UserCode   ::= ('x' | 'X') '-' ([a-z] | [A-Z])+
[38] Subcode    ::= ([a-z] | [A-Z])+
```

The Langcode may be any of the following:

✦ a two-letter language code as defined by [ISO 639], "Codes for the representation of names of languages"

✦ a language identifier registered with the Internet Assigned Numbers Authority [IANA]; these begin with the prefix "i-" (or "I-")

✦ a language identifier assigned by the user, or agreed on between parties in private use; these must begin with the prefix "x-" or "X-" in order to ensure that they do not conflict with names later standardized or registered with IANA.

There may be any number of Subcode segments; if the first subcode segment exists and the Subcode consists of two letters, then it must be a country code from [ISO 3166], "Codes for the representation of names of countries." If the first subcode consists of more than two letters, it must be a subcode for the language in question registered with IANA, unless the Langcode begins with the prefix "x-" or "X-".

It is customary to give the language code in lower case, and the country code (if any) in upper case. Note that these values, unlike other names in XML documents, are case insensitive.

For example:

```
<p xml:lang="en">The quick brown fox jumps over the lazy dog.</
p>
<p xml:lang="en-GB">What colour is it?</p>
<p xml:lang="en-US">What color is it?</p>
<sp who="Faust" desc='leise' xml:lang="de">
<l>Habe nun, ach! Philosophie,</l>
<l>Juristerei, und Medizin</l>
  <l>und leider auch Theologie</l>
  <l>durchaus studiert mit heißem Bemüh'n.</l>
  </sp>
```

The intent declared with xml:lang is considered to apply to all attributes and content of the element where it is specified, unless overridden with an instance of xml:lang on another element within that content.

A simple declaration for xml:lang might take the form:

```
xml:lang  NMTOKEN  #IMPLIED
```

but specific default values may also be given, if appropriate. In a collection of French poems for English students, with glosses and notes in English, the xml:lang attribute might be declared this way:

```
<!ATTLIST poem   xml:lang NMTOKEN 'fr'>
<!ATTLIST gloss  xml:lang NMTOKEN 'en'>
<!ATTLIST note   xml:lang NMTOKEN 'en'>
```

3. Logical Structures

Each XML document contains one or more **elements**, the boundaries of which are either delimited by start-tags and end-tags, or, for empty elements, by an empty-element tag. Each element has a type, identified by name, sometimes called its "generic identifier" (GI), and may have a set of attribute specifications. Each attribute specification has a name and a value.

Element

```
[39] element ::= EmptyElemTag | STag content ETag
             [ WFC: Element Type Match ]
             [ VC: Element Valid ]
```

This specification does not constrain the semantics, use, or (beyond syntax) names of the element types and attributes, except that names beginning with a match to (('X'|'x')('M'|'m')('L'|'l')) are reserved for standardization in this or future versions of this specification.

Well-Formedness Constraint: Element Type Match: The Name in an element's end-tag must match the element type in the start-tag.

Validity Constraint: Element Valid: An element is valid if there is a declaration matching `elementdecl` where the Name matches the element type, and one of the following holds:

1. The declaration matches EMPTY and the element has no content.

2. The declaration matches `children` and the sequence of child elements belongs to the language generated by the regular expression in the content model, with optional white space (characters matching the nonterminal S) between each pair of child elements.

3. The declaration matches Mixed and the content consists of character data and child elements whose types match names in the content model.

4. The declaration matches ANY, and the types of any child elements have been declared.

3.1 Start-Tags, End-Tags, and Empty-Element Tags

The beginning of every non-empty XML element is marked by a **start-tag**.

Start-tag

```
[40] STag ::= '<' Name (S Attribute)* S? '>'
             [ WFC: Unique Att Spec ]
[41] Attribute ::= Name Eq AttValue
             [ VC: Attribute Value Type ]
             [ WFC: No External Entity References ]
             [ WFC: No < in Attribute Values ]
```

The `Name` in the start- and end-tags gives the element's **type**. The `Name`-`AttValue` pairs are referred to as the **attribute specifications** of the element, with the `Name` in each pair referred to as the **attribute name** and the content of the `AttValue` (the text between the ' or " delimiters) as the **attribute value**.

Well-Formedness Constraint: Unique Att Spec: No attribute name may appear more than once in the same start-tag or empty-element tag.

Validity Constraint: Attribute Value Type: The attribute must have been declared; the value must be of the type declared for it. (For attribute types, see "3.3 Attribute-List Declarations".)

Well-Formedness Constraint: No External Entity References: Attribute values cannot contain direct or indirect entity references to external entities.

Well-Formedness Constraint: No < in Attribute Values: The replacement text of any entity referred to directly or indirectly in an attribute value (other than "<") must not contain a <.

An example of a start-tag:

```
<termdef id="dt-dog" term="dog">
```

The end of every element that begins with a start-tag must be marked by an **end-tag** containing a name that echoes the element's type as given in the start-tag:

End-tag

```
[42] ETag ::= '</' Name S? '>'
```

An example of an end-tag:

```
</termdef>
```

The text between the start-tag and end-tag is called the element's **content**:

Content of Elements

```
[43] content ::= (element | CharData | Reference | CDSect | PI
                  | Comment)*
```

If an element is **empty**, it must be represented either by a start-tag immediately followed by an end-tag or by an empty-element tag. An **empty-element tag** takes a special form:

Tags for Empty Elements

```
[44] EmptyElemTag ::= '<' Name (S Attribute)* S? '/>'
                      [ WFC: Unique Att Spec ]
```

Empty-element tags may be used for any element which has no content, whether or not it is declared using the keyword EMPTY. For interoperability, the empty-element tag must be used, and can only be used, for elements which are declared EMPTY.

Examples of empty elements:

```
<IMG align="left"
 src="http://www.w3.org/Icons/WWW/w3c_home" />
<br></br>
<br/>
```

3.2 Element Type Declarations

The element structure of an XML document may, for validation purposes, be constrained using element type and attribute-list declarations. An element type declaration constrains the element's content.

Element type declarations often constrain which element types can appear as children of the element. At user option, an XML processor may issue a warning when a declaration mentions an element type for which no declaration is provided, but this is not an error.

An **element type declaration** takes the form:

Element Type Declaration

```
[45] elementdecl ::= '<!ELEMENT' S Name S contentspec S? '>'
                     [ VC: Unique Element Type Declaration ]
[46] contentspec ::= 'EMPTY' | 'ANY' | Mixed | children
```

where the Name gives the element type being declared.

Validity Constraint: Unique Element Type Declaration: No element type may be declared more than once.

Examples of element type declarations:

```
<!ELEMENT br EMPTY>
<!ELEMENT p (#PCDATA|emph)* >
<!ELEMENT %name.para; %content.para; >
<!ELEMENT container ANY>
```

3.2.1 Element Content

An element type has **element content** when elements of that type must contain only child elements (no character data), optionally separated by white space (characters matching the nonterminal S). In this case, the constraint includes a content model, a simple grammar governing the allowed types of the child elements and the order in which they are allowed to appear. The grammar is built on content particles (cps), which consist of names, choice lists of content particles, or sequence lists of content particles:

Element-content Models

```
[47] children ::= (choice | seq) ('?' | '*' | '+')?
[48] cp       ::= (Name | choice | seq) ('?' | '*' | '+')?
[49] choice   ::= '(' S? cp ( S? '|' S? cp )* S? ')'
                  [ VC: Proper Group/PE Nesting ]
[50] seq      ::=  '(' S? cp ( S? ',' S? cp )* S? ')'
                  [ VC: Proper Group/PE Nesting ]
```

where each Name is the type of an element which may appear as a child. Any content particle in a choice list may appear in the element content at the location where the choice list appears in the grammar; content particles occurring in a sequence list must each appear in the element content in the order given in the list.

The optional character following a name or list governs whether the element or the content particles in the list may occur one or more (+), zero or more (*), or zero or one times (?). The absence of such an operator means that the element or content particle must appear exactly once. This syntax and meaning are identical to those used in the productions in this specification.

The content of an element matches a content model if and only if it is possible to trace out a path through the content model, obeying the sequence, choice, and repetition operators and matching each element in the content against an element type in the content model. For compatibility, it is an error if an element in the document can match more than one occurrence of an element type in the content model. For more information, see "E. Deterministic Content Models".

Validity Constraint: Proper Group/PE Nesting: Parameter-entity replacement text must be properly nested with parenthesized groups. That is to say, if either of the opening or closing parentheses in a choice, seq, or Mixed construct is contained in the replacement text for a parameter entity, both must be contained in the same replacement text. For interoperability, if a parameter-entity reference appears in a choice, seq, or Mixed construct, its replacement text should not be empty, and neither the first nor last non-blank character of the replacement text should be a connector (I or ,).

Examples of element-content models:

```
<!ELEMENT spec (front, body, back?)>
<!ELEMENT div1 (head, (p | list | note)*, div2*)>
<!ELEMENT dictionary-body (%div.mix; | %dict.mix;)*>
```

3.2.2 Mixed Content

An element type has **mixed content** when elements of that type may contain character data, optionally interspersed with child elements. In this case, the types of the child elements may be constrained, but not their order or their number of occurrences:

Mixed-content Declaration

```
[51] Mixed ::= '(' S? '#PCDATA' (S? '|' S? Name)* S? ')*'
             | '(' S? '#PCDATA' S? ')'
             [ VC: Proper Group/PE Nesting ]
             [ VC: No Duplicate Types ]
```

where the Names give the types of elements that may appear as children.

Validity Constraint: No Duplicate Types: The same name must not appear more than once in a single mixed-content declaration.

Examples of mixed content declarations:

```
<!ELEMENT p (#PCDATA|a|ul|b|i|em)*>
<!ELEMENT p (#PCDATA | %font; | %phrase; | %special; | %form;)*
 >
<!ELEMENT b (#PCDATA)>
```

3.3 Attribute-List Declarations

Attributes are used to associate name-value pairs with elements. Attribute specifications may appear only within start-tags and empty-element tags; thus, the productions used to recognize them appear in "3.1 Start-Tags, End-Tags, and Empty-Element Tags". Attribute-list declarations may be used:

+ To define the set of attributes pertaining to a given element type.

+ To establish type constraints for these attributes.

+ To provide default values for attributes.

Attribute-list declarations specify the name, data type, and default value (if any) of each attribute associated with a given element type:

Attribute-list Declaration

```
[52] AttlistDecl ::= '<!ATTLIST' S Name AttDef* S? '>'
[53] AttDef      ::= S Name S AttType S DefaultDecl
```

The Name in the AttlistDecl rule is the type of an element. At user option, an XML processor may issue a warning if attributes are declared for an element type not itself declared, but this is not an error. The Name in the AttDef rule is the name of the attribute.

When more than one AttlistDecl is provided for a given element type, the contents of all those provided are merged. When more than one definition is provided for the same attribute of a given element type, the first declaration is binding and later declarations are ignored. For interoperability, writers of DTDs may choose to provide at most one attribute-list declaration for a given element type, at most one attribute definition for a given attribute name, and at least one attribute definition in each attribute-list declaration. For interoperability, an XML processor may at user option issue a warning when more than one attribute-list declaration is provided for a given element type, or more than one attribute definition is provided for a given attribute, but this is not an error.

3.3.1 Attribute Types

XML attribute types are of three kinds: a string type, a set of tokenized types, and enumerated types. The string type may take any literal string as a value; the tokenized types have varying lexical and semantic constraints, as noted:

Attribute Types

```
[54] AttType ::= StringType | TokenizedType | EnumeratedType
[55] StringType ::= 'CDATA'
[56] TokenizedType ::= 'ID'          [ VC: ID ]
                                     [ VC: One ID per Element
Type ]
                                     [ VC: ID Attribute Default
]
                     | 'IDREF'       [ VC: IDREF ]
                     | 'IDREFS'      [ VC: IDREF ]
                     | 'ENTITY'      [ VC: Entity Name ]
                     | 'ENTITIES'    [ VC: Entity Name ]
                     | 'NMTOKEN'     [ VC: Name Token ]
                     | 'NMTOKENS'    [ VC: Name Token ]
```

Validity Constraint: ID: Values of type ID must match the Name production. A name must not appear more than once in an XML document as a value of this type; i.e., ID values must uniquely identify the elements which bear them.

Validity Constraint: One ID per Element Type: No element type may have more than one ID attribute specified.

Validity Constraint: ID Attribute Default: An ID attribute must have a declared default of #IMPLIED or #REQUIRED.

Validity Constraint: IDREF: Values of type IDREF must match the Name production, and values of type IDREFS must match Names; each Name must match the value of an ID attribute on some element in the XML document; i.e. IDREF values must match the value of some ID attribute.

Validity Constraint: Entity Name: Values of type ENTITY must match the `Name` production, values of type ENTITIES must match `Names`; each Name must match the name of an unparsed entity declared in the DTD.

Validity Constraint: Name Token: Values of type NMTOKEN must match the `Nmtoken` production; values of type NMTOKENS must match `Nmtokens`.

Enumerated attributes can take one of a list of values provided in the declaration. There are two kinds of enumerated types:

Enumerated Attribute Types

```
[57] EnumeratedType ::= NotationType | Enumeration
[58] NotationType ::= 'NOTATION' S '(' S? [ VC: Notation
Attributes]
                     Name (S? '|' S? Name)* S? ')'
[59] Enumeration  ::= '(' S? Nmtoken (S?   [ VC: Enumeration ]
                     '|' S?Nmtoken)* S? ')'
```

A NOTATION attribute identifies a notation, declared in the DTD with associated system and/or public identifiers, to be used in interpreting the element to which the attribute is attached.

Validity Constraint: Notation Attributes: Values of this type must match one of the notation names included in the declaration; all notation names in the declaration must be declared.

Validity Constraint: Enumeration: Values of this type must match one of the Nmtoken tokens in the declaration.

For interoperability, the same Nmtoken should not occur more than once in the enumerated attribute types of a single element type.

3.3.2 Attribute Defaults

An attribute declaration provides information on whether the attribute's presence is required, and if not, how an XML processor should react if a declared attribute is absent in a document.

Attribute Defaults

```
[60] DefaultDecl ::= '#REQUIRED' | '#IMPLIED'
                   | (('#FIXED' S)? AttValue)
                     [ VC: Required Attribute ]
                     [ VC: Attribute Default Legal ]
                     [ WFC: No < in Attribute Values ]
                     [ VC: Fixed Attribute Default ]
```

In an attribute declaration, #REQUIRED means that the attribute must always be provided, #IMPLIED that no default value is provided. If the declaration is neither #REQUIRED nor #IMPLIED, then the AttValue value contains the declared **default** value; the #FIXED keyword states that the attribute must always have the default value. If a default value is declared, when an XML processor encounters an omitted attribute, it is to behave as though the attribute were present with the declared default value.

Validity Constraint: Required Attribute: If the default declaration is the keyword #REQUIRED, then the attribute must be specified for all elements of the type in the attribute-list declaration.

Validity Constraint: Attribute Default Legal: The declared default value must meet the lexical constraints of the declared attribute type.

Validity Constraint: Fixed Attribute Default: If an attribute has a default value declared with the #FIXED keyword, instances of that attribute must match the default value.

Examples of attribute-list declarations:

```
<!ATTLIST termdef
          id      ID      #REQUIRED
          name    CDATA   #IMPLIED>
<!ATTLIST list
          type    (bullets|ordered|glossary)   "ordered">
<!ATTLIST form
          method  CDATA   #FIXED "POST">
```

3.3.3 Attribute-Value Normalization

Before the value of an attribute is passed to the application or checked for validity, the XML processor must normalize it as follows:

- ✦ a character reference is processed by appending the referenced character to the attribute value.

- ✦ an entity reference is processed by recursively processing the replacement text of the entity.

- ✦ a whitespace character (#x20, #xD, #xA, #x9) is processed by appending #x20 to the normalized value, except that only a single #x20 is appended for a "#xD#xA" sequence that is part of an external parsed entity or the literal entity value of an internal parsed entity.

- ✦ other characters are processed by appending them to the normalized value.

If the declared value is not CDATA, then the XML processor must further process the normalized attribute value by discarding any leading and trailing space (#x20) characters, and by replacing sequences of space (#x20) characters by a single space (#x20) character.

All attributes for which no declaration has been read should be treated by a non-validating parser as if declared CDATA.

3.4 Conditional Sections

Conditional sections are portions of the document type declaration external subset which are included in, or excluded from, the logical structure of the DTD based on the keyword which governs them.

Conditional Section

```
[61] conditionalSect   ::=  includeSect | ignoreSect
[62] includeSect   ::= '<![' S? 'INCLUDE' S? '[' extSubsetDecl
']]>'
[63] ignoreSect    ::= '<![' S? 'IGNORE' S? '['
ignoreSectContents*
                   ']]>'
```

```
[64] ignoreSectContents  ::= Ignore ('<![' ignoreSectContents
                              ']]>' Ignore)*
[65] Ignore               ::= Char* - (Char* ('<![' | ']]>')
Char*)
```

Like the internal and external DTD subsets, a conditional section may contain one or more complete declarations, comments, processing instructions, or nested conditional sections, intermingled with white space.

If the keyword of the conditional section is INCLUDE, then the contents of the conditional section are part of the DTD. If the keyword of the conditional section is IGNORE, then the contents of the conditional section are not logically part of the DTD. Note that for reliable parsing, the contents of even ignored conditional sections must be read in order to detect nested conditional sections and ensure that the end of the outermost (ignored) conditional section is properly detected. If a conditional section with a keyword of INCLUDE occurs within a larger conditional section with a keyword of IGNORE, both the outer and the inner conditional sections are ignored.

If the keyword of the conditional section is a parameter-entity reference, the parameter entity must be replaced by its content before the processor decides whether to include or ignore the conditional section.

An example:

```
<!ENTITY % draft 'INCLUDE' >
<!ENTITY % final 'IGNORE' >

<![%draft;[
<!ELEMENT book (comments*, title, body, supplements?)>
]]>
<![%final;[
<!ELEMENT book (title, body, supplements?)>
]]>
```

4. Physical Structures

An XML document may consist of one or many storage units. These are called **entities**; they all have **content** and are all (except for the document entity, see below, and the external DTD subset) identified by **name**. Each XML document has one entity called the document entity, which serves as the starting point for the XML processor and may contain the whole document.

Entities may be either parsed or unparsed. A **parsed entity's** contents are referred to as its replacement text; this text is considered an integral part of the document.

An **unparsed entity** is a resource whose contents may or may not be text, and if text, may not be XML. Each unparsed entity has an associated notation, identified by name. Beyond a requirement that an XML processor make the identifiers for the entity and notation available to the application, XML places no constraints on the contents of unparsed entities.

```
Parsed entities are invoked by name using entity references;
unparsed entities by name, given in the value of ENTITY or
ENTITIES attributes.
```

General entities are entities for use within the document content. In this specification, general entities are sometimes referred to with the unqualified term *entity* when this leads to no ambiguity. Parameter entities are parsed entities for use within the DTD. These two types of entities use different forms of reference and are recognized in different contexts. Furthermore, they occupy different namespaces; a parameter entity and a general entity with the same name are two distinct entities.

4.1 Character and Entity References

A **character reference** refers to a specific character in the ISO/IEC 10646 character set, for example one not directly accessible from available input devices.

Character Reference

```
[66] CharRef ::= '&#' [0-9]+ ';'
                | '&#x' [0-9a-fA-F]+ ';' [ WFC: Legal Character
]
```

Well-Formedness Constraint: Legal Character: Characters referred to using character references must match the production for Char.

If the character reference begins with "&#x", the digits and letters up to the terminating; provide a hexadecimal representation of the character's code point in ISO/IEC 10646. If it begins just with "&#", the digits up to the terminating ; provide a decimal representation of the character's code point.

An **entity reference** refers to the content of a named entity. References to parsed general entities use ampersand (&) and semicolon (;) as delimiters. **Parameter-entity references** use percent-sign (%) and semicolon (;) as delimiters.

Entity Reference

```
[67] Reference    ::= EntityRef | CharRef
[68] EntityRef    ::= '&' Name ';' [ WFC: Entity Declared ]
                                    [ VC: Entity Declared ]
                                    [ WFC: Parsed Entity ]
                                    [ WFC: No Recursion ]
[69] PEReference  ::= '%' Name ';' [ VC: Entity Declared ]
                                    [ WFC: No Recursion ]
                                    [ WFC: In DTD ]
```

Well-Formedness Constraint: Entity Declared: In a document without any DTD, a document with only an internal DTD subset which contains no parameter entity references, or a document with "standalone='yes'", the Name given in the entity reference must match that in an entity declaration, except that well-formed documents need not declare any of the following entities: amp, lt, gt, apos, quot. The declaration of a parameter entity must precede any reference to it. Similarly, the declaration of a general entity must precede any reference to it which appears in a default value in an attribute-list declaration. Note that if entities are declared in the external subset or in external parameter entities, a non-validating processor is not obligated to read and process their declarations; for such documents, the rule that an entity must be declared is a well-formedness constraint only if standalone='yes'.

Validity Constraint: Entity Declared: In a document with an external subset or external parameter entities with "standalone='no'", the Name given in the entity reference must match that in an entity declaration. For interoperability, valid documents should declare the entities amp, lt, gt, apos, quot, in the form specified in "4.6 Predefined Entities". The declaration of a parameter entity must precede any reference to it. Similarly, the declaration of a general entity must precede any reference to it which appears in a default value in an attribute-list declaration.

Well-Formedness Constraint: Parsed Entity: An entity reference must not contain the name of an unparsed entity. Unparsed entities may be referred to only in attribute values declared to be of type ENTITY or ENTITIES.

Well-Formedness Constraint: No Recursion: A parsed entity must not contain a recursive reference to itself, either directly or indirectly.

Well-Formedness Constraint: In DTD: Parameter-entity references may only appear in the DTD.

Examples of character and entity references:

```
Type <key>less-than</key> (&#x3C;) to save options.
This document was prepared on &docdate; and
is classified &security-level;.
```

Example of a parameter-entity reference:

```
<!— declare the parameter entity "ISOLat2"... —>
<!ENTITY % ISOLat2
        SYSTEM "http://www.xml.com/iso/isolat2-xml.entities" >
<!— ... now reference it. —>
%ISOLat2;
```

4.2 Entity Declarations

Entities are declared thus:

Entity Declaration

```
[70] EntityDecl ::= GEDecl | PEDecl
[71] GEDecl     ::= '<!ENTITY' S Name S EntityDef S? '>'
[72] PEDecl     ::= '<!ENTITY' S '%' S Name S PEDef S? '>'
[73] EntityDef  ::= EntityValue | (ExternalID NDataDecl?)
[74] PEDef      ::= EntityValue | ExternalID
```

The Name identifies the entity in an entity reference or, in the case of an unparsed entity, in the value of an ENTITY or ENTITIES attribute. If the same entity is declared more than once, the first declaration encountered is binding; at user option, an XML processor may issue a warning if entities are declared multiple times.

4.2.1 Internal Entities

If the entity definition is an EntityValue, the defined entity is called an **internal entity**. There is no separate physical storage object, and the content of the entity is given in the declaration. Note that some processing of entity and character references in the literal entity value may be required to produce the correct replacement text: see "4.5 Construction of Internal Entity Replacement Text".

An internal entity is a parsed entity. Example of an internal entity declaration:

```
<!ENTITY Pub-Status "This is a pre-release of the
specification.">
```

4.2.2 External Entities

If the entity is not internal, it is an **external entity**, declared as follows:

External Entity Declaration

```
[75] ExternalID ::= 'SYSTEM' S SystemLiteral
                  | 'PUBLIC' S PubidLiteral S SystemLiteral
[76] NDataDecl  ::= S 'NDATA' S Name [ VC: Notation Declared ]
```

If the NDataDecl is present, this is a general unparsed entity; otherwise it is a parsed entity.

Validity Constraint: Notation Declared: The Name must match the declared name of a notation.

The SystemLiteral is called the entity's **system identifier**. It is a URI, which may be used to retrieve the entity. Note that the hash mark (#) and fragment identifier frequently used with URIs are not, formally, part of the URI itself; an XML processor may signal an error if a fragment identifier is given as part of a system identifier. Unless otherwise provided by information outside the scope of this specification (e.g. a special XML element type defined by a particular DTD, or a processing instruction defined by a particular application specification), relative URIs are relative to the location of the resource within which the entity declaration occurs. A URI might thus be relative to the document entity, to the entity containing the external DTD subset, or to some other external parameter entity.

An XML processor should handle a non-ASCII character in a URI by representing the character in UTF-8 as one or more bytes, and then escaping these bytes with the URI escaping mechanism (i.e., by converting each byte to %HH, where HH is the hexadecimal notation of the byte value).

In addition to a system identifier, an external identifier may include a **public identifier**. An XML processor attempting to retrieve the entity's content may use the public identifier to try to generate an alternative URI. If the processor is unable to do so, it must use the URI specified in the system literal. Before a match is attempted, all strings of white space in the public identifier must be normalized to single space characters (#x20), and leading and trailing white space must be removed.

Examples of external entity declarations:

```
<!ENTITY open-hatch SYSTEM
    "http://www.textuality.com/boilerplate/OpenHatch.xml">
<!ENTITY open-hatch
    PUBLIC "-//Textuality//TEXT Standard open-
hatch boilerplate//EN"
    "http://www.textuality.com/boilerplate/OpenHatch.xml">
<!ENTITY hatch-pic SYSTEM "../grafix/OpenHatch.gif" NDATA gif >
```

4.3 Parsed Entities

4.3.1 The Text Declaration

External parsed entities may each begin with a **text declaration**.

Text Declaration

```
[77] TextDecl ::= '<?xml' VersionInfo? EncodingDecl S? '?>'
```

The text declaration must be provided literally, not by reference to a parsed entity. No text declaration may appear at any position other than the beginning of an external parsed entity.

4.3.2 Well-Formed Parsed Entities

The document entity is well-formed if it matches the production labeled document. An external general parsed entity is well-formed if it matches the production labeled extParsedEnt. An external parameter entity is well-formed if it matches the production labeled extPE.

Well-Formed External Parsed Entity

```
[78] extParsedEnt ::= TextDecl? content
[79] extPE        ::= TextDecl? extSubsetDecl
```

An internal general parsed entity is well-formed if its replacement text matches the production labeled content. All internal parameter entities are well-formed by definition.

A consequence of well-formedness in entities is that the logical and physical structures in an XML document are properly nested; no start-tag, end-tag, empty-element tag, element, comment, processing instruction, character reference, or entity reference can begin in one entity and end in another.

4.3.3 Character Encoding in Entities

Each external parsed entity in an XML document may use a different encoding for its characters. All XML processors must be able to read entities in either UTF-8 or UTF-16.

Entities encoded in UTF-16 must begin with the Byte Order Mark described by ISO/IEC 10646 Annex E and Unicode Appendix B (the ZERO WIDTH NO-BREAK SPACE character, #xFEFF). This is an encoding signature, not part of either the markup or the character data of the XML document. XML processors must be able to use this character to differentiate between UTF-8 and UTF-16 encoded documents.

Although an XML processor is required to read only entities in the UTF-8 and UTF-16 encodings, it is recognized that other encodings are used around the world, and it may be desired for XML processors to read entities that use them. Parsed entities which are stored in an encoding other than UTF-8 or UTF-16 must begin with a text declaration containing an encoding declaration:

Encoding Declaration

```
[80] EncodingDecl ::= S 'encoding' Eq ('"' EncName '"'
                      | "'" EncName "'" )
[81] EncName       ::= [A-Za-z] ([A-Za-z0-9._] | '-')*
/* Encoding name contains only Latin characters */
```

In the document entity, the encoding declaration is part of the XML declaration. The EncName is the name of the encoding used.

In an encoding declaration, the values "UTF-8", "UTF-16", "ISO-10646-UCS-2", and "ISO-10646-UCS-4" should be used for the various encodings and transformations of Unicode / ISO/IEC 10646, the values "ISO-8859-1", "ISO-8859-2", ... "ISO-8859-9" should be used for the parts of ISO 8859, and the values "ISO-2022-JP", "Shift_JIS", and "EUC-JP" should be used for the various encoded forms of JIS X-0208-1997. XML processors may recognize other encodings; it is recommended that character encodings registered (as *charset*s) with the Internet Assigned Numbers Authority [IANA], other than those just listed, should be referred to using their registered names. Note that these registered names are defined to be case-insensitive, so processors wishing to match against them should do so in a case-insensitive way.

In the absence of information provided by an external transport protocol (e.g. HTTP or MIME), it is an error for an entity including an encoding declaration to be presented to the XML processor in an encoding other than that named in the declaration, for an encoding declaration to occur other than at the beginning of an external entity, or for an entity which begins with neither a Byte Order Mark nor an encoding declaration to use an encoding other than UTF-8. Note that since ASCII is a subset of UTF-8, ordinary ASCII entities do not strictly need an encoding declaration.

It is a fatal error when an XML processor encounters an entity with an encoding that it is unable to process.

Examples of encoding declarations:

```
<?xml encoding='UTF-8'?>
<?xml encoding='EUC-JP'?>
```

4.4 XML Processor Treatment of Entities and References

The table below summarizes the contexts in which character references, entity references, and invocations of unparsed entities might appear and the required behavior of an XML processor in each case. The labels in the leftmost column describe the recognition context:

Reference in Content as a reference anywhere after the start-tag and before the end-tag of an element; corresponds to the nonterminal content.

Reference in Attribute Value as a reference within either the value of an attribute in a start-tag, or a default value in an attribute declaration; corresponds to the nonterminal AttValue.

Occurs as Attribute Value as a Name, not a reference, appearing either as the value of an attribute which has been declared as type ENTITY, or as one of the space-separated tokens in the value of an attribute which has been declared as type ENTITIES.

Reference in Entity Value as a reference within a parameter or internal entity's literal entity value in the entity's declaration; corresponds to the nonterminal EntityValue.

Reference in DTD as a reference within either the internal or external subsets of the DTD, but outside of an EntityValue or AttValue.

Entity Type	Character	Parameter	Internal General	External Parsed General	Unparsed
Reference in Content	Not recognized	Included	Included if validating	Forbidden	Included
Reference in Attribute Value	Not recognized	Included in literal	Forbidden	Forbidden	Included
Occurs as Attribute Value	Not recognized	Forbidden	Forbidden	Notify	Not recognized
Reference in Entity Value	Included in literal	Bypassed	Bypassed	Forbidden	Included
Reference in DTD	Included as PE	Forbidden	Forbidden	Forbidden	Forbidden

4.4.1 Not Recognized

Outside the DTD, the % character has no special significance; thus, what would be parameter entity references in the DTD are not recognized as markup in content. Similarly, the names of unparsed entities are not recognized except when they appear in the value of an appropriately declared attribute.

4.4.2 Included

An entity is **included** when its replacement text is retrieved and processed, in place of the reference itself, as though it were part of the document at the location the reference was recognized. The replacement text may contain both character data and (except for parameter entities) markup, which must be recognized in the usual way, except that the replacement text of entities used to escape markup delimiters (the entities amp, lt, gt, apos, quot) is always treated as data. (The string "AT&T;" expands to "AT&T;" and the remaining ampersand is not recognized as an entity-reference delimiter.) A character reference is **included** when the indicated character is processed in place of the reference itself.

4.4.3 Included If Validating

When an XML processor recognizes a reference to a parsed entity, in order to validate the document, the processor must include its replacement text. If the entity is external, and the processor is not attempting to validate the XML document, the processor may, but need not, include the entity's replacement text. If a non-validating parser does not include the replacement text, it must inform the application that it recognized, but did not read, the entity.

This rule is based on the recognition that the automatic inclusion provided by the SGML and XML entity mechanism, primarily designed to support modularity in authoring, is not necessarily appropriate for other applications, in particular document browsing. Browsers, for example, when encountering an external parsed entity reference, might choose to provide a visual indication of the entity's presence and retrieve it for display only on demand.

4.4.4 Forbidden

The following are forbidden, and constitute fatal errors:

- ✦ the appearance of a reference to an unparsed entity.
- ✦ the appearance of any character or general-entity reference in the DTD except within an EntityValue or AttValue.
- ✦ a reference to an external entity in an attribute value.

4.4.5 Included in Literal

When an entity reference appears in an attribute value, or a parameter entity reference appears in a literal entity value, its replacement text is processed in place of the reference itself as though it were part of the document at the location the reference was recognized, except that a single or double quote character in the replacement text is always treated as a normal data character and will not terminate the literal. For example, this is well-formed:

```
<!ENTITY % YN '"Yes"' >
<!ENTITY WhatHeSaid "He said &YN;" >
```

while this is not:

```
<!ENTITY EndAttr "27'" >
<element attribute='a-&EndAttr;>
```

4.4.6 Notify

When the name of an unparsed entity appears as a token in the value of an attribute of declared type ENTITY or ENTITIES, a validating processor must inform the application of the system and public (if any) identifiers for both the entity and its associated notation.

4.4.7 Bypassed

When a general entity reference appears in the EntityValue in an entity declaration, it is bypassed and left as is.

4.4.8 Included as PE

Just as with external parsed entities, parameter entities need only be included if validating. When a parameter-entity reference is recognized in the DTD and included, its replacement text is enlarged by the attachment of one leading and one following space (#x20) character; the intent is to constrain the replacement text of parameter entities to contain an integral number of grammatical tokens in the DTD.

4.5 Construction of Internal Entity Replacement Text

In discussing the treatment of internal entities, it is useful to distinguish two forms of the entity's value. The **literal entity value** is the quoted string actually present in the entity declaration, corresponding to the non-terminal EntityValue. The **replacement text** is the content of the entity, after replacement of character references and parameter-entity references.

The literal entity value as given in an internal entity declaration (EntityValue) may contain character, parameter-entity, and general-entity references. Such references must be contained entirely within the literal entity value. The actual replacement text that is included as described above must contain the *replacement text* of any parameter entities referred to, and must contain the character referred to, in place of any character references in the literal entity value; however, general-entity references must be left as-is, unexpanded. For example, given the following declarations:

```
<!ENTITY % pub     "&#xc9;ditions Gallimard" >
<!ENTITY   rights "All rights reserved" >
<!ENTITY   book   "La Peste: Albert Camus,
&#xA9; 1947 %pub;. &rights;" >
```

then the replacement text for the entity "book" is:

```
La Peste: Albert Camus,
(c) 1947 ∞ditions Gallimard. &rights;
```

The general-entity reference "&rights;" would be expanded should the reference "&book;" appear in the document's content or an attribute value.

These simple rules may have complex interactions; for a detailed discussion of a difficult example, see "D. Expansion of Entity and Character References".

4.6 Predefined Entities

Entity and character references can both be used to **escape** the left angle bracket, ampersand, and other delimiters. A set of general entities (amp, lt, gt, apos, quot) is specified for this purpose. Numeric character references may also be used; they are expanded immediately when recognized and must be treated as character data, so the numeric character references "<" and "&" may be used to escape < and & when they occur in character data.

All XML processors must recognize these entities whether they are declared or not. For interoperability, valid XML documents should declare these entities, like any others, before using them. If the entities in question are declared, they must be declared as internal entities whose replacement text is the single character being escaped or a character reference to that character, as shown below.

```
<!ENTITY lt     "&#38;#60;">
<!ENTITY gt     "&#62;">
<!ENTITY amp    "&#38;#38;">
<!ENTITY apos   "&#39;">
<!ENTITY quot   "&#34;">
```

Note that the < and & characters in the declarations of "lt" and "amp" are doubly escaped to meet the requirement that entity replacement be well-formed.

4.7 Notation Declarations

Notations identify by name the format of unparsed entities, the format of elements which bear a notation attribute, or the application to which a processing instruction is addressed.

Notation declarations provide a name for the notation, for use in entity and attribute-list declarations and in attribute specifications, and an external identifier for the notation which may allow an XML processor or its client application to locate a helper application capable of processing data in the given notation.

Notation Declarations

```
[82] NotationDecl  ::= '<!NOTATION' S Name S (ExternalID
                         | PublicID) S? '>'
[83] PublicID      ::= 'PUBLIC' S PubidLiteral
```

XML processors must provide applications with the name and external identifier(s) of any notation declared and referred to in an attribute value, attribute definition, or entity declaration. They may additionally resolve the external identifier into the system identifier, file name, or other information needed to allow the application to call a processor for data in the notation described. (It is not an error, however, for XML documents to declare and refer to notations for which notation-specific applications are not available on the system where the XML processor or application is running.)

4.8 Document Entity

The **document entity** serves as the root of the entity tree and a starting-point for an XML processor. This specification does not specify how the document entity is to be located by an XML processor; unlike other entities, the document entity has no name and might well appear on a processor input stream without any identification at all.

5. Conformance

5.1 Validating and Non-Validating Processors

Conforming XML processors fall into two classes: validating and non-validating.

Validating and non-validating processors alike must report violations of this specification's well-formedness constraints in the content of the document entity and any other parsed entities that they read.

Validating processors must report violations of the constraints expressed by the declarations in the DTD, and failures to fulfill the validity constraints given in this specification. To accomplish this, validating XML processors must read and process the entire DTD and all external parsed entities referenced in the document.

Non-validating processors are required to check only the document entity, including the entire internal DTD subset, for well-formedness. While they are not required to check the document for validity, they are required to **process** all the declarations they read in the internal DTD subset and in any parameter entity that they read, up to the first reference to a parameter entity that they do *not* read; that is to say, they must use the information in those declarations to normalize attribute values, include the replacement text of internal entities, and supply default attribute values. They must not process entity declarations or attribute-list declarations encountered after a reference to a parameter entity that is not read, since the entity may have contained overriding declarations.

5.2 Using XML Processors

The behavior of a validating XML processor is highly predictable; it must read every piece of a document and report all well-formedness and validity violations. Less is required of a non-validating processor; it need not read any part of the document other than the document entity. This has two effects that may be important to users of XML processors:

✦ Certain well-formedness errors, specifically those that require reading external entities, may not be detected by a non-validating processor. Examples include the constraints entitled Entity Declared, Parsed Entity, and No Recursion, as well as some of the cases described as forbidden in "4.4 XML Processor Treatment of Entities and References".

✦ The information passed from the processor to the application may vary, depending on whether the processor reads parameter and external entities. For example, a non-validating processor may not normalize attribute values, include the replacement text of internal entities, or supply default attribute values, where doing so depends on having read declarations in external or parameter entities.

For maximum reliability in interoperating between different XML processors, applications which use non-validating processors should not rely on any behaviors not required of such processors. Applications which require facilities such as the use of default attributes or internal entities which are declared in external entities should use validating XML processors.

6. Notation

The formal grammar of XML is given in this specification using a simple Extended Backus-Naur Form (EBNF) notation. Each rule in the grammar defines one symbol, in the form

```
symbol ::= expression
```

Symbols are written with an initial capital letter if they are defined by a regular expression, or with an initial lower case letter otherwise. Literal strings are quoted.

Within the expression on the right-hand side of a rule, the following expressions are used to match strings of one or more characters:

```
#xN
```

where N is a hexadecimal integer, the expression matches the character in ISO/IEC 10646 whose canonical (UCS-4) code value, when interpreted as an unsigned binary number, has the value indicated. The number of leading zeros in the #xN form is insignificant; the number of leading zeros in the corresponding code value is governed by the character encoding in use and is not significant for XML.

```
[a-zA-Z], [#xN-#xN]
```

matches any character with a value in the range(s) indicated (inclusive).

```
[^a-z], [^#xN-#xN]
```

matches any character with a value *outside* the range indicated.

```
[^abc], [^#xN#xN#xN]
```

matches any character with a value not among the characters given.

```
"string"
```

matches a literal string matching that given inside the double quotes.

```
'string'
```

matches a literal string matching that given inside the single quotes.

These symbols may be combined to match more complex patterns as follows, where A and B represent simple expressions:

```
(expression)
```

expression is treated as a unit and may be combined as described in this list.

```
A?
```

matches A or nothing; optional A.

```
A B
```

matches A followed by B.

```
A | B
```

matches A or B but not both.

```
A - B
```

matches any string that matches A but does not match B.

```
A+
```

matches one or more occurrences of A.

```
A*
```

matches zero or more occurrences of A.

Other notations used in the productions are:

```
/* ... */
```

comment.

```
[ wfc: ... ]
```

well-formedness constraint; this identifies by name a constraint on well-formed documents associated with a production.

```
[ vc: ... ]
```

validity constraint; this identifies by name a constraint on valid documents associated with a production.

Appendices

A. References

A.1 Normative References

IANA (Internet Assigned Numbers Authority). *Official Names for Character Sets*, ed. Keld Simonsen et al. See ftp://ftp.isi.edu/in-notes/iana/assignments/character-sets.

IETF RFC 1766 IETF (Internet Engineering Task Force). *RFC 1766: Tags for the Identification of Languages*, ed. H. Alvestrand. 1995.

ISO 639 (International Organization for Standardization). *ISO 639:1988 (E). Code for the representation of names of languages.* [Geneva]: International Organization for Standardization, 1988.

ISO 3166 (International Organization for Standardization). *ISO 3166-1:1997 (E). Codes for the representation of names of countries and their subdivisions — Part 1: Country codes* [Geneva]: International Organization for Standardization, 1997.

ISO/IEC 10646 ISO (International Organization for Standardization). *ISO/IEC 10646-1993 (E). Information technology — Universal Multiple-Octet Coded Character Set (UCS) — Part 1: Architecture and Basic Multilingual Plane.* [Geneva]: International Organization for Standardization, 1993 (plus amendments AM 1 through AM 7).

Unicode The Unicode Consortium. *The Unicode Standard, Version 2.0.* Reading, Mass.: Addison-Wesley Developers Press, 1996.

A.2 Other References

Aho/Ullman Aho, Alfred V., Ravi Sethi, and Jeffrey D. Ullman. *Compilers: Principles, Techniques, and Tools.* Reading: Addison-Wesley, 1986, rpt. corr. 1988.

Berners-Lee et al. Berners-Lee, T., R. Fielding, and L. Masinter. *Uniform Resource Identifiers (URI): Generic Syntax and Semantics.* 1997. (Work in progress; see updates to RFC1738.)

Brüggemann-Klein Brüggemann-Klein, Anne. *Regular Expressions into Finite Automata.* Extended abstract in I. Simon, Hrsg., LATIN 1992, S. 97-98. Springer-Verlag, Berlin 1992. Full Version in Theoretical Computer Science 120: 197-213, 1993.

Brüggemann-Klein and Wood Brüggemann-Klein, Anne, and Derick Wood. *Deterministic Regular Languages.* Universität Freiburg, Institut für Informatik, Bericht 38, Oktober 1991.

Clark James Clark. Comparison of SGML and XML. See `http://www.w3.org/TR/NOTE-sgml-xml-971215`.

IETF RFC1738 IETF (Internet Engineering Task Force). *RFC 1738: Uniform Resource Locators (URL)*, ed. T. Berners-Lee, L. Masinter, M. McCahill. 1994.

IETF RFC1808 IETF (Internet Engineering Task Force). *RFC 1808: Relative Uniform Resource Locators*, ed. R. Fielding. 1995.

IETF RFC2141 IETF (Internet Engineering Task Force). *RFC 2141: URN Syntax*, ed. R. Moats. 1997.

ISO 8879 ISO (International Organization for Standardization). *ISO 8879:1986(E). Information processing — Text and Office Systems — Standard Generalized Markup Language (SGML)*. First edition — 1986-10-15. [Geneva]: International Organization for Standardization, 1986.

ISO/IEC 10744 ISO (International Organization for Standardization). *ISO/IEC 10744-1992 (E). Information technology — Hypermedia/Time-based Structuring Language (HyTime)*. [Geneva]: International Organization for Standardization, 1992. *Extended Facilities Annexe*. [Geneva]: International Organization for Standardization, 1996.

B. Character Classes

Following the characteristics defined in the Unicode standard, characters are classed as base characters (among others, these contain the alphabetic characters of the Latin alphabet, without diacritics), ideographic characters, and combining characters (among others, this class contains most diacritics); these classes combine to form the class of letters. Digits and extenders are also distinguished.

Characters

```
[84] Letter    ::= BaseChar | Ideographic
[85] BaseChar ::= [#x0041-#x005A] | [#x0061-#x007A]
                | [#x00C0-#x00D6] | [#x00D8-#x00F6]
                | [#x00F8-#x00FF] | [#x0100-#x0131]
                | [#x0134-#x013E] | [#x0141-#x0148]
                | [#x014A-#x017E] | [#x0180-#x01C3]
                | [#x01CD-#x01F0] | [#x01F4-#x01F5]
                | [#x01FA-#x0217] | [#x0250-#x02A8]
                | [#x02BB-#x02C1] | #x0386 | [#x0388-#x038A]
                | #x038C | [#x038E-#x03A1] | [#x03A3-#x03CE]
                | [#x03D0-#x03D6] | #x03DA | #x03DC | #x03DE
                | #x03E0 | [#x03E2-#x03F3] | [#x0401-#x040C]
                | [#x040E-#x044F] | [#x0451-#x045C]
                | [#x045E-#x0481] | [#x0490-#x04C4]
```

```
| [#x04C7-#x04C8] | [#x04CB-#x04CC]
| [#x04D0-#x04EB] | [#x04EE-#x04F5]
| [#x04F8-#x04F9] | [#x0531-#x0556] | #x0559
| [#x0561-#x0586] | [#x05D0-#x05EA]
| [#x05F0-#x05F2] | [#x0621-#x063A]
| [#x0641-#x064A] | [#x0671-#x06B7]
| [#x06BA-#x06BE] | [#x06C0-#x06CE]
| [#x06D0-#x06D3] | #x06D5 | [#x06E5-#x06E6]
| [#x0905-#x0939] | #x093D | [#x0958-#x0961]
| [#x0985-#x098C] | [#x098F-#x0990]
| [#x0993-#x09A8] | [#x09AA-#x09B0]
| #x09B2 | [#x09B6-#x09B9] | [#x09DC-#x09DD]
| [#x09DF-#x09E1] | [#x09F0-#x09F1]
| [#x0A05-#x0A0A] | [#x0A0F-#x0A10]
| [#x0A13-#x0A28] | [#x0A2A-#x0A30]
| [#x0A32-#x0A33] | [#x0A35-#x0A36]
| [#x0A38-#x0A39] | [#x0A59-#x0A5C]
| #x0A5E | [#x0A72-#x0A74] | [#x0A85-#x0A8B]
| #x0A8D | [#x0A8F-#x0A91] | [#x0A93-#x0AA8]
| [#x0AAA-#x0AB0] | [#x0AB2-#x0AB3]
| [#x0AB5-#x0AB9] | #x0ABD | #x0AE0
| [#x0B05-#x0B0C] | [#x0B0F-#x0B10]
| [#x0B13-#x0B28] | [#x0B2A-#x0B30]
| [#x0B32-#x0B33] | [#x0B36-#x0B39]
| #x0B3D | [#x0B5C-#x0B5D] | [#x0B5F-#x0B61]
| [#x0B85-#x0B8A] | [#x0B8E-#x0B90]
| [#x0B92-#x0B95] | [#x0B99-#x0B9A] | #x0B9C
| [#x0B9E-#x0B9F] | [#x0BA3-#x0BA4]
| [#x0BA8-#x0BAA] | [#x0BAE-#x0BB5]
| [#x0BB7-#x0BB9] | [#x0C05-#x0C0C]
| [#x0C0E-#x0C10] | [#x0C12-#x0C28]
| [#x0C2A-#x0C33] | [#x0C35-#x0C39]
| [#x0C60-#x0C61] | [#x0C85-#x0C8C]
| [#x0C8E-#x0C90] | [#x0C92-#x0CA8]
| [#x0CAA-#x0CB3] | [#x0CB5-#x0CB9] | #x0CDE
| [#x0CE0-#x0CE1] | [#x0D05-#x0D0C]
| [#x0D0E-#x0D10] | [#x0D12-#x0D28]
| [#x0D2A-#x0D39] | [#x0D60-#x0D61]
| [#x0E01-#x0E2E] | #x0E30 | [#x0E32-#x0E33]
| [#x0E40-#x0E45] | [#x0E81-#x0E82] | #x0E84
| [#x0E87-#x0E88] | #x0E8A | #x0E8D
| [#x0E94-#x0E97] | [#x0E99-#x0E9F]
| [#x0EA1-#x0EA3] | #x0EA5 | #x0EA7
| [#x0EAA-#x0EAB] | [#x0EAD-#x0EAE] | #x0EB0
| [#x0EB2-#x0EB3] | #x0EBD | [#x0EC0-#x0EC4]
| [#x0F40-#x0F47] | [#x0F49-#x0F69]
| [#x10A0-#x10C5] | [#x10D0-#x10F6] | #x1100
| [#x1102-#x1103] | [#x1105-#x1107] | #x1109
| [#x110B-#x110C] | [#x110E-#x1112] | #x113C
| #x113E | #x1140 | #x114C | #x114E | #x1150
| [#x1154-#x1155] | #x1159 | [#x115F-#x1161]
```

```
                                  #x1163 |  #x1165    #x1167 |  #x1169
                                 [#x116D-#x116E]    [#x1172-#x1173] |  #x1175
                                  #x119E |  #x11A8    #x11AB   [#x11AE-#x11AF]
                                 [#x11B7-#x11B8]     #x11BA   [#x11BC-#x11C2]
                                  #x11EB |  #x11F0    #x11F9 |  [#x1E00-#x1E9B]
                                 [#x1EA0-#x1EF9]    [#x1F00-#x1F15]
                                 [#x1F18-#x1F1D]    [#x1F20-#x1F45]
                                 [#x1F48-#x1F4D]    [#x1F50-#x1F57] |  #x1F59
                                  #x1F5B |  #x1F5D   [#x1F5F-#x1F7D]
                                 [#x1F80-#x1FB4]    [#x1FB6-#x1FBC] |  #x1FBE
                                 [#x1FC2-#x1FC4]    [#x1FC6-#x1FCC]
                                 [#x1FD0-#x1FD3]    [#x1FD6-#x1FDB]
                                 [#x1FE0-#x1FEC]    [#x1FF2-#x1FF4]
                                 [#x1FF6-#x1FFC]     #x2126   [#x212A-#x212B]
                                  #x212E |  [#x2180-#x2182] |  [#x3041-#x3094]
                                 [#x30A1-#x30FA] |  [#x3105-#x312C]
                                 [#xAC00-#xD7A3]
[86] Ideographic    ::= [#x4E00-#x9FA5] |  #x3007
                      | [#x3021-#x3029]
[87] CombiningChar ::= [#x0300-#x0345]    [#x0360-#x0361]
                     | [#x0483-#x0486]    [#x0591-#x05A1]
                     | [#x05A3-#x05B9]    [#x05BB-#x05BD]
                     | #x05BF |  [#x05C1-#x05C2] |  #x05C4
                     | [#x064B-#x0652]     #x0670
                     | [#x06D6-#x06DC]    [#x06DD-#x06DF]
                     | [#x06E0-#x06E4]    [#x06E7-#x06E8]
                     | [#x06EA-#x06ED]    [#x0901-#x0903]
                     | #x093C |  [#x093E-#x094C] |  #x094D
                     | [#x0951-#x0954]    [#x0962-#x0963]
                     | [#x0981-#x0983]     #x09BC |  #x09BE
                     | #x09BF |  [#x09C0-#x09C4]
                     | [#x09C7-#x09C8]    [#x09CB-#x09CD]
                     | #x09D7 |  [#x09E2-#x09E3] |  #x0A02
                     | #x0A3C |  #x0A3E    #x0A3F
                     | [#x0A40-#x0A42]    [#x0A47-#x0A48]
                     | [#x0A4B-#x0A4D]    [#x0A70-#x0A71]
                     | [#x0A81-#x0A83]     #x0ABC
                     | [#x0ABE-#x0AC5]    [#x0AC7-#x0AC9]
                     | [#x0ACB-#x0ACD]    [#x0B01-#x0B03]
                     | #x0B3C |  [#x0B3E-#x0B43]
                     | [#x0B47-#x0B48]    [#x0B4B-#x0B4D]
                     | [#x0B56-#x0B57]    [#x0B82-#x0B83]
                     | [#x0BBE-#x0BC2]    [#x0BC6-#x0BC8]
                     | [#x0BCA-#x0BCD]     #x0BD7
                     | [#x0C01-#x0C03]    [#x0C3E-#x0C44]
                     | [#x0C46-#x0C48]    [#x0C4A-#x0C4D]
                     | [#x0C55-#x0C56]    [#x0C82-#x0C83]
                     | [#x0CBE-#x0CC4]    [#x0CC6-#x0CC8]
                     | [#x0CCA-#x0CCD]    [#x0CD5-#x0CD6]
                     | [#x0D02-#x0D03]    [#x0D3E-#x0D43]
                     | [#x0D46-#x0D48]    [#x0D4A-#x0D4D]
```

```
                                 #x0D57 | #x0E31 | [#x0E34-#x0E3A]
                                 [#x0E47-#x0E4E] | #x0EB1
                                 [#x0EB4-#x0EB9] | [#x0EBB-#x0EBC]
                                 [#x0EC8-#x0ECD] | [#x0F18-#x0F19]
                                 #x0F35 | #x0F37 | #x0F39 | #x0F3E
                                 #x0F3F | [#x0F71-#x0F84]
                                 [#x0F86-#x0F8B] | [#x0F90-#x0F95]
                                 #x0F97 | [#x0F99-#x0FAD]
                                 [#x0FB1-#x0FB7] | #x0FB9
                                 [#x20D0-#x20DC] | #x20E1
                                 [#x302A-#x302F] | #x3099 | #x309A
   [88] Digit ::=               [#x0030-#x0039] | [#x0660-#x0669]
                                 [#x06F0-#x06F9] | [#x0966-#x096F]
                                 [#x09E6-#x09EF] | [#x0A66-#x0A6F]
                                 [#x0AE6-#x0AEF] | [#x0B66-#x0B6F]
                                 [#x0BE7-#x0BEF] | [#x0C66-#x0C6F]
                                 [#x0CE6-#x0CEF] | [#x0D66-#x0D6F]
                                 [#x0E50-#x0E59] | [#x0ED0-#x0ED9]
                                 [#x0F20-#x0F29]
   [89] Extender ::=            #x00B7 | #x02D0 | #x02D1 | #x0387
                                 #x0640 | #x0E46 | #x0EC6 | #x3005
                                 [#x3031-#x3035] | [#x309D-#x309E]
                                 [#x30FC-#x30FE]
```

The character classes defined here can be derived from the Unicode character database as follows:

- ✦ Name start characters must have one of the categories Ll, Lu, Lo, Lt, Nl.

- ✦ Name characters other than Name-start characters must have one of the categories Mc, Me, Mn, Lm, or Nd.

- ✦ Characters in the compatibility area (i.e. with character code greater than #xF900 and less than #xFFFE) are not allowed in XML names.

- ✦ Characters which have a font or compatibility decomposition (i.e. those with a "compatibility formatting tag" in field 5 of the database — marked by field 5 beginning with a "<") are not allowed.

- ✦ The following characters are treated as name-start characters rather than name characters, because the property file classifies them as Alphabetic: [#x02BB-#x02C1], #x0559, #x06E5, #x06E6.

- ✦ Characters #x20DD-#x20E0 are excluded (in accordance with Unicode, section 5.14).

- ✦ Character #x00B7 is classified as an extender, because the property list so identifies it.

- ✦ Character #x0387 is added as a name character, because #x00B7 is its canonical equivalent.

- ✦ Characters ':' and '_' are allowed as name-start characters.

- ✦ Characters '-' and '.' are allowed as name characters.

C. XML and SGML (Non-Normative)

XML is designed to be a subset of SGML, in that every valid XML document should also be a conformant SGML document. For a detailed comparison of the additional restrictions that XML places on documents beyond those of SGML, see [Clark].

D. Expansion of Entity and Character References (Non-Normative)

This appendix contains some examples illustrating the sequence of entity- and character-reference recognition and expansion, as specified in "4.4 XML Processor Treatment of Entities and References".

If the DTD contains the declaration

```
<!ENTITY example "<p>An ampersand (&#38;#38;) may be escaped
numerically (&#38;#38;#38;) or with a general entity
(&amp;amp;).</p>" >
```

then the XML processor will recognize the character references when it parses the entity declaration, and resolve them before storing the following string as the value of the entity "example":

```
<p>An ampersand (&#38;) may be escaped
numerically (&#38;#38;) or with a general entity
(&amp;amp;).</p>
```

A reference in the document to "&example;" will cause the text to be reparsed, at which time the start- and end-tags of the "p" element will be recognized and the three references will be recognized and expanded, resulting in a "p" element with the following content (all data, no delimiters or markup):

```
An ampersand (&) may be escaped
numerically (&#38;) or with a general entity
(&amp;).
```

A more complex example will illustrate the rules and their effects fully. In the following example, the line numbers are solely for reference.

```
1 <?xml version='1.0'?>
2 <!DOCTYPE test [
3 <!ELEMENT test (#PCDATA) >
4 <!ENTITY % xx '&#37;zz;'>
5 <!ENTITY % zz '&#60;!ENTITY tricky "error-prone" >' >
6 %xx;
7 ]>
8 <test>This sample shows a &tricky; method.</test>
```

This produces the following:

in line 4, the reference to character 37 is expanded immediately, and the parameter entity "xx" is stored in the symbol table with the value "%zz;". Since the replacement text is not rescanned, the reference to parameter entity "zz" is not recognized. (And it would be an error if it were, since "zz" is not yet declared.)

in line 5, the character reference "<" is expanded immediately and the parameter entity "zz" is stored with the replacement text "<!ENTITY tricky "error-prone" >", which is a well-formed entity declaration.

in line 6, the reference to "xx" is recognized, and the replacement text of "xx" (namely "%zz;") is parsed. The reference to "zz" is recognized in its turn, and its replacement text ("<!ENTITY tricky "error-prone" >") is parsed. The general entity "tricky" has now been declared, with the replacement text "error-prone".

in line 8, the reference to the general entity "tricky" is recognized, and it is expanded, so the full content of the "test" element is the self-describing (and ungrammatical) string This sample shows a error-prone method.

E. Deterministic Content Models (Non-Normative)

For compatibility, it is required that content models in element type declarations be deterministic.

SGML requires deterministic content models (it calls them "unambiguous"); XML processors built using SGML systems may flag non-deterministic content models as errors.

For example, the content model ((b, c) | (b, d)) is non-deterministic, because given an initial b the parser cannot know which b in the model is being matched without looking ahead to see which element follows the b. In this case, the two references to b can be collapsed into a single reference, making the model read (b, (c | d)). An initial b now clearly matches only a single name in the content model. The parser doesn't need to look ahead to see what follows; either c or d would be accepted.

More formally: a finite state automaton may be constructed from the content model using the standard algorithms, e.g. algorithm 3.5 in section 3.9 of Aho, Sethi, and Ullman [Aho/Ullman]. In many such algorithms, a follow set is constructed for each position in the regular expression (i.e., each leaf node in the syntax tree for the regular expression); if any position has a follow set in which more than one following position is labeled with the same element type name, then the content model is in error and may be reported as an error.

Algorithms exist which allow many but not all non-deterministic content models to be reduced automatically to equivalent deterministic models; see Brüggemann-Klein 1991 [Brüggemann-Klein].

F. Autodetection of Character Encodings (Non-Normative)

The XML encoding declaration functions as an internal label on each entity, indicating which character encoding is in use. Before an XML processor can read the internal label, however, it apparently has to know what character encoding is in use—which is what the internal label is trying to indicate. In the general case, this is a hopeless situation. It is not entirely hopeless in XML, however, because XML limits the general case in two ways: each implementation is assumed to support only a finite set of character encodings, and the XML encoding declaration is restricted in position and content in order to make it feasible to autodetect the character encoding in use in each entity in normal cases. Also, in many cases other sources of information are available in addition to the XML data stream itself. Two cases may be distinguished, depending on whether the XML entity is presented to the processor without, or with, any accompanying (external) information. We consider the first case first.

Because each XML entity not in UTF-8 or UTF-16 format *must* begin with an XML encoding declaration, in which the first characters must be '<?xml', any conforming processor can detect, after two to four octets of input, which of the following cases apply. In reading this list, it may help to know that in UCS-4, '<' is "#x0000003C" and '?' is "#x0000003F", and the Byte Order Mark required of UTF-16 data streams is "#xFEFF".

- ✦ 00 00 00 3C: UCS-4, big-endian machine (1234 order)
- ✦ 3C 00 00 00: UCS-4, little-endian machine (4321 order)
- ✦ 00 00 3C 00: UCS-4, unusual octet order (2143)
- ✦ 00 3C 00 00: UCS-4, unusual octet order (3412)
- ✦ FE FF: UTF-16, big-endian
- ✦ FF FE: UTF-16, little-endian
- ✦ 00 3C 00 3F: UTF-16, big-endian, no Byte Order Mark (and thus, strictly speaking, in error)
- ✦ 3C 00 3F 00: UTF-16, little-endian, no Byte Order Mark (and thus, strictly speaking, in error)
- ✦ 3C 3F 78 6D: UTF-8, ISO 646, ASCII, some part of ISO 8859, Shift-JIS, EUC, or any other 7-bit, 8-bit, or mixed-width encoding which ensures that the characters of ASCII have their normal positions, width, and values; the actual encoding declaration must be read to detect which of these applies, but since all of these encodings use the same bit patterns for the ASCII characters, the encoding declaration itself may be read reliably
- ✦ 4C 6F A7 94: EBCDIC (in some flavor; the full encoding declaration must be read to tell which code page is in use)
- ✦ other: UTF-8 without an encoding declaration, or else the data stream is corrupt, fragmentary, or enclosed in a wrapper of some kind

This level of autodetection is enough to read the XML encoding declaration and parse the character-encoding identifier, which is still necessary to distinguish the individual members of each family of encodings (e.g. to tell UTF-8 from 8859, and the parts of 8859 from each other, or to distinguish the specific EBCDIC code page in use, and so on).

Because the contents of the encoding declaration are restricted to ASCII characters, a processor can reliably read the entire encoding declaration as soon as it has detected which family of encodings is in use. Since in practice, all widely used character encodings fall into one of the categories above, the XML encoding declaration allows reasonably reliable in-band labeling of character encodings, even when external sources of information at the operating-system or transport-protocol level are unreliable.

Once the processor has detected the character encoding in use, it can act appropriately, whether by invoking a separate input routine for each case, or by calling the proper conversion function on each character of input.

Like any self-labeling system, the XML encoding declaration will not work if any software changes the entity's character set or encoding without updating the encoding declaration. Implementors of character-encoding routines should be careful to ensure the accuracy of the internal and external information used to label the entity.

The second possible case occurs when the XML entity is accompanied by encoding information, as in some file systems and some network protocols. When multiple sources of information are available, their relative priority and the preferred method of handling conflict should be specified as part of the higher-level protocol used to deliver XML. Rules for the relative priority of the internal label and the MIME-type label in an external header, for example, should be part of the RFC document defining the text/xml and application/xml MIME types. In the interests of interoperability, however, the following rules are recommended.

+ If an XML entity is in a file, the Byte-Order Mark and encoding-declaration PI are used (if present) to determine the character encoding. All other heuristics and sources of information are solely for error recovery.

+ If an XML entity is delivered with a MIME type of text/xml, then the charset parameter on the MIME type determines the character encoding method; all other heuristics and sources of information are solely for error recovery.

+ If an XML entity is delivered with a MIME type of application/xml, then the Byte-Order Mark and encoding-declaration PI are used (if present) to determine the character encoding. All other heuristics and sources of information are solely for error recovery.

These rules apply only in the absence of protocol-level documentation; in particular, when the MIME types text/xml and application/xml are defined, the recommendations of the relevant RFC will supersede these rules.

G. W3C XML Working Group (Non-Normative)

This specification was prepared and approved for publication by the W3C XML Working Group (WG). WG approval of this specification does not necessarily imply that all WG members voted for its approval. The current and former members of the XML WG are:

Jon Bosak, Sun (Chair); James Clark (Technical Lead); Tim Bray, Textuality and Netscape (XML Co-editor); Jean Paoli, Microsoft (XML Co-editor); C. M. Sperberg-McQueen, U. of Ill. (XML Co-editor); Dan Connolly, W3C (W3C Liaison); Paula Angerstein, Texcel; Steve DeRose, INSO; Dave Hollander, HP; Eliot Kimber, ISOGEN; Eve Maler, ArborText; Tom Magliery, NCSA; Murray Maloney, Muzmo and Grif; Makoto Murata, Fuji Xerox Information Systems; Joel Nava, Adobe; Conleth O'Connell, Vignette; Peter Sharpe, SoftQuad; John Tigue, DataChannel.

✦   ✦   ✦

What's on the CD-ROM

The CD that comes with this book should be readable on a Mac, Solaris, Windows 95, and Windows NT 4.0. Just put the CD in the drive, and mount it using whatever method you normally use on your platform, probably filemanager in Solaris, and just stick it in the drive if you're using a Mac and Windows. There's no fancy installer. You can browse the directories as you would a hard drive.

All CD-ROM files are read-only. Therefore, if you open a file from the CD-ROM and make any changes to it, you'll need to save it to your hard drive. Also, If you copy a file from the CD-ROM to your hard drive, the file retains its read-only attribute. To change this attribute after copying a file, right-click the file name or icon and select Properties from the shortcut menu. In the Properties dialog box, click the General tab and remove the checkmark from the Read-only checkbox.

There are seven main directories:

1. Browsers
2. Parsers
3. Specifications
4. Examples
5. Source Code
6. Utilities
7. PDFs

Browsers

This directory has a number of Web browsers that support XML to a greater or lesser extent including:

+ Microsoft Internet Explorer 5.0 for Windows
+ Microsoft Internet Explorer 4.5 for the Mac
+ Netscape Navigator 4.0.8 for the Mac
+ Netscape Navigator 4.0.4 for Windows
+ Amaya 1.4b (various platforms)

Of these, only Internet Explorer 5.0 for Windows can directly display XML files. The remainder use XML internally for various functions, such as Netscape's What's Related or Amaya's MathML support.

Parsers

This directory contains version 0.86 of the Silfide XML Parser (SXP), a parser and a complete XML API in Java. . The latest version is available at `http://www.loria.fr/projets/XSilfide/EN/index.html`.

Specifications

This directory contains the official specification documents for many of the technologies discussed in this book including:

+ XML 1.0
+ Namespaces in XML
+ CSS Level 1
+ CSS Level 2
+ Document Object Model
+ HTML 4.0
+ XHTML
+ MathML
+ The Resource Description Framework
+ SMIL

These are all included in HTML format. Some are provided in other formats like XML and PDF as well. Many technologies discussed in this book are not yet finalized (for example, XSL). You can find the current draft specifications for these on the W3C Web site at http://www.w3.org/TR/.

Examples

This directory contains several examples of large XML files and large collections of XML documents. Some (but not all) of these are based on smaller examples printed in the book. For instance, you'll find complete statistics for the 1998 major league baseball season including all players and teams. Examples include:

- ✦ The 1998 major league season
- ✦ The complete works of Shakespeare (courtesy of Jon Bosak)
- ✦ The Old Testament (courtesy of Jon Bosak)
- ✦ The New Testament (courtesy of Jon Bosak)
- ✦ The Koran (courtesy of Jon Bosak)
- ✦ The Book of Mormon (courtesy of Jon Bosak)
- ✦ The Periodic Table of the Elements

Source Code

All complete numbered code listings from this book are on the CD-ROM in a directory called source. They are organized by chapter. Very simple HTML indexes are provided for the examples in each chapter. However, because most of the examples are raw XML files, current Web browsers won't display them very well. You're probably better off just opening the directories in Windows Explorer or the equivalent on your platform of choice, and reading the files with a text editor.

Most of the files are named according to the listing number in the book (for example, 6-1.xml, 21-1.cdf). However, in a few cases where a specific name is used in the book, such as family.dtd or family.xml, then that name is also used on the CD. The files on the CD appear exactly as they do in the book's listings.

Utilities

The utilities directory contains a single program — Tidy, compiled for a variety of platforms. Tidy can clean up most HTML files so that they become well-formed

XML.Tidy can correct many common problems and warn you about the ones you need to fix yourself. Tidy was written for the W3C by Dave Raggett. The latest version can be found at `http://www.w3.org/People/Raggett/tidy`.

PDF

The PDF directory contains Acrobat PDF files for this entire book. To read them, you'll need the free Acrobat reader software which is included on the CD-ROM. Feel free to put them on your local hard disk for easy access. And I don't really care if you loan the CD-ROM to some cash-strapped undergrad who finds it cheaper to tie up a school printer for a few hours printing all 1000+ pages rather than spend $49.95 for a printed copy. (If you're using your own printer, toner, and paper, it's *much* cheaper to buy the book.)

However, I would very much appreciate it if you do not place these files on *any* Web or FTP servers. This includes intranet servers, password-protected sites, and other things that aren't meant for the public as large. Most local sites and intranets are far more exposed to the broader Net that most people think. Today's search engines are *very* good at locating content that is supposed to be hidden. Putting mirror copies of these files around the Web makes it extremely difficult to keep all the files up to date and to make sure that search engines find the right copies.

✦   ✦   ✦

Index

continued

continued

IDG Books Worldwide, Inc.
End-User License Agreement

4. **Restrictions on Use of Individual Programs.** You must follow the individual requirements and restrictions detailed for each individual program in Appendix C of this Book. These limitations are also contained in the individual license agreements recorded on the Software Media. These limitations may include a requirement that after using the program for a specified period of time, the user must pay a registration fee or discontinue use. By opening the Software packet(s), you will be agreeing to abide by the licenses and restrictions for these individual programs that are detailed in Appendix C and on the Software Media. None of the material on this Software Media or listed in this Book may ever be redistributed, in original or modified form, for commercial purposes.

5. **Limited Warranty.**

   (a) IDGB warrants that the Software and Software Media are free from defects in materials and workmanship under normal use for a period of sixty (60) days from the date of purchase of this Book. If IDGB receives notification within the warranty period of defects in materials or workmanship, IDGB will replace the defective Software Media.

   (b) IDGB AND THE AUTHOR OF THE BOOK DISCLAIM ALL OTHER WARRANTIES, EXPRESS OR IMPLIED, INCLUDING WITHOUT LIMITATION IMPLIED WARRANTIES OF MERCHANTABILITY AND FITNESS FOR A PARTICULAR PURPOSE, WITH RESPECT TO THE SOFTWARE, THE PROGRAMS, THE SOURCE CODE CONTAINED THEREIN, AND/OR THE TECHNIQUES DESCRIBED IN THIS BOOK. IDGB DOES NOT WARRANT THAT THE FUNCTIONS CONTAINED IN THE SOFTWARE WILL MEET YOUR REQUIREMENTS OR THAT THE OPERATION OF THE SOFTWARE WILL BE ERROR FREE.

   (c) This limited warranty gives you specific legal rights, and you may have other rights that vary from jurisdiction to jurisdiction.

6. **Remedies.**

   (a) IDGB's entire liability and your exclusive remedy for defects in materials and workmanship shall be limited to replacement of the Software Media, which may be returned to IDGB with a copy of your receipt at the following address: Software Media Fulfillment Department, Attn.: XML(tm) Bible, IDG Books Worldwide, Inc., 7260 Shadeland Station, Ste. 100, Indianapolis, IN 46256, or call 1-800-762-2974. Please allow three to four weeks for delivery. This Limited Warranty is void if failure of the Software Media has resulted from accident, abuse, or misapplication. Any replacement Software Media will be warranted for the remainder of the original warranty period or thirty (30) days, whichever is longer.

   (b) In no event shall IDGB or the author be liable for any damages whatsoever (including without limitation damages for loss of business profits, business interruption, loss of business information, or any other pecuniary loss) arising from the use of or inability to use the Book or the Software, even if IDGB has been advised of the possibility of such damages.

(c) Because some jurisdictions do not allow the exclusion or limitation of liability for consequential or incidental damages, the above limitation or exclusion may not apply to you.

7. **<u>U.S. Government Restricted Rights</u>.** Use, duplication, or disclosure of the Software by the U.S. Government is subject to restrictions stated in paragraph (c)(1)(ii) of the Rights in Technical Data and Computer Software clause of DFARS 252.227-7013, and in subparagraphs (a) through (d) of the Commercial Computer — Restricted Rights clause at FAR 52.227-19, and in similar clauses in the NASA FAR supplement, when applicable.

8. **<u>General</u>.** This Agreement constitutes the entire understanding of the parties and revokes and supersedes all prior agreements, oral or written, between them and may not be modified or amended except in a writing signed by both parties hereto that specifically refers to this Agreement. This Agreement shall take precedence over any other documents that may be in conflict herewith. If any one or more provisions contained in this Agreement are held by any court or tribunal to be invalid, illegal, or otherwise unenforceable, each and every other provision shall remain in full force and effect.